Longman Annotated

GENERAL EDITOR: F.

D0541630

JOHN MILTON

PARADISE LOST

EDITED BY
ALASTAIR FOWLER

LONGMAN

LONGMAN GROUP LIMITED

London

Associated companies, branches and representatives
throughout the world

© *Longman Group Limited*
(*formerly Longmans, Green and Co Ltd*) *1968, 1971*

The complete poems of Milton
first issued in one volume in the
Longman Annotated English Poets Series 1968.
Paradise Lost first published separately in
paperback with minor corrections 1971.

ISBN 0 582 48455 3

Printed in Hong Kong by
The Continental Printing Co Ltd

Contents

Preface

In preparing the text I have throughout this volume followed a somewhat unusual plan. I have modernized old spelling, but have reproduced old punctuation with diplomatic faithfulness. Usually a different, even an opposite, plan is followed. A modernized text is commonly modernized throughout; and it is even possible to find cases where an editor has retained old spelling but modernized the punctuation. But I believe that if the matter is considered in the light of linguistic theory the plan adopted in the present edition will normally appear preferable. Of course some readers need freely modernized texts, just as scholars for certain purposes need texts scrupulously diplomatic. In general, however, it is best to modernize only the spelling.

Spelling and punctuation present quite separate problems to an editor for the good reason that they have quite different functions linguistically. Punctuation, like word order, inflection and function words, is a class of grammatical symbols. It is an organic part of the grammatical system, and as such its mode of operation is subtle and complex. Not only does it obey conventions of logic but also others whereby it renders the pauses and junctures and tones of spoken language (see the emphasis laid in, e.g., D. W. Brown, W. C. Brown, and D. Bailey, *Form in Modern English* (1958) or H. Whitehall, *Structural Essentials of English* (New York 1956)). Consequently we ought to be almost as reluctant to alter the punctuation of an old text as we would be to alter, say, its word order. Moreover, punctuation is less standardized than the other types of grammatical symbol; which means that the gain from modernizing is reduced, while the difficulty of finding exactly equivalent modern conventions is increased. And unless he finds exact equivalents the modernizing editor must continually falsify the meaning (not to mention the rhythm) of the text. With subtle complex poetry such as Milton's, decisions have to be made about tone, juncture and logical structure for which there is no basis in the punctuation of the early editions, and distinctions introduced that the poet himself may have taken care to exclude. Time and again ambiguities will have to be removed and enhancing suggestions lost. Yet even these are not all the problems with which the modernizing editor is faced. For he has next to maintain a sensible rank-ordering or relative frequency among the modern punctuation points he uses. He could make some sort of version of the meaning of *Paradise Lost*, for example, if he allowed himself a very high relative incidence of dashes or of commas. But this he may not do; since the overall effect would be breathy and talkative in the one instance, unrhythmical and pedantic in the other.

My aim, then, has been to provide a text that retains evidential value with respect to punctuation, equally with word order and the other grammatical symbols. The cost that has to be paid for this (and I regard it as a relatively low cost) is that the reader may at first experience an occasional temporary difficulty in making out Milton's syntax. But when he overcomes the difficulty it will at least be Milton's syntax he has understood, and not the editor's.

The linguistic function of spelling is by comparison much cruder and simpler. It is not a grammatical symbol but a vocabulary symbol. That is to say, all that can generally be expected of orthographic signals is that they should enable the reader to make the right vocabulary selection. Now modern spelling is perfectly well able to do this for a seventeenth-century text. It is usually easy to find exact modern equivalents for old spellings, because orthographic signals are essentially simple binary signals. True, spelling also conveys some information about how words sound. But in English the relation between orthography and the phonetic pattern it renders is remote. Certainly with our knowledge of the pronunciation of the seventeenth century in its present state there can be few instances where the old spelling indicates the sound to a modern reader better than the new. (I have drawn attention to some of these instances in the notes.) The typical case, on which editorial practice must be based, is instead exemplified by *eternity*, *PL* viii 406, where the early editions have *eternitie*. It is probable that Milton intended a pronunciation something like *etarnity*: or perhaps even *etarrnity*, since (according to Aubrey) 'he pronounc'd the letter R very hard'. But how are we to tell this from the old spelling?

Some will object that while in general it may be all very well to treat punctuation and spelling differently, it will not do for Milton. What about his special orthographic rules and his preferences for certain current forms rather than others? A great deal of attention was focused on these matters by Helen Darbishire's and Bernard Wright's editions, in which the spelling purported to be normalized in accordance with Milton's wishes. Each text was based upon an ingenious system of idiosyncratic spellings; and between the two systems there was an impressive area of agreement. If either could be mastered, it seemed reasonable to hope for a better grasp of the intentions of the author of the spellings. The special rules of spelling and capitalization fell into five main groups (1) those distinguishing homophones; (2) those making grammatical distinctions, especially between the preterites (ending in *-d*) and past participles (in *-t*) of certain weak verbs; (3) those indicating prosodic stress; (4) those preferred for their phonetic value, etymological value, modernity, or cultural flavour; and (5) those distinguishing emphatic forms of the personal pronouns—*mee, hee, wee, yee* or *you, their*—from unemphatic *me, he, we, ye, thir*. Much of the information that could be gleaned from the special rules was, it is true, redundant; and almost all of it was complicated by doubts as to whether one was dealing with a blunder on the printer's part or a finesse on Milton's. But there were a good many places where the special rules had some bearing, even a bearing on interpretation of the meaning.

Miss Darbishire's edition, of which the first volume appeared in 1953, provoked controversy. Uneasiness was expressed at the readiness with which she attributed to Milton's printer or amanuenses only the many exceptions to the spelling rules, and not the rules themselves. Then in 1955 Robert Martin Adams's *Ikon: John Milton and the Modern Critics* questioned the whole theory of special orthography. Arguing closely on the basis of internal evidence, he seemed to many to demolish the theory, particularly with respect to the distinction between emphatic and unemphatic pronoun spellings (Adams 61–76). However, the Preface to Professor Wright's edition in 1959 set out a modified, and in some ways even more complex, system of idiosyncratic spellings. The *coup de grâce* to the special orthography theory was not delivered until 1963, by John T. Shawcross's modestly titled 'One aspect of Milton's spelling: idle final "E",' *PMLA* lxxviii (1963) 501–10. Neither Miss Darbishire nor Professor Wright had cared to test the statistical bases of their theories. But Shawcross's statistical comparison of Milton's own holograph spellings and the spellings of the printed editions showed that the latter could only reasonably be attributed to amanuenses or compositors, since they were completely at variance with Milton's own practice. The same applies to the spelling corrections at the press, including the notorious alteration of *we* to *wee* at *Paradise Lost* ii 414. The issue seems as settled now as any in literary criticism.

Accordingly I have paid no attention in the present edition to spelling variants in the early editions. The early punctuation, on the other hand, for reasons explained above, is reproduced with diplomatic faithfulness; though this should not be taken to imply that it is necessarily Milton's punctuation. In the few instances where a clear misprint in the early editions has had to be corrected, a note calls attention to the emendation.

For the rest, I have retained the early spelling of proper names, as well as of other words that have changed their form in a way that might have a bearing on sound or sense (e.g. *ammiral; highth*), even if the obsolete form is probably only a spelling variant. A very few obsolete words and words intended by Milton as archaisms are also inevitably given in old spelling; but the forms are those selected as commonest in *OED*, and have no evidential value. Similarly with obsolete verb terminals, which for uniformity and intelligibility are given in standard spelling, regardless of contractions and elisions, unless the modern spelling is likely to confuse the reader by suggesting an extra-metrical syllable: thus *didst* is printed for 'di'st' (vii 544), *urged* for 'urg'd' (ii 120); but *revisit'st* (iii 23) and *sat'st* (i 21). Similarly *the* is printed for 'th''. Old hyphenated words now amalgamated are given their new form. Where old spelling indicates two words and modern spelling one, however, the old word division is kept for its potential prosodic or other interest (e.g. *mean while*). Italicization of proper names is not retained: it is a typographical accidental not found in the MSS. But a note is given where its presence or absence may have a bearing on, for example, personification.

(The above refers only to the text, and to quotations from M.'s poems. In the notes generally, the spelling and italicization of the edition cited are retained, with *v*, *u*, *i*, *j*, *s*, and *ſ* normalized in the usual way.)

My textual policy may seem an oversimplification. But editorial policy is bound to be decided in terms of broad simple issues; even though it is a different matter with editorial practice in individual cases. And if the policy seems a compromise, this too is inevitable. For no text is completely modern unless the editor is prepared to change word order and vocabulary; and none is completely diplomatic unless he resorts to photographic facsimile (perhaps not even then). I have tried to arrive at the best practicable compromise between the demand for evidential value and the demand for readability.

In the headnotes and footnotes, the titles of works that I have had to cite fairly frequently have been abbreviated to the author's or editor's surname. Where similar abbreviation has been needed for a second, third or fourth work by the same author or editor, I have used the surname followed by the appropriate arabic numeral above the line. A list of these abbreviations will be found at pp. 643–49. For other abbreviations, see pp. xiii–xiv.

Reference-books that we have used include: D. H. Stevens, *A Reference Guide to Milton* (Chicago, Ill. 1930); Harris F. Fletcher, *Contributions to a Milton Bibliography 1800–1930*, University of Illinois Studies in Language and Literature xvi (1931); Calvin Huckabay, *John Milton. A Bibliographical Supplement 1929–1957*, Duquesne Studies Philological Series i (1960); John Bradshaw, *A Concordance to the Poetical Works of John Milton* (1894); A. H. Gilbert, *A Geographical Dictionary of Milton* (New Haven, Conn. 1919); E. S. Le Comte, *A Milton Dictionary* (1961); J. Milton French, *The*

Life Records of John Milton (New Brunswick, N. J. 1949–58); and Harris
F. Fletcher, *The Intellectual Development of John Milton*, Vols. i and ii
(Urbana, Ill. 1956–61).

In preparing this edition I have greatly profited from the pertinent
observations of Mr F. W. Bateson, general editor of the series of Anno-
tated English Poets. Learned advice as well as kindly interest was offered
by Mr George Merton; Mr B. D. H. Miller, the Revd L. M. Styler, Mr
L. L. Stockton and Mr J. V. Peach of Brasenose College; and Mr J. C.
Maxwell of Balliol College. I should like to express gratitude to each.
The remaining errors, needless to say, are my own.

Brasenose College   A. D. S. F.
Oxford
August 1966

In the present paperback edition I have had an opportunity to make some
corrections. These affect the text at i 294 and iv 174.

                                                                        A. D. S. F.

September 1970

Abbreviations

The following abbreviations will be found, in addition to standard abbreviations for books of the Bible, classical works and literary periodicals.

Ed I = *Paradise Lost.* First edition (1667).
Ed II = *Paradise Lost.* Second edition (1674).
Trin. MS = The Trinity Manuscript.
MS = The Manuscript of *Paradise Lost* i.

Ad Pat = *Ad Patrem.*
Dam = *Epitaphium Damonis*
Id Plat = *De Idea Platonica quemadmodum Aristoteles intellexit.*
Leon = *Ad Leonoram Romae canentem.*
Natur = *Naturam non pati senium.*
PL = *Paradise Lost.*
PR = *Paradise Regained.*
Prae E = *In obitum Praesulis Eliensis.*
Proc Med = *In obitum Procancellarii medici.*
Prod Bomb = *In Proditionem Bombardicam.*
Prol = *Prolusion.*
Q Nov = *In quintum Novembris.*
SA = *Samson Agonistes.*
Salsill = *Ad Salsillum poetam Romanum aegrotantem. Scazontes.*

Columbia = *The Works of John Milton,* ed. F. A. Patterson *et al.* (New York 1931–8).
EB = *Encyclopaedia Britannica.* Eleventh edition (1910–11).
F.Q. = *The Faerie Queene.*
Migne = *Patrologia Latina,* ed. J. P. Migne (Paris 1844–55).
Migne *P. G.* = *Patrologia Graeca,* ed. J. P. Migne (Paris 1857–66).
Yale = *The Complete Prose Works of John Milton,* ed. Douglas Bush *et al.* (New Haven 1953–).

Selected Journal Abbreviations

AR	*American Review*
CQ	*Classical Quarterly*
E & S	*Essays and Studies by Members of the English Association*
EC	*Essays in Criticism*
ELH	*A Journal of English Literary History*
EM	*English Miscellany*
HLQ	*Huntington Library Quarterly*
JEGP	*Journal of English and Germanic Philology*
JHI	*Journal of the History of Ideas*
JWI	*Journal of the Warburg and Courtauld Institutes*
KR	*Kenyon Review*
MLN	*Modern Language Notes*
MLQ	*Modern Language Quarterly*
MLR	*Modern Language Review*
N & Q	*Notes and Queries*
PMLA	*PMLA: Publications of the Modern Language Association of America*
PQ	*Philological Quarterly*
RES	*Review of English Studies*
SP	*Studies in Philology*
TLS	*The Times Literary Supplement*
TRSL	*Transactions of the Royal Society of Literature*
UTQ	*University of Toronto Quarterly*
UTSE	*University of Texas Studies in English*

Chronological Table of Milton's Life and Chief Publications

1608   (*9 December*) Born at his father's house, The Spreadeagle, Bread St, London.

1615   (*24 November*) Brother Christopher born.

1618   Portrait painted by Cornelius Janssen.

1620   Enters St Paul's School, under Alexander Gill. The date is uncertain: some would put it as early as 1615, but see *Defensio Secunda* 'after I was 12 years old I rarely retired to bed from my studies till midnight' (Columbia viii 119). Friendship with Charles Diodati begins. Either now, or earlier, begins to receive tuition at home from, among others, Thomas Young.

1625   (*12 February*) Admitted to Christ's College, Cambridge, under tutorship of Chappell.

1626   Perhaps rusticated temporarily. Removed to tutorship of Tovell.

1627   Unpopular with fellow-students: dissatisfied with Cambridge syllabus (see *Prolusions* i, iii and iv, Columbia xii 118–49, 158–99 Yale i 218–33, 240–56).

      (*11 June*) Lends future father-in-law, Richard Powell, £500.

1628   (*June*) Writes verses for one of his College fellows (*Id Plat*?).

1629   So-called Onslow-portrait painted, also portrait painted by unknown artist (now in Christ's College).

      (*26 March*) Takes B.A.

1630   Portrait, said to be M., painted by Daniel Mytens (now in St Paul's School: the date is uncertain).

      (*16 April*) Charles Diodati matriculates at Geneva.

      (*10 June*) Edward King given a fellowship which it has been assumed (without evidence) M. expected or desired.

1631   (*November*) Brother Christopher admitted to Inner Temple.

1632   *On Shakespeare* published.

      (*3 July*) Takes M.A.

      Retires to Horton for life of study; see *Defensio Secunda* 'I left with most of the fellows of the College, by whom I had been cultivated with more than indifference, a regretful desire for my presence. At my father's house in the country, to which he had gone to pass his old age, I gave myself up with the most complete leisure to reading through the Greek and Latin writers; with this proviso, however, that I occasionally exchanged the country for the town, for the sake of buying books or of learning something new in mathematics or music, in which I then delighted' (Columbia viii 120).

1634 (*29 September*) *Comus* acted.

1637 *Comus* published.

(*3 April*) Mother dies.

(*September*) Thinking of entering an Inn of Court (see letter to Diodati dated 29 September, Columbia xii 28, Yale i 327).

1638 *Lycidas* printed in *Justa Edouardo King Naufrago*.

(*1 February*) Lends Sir John Cope and others £150 at 8 per cent.

(*April*) Meets Sir Henry Wotton; is kindly treated (see Wotton's letter to M., Columbia i 476–7, Yale i 339–43).

(*May*) Sails for France; meets John, Viscount Scudamore, in Paris; calls on Hugo Grotius.

(*June–July*) To Nice, Genoa, Leghorn, Pisa.

(*27 August*) Charles Diodati buried.

(*August–September*) Arrives in Florence; makes friends (see *Defensio Secunda* 'There I quickly contracted intimacy with many truly noble and learned men. I also assiduously attended their private academies, an institution which is most highly to be praised there ... Time shall never efface the memory of you, James Gaddi, Charles Dati, Frescobaldi, Cultellino, Bonmatthei, Clementillo, Francini, and numerous others', Columbia viii 122). Visits Galileo (see *Areopagitica*, Columbia iv 329–30).

(*October*) To Siena, Rome. Meets Lucas Holstein, one of the Vatican librarians. Attends Barberini concert. Entertained in English College.

(*December*) To Naples. Meets Manso.

1639 Receives news of Diodati's death. Gives up plan of crossing to Sicily and Greece (see *Defensio Secunda* 'The sad news of the English civil war recalled me; for I thought it shameful, while my countrymen were fighting for their liberty at home, that I should be peacefully travelling for culture', Columbia viii 124).

(*January–February*) Revisits Rome; hears Leonora Baroni sing.

(*March*) Returns to Florence. Again reads poems at Svogliati academy.

(*April*) Excursion to Lucca (home of Diodati family). To Bologna, Ferrara, Venice (stays a month, and ships parcel of books home).

(*May*) To Verona and Milan. Travels through Lombardy.

(*June*) Visits theologian John Diodati in Geneva (uncle of Charles)

(*July*) Returns home.

1640 Moves to St Bride's churchyard: begins tutoring nephews. Takes 'a large house' to contain self, books and pupils, who include 'the Earl of Barrimore ... Sir Thomas Gardiner of Essex, and others' (Darbishire 24–5).

Occasionally leaves this secluded 'pretty Garden-House ... in Aldersgate-Street, at the end of an Entry' and drops 'into the society of some young sparks of his acquaintance, the chief whereof were Mr Alphry, and Mr Miller, two Gentlemen of Gray's-Inn, the Beaus of those times,' with whom he likes to 'keep a Gawdy-day' (Darbishire 62).

Poem on Hobson printed in *A Banquet of Jests.*

Epitaphium Damonis printed? The first edition is undated but probably belongs to 1640.

(*30 June*) Takes Powell's lands in Wheatley by mortgage.

1641 (*May*) *Of Reformation* published.

Of Prelatical Episcopacy published.

(*July*) *Animadversions* published.

1642 (*February*) *The Reason of Church Government* published.

(*May?*) *Apology For Smectymnuus* published. Marries Mary Powell ('At Whitsuntide it was, or a little after, that he took a Journey into the Country; no body about him certainly knowing the Reason: ... after a Month's stay, home he returns a Married-man, that went out a Batchelor', Darbishire 63).

(*July?*) Mary returns home.

(*October?*) M. sends for her without success.

(*21 October*) Brother Christopher's name on Reading muster-roll: supporting Royal cause.

1643 Brother-in-law Richard Powell doing intelligence work for Royalists.

(*1 August*) *Doctrine and Discipline of Divorce* published.

1644 (*2 February*) *Doctrine and Discipline of Divorce* (second edition) published.

(*5 June*) Tract *Of Education* published. About this time M.'s attempts to seize the Powell property for debt begin: they continue till 16 July 1647, when he obtains the writ he requires.

(*6 August*) *Judgment of Martin Bucer Concerning Divorce* published.

(*13 August*) Divorce books attacked by Herbert Palmer in sermon before Parliament.

(*24–26 August*) Stationers petition against his divorce books.

(*September*) Begins to notice failure of sight (cp. letter to Philaras, 28 September 1654, Columbia xii 66).

(*23 November*) *Areopagitica* published.

(*28 December*) Summoned before the House of Lords for examination: 'soon dismissed' (Darbishire 24).

1645 Plans to marry 'one of Dr Davis's Daughters, a very Handsome and Witty Gentlewoman' (Darbishire 66). Wife returns.
(*4 March*) *Tetrachordon* and *Colasterion* published.
(*September?*) Moves to larger house at Barbican.
(*6 October*) *Poems of Mr John Milton, Both English and Latin . . . 1645* registered for publication.

1646 (*2 January*) *Poems . . . 1645* published.
(*29 July*) Daughter Anne born.

1647 (*1 January*) Father-in-law Richard Powell dies.
(*13 March*) Father dies, leaving M. the Bread St house and a 'moderate Estate' (Darbishire 32–3).
(*16 July*) Obtains extent on Powell's property in Oxfordshire.
(*September–October*) Moves from Barbican to a smaller house in High Holborn 'among those that open backward into Lincolns-Inn Fields, here he liv'd a private and quiet Life, still prosecuting his Studies and curious Search into Knowledge' (Darbishire 68).
(*20 November*) Takes possession of Powell property at Wheatley.

1648 (*25 October*) Daughter Mary born.

1649 (*13 February*) *Tenure of Kings and Magistrates* published.
(*13 March*) Invited to be Secretary for the Foreign Tongues by the Council of State.
(*15 March*) Appointed Secretary (at £288 p.a.). Ordered to answer *Eikon Basilike*.
(*11 May*) Salmasius's *Defensio Regia* appears in England.
(*16 May*) *Observations on the Articles of Peace* published.
(*6 October*) *Eikonoklastes* published.
(*19 November*) Given lodgings for official work in Scotland Yard.

1650 (*8 January*) Ordered by Council of State to reply to Salmasius.

1651 (*24 February*) *Defensio pro populo Anglicano* published.
(*16 March*) Son John born.
(*17 December*) Moves, for the sake of health, to 'a pretty Garden-house in Petty-France in Westminster . . . opening into St James's Park' (Darbishire 71).

1652 (*28 February*) Becomes totally blind at about this date.
(*2 May*) Daughter Deborah born.
(*5 May*) Wife dies.
(*16 June*) Son John dies on or about this date.
(*August*) Pierre du Moulin's *Regii Sanguinis Clamor* published, in reply to M.'s *Defensio*. M. ordered to reply by Council of State.

1653 (*21 February*) Writes letter recommending Andrew Marvell to John Bradshaw (this is the first evidence of M.'s acquaintance with Marvell).

(*3 September*) Salmasius dies.

1654 (*30 May*) *Defensio Secunda* published.

1655 Allowed substitute in Secretaryship (Darbishire 28). Takes up private studies again. Starts compiling Latin dictionary and Greek lexicon; works on *De Doctrina*, and possibly on *Paradise Lost* (Darbishire 29).

(*17 April*) Salary reduced from £288 to £150, but made pension for life.

(*8 August*) *Defensio Pro Se* published.

1656 (*12 November*) Marries Katherine Woodcock.

1657 (*19 October*) Daughter Katherine born.

1658 (*14 January*) Lends Thomas Maundy £500 and takes mortgage on property in Kensington as security.

(*3 February*) Wife dies.

(*17 March*) Daughter Katherine dies.

(*May?*) Edits and publishes his MS of Sir Walter Raleigh's *Cabinet Council*.

1659 (*16 February?*) *A Treatise of Civil Power* published.

(*August*) *The Likeliest Means to Remove Hirelings out of the Church* published.

(*20 October*) Writes *Letter to a Friend, Concerning the Ruptures of the Commonwealth* (not published until 1698).

(*3 March*) *Ready and Easy Way to Establish a Free Commonwealth* published.

(*April*) Publishes *Brief Notes Upon a late Sermon* in reply to Matthew Griffith's *Fear of God and the King*.

(*May*) Goes into hiding in friend's house in Bartholomew Close to escape retaliation (Darbishire 74).

(*16 June*) Parliament takes steps to have M. arrested and *Defensio pro populo Anglicano* and *Eikonoklastes* burned.

(*27 August*) Copies of M.'s books burned by hangman in London.

(*29 August*) Act of Indemnity does not exclude M.

(*September*) Takes house in Holborn, near Red Lion Fields. Moves from there to Jewin St (Darbishire 74-5).

(*October?*) Arrested, and imprisoned.

(*15 December*) Parliament orders that M. should be released.

(*17 December*) Andrew Marvell protests in Parliament about M.'s excessive jail fees (£150).

1662 Becomes acquainted with Thomas Ellwood: begins tutoring him (see *The History of the Life of Thomas Ellwood*, ed. C. G. Crump (1900) 88–90).

(*June?*) Sonnet to Sir Henry Vane published.

1663 On bad terms with children: 'a former Maidservant of his told Mary one of the deceased's [M.'s] Daughters ... that shee heard the deceased was to be marryed, to which the said Mary replyed ... that that was noe News to Heare of his wedding but if shee could heare of his death that was something, – and further told this Respondent that all his said Children did combine together and counsell his Maidservant to cheat him ... in her Markettings, and that his said children had made away some of his bookes and would have sold the rest of his bookes to the Dunghill women' (from Elizabeth Fisher's deposition on M.'s will, 15 December 1674, French iv 374–5).

(*24 February*) Marries Elizabeth Minshull.

(*February?*) Moves from Jewin St to 'a House in the Artillery-walk leading to Bunhill Fields' (Darbishire 75). New wife allegedly severe to M.'s daughters, 'the two eldest of whom she bound prentices to Workers in Gold-Lace, without his knowledge; and forc'd the younger to leave his Family' (from a letter of Thomas Birch, 17 November 1750, French iv 388).

1665 (*June?*) Thomas Ellwood takes house for M. in Chalfont St Giles, to avoid plague.

1666 (*2–6 September*) House in Bread St destroyed by fire.

1667 (*August?*) *Paradise Lost* published.

1669 (*June*) *Accedence Commenced Grammar* published.

1670 Portrait by William Faithorne.

(*November?*) *History of Britain* published.

1671 *Paradise Regained* and *Samson Agonistes* published.

1672 (*May?*) *Art of Logic* published.

1673 (*May?*) *Of True Religion* published.

(*November?*) *Poems, &c. upon Several Occasions . . . 1673* published.

1674 (*May*) *Epistolae Familiares* and *Prolusiones* published.

(*6 July?*) Second edition of *Paradise Lost* published.

(*8–10 November*) Dies in Bunhill house. The exact date is not known.

(*12 November*) Buried in St Giles, Cripplegate.

Paradise Lost

INTRODUCTION

Composition

It is very likely that at an early stage of its composition *Paradise Lost* was conceived not as an epic but as a tragedy. Edward Phillips says so in his *Life* (1694); where he quotes *PL* iv 32–41 as having been shown to him several (Aubrey says, fifteen or sixteen) years before the epic was begun, as the 'very beginning' of a tragedy (Darbishire 13, 72f). Moreover, the Trinity College Cambridge MS contains four drafts – written perhaps in 1640 – of an outline for a tragedy on Paradise Lost, which bear many suggestive resemblances to the epic. This outline is of such interest that it deserves to be given here in full (spelling is modernized, punctuation unaltered, cancellations omitted):

Draft i		*Draft ii*	
The Persons		The Persons	
Michael.		Moses	
Heavenly love		Justice	
Chorus of angels		Mercy	
Lucifer		Wisdom	
Adam	with the serpent	Heavenly love	
Eve		Hesperus the evening star	
Conscience		Chorus of angels	
Death		Lucifer	
Labour		Adam	
Sickness		Eve	
Discontent	mutes.	Conscience	
Ignorance		Labour	
with others		Sickness	
Faith		Discontent	
Hope		Ignorance	mutes
Charity.		Fear	
		Death	
		Faith	
		Hope	
		Charity.	

Draft iii

PARADISE LOST
The Persons

Moses προλογίζει recounting how he assumed his true body, that it corrupts not because of his [being] with God in the mount declares the like of Enoch and Eliah, besides the purity of the place that certain pure winds, dews, and

3

clouds preserve it from corruption whence he hastes to the sight of God, tells
they cannot see Adam in this state of innocence by reason of their sin
Justice ⎫
Mercy ⎬ debating what should become of man if he fall
Wisdom ⎭
Chorus of angels sing a hymn of the Creation

Act 2

Heavenly love
Evening star
Chorus sing the marriage song and describe Paradise

Act 3

Lucifer contriving Adam's ruin
Chorus fears for Adam and relates Lucifer's rebellion and fall.

Act 4

Adam ⎫ fallen
Eve ⎭
Conscience cites them to God's examination
Chorus bewails and tells the good Adam hath lost

Act 5

Adam and Eve, driven out of Paradise presented by an angel with
Labour ⎫
Grief
Hatred
Envy
War
Famine   ⎬ mutes to whom he gives their names
Pestilence ⎰ likewise Winter, Heat Tempest &c.
Sickness
Discontent
Ignorance
Fear
Death ⎭ entered into the world
Faith ⎫
Hope ⎬ comfort him and instruct him
Charity ⎭
Chorus briefly concludes.

Draft iv

ADAM UNPARADIZED

The angel Gabriel, either descending or entering, showing since this globe
was created, his frequency as much on earth, as in heaven, describes Paradise.
Next the Chorus showing the reason of his coming to keep his watch in
Paradise after Lucifer's rebellion by command from God, and withal
expressing his desire to see, and know more concerning this excellent new
creature man. The angel Gabriel as by his name signifying a prince of power
tracing paradise with a more free office passes by the station of the chorus
and desired by them relates what he knew of man as the creation of Eve
with their love, and marriage. After this Lucifer appears after his overthrow,
bemoans himself, seeks revenge on man the Chorus prepare resistance at his

first approach at last after discourse of enmity on either side he departs whereat the chorus sings of the battle, and victory in heaven against him, and his accomplices, as before after the first act was sung a hymn of the creation. Here again may appear Lucifer relating, and insulting in what he had done to the destruction of man. Man next and Eve having by this time been seduced by the serpent appears confusedly covered with leaves conscience in a shape accuses him, Justice cites him to the place whither Jehova called for him in the mean while the chorus entertains the stage, and is informed by some angel the manner of his fall here the chorus bewails Adam's fall. Adam then and Eve return accuse one another but especially Adam lays the blame to his wife, is stubborn in his offence Justice appears reasons with him convinces him the chorus admonisheth Adam, and bids him beware by Lucifer's example of impenitence the angel is sent to banish them out of Paradise but before causes to pass before his eyes in shapes a mask of all the evils of this life and world he is humbled relents, despairs. At last appears Mercy comforts him promises the Messiah, then calls in Faith, Hope, and Charity, instructs him he repents gives God the glory, submits to his penalty the chorus briefly concludes. Compare this with the former draft.

The significance of the drafts is that they prepare us for seeing *Paradise Lost* as in certain respects a tragic work. We should even, perhaps, consider it a tragical epic rather than a pure epic. It is not so much that it has too much dialogue for an ordinary epic; though this may be true of Books ii, iii, viii, and ix. It is more that the characters have always the choice of falling into a tragic role–of becoming, as it were, tragic characters. Satan, who quite often soliloquizes, can be thought of as one who has in fact chosen to be an Elizabethan villain-hero. (A line of thought opened up by Helen Gardner in 'Milton and the Tragedies of Damnation', *E & S* i (1948) and developed by Dennis Burden in *The Logical Epic*.) Milton announces at the beginning of Book ix 'I now must change / Those notes to tragic' (5f); and it is in fact the subsequent portion of the poem that approximates to tragedy most closely. Its action very nearly obeys the Unity of Time; for it is only the visions shown by Michael that take us beyond the 24 hours proper to neo-classic tragedy. There are even fully developed *peripeteias* or discoveries, when events reveal to Adam new meanings in the terms both of God's prohibition against eating the forbidden fruit and of his promise about the seed of Eve. These *peripeteias* are broken up into series of partial discoveries (rather like the ones in *Oedipus Tyrannus*), in such a way as to communicate wonderfully a sense of life's unfathomable capacity to keep disclosing new truths and new ironies. According to the prohibition, for example, Adam is to die on 'the day' he eats the forbidden fruit; and right up to the end of the poem new facets of this word go on emerging (see x 49–53n, 773n, 1050n; xii 588–9n).

It might be added that the visions Michael shows to Adam in Book xi are like brief tragedies, some of them with subjects that figure among the 53 Old Testament tragedies projected in the Trinity MS. Not that there is any question of *Paradise Lost* being tragedy imperfectly adapted for epic. But neither will it quite do to speak of tragedy as one of a number of similar formal ingredients–though it is true that epic can embrace many different modes. (This is a fruitful line of thought about *Paradise Lost* in particular, which has pastoral, lyrical, philosophical, historical, and devotional, as well as tragical, passages.) For it is possible to regard the loss of Paradise as the tragedy *par excellence*, the tragedy underlying all tragedies; so that the tragic mode must have a special place among those used. Certainly it is far from being confined to the last books. The whole poem can be seen as tragic, because of our knowledge of the fatal conclusion. Milton so often utilizes this knowledge to produce effects of dramatic irony that the latter becomes almost a permanent property of the style of *Paradise Lost*. At the same time, the tragedy is not tragedy *simpliciter*. And this fact, that the tragic possi-bilities can be seen, if one so wills it, as outweighed by epic actuality–by the creativity and triumph of Messiah, by the prophecies of Paradise regained– is perhaps the first critical observation to be made about the poem. As epic, it presents a world; but a world that can be viewed either as tragic or (if we can reach Adam's instructed vision) as heroic. Thus Milton's decision to change one form for another may have been in more ways than one an act of faith.

About the order in which the different parts of *Paradise Lost* were com-posed, we know nothing. A. H. Gilbert's *On the Composition of 'Paradise Lost'* (Chapel Hill 1947) sets out an elaborate theory of six stages of compo-sition (iv 8–31, e.g., belongs to the first, ii 1–520 to the last), and at least merits praise for its rejection of the common false assumption that compo-sition has to be *seriatim*. But the theory is based on a long list of internal dis-crepancies, only two of which are established at all persuasively (see iv 712n and ix 163–7n). Nevertheless some have hoped to use it against the position that Milton's power declined during his work on the poem; or even against A. J. A. Waldock's more plausible view that in the later books Milton tries to correct the early blunder of making Satan too magnificent. If Gilbert's speculation can help anyone to see the falsity of these others, it may have served some purpose. It is naive, however, to suppose (as Gilbert does, no less than Waldock) that the author of such a poem as *Paradise Lost* can have failed to revise his work carefully. The question of the order of composition needs fresh consideration; but in the present state of our ignorance we can only regard the poem as composed *in toto* at one moment of time, at least in the only sense that matters critically. This moment was when Milton de-cided to stop revising and to leave the poem as it is. He became responsible at that moment for the whole text we know: if it has inconsistencies, he allowed them, then, to remain.

Of the time and manner of composition we know a little. Milton seems to have contemplated writing *some* epic from the beginning of his adult life; though at one stage the subject envisaged was the matter of Britain (see *Vacation Exercise*; *Mans*; *Dam*; and *Reason of Church-Govern-ment* ii Pref., Yale i 812ff). There are many speculations as to why Milton chose a scriptural theme, but no firm knowledge. It is fairly certain that he took some years over the poem we have; that he mostly composed during the winter, usually in the night or early morning; that he sometimes lay awake unable to write a verse, and at other times was inspired easily 'with a certain *impetus* and *oestro* [frenzy, *furor poeticus*]'; that he dictated in the first part of the day to whatever amanuensis happened to be available; that after dictating perhaps as much as 40 lines he would 'reduce them to half the Number'; and that he had his nephew Edward Phillips in from time to time to correct the orthography and pointing of the last part written, 'a Parcel of Ten, Twenty, or Thirty Verses at a Time' (see *PL* iii 22ff, vii 25ff, and ix 21ff; Aubrey, Edward Phillips, and Richardson in Darbishire 13, 73 and 291). According to Edward Phillips and Aubrey, the poem was written in four or five years, about 1658–63; Thomas Elwood says he saw it complete in 1665.

Printing history

Milton's contract with the printer Samuel Simmons is dated 27 April 67; and *Paradise Lost* was licensed (after some difficulty, according to John Toland) on 20 August of the same year. A MS of the first book (*MS*) has survived, which printers' marks show to be the one actually used in setting up the first edition. It is a final fair copy written by an amanuensis with a somewhat old-fashioned taste in orthography, but corrections in other hands indicate that its punctuation and spelling may have been revised under Milton's directions. The MS is now in the Pierpont Morgan Library, New York. There is a careful edition of it, with a facsimile, by Helen Darbishire (Oxford 1931). An examination of the MS makes one aware of the difficulties under which Milton worked because of his blindness. It reveals a concern about textual accuracy in *minutiae*, but also an inevitable and tantalizing failure to achieve the uniformity that might have made the special orthographic rules invaluable to an interpretative critic. The MS has disappointingly little textual interest, however: the readings peculiar to it are insignificant. Only in its punctuation (which is very light indeed) does it differ much from the first printed edition.

There were two editions of *Paradise Lost* in Milton's lifetime, both printed by Simmons. The first edition, a quarto (*Ed I*), appeared in 1667, 1668, and 1669, in six issues marked by six different title-pages. The title itself reads, with insignificant variants, *Paradise Lost. A poem in ten books*. From the fourth issue onwards the text is accompanied by preliminaries: 'The Printer to the Reader'; the 'Argument' (which stood all together, not distributed through the books); Milton's note on 'The Verse'; and the 'Errata'. In spite of his blindness Milton seems to have supervised the printing of *Ed I* very carefully–so carefully, indeed, that its authority is in general greater than that of *MS*. Corrections were made, as *Ed I* went through the press, for which he himself, or his agent, may have been responsible: these are studied in H. F. Fletcher's facsimile edition, and in Darbishire[2] i 314–22.

The second, octavo edition (*Ed II*) appeared in 1674, under the title

Paradise Lost. A poem in twelve books. To the preliminaries are added S[am-uel] B[arrow]'s Latin verses 'In Paradisum Amissam summi poetae Jo-hannis Miltoni' and A[ndrew] M[arvell]'s verses 'On Paradise Lost'; while the Argument is now distributed through the books, and the Errata assimi-lated (or forgotten). The poem itself is redivided into twelve books, by a simple dichotomy of *Ed I* vii and x (which become *Ed II* vii, viii and xi, xii). Minor additions or alterations of up to five lines are also made, at i 504–5, v 636–9, viii 1–4, xi 485–7, 551–2, and xii 1–5. Naturally enough, *Ed II* underwent less correction at the press than *Ed I.* In some cases it follows uncorrected sheets of the latter; and it will occasionally introduce new errors of its own. Nevertheless, on the whole *Ed II* represents an improve-ment. We may agree with B. A. Wright that its authority is usually to be preferred to that of *Ed I.*

After a slow start, *Ed I* went quickly, selling 1300 copies–a large sale for the period, even if the author only received £10. After Milton's death there were three unimportant editions (1678, 1688, 1691), then a sixth with full-scale commentary by Patrick Hume (1695). Of many subsequent editions the most notable have been Richard Bentley's, an eccentric emen-dation-list that has been valued for the rebuttals it provoked (1732); Thomas Newton's fine edition incorporating many of Pearce's strong replies to Bentley (1749); J. H. Todd's variorum edition (1809); and A. W. Verity's solid commentary (revised edn 1910). More recently, M. Y. Hughes's is the only considerable annotated edition of the whole poem (New York 1957); though the first two books have been well edited by B. Rajan (1964). Of textual interest are H. C. Beeching's decent text (1900); the Columbia University edition, a reprint of *Ed II* (New York 1931); H. F. Fletcher's photographic facsimile edition of both *Ed I* and *Ed II*, with very elaborate apparatus (Urbana, Ill. 1943–8); Helen Darbishire's synthetic normalized text (Oxford 1952), as well as her reprint of *Ed II* (1961; not to be confused with her 1958 Oxford Standard Authors edition); and B. A. Wright's edition, also with normalized spelling and punctuation (1956). The com-mentaries from Hume to Todd are shrewdly studied in Ants Oras, *Milton's Editors and Commentators* (Tartu [Yuriev] 1930).

Text

Although the primary purpose of this edition is not textual, the text is in large part freshly prepared. The printed copies followed–apart from sup-plementation in the case of the corrected sheets of *Ed I*–were BM C 14 a 9 (*Ed I*) and BM 1076 f 20 (*Ed II*). Other copies collated, however, were all within the range of copies already covered by Miss Darbishire. Since ortho-graphic accidentals were to be modernized, and since the texts of *Ed I* and *Ed II* differ very seldom in other respects, the choice of copy-text scarcely mattered. For the sake of consistency and for the evidential value the readings of *Ed II* have been printed throughout, except where they are palpably in error. Unless it is otherwise stated, *Ed I* and *Ed II* agree in punc-tuation and in all features of their spelling that seem of any interest. Punctuation variants and significant spelling variants are recorded in the notes. The treatment of *MS* readings is similar; except that in this case some insignificant punctuation variants are omitted (the *MS* punctuation is generally lighter overall than that of the printed editions). The present text will be found to differ very little from the received text; but see, e.g., iii 592*n*, vii 588–90*n*, viii 332*n*, ix 394*n*, 944*n*, and x 989–90*n*.

Punctuation

Punctuation is unusually important in Milton's *Paradise Lost*. For the long verse paragraphs to have their full effect must be sustained grammatically and rhythmically beyond the limits of the ordinary syntactic breath, with the sense drawn out in such a way as to require light punctuation. On the other hand Milton's temperament, as well as the particular character of his subject, lead him to make many nice logical discriminations; which calls for somewhat closer, 'slower', pointing. Finally there are countless ambiguities in which more than one chain of discourse has to be left so far as possible open; and this needs very judiciously chosen points or none at all. Reconciling these demands would have been impossible if the pointing rules of the time had not given Milton a certain room for manoeuvre.

In the seventeenth century punctuation was often rhetorical: i.e. it was apt to reflect the physical pauses and stresses of speech directly and simply, rather than to signpost the sentence structure logically or grammatically. B. A. Wright even goes so far as to say that the punctuation of *Paradise Lost* 'is strictly rhetorical inasmuch as it always conforms to the prosody'. But in a good poet such as Milton, prosody is the handmaid of rhetoric, not rhetoric of prosody. Besides, Milton and his intermediaries seem to have paid unusually close attention to the grammatical operation of pointing. The main differences from modern punctuation are as follows:

1. While the full stop is sometimes used like ours (though more seldom), it is also used before comparisons (i 768) and before direct speech (i 272).
2. The colon can be much heavier than ours; so that we often find it where we would have put a full stop. But it also has a great variety of uses, of different rhetorical weights: namely to mark logical divisions, and to introduce alternatives, reasons, concessions, comparisons, defining clauses, afterthoughts, interruptions, and direct speech.
3. The lighter semicolon often separates stages in a narrative sequence or items in a catalogue (ii 959, 961, 963, 965).
4. Exclamation and question marks occasionally seem to us transposed (i 183).
5. The comma is like ours, but may be omitted before a defining relative clause, before a vocative (v 388), before and after an appositional phrase (iv 270), and at one end of a qualifying or parenthetic phrase (ix 1037–9).

The punctuation of *Paradise Lost* will not give much trouble if a fast enough reading pace is kept up to allow the movement of thought on the scale of the paragraph to assert itself and if allowance is made for rhetorical and economical use of the points. Some difficulties will be experienced, however, particularly with the colon and semicolon, which have no exact modern equivalents. It may be some consolation, therefore, to glance at the terrible effect that modernization would have had, if the alternative course had been adopted. It goes without saying that heavy modern pointing must impede the flow of the blank verse. But that is the least of it. Even Verity, who modernizes far more leniently and sporadically than Masson, will render a passage such as

> a flame,
> Which oft, they say, some evil spirit attends
> Hovering and blazing with delusive light . . .
>   (ix 637–9)

like this:

> a flame
> (Which oft, they say, some evil spirit attends),
> Hovering and blazing with delusive light. . . .

The old punctuation of these lines allows us to think of the *spirit* hovering and deluding; and this ambiguity may well have been intentional on Milton's part, in view of the superstition that held the *ignis fatuus* to be a spirit. But with modern punctuation the editor opts for a single chain of discourse, allowing other possibilities to be bitten off by a parenthesis whose jaw closes either after *attends* (with only the *flame* hovering) or after *light* (with only the *spirit* hovering). And such passages abound: there is another within a few lines, at ix 650.

Sources and Models

The principal source of *Paradise Lost* is the Bible, with which it has a closer and more intimate relation than with any other work, ancient or modern. Naturally the scriptural allusions in many individual passages have long been editorial stock. But in the present edition it has been possible to add a surprising number of new scriptural parallels, echoes and allusions; in many cases thanks to James H. Sims's *The Bible in Milton's Epics* (Gainesville, Fla. 1962). It is beginning to be understood that the Bible for Milton meant the Bible glossed by commentators. For this reason Milton's modern reader would do well to consult Arnold Williams's *The Common Expositor* (Chapel Hill, N.C. 1948), which gives some indication of the interest and relevance of this neglected body of writing. In preparing the notes that follow, extensive use was made of Willet's *Hexaplus* on *Genesis*, an unoriginal commentary summarising a fairly broad spectrum of contemporary and earlier opinion. An important set of sources intersecting with the last are the Patristic. Sister M. I. Corcoran's *Milton's Paradise with Reference to the Hexaemeral Background* opened this territory as early as 1945, but it shows little sign of becoming a built-up area. Rabbinical sources, on the other hand, have probably been over-exploited, as a result of H. F. Fletcher's *Milton's Rabbinical Readings* (Urbana, Ill. 1930). The same author's series of volumes on *The Intellectual*

Development of John Milton (Urbana, Ill. 1956–) promises to be more balanced, and to contain a great deal of useful information on sources and potential sources; but so far it is not very accurate. Milton's ideas about angels are studied at length in Robert H. West's *Milton and the Angels*, (Athens, Ga. 1955); the sources are found to be numerous and the angelology unsystematic. It is to be suspected that Milton's angels will come still more sharply into focus, however, when they are looked at through the spectacles of the sacred iconographer. The iconographical sources of *Paradise Lost* have not been studied.

Not neglected, but requiring further study, are Milton's classical models— particularly the Homeric epics and Virgil's *Aeneid*. Such articles as Condee's have shown that the study of these models can mean much more than cataloguing verbal and narrative echoes. Milton's allusions to earlier epics are so consistent as to constitute a distinct strand of meaning in the poem: even, sometimes, a kind of critical accompaniment. What still remains to be investigated is the extent to which *Paradise Lost* allegorizes the inherited epic images, in the Neoplatonic manner of a Landino or a Spenser–that is, the extent to which the poem is tertiary rather than secondary epic.

The mention of Spenser gives occasion to remark that *The Faerie Queene* (contrary, perhaps, to expectation) is the most important, even if not the most obvious, vernacular model of *Paradise Lost*. Naturally Milton had studied earlier literary treatments of the Fall, such as the dramas of Grotius (*Adamus exul*, 1601) and Andreini (*L'Adamo*, 1613); and, in the Ninth Book of *Paradise Lost*, at least, they must be considered as main sources and perhaps even as models, in a certain sense. They may be conveniently studied in Watson Kirkconnell's splendid collection of analogues, *The Celestial Cycle* (Toronto 1952). But, from a critical point of view, the study proves on the whole unrewarding. Milton had the taste not to allude to these works in quite the same way that he alluded to Homer and Virgil. The situation is similar with respect to the hexaemeral parts of the poem, with Tasso's *Sette Giornate del Mondo Creato* (1607) as the model with literary worth. But here for once one must allow that Milton's taste erred. The quality of Du Bartas's *Sepmaines*, even in Sylvester's translation, does not seem to us to justify the extensiveness of Milton's allusions to it. Or was it that even in his fit audience there were limitations of taste and learning, within which he had to work?

Language and style

We are fortunate in now having a statistical analysis of Milton's language: R. D. Emma's *Milton's Grammar* (The Hague 1964). Though Emma's samples are too small to support those of his conclusions which concern rare phenomena, many of his results are convincing and of interest to the critic. We learn that Milton was outstandingly modern in his diction and even in his accidence (e.g., the avoidance of obsolescent verb terminals). And it seems that the diction of *Paradise Lost* is characterised by a very high incidence of words qualifying substantives; in spite of the fact that the use of adjectives is restrained compared with, say, Spenser's (Emma 26, 70). There is also a high incidence of conjunctions – nearly double their frequency in T. S. Eliot's poetry (Emma 87n, 129f). Both these features correlate with Milton's tendency in *Paradise Lost* to develop fine discriminations, and to introduce qualifications in an oblique or indirect way. The frequency of conjunctions of a coordinating kind has also of course to be seen in relation to the needs of Milton's sentence structure, which is markedly paratactic. But the complicated paratactic structure seems itself to result from a compromise between Milton's desire on the one hand to achieve fluent continuity and energy of movement, on the other to interpose continual corrections and qualifications.

It is to be hoped that this work of Emma's may be the first of a series of more objective and descriptive studies of Milton's style. For a long time, now, the emphasis has been dogmatic and polemical. F. R. Leavis began the present trend, with an essay in *Scrutiny* in 1933, in which he spoke of Milton's verse as monotonously ritualistic, 'not doing as much as its impressive pomp and volume seem to be asserting'; of his grand style as compelling an attitude 'incompatible with sharp, concrete realization'. Three years later T. S. Eliot also attacked Milton, in *Essays and Studies*; though his attack (as he explained in his Henriette Hertz Lecture to the British Academy in 1947) was somehow directed against the influence of Milton's verse without being directed against the verse itself. It is not necessary to accept all of Herbert Howarth's interesting suggestions about private motives for attacking Milton ('Eliot and Milton: the American Aspect', *UTQ* xxx (1961)), but we can hardly help feeling that Eliot's tactical warfare against the Georgians got disastrously out of hand. His influence on subsequent Milton criticism has been bad. And his criticism was bad too: like Leavis's it was dogma, built on unexamined premises and unsupported by demonstration. There have since been several sympathetic accounts of Milton's style; notably in C. S. Lewis, *A Preface to Paradise Lost* (1942), in Arnold Stein, *Answerable Style* (Minneapolis, Minn. 1953), and in Isabel G. MacCaffrey, *Paradise Lost as 'Myth'* (Cambridge, Mass. 1959). What was left of the attack has been routed – surely with finality – by Christopher Ricks in *Milton's Grand Style* (Oxford 1963), which shows how superlatively good Milton's style is, even judged by Leavis's criteria.

Perhaps the most notorious feature of the style of *Paradise Lost* has been its Latinity. An early comment was Jonathan Richardson's: '*Milton's* Language is English, but 'tis *Milton's* English; 'tis Latin, 'tis Greek English; not only the Words, the Phraseology, the Transpositions, but the Ancient Idiom is seen in All he Writes, So that a Learned Foreigner will think *Milton* the Easiest to be Understood of All the English Writers' (Darbishire 313). He adds a comparison of the language of *Paradise Lost* with that of New Testament Greek (colloquial, but affected by 'Oriental Dialects') and with that of Shakespeare. Even this view is a far cry from the contrast between Milton's and Shakespeare's use of English in the essay by Leavis, or from Eliot's emphasis on 'the remoteness of Milton's verse from ordinary speech'.

Now the sentence structure of *Paradise Lost* has nothing overtly neo-classical about it. It is a native English coordinate structure, loose rather than periodic, paratactic rather than syntactic. The verse paragraphs do not keep us waiting, perplexed, for the sense, or force us to traverse a single long syntactic line of subordinated parts. Instead the sense is 'diffused throughout a larger block of words' than is common (Prince 122). Usually there is a series of very temporary stopping-places, from which the thought darts off in unforeseen directions. And it is characteristic that any new phrase may introduce a modification, or show that a syntactic schema earlier applied was wrong or partial. Thus 'Of man's first disobedience, and the fruit [of that disobedience]' passes to 'Of man's first disobedience, and the fruit / Of that forbidden tree . . .' This unexpectedly sustained syntactic breath not only has continuity and force, but also communicates a strong effect of passion, or of thought in process. It is anything but an ordinary sentence structure; but it is not extraordinary in a manner foreign to the genius of English. In a more essential way, of course, the built order and flowing mass of the verse paragraphs are profoundly classical. Classicism in that sense, however, is only a virtue.

If the sentence structure is native, there are nevertheless many individual clauses or phrases that could be described as having a Latin or Greek construction; though information on this point is surprisingly scanty. Lewis (45f) thought Milton's Latin constructions justified by the freedom of word order they secure. But this point ought perhaps to be made another way round. At their best the arrangements of words in *Paradise Lost* have their own poetic reasons. If (subsequently, as it were) they can be made to correspond to Latin constructions, so much the better. Milton naturally preferred his poetic dislocations of conventional English syntax to have the additional value of corresponding to ancient usage. Thus the common omission of the article, and the occasional use of *after* with a past participle (e.g. iii 552 'after heaven seen') produce effects that are first concise, spare and pungent; then Latinate. Latinate constructions, we notice, are commonest in the transitions, where they give a sense of command and artistic detachment (e.g. x 229).

Perhaps the word order of *Paradise Lost* has lent as much support as anything to the charge of unidiomatic remoteness; for about one quarter of its clauses are inverted. We are now coming to understand, however, that the word order of Milton's time was very much freer than that permissible with us (see Emma 140ff). The best recent work on Milton's diction is probably F. T. Prince's *The Italian Element in Milton's Verse* (Oxford 1954), which isolates many of the features we consider most characteristic of *Paradise Lost*, and assigns them their context in contemporary literary practice. (Professor Prince is especially interesting on the disposition of epithets–e.g. the device adjective+noun+*and*+adjective, as in 'sad task and hard' v 564.) But even this fine book requires to be rewritten on a statistical basis, so as to make clear which features of Milton's word order were non-standard. What statistical information there is about Milton's word order is of doubtful value, partly because of the uncertainty with which parameters have been set and partly because of the inadequacy of samples. Emma, e.g., working with a sample of only 140 lines of *Paradise Lost* (and about three times as much of the other poetry) finds the Subject–Object–Verb inversion ('She . . . Her unadorned golden tresses wore', iv 304f) to be the commonest; whereas if one works with a sample of about 1400 lines of *Paradise Lost* it turns out to be comparatively rare. Similarly the Object–Subject–Verb inversion ('the companions of his fall . . . He soon discerns', i 76–8) is more frequent than Emma's figures imply; and the Verb–Subject inversion ('So spake the apostate angel', i 125) much more frequent. Verb–Subject 'inversion', however, can hardly be described as alien to the genius of the language. Not only was it a common alternative in seventeenth-century English, but it was the regular order at an earlier stage. (See R. Quirk and C. L. Wrenn, *An Old English Grammar* (1957) 94; Otto Jespersen, *A Modern English Grammar*, vol. vii (1961) pp. 59, 78f; and–with many examples–E. Mätzner, *Englische Grammatik* (Berlin 1885) pp. 587ff, 627.) For poetic purposes Milton followed one indigenous alternative to an extent that was unusual: that is all we are entitled to say. And it is the same with other forms of inversion. We should never assume them to be simply Italianate or Latinate, until seventeenth-century English colloquial and literary usage has been examined with some care statistically.

In much the same way, the Latinity of Milton's choice of diction has generally been assumed, without recourse to a good English dictionary. An honourable exception is Lalia Phipps Boone, who arrives at the conclusion that Milton's Latinity has been exaggerated, in 'The Language of Book VI, *PL*' in *S.A.M.L.A. Studies in Milton*, ed. J. Max Patrick (Gainesville, Fla. 1953). On closer inspection it turns out that the general assumption is in need of many qualifications. Often what has been taken for imitation of Latin or Greek is really only poetic departure from ordinary usage; often, too, even when the ancient idiom is really present it contributes no more than an Empsonian ambiguity. Hence innumerable ghost Latinisms, which were raised by early editors and superstitiously believed in by their successors.

There is a spectrum of possible Latinity of diction in which four bands may be distinguished:

1. The Latin usage is the primary sense or chain of discourse; and is completely new in English. Milton very seldom innovates so extremely, but *omnific* (vii 217) and *recline* (iv 333, 'they sat recline') are probably instances of this kind of Latinizing coinage.
2. The Latin usage is the primary sense; and occurs in English only or mostly in poetic contexts: i.e. the familiar Augustan 'gradus diction' (viii 263, 'liquid lapse of murmuring streams', where *liquid*,= 'flowing', is poetic diction). *Paradise Lost* has few Latinisms of this kind.
3. The Latin usage is a secondary sense only. The primary sense is an ordinary English usage, but a Latin usage is present in addition, as an allusion or ambiguity (e.g. vii 264f, 'The firmament, expanse of liquid . . . air', which

may well allude to Latin *expansum*, supposed a better translation than *firmamentum* of the Hebrew word in *Gen.* i 6). There are many 'Latinisms' of this type; but they could never be said to weaken the native sinews of anyone's style. Such effects enrich and deepen.

4. The primary sense is an ordinary English usage, occurring in prose contexts, which happens also to be a Latin usage. This, if it were to be considered Latinism at all, would be Latinism at its faintest and least objectionable. Examples of this type naturally occur throughout *Paradise Lost* in great numbers.

By any reasonable criterion the term Latinism should only be applied to forms recognizable in Milton's time as in some way non-standard usage – i.e. Types 1-2, or at most Types 1-3. It follows that most of the supposed Latinisms in *Paradise Lost* are really nothing of the sort. Thus x 155-6, 'to bear rule, which was thy part / And person', which was hailed by Newton as 'a pure Latinism', had been perfectly good English back in Milton's time (*OED* gives six instances in non-technical prose, earlier than 1667, of *person*='role'). And it is the same with vii 93, *absolved*='completed', which is treated as a Latinism even by Ricks (six earlier instances in prose). There are, of course, difficult borderline cases. But this does not excuse us from doing what we can to distinguish the extremes. In some respects we are actually better equipped than Richardson and Dr Johnson to estimate the degree of Latinity of Milton's diction.

If therefore a usage occurs in English, in non-technical non-fiction prose contexts earlier than *Paradise Lost*, it may ordinarily be assumed not to be a Latinism. In such cases only the meaning has been given in the notes, with perhaps an indication of the relevant section in *OED*, where citations of earlier instances will be found. A simple gloss of this type is to be taken to imply that the word has more or less its standard seventeenth-century English sense. Milton would of course know the etymology of many of the words in *Paradise Lost* (though not as many as Verity). But unless he used them in such a way as to draw attention to and exploit the derivation, it is hard to see how that knowledge concerns us. Naturally the interplay between words of Romance and of Anglo-Saxon origin is an important feature of Milton's style, as of most English styles. But that is a matter for the critic, not the editor. In consequence, many 'Latinisms' have been ignored in the notes to the present edition, and the diction of the poem has been allowed to resume its original strongly colloquial character. True, it is only colloquial in a comparative sense; for much of it is in high style rhetorically. But it remains, nevertheless, the most colloquial secondary epic ever written – a fact that ignorant emphasis on its Latinity has done much to obscure.

If the Latinisms in *Paradise Lost* have been overestimated, it is quite the reverse with the ambiguities and ironies. There are far more instances of such effects than any critic has led us to expect. They may almost be said, indeed, to form the general texture of the style. The effects range from what I shall call double syntax, through puns, ironies and *doubles entendres*, to outright radical ambiguities challenging a choice of attitude on the part of the reader. Double syntax occurs when three word groups *a, b, c* are connected in such a manner that *ab* forms one chain of discourse and *bc* another (to which *a* may or may not belong), e.g. in

> That shepherd, who first taught the chosen seed,
> In the beginning how the heavens and earth
> Rose out of chaos   (i 8–10)

In the beginning seems linked with *first taught*, until we find a better connection with *rose*. (Notice how the effect is assisted by the inversion in l. 9, which is as far as possible from existing for its own sake.) Such double syntax has a large role in the drawing out of the sense through the poem's verse paragraphs. The reader is constantly led on by the fluid movement of phrases or even clauses that relate first retrospectively and then prospectively. But this grammatical illusionism is not so emphatic as to constitute full ambiguity. In fact, if its mechanism is noticed at all, the alternatives will usually be dismissed as trivial.

At the other extreme are radical ambiguities which present real alternatives of value. These constitute one of the most characteristic features of Milton's style, giving it much of its surprising sharpness and subtlety. Yet they have often been regarded as mere troublesome cruxes. Thus Miss Darbishire is so annoyed with iv 410, where Adam 'Turned him all ear to hear new utterance flow'–*him* being either Adam or Satan–that she adds a pair of commas in her normalized text, 'to make the sense clear'. But the way in which Adam and Satan share the pronoun *him* can seem positively effective, if the passage is related to others in which Satan takes Adam's place (see e.g. v 40f and *n*). A more typical ambiguity, perhaps, is Satan's soliloquizing address to Adam and Eve: 'League with you I seek, / And mutual amity so strait . . .' (iv 375f). If we are of the devil's gullible party, we shall take *strait* to mean only 'intimate' (*OED* 14); for the pun with *straight* (= 'honest') is almost excluded by the appositional phrase *so close* and by the consequence that follows. But if we have our wits about us we recall that *strait* could also mean 'involving privation'. Similarly, at iii 397f the choice of syntactical connections in

> Back from pursuit thy powers with loud acclaim
> Thee only extolled, Son of thy Father's might,

is related to the choice between Satan's and Raphael's accounts of the expulsion of the rebel angels. In a high proportion of instances, the ambiguities in *Paradise Lost* call for discrimination of this kind on the reader's part.

If discrimination is challenged by the ambiguities, it is almost forced on us by the similes. After all, Milton had lived through a vogue for difficult and witty comparisons; so that we may expect him to engage our attention especially strenuously in this area. At one level, of course, the similes are easy and pleasant: so much so that to earlier generations of critics they were oases where a reader could refresh himself, as one who in his journey bates.

More recently the similes have been studied by James Whaler, in *PMLA* xlvi
(1931); by William Empson, in *Some Versions of Pastoral* (1935); by Laurence
Lerner, in *EC* iv (1954); and by Christopher Ricks, in *Milton's Grand Style*
(Oxford 1963). They have disclosed many beauties, but also many difficul-
ties. The most serious problem is that the comparisons sometimes seem cu-
riously thin, with only slender grounds of resemblance between tenor and
vehicle. Consequently the doctrine has been developed that Milton often
uses similes 'with a clear sense of the fact that they don't fit exactly' (Ricks
127). Now it is certainly true sometimes that an element of disparity is
present–particularly in the similes relating to Satan, whom we may agree
with Ricks in regarding as a hideous parody of the good (e.g. i 338–44,
discussed Ricks 128f). But it is much more often the case that the comparison
is positive but difficult. We may perhaps be invited to discriminate between
right and wrong ways of applying the simile, or to catch an allusion and read
with the eyes of faith. The typical case is iii 510–25, where Satan, looking
up at the entrance to heaven, is compared at some length with Jacob:

> The stairs were such as whereon Jacob saw
> Angels ascending and descending, bands
> Of guardians bright, when he from Esau fled
> To Padan-Aram in the field of Luz,
> Dreaming by night under the open sky,
> And waking cried, *This is the gate of heaven.*

If the only resemblance between Jacob and Satan were that each saw steps
leading to heaven's gate it might be right to conclude that the point of the
simile lay in the disparity betwen them. But we are meant to see a deeper
similarity of situation. Satan, like Jacob, is escaping from retribution and
has come to a critical turning-point. He will go on, after his vision of the
cosmos, to harden his heart; whereas Jacob was awed and repentant and
'vowed a vow' (*Gen.* xxviii 20f). For the moment, however, the resem-
blance holds.

It will have been noticed that in the last example an important element
on the vehicle side of the comparison–the moral significance of the vision
to Jacob–is present only by implication. This type of simile, in which the
vehicle is partially suppressed or compressed into allusive form, is common
in *Paradise Lost*: a fairly extreme instance is the group of three similes at
ix 439–43. The notes that follow achieve some increase in the number of
similes whose resonant or allusive character has been recognized. And it is
likely that the number will be increased still further as our understanding of
the structure of poetic analogy grows. For one of the difficulties with Mil-
ton's similes lies in the astonishing complexity and variety of their logical
forms. There are comparisons within comparisons; comparisons cast in
negative form; comparisons with double or triple vehicles (e.g. ix 670–6);
and even a few comparisons that appear to have double tenors (e.g. x 289–
93).

What might be called ideological awareness is in evidence not only in the

first part of Book vi, where we get a remarkably high concentration of such figures as puns, which were considered low and easily liable to excess. Paradoxically, the frequent 'indecorum' of this passage is appropriate to the subject, the 'wild work' of the angelic war: see vi 498n, 578–94n, 566n, 698–9n. Thus, from a rhetorical point of view, the description of the devils' cannon at vi 572–84 is viciously inflated (bomphiologia); while immediately afterwards the diction is at the other extreme of indecorum, when the firing is described in such low terms as *belched*, *embowelled*, *entrails*, *disgorging*, *glut*. A very different example is Eve's lyrical expression of her love at iv 639–56. The major scheme of these verses, a kind of large-scale *epanalepsis* or *enumeratio*, is itself a mimetic repetition rendering Eve's responsiveness to Adam. From its intricate magic circle all schemes are excluded but those of completeness and varied reflection; though at the semantic level this expansive repose is made to rest on Eve's sustained rejection of the world of separation from Adam. The smooth returning flow of *epanalepsis* and *epanodos*, the copiousness of *merismus* within *merismus*, and the exquisite balance of similarity against variety in the poignant negative repetition, put the passage among the most satisfying, from a formal point of view, ever composed in this mode.

On occasion Milton could carry the patterning of his language to astonishing lengths. We find it, for example, even in enumerative passages. He seldom *just* gives a catalogue of names or a list of like items: usually he is simultaneously at work ordering and informing the arrangement with silent meaning. Thus by a neat irony the very catalogue of place-names that T. S. Eliot dismissed as 'a solemn game' has a pattern that shows Milton's creative intellect at its most energetic, shaping almost pure form into a body of thought:

> Of Cambalu, seat of Cathaian khan
> And Samarchand by Oxus, Temir's throne,
> To Paquin of Sinaean kings, and thence
> To Agra and Lahor of great mogul
> Down to the golden Chersonese, or where
> The Persian in Ecbatan sat, or since
> In Hispahan, or where the Russian czar
> In Mosco, or the sultan in Bizance,
> Turchestan-born. . . .   (xi 388–96)

The Asian names sound out their exotic grandeur with a power, a magic, that no sensible person will despise (for its particularity lies close to the heart of poetry). But the names do something else besides. By their disposition they tacitly confer upon one of their members, golden Chersonese (Ophir), the sovereignty that accords with its central position. The same pattern is repeated in the vista of African principalities, with 'Sofala thought Ophir' in the central position. Ophir rules, because the gold of Ophir is the gold of Christ's sovereignty (*Is.* xiii 12: 'I will make a man more precious than fine gold; even a man than the golden wedge of Ophir'). And about this centre, various symmetrical patterns are formed (see xi 388–95n, 396–407n). This may seem to some a strange, even an alien, poetic form; but it is not one that much suggests vague aestheticism.

Prosody

The standard line in *Paradise Lost* has ten syllables, with stresses on those of even number: 'United thoughts and counsels, equal hope' (i 88). Naturally such lines are not in an overwhelming majority; but departures from the norm are subject to certain restrictions. Most scholars agree that the verse is syllabic, not accentual; which is to say that while the number of heavy speech accents a line contains is variable, the number of theoretical syllables is not. (In accentual verse, on the contrary, there is a fixed complement of accents, but the number of unaccented syllables may vary widely.) It is probable, though not certain, that a distinction has to be made, in the verse of *Paradise Lost*, between accent and stress. The line 'Stirred up with envy and revenge, deceived' (i 35) has only four heavy accents; while 'Fallen cherub, to be weak is miserable' (i 157) has only three. But *and, to*, and *-able*, though they bear little accent, seem either to have had actual quantitative length, or to have been regarded as bearing 'theoretical' stress. Thus the line always has five *stresses*, but may have fewer than five *accents*.

As for the number of syllables, it is very often greater than ten. But it has to be reducible to a theoretical ten by one or other of the customary procedures that had been imported into English prosody from Italian. By far the most usual of these are elision, synaloepha, and contraction. In the line 'Till, as a signal given, the uplifted spear' (i 347) *given* is contracted to a monosyllable, while *the uplifted* is run together by synaloepha to give *th'uplifted*; so that the syllables theoretically number ten. Synaloepha may or may not involve the complete loss of one of the vowels concerned; in the former case it is often called elision. It can occur within a word ('Of man's first disobed*ie*nce'); also when the vowels are separated by *h*. One exception to the theoretical limit of ten syllables should be mentioned: namely the occasional excess of a final extrametrical syllable. Milton seems to have regarded this variation as a definite licence; and Ernest Sprott plausibly suggests that the licence is introduced mimetically. Thus it is most frequent at the end of Book ix, where Adam is 'estranged in look and altered style' (ix 1132; see Sprott 58f).

A great many other 'rules' governing Milton's prosodic freedom have from time to time been formulated. But they are all either illusory, or merely statistical and not invariable, or trivial, or irrelevant to literary criticism. Who but a prosodist cares how often Milton allowed himself an inverted *n*th foot? Even the famous rule about the fourth syllable always being stressed is probably not a rule at all. As Sprott (102) suggests, the statistical predominance of stressed fourth syllables may only be a consequence of the need to compensate for the inversion in the opening foot of which Milton was so fond.

Robert Bridges's *Milton's Prosody* (revised edn, Oxford 1921) is still worth reading for incidental felicities, but has been replaced by S. E. Sprott's more systematic and sensitive *Milton's Art of Prosody* (Oxford 1953). Both are, up to a point, clear and convincing. But both shy away from the topic of quantity–indeed, from the whole question of what (if anything) decided heavy stress on unaccented syllables. Yet the poetic of, e.g., Alexander Gill (Milton's old headmaster at St Paul's) goes into this subject in some detail. Gill discusses how syllable length is affected by vowel length, internal accent and position; also how these considerations are overriden by rhetorical accent, our grammatical accent (*Logonomia anglica* (revised edn, 1621) 132ff). Thus, in the opening line of *Paradise Lost*, if Milton were following Gill's system (or a system like it), in which prefixes such as *dis*– had to be short whenever position allowed, we would get the scansion: 'Of mán's fírst disobédience, ánd the frúit'– always supposing that the grammatical accents didn't decide the matter otherwise. The inverted second foot here is of some interest; for strong grammatical accent on *first* is in fact by no means inevitable. Obviously this is a matter that calls for early enquiry. Until more is known about the rules governing syllable length, indeed, it is probably vain to bother with more difficult and delicate problems of scansion.

Not that we need be shut out from all appreciation of the prosodic effects in *Paradise Lost*. Fortunately in the majority of lines the grammatical accent–*pace* Albert Cook in *UTQ* xxix (1960)–is strong and dominant. And in some others where this is not the case, the effect Milton intends is nevertheless clear enough: e.g. in 'O'er bog or steep, through straight, rough, dense, or rare,' (ii 948) most readers will agree that the stress and accent gradients from *rough* to *dense* and from, say, *or* to *steep* are different; and that this difference somehow mimes the roughness of the rough patch. Commenting on this line Sprott for once grasps the nettle of quantity, and says the effect is due to the length of *rough* 'because of the labial spirant'. Well, perhaps. But it seems to me that we have to know much more about what Milton meant by 'fit quantity of syllables' before we can explain the *mechanism* of the effect. (We would also have to allow for such other factors as the contrasting extraordinarily smooth liaison in *or rare*, and the interruption of the sequence preposition / noun / conjunction / noun at the terms *rough, dense*.) Nevertheless, the existence of the effect itself is beyond doubt.

Similarly, there is no obstacle to our enjoyment of Milton's skilful variation of caesura position. This variation is almost certainly what is meant, in the Note on the Verse, by 'the sense variously drawn out from one verse into another'.

Numerology
Still more doubtful, at present, is the question of the numerical organization of *Paradise Lost*. The first work on the subject, James Whaler's *Counterpoint and Symbol* (Copenhagen 1956) dealt with elaborate patterns formed by the

numbers of beats intervening between breaks in the sense. Numerology based on units so elusive and debatable, even if it existed, could only be a private method of the poet's. And in any case, the symbolisms Whaler assigns to numbers are often arbitrary meanings, without foundation in seventeenth-century arithmology (3, e.g., simply was not the number of justice). It is possible, however, that some of the patterns really exist. Whaler may have stumbled on something quite different from numerology: namely, organic laws governing enjambement in blank verse.

Gunnar Qvarnström's *Dikten och den nya vetenskapen. Det astronautiska motivet* (Lund 1961) (now in a modified English version: *Poetry and Numbers*, Scripta minora Regiae Societatis Humaniorum Litterarum Lundensis (1964–5)) more convincingly argues for the existence of a line-count numerology governing the length of speeches throughout the poem. Qvarnström (93) draws attention, e.g., to Christ's two speeches at the very centre of the poem (vi 723–45, 801–23), both of them 23 lines long. Between the speeches Christ ascends his chariot to drive the rebel angels from heaven. Now in the number symbolism of the time 23 sometimes signified the fulness of Christ's redemption, sometimes vengeance upon the heathen (see Bongo 442, Fowler 247*n*). Qvarnström's most impressive result is that in *Ed I* the numerological centre of the whole poem by line-count falls between vi 761 and 762, i.e., precisely where Christ ascends his triumphal chariot:

> He in celestial panoply all armed
> *761* Of radiant urim, work divinely wrought,
> *762* Ascended, at his right hand victory
> Sat, eagle-winged. . . .

It would be hard to exaggerate the importance of this observation, which lends point to a whole series of other symmetries about the midpoint of the poem (see, e.g., vi 761*n* and viii 249*n*). Some of these symmetries have been independently studied (though not from a numerological point of view) by J. R. Watson in 'Divine providence and the structure of *Paradise Lost*', *EC* xiv (1964) 148–55, an excellent article which nevertheless fails to notice the centre of the symmetry in the triumphal chariot of Christ. Watson speaks of a tension between the poem's dramatic effects – especially the apparent climax in Bk ix – and its enclosing symmetrical pattern. He rightly sees in this an analogy with the characteristic contrasting movements of Baroque architecture.

There is the difficulty, of course, that the additions made in *Ed II* have the net effect of moving the centre point $4\frac{1}{2}$ lines later, to vi 766. (It may be relevant that the lines are numbered in the margin – sometimes erratically – in *Ed I*, but not numbered in *Ed II*.) This is partly offset, however, by the simultaneous reordering of the book division; which as Mrs MacCaffrey 57*n* remarks makes the poem more obviously symmetrical about its midpoint:

Ed I Book	(1667) Lines	*Ed II* Book	(1674) Lines	
i	798	i	798	
ii	1055	ii	1055	
iii	742	iii	742	
iv	1015	iv	1015	
v	904	v	907	(3 lines added at 636–9)
vi	912	vi	912	
vii	1290	vii	640	
		viii	653	(3 lines added at 1–4)
viii	1189	ix	1189	
ix	1104	x	1104	
x	1541	xi	901	(3 lines added at 485–7 and 1 at 551–2)
		xii	649	(5 lines added at 1–5)
	10550		10565	

There is no external evidence as to why Milton made the change. Whaler (165) suggests that he wanted to draw attention to the poem's number symbolism without forgoing conformity to the Virgilian twelve-book pattern. (In the Pythagorean system, Ten was the divine tetractys, the fountain of number from which all created being arises.) Barker, however, thinks that the change is essentially one from a dramatic structure – with five two-book acts – to an epic structure. In any case, the extreme length of *Ed I* Bk x (= *Ed II* xi and xii) certainly suggests that the subsequent division was planned from the start. The same conclusion might be drawn from vii 21, 'Half yet remains unsung', which in *Ed I* came in the seventh of ten books.

In *Ed II*, 'Half yet remains' is not only true, but also a useful structural signpost. For the two six-book halves of the poem match one another formally with some precision. Thus, each is divided by renewed invocations of the Muse into two parts bearing the octave proportion of harmony, 1 : 2, the proportion that according to Pico della Mirandola ought to exist between reason and concupiscence in the well-tempered soul; i.e., each half consists of two followed by four books: 2/4//2/4 (see ix 1–47*n* below, and Fowler 281*n*). Cutting across this division in the Baroque manner is a more emphatic upward movement to a double centre in Bks vi and vii (both editions). The first and more important of these centres is where Messiah, the *Sol iustitiae*, ascends his triumphal throne; the second is the 'crowned' central day of creation, when his image the sun is set to rule the day (see below, p. 445). In *Ed II*, which has more obvious symmetry, the point of bisection of twelve books falls between the two 'centres'. Moreover, as we work inwards from the outside books we find a series of connections between the matter of the first half and the answering matter in corresponding books of the second half. A few examples must suffice. The outermost two books in each case are concerned with the consequences of a fall:

i–ii portray the evil consequences of the fall of the angels, xi–xii the mixed consequences of the Fall of man. Next comes a divine council of deliberation on man's fall, and Christ's offer of mediation (iii); this is answered by a council of judgment, and by Christ's descent to judge and clothe fallen man (x). Similarly, in iii Satan enters the universe, in x he leaves it. Bk iv has the first temptation, which is answered in ix by the second. Then in the centre four books v–viii we have the 'episode' of Raphael, elevating Christ first in war then in creation.

A subsidiary pattern in *Ed II* is the correspondence between hell and chaos at the beginning of the first half, and the chaotic war of the angels at the end of the first half. In the same way the second half is flanked by pairs of books setting out the Mirror of Nature (vii–viii) and the Mirror of History (xi–xii).

In *Ed I*, 'Half yet remains unsung' refers to the line-count, not to the book-division. But there too the invocations have their significance. They mark the inceptions of groups of 2, 4, 1, and 3 books. Just as the book-totals of these four parts denote the tetractys in its expanded form (1, 2, 3, 4), so the total number of books in the whole of *Ed I* denotes the tetractys in its summed form (10 = 1 + 2 + 3 + 4).

Numerology may prove an even more useful tool to the interpretative critic of *Paradise Lost* when more is known about the particular sources of number symbolism on which Milton drew. Some steps have already been taken in this direction by Maren-Sofie Röstvig ('The Hidden Sense' in *Norwegian Studies in English* ix (Oslo 1963)).

Chronology

Newton thought Milton 'not very exact in the computation of time' (see his note to *PL* xi 135): a judgment that seems to have discouraged critics from bothering with the time scheme of the poem. (Even Grant McColley, who gives much interesting information about patristic ideas as to the timing of the Fall relative to the Creation, largely ignores the chronological indications in *Paradise Lost* itself.) With more justice Ricks 19 speaks of 'characteristic pedantry about the passage of time'. Milton does in fact take pains to arrange precise indications of the passage of time; dwelling fondly on *chronologiae* and giving long-drawn-out descriptions of sunset and sunrise (e.g. the especially elaborate nightfall at iv 352–633). But the indication of time is with him by no means an end in itself. For important thematic ideas are set out formally and structurally through the medium of the poem's chronology. These ideas will be better understood when work in progress by Qvarnström and Miss Röstvig is published. The present account agrees with theirs in the main, though not in all details.

Current confusion about the temporal scheme of *Paradise Lost* arises in part from a false conception of what Milton meant by 'day'. It is assumed that he meant a 24-hour period beginning and ending at midnight. Milton's fit audience, however, would be familiar with several different ways of reckoning days–from sunrise or noon or sunset, for example (see Riccioli i 31ff). It is clear, especially from Raphael's narration, that in *Paradise Lost* Milton in general follows the Biblical practice of reckoning the day from evening to evening (e.g. v 227, vii 260, 338). The Biblical 'evening' was itself a term of debated meaning (see Willet 4 on *Gen.* i 4); but that Milton agreed with St Jerome in reckoning evening from sunset is certain from vii 582f: 'Evening arose in Eden, for the sun / Was set'. Time is thus divided ordinally or calendrically into Biblical days consisting each of an evening followed by a morning. On the other hand, *duration* of time may be reckoned in 24-hour periods, also called days, beginning at any point (e.g. vi 871). The resultant ambiguity is exploited when Adam waits for judgment to descend on 'the day' he ate the forbidden fruit (see x 773n).

With this in mind it is not very difficult to determine the main lines of the poem's chronology:

EVENING AND MORNING	EVENT	INDICATION IN TEXT
1	First exaltation of Christ	v 582f, 618
2–4	War in heaven	v 642, vi 406, 524, 684–6, 748
4–13	Rebel angels' 9-day pursuit through chaos	vi 871
13–22	Rebel angels' 9-day stupor in hell	i 50
14–20	The creation	vi 715f, vii 131ff
17	Creation of sun and moon	vii 386
19	Creation of man	vii 550
22	Rebel angels' awakening; building of Pandaemonium (1 hour); council; Satan's departure	i 697
23	Satan's observation of the universe (midnight); his conversation with Uriel (noon)	iii 555–61, iv 564
24	First temptation of Eve; Satan's expulsion (midnight); Raphael's visit (noon to sunset)	iv 1015, v 311, viii 630
24–31	Satan's 7-day encompassing of earth	ix 58–67
32	Satan's reentry (midnight); the Fall (noon); Messiah's judgement of man (late afternoon)	ix 739, x 92f
33	Michael's visit (sunrise to noon); the Expulsion of man (noon)	xi 184, xii 589

NOTES: (*a*) Additional time could be interposed if one were to speculate about what happens outside the poem (e.g. while Satan 'long . . . wandered' on the surface of the universe, iii 499). But I think Milton means us only to reckon days necessarily expended in the action actually presented.

(*b*) The duration assigned to Satan's journey to earth finds some additional confirmation in the time Raphael took to fly to hell gate (viii 229–46).

(c) The critical chronology of the events assigned to Days 32–3 is established in more detail in the notes. See x 49–53n, 92–102n, 328–9n, 342n, 1050n, and especially 773n.

(d) It seems reasonable to assume that Messiah went straight on to create after driving the rebel angels down to hell. This would put the week of creation on Days 14–20, and the creation of man on Day 19, as shown in the accompanying Table. Raphael's finding the gate of hell barred on the 6th day of creation (viii 240) would tally with this scheme; for the gate was barred from the 13th to the 22nd. Some, it is true, infer from the sounds of torment Raphael heard on this occasion that the devils had risen from their stupor; which would fix the creation of man on the opening day of the poem, Day 22. But the sounds Raphael heard are chronologically irrelevant, since they may be explained as the noise of Sin and her hell hounds at the gate (ii 862), and since in any case devils were believed to undergo torment during their sleep (viii 242–4n). Moreover, such passages as v 3, 31, and especially iv 449–50 ('That day I oft remember, when from sleep / I first awaked', spoken on Day 23), seem to rule out a creation of man on the 22nd.

From the above analyses, several numerological patterns emerge. (It is very natural that Milton should have organized his poem in this way; for speculation about the number symbolism underlying the sequence of the days of creation had long been a prominent element in the hexaemeral tradition.) We note that in *Ed I* the action of the first 3 books takes place off the earth and ends with an account of creation; while the first-order action of the remaining 7 books (iv–x; *Ed II* iv–xii) is almost exclusively terrestrial. If we recall that 7 was the number of the world and of the week of creation, it may well seem significant that in *Ed I* the centre book of these terrestrial 7 is Bk vii (*Ed II* vii–viii); and that the content of that book is an account of the creation and a discussion of the 7 planetary spheres. In the course of the hexaemeron itself, moreover, the central day of the week, which is also the central day of the poem's whole action, is said to be 'crowned' (vii 386), i.e., to occupy the central position of sovereignty. On that day (Day 17) is created the sun, whose centrality is suggested by Raphael in the central line of a long paragraph in the dialogue on astronomy. The simplest diagram of the poem's action would be:

FALL OF THE ANGELS	CREATION	FALL OF MAN
13 days	7 days	13 days

In both editions, the direct action of the poem occupies 11 days, i.e., Days 23–33. There is an obvious number symbolism in this, since 11 signified sin–transgressing the 10 of the Decalogue. (See St Augustine, *Civ. Dei* xv 20; Hopper 87, 101, 152; Fowler 54; Qvarnström 90.) Less obviously, the 11 days of action directly represented are in a ratio of 11:22 or 1:2 with the remaining days of retrospectively narrated action. Now the ratio 1:2, the octave proportion, signified the ideal relation between the reason and the concupiscible faculty. (See Pico della Mirandola, *Conclusiones secundum mathematicam Pythagorae* in *Opera omnia* (Basel 1573) i 79; Fowler 281n. The same ratio is used in *Paradise Lost* for the proportions of the universe: see i 73–4n.) Thus the form of the action repeats, but also repairs, man's first concupiscence. A similar symbolism governs the detailed arrangement of the 11 days of direct action. Satan's briefly recounted week of miscreation is framed or contained by the remaining 4 days–

Bks i–iv	Bk ix 48–66	Bks ix–xii
	week of miscreation	
23rd, 24th	25th–31st	32nd, 33rd

–so that the 7 of mutability is ordered and raised by the 4 of concord and virtue, the holy tetractys.

Finally, there is significance in the ordinal numbers denoting certain days of the action. For example, the first day, the only unfallen 'undivided' day, the only day without a preceding night, is appropriately denoted by the monad. The sole event that takes place on this unique day is the generation of God's only Son, under whose reign the angels are to abide 'United as one individual soul'. Again, it is on the day denoted by the evil and rebellious dyad that war breaks out in heaven. The Fall itself and the judgment of man take place on Day 32: appropriately, since 32 was a number symbolizing pleasure, whose Pythagorean name was Justice (Bongo 486). The last day of the poem's action, when Adam is shown visions of the Fall's consequences and of the redemptive history, and when he himself leaves Paradise to enter that history, is denoted by 33. This number, the number of man's earthly suffering and of the life of Christ, was a very familiar symbol, which had already been used as the numerological basis of Dante's *Divina commedia*.

We conclude that the prominence given to the succession of day and night is entirely justified on thematic grounds. Seen with the eyes of faith, that succession sets out the divine nature, our covenant with whom must be as sure 'as the days of heaven' (xii 344–7n). It is not only Adam who discovers, in the peripeteias of x–xii, that God's judgment is numerically sure. The reader, too, learns to say with the Psalmist 'teach us to number our days'. For the whole form of the poem is designed to lead us up to the mount of God, where a cave is alternately inhabited by light and darkness (vi 4–12) to image his transcendence over time, as over good and evil. Isabel Mac-Caffrey puts it well when she speaks of the alternation of day and night in heaven as 'an elaborate kind of changelessness'. The imagery is in keeping with a seventeenth-century fashion for philosophical optics and astronomical mysticism. But it would be a mistake to think of it as the result of easy or impersonal choices on Milton's part. It is more like a confession of his faith in the justice of the God who had made darkness succeed light for him so unnaturally.

Milton's Universe
If the God of *Paradise Lost* can be said to contain and yet transcend light and darkness and the time they divide, the same is true of his relation to physical

space. In an obvious way he is 'high throned above all height' (iii 58); more mysteriously, the spatial universe is imagined throughout as his Son's *vehicle*. The central image of the poem, physically, is that of a triumphal chariot, formed by cherubs, on which is carried the throne of Christ (see vi 749–59*n*). Ranged around this centre are ten thousand stellar beings, all praising and acknowledging his transcendent sovereignty. For the stars lighting the heavens are identified–sometimes metaphorically (v 700–16), sometimes almost literally (iii 622ff)–with angels. Their revolutions are a sacred *choresis*, a 'starry dance' (iii 580), that 'resembles nearest' the 'mystical dance' of the angels 'about the sacred hill' (v 619–22). Thus the poem's world can be regarded as expanding and developing the terrific idea concentrated in its central image, the *machina mundi* enthroning Christ. Like the universe imagined in Plato's *Timaeus* it is a living creature, a being animate throughout. It has motion; it engages in continual metabolic exchanges (v 414ff); and it exhales, transpiring fragrance and spirit up to God in prayer. This world with its celestial canopy was not of course one whose fabric Milton cut out of whole cloth. It is patched together from Neoplatonic pieces, or from worn canonicals handed down by medieval Christian Platonists. But the way in which the world is imaged, in passionate fullness of detail, is original. Instinct as it is with life, Milton's cosmos, however orderly, has always something of life's capacity to surprise.

This quality of unexpectedness is nowhere more striking than in the panoramic vistas, on which Mrs MacCaffrey has written so well. Whenever you move your eye over one of these vistas, or follow out any of the poem's innumerable flights through space, or trace out its chartings of the movements of heavenly bodies, you are constantly astonished by the power of spatial realization and by the sustained inventiveness with which natural phenomena are imaged more fully than ever before. Milton was the first Englishman, for example, to describe a sunset in detail. Everything we see in his poem tells us that Miss M. M. Mahood (*Poetry and Humanism* (1950) pp. 199–201) is right and T. S. Eliot ('A Note on the Verse of John Milton,' *Essays and Studies* (1936)) wrong: Milton had a strong spatial imagination. The surprise, then, is first at the unexpected sharpness of the perspectives. The space opened up has not only the amplitude of Poussin's space but also the dramatic force of the Mannerists' or Piranesi's.

And then a further surprise comes, when we notice to what extent each of Milton's perspectives is a 'legitimate construction': an exact reproduction, correct in every geographical or astronomical detail, of the actual world as it appears from a unique point of view. (This strong indication of a single distinctive physical standpoint can perhaps be regarded as a formal correlate of the poem's ideological engagement, of its constant discrimination between theological 'points of view'.) This is not just a matter of neatness or prosaic thoroughness. The details of Milton's astronomy are always significant, and almost always in more ways than one. Thus, when Satan leaves earth after the Fall 'Betwixt the Centaur and the Scorpion steering / His zenith, while the sun in Aries rose:' (x 328–9), we may at first be inclined to see only a magnificent visual image. Between the Centaur and the Scorpion stretches a starry serpent, the constellation Anguis. But then the details assert themselves, and the lines can be seen as a *chronographia*. A point between Sagittarius and Scorpio will be 120°–150° from Aries, so that, if the zenith at Paradise is such a point, it must there be between 2.00 and 4.00 am. This has a crucial significance for the chronology of the day of judgment after the Fall, the day whose termination is repeatedly delayed (see x 773*n*). But even this does not exhaust the content of the image. For there is also a dramatic irony, if we remember that the sun will not rise always in Aries. This sole occasion on which the sun's position in the *thema coeli* of creation is explicitly stated occurs almost immediately before it is displaced as a result of the Fall (x 668ff).

It would be inappropriate here to attempt an account of the Ptolemaic, Copernican and other planetary systems available to Milton. For that the reader must be referred to the Introduction to D. J. Price, ed., *The Equatorie of the Planetis* (Cambridge 1955); F. R. Johnson, *Astronomical Thought in Renaissance England* (Baltimore, Md. 1937); J. L. E. Dreyer, *A History of Astronomy from Thales to Kepler* (1953); or P. Duhem, *Le Système du Monde* (Paris 1913). There are also numerous articles and books on Milton's astronomy, such as A. H. Gilbert's in *SP* xix (1922), *SP* xx (1923) and *PMLA* xxxviii (1923); G. McColley's in *MLN* xlvii (1932), *SP* xxxiv (1937) and *PMLA* lii (1937); Marjorie Nicolson's in *ELH* ii (1935) and *SP* xxxii (1935); her *The Breaking of the Circle* (Evanston 1950); and Chs ii–iii of Kester Svendsen's *Milton and Science* (Cambridge, Mass. 1956). The theory that Milton was a Ptolemaist who rejected the new science of his day, like the theory that he was a Copernican who cynically used the Ptolemaic universe for poetic purposes, has now been abandoned. McColley's articles, in particular, have shown that there was a wide choice of planetary systems available to Milton, and that he alludes to many of these in his poem. The universe of *Paradise Lost* is a more subtly considered one than could have been devised by anyone with a naive belief in the exclusive truth of a scientific model. Not only does it combine elements of several systems but it even sometimes contrives (as at iv 592–7) to be geocentric and heliocentric simultaneously. Always it avoids unambiguous resolution of such uncertainties as the order of proximity of the planets to the earth.

This is not the result of a disinclination to risk backing a theory that might promptly be invalidated by some new Galileo; though this was a real consideration at a time when planetary systems were ten-a-penny. It is rather that Milton is using astronomical controversy as a symbol of all enquiry into knowledge hidden beyond the verge of man's capacities and limitations. The heliocentric and geocentric alternatives have to be kept open so that the seventeenth-century Adam of the poem may be only just at the point of beginning, with Raphael's help, to realize the inadequacies of the Ptolemaic system. Milton would want to relate the Fall to actual processes of cultural development, actual exchanges of new knowledge for simpler happiness. At such junctures, orientation and moral awareness matter as much as the capacity to choose the next scientific model. But there is also, one suspects, a deeper and less complicated reason for the carefully sustained uncertainty about the order of the planets (an uncertainty that in 1667 must almost have had a historical flavour). It goes without saying that Milton is trying to render something of the elusiveness and mystery of nature herself, who is not always as committed as we would wish her to be. The world of *Paradise Lost* is also, however, an attempt to render a visionary and perfected nature. She will not fit the girdling circles of Ptolemy, or Copernicus, or Galileo, or Brahe, because these were all devised, new and old alike, to describe our own fallen world.

By contrast, the universe of *Paradise Lost* is an ideal universe. For, in a remarkably original way, Milton has constructed a complete imaginary astronomy, based on a premise that does not hold for the existing world. The premise is that the ecliptic and equatorial planes coincide. The astronomical implications of this axiom are worked out with an almost science-fictional inventiveness: see, e.g., iii 555–61, iv 209–16, 354f, v 18–25, x 328f below. (Milton seems to have believed, like Plato and St Augustine, that creation has to be by number and measure.) Thus a world is generated that is beautifully simple and symmetrical—and exhilaratingly easy for a reader to imagine. It is one where day and night are always equal, where the sun remains always in the same sign, and where the positions of the constellations at any given time can easily be determined without recourse to an astrolabe. There are no variations in the declination of the sun, no equinoctial points, no precession and no distinction between sidereal, natural and civil days. The loss of this simple world is from one point of view a physical expression of the consequences of the Fall. The prelapsarian stasis of the Golden Age passes, then, into oblique movement; the sun starts his seasonal and precessional journeys; a new Platonic Great Year, a cycle of decay, sets in (v 583, x 651–706). But the original coincidence of ecliptic and equatorial does not exist just to provide, in its passing, another symbol of the Fall—any more than it is an aetiological myth to explain away bad weather. Rather is it part of Milton's offering of a purified integral pristine world, a macrocosmic setting for his righteous Adam. Like the removal of hell outside the universe, the rectifying of the zodiac allows a revaluation of nature and an aspiration towards unflawed beauty. Milton's golden world is just in its division of light and darkness where ours, in the short run, is not: it remains always constant where ours decays: it has a clockwork regularity, emblematic of its temperance, where ours is inordinate and mutable. But all the same it is the most naturalistic golden world to be found in the whole epic tradition.

Milton was the last great poet to work within a Christian world-picture frame, interpreting nature as endowed in all her features with significance. After him the capacity (or the wish) to give literary expression to such a reverence for nature was almost entirely lost, and when it was recovered, more than a century later, the sensibility had assumed a much altered form. Nevertheless it is right to think of Milton as a nature poet; and to attend to the tradition that extends from him through James Thomson to the Romantic poets, especially Wordsworth and Shelley.

Milton's God

When Johnson said that 'the want of human interest is always felt' in *Paradise Lost*, he betrayed his blindness to the metaphorical activity of the poem, whereby angels, devils, and even Sin and Death–not to say the divine persons–all convey insights into the psychology of man. Nor do Adam and Eve themselves simply portray before the Fall all that is virtuous, after it all that is not. For, without being quite naturalistic in his portrayal of character, Milton is nevertheless very well able to render stages of transition from innocence to experience. And there is besides something elusive about prelapsarian psychology and morality that has interested critics during the last two decades. For example, there is uncertainty about the point at which temptation begins, and at which the Fall becomes inevitable. The tendency to regard these points as lying earlier than Bk ix is exemplified in Millicent Bell's 'The Fallacy of the Fall in *Paradise Lost*', *PMLA* lxviii (1953), which reaches the extreme view that prelapsarian man was pretty much like the passionate, sinful, post-lapsarian man we are familiar with. There is something to be said for this view. At least, such passages as viii 530ff and 588ff show clearly enough that Johnson was wrong to say that 'human passions did not enter the world before the Fall'. The evidences of temptation, however, do not go back before Eve's dream. And the doctrine that the Fall was gradual was after all quite a familiar and venerable one. (Burden quotes, in this connection, William Ames's popular work *The Marrow of Sacred Divinity* (1642) 56: 'man was a sinner before he had finished that outward act of eating'; while Broadbent (197) quotes St Augustine: 'our first parents fell into open disobedience because already they were secretly corrupted'.) Certainly to conclude, as Mrs Bell does, that Milton is interested in showing the effects rather than the causes of the Fall, seems quite without warrant.

It would be more obedient to the main movement of the poem to say that Milton is throughout concerned with the causes of evil *as the term cause was then understood*; and that he pushes this enquiry as far back, and as deeply, as he can. For the action moves from the already fallen society of the devils, sunk in darkness and falsehood, up through confusion, to the clarity of heaven; then back through a universe with Satan already in it, back through a Fall, to the creation of a pristine universe. In iii we are taken to an ultimate point of origin: the mind of God, who not only foresees that evil is inevitably bound up with the freedom of created spirits but also carefully avoids doing anything to curtail that freedom. But however sceptical the enquiry may at times become, however difficult the ground it invades, the end is unquestionably intended to be justification: 'Evil into the mind of God . . . / May come and go, so unapproved, and leave / No spot or blame behind . . .' (v 117-9). For we should not for a moment assume that Milton was preoccupied by causation in our own sense of the term; far less that his artistic purpose was to set out a single naturalistic series of cause-effect relations leading up to and 'explaining' the Fall.

There is also some uncertainty about the motives of Adam and Eve at the time of the Fall itself. A. J. A. Waldock in *Paradise Lost and its Critics* (Cambridge 1947) and William Empson in *Milton's God* both try to exonerate Eve and lay blame instead on Adam or Raphael or God. But anyone who has been sensitive to the painfulness of Adam's experience of moral dilemma-of the difficulty of a world fast losing its simplicity-will think it a shallow response merely to blame Adam for allowing Eve to go off to work by herself. Book ix is presented by Milton as tragic; it is tragic action, therefore, and tragic moral predicaments that we should expect to find portrayed there. Adam makes himself in a sense responsible for the Fall by giving Eve permission to go. Yet he could hardly, without degrading her, have acted differently at that time-an inevitability that distantly echoes the inevitability of God's supra-tragic decision in Bk iii. As for Eve, at the separation she is 'sinless' (as she still is at ix 659); but she is sufficiently influenced by her dream for the epithet to be no longer superfluous. Of course Eve's motives, even in her fall, are often lofty. That she would act from motives that seem high to wretches like ourselves is only to be expected. And in any case it would hardly have justified God to show only his dealings with low people; for that would have left a way open for the objection that his unfairness to noble souls remained unjustified. Nevertheless, to pretend that Eve was not wrong to eat the fruit is to loosen the moral nexus of the whole poem. Cowley might think that 'Less hard 'tis not to err ourselves than know / If our forefathers erred or no' ('Reason')-but Milton was of a different temper.

A contrary tendency, which seems in the long run much more promising, is observable in J. S. Diekhoff, *Milton's 'Paradise Lost': A Commentary on the Argument* (New York 1964); Leon Howard, '"The Invention" of Milton's "Great Argument": A Study of the Logic of "God's Ways to Men"', *HLQ* ix (1945); J. Steadman, 'Heroic Virtue and the Divine Image in *Paradise Lost*', *JWI* xxii (1959) and 'Man's First Disobedience', *JHI* xxi (1960); and Dennis Burden, *The Logical Epic* (1967).

All of these show, in their different ways, a new respect for the logical structure of *Paradise Lost*. When the poem is approached by this admittedly arduous route it takes on an authentic, challenging aspect. Details of the action no longer seem confusingly ambiguous attempts at naturalism, but work together to unfold the logical 'causes' of the fallen world, and the nature of true virtue. No longer the pawns of controversial critics, the most trivial events show moving reasons of their own for being precisely what they are. Some belong to an elaborate portrayal of the various stages of repentance (e.g. x 1073n, 1088-92n); others constitute graded exercises in moral discrimination (e.g. the different accounts of the size of Satan's army, and of the pursuit of the devils after the war in heaven). Others again have to be taken with their counterparts for their function to be appreciated. Thus, the portrayals of Paradise before and after the Fall are in minutely organized opposition, and so are those of heaven and hell. It would hardly be exaggeration to say that everything in heaven has its devilish counterpart. There is an infernal Creation, an infernal Trinity, even a Satanic travesty of the Incarnation.

When once the fruits of this kind of criticism have been tasted, and the extent to which *Paradise Lost* is organized around 'that right Porphyrian tree which did true Logic shew' has been glimpsed, there can never be uncertainty about Milton's overall artistic intention. Questions about whether Satan is the hero of the poem come to seem childish, or else excessively concerned with one phase of the poem's argument. It is not just that we come to be sure of Milton's moral intention, his intention to justify the ways of God, but that we come to see this intention as worked out in the structure of *Paradise Lost* and in the details of its action. Almost throughout its extent, the poem is found to be theologically informed to a remarkable degree. This should not much surprise any student of the period. Anyone who has read the notes Cowley appended to his *Davideis* knows that quite minute physical particulars could at any time involve a seventeenth-century poet in exegetical controversy. Milton is so involved very frequently indeed in *Paradise Lost*, and invariably he takes up a position that has good Scriptural or patristic authority. This point finds confirmation of a sort in the many close parallels with the *De doctrina Christiana*; some of which are carefully listed by Maurice Kelley in *This Great Argument* (Princeton 1941).

But if Milton's conscious intentions are broadly speaking unambiguous, this need not be true of his unconscious intentions. Indeed, several critics besides Waldock have argued that what Milton actually performs in *Paradise Lost* is something radically different from what he intends and professes to perform. The most brilliant work in this tradition is *Milton's God*, which sets out the theory of a contradiction between intention and performance in an unusually subtle form. Empson imagines a Milton who grappled consciously with the most difficult theological problems, and searched sincerely for ways to present God in the best light possible. Unfortunately God was too nasty for this to work, so that contradictions kept creeping into the poem, and it ended up better (and more antitheistic) than Milton ever knew. Empson's book contains much with which we can agree, or at least sympathize. It is true, for example, that Milton focuses penetratingly on some awkward or weak parts of the doctrine of the Fall. And it is in a sense wonderful that he could go on being a Christian after expressing some of the objections to belief raised in the poem. But the fact remains that, after allowing these objections their say, he came to a Christian conclusion; whereas *Milton's God* is propaganda in the interest of a different conclusion. The points made in that work deserve separate consideration at the relevant places in the notes. Here we can only speculate whether Milton may not have been even more conscious of the complexities of the God of *Paradise Lost* than Empson gives him credit for being. Not that he would have understood them at all in the terms of our quaint opinions wide. But he could have formulated his awareness of the objections to belief well enough theologically. For such topics as God's responsibility for evil were discussed in the seventeenth century with a hardihood that would shock many a liberal theologian of our own day. It is hard for us to imagine – yet it seems to have been the case–that Milton could seriously be concerned about what the world is really like, and still be able most of the time to conduct the enquiry in the classic terms of theology. Indeed, what makes *Paradise Lost* perhaps the most serious epic ever written is largely the refusal to take the character of the divine protagonist for granted. But, for that very reason, if the poem leaves us at the end in any doubt about God's justice and love, then it has failed in its communication, not merely in one respect, but altogether.

Critics often call the portrayal of God in *Paradise Lost* a failure, without adequately considering how ludicrous it would be to call any such portrayal a complete success, or even a good likeness. For it would not be a wholly extra-literary judgment to say that Milton was bound to overreach himself, from the time when he decided to introduce a divine character. Nevertheless, it should be the business of the critic not to deplore the attempt but rather to weigh performance against possibility by the standards proper to literature. If this is done, a somewhat different verdict from Waldock's may be arrived at. The sacred conversations, for example, seem to me better than has ever been allowed. Stylistically, almost all the passages concerned are vigorous and intelligent. Indeed, the effects of poetic syntax, whereby the timelessness of God's thoughts and his reflective relationship with Messiah are rendered, must rank among Milton's finest (see iii 125n, 261n). The high level of abstraction: the sustained abstention from imagery, except the very simplest and least sensuous: the calm freedom from unresolved emotional expressions: all these qualities now arouse distaste in readers whose formal demands are at once narrow and sensational. But Milton's fit audience would see the aptness of these qualities in speeches that are not intended to be merely human.

For, in spite of all that Waldock says to the contrary, it is not the human impression left by the God of *Paradise Lost* that matters. He is not human, though he is personal: he is not a character, though he thinks and speaks. He sees the world of events, and also the world in which agents are themselves events–'His own works and their works at once to view' (iii 59); and his mere looking upon them confers bliss. The conception of such a divine point of view deserves to be admired as a feat of imagination, at the same time as we acknowledge the inevitability of its failure. Even the comprehensible difficulties in the way of this achievement were staggering. Milton had not only to assimilate and condense a vast mass of theological erudition but also to transcend it, incorporating the whole tradition in personal terms in the speeches of a consistent being. On top of this he must add his own contribution; for he was himself a theologian. It would perhaps be enough to defend the position that Milton in the face of these difficulties has managed to convey the impression of a distinct divine person–one with a presence so strong that we come to detect his unseen hand in the earthly events and visions, and to hear echoes of his subtleties in the poem's dramatic ironies. But we can say more than this. For Milton's God can be taken seriously both as a theological and as an imaginative construct, in a way that almost no other in our literature can.

From a literary point of view what should be noticed is not so much the direct representation of God, which has already received disproportionate attention, as the indirect. I refer to the formal symbolism—if a category of presentation may be distinguished, complementary to Ian Watt's formal realism (*The Rise of the Novel* (1957) pp 32f)—whereby Milton makes God and Messiah the only agents in the poem who have full consciousness of what they are doing. Only they participate in the dramatic ironies, only they express themselves in interior monologues that are not self-dramatising. On a smaller scale, the indirect presentation of God's attributes is accomplished in such formal dispositions as the order in which, during the first divine exchanges, traditional theological doctrines are introduced. By dealing with Predestination to salvation before even Atonement, for example, Milton implies that his God's thought is 'mercy first and last' (iii 134; see 173–202n).

The question whether the God of *Paradise Lost* obeys the rules of classical theology is declining in interest; so that his personal qualities (as distinct both from the doctrinal and from the human) can be better appreciated. As it happens, however, the poem is also coming more and more to be seen as substantially orthodox in its theology. Its account of creation, for example, in which Denis Saurat saw a *recherché* heresy of divine 'withdrawal', is now understood to be Christian-Platonic theistic materialism; see R. J. Z. Werblowski in *JWI* xviii (1955); A. S. P. Woodhouse in *PQ* xxviii (1949); and W. C. Curry, Milton's *Ontology, Cosmogony, and Physics* (Lexington, Ky. 1957). It is the same with the christology. Milton has been thought Arian, yet *Paradise Lost* accords the Son as supreme a transcendence as any poem in the language. William B. Hunter ('Milton's Arianism Reconsidered', *Harvard Theological Review* lii (1959) 9–35; cp. C. A. Patrides in *JEGP* lxiv (1965)) is probably right in his view that Milton is Subordinationist rather than Arian. The 'Arianism' is perhaps to be seen as an attempt—characteristic of his time—to get beyond the scholasticism of Trinitarian theology to the pure doctrine of the ante-Nicene Fathers. Even if H. F. Robins does not quite convince us of the rightness of concentrating exclusively on Milton's debt to Origen, his *If This Be Heresy: A Study of Milton and Origen* (Urbana, Ill. 1963) remains the best study so far of the theology of *Paradise Lost*. It is clear that Milton was not content with the amalgam of Christianity and Platonism inherited from the Middle Ages, but preferred to attempt a fresh synthesis in the manner of the early Fathers. The *De doctrina* shows that this attempt could involve him in controversy. But *Paradise Lost* expresses rather the impulse behind the controversy: namely, a desire to understand the Trinity as a rational description of the activity of a living and creative God. Thus at the divine level the action of the poem moves from scenes in which Father and Son appear together (iii, v) to others in which the Son emerges separately in the creation and judgment of the universe (vii, x).

Though Milton was not so religious a man as Dante, he has succeeded, by honesty and faith, in constructing an image of deity no less marvellous than that of the *Divina Commedia*. Milton's God is surprising enough to be a universal father figure; enigmatic enough to be the subject of interminable scholastic debates; sublime enough to be awe-inspiring; remote enough from our wishes to be partly true. And certainly there is no divine image in English literature half so interesting.

THE PRINTER TO THE READER

Added in 1668 to the remaining copies of *Ed I*: the text is that of the slightly revised form used in the fifth issue and in some copies of the fourth.

Courteous reader, there was no argument at first intended to the book, but for the satisfaction of many that have desired it, I have procured it, and withal a reason of that which stumbled many others, why the poem rhymes not.

S. Simmons

ON *PARADISE LOST*

Added in *Ed II*. The text is that of 1674: there are no significant variants in the text printed in the 1681 edn of Marvell's *Miscellaneous Poems* and followed by Margoliouth. Lines 18–26 have been taken to refer to Dryden's opera *The Fall of Angels and Man in Innocence*, which was licensed 17 April 1674 but apparently never performed. (Aubrey says that Dryden 'went to him to have leave to putt his Paradise Lost into a drama in rhymne. Mr. Milton received him civilly, and told him he would give him leave to tagge his verses'.) Line 47 certainly refers to Dryden, who was satirized in Buckingham's *Rehearsal* (1674) under the character of Bayes. Lines 51f allude with gentle irony to a passage in the immediately following Note on 'The Verse': 'modern poets, carried away by custom, but much to their ... constraint to express many things otherwise, and for the most part worse then else they would have expressed them.'

> When I beheld the poet blind, yet bold,
> In slender book his vast design unfold,
> Messiah crowned, God's reconciled decree,
> Rebelling angels, the forbidden tree,
> 5   Heaven, hell, earth, chaos, all; the argument
> Held me a while misdoubting his intent,
> That he would ruin (for I saw him strong)
> The sacred truths to fable and old song
> (So Sampson groped the Temple's post in spite)
> 10   The world o'erwhelming to revenge his sight.
>   Yet as I read, soon growing less severe,
> I liked his project, the success did fear;
> Through that wide field how he his way should find

O'er which lame faith leads understanding blind;
15 Lest he perplexed the things he would explain,
And what was easy he should render vain.
    Or if a work so infinite he spanned,
Jealous I was that some less skilful hand
(Such as disquiet always what is well,
20 And by ill imitating would excell)
Might hence presume the whole creation's day
To change in scenes, and show it in a play.
    Pardon me, mighty poet, nor despise
My causeless, yet not impious, surmise.
25 But I am now convinced, and none will dare
Within thy labours to pretend a share.
Thou hast not missed one thought that could be fit,
And all that was improper dost omit:
So that no room is here for writers left,
30 But to detect their ignorance or theft.
    That majesty which through thy work doth reign
Draws the devout, deterring the profane.
And things divine thou treatest of in such state
As them preserves, and thee, inviolate.
35 At once delight and horror on us seize,
Thou singest with so much gravity and ease;
And above human flight dost soar aloft
With plume so strong, so equal, and so soft.
The bird named from that Paradise you sing
40 So never flags, but always keeps on wing.
    Where couldst thou words of such a compass find?
Whence furnish such a vast expense of mind?
Just heaven thee like Tiresias to requite
Rewards with prophecy thy loss of sight.
45   Well mightest thou scorn thy readers to allure
With tinkling rhyme, of thy own sense secure;
While the town-Bayes writes all the while and spells,
And like a pack-horse tires without his bells:
Their fancies like our bushy-points appear,
50 The poets tag them, we for fashion wear.
I too transported by the mode offend,
And while I meant to praise thee must commend.
Thy verse created like thy theme sublime,
In number, weight, and measure, needs not rhyme.
                            A[ndrew]. M[arvell].

THE VERSE

Added in *Ed II*. For explanations of the meanings of the technical terms
used, see Sprott 39ff, and Introd., 'Prosody', above.

The measure is English heroic verse without rhyme, as that of Homer in
Greek, and of Virgil in Latin; rhyme being no necessary adjunct or true
ornament of poem or good verse, in longer works especially, but the invention
of a barbarous age, to set off wretched matter and lame metre; graced indeed

since by the use of some famous modern poets, carried away by custom, but
much to their own vexation, hindrance, and constraint to express many
things otherwise, and for the most part worse than else they would have
expressed them. Not without cause therefore some both Italian and Spanish
poets of prime note have rejected rhyme both in longer and shorter works,
as have also long since our best English tragedies, as a thing of it self, to all
judicious ears, trivial and of no true musical delight; which consists only in
apt numbers, fit quantity of syllables, and the sense variously drawn out from
one verse into another, not in the jingling sound of like endings, a fault
avoided by the learned ancients both in poetry and all good oratory. This
neglect then of rhyme so little is to be taken for a defect, though it may seem
so perhaps to vulgar readers, that it rather is to be esteemed an example set,
the first in English, of ancient liberty recovered to heroic poem from the
troublesome and modern bondage of rhyming.

Paradise Lost

BOOK I

The Argument

This first book proposes, first in brief, the whole subject, man's disobedience,
and the loss thereupon of Paradise wherein he was placed: then touches the
prime cause of his fall, the serpent, or rather Satan in the serpent; who
revolting from God, and drawing to his side many legions of angels, was by
the command of God driven out of heaven with all his crew into the great
deep. Which action passed over, the poem hastes into the midst of things,
presenting Satan with his angels now fallen into hell, described here, not in
the centre[1] (for heaven and earth may be supposed as yet not made,[2]

¶ 94. i *Argument*[1]. *described here, not in the centre*] The obvious meaning is that
hell is here described not at the centre of the earth, but at another situation.
As MacCaffrey 54 implies, however, there is a secondary sense in which M.,
still discussing his *in medias res* narrative method, is telling us that we shall
not find hell at the centre of *PL*. On the symbolic importance of the mid-
point of the poem, which is occupied by Christ in his triumphal chariot,
see vi 749–59*n*. M. displaces hell from the centre of the earth for theological
reasons: namely, that when hell was formed the earth was not yet cursed;
and that the earth is to be destroyed at the last (*De doctrina* i 33, Columbia
xvi 372–4). Cp. Cowley's note 11 to *Davideis* i: 'making *Hell* to be in the
Center of the Earth, it is far from infinitely large, or deep; yet, on my con-
science, where e're it be, it is not so strait, as that *Crowding* and sweating
should be one of the *Torments* of it, as is pleasantly fancied by *Bellarmin*.'
i *Argument*[2]. *yet not made*] Earth was not yet made when Satan and his angels

certainly not yet accursed) but in a place of utter[3] darkness, fitliest called
Chaos: here Satan with his angels lying on the burning lake, thunderstruck
and astonished, after a certain space recovers, as from confusion, calls up
him who next in order and dignity lay by him; they confer of their miserable
fall. Satan awakens all his legions, who lay till then in the same manner
confounded; they rise, their numbers, array of battle, their chief leaders
named, according to the idols known afterwards in Canaan and the countries
adjoining. To these Satan directs his speech, comforts them with hope yet
of regaining heaven, but tells them lastly of a new world and new kind of
creature to be created, according to an ancient prophecy or report in heaven;
for that angels were long before this visible creation, was the opinion of many
ancient Fathers.[4] To find out the truth of this prophecy, and what to determine
thereon he refers to a full council. What his associates thence attempt.[5] Pan-
demonium the palace of Satan rises, suddenly built out of the deep: the
infernal peers there sit in council.

> Of man's first disobedience, and the fruit
> Of that forbidden tree, whose mortal taste
> Brought death into the world, and all our woe,

fell into hell; but it is made *now*: see Introduction, 'Chronology', pp. 443–
45 above.
i *Argument*[3]. *utter*] Either 'outer' or 'utter.'
i *Argument*[4]. *De doctrina* i 7 (Columbia xv 33–5): 'Many at least of the Greek,
and some of the Latin Fathers, are of opinion that angels, as being spirits,
must have existed long before the material world; and it seems even prob-
able, that the apostasy which caused the expulsion of so many thousands
from Heaven, took place before the foundations of this world were laid.'
In M.'s own day, however, the commoner belief was that the angels were
created at the same time with the world.
i *Argument*[5]. *What his associates thence attempt*] The building of Pandaemo-
nium, as the next sentence explains.
i *1–49*. Rhetorically, the *invocatio*, consisting of an address to the Muse;
1–26 is also the *principium* that states the whole scope of the poem's action.
M.'s particular overlapping arrangement of the opening parts traditional
in epic combines the Virgilian and Homeric plans; so that, without the
interruption of direct allusion, *PL* is silently related to its three principal
analogues. A metaphorical comparison is set up between Adam and Achil-
les, Odysseus and Aeneas, and between the loss of Paradise and the loss of
Troy (Condee). On the placing of the poem's four invocations, see ix 1–47*n*
below.
i *1–13*. As Sims 11 points out, the widely separated persons and events
referred to in these lines have a typological or figural connection that M.
assumes his readers will grasp: 'the disobedience of Adam in Eden, the
receiving of the Law by Moses on Sinai, and the placing of the Ark of the
Covenant in the Temple on '*Sion* Hill' are not causally connected as a hori-
zontal chain of events, but the divine scheme of salvation as seen by centuries
of Christians seeking to align the Old Testament with the New had vertically

> With loss of Eden, till one greater man
> 5 Restore us, and regain the blissful seat,
> Sing heavenly Muse, that on the secret top

connected these events as successive stages in God's plan for man's redemption.' See, however, Lewis 40f for the view that the true function of the opening 'is to give us the sensation *that some great thing is now about to begin*'.

i *1–5*. The sequence *disobedience–loss of Eden–regain the blissful seat* corresponds to the sequence in Virgil's *principium*, from the fall of Troy through a journey to the founding of Rome. See Arthur Barker in *PQ* xxviii (1949) 17f, MacCaffrey 83f.

i *1–2*. This definition of the first sin follows exactly that given in Calvin's Catechism, in its familiar Ursinian form: see Fletcher ii 95f. Daiches (56f) finds in the alliterative connection between *first*, *fruit* and *forbidden* an 'acoustical' allusion to the oblation of firstfruits, prescribed in *Lev.* xxiii. More obviously, the metrical pause between the lines invites us to connect *fruit* with *disobedience*–'disobedience and its organic consequences'–until *Of* (2) shows that the grammatical link is with the words that follow. Such double syntactical or lexical sequences are ubiquitous in *PL*, but will not be noticed below unless some special difficulty is involved. The *taste* of the fruit is *mortal* in a derivative sense: 'deadly', 'death-bringing' (Latin *mortalis*). On the strict logical structure of these lines, and on M.'s concern with the *causes* of the Fall, see Howard, especially 152.

i *3. all our woe*] A key phrase in *PL*; see MacCaffrey 84.

i *4–5. loss of Eden*] By a synecdoche, the whole is put for the part; Eden is not lost, though Paradise is. The *greater man* is Christ, in Pauline theology the second Adam (see especially *Rom.* v 19). M.'s repetition of *man* is mainly intended to make this point, though it also glances at Virgil's *virumque* (*Aen.* i 1) and Homer's ἄνδρα (*Od.* i 1). Virgil sings one man, but M. will sing two: setting the supernatural Christ over against the natural man, he deliberately departs from pagan epic tradition. There were, however, precedents for having two heroes; see Spenser's Letter to Raleigh on Tasso's practice in this respect.   *Restore*] Both 'replace in a state of grace; free from the effects of sin' (*OED* 4 a) and 'make amends for' (*OED* 2). In the latter sense, *Restore* is followed by an ethic dative (Emma 54*n*).

i *6–22*. The *heavenly Muse*, later addressed as *Urania* (vii 1), is here apparently identified as the divine Logos, the second person of the Trinity, who inspires both the prophetic vision of a Moses on Mount *Oreb* and the sacerdotal wisdom and Temple ritual of *Sion hill*, but who is not confined to these localities (ll. 17f). M. is signifying his readiness to assume either the prophetic or the priestly role, as the Spirit wills (Daiches² 61). M.'s opening was particularly bold in view of contemporary attacks on invocation. Davenant, e.g., condemned the invoking of the Holy Ghost in poetry as 'saucy familiarity with a true God'; see Broadbent 67, also ll. 17–22*n* below.

i *6–8*. The form of this allusion, with its casual assumption of common

> Of Oreb, or of Sinai, didst inspire
> That shepherd, who first taught the chosen seed,
> In the beginning how the heavens and earth
> 10   Rose out of chaos: or if Sion hill
> Delight thee more, and Siloa's brook that flowed
> Fast by the oracle of God; I thence
> Invoke thy aid to my adventurous song,
> That with no middle flight intends to soar

ground with the reader, resembles Dante's periphrastic references to historical personages. As *shepherd* of Jethro's flock, Moses was granted the vision of the burning bush on Mount Horeb (*Exod.* iii: for euphony, the Vulgate form, *Oreb*, is preferred); as pastor, he received the Law, either on Mount Horeb (*Deut.* iv 10) or on its lower part, Mount Sinai (*Exod.* xix 20). The *top* is *secret* because set apart (Latin *secretus*) and concealed by storm clouds (*Exod.* xix; cp. *PL* xii 227–9).

i 7. *MS* omits both commas.

i 8. *the chosen seed*] The children of Israel, whom Moses, the *first* (note the emphatic repetition of this word, in ll. 1, 19, 27, 28, 33) Jewish writer, taught about the *beginning* of the world in *Genesis*, the principal source of the mythos of *PL*. Cp. Gabriel Harvey, *Marginalia*, ed. Smith (Stratford-upon-Avon 1913) 209, where the Pentateuch is called the root and fountain of all books in the world. Moses should not be regarded merely as M.'s authority, but as his original. For the reference is no mere literary artifice: M. believed himself 'possessed', in the Platonic sense, by Moses; as his successor, he was similarly animated by divine afflatus (Hanford 414f).

i 9. *In the beginning*, the opening words of the Bible, are mimetically moved earlier by the inversion.

i 10. *Sion hill*] The sanctuary, a place of ceremonial song, but also (*Is.* ii 3) of oracular pronouncements.

i 11. *Siloa*] A spring immediately west of Mount Zion and beside Calvary, often used as a symbol of the operation of the Holy Ghost 'in gentle mild manner' (Lancelot Andrewes, *Sermons*, Libr. of Anglo-Cath. Theol., iii (1841) 267f) or in a manner not obvious (e.g. Calvin's Comm. on *Is.* viii 6). But M. may have in mind the curative and purificatory pool of Siloam ('which is by interpretation, Sent': *John* ix 7). If so, an analogy would seem to be implied between the poet, and the blind disciple given sight and insight by Jesus and sent to wash in the pool (*John* ix 1–11, 30–9; see Paul Lauter, *N & Q* cciii (1958) 204f). As *PL* iii 26–32 shows, M. intends, in the brook flowing beside the Temple Mount, a complete sacred counterpart to the brook frequented by the pagan Muses: Aganippe, that 'from beneath the seat of Jove doth spring' (*Lycidas* 16, following Hesiod). *Sion* and *Siloa* are again Vulgate forms.

i 13. *adventurous*] 'adventrous' in *MS* and the early edns; probably pronounced as a trisyllable. See *Comus* 79n.

15 Above the Aonian mount, while it pursues
Things unattempted yet in prose or rhyme.
And chiefly thou O Spirit, that dost prefer
Before all temples the upright heart and pure,
Instruct me, for thou know'st; thou from the first
20 Wast present, and with mighty wings outspread
Dove-like sat'st brooding on the vast abyss

i *15. the Aonian mount*] Helicon, sacred to the Muses. M. believes his source
of inspiration and the matter he *pursues* (i.e. treats: Latin *sequor*) to be
higher than any possible in the pagan world. Appropriately, he makes the
Biblical mountains – sources of inspiration – more numerous than the classi-
cal (Daiches[2] 63). The spelling in *MS* and the early edns indicates the syna-
loepha: th'Aonian. *MS* has semicolon after *mount*.

i *16*. Ironically translating Ariosto's boast in *Orl. Fur.* i 2: *Cosa non detta in
prosa mai, né in rima*; cp. ix 27–47 below. On the claim to novelty as a tradi-
tional opening topic, see Curtius 85f.   *unattempted*] 'Unattempted even
in the Bible? . . . "unattempted in English literature"?' asks Daiches[2] 63.

i *17–22*. If not before, surely now it is the Holy Spirit who is addressed; in
spite of M.'s argument in *De doctrina* i 6 (Columbia xiv 392–4), that invo-
cation of the Holy Spirit as a separate person has no Biblical foundation.
Unlocalised and operating inwardly, the Spirit provides the impulse of every
creative act, divine or human. The analogy M. implies between creation
and poetic making is examined by Cormican (178f), who finds it to be de-
veloped in a Metaphysical manner; and by Daiches ([2] 66f), who traces its
theological content. An unnoticed analogue is Sylvester's Du Bartas 9f:
'As a good Wit . . . on his Book still muses: / . . . Or, as a Hen that fain
would hatch a Brood / . . . Even in such sort seemed the Spirit Eternall / To
brood upon this Gulf.' In visual art of the period, chaos was often depicted
as an egg-shaped mass.   *temples*] Cp. the Pauline idea of the body as the
'temple of the Holy Ghost' (*1 Cor.* vi 19). St Paul also regarded the Spirit
as the only instructor about the things of God (Sims 17).   *Dove-like*]
Identifying the Spirit present at the creation with the Spirit in the form of a
dove that descended on Jesus at the beginning of his ministry (*John* i 32).
brooding] rendering the Heb. word in *Gen.* i 2 that is translated in A.V. as
'moved', but in St Basil and other patristic authors as *incubabat* (brooded).
brooding . . . madest it pregnant] Not a mixed metaphor, but a deliberate
allusion to the Hermetic doctrine that God is both masculine and feminine.
Cp. Nicolas Cusanus, *De docta ignorantia* i 25; tr. G. Heron, ed. D. J. B.
Hawkins (1954) 57.   *vast*] In addition to the primary sense ('large')
there is a Latinizing secondary sense, 'waste, deserted, unformed' (Lat.
vastus).

i *17*. *MS* has no point after *Spirit*.
i *18*. *MS* has no point after *pure*.
i *19*. Cp. Homer, *Il.* ii 484: 'Tell me, Muses . . . since you are goddesses and
are present and know all things.'

And madest it pregnant: what in me is dark
Illumine, what is low raise and support;
That to the highth of this great argument
25 I may assert eternal providence,
And justify the ways of God to men.
    Say first, for heaven hides nothing from thy view
Nor the deep tract of hell, say first what cause
Moved our grand parents in that happy state,
30 Favoured of heaven so highly, to fall off
From their creator, and transgress his will
For one restraint, lords of the world besides?
Who first seduced them to that foul revolt?
The infernal serpent; he it was, whose guile
35 Stirred up with envy and revenge, deceived
The mother of mankind, what time his pride

i 22–6. Both in sense and in rhetorical form, this prayer of invocation echoes
the celebrated 'Golden Sequence', *Veni sancte Spiritus*: '*Veni, lumen cor-
dium.* / ... *Lava quod est sordidum,* / ... *Rege quod est devium.*'   *argument*]
subject, theme.   *justify* does not mean merely 'demonstrate logically' but
has its Biblical meaning and implies spiritual rather than rational understan-
ding (Cormican 175).   *to men*] The plural contrasts with the generalising
singular of *man* (1): the Fall is universal, but M. writes for the elect, a 'fit
audience ... though few' (Daiches[2] 57).
i 25. *eternal*] th'eternal *Ed I*; corr. in 1668 *Errata. MS* originally had 'th'eter-
nal', and the deletion of *th*' seems to have been ignored by the *Ed I* printer.
i 27–49. Rhetorically the *initium*, introducing the first scene and giving the
cause of the action. With l. 28, cp. the *initium* of Virgil's *Aen.* (i 8: '*Musa mihi
causas memor*); and with 33 cp. Homer's question about the source of discord
between Achilles and Agamemnon (*Il.* i 8). M.'s formulaic method assists
the involvement of 'a whole segment of western culture', and counterpoints
the deeds of classical heroes with those of Adam (Condee 507). The counter-
point emerges here as a strong contrast, for in Virgil it is the cause of divine
wrath that seems inexplicable.
i 28–31. *cause*] M. turns at once to the instrumental cause of the Fall (Howard
159).
i 29. *grand*] Implies not only titular greatness, but also inclusiveness or
generality of parentage–a meaning that now survives only in the phrase
'grand total'.
i 32. i.e. because of a single restraint; even though their autonomy in all
other respects was unrestricted.
i 34. *The infernal serpent*] 'That old serpent, called the Devil, and Satan'
(*Rev.* xii 9) both because Satan entered the body of a serpent to tempt Eve,
and because his nature is guileful and dangerous to man. See also x 506–47,
where the devils are metamorphosed into serpents.
i 36–7. *MS* has colon, altered to semicolon, after *mankind,* and semicolon

Had cast him out from heaven, with all his host
Of rebel angels, by whose aid aspiring
To set himself in glory above his peers,
40 He trusted to have equalled the most high,
If he opposed; and with ambitious aim
Against the throne and monarchy of God
Raised impious war in heaven and battle proud
With vain attempt. Him the almighty power
45 Hurled headlong flaming from the ethereal sky
With hideous ruin and combustion down
To bottomless perdition, there to dwell
In adamantine chains and penal fire,

after *heaven*.   *what time*] Usually compared with Lat. *quo tempore*–need-
lessly, since the phrase was perfectly idiomatic English; see *OED* s.v. *What*
C II 10. Cp. *Comus* 291, *Lycidas* 28.

i *38*. *aspiring*] The first of the poem's comparatively rare feminine line-
endings. The only other certain instances in Bk i are at ll. 98, 102 and 606.
On the theory underlying M.'s practice in this respect, see Prince 135.

i *39*. Satan's crime was not his aspiring *above his peers*–he was already
'high above' them (v 812)–but aspiring *To set himself in* [divine] *glory*.

i *40–8*. Numerous verbal echoes relate these lines to the Biblical accounts of
the fall and binding of Lucifer, in *2 Pet*. ii 4, *Jude* 6, *Rev*. xx 1–2, and *Is*.
xiv 12–15: 'Thou hast said . . . I will exalt my throne above the stars of God
. . . I will be like the most High. Yet thou shalt be brought down to hell.'

i *40*. The construction with a past infinitive was standard English.

i *42*. *MS* has comma after *God*.

i *43*. *impious war*] Perhaps has a secondary Latinate sense; *bellum impium*
means internecine war.

i *44*. *With vain attempt*] 'The typically Miltonic half-line of derision' (Broad-
bent 69). Cp. ll. 746f below.

i *44–5*. *Him . . . Hurled*] Object–subject–verb inversions constitute one of the
two types of inversion commonest in *PL*, according to Emma (143ff). But
larger samples than his show this to be the only common form of inversion.
(Subject–object–verb inversions, Emma's other common type, are in fact
rare.)

i *45*. Characteristically mingling a Biblical allusion (to *Luke* x 18, 'I beheld
Satan as lightning fall from heaven') with a classical (to Homer, *Il*. i 591,
Hephaistos 'hurled from the ethereal threshold').

i *46*. *ruin*] falling, downfall. Not a Latinism, except etymologically.
combustion] M. may intend an ambiguity; in astronomical contexts the
word meant 'obscuration of a planet due to near conjunction with the sun'.

i *48*. Cp. *Jude* 6 and *2 Pet*. ii 4; 'God spared not the angels that sinned, but . . .
delivered them into chains of darkness.' The *adamantine* chains, however,
perhaps also allude to Aeschylus, *Prom*. 6. *MS* omits comma after *fire*.

> Who durst defy the omnipotent to arms.
> 50   Nine times the space that measures day and night
>   To mortal men, he with his horrid crew
>   Lay vanquished, rolling in the fiery gulf
>   Confounded though immortal: but his doom
>   Reserved him to more wrath; for now the thought
> 55   Both of lost happiness and lasting pain
>   Torments him; round he throws his baleful eyes
>   That witnessed huge affliction and dismay
>   Mixed with obdurate pride and steadfast hate:
>   At once as far as angels' ken he views
> 60   The dismal situation waste and wild,

i 49. The elliptic *Who* (= He who) is common in Spenser, Shakespeare and Donne (see Emma 57). It is not a Latinism. Empson 37 brings out the implication that 'though Milton believes God to be omnipotent, Satan dared to hope he could be defeated'. Note how M. gives an early signal to prepare the reader to recognize this as one of the many things about which Satan deludes himself.

i 50–83. In rhetorical terminology, the *exordium*, which supplies the setting and stage directions of the opening scene (Condee 507f). The nine days during which the devils *Lay vanquished* (Days 13–22) immediately follow the nine days of their fall from Heaven (Days 4–13; see vi 871, also Introduction, 'Chronology', pp. 25–28 above. The choice of this particular time interval points up the analogy between the fall of the devils and the fall of the defeated Titans (also lasting nine days: see Hesiod, *Theog.* 664–735). Throughout, M. makes extensive use of this mythological parallel; it was important to him, since it justified treating the brief Biblical references to a war in heaven as more than allegory.

i 55. The fallen angels became vulnerable to pain when their natures were 'impaired' by sin (vi 327 and 691).

i 56. *MS* has comma after *him*.   *baleful*] 'full of evil'; but also 'full of suffering'. On the change of tense, see MacCaffrey 43; also Broadbent 69f: 'the tenses shift imperceptibly into an immediate Hell.'

i 57. *witnessed*] bore witness to.

i 58. *obdurate*] Stressed on the second syllable.

i 59. *Angels' ken*] the field of vision of angels (*OED* 2). As was common seventeenth-century orthographical practice, however, the apostrophe is omitted in *MS*, *Ed I* and *Ed II*, so that *Angels ken* is also a possible reading. Both uses of *ken* (i.e., as noun or as verb) can be matched in *PL* (e.g. xi 379 and 396).

i 60. *MS* has no stop after *wild*. It is usually said that the sense demands a colon. This is not so, however, if 'flamed' (l. 62) is understood as a past participle= 'aflame' (see *OED* s.v. *Flamed* 1).   *dismal*] A stronger word than it has since become: 'dreadful' or 'sinister', rather than merely 'gloomy'. Emma 73 finds the epithet–noun–epithet scheme infrequent in M. But this

A dungeon horrible, on all sides round
As one great furnace flamed, yet from those flames
No light, but rather darkness visible
Served only to discover sights of woe,
65   Regions of sorrow, doleful shades, where peace
And rest can never dwell, hope never comes

extraordinary conclusion may be the result of taking an inadequate sample, or of underestimating the rarity of the scheme in the corpus of literature at large. Until we have rank-ordered rhetorical tables, one can only record the guess that this will in fact be found to be a favourite device of M.'s. Cp. ll. 69, 180, 304f; and for a discussion of earlier uses of the device by the Italian poets, see Prince 112–9.

i *61. dungeon horrible*] M. customarily avoided inversion of the normal noun–adjective order; see Emma (69f), who finds an incidence of only 4·7 per cent of the adjectives in his poetry. On the symbolic nature of M.'s hell, see Joseph E. Duncan in *HLQ* xx (1957); Merritt Y. Hughes in *MP* liv (1956); Ernest Schanzer in *UTQ* xxiv (1955); and Broadbent Ch. ii.

i *62–4.* Oddly censured by T. S. Eliot as 'difficult to imagine'; but of course the passage is not intended merely as physical description. Cp. the account of the land of the dead in *Job* x 22: 'the light is as darkness'; and see Ann Gossman *N & Q* ccvi (1961) 182 on Plutarch's affirmative answer to the question 'Whether darkness can be visible to us'. The paradoxes M. alludes to would be familiar to his contemporaries, for they were the subject of much theological speculation. Thus, the notion of flames without light had its classic statement in St Basil's *Homil. in Ps. xxviii*, where we are told that God separates the brightness of fire from its burning power, in such a way that the brightness works to the joy of the blessed, the burning to the torture of the damned; cp. Herrick 387, 'The fire of Hell this strange condition hath' / To burn, not shine (as learned *Basil* saith.)'; and see further Hughes 183 and John M. Steadman, 'John Collop and the flames without light', *N & Q* cc (1955) 382–3. Discussing the paradox of *sights of woe* visible in darkness, Edgar F. Daniels ('Thomas Adams and "Darkness Visible"("Paradise Lost", I, 62–3)', *N & Q* cciv (1959)) finds authority in Adams for the idea of a special visory power granted to devils. But a more obvious source is Aquinas *Summa theol.* Supple. xcvii 4, where it is debated whether the damned have any light and can see, and where the Basilian passage is cited. Among literary analogues to M.'s description, the best known is the O.E. *Genesis B*, 333: 'þæt wæs leohtes leas | and wæs liges full'. Broadbent 71 notes that i and ii 'are full of paradoxical expressions–antithesis, antimetabole, oxymoron, etc.' This is the case with almost all those parts of the poem where the devils appear. See vi 498*n* on the extravagant rhetoric used to portray the angelic war.

i *66.* Cp. Dante, *Inf.* iii 9, 'All hope abandon, you who enter here'; also Euripides, *Troades* 681, 'to me even hope, that remains to all mortals, never comes'.

That comes to all; but torture without end
Still urges, and a fiery deluge, fed
With ever-burning sulphur unconsumed:
70   Such place eternal justice had prepared
For these rebellious, here their prison ordained
In utter darkness, and their portion set
As far removed from God and light of heaven
As from the centre thrice to the utmost pole.
75   O how unlike the place from whence they fell!
There the companions of his fall, o'erwhelmed
With floods and whirlwinds of tempestuous fire,
He soon discerns, and weltering by his side
One next himself in power, and next in crime,
80   Long after known in Palestine, and named
Beelzebub. To whom the arch-enemy,

i 68. *urges*] presses.

i 69. *sulphur*] The sulphurousness of the *deluge* goes back at least to Statius, who speaks of Cocytus' *sulfureas undas* (*Theb.* i 91).

i 71. *those*] these *MS*.   *prison*] In *MS* an apostrophe over the *o* indicates elision, by a convention common at the time.

i 72. *utter*] Both 'outer' and 'utter'.

i 73–4. See iv 20–3n. For the association of heaven with the celestial pole, see Cicero, *De nat.* ii 40f, rendering Aratus, *Phainomena*. Whereas Homer simply places Hades as far below earth as heaven is above it (*Il.* viii 16), and Virgil places Tartarus 'twice' as far below (*Aen.* vi 577), M. gives a more intricate formulation: a 'typically "geometrical" statement of relationships', as MacCaffrey 78 calls it. By so doing, he draws attention to the numerical proportion, heaven–earth: earth–hell :: 1 : 2, i.e., earth divides the interval between heaven and hell in the proportion that Neoplatonists believed should be maintained between reason and concupiscence: the harmonious diapason. See, e.g., Pico della Mirandola, *Conclusiones*, 'secundum mathematicam Pythagorae', *Opera omnia* (Basel 1573) i 79. For the view that 'thrice' is merely an intensive, see B. A. Wright in *RES* xxi (1945) 43.

i 76. *MS* omits comma after *fall*.

i 79. *MS* omits comma after *power*.

i 81. *Beelzebub*] Hebrew 'Lord of the flies'; *Matt.* xii 24, 'the prince of the devils'; cp. *Mark* iii 22, *Luke* xi 15, etc. Although M. would know that Beelzebub's name had an anthropological background in the cults of deliverers from insect pests (see John Selden, *De dis Syris* ii 6), his portrayal of the devil seems rather to be based on an allegorization invented by St Jerome and cited by Valeriano in his discussion of the fly as a symbol of pertinacity. Beelzebub is god of flies 'because he never ceases to infest the human race in every way, and to lay now this snare, now that, for our destruction' (Valeriano 320). It is in keeping with his pertinacious malignity

> And thence in heaven called Satan, with bold words
> Breaking the horrid silence thus began.
> 　　If thou beest he; but O how fallen! how changed
> 85　From him, who in the happy realms of light
> Clothed with transcendent brightness didst outshine
> Myriads though bright: if he whom mutual league,
> United thoughts and counsels, equal hope
> And hazard in the glorious enterprise,
> 90　Joined with me once, now misery hath joined
> In equal ruin: into what pit thou seest
> From what highth fallen, so much the stronger proved
> He with his thunder: and till then who knew
> The force of those dire arms? Yet not for those,

towards mankind that Beelzebub should be made the spokesman of Satan's plan to ruin the 'new race' (ii 345–76).　　*arch-enemy*,] *MS* omits comma.
i *82*. *Satan*] Hebrew, 'enemy'. After his rebellion, Satan's 'former name' (according to patristic tradition, Lucifer) was no longer used (v 658).
i *84*. Rhetorically, the *ianua narrandi* or opening of the action proper. Satan's exclamation echoes Aeneas' at the appearance of Hector's ghost during the fall of Troy: *ei mihi, qualis erat! quantum mutatus ab illo / Hectore* (*Aen.* ii 274). But cp. also *Is.* xiv 12: 'How art thou fallen from heaven, O Lucifer.' The 41-line speech beginning here, the first speech in the book, exactly balances the last, which also is spoken by Satan and also consists of 41 lines (i 622–62). For the numerological significance of speech-lengths in *PL*, see Introduction, 'Numerology', p. 23 above.　　*he*;] he? *MS*, question mark altered to comma.　　*fallen!*] *MS* no point.
i *85*. *him*,] *MS* omits comma.
i *86*. *didst*] The break in grammatical concord reflects Satan's doubt whether Beelzebub is present and so whether second-person forms are appropriate. In *PL*, such incomplete grammar usually implies agitation in the speaker.
i *87*. *If he*] Ellipsis for 'If thou beest he' as in l. 84. For the closeness of Beelzebub's alliance with Satan, see v 673–96.
i *88–9*. *MS* comma after *hope* is transferred to the end of the line following in *Ed I* and *Ed II*, probably correctly.
i *91–2*. *into what . . . From what*] Possibly imitating the Greek construction οἷος . . . οἷος. Cp. v 543 and *PR* ii 30.
i *94–8*. Perhaps echoing Aeschylus, *Prom.* 987–96, or Dante, *Inferno* xiv 52–60, the boast of Capaneus (one of the Violent against God) that all Jove's thunderbolts will never crush his spirit.　　*fixed mind*] Cp. *Il Penseroso* 4 and Spenser, *F.Q.* IV vii 16: 'nothing could [Aemylia's] fixed mind remove'.
high disdain] A common phrase in Elizabethan poetic diction, rendering the Italian *alto sdegno*, and not necessarily implying adverse criticism of the aristocratic sentiment. So Satan intends it here; but M. means it to betray the speaker's contemptuous pride, as 'fixed' does his rigidity.
i *94*. *MS* and *Ed I* omit comma.

95   Nor what the potent victor in his rage
     Can else inflict, do I repent or change,
     Though changed in outward lustre, that fixed mind
     And high disdain, from sense of injured merit,
     That with the mightiest raised me to contend,
100 And to the fierce contention brought along
     Innumerable force of spirits armed
     That durst dislike his reign, and me preferring,
     His utmost power with adverse power opposed
     In dubious battle on the plains of heaven,
105 And shook his throne. What though the field be lost?
     All is not lost; the unconquerable will,
     And study of revenge, immortal hate,
     And courage never to submit or yield:
     And what is else not to be overcome?
110 That glory never shall his wrath or might
     Extort from me. To bow and sue for grace
     With suppliant knee, and deify his power,

i 96. MS and Ed I omit comma after *inflict*.

i 97. *Though . . . lustre*] A parenthesis, so that MS comma after *lustre* at first
seems preferable to Ed I and Ed II semicolon. But semicolon dividing a
verb from its object was common seventeenth-century rhetorical punctu-
ation.

i 98–9. Contrast iii 309–11; Satan conceives 'merit' in terms of might,
but Christ's merit consists in being good. See vi 820*n*.

i 105. *shook his throne*] Untrue, as we learn at vi 834. 'In fact it is the Son's
chariot rather than Satan's armies which shake heaven to its foundations
(vi 710–2)' (Rajan² 12). Cp. Cowley, *Davideis* i, *n* 15, 'it were improper for a
Devil to make a whole speech without some lies in it; such are those pre-
cedent exaltations of the *Devils* power, which are most of them false, but
not *All*.' Throughout the present passage Satan sees himself as the hero of the
sort of Satanic or pagan epic that the devils show a taste for at ii 549ff (Bur-
den 64). Empson 44 defends the difficult position that Satan's argument is
false, yet his defiant belief in it somehow creditable.

i 105–6. Enlarging on the speech of Satan in Fairfax's translation of Tasso
Gerusalemme liberata iv 15: 'We lost the field, yet lost we not our heart.'

i 106–10. The question mark after l. 109 shows the primary chain of dis-
course to be 'what else is it, not to be overcome?' But in a secondary chain
And what is else corresponds to the Latin construction *Et si quid sit*: 'And if
there is anything else (besides *will . . . study of revenge . . . hate . . . courage*)
that is not to be overcome.'   *That glory*] Either 'the glory of overcoming
me' or 'my glory of *will*, etc.'

i 107. *study*] pursuit of.

i 112. MS and Ed I omit comma after *power*.

> Who from the terror of this arm so late
> Doubted his empire, that were low indeed,
115 That were an ignominy and shame beneath
> This downfall; since by fate the strength of gods
> And this empyreal substance cannot fail,
> Since through experience of this great event
> In arms not worse, in foresight much advanced,
120 We may with more successful hope resolve
> To wage by force or guile eternal war
> Irreconcilable, to our grand foe,
> Who now triumphs, and in the excess of joy
> Sole reigning holds the tyranny of heaven.
125   So spake the apostate angel, though in pain,
> Vaunting aloud, but racked with deep despair:

i *114. Doubted*] feared for. *MS* has semicolon after *empire*.

i *115. ignominy*] Possibly pronounced 'ignomy', as it was often spelled.
But the word has four syllables at vi 383, and may have here, if we assume
synaloepha or coalescence between –*y* and *and*.

i *116–7.* Implying not only that as angels they are immortal (which M.
himself believed, on the basis of *Luke* xx 36: see *De doctrina* i 7 (Columbia
xv 34), but also that the continuance of their strength (another quality of
angels: see *Ps.* ciii 20 and *De doctrina* i 7) is assured *by fate*, in accordance
with which, Satan thinks, he was self-begotten in his own 'puissance'
(v 864). Contrast Moloch's and Belial's doubts at ii 92–100 and 142–54.
Throughout, the devils acknowledge the ultimate power of fate; yet like
the Stoics of *PR* iv 317 they avoid the identification of it with the will of God
that is stated at vii 137.   *gods*] As used by God the Father in iii 341, this is
merely another term for angels; but as Satan uses it here, and as it is used in
his temptations of Eve (v 70–81); ix 708–18), it is more ambiguous, im-
plying the pagan illusion of a pantheon. Cp. v 853–64, where Satan asserts
that the angels are uncreated. *MS* has full stop after *downfall*.   *empyreal
substance*] Contrast Raphael's 'intelligential substances' (v 408); Satan's
phrase obscures the fact that the qualities of the substance depend on con-
tinuing rationality.

i *122. foe*] Note how the devils studiously avoid naming God directly; cp.
ll. 95, 131.

i *123. triumphs*] Stressed on the second syllable.

i *124. tyranny*] An obvious instance of devilish partiality, exposed in advance
by 'monarchy of God' in l. 42 and 'joy' in l. 123. Less obvious is Beelzebub's
careful choice of *perpetual* rather than 'eternal' in l. 131.

i *126.* Empson (31) tries to excuse Satan's despair by saying it is not despair
in the religious sense, but the feeling of a defeated general. But it is hard to
imagine any sense in which fighting against God is not a religious exper-
ience.

And him thus answered soon his bold compeer.
O prince, O chief of many throned powers,
That led the embattled seraphim to war
130 Under thy conduct, and in dreadful deeds
Fearless, endangered heaven's perpetual king;
And put to proof his high supremacy,
Whether upheld by strength, or chance, or fate,
Too well I see and rue the dire event,
135 That with sad overthrow and foul defeat
Hath lost us heaven, and all this mighty host
In horrible destruction laid thus low,
As far as gods and heavenly essences
Can perish: for the mind and spirit remains
140 Invincible, and vigour soon returns,
Though all our glory extinct, and happy state
Here swallowed up in endless misery.
But what if he our conqueror, (whom I now
Of force believe almighty, since no less

i *127*. MS colon after *compeer* is probably an error, for M. regularly uses period before direct speech.

i *128-9*. *throned powers*] Obliquely evokes thrones and powers–orders, like the seraphim, in Dionysius' angelic hierarchies. But the direct meaning is less specific: 'exalted and powerful beings'. The seraphim are mentioned as one of the offices or degrees that distinguish the angels, in *De doctrina* i 7 (Columbia xv 36f). See also 324n, ii 512n. Seraphim receive mention at i 539, 794; ii 750; iii 381, 667; v 277, 749, 804, 875, 896; vi 249, 579, 604, 841; vii 113, 198.

i *131*. *endangered . . . king*] As Empson 38 hints, this verges on paradox. *MS* has semicolon after *Fearless*. For the medieval and Renaissance concept of a metaphysical perpetuity or continuity of kingship, consult Ernst H. Kantorowicz, *The King's Two Bodies: A Study in Mediaeval Political Theology* (Princeton 1957) chs vi, vii. But there is an allusion also to Boethius' distinction between *aeternus* and *perpetuus* in *De consolatione* v, Prose 6: 'If we would apply proper epithets to those subjects, we can say, following Plato, that God is eternal, but the universe is continual.'

i *133*. The main powers recognized in the devils' ideology. All the explanations of God's supremacy miss the mark: the loyal angels were unable to win by *strength*; and, as Raphael tells Adam at v 534, God never exacts obedience by destiny (*fate*). God's power rests on a quality that does not occur to Beelzebub: goodness. *MS* has semicolon after *fate*.

i *141*. *extinct*] 'put out, as a Flame, or any thing that burns and shines' (Patrick Hume, *cit*. Ricks 61).

i *144*. Empson 38 notes that as Beelzebub uses it *almighty* means only 'able to defeat any opposing combination in battle'. From the defeat of the devils

145   Than such could have o'erpowered such force as ours)
        Have left us this our spirit and strength entire
        Strongly to suffer and support our pains,
        That we may so suffice his vengeful ire,
        Or do him mightier service as his thralls
150   By right of war, whate'er his business be
        Here in the heart of hell to work in fire,
        Or do his errands in the gloomy deep;
        What can it then avail though yet we feel
        Strength undiminished, or eternal being
155   To undergo eternal punishment?
        Whereto with speedy words the arch-fiend replied.
            Fallen cherub, to be weak is miserable
        Doing or suffering: but of this be sure,
        To do aught good never will be our task,
160   But ever to do ill our sole delight,

Beelzebub concludes that the supremacy of heaven's king is upheld by
strength (l. 133), not *chance*. See ll. 116–7n and ii 232–3n.   *Of force*] perforce.
i *148. suffice*] satisfy (*OED* 5); not a Latinism.
i *149–52.* 'The evil angels are reserved for punishment. They are sometimes,
however, permitted to wander throughout the whole earth, the air, and
heaven itself, to execute the judgments of God' (*De doctrina* i 9; Columbia
xv 106–9).
i *154–5.* i.e., 'being that is eternal, merely so that our punishment may also
be eternal'. A secondary connection between *avail* (153) and *To undergo*
is not out of the question, *pace* Verity.
i *156. the Fiend*] MS corr. to 'th'Arch-fiend' by a different hand.
i *157. cherub*] The cherubim were the second order of the angels, who ex-
celled in knowledge. See l. 128–9n and vi 102n.
i *158. Doing or suffering*] Some will choose to hear an echo of Livy ii 12: *Et
facere et pati fortia Romanum est*, the famous words of Mutius Scaevola when
he demonstrated Roman fortitude by voluntarily burning his right hand,
and thus frightened the Etruscan Porsenna into withdrawing his army.
But the phrase also recalls Horace, *Odes* III xxiv 43, where it is covetousness
that impels men 'to do and to suffer' anything, and to desert the path of
virtue. In any case the idiom was not uncommon, both in Latin and in
English. Cp. *PL* ii 199. Broadbent 76–8 gives an account of the theological
process whereby in this passage Satan's heart is hardened into a demonic
nihilism.
i *159–68.* This fundamental disobedience and disorientation makes Satan's
heroic virtue into the corresponding excess of vice (Steadman 94). 163–5
looks forward to xii 470–8 and Adam's wonder at the astonishing reversal
whereby God will turn the Fall into an occasion for good. For 'the inmost
counsel of God was the Fortunate Fall of man' (Empson 39).

As being the contrary to his high will
Whom we resist. If then his providence
Out of our evil seek to bring forth good,
Our labour must be to pervert that end,
165   And out of good still to find means of evil;
Which oft-times may succeed, so as perhaps
Shall grieve him, if I fail not, and disturb
His inmost counsels from their destined aim.
But see the angry victor hath recalled
170   His ministers of vengeance and pursuit
Back to the gates of heaven: the sulphurous hail
Shot after us in storm, o'erblown hath laid
The fiery surge, that from the precipice
Of heaven received us falling, and the thunder,
175   Winged with red lightning and impetuous rage,
Perhaps hath spent his shafts, and ceases now
To bellow through the vast and boundless deep.
Let us not slip the occasion, whether scorn,
Or satiate fury yield it from our foe.
180   Seest thou yon dreary plain, forlorn and wild,
The seat of desolation, void of light,
Save what the glimmering of these livid flames
Casts pale and dreadful? Thither let us tend
From off the tossing of these fiery waves,

i *167. if I fail not*] unless I am mistaken; err (*OED* s.v. *Fail* III 11). Not a Latinism.

i *169–71.* Although Messiah was 'sole victor' at the expulsion (vi 880), it is just possible that he subsequently sent loyal detachments in pursuit of the falling rebels. At least, Chaos confirms Satan's account in this respect, at ii 997–8 (*q.v.*). Raphael, however, omits any mention of an immediate pursuit. This could be due to modesty on his part, or oversight on M.'s. But if the discrepancy is intentional it presumably means that Satan is reluctant to admit that Christ won singlehanded. Or is M. more subtly implying that to encounter Messiah's power is not to have his kingship irresistibly proved, but only to be 'thunderstruck' (vi 858); so that memory is confused and the problem of belief remains? At any rate, as Empson (43) perceives, 'the rebels are as if emerging from a drug, and remember nothing of the intervening period' between the war and their release from chains.

i *172. laid*] caused to subside.

i *173. The fiery*] This fiery *MS*.

i *178. MS* has colon after *occasion*.

i *181–3.* See ll. 62–4n.   *livid*] Cp. the address of the damned Oedipus to the Styx, which he 'sees' with sightless eyes: *umbrifero Styx livida fundo* (Statius, *Theb.* i 57). *MS* erroneously has exclamation mark after *dreadful*.

185   There rest, if any rest can harbour there,
      And reassembling our afflicted powers,
      Consult how we may henceforth most offend
      Our enemy, our own loss how repair,
      How overcome this dire calamity,
190   What reinforcement we may gain from hope,
      If not what resolution from despair.
         Thus Satan talking to his nearest mate
      With head uplift above the wave, and eyes
      That sparkling blazed, his other parts besides
195   Prone on the flood, extended long and large
      Lay floating many a rood, in bulk as huge
      As whom the fables name of monstrous size,
      Titanian, or Earth-born, that warred on Jove,

i *185.* The allusion to *Richard II* V i 5–6, 'Here let us rest, if this rebellious
Earth / Have any resting for her true king's queen', is particularly appro-
priate, since Earth was rebellious because mother of the Giants, the 'Earth-
born' of l. 198 below.

i *186–7. afflicted*] downcast.   *offend*] strike at so as to hurt; harm, injure
(*OED* II 6).

i *191. If not*] This may be elliptical ('If we may not gain such reinforcement'),
or it may imply that for Satan despair is preferable to hope (cp. vi 787–8)–
'. . . from hope if not . . . from despair'. The comma after *not* which would
have singled out the first line of meaning is not found in *MS, Ed I*, or *Ed II*.

i *193–5.* Anticipating Satan's later metamorphosis into a serpent, these
lines are modelled on Virgil's description of the sea-serpents swimming
towards Laocoon; cp. esp. *pectora quorum inter fluctus arrecta iubaeque /
sanguineae superant undas*; *pars cetera pontum / pone legit* and *ardentisque oculos
suffecti* (*Aen.* ii 206–8, 210). Burden 56 notes that in the last glimpse we have
of Satan he is again a sea-serpent. For the periodic conversion of devils to
serpent form see x 556*n.*

i *196.* So Virgil makes the body of the Giant Tityos cover an area of nine
iugera, as he lies suffering the tortures of Tartarus (*Aen.* vi 596); while Spen-
ser's 'old Dragon', a descendant of the dragon of *Revelation*, 'with his large-
nesse measured much land' (*F.Q.* I xi 8).

i *197–200.* According to most accounts, the serpent-legged *Briareos* was a
Titan, the serpent-headed *Typhon* (= Typhoeus) a Giant; though often
the two races were confused. Each was a son of Earth; each fought against
Jupiter; and each was eventually confined beneath Aetna (in this connect-
tion, note the comparison of the 'dry land' of hell to the shattered side of
Aetna, at ll. 232–7). Typhon was so powerful that when he first made war
on the Olympians they had to resort to metamorphoses to escape (Ovid,
Met. v 325–31 and 346–58); thus M.'s choice of simile prepares for the devils'
assumption of new shapes at ll. 392–521 below. The main force of the simile,
however, is to continue the rebel angel / Giant analogy (see ll. 50–83*n*).

Briareos or Typhon, whom the den
200   By ancient Tarsus held, or that sea-beast
Leviathan, which God of all his works
Created hugest that swim the ocean stream:
Him haply slumbering on the Norway foam
The pilot of some small night-foundered skiff,
205   Deeming some island, oft, as seamen tell,
With fixed anchor in his scaly rind
Moors by his side under the lea, while night
Invests the sea, and wished morn delays:

Here the analogy is not only a matter of size: Conti and others had inter-
preted the myth of Typhon's attack on Jupiter allegorically, taking it to
mean that 'there is no religion, no humanity, no justice, where the fury of
ambition rears itself' (*Mythologiae* vi 22). At *Nativity Ode* 226 M. conflates
this snaky Typhon with the Typhon of Egyptian mythology, an important
deity representing the cosmic principle of divisive evil (see Plutarch, *De
Iside*); and in *Areopagitica* he interprets the Egyptian Typhon as a type of
those who dismember truth (Yale ii 549).   *den / By ancient Tarsus*] The
Biblical Tarsus was the capital of Cilicia, and both Pindar and Aeschylus
describe Typhon's habitat as a Cilician cave or 'den' (*Pyth.* i 17; *Prom.*
351–4).

i *200–8. Leviathan*] The monster of *Job* xli, identified in Isaiah's prophecy
of judgment as 'the crooked serpent' (*Is.* xxvii 1), but also sometimes
thought of as a whale. The anecdote of the illusory island is from the *Phy-
siologus*, where the moral drawn is that the devil is similarly deceitful (see
J. H. Pitman, 'Milton and the Physiologus', *MLN* xl (1925) 439). It was a
familiar story, which was not only repeated in Renaissance encyclopae-
dias, but even achieved the currency of visual representation. At Hardwick
House, e.g., there is an emblematic mural showing a ship anchored to a
whale, with the legend *Nusquam tuta fides* (see Freeman 92). On the tradition-
al comparison of Satan to a whale-island Ricks (6) cites James Whaler in
PMLA xlvi (1931) 1050; Svendsen 33–5; and D. M. Hill in *N & Q* cci (1956)
158. Other refs. will be found in White 197f; E. G. Millar, ed., *A Thir-
teenth Century Bestiary* (Oxford 1958) 38f and Pl. 76; and Jurgis Baltrušaitis,
Réveils et Prodiges (Paris 1960) 130f and Fig. 20A. T. S. Eliot (*Proc. of the
Brit. Acad.* xxxiii (1947) 74) thought the simile an extraneous digression; but
it illustrates the delusiveness of Satan and the danger of trusting his false
appearance of greatness in the early books of the poem.
i *202. ocean stream*] A Homeric phrase (ῥόος ὠκεάνοιο).
i *203. foam*] Bentley thought this an unhappily inadequate support for a
whale; but Ricks 16 defends the synecdoche, on the ground that M. intends
a mysterious, sinister effect. Cp. ll. 226f below.
i *204. night-foundered*] sunk in night, benighted; as in *Comus* 483.
i *208. Invests*] wraps, covers; but also 'night beleaguers, and morn is slow
to raise the siege'.

So stretched out huge in length the arch-fiend lay
210 Chained on the burning lake, nor ever thence
Had risen or heaved his head, but that the will
And high permission of all-ruling heaven
Left him at large to his own dark designs,
That with reiterated crimes he might
215 Heap on himself damnation, while he sought
Evil to others, and enraged might see
How all his malice served but to bring forth
Infinite goodness, grace and mercy shown
On man by him seduced, but on himself
220 Treble confusion, wrath and vengeance poured.
Forthwith upright he rears from off the pool
His mighty stature; on each hand the flames
Driven backward slope their pointing spires, and rolled
In billows leave i' the midst a horrid vale.
225 Then with expanded wings he steers his flight
Aloft, incumbent on the dusky air
That felt unusual weight, till on dry land
He lights, if it were land that ever burned
With solid, as the lake with liquid fire;

i *209–13.* See *De doctrina* i 9 (Columbia xv 108f): the 'proper place' of the devils is the pit, 'from which they cannot escape without permission'. In *De doctrina* i 8 M. explains why God is blameless, even though he permits, and even tempts, the wicked to sin. Lewis 66 cites St Augustine on God's exploitation of evil wills: *voluntatum malarum iustissimus ordinator.* Empson 42f dwells on the horror of God's leading Satan into evil; but it is wayward to take the first part of the sentence without the second. God's purpose is not that Satan should damn himself, but that grace should be shown to man (in spite of all Satan's malice, which only redounds on himself).   *heaved*] raided.

i *217–20.* Cp. 163–5 and xii 470–8; also *De doctrina* i 8 (Columbia xv 72–5): 'The will being already in a state of perversion, he [God] influences it in such a manner, that out of its own wickedness it either operates good for others, or punishment for itself.'

i *224. horrid*] bristling (with *spires*).

i *226–7. incumbent*] 'pressing with his weight', then a common use of the word. The conceit of the air oppressed by Satan's weight recalls Spenser, *F.Q.* I xi 18, where the burden is a similar one: the old dragon.

i *229–30.* Darbishire[2] i 285 prefers the punctuation of *MS* (comma after *fire*, semicolon after *hue*), since it throws the volcano simile 'into relation with the whole phenomenon of the fiery liquid–solid land of Hell, while the punctuation of the first edition [and one might add, the second also] relates it erroneously to the one aspect of colour'. But 'hue' means far more

230　And such appeared in hue, as when the force
　　　Of subterranean wind transports a hill
　　　Torn from Pelorus, or the shattered side
　　　Of thundering Aetna, whose combustible
　　　And fuelled entrails thence conceiving fire,
235　Sublimed with mineral fury, aid the winds,
　　　And leave a singed bottom all involved
　　　With stench and smoke: such resting found the sole
　　　Of unblessed feet. Him followed his next mate,
　　　Both glorying to have scaped the Stygian flood
240　As gods, and by their own recovered strength,
　　　Not by the sufferance of supernal power.
　　　　　Is this the region, this the soil, the clime,
　　　Said then the lost archangel, this the seat
　　　That we must change for heaven, this mournful gloom
245　For that celestial light? Be it so, since he

than colour. It was a complex word in the seventeenth century, referring to both surface appearance and texture.

i *230–7*. For a full exposition of the seismological theory that attributed earthquakes and volcanoes to the action of imprisoned winds swelling the body of the earth, see Gabriel Harvey's 'Discourse, of the Earthquake' (Spenser, *The Prose Works*, ed. R. B. Gottfried (Baltimore, Md. 1949), pp. 449–59). The same anthropomorphic notion underlies Virgil's and Ovid's descriptions of Aetna, the main sources of the present passage: *Aen.* iii 571–7 (note esp. *viscera montis*; cp. M.'s image of *entrails*) and *Met.* xv 297–306, 340–55 (note the mention of combustible material 'containing the seeds of flame'). The passage continues the Typhon allusion of 199, for, according to one theory, Typhon symbolised the power of volcanoes (see Conti, *Mythologiae* vi 22). See further in vi 195–8n below. It may be relevant that Raban Maur interprets the 'great mountain burning with fire' of *Rev.* viii 8 as the devil himself (Migne cxi 365).

i *232–3*. *Pelorus*] Cape Faro, the north-eastern promontory of Sicily, near Aetna. The allusion is to Virgil, *Aen.* iii 570ff, a description of the uptorn entrails of the volcano, with a version of the myth that the Giant Enceladus lies beneath the mountain.

i *235*. *Sublimed*] converted directly from solid to vapour by volcanic heat in such a way as to resolidify on cooling.　　*mineral fury*] disorder of minerals, or subterranean disorder.

i *236*. *involved*] wreathed.

i *239*. *Stygian flood*] the 'gulf' of l.52. The epithet perhaps also implies darkness, as in *Elegia iv* 95 *Stygiis . . . tenebris*.

i *240–1*. This is illusion, as ll. 210–20 has enabled us to recognize.

i *244*. *change for*] have instead of.

Who now is sovereign can dispose and bid
What shall be right: furthest from him is best
Whom reason hath equalled, force hath made supreme
Above his equals. Farewell happy fields
250 Where joy for ever dwells: hail horrors, hail
Infernal world, and thou profoundest hell
Receive thy new possessor: one who brings
A mind not to be changed by place or time.
The mind is its own place, and in itself
255 Can make a heaven of hell, a hell of heaven.
What matter where, if I be still the same,
And what I should be, all but less than he
Whom thunder hath made greater? Here at least
We shall be free; the almighty hath not built
260 Here for his envy, will not drive us hence:
Here we may reign secure, and in my choice
To reign is worth ambition though in hell:
Better to reign in hell, than serve in heaven.

i 246. *sovereign*] M. customarily used the Italianate spelling 'sovran', in his later poetry – possibly to ensure a disyllabic reading.

i 255. The view that heaven and hell are states of mind was held by Amaury de Bene, a medieval heretic often cited in seventeenth-century accounts of atheism; it is to be distinguished from the Ubiquism of Marlowe's Mephistophilis in *Doctor Faustus* l. 316 (D. C. Allen, *MLN* lxxi (1956) 325). As MacCaffrey 70f points out, this passage has a strong irony that has generally been missed. Satan's specious denial of the effects of the fall of the angels is belied by his shock at the change in Beelzebub (84 above), and almost verbally contradicted at iv 75ff, 'Which way I fly is hell'.

i 257. *all but less than*] The confusion of the idioms 'all but equal to' and 'only less than' reflects Satan's self-deception about his status.

i 258. In Satan's view it is only God's power that makes him greater. See vi 820–3n.

i 259. As Empson 40 notes, Satan is here speaking with an ironic tone, sneering at the metaphysical sense of 'almighty'.

i 262. *worth ambition*] worth striving for (Latin *ambitio*). Satan refers, not merely to a mental state, but to an active effort that is the price of power (B. A. Wright, *N & Q* cciii (1958) 200).

i 263. An almost proverbial commonplace: cp. *Ps.* lxxxiv 10; Homer, *Od.* xi 488 (better a living swain than king of the dead); Aeschylus, *Prom.* 965; Plutarch, *Life of Julius Caesar* xi 2 ('I would rather be first here [in a miserable barbarian village] than second in Rome'); Serafino della Salandra, *Adamo caduto* ii 1; and Phineas Fletcher, *The Purple Island* vii 10: 'In heav'n they scorn'd to serve, so now in hell they reigne.' And contrast *PL* vi 183–4, where Abdiel, who prefers to serve in heaven, points out that hell is a prison, not a kingdom.

But wherefore let we then our faithful friends,
265   The associates and copartners of our loss
Lie thus astonished on the oblivious pool,
And call them not to share with us their part
In this unhappy mansion, or once more
With rallied arms to try what may be yet
270   Regained in heaven, or what more lost in hell?
    So Satan spake, and him Beelzebub
Thus answered. Leader of those armies bright,
Which but the omnipotent none could have foiled,
If once they hear that voice, their liveliest pledge
275   Of hope in fears and dangers, heard so oft
In worse extremes, and on the perilous edge
Of battle when it raged, in all assaults
Their surest signal, they will soon resume
New courage and revive, though now they lie
280   Grovelling and prostrate on yon lake of fire,
As we erewhile, astounded and amazed,
No wonder, fallen such a pernicious highth.
    He scarce had ceased when the superior fiend
Was moving toward the shore; his ponderous shield
285   Ethereal temper, massy, large, and round,
Behind him cast; the broad circumference

i 266. *oblivious pool*] the pool attended by oblivion; the 'forgetful lake' of ii 74. Unlike the river Lethe of the classical underworld and of M.'s hell (ii 583–614), with which Merritt Hughes wrongly identifies it, this pool lacks the power to wash out memory and woe completely. In ii 606–14 the devils are tortured by their inability to drink from the Lethe: a torture they would be oblivious to, if they had already drunk.   *astonished*] stunned; dismayed; stupefied.

i 268. *MS* has semicolon after *mansion*.

i 276. *edge*] critical position; also 'front line', rendering the related Latin word *acies* (though not necessarily felt as a Latinism – *OED* cites Coverdale). cp. vi 108.

i 282. *fallen . . . highth*] As often in *PL*, the preposition is by an ellipsis omitted.

i 284. *Was moving*] Poetic syntax, rendering Satan's haste by the use of a continuative tense, where some such phrase as 'started to move', describing the inception of the movement, would have been more ordinary. A similar graphic use of the imperfect tense is common in Latin and Greek.

i 285. *Ethereal temper*] tempered in celestial fire; cp. ii 139 and 813. Syntactically elusive, the phrase is an ellipsis for 'Ethereal in its temper' or 'Of ethereal temper'.

i 286–91. Homer compares Achilles' shield to the moon in *Il.* xix 373, but

Hung on his shoulders like the moon, whose orb
Through optic glass the Tuscan artist views
At evening from the top of Fesole,
290   Or in Valdarno, to descry new lands,
Rivers or mountains in her spotty globe.
His spear, to equal which the tallest pine
Hewn on Norwegian hills, to be the mast
Of some great ammiral, were but a wand,

there the comparison is one of brightness, not of size. Cp. also the shield of
the proud Radigund in Spenser, *F.Q.* V v 3, 'that shined wide, / As the
faire Moone in her most full aspect'. In *Areopagitica* M. mentions having
visited Galileo, the *Tuscan artist*–i.e., scientist–who first studied the moon
with a telescope powerful enough to resolve its surface features. At the time
Galileo had been placed under house arrest by the Inquisition, near Florence,
which is in the 'Valdarno' or Valley of the Arno, overlooked by the hills of
Fesole or Fiesole (Latin *Faesulae*). (The apparently supererogatory geo-
graphical details may be M.'s indulgence of fond memories; or they may be
intended to supply terrestrial counterparts to the lunar *Rivers or mountains*
of l. 291.) For a review of the controversy as to whether M. did actually
visit Galileo, see Yale ii 538*n*; and for his fascination with Galileo's re-
searches–which is reflected also in iii 588–90 and v 261–3–see Grant Mc-
Colley in *PMLA* lii (1937) 728–62, and Nicolson[2]. The mountainous for-
mation of the moon's surface was described in Galileo's *Siderius nuncius*
(Venice 1610). In his reference to the telescope M. as it were lays in advance
the evidential basis for the world in which the action of this 'first modern
cosmic poem' (Nicolson[4] 81) is to take place. As Cope (50ff) argues, how-
ever, space in *PL* is much more than topical scientific reality: it is also 'the
aesthetic shape of the myth'. And in any case it is possible that Galileo is
introduced here as the representative of 'a culture quite different from, and
implicitly superior to, the military heroism' of Satan (Broadbent 72).
optic glass] telescope (not poetic diction).
i *292–4*. The comparison of a weapon to a mast was common; e.g. the club
of Polyphemus (Homer, *Od.* ix 322) and the lances of Tancredi and Argante
(Tasso, *Gerus. lib.* vi 40 and–in Fairfax's translation only–iii 17). But the
comparison to a tree suggests more particularly the rude weapon that was
a conventional attribute of the lawless Wild Man: cp. the 'lopped pine' of
Polyphemus in Virgil, *Aen.* iii 659 and the 'snaggy Oke' of the proud Orgo-
glio in Spenser, *F.Q.* I vii 10; and see Richard Bernheimer, *Wild Men in the
Middle Ages: A Study in Art, Sentiment and Demonology* (Cambridge, Mass.
1952). A famous engraving by Melchior Lorch (illus. Cohn, Fig. 2) shows
Satan–Antichrist with a roughly lopped tree.   *equal*] compare with.
Norwegian] Ships' masts were commonly made from imported Norwegian
fir.   *ammiral*] flagship; a spelling current in M.'s time.

295   He walked with to support uneasy steps
       Over the burning marl, not like those steps
       On heaven's azure, and the torrid clime
       Smote on him sore besides, vaulted with fire;
       Natheless he so endured, till on the beach
300   Of that inflamed sea, he stood and called
       His legions, angel forms, who lay entranced
       Thick as autumnal leaves that strew the brooks
       In Vallombrosa, where the Etrurian shades
       High overarched imbower; or scattered sedge
305   Afloat, when with fierce winds Orion armed
       Hath vexed the Red Sea coast, whose waves o'erthrew
       Busiris and his Memphian chivalry,

i *296. marl*] rich clay soil, but probably used here as a sensuously rich synonym for 'ground'.

i *297. MS* semicolon after *azure*.

i *299. Natheless*] nevertheless. Perhaps already archaic-poetic.

i *302-4.* Cp. *Is.* xxxiv 4: 'And all the host of heaven shall be dissolved, and the heavens shall be rolled together as a scroll: and all their host shall fall down, as the leaf falleth off from the vine, and as a falling fig from the fig tree.' Fallen leaves were an enduring simile for the numberless dead: see Homer, *Il.* vi 146, Virgil, *Aen.* vi 309-10 ('multitudinous as the leaves of the forest that in the first frost of autumn fall away and drop') and Dante, *Inf.* iii 112-5. But M. adds the concrete precision of an actual locality, again near Florence. If he visited *Vallombrosa* he would know that (as its name partly suggests) it was shaded by extensive deciduous woods. The use of *shades*, by metonymy, for foliage or woods is a characteristic of M.'s diction (B. A. Wright, *N & Q* cciii (1958) 205-8). Broadbent 86 notes the correspondence between the 'Etrurian shades / High overarched' and hell's fiery vault. MacCaffrey 124ff explores the implication that Satan's legions are morally unfruitful and withering.

i *304-6.* The acronychal rising of Orion's belt was anciently supposed to mark the season of storms (see Pliny xviii 223; Virgil, *Aen.* i 535; and Riccioli i 473). But the point of the simile depends on Orion's force as a Biblical symbol. Commentators on *Job* ix 9 and *Amos* v 8 interpreted the creation of Orion as a symbol of God's power to raise tempests and floods to execute his judgments (Riccioli i 408). Thus M.'s transition to the Egyptians overwhelmed by God's judgment in ll. 306-11 is a natural one.   *sedge*] The Hebrew name for the Red Sea was 'Sea of Sedge'.   *armed*] Cp. Virgil, *Aen.* iii 517, *armatumque auro . . . Oriona.*   *vexed*] tossed about.

i *306-11.* Contrary to his promise, the Pharaoh with his *Memphian* (i.e. Egyptian; a favourite word in Sylvester's Du Bartas) charioteers pursued the Israelites–who had been in captivity in *Goshen*–across the Red Sea. The Israelites passed over safely; but the Egyptians' *chariot wheels* were broken (*Exod.* xiv 25), and the rising sea engulfed them and cast their corpses on the

                    While with perfidious hatred they pursued
                    The sojourners of Goshen, who beheld
310   From the safe shore their floating carcasses
                    And broken chariot wheels, so thick bestrewn
                    Abject and lost lay these, covering the flood,
                    Under amazement of their hideous change.
                    He called so loud, that all the hollow deep
315   Of hell resounded. Princes, potentates,
                    Warriors, the flower of heaven, once yours, now lost,
                    If such astonishment as this can seize
                    Eternal spirits; or have ye chosen this place
                    After the toil of battle to repose
320   Your wearied virtue, for the ease you find
                    To slumber here, as in the vales of heaven?
                    Or in this abject posture have ye sworn
                    To adore the conqueror? who now beholds
                    Cherub and seraph rolling in the flood
325   With scattered arms and ensigns, till anon

shore (*ibid.* 30). Traditionally, the Pharaoh was interpreted as a type of the
Devil (Rabanus Maurus, in Migne cxi 51). The mythical tyrant *Busiris* was
commonly identified with the Pharaoh of *Exod.* i (see, e.g., George Sandys[2]
321, commenting on Ovid, *Met.* ix 183 and citing Reinerus Reineccius:
'Busiris . . . is held to be that king of Aegipt who so grievously oppressed
the Israelites: and the author of that inhumane Edict of drowning their
male-children; whence arose the tradition of his sacrificing strangers'); but
naming the later Pharaoh of Exod. xiv Busiris was less usual, and shows,
according to D. C. Allen, *MLN* lxv (1950) 115, that M. had learned from the
Chronicle of Carion, as rewritten by Melancthon, that 'there were many
kings with the same name, Busirises'. Perhaps, however, M. simply con-
flates the two Pharaohs, in the interests of dramatic concentration; as he
may be thought to do also at xii 165–96.
i *311*. MS has full stop after *wheels*, as in seven other places before 'So' or
'As' beginning a simile.
i *313*. *amazement*] consternation, stupefaction.
i *314*. *deep*] In view of iv 76, many will prefer the MS reading 'deeps'.
i *317*. *astonishment*] mental prostration; cp. 313*n*. Note the double lines of
discourse: 'If indeed you are the flower of heaven, when such astonish-
ment can seize you' and 'Heaven lost indeed, if you are susceptible to such
astonishment'.
i *318*. MS colon after *spirits* may be preferable.
i *320*. *virtue*] strength, power, courage.
i *322*. Alluding to the conspirators' oath sworn by the rebel angels; see ii
693.
i *324*. *seraph*] See i 128–9*n*. The singular form may be M.'s own coinage;
earlier only *seraphim* was used, the form with the Hebrew plural inflection.

His swift pursuers from heaven gates discern
The advantage, and descending tread us down
Thus drooping, or with linked thunderbolts
Transfix us to the bottom of this gulf.
330 Awake, arise, or be for ever fallen.
   They heard, and were abashed, and up they sprung
Upon the wing, as when men wont to watch
On duty, sleeping found by whom they dread,
Rouse and bestir themselves ere well awake.
335 Nor did they not perceive the evil plight
In which they were, or the fierce pains not feel;
Yet to their general's voice they soon obeyed
Innumerable. As when the potent rod
Of Amram's son in Egypt's evil day
340 Waved round the coast, up called a pitchy cloud
Of locusts, warping on the eastern wind,
That o'er the realm of impious Pharaoh hung
Like night, and darkened all the land of Nile:
So numberless were those bad angels seen
345 Hovering on wing under the cope of hell
'Twixt upper, nether, and surrounding fires;
Till, as a signal given, the uplifted spear
Of their great sultan waving to direct
Their course, in even balance down they light
350 On the firm brimstone, and fill all the plain;
A multitude, like which the populous north

i *328. linked thunderbolts*] The weapon used by Jupiter and Minerva against
the rebel Giants.
i *332.* MS has semicolon after *wing*.
i *335. nor did they not*] Simulating the Latin idiom *neque non*.
i *337.* M.'s use of the somewhat unusual construction 'obey to' may be
meant to recall *Rom.* vi 16 (its sole occurrence in A.V.), and thus to imply
that Satan's followers are 'servants . . . of sin unto death'.
i *338–44. Amram's son*] Moses, who used his *rod* to bring down on the Egyp-
tians a plague of locusts that 'covered the . . . earth, so that the land was
darkened' (*Exod.* x 12–15; cp. *PL* xii 185–8). M.'s comparison of devils
to locusts is based on allegorisations of this passage and of *Rev.* ix 3 (e.g.
Raban Maur's, Migne cxi 257), which had become so familiar that Phineas
Fletcher could allude to them in the title of his poem *Locustae*. Callot used
the locust schema–on which see E. H. Gombrich, *Art and Illusion* (1962) 68f–
for some of the devils in his engraving *The Temptation of St Anthony* (1617).
warping] floating or turning through the air.
i *345. cope*] canopy, as in iv 992 and vi 215.
i *351–5.* Completing the series of three similes (arranged in ascending order
of cosmic degree), whereby M. successively compares the numerousness of

Poured never from her frozen loins, to pass
Rhene or the Danaw, when her barbarous sons
Came like a deluge on the south, and spread
355   Beneath Gibralter to the Lybian sands.
Forthwith from every squadron and each band
The heads and leaders thither haste where stood
Their great commander; godlike shapes and forms
Excelling human, princely dignities,
360   And powers that erst in heaven sat on thrones;
Though of their names in heavenly records now
Be no memorial blotted out and razed
By their rebellion, from the books of life.
Nor had they yet among the sons of Eve
365   Got them new names, till wandering o'er the earth,
Through God's high sufferance for the trial of man,

the fallen angels to that of plants, insects, and human armies. In *Prol v*, M.
uses barbarian hordes as a symbol for the multitude of errors that threaten
truth. Certain particulars in the present passage, such as the mention of the
Rhine and the Danube, may possibly be drawn from the first few sentences
in Macchiavelli's *Istorie Fiorentine*. See also v 689*n*. The effect of the series
of similes is a complex one: the devils are raised, necromantically; but at the
same time the comparisons are all, in one way or another, morally unfavour-
able.

i *352. frozen loins*] Bentley thought frozen loins unsuitable for generation;
but as MacCaffrey 129 notices, the image is deliberately unnatural and in-
fertile.

i *358. godlike*] Frequently used in *PL* as a synonym for 'heroic'; heroic virtue
being essentially a reflection of the divine (Steadman 95–6).

i *361–3*. Cp. i 82*n* and v 658–9.   *books of life*] The allusion is principally
to *Rev.* iii 5 ('He that overcometh . . . I will not blot out his name out of the
book of life') and *Exod.* xxxii 32–3. 'The emphasis upon the names has an
ironic effect when one remembers that the Biblical overcomers of evil are
given new names in Heaven (*Rev.* iii 12), while these fallen angels 'Got them
new Names' upon earth through the evil of pagan idolatry'' (Sims 13).

i *364–75*. Cp. Hooker, *Laws of Eccles. Pol.* I iv 3: 'These wicked spirits the
Heathens honoured instead of Gods, both generally under the name of
Dii inferi, Gods infernal; and particularly, some in Oracles, some in Idols,
some as household Gods, some as Nymphs.' The origins of the doctrine
that the fallen angels came to earth and deceived men into worshipping
them as gods are traced in Verity 672–4. It was authorized by such texts as
1 Cor. x 20 and *Deut.* xxxii 17 ('They sacrificed unto devils, not to God';
see Sims 14); but a Platonic influence is more conspicuous in such versions
as St Augustine's (*Civ. Dei* vii–x). Broadbent (88f) sees this passage, and
indeed the whole catalogue of devils, as a liberal and aggressively Reformist
attack on the 'multiplex superstition' of Rome.

By falsities and lies the greatest part
Of mankind they corrupted to forsake
God their creator, and the invisible
370   Glory of him that made them, to transform
Oft to the image of a brute, adorned
With gay religions full of pomp and gold,
And devils to adore for deities:
Then were they known to men by various names,
375   And various idols through the heathen world.
Say, Muse, their names then known, who first, who
                   last,
Roused from the slumber, on that fiery couch,
At their great emperor's call, as next in worth
Came singly where he stood on the bare strand,
380   While the promiscuous crowd stood yet aloof?
The chief were those who from the pit of hell
Roaming to seek their prey on earth, durst fix
Their seats long after next the seat of God,
Their altars by his altar, gods adored
385   Among the nations round, and durst abide
Jehovah thundering out of Sion, throned

i *368–71*. Cp. *Rom.* i 23: the Gentiles 'changed the glory of the uncorruptible
God into an image made like to corruptible man, and to birds, and four-
footed beasts, and creeping things'.

i *370*. *Ed I* has comma after *him*.

i *372*. *religions*] rites.

i *376*. Echoing Virgil, *Aen.* xi 664 (*Quem... primum, quem postremum*),
itself an echo of Homer, *Il.* v 703; while the list of heathen deities that
follows (ll. 392–522) is M.'s counterpart to Homer's catalogue of the cap-
tains and ships of the Greeks in *Il.* ii 484–877.   *then known*] By a kind of
prolepsis, M. anticipates the names given to the fallen angels in later ages.

i *377*. *MS* omits comma after *slumber*.

i *380*. *MS* has full stop after *aloof*.

i *381–91*. Introducing the first group of angels (ll. 392–506), those who
later became the gods of nations in contact with the Israelites, and for whom
there is therefore direct Biblical authority. M. imagines their geographical
proximity to Jehovah in his sanctuary to be evidence of their special bold-
ness. On the classification of the devils according to the authority for their
early existence, see Sims 14. Thammuz-Adonis, e.g., is accorded a promi-
nent place on the strength of Ezekiel's reference to him.   *Between the
cherubim*] A formulaic description, frequent in the O.T. (e.g. 2 *Sam.* vi 2,
Is. xxxvii 16), that gains fresh point in the present context. Jehovah is so
throned in his sanctuary, because images of cherubim flanked the ark in the
tabernacle (*Exod.* xxv 18–21).

i *383*. *MS* has commas after *seats* and *after*.

Between the cherubim; yea, often placed
Within his sanctuary itself their shrines,
Abominations; and with cursed things
390   His holy rites, and solemn feasts profaned,
And with their darkness durst affront his light.
First Moloch, horrid king besmeared with blood
Of human sacrifice, and parents' tears,
Though for the noise of drums and timbrels loud
395   Their children's cries unheard, that passed through fire
To his grim idol. Him the Ammonite
Worshipped in Rabba and her watery plain,
In Argob and in Basan, to the stream
Of utmost Arnon. Nor content with such

i *387-91*. M. refers to apostasies of the kings of Judah, such as that of Manasseh, who followed 'the abominations [i.e., unclean practices] of the heathen' and 'built altars for all the host of heaven in ... the house of the Lord' (*2 Kings* xxi 2–7).   *affront*] confront, insult.

i *392-521*. Satan gathers twelve disciples: Moloch, Baal, Ashtoreth, Tammuz, Dagon, Osiris, Isis, Horus, Belial, Titan, Saturn, Jupiter. This travesty of Christ's calling of his disciples may have been suggested to M. by various traditional schemes, such as the Manilian astrological system of twelve Olympian Guardians, or the many attempts to introduce the twelve apostles into the solar zodiac (*EB* vii 13).

i *392-6*. Here and at ii 43, vi 357, M. refers to *Moloch* as *king* because this is the literal meaning of his name. He comes first as the 'strongest and fiercest' (ii 44) of the rebel angels. With the account of his cult, cp. *Nat* 205–10. *passed through fire*] Cp. *2 Kings* xxiii 10: 'that no man might make his son or daughter to pass through fire to Molech'. George Sandys describes the idol of Moloch as hollow, filled with fire; and explains that 'least [the children's] lamentable shreeks should sad the hearts of their parents, the Priests of *Molech* did deafe their eares with the continuall clang of trumpets and timbrels' (*A relation of a journey* (1637) 186); cp. Fuller IV vii 34.

i *397-9*. Though ostensibly magnifying Moloch's empire, these lines look forward to his eventual defeat; for *Rabba*, the Ammonite royal city, is best known for its capture by David after his repentance (*2 Sam.* xii), while the Israelite conquest of the regions of *Argob* and *Basan*, as far as the boundary river *Arnon*, is recalled by Moses as particularly crushing (*Deut.* iii 1–13). *watery plain*] From *2 Sam.* xii 27. *Basan* is the Septuagint and Vulgate form; as usual, M. avoids the *sh* sound.

i *399-403*. Solomon's wives drew him into idolatry (*1 Kings* xi 5–7); but the 'high places that were before Jerusalem ... on the right hand of the mount of corruption which Solomon ... had builded for Ashtoreth the abomination of the Zidonians, and for Chemosh the abomination of the Moabites, and for Milcom the abomination of the children of Ammon' were later destroyed by Josiah (*2 Kings* xxiii 13–4; and see l. 418).

400   Audacious neighbourhood, the wisest heart
       Of Solomon he led by fraud to build
       His temple right against the temple of God
       On that opprobrious hill, and made his grove
       The pleasant valley of Hinnom, Tophet thence
405   And black Gehenna called, the type of hell.
       Next Chemos, the obscene dread of Moab's sons,
       From Aroar to Nebo, and the wild
       Of southmost Abarim; in Hesebon
       And Horonaim, Seon's realm, beyond
410   The flowery dale of Sibma clad with vines,
       And Eleale to the Asphaltic Pool.

i 403. *opprobrious hill*] The Mount of Olives, because of Solomon's idolatry called 'mount of corruption' (A.V.) or *mons offensionis* (Vulgate). M. approximates even more closely to the Vulgate form at 416 and 443. Throughout the poem, Solomon functions as a type both of Adam and of Christ. Here Solomon's uxoriousness foreshadows Adam's. Cp. vi 833–4*n*, ix 439–43*n*, xi 396–407*n*, xii 332–4*n*.

i 403–5. To abolish sacrifice to Moloch, Josiah 'defiled Topheth, which is in the valley of the children of Hinnom' (*2 Kings* xxiii 10). Fuller treats Tophet as a synonym for 'the *Valley of* the sons of *Hinnom*', deriving it from *toph*, a drum (an allusion to Moloch's ritual music) (*Pisgah-Sight* IV vii 34). *Gehenna*] 'Valley of Hinnom': not an O.T. form, but used in *Matt.* x 28 as a name for hell. St Jerome explains that because it was a place of sacrifice, known as 'the Graveyard', the Valley of Hinnom became a type of the 'everlasting punishments with which sinners were afflicted' (*Comm. in Matt.*; Migne xxvi 68). The *grove* of Moloch, which is not mentioned in the Bible, also comes from St Jerome. George Sandys remarks that before the grove was hewn down it was 'most delightful' and 'a Paradise' (*Relation* 186).

i 406. *Chemos*, 'the abomination of Moab', is associated with the neighbouring god Moloch in *1 Kings* xi 7, and follows naturally therefore in M.'s catalogue.

i 407–11. Most of these places are named in *Num.* xxxii as the formerly Moabite inheritance assigned by Moses to the tribes of Reuben and Gad (see also Fuller's map in *Pisgah-Sight*).   *Aroar*] Aroer *MS* and *Ed I*, as A.V. A town in the extreme north of the territory.   *Nebo*] A town in the south, near the *Abarim* mountains. *Num.* xxi 25–30 rejoices at the Israelite capture of *Hesebon* (Heshbon), a Moabite city which had been taken by the Amorite King *Seon* or Sihon. Heshbon, Horonaim, 'the vine of Sibmah', and Elealeh all figure in Isaiah's sad prophecy of the destruction of Moab (*Is.* xv 5, xvi 8f).   *Horonaim*] *MS, Errata* and *Ed II*; Heronaim *Ed I*.   *Asphaltic Pool*] The Dead Sea or *lacus Asphaltites*, so called because of its bituminous scum; the south-west Moabite boundary.

> Peor his other name, when he enticed
> Israel in Sittim, on their march from Nile,
> To do him wanton rites; which cost them woe.
> 415   Yet thence his lustful orgies he enlarged
> Even to that hill of scandal, by the grove
> Of Moloch homicide, lust hard by hate;
> Till good Josiah drove them thence to hell.
> With these came they, who from the bordering flood
> 420   Of old Euphrates to the brook that parts
> Egypt from Syrian ground, had general names
> Of Baalim and Ashtaroth; those male,
> These feminine. For spirits when they please
> Can either sex assume, or both; so soft
> 425   And uncompounded is their essence pure,

i *412–4. Num.* xxv 1–3 and *Hos.* ix 10.   *woe*] A plague that killed 24,000 (*Num.* xxv 9).

i *415–7. hill of scandal*] See 399–403n. The *orgies* (ὄργια, rites) are called lustful on the authority of *Num.* xxv 1, and of the Fathers, especially St Jerome, who identified the Moabite deity Chemosh or Baal-Peor with the Latin Priapus (Migne xxv 896).

i *418. Josiah*] Always a favourite with the Reformers, because of his destruction of idolatrous images; see Broadbent 88.

i *419–21.* An area stretching from the north-east limit of Syria to the south-west limit of Canaan, the river Besor. The Euphrates is *old* because mentioned in *Gen.* ii 14.

i *421–3. Baal*] 'Baal. That is, a lord, being the name general for most idols' (Fuller, *Pisgah-Sight* IV vii 23). The Phoenician and Canaanite sun-gods were collectively called *Baalim* (plural form), each local cult being particularised by a further surname, as Baal-Peor. Similarly the variants of the moon goddess Ashtoreth were *Ashtaroth.* 'Milton proves his control over the devils by sophisticated anthropological manipulation, and invites us to stand back from them without necessity of belief' (Broadbent 88).

i *423–31.* Cp. vi 344–53 and see vi 328–34n. In *Anatomy of Melancholy* I ii 1 ii, Burton gathers authorities for and against the view that devils are corporeal; but 'that they can assume other aerial bodies, all manner of shapes at their pleasures, appear in what likeness they will themselves', most angelologists, he reports, 'credibly believe'. Todd and McColley cite various sources and analogues; but R. H. West in *PQ* xxvii (1949) argues that M. is dependent on Michael Psellus. M.'s Satan is later to assume many different forms; see, e.g., his metamorphosis into a young cherub at iii 636. Such instability of form is in Renaissance poetry almost always evil: one thinks in particular of Spenser's Archimago (esp. *F.Q.* I ii 10). The last metamorphosis of the devils in *PL*, however, is punitive and perhaps subordinated to a cyclic pattern (see x 575f).   *dilated*] expanded.

i *425. MS* has semicolon after *pure.*

Not tied or manacled with joint or limb,
Nor founded on the brittle strength of bones,
Like cumbrous flesh; but in what shape they choose
Dilated or condensed, bright or obscure,
430   Can execute their airy purposes,
And works of love or enmity fulfil.
For those the race of Israel oft forsook
Their living strength, and unfrequented left
His righteous altar, bowing lowly down
435   To bestial gods; for which their heads as low
Bowed down in battle, sunk before the spear
Of despicable foes. With these in troop
Came Astoreth, whom the Phoenicians called
Astarte, queen of heaven, with crescent horns;
440   To whose bright image nightly by the moon
Sidonian virgins paid their vows and songs,
In Sion also not unsung, where stood
Her temple on the offensive mountain, built
By that uxorious king, whose heart though large,
445   Beguiled by fair idolatresses, fell
To idols foul. Thammuz came next behind,

i *432. those*] these MS.
i *433.* Cp. *1 Sam.* xv 29: 'Strength of Israel', a formulaic periphrasis for Jehovah.
i *438.* The image of *Astoreth* or *Astarte*, the *Sidonian* (Phoenician) moon-goddess and Venus, was 'the statue of a woman, having on her own head the head of a bull, where the horns erected resembled the crescent moon' (Fuller, *Pisgah-Sight* IV vii 22, drawing on Selden *De Dis Syris* ii 2). Cp. *Nativity Ode* 200, 'mooned Ashtaroth'.   *queen of heaven*] from *Jer.* xliv 17–19; cp. *Comus* 1002, 'Assyrian queen'.
i *442–6.* See 399–403n.   *large*] Alluding to *1 Kings* iv 29: 'God gave Solomon . . . largeness of heart' (i.e., capaciousness of intellect).
i *446. Thammuz* follows appropriately, as the lover of Astarte (Cicero, *De nat. deor.* iii 23). His identification with Adonis was based on St Jerome's commentary on the passage in Ezekiel drawn on by M. in 454–6: 'Then he brought me to the door of the gate of the Lord's house which was toward the north; and, behold, there sat women weeping for Tammuz' (*Ezek.* viii 14). The Syrian festival of Tammuz was celebrated after the summer solstice: the slaying of the young god by a boar was mourned as a symbol of the southward withdrawal of the sun and the death of vegetation (Macrobius, *Saturn.* i 21, Selden ii 11). Each year when the River Adonis became discoloured with red mud it was regarded as a renewed sign of the god's wound (Conti, *Mytholog.* v 26). Literary treatments of this myth and popular accounts of the cult (such as Fuller's and Sandys's) had made the story of Tammuz very familiar: see Fuller IV vii 43: 'the poets are almost hoarse

Whose annual wound in Lebanon allured
The Syrian damsels to lament his fate
In amorous ditties all a summer's day,
450 While smooth Adonis from his native rock
Ran purple to the sea, supposed with blood
Of Thammuz yearly wounded: the love-tale
Infected Sion's daughters with like heat,
Whose wanton passions in the sacred porch
455 Ezekiel saw, when by the vision led
His eye surveyed the dark idolatries
Of alienated Judah. Next came one
Who mourned in earnest, when the captive ark
Maimed his brute image, heads and hands lopped off
460 In his own temple, on the groundsel edge,
Where he fell flat, and shamed his worshippers:
Dagon his name, sea monster, upward man
And downward fish: yet had his temple high
Reared in Azotus, dreaded through the coast
465 Of Palestine, in Gath and Ascalon
And Accaron and Gaza's frontier bounds.
Him followed Rimmon, whose delightful seat
Was fair Damascus, on the fertile banks
Of Abbana and Pharphar, lucid streams.
470 He also against the house of God was bold:

with singing the sad elegies. . . .' For other mentions by M., see *Nativity Ode* 204, *Mans* 11.

i *455. Ezekiel*] Ezechiel *MS.*

i *457–63.* When the Philistines put the ark of the Lord, which they had captured, into the temple of Dagon, 'on the morrow morning, behold, Dagon was fallen upon his face to the ground . . . and the head of Dagon and both the palms of his hands were cut off upon the threshold' (*1 Sam.* v 4).   *groundsel*] threshold. The name *Dagon* was sometimes referred to the Hebrew word for 'corn'; but M. prefers to follow Selden's authority (*De dis Syris* ii 3) in deriving it from Heb. *dag*, 'fish', and in representing the god as half fish. Cp. Fuller, *Pisgah-Sight* II x 32: 'Upwards man-like he ascended, / Downwards like a fish he ended.'

i *464–6. Azotus, Ascalon, Accaron*] Vulgate forms (A.V. Ashdod, Askelon, Ekron) current in the seventeenth century. Divine vengeance on these Philistine cities is prophesied in *Zeph.* ii 4. *MS* has semicolon after *Azotus.*

i *467–71.* When Elisha told Naaman that his leprosy would be cured if he washed in the Jordan, the Syrian was at first angry (*2 Kings* v 12: 'Are not Abana and Pharpar, rivers of Damascus, better than all the waters of Israel?'), but then humbled himself and was cured. On Naaman as a type of the regenerate sinner, see Tuve 198.

A leper once he lost and gained a king,
Ahaz his sottish conqueror, whom he drew
God's altar to disparage and displace
For one of Syrian mode, whereon to burn
475   His odious offerings, and adore the gods
Whom he had vanquished. After these appeared
A crew who under names of old renown,
Osiris, Isis, Orus and their train
With monstrous shapes and sorceries abused
480   Fanatic Egypt and her priests, to seek
Their wandering gods disguised in brutish forms
Rather than human. Nor did Israel scape
The infection when their borrowed gold composed
The calf in Oreb: and the rebel king
485   Doubled that sin in Bethel and in Dan,
Likening his maker to the grazed ox,
Jehovah, who in one night when he passed
From Egypt marching, equalled with one stroke
Both her first born and all her bleating gods.
490   Belial came last, than whom a spirit more lewd

i *471–6.* After successfully engineering the overthrow of Damascus by the Assyrians, the *sottish* (foolish) King Ahaz became interested in the cult of Rimmon, and had an altar of the Syrian type put in the temple of the Lord (*2 Kings* xvi 9–17).

i *476–506.* Gods 'whose Scriptural authority is not so clear' (Sims 14).

i *477–82.* Cp. the flight of 'the brutish gods of Nile' in *Nativity Ode* 211–28. *wandering gods*] M. alludes to the myth–highly appropriate to this context–of the Olympian gods fleeing from the Giant Typhoeus into Egypt, and hiding in bestial forms (Ovid, *Met.* v 319–31) afterwards worshipped by the Egyptians.   *abused*] deceived.

i *482–4.* Perhaps the most familiar of all Israelite apostasies was their worship of 'a calf in Horeb' (*Ps.* cvi 19) made by Aaron while Moses was away receiving the tables of the Law (*Exod.* xxxii). The calf is identified by Fuller as the golden ox image of the Egyptian deity Apis (*Pisgah-Sight* IV vii 20).

i *484–5. rebel king*] Jeroboam, who led the revolt of the ten tribes of Israel against Rehoboam, Solomon's successor; he 'doubled' Aaron's sin, since he made 'two calves of gold', placing one in Bethel and the other in Dan (*1 Kings* xii 28–9).

i *486.* 'Thus they changed their glory into the similitude of an ox that eateth grass' (*Ps.* cvi 20).

i *488–9.* At the passover, Jehovah smote all the Egyptian firstborn, 'both man and beast' (*Exod.* xii 12); presumably this stroke would extend to their sacred animals. Calves could be described as *bleating*, though the main force of the word is in its contemptuousness.

i *490–3.* Of the devils treated at length Belial comes last, both because he

Fell not from heaven, or more gross to love
Vice for itself: to him no temple stood
Or altar smoked; yet who more oft than he
In temples and at altars, when the priest
495 Turns atheist, as did Ely's sons, who filled
With lust and violence the house of God.
In courts and palaces he also reigns
And in luxurious cities, where the noise
Of riot ascends above their loftiest towers,
500 And injury and outrage: and when night
Darkens the streets, then wander forth the sons
Of Belial, flown with insolence and wine.
Witness the streets of Sodom, and that night
In Gibeah, when the hospitable door
505 Exposed a matron to avoid worse rape.
These were the prime in order and in might;
The rest were long to tell, though far renowned,

had no local cult, and because in the poem he is 'timorous and slothful'
(ii 117). Properly, 'Belial' is an abstract noun meaning 'iniquity'; though
the personification in *2 Cor.* vi 15, and the common Biblical and pro-
verbial phrase 'sons of Belial', encouraged the notion that it was a name.
Burton makes Belial prince of the third order of devils, the 'inventors of
all mischief' (*Anatomy of Melancholy* I ii 1 ii). Cp. *PR* ii 150–224 where
Belial is again portrayed as lustful. Rajan (² 35) sees Belial as 'the cavalier
type in Puritan eyes–suave, dilettante, dissolute and lacking in courage'.
i *494–6.* The impiety and fornication of *Ely's* sons are described in *1 Sam.*
ii 12–24.
i *497–8.* Cp. the similar touch of satire at *PR* ii 183.
i *498–502. flown*] Literally 'swollen, in flood', but in the seventeenth century
used metaphorically of people. Cp. James Ussher, *Annals* (1658) vi 250:
'Being somewhat high flowen with wine'.
i *504–5. Gen.* xix helps to account for the *MS* and *Ed I* reading, 'In Gibeah,
when hospitable doors / Yielded their matrons to prevent[*MS* avoid] worse
rape'. In *Ed II* the allusion is more clearly to Judges xix, where we are told
of a Levite lodging in Gibeah, whose concubine was put outside the door
and given up to the 'sons of Belial' in order to save him from homosexual
rape. She herself was raped to death. Cp. M.'s draft of a tragedy on the
burning of Sodom: 'The first Chorus beginning may relate the course of
the citty each evening every one with mistresse, or Ganymed, gitterning
along the streets, or solacing on the banks of Jordan, or down the stream'
(*Trin. MS*; Columbia xviii 234).
i *506–7.* See ll. 381–7n.
i *507–21.* Gods, enumerated much more perfunctorily, for whom there is
little or no Scriptural authority. The *Ionian* (Greek) people were by some
held to be the issue of *Javan* the son of Japhet the son of Noah, on the basis

The Ionian gods, of Javan's issue held
Gods, yet confessed later than Heaven and Earth
510 Their boasted parents; Titan Heaven's first born
With his enormous brood, and birthright seized
By younger Saturn, he from mightier Jove
His own and Rhea's son like measure found;
So Jove usurping reigned: these first in Creet
515 And Ida known, thence on the snowy top
Of cold Olympus ruled the middle air
Their highest heaven; or on the Delphian cliff,
Or in Dodona, and through all the bounds
Of Doric land; or who with Saturn old
520 Fled over Adria to the Hesperian fields,
And o'er the Celtic roamed the utmost isles.
All these and more came flocking; but with looks
Down cast and damp, yet such wherein appeared
Obscure some glimpse of joy, to have found their chief
525 Not in despair, to have found themselves not lost
In loss itself; which on his countenance cast
Like doubtful hue: but he his wonted pride
Soon recollecting, with high words, that bore

of the Septuagint version of *Gen.* x 1f (also *Is.* lxvi 19). Cp. iv 717 and *SA* 715-6. Hesiod and other ancient authors make *Heaven* (Uranus, Coelus) and *Earth* (Ge, Terra, Thea) the parents of *Saturn* and the other Titans, but the story of *Titan* the eldest child and of his war against *Saturn* (Cronos) is transmitted only by the Christian author Lactantius. Saturn was rescued and enthroned by his son *Jove*, who later banished him, however, so that he had to flee across *Adria* (the Adriatic).   *enormous*] monstrous.
i 514-5. Cp. *Il Penseroso* 29. On Mt *Ida*, in *Creet* (Crete), *Jove* was born and secretly reared.
i 515-6. 'Snow-capped Olympus' is a Homeric formula (cp. *Il.* i 420, xviii 615).   *middle air*] the cold vaporous *media regio*, the second, only, of the three layers into which the Schoolmen divided the atmosphere. See Sylvester's Du Bartas 35, Verity 674-6 and Svendsen 88.
i 517. *Delphian cliff*] Cp. *Nativity Ode* 178 'steep of Delphos'. Delphi was famed as the site of the Pythian oracle of Apollo, but cults of Ge, Poseidon, and Artemis were also celebrated there.
i 518. The oracle of Zeus at Dodona in Epirus was thought to be the most ancient in Greece.
i 519-21. *Doric land* is Greece; *the Hesperian fields* Italy; the *Celtic* fields France; and *the utmost isles* the British Isles (*ultima Thule*: Virgil, *Georg.* i 30), or else Britain, Ireland and Iceland.
i 523. *damp*] depressed or stupefied; cp. xi 293.
i 528. recollecting] recovering (*OED* s.v. *Recollect* v.¹4). Perhaps ironic, in view of the common use of the word in devotional contexts, to mean

Semblance of worth, not substance, gently raised
530   Their fainting courage, and dispelled their fears.
Then straight commands that at the warlike sound
Of trumpets loud and clarions be upreared
His mighty standard; that proud honour claimed
Azazel as his right, a cherub tall:
535   Who forthwith from the glittering staff unfurled
The imperial ensign, which full high advanced
Shone like a meteor streaming to the wind
With gems and golden lustre rich imblazed,
Seraphic arms and trophies: all the while
540   Sonorous metal blowing martial sounds:
At which the universal host upsent

'concentrating the mind in mystical contemplation' (*OED* s.v. *Recollect* v.² 4).

i *529*. M. sometimes signposts an obvious moral intention; here this is occasioned, no doubt, by Satan's attractive tenderness towards his troops.

i *530. fainting*] Darbishire prefers *MS* and *Ed I* 'fainted': 'The context supports *fainted*: the collapse is over, their courage is not fainting, it begins to revive.' But 'fainting' could mean 'drooping, feeble'; and is stylistically preferable, in such close proximity to two preterites in *–ed*.

i *531–53*. Eisenstein 58f draws attention to the 'audio-visual distribution of images' in this passage.

i *532. clarions*] shrill narrow-tubed trumpets.

i *533–4. Azazel* figures as one of the chief of the fallen angels who are the object of God's avenging wrath in the apocryphal apocalypse *The Book of Enoch* (see esp. Chs viii, x, xiii, liv, lv, and lxix; Charles ii 192–4, 196, 220–1, 233). For the healing of the earth he is bound and cast into the same wilderness where the scapegoat was led (*Enoch* x 4–8; see also *Lev.* xvi, where the word *azazel* is again associated with the scapegoat). *Enoch* was not directly accessible in the seventeenth century; but cabbalistic tradition made Azazel one of the four standard-bearers in Satan's army. M. could have learned this from Reuchlin or Archangelus of Borgo Nuovo, or Fludd; see West 155f (we need not, however, imitate West's contortions to avoid the natural conclusion, that M. was interested in cabbalistic ideas).

i *537. meteor*] comet; appropriate not only visually, but also because it is ominous to man.

i *538. imblazed*] adorned with heraldic devices.

i *539*. Contrast the 'ensigns high advanced' in heaven, which are emblazoned with 'holy memorials, acts of zeal and love' (v 593; see Rajan 47). The ancient Roman practice in triumphal processions of carrying memorials of battles had been revived in the secular processions of the Renaissance. See, e.g., *The Triumph of Maximilian I*, ed. S. Appelbaum (New York 1964) 10ff.

i *541. upsent*] sent or discharged upwards (first instance in *OED*).

A shout that tore hell's concave, and beyond
Frighted the reign of Chaos and old Night.
All in a moment through the gloom were seen
545   Ten thousand banners rise into the air
With orient colours waving: with them rose
A forest huge of spears: and thronging helms
Appeared, and serried shields in thick array
Of depth immeasurable: anon they move
550   In perfect phalanx to the Dorian mood
Of flutes and soft recorders; such as raised
To highth of noblest temper heroes old
Arming to battle, and in stead of rage
Deliberate valour breathed, firm and unmoved
555   With dread of death to flight or foul retreat,
Nor wanting power to mitigate and swage,

i *542. concave*] A common term for the vault of heaven.

i *543. reign*] realm (*OED* 2; not a Latinism). See ii 894–909 and 959–70, where Chaos and Night are portrayed as rulers of the region of unformed matter between heaven and hell.

i *546. orient*] brilliant, resplendent; also, perhaps, 'rising': on the vertical movement throughout this passage (*raised* 529, *upreared* 532, *high advanced* 536, *upsent* 541, *rise* 545, *rose* 546, *raised* 551), which belong to a repeated pattern of ascents and falls, see Allen 108 and Cope 97–9.

i *550. phalanx*] A square battle formation common in M.'s time. Cp. the 'quadrate' of faithful angels at vi 62; also *Reason of Church-Government* i 6 (Yale i 789): 'as those smaller squares in battell unite in one great cube, the main phalanx, an embleme of truth and stedfastnesse'. On the cube as an iconographical symbol of virtue and stability, see Tervarent cols. 136f; there is a good example in Achille Bocchi's beautiful emblem book *Symbolicae quaestiones* (Bologna 1555). On the meanings of the square and the quadrate (Virtue, Justice, etc.) see Fowler, App. i. Note that at vi 552–5 the devils' square is a deceptive and hollow one.

i *550–61*. A parody of the 'instrumental harmony that breathed / Heroic ardour' into the loyal angels (vi 65–6); though M. allows the devils to use the best *mood* (mode) for encouraging calm and heroic firmness–the Doric mode, contrasted in this respect with the soft and indolent Ionian and Lydian modes, in Plato, *Republic*, iii 398–9. On 'grave and Dorick' music see *Areopagitica* (Yale ii 523) and *Lycidas* 189; and on the assuaging effect of music, *Of Education* (Yale ii 410–1).

i *551–2*. Unlike the Romans, who used trumpets, the Spartans went into battle, as many ancient authors remark, to the sound of flutes. The evocation of noble courage is one of several 'consciously designed to suggest the idea of heroic virtue' in the fallen angels (Steadman 91).

i *555. MS* has semicolon after *retreat*.

i *556. swage*] assuage.

With solemn touches, troubled thoughts, and chase
Anguish and doubt and fear and sorrow and pain
From mortal or immortal minds. Thus they
560 Breathing united force with fixed thought
Moved on in silence to soft pipes that charmed
Their painful steps o'er the burnt soil; and now
Advanced in view, they stand, a horrid front
Of dreadful length and dazzling arms, in guise
565 Of warriors old with ordered spear and shield,
Awaiting what command their mighty chief
Had to impose: he through the armed files
Darts his experienced eye, and soon traverse
The whole battalion views, their order due,
570 Their visages and stature as of gods,
Their number last he sums. And now his heart
Distends with pride, and hardening in his strength
Glories: for never since created man,
Met such embodied force, as named with these
575 Could merit more than that small infantry
Warred on by cranes: though all the Giant brood

i 560–1. At vi 64 the loyal angels also 'moved on / In silence'; cp. Homer, *Il.* iii 8: 'The Achaians marched in silence breathing courage.'

i 563. *horrid*] bristling (with spears). A poetic word, perhaps felt as a Latinism, though it had been used by Spenser (*F.Q.* I vii 31), Burton (I ii 3 xiv), and Evelyn (27 June 1654).

i 568. *traverse*] across.

i 569. *MS* has semicolon after *views*, and so has at least one copy of *Ed I*.

i 573. *since created man*] since man was created; a Latin construction.

i 574. *embodied*] united into one body.

i 575. *small infantry*] The Pygmies (see l. 780), whose smallness tradition much exaggerated. The image may have been suggested by Homer's simile (*Il.* iii 5) in the passage M. used for 561. Addison suspected *infantry* to be a pun; probably with justice (*Spectator* No. 297; 9 Feb. 1712). The same pun is perpetrated by Jonson; see *Time Vindicated* 176ff.

i 576–90. To amplify the heroic stature of the angels, and *a fortiori* of their leader, M. dismisses only to mention a series of armies that had been thought worthy of epic treatment. Successively he evokes the 'matter of Rome the great', the 'matter of Britain' and the 'matter of France'–all pygmy arguments compared with his own.

i 576–7. See 197–200n. Ovid (*Met.* x 151) and Statius (*Theb.* vi 358) and others locate the warfare of the Giants with the Olympian gods on the Phlegraean plains. The combat was supposed to have been begun at Phlegra in Macedonia (Pallene) and renewed at Phlegra in Italy, near Cumae. See 713–7n below.

Of Phlegra with the heroic race were joined
That fought at Thebes and Ilium, on each side
Mixed with auxiliar gods; and what resounds
580   In fable or romance of Uther's son
Begirt with British and Armoric knights;
And all who since, baptized or infidel
Jousted in Aspramont or Montalban,
Damasco, or Marocco, or Trebisond,
585   Or whom Biserta sent from Afric shore
When Charlemain with all his peerage fell
By Fontarabbia. Thus far these beyond

i *577-9*. Two of the principal ancient epic cycles centred on the strife of
the Theban brothers and on the siege of Troy. Conventionally, the gods
assisted their mortal protégés in battle – as they do, e.g., in Homer's *Iliad* and
Statius' *Thebaid*.

i *579-87*. Omitted by Bentley as 'Romantic Trash'.

i *580-1*. *Uther's son*] King Arthur. M. once projected an Arthurian epic (see
Mans 81, *Dam* 165-70 and Hanford² 179-81); though in *PR* ii 359-61 such
fables are represented as a temptation.   *Armoric*] from Brittany.

i *582*. The diction is Ariostan; cp. *Orlando Furioso* xviii 56: *Non men de le
'nfedel le battezzate.*

i *583*. *Aspramont*] A castle near Nice. M. may have in mind Andrea da
Barberino's popular romance *Aspromonte* (but see also Ariosto, *Orlando
Furioso* xvii 14).   *Montalban*] The castle of Rinaldo, which figures in
Luigi Pulci's *Morgante Maggiore*, Boiardo's *Orlando Innamorato* and Ariosto's
Orlando Furioso. All these romances are concerned with chivalric wars
between Christians and Saracens.

i *584*. Ariosto describes jousting of *baptized* and *infidel* at *Damasco* (Damas-
cus) in *Orlando Furioso* xvii. The splendid Byzantine city of Trebizond was
known for its tournaments, both from Bessarion's *Encomion Trapezountos*
(fifteenth century) and from Giovanni Ambrosio Marini's widely popular
romance, the *Caloandro Fedele* (1640).

i *585*. In *Orlando Innamorato* ii, Boiardo tells how the Saracens gathered at
Bizerta in Tunis for their invasion of Spain.

i *586-7*. M. would know late versions of the Charlemagne legend, such as
Barberino's *Reali di Francia* (*c.* 1400). Charlemagne's whole rearguard, led
by Roland, one of the twelve peers or paladins, was massacred at Ronces-
valles, about forty miles from *Fontarabbia* (mod. Fuenterrabia). One Spanish
author, Mariana, put the defeat at Fontarabbia itself; but there was no ver-
sion in which Charlemagne fell. Is it pure coincidence that, when the
royalist rising of August 1659 failed, Fuenterrabia was where Charles went,
to seek support from both French and Spanish? M. may have seen a sym-
bolic contrast between this treating with friend and foe, and the uncom-
promising chivalry of the greater Charles.

Compare of mortal prowess, yet observed
Their dread commander: he above the rest
590   In shape and gesture proudly eminent
Stood like a tower; his form had yet not lost
All her original brightness, nor appeared
Less than archangel ruined, and the excess
Of glory obscured: as when the sun new risen
595   Looks through the horizontal misty air
Shorn of his beams, or from behind the moon
In dim eclipse disastrous twilight sheds
On half the nations, and with fear of change
Perplexes monarchs. Darkened so, yet shone
600   Above them all the archangel: but his face
Deep scars of thunder had intrenched, and care
Sat on his faded cheek, but under brows
Of dauntless courage, and considerate pride
Waiting revenge; cruel his eye, but cast
605   Signs of remorse and passion to behold
The fellows of his crime, the followers rather
(Far other once beheld in bliss) condemned
For ever now to have their lot in pain,
Millions of spirits for his fault amerced
610   Of heaven, and from eternal splendours flung
For his revolt, yet faithful how they stood,

i 588. observed] honoured.

i 591. 'Satan's stature is self-reductive if we recall that, as we earlier found it on the lips of George Fox the Quaker, the "Tower" is a traditional epithet for Christ' (Cope 98, and see 39). 'Good and bad angels have the same Nature. . . . If no good (that is, no being) remained to be perverted, Satan would cease to exist' (Lewis 66).

i 596–9. The comparison is ironically double-edged; for the ominous solar eclipse presages not only disaster for creation, but also the doom of the Godlike ruler for whom the sun was a traditional symbol. (Thus Charles II's Licenser for the Press is said by Toland (Darbishire[3] x) to have regarded these lines as politically subversive.) See Broadbent[2] 166f, where a parallel is found with the shorn Samson; also Svendsen 69f, MacCaffrey 173f and Cope 98f. Cp. the solar eclipse at xi 183f, 203–7, an early sign of the changes produced in nature by man's fall.

i 603. courage] valour MS. Darbishire plausibly suggests that the change was made in the interests of melopoeia–to get in another hard consonant. considerate] deliberate.

i 609. amerced] punished by deprivation. The slightly unusual construction may have been resorted to for the sake of the ambiguity: 'deprived of heaven' and 'punished by God'.

i 611. yet . . . stood] Goes with 'behold' (l. 605).

Their glory withered. As when heaven's fire
Hath scathed the forest oaks, or mountain pines,
With singed top their stately growth though bare
615   Stands on the blasted heath. He now prepared
To speak; whereat their doubled ranks they bend
From wing to wing, and half enclose him round
With all his peers: attention held them mute.
Thrice he essayed, and thrice in spite of scorn,
620   Tears such as angels weep, burst forth: at last
Words interwove with sighs found out their way.
    O myriads of immortal spirits, O powers
Matchless, but with the almighty, and that strife
Was not inglorious, though the event was dire,
625   As this place testifies, and this dire change
Hateful to utter: but what power of mind
Foreseeing or presaging, from the depth
Of knowledge past or present, could have feared,
How such united force of gods, how such
630   As stood like these, could ever know repulse?
For who can yet believe, though after loss,
That all these puissant legions, whose exile
Hath emptied heaven, shall fail to re-ascend
Self-raised, and repossess their native seat?
635   For me be witness all the host of heaven,

i *620.* Probably meant to recall the famous tears of the proud Persian King
Xerxes, on reflecting that the vast army he was reviewing would some day
all be dead; see x 307–11*n* below. The hardening of Satan's heart is not yet
complete. There has been a good deal of discussion as to whether the present
passage is sublime or matter-of-fact (Davie² 81f, Rajan² 44). Peter is pro-
bably right in thinking that M. means to imply that angels are corporeal
and therefore capable of weeping. But the line would nevertheless have had
a strong shocking effect. Contrast Marvell, 'Eyes and Tears' 48: 'only
humane Eyes can weep'. On the other hand, there was a strong icono-
graphical traditon of angels *mourning*; see, e.g., Réau II ii 491.
i *623–4. almighty*] Satan 'cannot intend the metaphysical sense of the word',
because he congratulates his followers on 'having stood against him for a
time' (Empson 41). However, the not inglorious strife was hardly with the
almighty himself: see vi 423–8*n*.   *event*] result.
i *628. MS* has no point after *feared*.
i *632–3.* A rhetorical exaggeration: see ii 692*n*.   *exile*] Stressed on the
second syllable.
i *634. seat?*] *MS* has no point, *Ed I* full stop.
i *635. MS* and *Ed I* have comma after *me*.

If counsels different, or danger shunned
By me, have lost our hopes. But he who reigns
Monarch in heaven, till then as one secure
Sat on his throne, upheld by old repute,
640   Consent or custom, and his regal state
Put forth at full, but still his strength concealed,
Which tempted our attempt, and wrought our fall.
Henceforth his might we know, and know our own
So as not either to provoke, or dread
645   New war, provoked; our better part remains
To work in close design, by fraud or guile
What force effected not: that he no less
At length from us may find, who overcomes
By force, hath overcome but half his foe.
650   Space may produce new worlds; whereof so rife
There went a fame in heaven that he ere long
Intended to create, and therein plant
A generation, whom his choice regard
Should favour equal to the sons of heaven:
655   Thither, if but to pry, shall be perhaps
Our first eruption, thither or elsewhere:
For this infernal pit shall never hold
Celestial spirits in bondage, nor the abyss
Long under darkness cover. But these thoughts
660   Full counsel must mature: peace is despaired,

i 636. *different*] differing; see B. A. Wright, *N & Q* cciii (1958) 205. Florence M. Stewart, *N & Q* clxvi (1934) 79, argues for the sense 'procrastinating, deferring'.

i 641-2. In Empson's arraignment of M.'s God, one of the principal accusations is the one implied in these lines: that Satan was deliberately deceived into thinking that a rebellion might come off (see, e.g., Empson 47). But if God *had* displayed his strength earlier, no doubt that would have been intimidation. The error here lies in accepting Satan's reduction of life to power politics.

i 646. *close*] secret.

i 650. *Space may produce*] 'The first hint to the reader (not of course to the rebels) of Satan's doubt whether God can really create anything' (Empson 48).

i 651. MS has comma after *heaven*. For other mentions of the *fame* or rumour, see ii 345-53, 830-5, and x 481-2. Cp. Dryden, *Aeneis* i 27f, where Juno has heard an 'ancient Rumour ... Long cited by the People of the Sky' that Rome will displace Carthage. Throughout *PL* Rome corresponds to mankind as Carthage to the fallen angels.

i 656. MS has semicolon after *eruption*.

For who can think submission? War then, war
Open or understood must be resolved.
     He spake: and to confirm his words, out flew
Millions of flaming swords, drawn from the thighs
665 Or mighty cherubim; the sudden blaze
Far round illumined hell; highly they raged
Against the highest, and fierce with grasped arms
Clashed on their sounding shields the din of war,
Hurling defiance toward the vault of heaven.
670   There stood a hill not far whose grisly top
Belched fire and rolling smoke; the rest entire
Shone with a glossy scurf, undoubted sign
That in his womb was hid metallic ore,
The work of sulphur. Thither winged with speed
675 A numerous brigade hastened. As when bands
Of pioneers with spade and pickaxe armed
Forerun the royal camp, to trench a field,
Or cast a rampart. Mammon led them on,
Mammon, the least erected spirit that fell

i *661–2*. According to Broadbent 73f Satan began the speech in his tragic
hero role, but now in the peroration reverts to 'extraordinary epical crudity'.
i *666–7*. With the play on *highly* (proudly, overbearingly) and *highest*,
cp. 642 ('tempted our attempt'), etc. In *PL* such puns often have a sardonic
flavour. They were in the fashion of seventeenth-century poetic wit, but
were not generally appreciated by M.'s eighteenth-century editors: see
Empson² 157–9.
i *670–90*. Broadbent 73 suggests that the traditional physiognomy of the
fiend is in M.'s hell displaced on to the landscape. And it is a dead or corrupt
body imaged as scurf, belching, ransacked womb, bowels, entrails, and
ribs (cp. *ibid.* 84f).
i *670–5*. Cp. the mining of the materials of war in vi 507–15.
i *674*. *sulphur*] Regarded, because of its active nature, as the father of metals;
see Caron 161.
i *675*. *brigade*] Stressed on the first syllable.
i *678*. In *Matt.* vi 24 and *Luke* xvi 13, 'Mammon' is an abstract noun meaning
wealth, but later it was used as the name of 'the prince of this world' (*John*
xii 31). Medieval and Renaissance tradition often associated Mammon with
Plutus, the Greek god of riches, and so, by confusion, with Pluto. M. had a
special admiration for Spenser's account of the Cave of Mammon in *F.Q.*
II vii, where the god presides, as here, over the mining of gold (see Yale
ii 516, also i 719). Burton makes Mammon prince of the lowest order of
devils (*Anat. of Mel.* I ii 1 ii).
i *679–84*. Mammon is the reverse of the Senecan ideal of the astral con-
templative, who despised terrestrial things, and 'wandering among the
heavens enjoyed laughing at the pavements of the rich' (*divitùm pavimenta*);

680 From heaven, for even in heaven his looks and thoughts
       Were always downward bent, admiring more
       The riches of heaven's pavement, trodden gold,
       Than aught divine or holy else enjoyed
       In vision beatific: by him first
685 Men also, and by his suggestion taught,
       Ransacked the centre, and with impious hands
       Rifled the bowels of their mother earth
       For treasures better hid. Soon had his crew
       Opened into the hill a spacious wound
690 And digged out ribs of gold. Let none admire
       That riches grow in hell; that soil may best
       Deserve the precious bane. And here let those
       Who boast in mortal things, and wondering tell

see John M. Steadman in *N & Q* ccv (1960) 220. With the emphasis on Mammon's limited vision, cp. *Animadversions* (Yale i 697): 'a pearle [cataract] in your eye, Mammons Praestriction'.

i *679. erected*] uplifted.

i *682. gold*] In *Rev.* xxi 21 the street of the City of God is described as 'pure gold'.

i *684. vision beatific*] The Scholastic term for the mystical sight of heaven's glories: the 'Sabbath's sight' that every Christian longed to share with the angels. Cp. iii 61–2, v 613 ('blessed vision'), *Time* 18 ('happy-making sight'), and *Of Reformation* (Yale i 616).

i *684–92.* Ovid, *Met.* i 125–42 is the *locus classicus* for the commonplace that the impious age began when men first delved into the bowels of the earth for the wealth hid amidst 'Stygian shades'; cp. also Spenser, *F.Q.* II vii 17 and Sidney, *Arcadia* (1590), ed. Feuillerat (Cambridge 1939) 135. But M.'s version is nearest, especially in the oxymoron *precious bane*, to Boethius' in *De consolat.* II metre v: 'the anguysschous love of havynge brenneth in folk more cruely than the fyer of the mountaigne of Ethna that ay brenneth [cp. M.'s hill belching smoke, 670f]. Allas! what was he that first dalf up the gobbettes or the weyghtes of gold covered undir erthe and the precyous stones that wolden han be hydd? He dalf up precious periles' (Chaucer's transl.). Cp. vi 470–520.   *ribs*] veins of ore (a common usage then), but also carrying on the anatomical image. Empson[2] 175f salutes as 'profound' Pearce's comment that the phrase 'alludes to the formation of Eve viii 463 he *Open'd my Left, and took from thence a Rib:– wide was the wound*' (cp. Ricks 141f). The observation is certainly a sensitive one, and could be shown to be just by tracing Eve's role as universal mother, as well as the connections between this figure and the concept *mother Earth* (687). Nevertheless, the allusion is not necessary to the primary sense of the passage. It main concern is with the aggression underlying the many human activities represented in the devils' mining and land development operation.

i *690. admire*] wonder; not a Latinism.

Of Babel, and the works of Memphian kings
695   Learn how their greatest monuments of fame,
And strength and art are easily outdone
By spirits reprobate, and in an hour
What in an age they with incessant toil
And hands innumerable scarce perform.
700   Nigh on the plain in many cells prepared,
That underneath had veins of liquid fire
Sluiced from the lake, a second multitude
With wondrous art founded the massy ore,
Severing each kind, and scummed the bullion dross:
705   A third as soon had formed within the ground
A various mould, and from the boiling cells
By strange conveyance filled each hollow nook,
As in an organ from one blast of wind
To many a row of pipes the sound-board breathes.
710   Anon out of the earth a fabric huge

i *694. Babel*] The Tower of Babel, built by the ambitious Nimrod (xii 38–62). The *works of Memphian* (Egyptian) *kings* are probably the Pyramids, which ancient and modern authors alike regarded as memorials of vanity (see Rajan[2] 48).

i *702. Sluiced*] led through sluices.

i *703. founded*] (*MS, Ed I*) melted. Preferable to the easier *Ed II* reading 'found out', though that is defended by B. A. Wright in *TLS*, 9 Aug. 1934, 553. As Darbishire[2] i 289 points out, the 'ribs of gold' have already been discovered and dug out by the first gang.

i *707. MS* has colon after *nook* (as often before comparisons).

i *708–9.* Cp. xi 560ff, where the arts of music and metal-working are again associated, and the skills of the fallen angels rediscovered by man. The connection depends on the fact that Jubal the inventor of music, and his half-brother Tubalcain the inventor of metal-working, were both descendants of Cain (*Gen.* iv). See xi 556–73*n* below.

709. *row of*] hundred *MS*, corr. to 'row of'.   *pipes*] pipe *MS*, corr. to 'pipes'.

i *710–2.* Pandaemonium rises to music, as Thebes to the sound of Amphion's lyre, since in the Renaissance it was believed that musical proportions governed the forms of architecture (see Wittkower *passim*). It rises *like an exhalation* because an exhalation can become a meteor or a comet or lightning, and so is ominous for man (Svendsen 87); but also because it 'suggests the insubstantial, elusive, mystifying, the edifice a façade for the ugly discomforts of Hell' (Broadbent 101f). Several scholars have suggested that 'the palace rises like the machinery of a masque – artificial, temporary, illusory' (*ibid.*) In view of ll. 728–30 below, we are probably meant to see the rising of Pandaemonium as a grotesque travesty of the rising of earth out of

Rose like an exhalation, with the sound
Of dulcet symphonies and voices sweet,
Built like a temple, where pilasters round
Were set, and Doric pillars overlaid
715   With golden architrave; nor did there want
Cornice or frieze, with bossy sculptures graven,
The roof was fretted gold. Not Babilon,

chaos at the Creation. The whole passage should be compared with Mar-
vell's attempt at a similar theme (with Cromwell as Amphion) in *The First
Anniversary of the Government under O.C.* (1655) 49–74.
i *712. MS* has colon after *sweet.*
i *713–7.* There is an ironic allusion to Ovid's description of the Palace of the
Sun built by Mulciber (*Met.* ii 1–4); but the main point is simply that Pan-
daemonium has a classical design, complete in every respect, like that of the
ancient (but still surviving) gilt-roofed Pantheon, the most admired build-
ing of M.'s time. Note that the *pillars*, like the music of l. 550, are Doric.
Cp. also l. 682: 'the *roof* of Pandaemonium is made of the same material as
the *pavement* of Heaven' (Rajan 47). Marjorie Nicolson suggests in 'Milton's
Hell and the Phlegraean Fields', *UTQ* vii (1938) that M. may have had in
mind as a model the Forum Vulcani near Naples. The features in common
include a volcanic landscape, abundance of pitch and the exploitation of
mineral resources. Miss R. W. Smith (*MP* xxix (1931) 187–98) makes the
interesting suggestion that Pandaemonium may be modelled on St Peter's
at Rome. The pilasters, the carved roof, the gilding, the brazen doors and
the adjacent council chamber: all these details fit. Even the bee simile is
appropriate, for bees appeared in the arms of the Barberini Pope Urban viii.
The *Doric pillars* (l. 714), however, would appear to be an insuperable ob-
stacle to this interpretation. Unless, that is, M.'s allusion extends to Alex-
ander vii, Pope from 1655 to 1667, who was famous for his patronage of
Bernini's colonnade in the piazza of St Peter's, the gigantic columns of
which are modified Doric.   *pilasters*] properly square engaged columns;
so that 'pilasters round' may have been felt to have the effect of a momen-
tary oxymoron, until the continuation showed that *round* could be taken as
an adverb. Similarly *overlaid* / *With golden* makes us think of gilding (*OED*
s.v. *Overlay* 2) until *architrave* shows that the reference is to the superimposed
spanning entablature (*OED* s.v. *Overlay* 1 and perhaps 1 b). The *frieze* is the
member of the entablature above the architrave, and the *cornice* is the mem-
ber above the frieze.   *bossy*] projecting in relief.   *fretted*] adorned with
carved work in decorative, perhaps interlaced, patterns in relief.
i *717–22.* In traditional Biblical exegesis *Babylon*, a place of proud iniquity,
was often a figure of Antichrist or of hell (see e.g., Raban Maur, in Migne
cxii 872).   *Alcairo*] Memphis (modern Cairo), the most splendid city of
heathen Egypt.   *Belus*] Bel, the Babylonian Baal, whose temple is
described by Herodotus; see 421–3*n* and *Jer.* li 44: 'I will punish Bel in
Babylon.'   *Serapis*] an Egyptian deity, often identified with Apis;

Nor great Alcairo such magnificence
Equalled in all their glories, to enshrine
720   Belus or Serapis their gods, or seat
Their kings, when Egypt with Assyria strove
In wealth and luxury. The ascending pile
Soon fixed her stately highth, and straight the doors
Opening their brazen folds discover wide
725   Within, her ample spaces, o'er the smooth
And level pavement: from the arched roof
Pendent by subtle magic many a row
Of starry lamps and blazing cressets fed
With naphtha and asphaltus yielded light
730   As from a sky. The hasty multitude
Admiring entered, and the work some praise
And some the architect: his hand was known
In heaven by many a towered structure high,
Where sceptred angels held their residence,
735   And sat as princes, whom the supreme king
Exalted to such power, and gave to rule,
Each in his hierarchy, the orders bright.
Nor was his name unheard or unadored
In ancient Greece; and in Ausonian land

see 482–4n. Broadbent (101f) draws attention to the irony underlying the
magnificence of Pandaemonium. For M., like George Sandys, regarded the
exotic wonders named in this passage as '"barbarous monuments of prodi-
gality and vain-glory". . . . The oriental similes place the building as a
citadel of barbaric despotism.'

i 728–9. The solid pieces of *asphaltus* (asphalt, pitch) would go in the *cressets*
or iron baskets, the *naphtha*, an oily constituent of asphalt, in the lamps. For
the significance of the choice of this material, see x 296–8 below. Broadbent
102 condemns the devils for the superficiality of this attempt to escape hell
by constructing a heaven with lamps that shine *As from a sky*. On chronolo-
gical grounds this is of course in a sense unfair; for the devils' roof cannot
imitate a sky they have never seen. But the moral point may stand: the
correspondence is a formal one, non-naturalistic and unmotivated. The
printer italicizes *naphtha* and *asphaltus*, either in error or as technical terms.

i 733. On the rhetorical scheme, see l. 69n.

i 735. *supreme*] Stressed on the first syllable.

i 737. See ll. 128–9n.

i 738–40. The Greek god Hephaistos, in Latin *Mulciber* or Vulcan, presided
over all arts, such as metal-working, that required the use of fire. He built
all the palaces of the gods (see ll. 713–7n).   *Ausonian land*] The old Greek
name for Italy.

740   Men called him Mulciber; and how he fell
      From heaven, they fabled, thrown by angry Jove
      Sheer o'er the crystal battlements; from morn
      To noon he fell, from noon to dewy eve,
      A summer's day; and with the setting sun
745   Dropped from the zenith like a falling star,
      On Lemnos the Aegaean isle: thus they relate,
      Erring; for he with this rebellious rout
      Fell long before; nor aught availed him now
      To have built in heaven high towers; nor did he scape
750   By all his engines, but was headlong sent
      With his industrious crew to build in hell.
      Mean while the winged heralds by command
      Of sovereign power, with awful ceremony
      And trumpet's sound throughout the host proclaim
755   A solemn council forthwith to be held
      At Pandaemonium, the high capital
      Of Satan and his peers: their summons called
      From every band and squared regiment
      By place or choice the worthiest; they anon
760   With hundreds and with thousands trooping came
      Attended: all access was thronged, the gates

i *740–8.* Terence Spencer ('John Milton: the Great Rival', *The Listener* lxx (1963) 123f) notes M.'s sophisticated wit in first magnificently emulating Homer's description of the daylong fall of Hephaistos (*Il.* i 591–5), then deflating it in the casual but commanding dismissal of ll. 746–8. The devastating position of *Erring* is possibly in imitation of Lucretius' similar use of *errat* (i 393). Cp. *Elegia VII* 81f; and the academic exercise *Natram non pati senium* 23f, where the story of Vulcan's fall is treated as a myth of cosmic destruction.

i *756.* The name *Pandaemonium* is formed from Gk. πᾶν, 'all' and δαιμόνιον 'demon, evil spirit' (N.T.); or, more classically, from δαίμων with the termination –ιον added to mean 'assembly' – cp. Παναθήναιον. Hughes compares Henry More's *Pandaemoniothen*, the mundane dominion of the devils, in *Psychozoia* I iii 23.   *capital*] MS at first 'Capitoll', later corr. in a different hand to 'Capitall'. *Ed I* and *Ed II* have 'Capital'. As Theobald and Darbishire recognize, the original reading had the virtue of precision. The Roman Capitol was a place of assembly for debates of peace or war; while at the level of verbal propriety M.'s 'high capitol' with its roof of 'fretted gold' (l. 717) recalls Virgil's *Capitolia . . . alta* (*Aen.* vi 836) *aurea nunc* (viii 348). But Adams 88 seems right in his view that M. meant this only as a secondary allusion, and that the correct reading is 'capital'.

i *758. squared*] See 550*n.*   *band and*] and band *Ed I*, corr. in *Errata.*
i *760. hundreds*] hundreds *MS* and *Ed I*, corr. in *Errata* to 'hunderds'.

And porches wide, but chief the spacious hall
(Though like a covered field, where champions bold
Wont ride in armed, and at the soldan's chair
765   Defied the best of paynim chivalry
To mortal combat or career with lance)
Thick swarmed, both on the ground and in the air,
Brushed with the hiss of rustling wings. As bees
In spring time, when the sun with Taurus rides,
770   Pour forth their populous youth about the hive
In clusters; they among fresh dews and flowers
Fly to and fro, or on the smoothed plank,
The suburb of their straw-built citadel,
New rubbed with balm, expatiate and confer
775   Their state affairs. So thick the airy crowd
Swarmed and were straitened; till the signal given,
Behold a wonder! they but now who seemed

i *763 covered field*] like a field, only covered. Perhaps punning also on French *champ clos* ('closed lists': the area prepared for a duel or judicial combat, as distinct from the ordinary 'listed field' of *SA* 1087). Cp. Dryden, *Aeneis* xii 1034, where Turnus and Aeneas fight in 'clos'd Field'.

i *766*. The two varieties of chivalric encounter, combat *a l'outrance* and the less dangerous exhibition joust. 'Milton makes chivalry almost peculiar to hell, and to earth as hell's satellite' (Broadbent 96).

i *768–75*. In Homer, *Il.* ii 87–90 the Achaians going to a council, in Virgil *Aen.* i 430–6 the busy Carthaginians, are compared to bees. But as the last phrase shows M. also glances at Virgil's mock-epic account of the ideal social organization of the hive (*Georg.* iv 149–227). D. P. Harding notes that at *Georg.* iv 170ff there is a comparison of the bees to labouring Cyclopes at Aetna (*JEGP* lx (1961)). For an elaborate discussion of the simile, with citation of many analogues, see James Whaler in *PMLA* xlvii (1932) 545ff. In the *First Defence* M. found it necessary to rebut Salmasius' argument that the loyalty of bees to their monarchs sets an example to mankind. Miss R. W. Smith notes that the bee was Pope Urban viii's emblem, and that his followers were nicknamed 'bees'; see ll. 713–7*n*. But Urban viii, founder of the new St Peter's, had died in 1644.

i *769*. *Taurus*] In M.'s time the sun entered the second sign of the zodiac in mid-April, according to the Julian calendar. Perhaps this chronographia is proleptic of the sun's movement from Aries into Taurus after the Fall (x 673).

i *774*. *expatiate*] walk about at large without restraint, roam (*OED* 1); not a Latinism – the literal sense continued in use until the nineteenth century.

i *777–92*. For the possibility that 'this is another of Milton's mockeries of the falsely epical, all the more convincing than French and Augustan mockery for occurring in a genuine epic', see Broadbent (105f), who cites Voltaire's comment that the metamorphosis 'heightens the ridicule of the whole

In bigness to surpass Earth's giant sons
Now less than smallest dwarfs, in narrow room
780   Throng numberless, like that pygmean race
Beyond the Indian mount, or faerie elves,
Whose midnight revels, by a forest side
Or fountain some belated peasant sees,
Or dreams he sees, while overhead the moon
785   Sits arbitress, and nearer to the earth
Wheels her pale course, they on their mirth and dance
Intent, with jocund music charm his ear;
At once with joy and fear his heart rebounds.
Thus incorporeal spirits to smallest forms
790   Reduced their shapes immense, and were at large,
Though without number still amidst the hall
Of that infernal court. But far within
And in their own dimensions like themselves
The great seraphic lords and cherubim

Contrivance to an unexpressible Degree. Methinks the true Criterion for
discerning what is really ridiculous in an *Epick* Poem, is to examine if the
same Thing would not fit exactly the Mock Heroick . . . . no-thing is so
adapted to that ludicrous way of writing, as the Metamorphosis of the
Devils into Dwarfs' (*Voltaire's Essay on Epic Poetry*, ed. Florence D. White
(Albany, N.Y. 1915) 137).

i *778. giant sons*] giant-sons *MS*.

i *780–1*. Cp. 575n. Pliny located the land of the Pygmies in the mountains
beyond the source of the Ganges (*Nat. hist.* vii 26); and *extra Imaum* (see
iii 421 below) was a common phrase on seventeenth-century maps.

i *781–7*. Echoing *Midsummer Night's Dream* II i 28f and 141. *the moon | Sits
arbitress* because the moon-goddess was queen of faery: cp. Horace, *Epodes*
v 49–52: 'O witnesses (*arbitrae*) not unloyal to my purposes, Night and
Diana, who rulest the silence when mystic rites are performed.' On faery
mythology in the Renaissance, consult I. E. Rathborne, *The Meaning of
Spenser's Fairyland* (New York 1937) and K. M. Briggs, *Pale Hecate's Team*
(1962).

i *783–4. sees, | Or dreams he sees*] Alluding to *Aen.* vi 451–4, Virgil's com-
parison of Dido's shade to the fleeting moon. The function of the simile
as a device to magnify the scale of Pandaemonium is discussed in Lewis 41.
Rajan[2] 53f compares 573ff above: 'The angels are giants in their poten-
tiality for destruction; they are equally pygmies in the presence of righteous-
ness.'

i *783. MS* has comma after *fountain*.

i *786. MS* has colon after *course*.

i *789–90*. The 'superbly contemptuous pun' is discussed in Ricks 15.

795 In close recess and secret conclave sat
     A thousand demi-gods on golden seats,
     Frequent and full. After short silence then
     And summons read, the great consult began.

THE END OF THE FIRST BOOK

Paradise Lost

BOOK II

The Argument

The consultation begun, Satan debates whether another battle be to be
hazarded for the recovery of heaven: some advise it, others dissuade: a
third proposal is preferred, mentioned before by Satan, to search the truth
of that prophecy or tradition in heaven concerning another world, and
another kind of creature equal or not much inferior to themselves, about this
time to be created: their doubt who shall[1] be sent on this difficult search:
Satan their chief undertakes alone the voyage, is honoured and applauded.
The council thus ended, the rest betake them several ways and to several
employments, as their inclinations lead them, to entertain the time till Satan
return. He passes on his journey to hell gates, finds them shut, and who sat
there to guard them, by whom at length they are opened, and discover to
him the great gulf between hell and heaven, with what difficulty he passes
through, directed by Chaos, the power of that place, to the sight of this
new world which he sought.

> High on a throne of a royal state, which far
> Outshone the wealth of Ormus and of Ind,

i *795. close*] secret.   *conclave*] Could refer to any assembly in secret
session, but had already the specifically ecclesiastical meaning on which M.'s
satire here depends.

i *797. Frequent*] crowded; not a Latinism. The phrase used here, *Frequent
and full*, was particularly idiomatic; see *OED* s.v. *Frequent* 1 for examples.

i *798. consult*] consultation.

ii *Argument*[1] *shall*] should *Ed I, 1669 issue*.

ii *1–4.* Cp. Spenser's description of the bright throne of the Phaethon-like
Lucifera, embodiment of pride: 'High above all a cloth of State was spred, /
And a rich throne, as bright as sunny day' (*F.Q.* I iv 8). Satan has already
been portrayed as an eastern tyrant at i 348.

Or where the gorgeous East with richest hand
Showers on her kings barbaric pearl and gold,
5   Satan exalted sat, by merit raised
To that bad eminence; and from despair
Thus high uplifted beyond hope, aspires
Beyond thus high, insatiate to pursue
Vain war with heaven, and by success untaught
10   His proud imaginations thus displayed,
     Powers and dominions, deities of heaven,
For since no deep within her gulf can hold
Immortal vigour, though oppressed and fallen,
I give not heaven for lost. From this descent
15   Celestial virtues rising, will appear
More glorious and more dread than from no fall,
And trust themselves to fear no second fate:
Me though just right, and the fixed laws of heaven
Did first create your leader, next free choice,
20   With what besides, in counsel or in fight,
Hath been achieved of merit, yet this loss
Thus far at least recovered, hath much more
Established in a safe unenvied throne
Yielded with full consent. The happier state

ii 2. *Ormus* (modern Ormuz), an island town in the Persian gulf, was famous as a jewel market.

ii 3. *gorgeous east*] Cp. Shakespeare's account of a different sort of idolatry, in *Love's Labour's Lost* IV iii 218ff: 'Who sees the heavenly Rosaline, / That, like a rude and savage man of Inde, / At the first opening of the gorgeous east, / Bows not his vassal head, and strooken blind, / Kisses the base ground with obedient breast?'

ii 4. *barbaric*] Italicized as a proper name in the early edns, perhaps through confusion with 'Barbarian' (=native of Barbary). Cp. Virgil, *Aen.* ii 504: *barbarico postes auro spoliisque superbi.* Also Euripides, *Iph. in Aul.* 74, where Paris' clothing is described as 'gleaming with gold, barbaric bravery'.

ii 5. Cp. 20f. On Satan's eminence through *merit*, see i 98n and vi 820n. There is an implicit parallel and contrast with the Messiah's throne (vi (758–72), to which he too is exalted by merit (vi 43).

ii 9. *success*] the result. So in l. 123; the modern sense is commoner in the later books and in *PR*.

ii 11. *powers and dominions*] Two of the angelic orders mentioned by St Paul in *Col.* i 16; see i 128–9n. On the description of angels as 'gods' or *deities*, see i 116–7n.

ii 14–16. In 'a kind of parody of the *felix culpa*', Satan's words 'describe what happens to man, but only through God's grace' (MacCaffrey 65).

ii 15. *virtues*] Perhaps a pun, in that the virtues are another of the angelic orders.

25   In heaven, which follows dignity, might draw
      Envy from each inferior; but who here
      Will envy whom the highest place exposes
      Foremost to stand against the thunderer's aim
      Your bulwark, and condemns to greatest share
30   Of endless pain? Where there is then no good
      For which to strive, no strife can grow up there
      From faction; for none sure will claim in hell
      Precedence, none, whose portion is so small
      Of present pain, that with ambitious mind
35   Will covet more. With this advantage then
      To union, and firm faith, and firm accord,
      More than can be in heaven, we now return
      To claim our just inheritance of old,
      Surer to prosper than prosperity
40   Could have assured us; and by what best way,
      Whether of open war or covert guile,
      We now debate: who can advise, may speak.
          He ceased, and next him Moloc, sceptred king
      Stood up, the strongest and the fiercest spirit
45   That fought in heaven; now fiercer by despair:
      His trust was with the eternal to be deemed
      Equal in strength, and rather than be less
      Cared not to be at all; with that care lost
      Went all his fear: of God, or hell, or worse
50   He recked not, and these words thereafter spake.
          My sentence is for open war: of wiles,
      More unexpert, I boast not: them let those
      Contrive who need, or when they need, not now.
      For while they sit contriving, shall the rest,

ii *28. thunderer's*] Cp. i 93, and see i 122*n* and i 258*n*. By identifying him
with thunder, the attribute of Jupiter, Satan reduces God to a mere Olym-
pian tyrant.
ii *30–8.* Empson 48 finds it a noble paradox in the high Roman manner that
Satan should praise the benefits of hell. While this is no doubt part of the
meaning, the desperate irrationality seems also a symptom of self-delusion:
note, e.g., how 32f is belied by ll. 471–3 below.
ii *43.* On *Moloc*, see i 392*n* and vi 357ff.   *sceptred*] in the Homeric councils,
kings are described formulaically as 'sceptred'; see *Il.* ii 86, *Od.* ii 231.
ii *50. thereafter*] accordingly.
ii *51. sentence*] opinion.
ii *52–6.* Eliot and Leavis find an inconsistency between *millions . . . stand*
and *sit lingering*; not noticing that *stand* is present, *sit* future. Moloch is being
contemptuous: 'the superb upward thrust of *sit, stand, ascend* is razed by
the deliberate bathos of *sit again*' (Ricks 13).   *unexpert*] inexperienced.

55 Millions that stand in arms, and longing wait
    The signal to ascend, sit lingering here
    Heaven's fugitives, and for their dwelling place
    Accept this dark opprobrious den of shame,
    The prison of his tyranny who reigns
60 By our delay? No, let us rather choose
    Armed with hell flames and fury all at once
    O'er heaven's high towers to force resistless way,
    Turning our tortures into horrid arms
    Against the torturer; when to meet the noise
65 Of his almighty engine he shall hear
    Infernal thunder, and for lightning see
    Black fire and horror shot with equal rage
    Among his angels; and his throne itself
    Mixed with Tartarean sulphur, and strange fire,
70 His own invented torments. But perhaps
    The way seems difficult and steep to scale
    With upright wing against a higher foe.
    Let such bethink them, if the sleepy drench
    Of that forgetful lake benumb not still,
75 That in our proper motion we ascend
    Up to our native seat: descent and fall
    To us is adverse. Who but felt of late
    When the fierce foe hung on our broken rear
    Insulting, and pursued us through the deep,
80 With what compulsion and laborious flight
    We sunk thus low? The ascent is easy then;

ii 61. *hell flames and fury*] The violent yoking of concrete and abstract words
(a kind of zeugma) is one of the most characteristic figures of M.'s style;
cp. l. 67.
ii 65. *engine*] machine of war. Used at vi 484, 586 of artillery, but probably
here referring to the Messiah's chariot with its 'whirlwind sound' (vi 749),
or perhaps to his thunder (vi 764).
ii 69. In the Renaissance manner, M. identifies the Christian hell with the
classical underworld, in which Tartarus was the place of the guilty.   *strange*
fire] Cp. *Lev.* x 1–2: 'Nadab and Abihu, the sons of Aaron ... offered
strange fire before the Lord, which he commanded them not. And there
went out fire from the Lord, and devoured them.'
ii 73–4. See note on the 'oblivious pool' of i 266.   *drench*] 'soporific
drink'; though Moloch may also intend the bad half-pun (*drench*, verb=
soak).
ii 79. *Insulting*] Both 'making assaults' and 'exulting'.
ii 81. *ascent is easy*] Given the lie through the allusion to Virgil, *Aen.* vi 126–9:
facilis descensus Averno: / ... / *sed revocare gradum superasque evadere ad*

The event is feared; should we again provoke
Our stronger, some worse way his wrath may find
To our destruction: if there be in hell
85 Fear to be worse destroyed: what can be worse
Than to dwell here, driven out from bliss, condemned
In this abhorred deep to utter woe;
Where pain of unextinguishable fire
Must exercise us without hope of end
90 The vassals of his anger, when the scourge
Inexorably, and the torturing hour
Call us to penance? More destroyed than thus
We should be quite abolished and expire.
What fear we then? what doubt we to incense
95 His utmost ire? which to the highth enraged,
Will either quite consume us, and reduce
To nothing this essential, happier far
Than miserable to have eternal being:
Or if our substance be indeed divine,
100 And cannot cease to be, we are at worst
On this side nothing; and by proof we feel
Our power sufficient to disturb his heaven,
And with perpetual inroads to alarm,
Though inaccessible, his fatal throne:
105 Which if not victory is yet revenge.
    He ended frowning, and his look denounced
Desperate revenge, and battle dangerous
To less than gods. On the other side up rose

auras, / hoc opus, hic labor est (B. A. Wright in N & Q cciii (1958) 208f). See i 633 and vi 856–77.

ii 82. event] outcome.

ii 87. utter] Primarily 'extreme; out-and-out' (OED a. II 4); but also indicating the verb, 'express' (OED v.[1] II 6 b), and perhaps even the word outer, as in i 72 above.

ii 89. exercise] subject to ascetic discipline (OED I 3); not a Latinism nor (as Highet and Rajan maintain) an un-English use of the word.

ii 90. vassals] slaves; cp. Spenser, Tears of the Muses 126: 'vassals of Gods wrath, and slaves of sin'. But there is also a half-suppressed allusion to Rom. ix 22: 'What if God, willing to shew his wrath, and to make his power known, endured with much longsuffering the vessels of wrath fitted to destruction . . .?'

ii 97. essential] essence (adj. for noun).

ii 100–1. i.e., already we are in the worst condition possible, short of being nothing, being annihilated.   proof] practical experience.

ii 104. fatal] Both 'destructive' and 'destined'; see i 116–7n.

Belial, in act more graceful and humane;
110 A fairer person lost not heaven; he seemed
For dignity composed and high exploit:
But all was false and hollow; though his tongue
Dropt manna, and could make the worse appear
The better reason, to perplex and dash
115 Maturest counsels: for his thoughts were low;
To vice industrious, but to nobler deeds
Timorous and slothful, yet he pleased the ear,
And with persuasive accent thus began.
       I should be much for open war, O peers,
120 As not behind in hate; if what was urged
Main reason to persuade immediate war,
Did not dissuade me most, and seem to cast
Ominous conjecture on the whole success:
When he who most excels in fact of arms,
125 In what he counsels and in what excels
Mistrustful, grounds his courage on despair
And utter dissolution, as the scope
Of all his aim, after some dire revenge.
First, what revenge? The towers of heaven are filled
130 With armed watch, that render all access

ii *109–17. Belial*] See i 490*n* and, for his witty jests during the war in heaven, vi 620–7. Starting, perhaps, from the tradition transmitted by Reginald Scot (*The discoverie of witchcraft* (1584) xv 2: 'This Beliall . . . taketh the forme of a beautifull angell . . . he speaketh faire'), M. has constructed a 'character' in the seventeenth-century Theophrastian manner. See E. E. Stoll, 'Belial as an Example', *MLN* xlviii (1933) 419–27.   *humane*] courteous, elegant.
ii *110–18*. Fletcher² 263 attempts to relate Belial's dialectically brilliant but empty speech to the travesties of disputation delivered by the Prevaricators at Cambridge Commencements. The relationship is not, however, very close. Empson 52 characterises Belial as a sober lawyer, in spite of the explicit warning in the present lines, which should have saved him from being gulled by appearances. M. is satirising the 'hollow', yet persuasively negative, reactionary. But l. 113f presents something of a problem: By what criterion, exactly, are Belial's reasons here *worse*?
ii *113–4. make . . . reason*] This was the claim of the Greek Sophists, and one of the charges against Socrates (Plato, *Apology* 18 B).   *reason*] argument.
ii *124. fact*] feat, deed.
ii *127. scope*] target.
ii *129*. Not only does Belial answer Moloch point by point, but he even takes up particular phrases, as here (cp. l. 62). For the opposition of Belial and Moloch M. had a model in the contrast between two Saracen ambassadors, the smooth rhetorician Aletes and the fierce Argantes, in Tasso, *Gerus. Lib.* ii 58–90.

Impregnable; oft on the bordering deep
Encamp their legions, or with obscure wing
Scout far and wide into the realm of night,
Scorning surprise. Or could we break our way
135   By force, and at our heels all hell should rise
With blackest insurrection, to confound
Heaven's purest light, yet our great enemy,
All incorruptible would on his throne
Sit unpolluted, and the ethereal mould
140   Incapable of stain would soon expel
Her mischief, and purge off the baser fire
Victorious. Thus repulsed, our final hope
Is flat despair: we must exasperate
The almighty victor to spend all his rage,
145   And that must end us, that must be our cure,
To be no more; sad cure; for who would lose,
Though full of pain, this intellectual being,
Those thoughts that wander through eternity,
To perish rather, swallowed up and lost
150   In the wide womb of uncreated night,
Devoid of sense and motion? and who knows,
Let this be good, whether our angry foe
Can give it, or will ever? How he can
Is doubtful; that he never will is sure.
155   Will he, so wise, let loose at once his ire,

ii *132. obscure*] Stressed on the first syllable.
ii *138–42.* Criticising Moloch's proposal to mix God's throne with sulphur
(ll. 68–9) and shoot 'black fire' among his angels. This *baser fire* Belial con-
trasts with the *ethereal* fire of the throne, or perhaps of the angels (whose
substance is called 'empyreal' at i 177). See *Dan.* vii 9: 'his throne was like
the fiery flame' and *Ps.* civ 4: 'Who maketh his angels spirits; his ministers
a flaming fire'. God, who is also a 'consuming fire' (*Deut.* iv 24) is described
as 'incorruptible' in the *De doctrina* (Columbia xiv 47), on the basis of *Rom.*
i 23.
ii *143. flat*] absolute; coloured perhaps by the meaning 'dull'.
ii *146–51.* Cp. Claudio's fear that death will make 'this sensible warm
motion to become / A kneaded clod' (*Measure for Measure* III i 120f).
Several Senecan passages describe the soul's power to range through
heaven: see *De consolat.* xi 4f, and cp. i 679–84*n* above.　　*wander*] Some-
thing of a key word in *PL* (see, e.g., i 365, xi 779, xii 648), often subsidiarily
implies 'err' (cp. Latin *erro*). So in *Areopagitica* (Yale ii 527f): 'God . . . gives
us minds that wander beyond all limit and satiety.' Belial is sensitive and
intellectual; but the idea that he is like M. himself should be scouted.

Belike through impotence, or unaware,
To give his enemies their wish, and end
Them in his anger, whom his anger saves
To punish endless? Wherefore cease we then?
160   Say they who counsel war, we are decreed,
Reserved and destined to eternal woe;
Whatever doing, what can we suffer more,
What can we suffer worse? Is this then worst,
Thus sitting, thus consulting, thus in arms?
165   What when we fled amain, pursued and struck
With heaven's afflicting thunder, and besought
The deep to shelter us? This hell then seemed
A refuge from those wounds: or when we lay
Chained on the burning lake? That sure was worse.
170   What if the breath that kindled those grim fires
Awaked should blow them into sevenfold rage
And plunge us in the flames? or from above
Should intermitted vengeance arm again
His red right hand to plague us? what if all

ii *156. Belike*] no doubt.   *impotence*] weakness of mind, lack of restraint, passion.

ii *159–61.* The endlessness of the devils' punishments was a commonplace. See, e.g., Sir T. Browne, *Christian Morals* ii 13 'evil Spirits, as undying Substances, are unseparable from their calamities . . . bound up with immortality can never get out of themselves' and *Religio medici* i 51; also *De doctrina* i 9 (Columbia xv 107) 'The evil angels are reserved for punishment.'

ii *160. they who*] Belial prefers to couch his reference to Moloch in a courteously impersonal form.

ii *165. What when*] 'What about when . . .'   *amain*] at full speed.   *struck*] M.'s spelling 'strook' records a common seventeenth-century form and the pronunciation he probably preferred; see the rhyme with 'took' at *Nativity Ode* 95.

ii *166. afflicting*] striking down.

ii *168–9.* See i 48*n* and 209–13*n*.

ii *170–86.* On the relentlessness with which Belial's argument drives on to a deliberately delayed conclusion, see Ricks 30.

ii *170.* Cp. *Is.* xxx 33: 'Tophet is ordained of old . . . the pile thereof is fire and much wood; the breath of the Lord, like a stream of brimstone, doth kindle it.' For Tophet as a type of hell, see i 403–5*n*.

ii *174–84.* Corresponding in general to classical accounts of the fate of the Giants, expecially Typhon: see i 197–200*n*, and Aeschylus, *Prometheus vinctus* 353–68.

ii *174. red right hand*] Horace, *Odes* I ii 1–4, recalling the horrors of civil war writes: 'Enough . . . hath the Father smiting with the bolt from his red right hand (*rubente dextera*) . . . struck panic into Rome'.

175   Her stores were opened, and this firmament
      Of hell should spout her cataracts of fire,
      Impendent horrors, threatening hideous fall
      One day upon our heads; while we perhaps
      Designing or exhorting glorious war,
180   Caught in a fiery tempest shall be hurled
      Each on his rock transfixed, the sport and prey
      Of racking whirlwinds, or for ever sunk
      Under yon boiling ocean, wrapped in chains;
      There to converse with everlasting groans,
185   Unrespited, unpitied, unreprieved,
      Ages of hopeless end; this would be worse.
      War therefore, open or concealed, alike
      My voice dissuades; for what can force or guile
      With him, or who deceive his mind, whose eye
190   Views all things at one view? He from heaven's highth
      All these our motions vain, sees and derides;

ii *176. cataracts*] Perhaps here 'flood-gates', the sense in which *cataractae* is used in Vulgate *Gen.* vii 11–as in Tremellius' Protestant version–in the account of the Flood: Cp. *King Lear* III ii 2: 'You cataracts and hurricanoes, spout.'

ii *180–1.* Cp. Virgil, *Aen.* i 44f: to punish the frenzy of Ajax, Pallas 'caught him in a whirlwind and impaled him on a spiky crag'.

ii *181–2.* Cp. the sufferings of the dead in Virgil, *Aen.* vi 740f: 'hung stretched out to the empty winds'; and in *Measure for Measure* III i 124: 'imprisoned in the viewless winds'.   *racking*] both 'torturing' and 'driving'.

ii *184. converse with*] A pun ('dwell with' and 'talk by means of').

ii *185.* M. is fond of this scheme, in which asyndeton (omission of grammatical connections) is combined with similarity or sameness of prefix; cp. iii 231, v 899 and *SA* 1422. He could have learned it from the Greek tragedians (e.g. Sophocles, *Antigone* 1071); from Spenser (*F.Q.* VII vii 46: 'Unbodied, unsoul'd, unheard, unseen'); or from Shakespeare (*Hamlet* I v 77: 'Unhousel'd, disappointed, unanel'd').

ii *187.* Exactly opposed to the conclusion of Satan's earlier speech, i 661–2.

ii *188–90.* Cp. *De doctrina* (Columbia xiv 57): 'So extensive is the prescience of God, that he knows beforehand the thoughts and actions of free agents as yet unborn, and many ages before those thoughts or actions have their origin.' Satan at least seems not to have believed God to be omniscient before the rebellion (see esp. v 682f); but perhaps the devils have been convinced by recent events (Empson 51f). On the synoptic character of the creator's vision, see iii 77*n*.

ii *190–1. Ps.* ii 4: 'He that sitteth in the heavens shall laugh: the Lord shall have them in derision.' M. did not believe in a detached impassible God, but in one who displays a whole range of emotions. See *De doctrina* (Columbia xiv 33–5) and Kelley 194.   *motions*] schemes.

Not more almighty to resist our might
Than wise to frustrate all our plots and wiles.
Shall we then live thus vile, the race of heaven
195 Thus trampled, thus expelled to suffer here
Chains and these torments? Better these than worse
By my advice; since fate inevitable
Subdues us, and omnipotent decree,
The victor's will. To suffer, as to do,
200 Our strength is equal, nor the law unjust
That so ordains: this was at first resolved,
If we were wise, against so great a foe
Contending, and so doubtful what might fall.
I laugh, when those who at the spear are bold
205 And venturous, if that fail them, shrink and fear
What yet they know must follow, to endure
Exile, or ignominy, or bonds, or pain,
The sentence of their conqueror: this is now
Our doom; which if we can sustain and bear,
210 Our supreme foe in time may much remit
His anger, and perhaps thus far removed,
Not mind us not offending, satisfied
With what is punished; whence these raging fires
Will slacken, if his breath stir not their flames.
215 Our purer essence then will overcome
Their noxious vapour, or enured not feel,

ii 199. *To suffer, as to do*] The affirmation of Mucius Scaevola; see i 158*n*.
ii 200. *law*] Not necessarily admitting that God's law is just: 'drawing as usual upon the classics for the thoughts of devils, Milton has him say that they have been defeated by . . . some kind of law of Nature which may be prior to God' (Empson 51). But perhaps the timorous Belial, fearing renewal of the pains of the fall (cp. Lewis 102), and really believing that he is overheard by God (189f), is unwilling to commit himself. He would like to trim a safe course between good and evil.
ii 207. *ignominy*] For pronunciation see i 115*n*.
ii 210. *supreme*] Often stressed on the first syllable, as here probably.
ii 211. See i 73–4*n*.
ii 213–6. St Augustine, *Civ. Dei* xxi 10, explains how devils suffer the everlasting fire – either through passible aery bodies, or through natures specially adapted so that they can feel pain without being destroyed.
ii 215–6. Empson 51 argues that Belial's description of the incorruptibility of the rebel angels and of God and the good angels (ii 138–41) by the same chemical metaphors means that he thinks of them as two comparable groups who 'should arrange co-existence'. But Belial only says that the devils' essence will overcome the vapour if God ceases to stir the flames, i.e., their incorruptibility is dependent on his will.

> Or changed at length, and to the place conformed
> In temper and in nature, will receive
> Familiar the fierce heat, and void of pain;
> 220 This horror will grow mild, this darkness light,
> Besides what hope the never-ending flight
> Of future days may bring, what chance, what change
> Worth waiting, since our present lot appears
> For happy though but ill, for ill not worst,
> 225 If we procure not to ourselves more woe.
>   Thus Belial with words clothed in reason's garb
> Counselled ignoble ease, and peaceful sloth,
> Not peace: and after him thus Mammon spake.
>   Either to disenthrone the king of heaven
> 230 We war, if war be best, or to regain
> Our own right lost: him to unthrone we then
> May hope when everlasting fate shall yield
> To fickle chance, and Chaos judge the strife:

ii *217–9.* A point taken up by Mammon at ll. 274–8.   *temper*] temperament, the mixture or adjustment of humours. Thus the phrase means 'adjusted psychologically and physically to the new environment'.

ii *220. light*] 'easy to bear', and 'illumination'. Bentley argued that only the first sense can apply, in view of the parallelism between *horror . . . mild* and *darkness* (in a moderate degree). But 'both . . . senses are present, and the combination allows Belial to suggest high hopes without obvious absurdity' (Empson[2] 159). If *light* is taken as 'luminous', the effect is oxymoron rather than hyperbole. Note the rhyme between l. 220 and l. 221–perhaps meant as a suitably jingling accompaniment to Belial's cheerful fantasy. The absurdity of the stoicism is far from obvious: I think we are meant to recognize not only the irrationality and self-contradiction of Belial's wish but also the fact that in a grim sense it has already been granted (cp. the 'darkness visible' of i 63).

ii *221. never-ending*] Compound adjectives are rare in *PL*; see Emma 70f.

ii *224. for happy*] as far as happiness is concerned.

ii *226.* Cp. *Comus* 759: 'false rules pranked in reason's garb'.

ii *228. Mammon's* character has been given at i 678–84.

ii *232–3.* Both Bentley's interpretation (strife between *fate* and *chance*) and Pearce's (strife between *the king of heaven* and the devils) are possible, but the former is preferable. If providence–which the devils call fate–yielded to chance, the result would be chaotic; so that the adjudication is appropriately by *Chaos*. There may also be an allusion to the Empedoclean notion of a universal Strife. M.'s devils on the whole concede more than Tasso's Satan, who claims to have been overthrown only by chance (*Gerus. Lib.* iv 15); see 551, i 116–7n, 133, and 144n. *Ed I* has comma after *hope*. The early edns give *Chaos* italics and initial capital, but *fate* and *chance* an initial capital only.

The former vain to hope argues as vain
235   The latter: for what place can be for us
Within heaven's bound, unless heaven's lord supreme
We overpower? Suppose he should relent
And publish grace to all, on promise made
Of new subjection; with what eyes could we
240   Stand in his presence humble, and receive
Strict laws imposed, to celebrate his throne
With warbled hymns, and to his Godhead sing
Forced hallelujahs; while he lordly sits
Our envied sovereign, and his altar breathes
245   Ambrosial odours and ambrosial flowers,
Our servile offerings? This must be our task
In heaven, this our delight; how wearisome
Eternity so spent in worship paid
To whom we hate. Let us not then pursue
250   By force impossible, by leave obtained
Unacceptable, though in heaven, our state
Of splendid vassalage, but rather seek
Our own good from ourselves, and from our own
Live to ourselves, though in this vast recess,
255   Free, and to none accountable, preferring

ii 243. The word *hallelujah* (Heb. 'praise Jehovah') occurred in so many psalms that it came to mean a song of praise to God. Cp. and contrast vi 744, where Messiah promises that once the rebellious angels are expelled, the remnant will sing 'unfeigned hallelujahs'.

ii 245. *Ambrosial*] fragrant and perfumed; immortal. Ambrosia was the fabled food, or drink, of the gods. It was, however, also identified by the herbalist with certain specific plants: see, e.g., Gerard, *Herball* (1597) p. 950: 'The fragrant smell that this kinde of *Ambrosia* or Oke of Cappadocia [sometimes 'Oak of Jerusalem'] yeeldeth, hath mooved the Poets to suppose that this herbe was meate and foode for the gods.'

ii 247. *Ed II*, probably wrongly, omits comma after *heaven*.

ii 249. *pursue*] seek to attain to. The interposition of the compressed phrases floating between the verb and its distant object *state* (e.g., either 'pursue by force' or 'pursue what is by force impossible to obtain') may be meant to mime the difficulty of access.

ii 254. *Live to ourselves*] Echoing Horace's isolationist resolve 'let me live to myself for what remains of life' (*Epodes* I xviii 107f), but omitting the sober continuation 'if the gods will that anything remain'.

ii 255-7. In *SA* 271 Samson condemns those who are fonder of 'bondage with ease than strenuous liberty'. The antithesis is from M.'s favourite Roman historian, Sallust, who puts it in the mouth of Aemilius Lepidus, an opponent of the dictator Sulla. But cp. also Jesus' words in *Matt.* xi 28-30: 'Come unto me. . . . For my yoke is easy.'

Hard liberty before the easy yoke
Of servile pomp. Our greatness will appear
Then most conspicuous, when great things of small,
Useful of hurtful, prosperous of adverse
260   We can create, and in what place so e'er
Thrive under evil, and work ease out of pain
Through labour and endurance. This deep world
Of darkness do we dread? How oft amidst
Thick clouds and dark doth heaven's all-ruling sire
265   Choose to reside, his glory unobscured,
And with the majesty of darkness round
Covers his throne; from whence deep thunders roar
Mustering their rage, and heaven resembles hell?
As he our darkness, cannot we his light
270   Imitate when we please? This desert soil
Wants not her hidden lustre, gems and gold;
Nor want we skill or art, from whence to raise
Magnificence; and what can heaven show more?
Our torments also may in length of time
275   Become our elements, these piercing fires
As soft as now severe, our temper changed
Into their temper; which must needs remove

ii *258–61*. Explicitly here, implicitly in ll. 252–7 and elsewhere, Mammon keeps up a juxtaposition of contraries which indicates his confused values and his hopes of an impossible compromise. Both Adam (xii 561–9) and Mammon recognize that if great things are to be accomplished from small beginnings, patience is needed. But to this Adam joins obedience, Mammon *liberty* (l. 256); see Mindele C. Treip, *N & Q* cciii (1958) 209f.

ii *264–5*. Ironically, the words come from 'unfeigned hallelujahs', *Ps.* xviii 11–13, 'He made darkness his secret place; his pavilion round about him were dark waters and thick clouds of the skies. . . . The Lord also thundered in the heavens', and xcvii 2, 'Clouds and darkness are round about him: righteousness and judgment are the habitation of his throne'. Cp. also *2 Chron.* v 13–vi 1.

ii *275*. Possibly referring to the belief that the fallen angels inhabit one or another of the four *elements*: 'being dispersed, some in the air, some on the earth, some in the water, some amongst the minerals, dens, and caves, that are under the earth' (Hooker, *Laws of Eccles. Pol.* I iv 3; cp. *Il Penseroso* 93–6: 'Daemons that are found / In fire, air, flood, or under ground' and have a 'true consent . . . with element'). But the point of the line more probably lies in the allusion (M.'s not Mammon's) to an idea of St Augustine's, that the devils are bound to tormenting fires as if to bodies (*Civ. Dei* xxi 10).

The sensible of pain. All things invite
To peaceful counsels, and the settled state
280   Of order, how in safety best we may
Compose our present evils, with regard
Of what we are and where, dismissing quite
All thoughts of war: ye have what I advise.
     He scarce had finished, when such murmur filled
285   The assembly, as when hollow rocks retain
The sound of blustering winds, which all night long
Had roused the sea, now with hoarse cadence lull
Seafaring men o'erwatched, whose bark by chance
Or pinnace anchors in a craggy bay
290   After the tempest: such applause was heard
As Mammon ended, and his sentence pleased,
Advising peace: for such another field
They dreaded worse than hell: so much the fear
Of thunder and the sword of Michael
295   Wrought still within them; and no less desire
To found this nether empire, which might rise
By policy, and long process of time,
In emulation opposite to heaven.
Which when Beelzebub perceived, than whom,
300   Satan except, none higher sat, with grave
Aspect he rose, and in his rising seemed
A pillar of state; deep on his front engraven
Deliberation sat and public care;
And princely counsel in his face yet shone,

ii *278. The sensible of pain*] the part of pain apprehended through the senses; see J. C. Maxwell in *RES*, n.s., v (1954) 268.

ii *281. Compose*] order, adjust.

ii *282. where*] *Ed I*. Since Mammon is exhorting the devils to accept and to exploit their present situation, *Ed II* 'were', which would make him direct their attention elsewhere, is obviously an error.

ii *291. sentence*] opinion.

ii *294.* In the war in Heaven, Michael's two-handed sword felled 'squadrons at once' and wounded even Satan (see vi 250ff and 320ff). *Michael* is here a trisyllable; cp. vi 411, but contrast xi 453.

ii *297. policy*] statesmanship; often in a bad sense, implying Machiavellian strategems. The earlier history of the word is traced in M. Praz, 'Machiavelli and the Elizabethans', *Proc. of the Brit. Acad.* xiii (1928)   *process*] stressed on the second syllable.

ii *299. Beelzebub*] Satan's closest associate; see i 81*n* and v 671*n*.

ii *301. Aspect*] Stressed on the second syllable.

ii *302. front*] forehead (*OED* I 1) or face (*OED* I 2). Neither sense would have been felt as a Latinism.

305   Majestic though in ruin: sage he stood
        With Atlantean shoulders fit to bear
        The weight of mightiest monarchies; his look
        Drew audience and attention still as night
        Or summer's noontide air, while thus he spake.
310   Thrones and imperial powers, offspring of heaven
        Ethereal virtues; or these titles now
        Must we renounce, and changing style be called
        Princes of hell? For so the popular vote
        Inclines, here to continue, and build up here
315   A growing empire; doubtless; while we dream,
        And know not that the king of heaven hath doomed
        This place our dungeon, not our safe retreat
        Beyond his potent arm, to live exempt
        From heaven's high jurisdiction, in new league
320   Banded against his throne, but to remain
        In strictest bondage, though thus far removed,
        Under the inevitable curb, reserved
        His captive multitude: for he, be sure
        In highth or depth, still first and last will reign
325   Sole king, and of his kingdom lose no part
        By our revolt, but over hell extend
        His empire, and with iron sceptre rule
        Us here, as with his golden those in heaven.
        What sit we then projecting peace and war?

ii *306.* Statesmen burdened by affairs of state were commonly compared to
Atlas (see, e.g., *Antony and Cleopatra* I v 23 and Spenser, Sonnet to Lord
Burleigh prefaced to *F.Q.*); but in the present context *Atlantean* functions
as one of a large set of allusions to the Titans. Atlas was forced by Jupiter to
carry the heavens on his shoulders specifically as a punishment for his part
in the rebellion.

ii *310–2.* On the angelic orders, see i 128–9*n* and ii 11*n*.   *style*] ceremonial
title.

ii *321.* Answering Belial's argument at ll. 211f.

ii *324.* Contrast v 165, where Adam and Eve in their morning hymn joy-
fully call on all creatures 'to extol / Him first, him last'. Both speakers
anticipate *Rev.* i 11 (cp. xxi 6, xxii 13): 'I am Alpha and Omega, the first and
the last.'

ii *327–8. Beelzebub* perhaps only intends the gold and iron sceptres that were
traditionally symbolic of merciful equity and rigorous justice. But the
specific allusion to *Ps.* ii 9 ('Thou shalt break them with a rod of iron') makes
the reader realise that Abdiel's warning of v 886–8 is coming true, and that
God will ultimately destroy evil. See Sims 16.

ii *329. What*] Why; idiomatic and colloquial: see *OED* III 19.

330 War hath determined us, and foiled with loss
    Irreparable; terms of peace yet none
    Vouchsafed or sought; for what peace will be given
    To us enslaved, but custody severe,
    And stripes, and arbitrary punishment
335 Inflicted? And what peace can we return,
    But to our power hostility and hate,
    Untamed reluctance, and revenge though slow,
    Yet ever plotting how the conqueror least
    May reap his conquest, and may least rejoice
340 In doing what we most in suffering feel?
    Nor will occasion want, nor shall we need
    With dangerous expedition to invade
    Heaven, whose high walls fear no assault or siege,
    Or ambush from the deep. What if we find
345 Some easier enterprise? There is a place
    (If ancient and prophetic fame in heaven
    Err not) another world, the happy seat
    Of some new race called Man, about this time
    To be created like to us, though less
350 In power and excellence, but favoured more
    Of him who rules above; so was his will

ii *330. determined*] finished (as in vi 318). But the context also activates a subsidiary meaning, 'war has given us a settled aim'.

ii *332. Vouchsafed*] M.'s spelling, 'Voutsaf't', indicates the seventeenth-century pronunciation he preferred.

ii *336. to our power*] to the limit of our power.

ii *337. reluctance*] resistance, not just 'unwillingness' (*OED* 1).

ii *346–52*. Clarifying the obscure passage at i 651ff about a rumour of a new race. The creation of man was the subject of a public oath by God, but the time of the creation was the subject of a rumour only ('it is not for you to know the times or seasons', *Acts* i 7). Beelzebub's use of the foreordinance to persuade the devils that God means to supplant them is dramatic irony; for the devils' spite makes this lie come true. To prevent their being supplanted they agree to the corruption of man, which in turn occasions Christ's incarnation and the elevation of manhood. On the other hand (so complex is the manner of God's foreknowledge), at iii 678–80 Uriel evidently thinks of man as created to fill the vacancies in heaven; as Raphael does at vii 150–61. God's 'foreknowledge prevents the two stories from being inconsistent; he would have known throughout all past time that he was going to want to spite [the devils]' (Empson 56). The Biblical authority for the relative status of man and angel was *Ps.* viii 5: 'thou hast made him a little lower than the angels, and hast crowned him with glory and honour' – developed and applied to Jesus in *Heb.* ii 6–9.

Pronounced among the gods, and by an oath,
That shook heaven's whole circumference, confirmed.
Thither let us bend all our thoughts, to learn
355   What creatures there inhabit, of what mould,
Or substance, how endued, and what their power,
And where their weakness, how attempted best,
By force or subtlety: though heaven be shut,
And heaven's high arbitrator sit secure
360   In his own strength, this place may lie exposed
The utmost border of his kingdom, left
To their defence who hold it: here perhaps
Some advantageous act may be achieved
By sudden onset, either with hell fire
365   To waste his whole creation, or possess
All as our own, and drive as we were driven,
The puny habitants, or if not drive,

ii *352–3*. Editors have treated this heaven-shaking oath as an instance of
M.'s obedience to epic formula (e.g. Homer, *Il.* i 530, Virgil, *Aen.* ix 106
totum nutu tremefecit Olympum). In fact the thought is much nearer to
Is. xiii 12–3: 'I will make a man more precious than fine gold; even a man
than the golden wedge of Ophir. Therefore I will shake the Heavens' (a key
verse in *PL*: see xi 396–407, vi 832f). Cp. *Heb.* vi 17, 'God, willing . . . to
shew . . . the immutability of his counsel, confirmed it by an oath', and
Heb. xii 26, 'Whose voice then shook the earth: but now he hath promised,
saying, Yet once more I shake not the earth only, but also heaven'; also
Gen. xxii 16 and *Is.* xlv 23.   gods] See i 116–7*n* and iii 341*n*.
ii *356. endued*] gifted. The *substance* of man is of the greatest practical im-
portance to the devils, for it is the Material Cause of the Fall. See Howard
161–3.
ii *357. attempt*] Both 'try to entice or seduce' and 'attack, overthrow,
rape'. Each meaning is further developed in ll. 366–8 below.
ii *359. arbitrator*] arbiter, judge, sole controller. Yet another of the many
antonomasias by which the devils desperately attempt 'to assert Dualistic
equality with [their] Creator' (Broadbent 130). Cp. 'conqueror' (l. 338
above), 'king of heaven' (l. 316), 'heaven's all-ruling sire' (l. 264), 'heaven's
lord' (l. 236), 'supreme foe' (l. 210), etc. *God* is always avoided.
ii *360.* To encourage the war-weary devils, Beelzebub here minimises the
danger; but later (ll. 410–3) he maximises it, to ensure the choice of a suffi-
ciently meritorious explorer.
ii *367. puny*] weak; but also, as Hume and Newton noted, 'born since us'
(the original meaning, from Fr. *puis né*). That men are puny 'superbly
compresses Beelzebub's contemptuous reasons for hating them (new fa-
vourites) *and* his reasons for revenge: they are weak' (Ricks 66).   *drive*]
put to flight. Hughes compares Joseph Beaumont, *Psyche* (1648) i 24:
'Was't not enough, against the righteous Law / Of Primogeniture, to

Seduce them to our party, that their God
May prove their foe, and with repenting hand
370 Abolish his own works. This would surpass
Common revenge, and interrupt his joy
In our confusion, and our joy upraise
In his disturbance; when his darling sons
Hurled headlong to partake with us, shall curse
375 Their frail original, and faded bliss,
Faded so soon. Advise if this be worth
Attempting, or to sit in darkness here
Hatching vain empires. Thus Beelzebub
Pleaded his devilish counsel, first devised
380 By Satan, and in part proposed: for whence,
But from the author of all ill could spring,
So deep a malice, to confound the race
Of mankind in one root, and earth with hell
To mingle and involve, done all to spite
385 The great creator? But their spite still serves
His glory to augment. The bold design

throw Us down / From that bright home, which all the world do's know /
Was by confest inheritance our own: / But, to our shame, Man, that vile
worm, must dwell / In our fair Orbs, and Heav'n with Vermin fill.'
ii *369–70*. Cp. *Gen*. vi 7: 'And the Lord said, I will destroy man whom I
have created from the face of the earth; both man, and beast ... for it
repenteth me that I have made them.'
ii *374. partake with us*] share in our condition; also, 'take sides with us'.
ii *375. original*] originals *Ed I*. Either reading is feasible. The *Ed II* reading
could mean 'origin, derivation' or 'parentage' or 'author, progenitor'
(*OED* s.v. *Original* sb. 1, 2); 'originals' could have only the last sense.
ii *376–8*. For the devils, this is merely sarcasm directed against Mammon;
but, for the reader, the allusion in *sit in darkness* to *Ps*. cvii 1of ('Such as sit
in darkness and in the shadow of death, being bound in affliction and iron;
Because they rebelled against the words of God') may suggest 'the ultimate
fate of all rebels against God' (Sims 16).   *Advise*] consider.
ii *383. one root*] Adam, the root of the genealogical tree of man. The Biblical
horticultural metaphor, which runs throughout *PL* (e.g. iii 288, ix 89, 645)
was very extensively used by the Reformers in their discussions of the doc-
trine of Original Sin. Rajan cites the Westminster Confession: Adam and
Eve 'being the root of all mankind, the guilt of this sin was imputed, and the
same death in sin and corrupted nature conveyed, to all their posterity'.
ii *384. involve*] entangle in trouble, implicate; perhaps also 'envelop'. On the
inextricable mingling of good and evil in the fallen world, see *Areopagitica*
(Yale ii 514): 'Good and evill we know in the field of this World grow up
together almost inseparably; and the knowledge of good is ... involv'd
and interwoven with the knowledge of evill.'

Pleased highly those infernal states, and joy
Sparkled in all their eyes; with full assent
They vote: whereat his speech he thus renews.
390   Well have ye judged, well ended long debate,
Synod of gods, and like to what ye are,
Great things resolved, which from the lowest deep
Will once more lift us up in spite of fate,
Nearer our ancient seat; perhaps in view
395   Of those bright confines, whence with neighbouring
        arms
And opportune excursion we may chance
Re-enter heaven; or else in some mild zone
Dwell not unvisited of heaven's fair light
Secure, and at the brightening orient beam
400   Purge off this gloom; the soft delicious air,
To heal the scar of these corrosive fires
Shall breathe her balm. But first whom shall we send
In search of this new world, whom shall we find
Sufficient? Who shall tempt with wandering feet
405   The dark unbottomed infinite abyss
And through the palpable obscure find out
His uncouth way, or spread his airy flight
Upborne with indefatigable wings
Over the vast abrupt, ere he arrive

ii *387. states*] estates of the realm, people of rank and authority.
ii *391. synod*] A carefully chosen term, since it could be used of the conjunction of stars as well as the meeting of councillors. We are not long allowed to forget that the devils were once 'sons of the morning'; see v 700–14*n*.
ii *400. Purge . . . gloom*] In one sense the meaning is psychological ('clear away this depression'); in another, it develops the same catachresis as 'palpable obscure' at l. 406 – the darkness is so thick that the devils think of washing it off.
ii *402. breathe*] *Ed I* wrongly has 'breath'.
ii *404. tempt*] try (*OED* I 3) or 'venture upon' (*OED* I 2 c, first instance); perhaps aphetic for *attempt*.
ii *405. unbottomed*] Points to the primary meaning of *abyss* (Greek ἄβυσσος bottomless); cp. *Rev.* xx 3, where the A.V. translation is 'bottomless pit'. The repeated delay of the noun may mime the infinite regression of the chasm.
ii *406. palpable obscure*] Cp. xii 188, 'Palpable darkness'; the allusion is to *Exod.* x 21: 'The Lord said unto Moses, Stretch out thine hand toward heaven, that there may be darkness over the land of Egypt, even darkness which may be felt [Vulgate *palpari queant*, Tremellius *palpet*].'
ii *407. uncouth*] unknown, and so unfrequented.
ii *409. abrupt*] The adjective (precipitous, broken off) is here used as a noun,

410   The happy isle; what strength, what art can then
      Suffice, or what evasion bear him safe
      Through the strict sentries and stations thick
      Of angels watching round? Here he had need
      All circumspection, and we now no less
415   Choice in our suffrage; for on whom we send,
      The weight of all and our last hope relies.
         This said, he sat; and expectation held
      His look suspense, awaiting who appeared
      To second, or oppose, or undertake
420   The perilous attempt: but all sat mute,
      Pondering the danger with deep thoughts; and each
      In other's countenance read his own dismay
      Astonished: none among the choice and prime
      Of those heaven-warring champions could be found
425   So hardy as to proffer or accept
      Alone the dreadful voyage; till at last
      Satan, whom now transcendent glory raised
      Above his fellows, with monarchal pride
      Conscious of highest worth, unmoved thus spake.

and refers to the *abyss* between hell and heaven.   *arrive*] arrive at, reach
(*OED* I 3).

ii *410*. Metaphors and similes in which Satan is a voyager or trader, and
earth an island, are extremely common in *PL*. Cp. ll. 426, 636–42, 919, 1011,
1042–4, in this book alone; and see iv 159–66*n*.   *happy isle*] Hints at the
Fortunate Isles, or Isles of the Blessed (Happy), from the antique descriptions
of which M. is to draw much of his imagery for Paradise. The suggestion
is taken up more firmly near the end of Satan's voyage: see iii 568–9*n*.

ii *411*. *evasion*] subterfuge, evasive action.

ii *412*. *sentries*] A trisyllable, spelt 'senteries'–a not unusual seventeenth-
century form.   *stations*] guard posts.

ii *414*. *we*] *Ed I* and *Ed II*. But a famous *erratum* in *Ed I* –'Lib. 2. v. 414 for
we read *wee*'–has wrongly been taken, since Richardson, as evidence that
M. meant to distinguish emphatic and unemphatic forms of the pronoun.
See Preface, p. ix.

ii *415*. *Choice . . . suffrage*] discrimination in our vote (to elect him).

ii *418*. *suspense*] attentive; in a state of suspense, waiting for the issue (*OED*
a. I, 2).

ii *423*. *Astonished*] dismayed.   *prime*] first in rank or importance.

ii *425*. Reflecting the irresolution of the devils, *proffer* hesitates between two
incomplete meanings: 'offer the voyage (to Satan)' and 'offer (to go on)
the voyage, volunteer'.

ii *427*. Contrasting with Messiah's 'meek' offering of himself at iii 227ff
where sovereignty is objectively present, but conferred by the Father.

430 O progeny of heaven, empyreal thrones,
    With reason hath deep silence and demur
    Seized us, though undismayed: long is the way
    And hard, that out of hell leads up to light;
    Our prison strong, this huge convex of fire,
435 Outrageous to devour, immures us round
    Ninefold, and gates of burning adamant
    Barred over us prohibit all egress.
    These passed, if any pass, the void profound
    Of unessential night receives him next
440 Wide gaping, and with utter loss of being
    Threatens him, plunged in that abortive gulf.
    If thence he scape into whatever world,
    Or unknown region, what remains him less
    Than unknown dangers and as hard escape.
445 But I should ill become this throne, O peers,
    And this imperial sovereignty, adorned
    With splendour, armed with power, if aught proposed
    And judged of public moment, in the shape
    Of difficulty or danger could deter
450 Me from attempting. Wherefore do I assume
    These royalties, and not refuse to reign,

ii *430–66.* Cp. Satan's speech, in a similar situation, in *PR* i 44–105.

ii *432–3.* See l. 81*n* and iii 20f. Cp. Virgil, *Aen.* vi 126–9, the Sibyl's warning to Aeneas before his descent into the world of the dead: 'easy is the descent to Avernus . . . but to recall your steps and pass out to the upper air, this is the task, this the toil'; and Dante, *Inf.* xxxiv 95: 'the way is long and the road is hard'. Rajan contrasts the 'smooth, easy' bridge built by Sin and Death at x 282ff below.

ii *434. convex*] vault; both a poetic and a scientific word.

ii *436.* Virgil's underworld is *immured* by the *ninefold* Styx (*Aen.* vi 439), and his Tartarus has a gate with pillars of *adamant* (*Aen.* vi 552).

ii *439. unessential*] without substance or being; cp. l. 150, 'uncreated night'.

ii *441. abortive*] A strong and difficult word. The gulf itself can hardly be 'aborted' or 'born prematurely', while, if it is abortion-causing in the sense of 'frustrating' (Hughes), this is weak beside the threat of l. 440, 'utter loss of being'. Perhaps Satan thinks of the gulf as a miscarrying womb (cp. l.150, 'wide womb of uncreated night') from which the traveller may never be born, or which may render him as if unborn. A rather arcane pun may also be intended (Latin *aborior* = set, disappear; used of heavenly bodies such as, e.g., Lucifer).

ii *444.* The fourth (1688) and subsequent edns have question mark after *escape*. But Satan may well be meant to amplify the dangers before him with an affirmatory rather than an interrogative tone.

Refusing to accept as great a share
Of hazard as of honour, due alike
To him who reigns, and so much to him due
455   Of hazard more, as he above the rest
High honoured sits? Go therefore mighty powers,
Terror of heaven, though fallen; intend at home,
While here shall be our home, what best may ease
The present misery, and render hell
460   More tolerable; if there be cure or charm
To respite or deceive, or slack the pain
Of this ill mansion: intermit no watch
Against a wakeful foe, while I abroad
Through all the coasts of dark destruction seek
465   Deliverance for us all: this enterprise
None shall partake with me. Thus saying rose
The monarch, and prevented all reply,
Prudent, lest from his resolution raised
Others among the chief might offer now
470   (Certain to be refused) what erst they feared;
And so refused might in opinion stand
His rivals, winning cheap the high repute
Which he through hazard huge must earn. But they
Dreaded not more the adventure than his voice
475   Forbidding; and at once with him they rose;
Their rising all at once was as the sound
Of thunder heard remote. Towards him they bend
With awful reverence prone; and as a god
Extol him equal to the highest in heaven:
480   Nor failed they to express how much they praised,
That for the general safety he despised

ii 452. *Refusing*] 'if I refuse'; the speech is unfortunately open however to an exactly contrary interpretation–'refusing as I do'.

ii 457. *intend*] consider, concentrate on; not a Latin sense.

ii 461. *respite*] rest, relieve.   *deceive*] beguile away.

ii 467. See i 348 and iv 393: Satan is 'a blend of oriental despot and Machiavellian prince' (Lewis 65).

ii 468. *raised*] encouraged.

ii 477. Rajan points out that just as the adoption of the scheme to ruin mankind is accompanied by thunder, so is the completion of the original sin at ix 1002.

ii 478. *awful*] respectful, reverent.   *prone*] grovelling. Contrast the loyal angel's obeisance at iii 349f.

ii 479. *highest*] 'the highest of the gods (angels) in heaven' and 'the highest, in heaven: God'. The second meaning belongs to the detailed parallel between Satan's self-sacrifice and Messiah's.

His own: for neither do the spirits damned
Lose all their virtue; lest bad men should boast
Their specious deeds on earth, which glory excites,
485   Or close ambition varnished o'er with zeal.
Thus they their doubtful consultations dark
Ended rejoicing in their matchless chief:
As when from mountain tops the dusky clouds
Ascending, while the north wind sleeps, o'erspread
490   Heaven's cheerful face, the louring element
Scowls o'er the darkened landscape snow, or shower;
If chance the radiant sun with farewell sweet
Extend his evening beam, the fields revive,
The birds their notes renew, and bleating herds
495   Attest their joy, that hill and valley rings.
O shame to men! Devil with devil damned
Firm concord holds, men only disagree
Of creatures rational, though under hope
Of heavenly grace: and God proclaiming peace,
500   Yet live in hatred, enmity, and strife
Among themselves, and levy cruel wars,
Wasting the earth, each other to destroy:
As if (which might induce us to accord)
Man had not hellish foes enow besides,
505   That day and night for his destruction wait.
        The Stygian council thus dissolved; and forth

ii *483. lest . . . boast*] so that men ought not to boast; cp. *Eph*. ii 8f: 'by grace
are ye saved. . . . Not of works, lest any man should boast.'
ii *485. close*] secret.
ii *488–95*. 'The volcanoes of Book i are charmed into pastoral hills' (Broad-
bent 121) by the deceiving elf of the devils' imagination. The north wind is
appropriate to Satan (see v 689*n*).
ii *490. element*] sky.
ii *491. scowls*] The transitive use is discussed as an instance of expressive
syntax by Ricks (81).   *landscape*] Early edns have the variant spelling
'lantskip', but there seems to have been no phonetic difference between the
two forms.
ii *492. If chance*] if it chance that.
ii *494. bleating*] Used of goats or calves, as well as of sheep.
ii *496–502*. 'The lines state an orthodox doctrine that is found in Antonio
Rusca's *De Inferno et Statu Daemonum* (Milan 1621), pp. 505–7. . . . The devils
avoid civil strife and maintain orders and ranks among themselves so as to
tempt mankind most efficiently' (Hughes).
ii *503. accord*] agree.
ii *504. enow*] enough.

In order came the grand infernal peers,
Midst came their mighty paramount, and seemed
Alone the antagonist of heaven, nor less
510 Than hell's dread emperor with pomp supreme,
And God-like imitated state; him round
A globe of fiery seraphim enclosed
With bright emblazonry, and horrent arms.
Then of their session ended they bid cry
515 With trumpets' regal sound the great result:
Toward the four winds four speedy cherubim
Put to their mouths the sounding alchemy
By herald's voice explained: the hollow abyss
Heard far and wide, and all the host of hell
520 With deafening shout returned them loud acclaim.
Thence more at ease their minds and somewhat raised
By false presumptuous hope, the ranged powers
Disband, and wandering, each his several way
Pursues, as inclination or sad choice
525 Leads him perplexed, where he may likeliest find
Truce to his restless thoughts, and entertain

ii *507*. A heavier stop seems to be required after *peers*.

ii *508*. *midst*] This adverbial use is peculiar to M. *OED* suggests it may be
a contracted form of 'middest'. *paramount*] lord paramount, ruler.

ii *510–20*. Broadbent (113) sees in these lines a portrayal of the English mob's
easy gullibility and of their passion (which M. detested) for the regalia of
monarchy.

ii *512*. *globe*] compact body (often of soldiers). The word had been used of
angels by Giles Fletcher: 'A globe of winged angels, swift as thought'
(*Christs triumph after death* 13). *fiery*] the word *seraphim* was connected
with the Heb. root *saraph*, to burn. Cp. Spenser, *Hymn to Heavenly Beauty*
94f: 'Those eternall burning Seraphins, / Which from their faces dart out
fierie light'. John Norris of Bemerton asks: 'What is it that makes the
Seraphin burn and flame above the rest of the Angelical Orders?' (*Practical
discourses* (1691) 298). See also i 129n.

ii *513*. *imblazonry*] heraldic devices. *horrent*] bristling; first instance in
OED; perhaps a Latinizing coinage based on *horrens*; but cp. M.E. *horrend*=
dreadful, also *horrendous*.

ii *515*. *result*] resolution, outcome of the *session*. Note M.'s use, in the passage,
of terms appropriate to an earthly parliament.

ii *517*. *alchemy*] alloy, brass (alchemy gold, imitation gold).

ii *521*. *raised*] encouraged.

ii *522*. *ranged powers*] armies drawn up in ranks.

ii *526*. *entertain*] while away.

> The irksome hours, till this great chief return.
> Part on the plain, or in the air sublime
> Upon the wing, or in swift race contend,
> 530   As at the Olympian games or Pythian fields;
> Part curb their fiery steeds, or shun the goal
> With rapid wheels, or fronted brigades form.
> As when to warn proud cities war appears
> Waged in the troubled sky, and armies rush
> 535   To battle in the clouds, before each van
> Prick forth the airy knights, and couch their spears
> Till thickest legions close; with feats of arms
> From either end of heaven the welkin burns.
> Others with vast Typhoean rage more fell
> 540   Rend up both rocks and hills, and ride the air
> In whirlwind; hell scarce holds the wild uproar.
> As when Alcides from Oechalia crowned

ii *527. this*] his *Ed I* – perhaps preferably, since it does not abandon the point of view of the individual devil.

ii *528–69.* Epic models include the sports of the Myrmidons during Achilles' absence from the war (Homer, *Il.* ii 774ff); the Greek funeral games of *Il.* xxiii and the Trojan of *Aen.* v; and – closest of all – the amusements of the blessed dead in Virgil's Elysium (*Aen.* vi 642–59).

ii *528. sublime*] uplifted, high (archaic).

ii *530.* The Pythian games at Delphi were next in importance after the Olympian.

ii *531–2.* Imitating Horace's image of the turning posts shunned by chariot-wheels (*Od.* I i 4–5: *metaque fervidis / evitata rotis.   fronted*] opposed, face to face.   *brigades*] Stressed on the first syllable. With the 'aggressive war-games' (Broadbent 118) of the devils contrast the 'unarmed' games of the good angels (iv 552 below).

ii *533–8.* Among portents of the burning of the Temple at Jerusalem, Josephus mentions chariots and troops of soldiers in their armour . . . running about among the clouds, and surrounding of cities (*De bellis* VI v 3).

ii *539. Typhoean rage*] See i 197–200n.

ii *541. whirlwind*] Brings out a mild pun in *Typhoean*, for 'typhon', besides being a name, was an English word meaning 'whirlwind'. Cp. the storm made by Satan in *PR* iv 409–19, though here the emphasis is on the whirlwind as a torment of the damned: see i 77, ii 180–2 and vi 749n. For the throwing of hills as a symbol of rebellion, see vi 639–66n.

ii *542–6. Alcides* (Hercules) returning *victor ab Oechalia* (Ovid, *Met.* ix 136) put on a ritual robe which had inadvertently been soaked by his wife in corrosive poison. Mad with pain, he blamed his friend Lichas, who had brought the robe, and hurled him far into the *Euboic* (Euboean) sea. Throughout M. follows Ovid rather than Seneca (*Hercules furens*) or Sophocles (*Trachiniae*). The rhythmic and syntactic organization of the passage,

With conquest, felt the envenomed robe, and tore
Through pain up by the roots Thessalian pines,
545   And Lichas from the top of Oeta threw
Into the Euboic sea. Others more mild,
Retreated in a silent valley, sing
With notes angelical to many a harp
Their own heroic deeds and hapless fall
550   By doom of battle; and complain that fate
Free virtue should enthral to force or chance.
Their song was partial, but the harmony
(What could it less when spirits immortal sing?)
Suspended hell, and took with ravishment
555   The thronging audience. In discourse more sweet
(For eloquence the soul, song charms the sense,)
Others apart sat on a hill retired,
In thoughts more elevate, and reasoned high
Of providence, foreknowledge, will and fate,

attacked in Davie 67, is defended in Ricks 43–5, where the separation of
tore from *up*, e.g., is noticed as an effect mimetic of violent effort. On the
uprooting of trees as a symbol of lawless wildness, see i 292–4n. M.'s use of
torn hills and uprooted trees as images of reversion to chaos is traced in
MacCaffrey 88f.   *Oechalia*] Oealia *Ed I* misprint.

ii *546–69*. Burden 58ff argues that M., not content to write divine poetry,
must also construct a refutation of ordinary, merely charming, poetry. The
rejected secular poetry has its place in hell, and is shown to have definite
satanic characteristics. Thus the satanic epic hero is not free, but subjected by
fate to chance. We notice the close correlation between satanic literature
and 'perplexed' satanic philosophy. For M., unideological literature is an
impossibility. According to Webster's *Displaying of witchcraft* (1677) 215–41,
it is the devils' custom 'to sing melodiously' and 'with their impure mouths'
to 'meditate and talk of holy scriptures' (Schultz 86).

ii *551–2. partial*] polyphonic; also 'prejudiced' (since they sang their own
version of the Fall, in which virtue is on their side, force or chance on God's,
and the ultimate power is fate). See 232–3n.

ii *554. Suspended*] held the attention of. The parenthesis delaying the verb
'suspends as it were the event' (Newton). It would be better still if the syn-
tactical effect echoed a 'play on *suspend*–suspension as a technical harmonic
term' (Ricks 79), but this term does not seem to have been used before about
1800.   *took*] charmed.

ii *557–69*. Cp. the Castle of Wisdom in Dante's Limbo (*Inf*. iv).

ii *557–8. retired*] In thought as well as on the hill (Ricks 88).

ii *559–61*. Eighteenth-century critics noticed a mimetic intricacy in the
rhetorical patterning of these lines. The devils, lacking the resources of
Scriptural authority, are lost among these labyrinthine preoccupations of
medieval and Reformation scholasticism. Dialectic itself is one of the results

560   Fixed fate, free will, foreknowledge absolute,
And found no end, in wandering mazes lost.
Of good and evil much they argued then,
Of happiness and final misery,
Passion and apathy, and glory and shame,
565   Vain wisdom all, and false philosophy:
Yet with a pleasing sorcery could charm
Pain for a while or anguish, and excite
Fallacious hope, or arm the obdured breast
With stubborn patience as with triple steel.
570   Another part in squadrons and gross bands,
On bold adventure to discover wide
That dismal world, if any clime perhaps
Might yield them easier habitation, bend
Four ways their flying march, along the banks
575   Of four infernal rivers that disgorge
Into the burning lake their baleful streams;
Abhorred Styx the flood of deadly hate,
Sad Acheron of sorrow, black and deep;

of the Fall: the devils have 'lost the power of intuitive reasoning which differentiates [angels] from men' (Rajan² 83, citing v 486–90).   *mazes*] Rajan contrasts the regular 'mazes intricate' of the loyal angels' dance at v 622, and compares Adam's attempt to escape from recognition of his guilt 'through mazes' of evasion and error at x 830. The heavenly maze is a cosmic labyrinth like the ones on medieval cathedral floors; whereas that of hell is a Labyrinth of Error.

ii *564–9.* Directed especially against Stoicism, the most formidable ethical challenge to . Christianity.   *apathy*] complete freedom from passion; a Stoic ideal, contrasted with true *patience* in *De doctrina* ii 10 (and see also *PR* iv 300–18). Henry More (*Immortality of the soul* III ix 2) held that 'Stoicks, Epicureans, and whatever other sects and humors are on the Earth, may in likelihood be met with there' (i.e. among aerial spirits).

ii *568. obdured*] hardened, made callous.

ii *569. stubborn patience*] contrast the 'true patience' of xi 361.

ii *570. gross*] large, or compact.

ii *575–81.* This description of the four rivers of hell takes its broad outline from Virgil's (esp. *Aen.* vi), Dante's (e.g. *Inf.* xiv), and Spenser's (e.g. *F.Q.* II vii 56f). M. adds the detail of confluence in the 'burning lake' (for which see i 210 and *Rev.* xix 20), perhaps to provide a counterpart to the common source of the four rivers of Paradise (iv 223–33 and *Gen.* ii 10). The epithet or description attached to each river translates its Greek name (e.g. Στύξ, hateful). These etymologies were familiar ones, easily accessible in dictionaries such as Calepinus'. The rivers had often been allegorised, notably by Cristoforo Landino (*Opera* (Basel 1596) 3038, 3044), but M. does not seem to pursue this possibility very far.   *baleful*] evil, painful, sorrowful.

Cocytus, named of lamentation loud
580   Heard on the rueful stream; fierce Phlegethon
Whose waves of torrent fire inflame with rage.
Far off from these a slow and silent stream,
Lethe the river of oblivion rolls
Her watery labyrinth, whereof who drinks,
585   Forthwith his former state and being forgets,
Forgets both joy and grief, pleasure and pain.
Beyond this flood a frozen continent
Lies dark and wild, beat with perpetual storms
Of whirlwind and dire hail, which on firm land
590   Thaws not, but gathers heap, and ruin seems
Of ancient pile; all else deep snow and ice,
A gulf profound as that Serbonian bog
Betwixt Damiata and Mount Casius old,
Where armies whole have sunk: the parching air
595   Burns frore, and cold performs the effect of fire.
Thither by harpy-footed Furies haled,

ii *583. Lethe*] Not the 'forgetful lake' of 74 above; see i *266n.*
ii *592–4. Serbonian bog*] Serbonis, a lake bordered by quicksands on the
Egyptian coast; Diodorus Siculus (I xxx 5–7) and Sandys (*A relation of a
journey* (1637) 137) speak of it devouring 'whole armies'. *Damiata* (mod.
Damietta, east of the Nile) and Mt *Casius* were both names that often oc-
curred in the Italian epics; and Dante made Damiata a symbol of mankind's
early, eastern past (*Inf.* xiv 104). M. probably introduces the Serbonian lake
because, according to one tradition, Typhon after his unsuccessful rebellion
against heaven lay overwhelmed beneath its waters. The name is a bad
omen for Satan's enterprise.
ii *594–5. parching*] drying, withering; as in xii 636 and *Lycidas* 13.   *frore*]
frozen, intensely cold. The idea that hell's torments include cold as well as
heat goes back to O.T. apocryphal writings (e.g. II *Enoch* x 2–3, Charles ii
435: 'frost and ice, thirst and shivering'), and had become well established
in medieval tradition. See Vulgate *Job* xxiv 19; Dante, *Inf.* iii 87 and xxxii;
St Thomas Aquinas, *Summa Theol.* Supple. xcvii 1; and, among later
writers, Shakespeare, *Measure for Measure* III i 121–2; and Giles Fletcher,
Christs victorie on Earth 22.
ii *596.* Dante had introduced Virgil's claw-handed Harpies (*Aen.* iii 211–8)
into his hell (*Inf.* xiii 10); and M. combines them with the *Furies* or Eume-
nides, daughters of Acheron and Night, and agencies of divine vengeance.
In Homer, the Harpies snatch souls off to death and to the ministrations of
the Erinyes or Furies: see *Od.* xx 77 and Jane Harrison, *Prolegomena to the
Study of Greek Religion* (New York 1957) 176–83.   *haled*] obviously
preferable to 'hailed'; though the spelling of the early edns, 'hail'd', could
indicate either word.

At certain revolutions all the damned
Are brought: and feel by turns the bitter change
Of fierce extremes, extremes by change more fierce,
600   From beds of raging fire to starve in ice
Their soft ethereal warmth, and there to pine
Immovable, infixed, and frozen round,
Periods of time, thence hurried back to fire.
They ferry over this Lethean sound
605   Both to and fro, their sorrow to augment,
And wish and struggle, as they pass, to reach
The tempting stream, with one small drop to lose
In sweet forgetfulness all pain and woe,
All in one moment, and so near the brink;
610   But fate withstands, and to oppose the attempt
Medusa with Gorgonian terror guards
The ford, and of itself the water flies
All taste of living wight, as once it fled
The lip of Tantalus. Thus roving on
615   In confused march forlorn, the adventurous bands
With shuddering horror pale, and eyes aghast
Viewed first their lamentable lot, and found
No rest: through many a dark and dreary vale
They passed, and many a region dolorous,
620   O'er many a frozen, many a fiery alp,
Rocks, caves, lakes, fens, bogs, dens, and shades of
      death,
A universe of death, which God by curse

ii *600. starve*] die lingeringly from cold.

ii *603–10*. Virgil's Lethe is drunk by those who, after the completion of *certain revolutions* or *periods of time*, have become purified (*Aen.* vi 745–51), but M.'s devils, unrepentant, only cross the river for another term of suffering.

ii *607. lose*] *Ed I* and *Ed II* 'loose' could indicate either 'lose' or 'loose'. 'Loose' is just possible, in the sense 'do away with' (*OED* 7).

ii *608*. On the reverberations in the word *woe*, which echoes i 3 and anticipates x 754, see MacCaffrey 85.

ii *611. Medusa*] One of the Gorgons; Odysseus during his visit to the dead is terrified of meeting her petrifying glance (*Od.* xi 634).

ii *614*. In Homer's hell *Tantalus* is tormented by thirst, standing in a pool that recedes whenever he tries to drink (*Od.* xi 582–92). According to one theory, he was so punished because he gave the food of the gods to mortal men (see Conti, *Mytholog.* vi 18); according to another, he was a type of ambition.

ii *617–8*. Echoing *Matt.* xii 43.

Created evil, for evil only good,
Where all life dies, death lives, and nature breeds,
625   Perverse, all monstrous, all prodigious things,
Abominable, inutterable, and worse
Than fables yet have feigned, or fear conceived,
Gorgons and Hydras, and Chimeras dire.
        Mean while the adversary of God and man,
630   Satan with thoughts inflamed of highest design,
Puts on swift wings, and towards the gates of hell
Explores his solitary flight; some times
He scours the right hand coast, some times the left,
Now shaves with level wing the deep, then soars
635   Up to the fiery concave towering high.
As when far off at sea a fleet descried
Hangs in the clouds, by equinoctial winds
Close sailing from Bengala, or the isles
Of Ternate and Tidore, whence merchants bring

ii *624. nature*] Ed I no initial capital. The degree of personification is uncertain.

ii *628.* Virgil's and Tasso's hells have similar shadowy horrors: see *Aen.* vi 287–9; *Gerus. Lib.* iv 5. The *Hydra* was many-headed; the *Gorgons* had serpents for hair; and the *Chimaera*, a composite monster, breathed flame. The last two are treated as the pains of a guilty conscience in *Prol i* (Yale i 231).

ii *631. towards*] toward *Ed I*.

ii *632. Explores*] puts to the proof; a Latinism (see Elizabeth Holmes in *Essays and Studies* x (1924) 106), though the construction probably also depends on the English idiom 'to fond one's flight' (make trial of one's powers). See *OED* s.v. *Flight* sb.[1] 1 b.

ii *635. towering*] 'rising aloft' is probably meant. But the spelling in *Ed I* and *Ed II*, 'touring', does not distinguish 'towering' from 'touring' (turning, making a circuitous journey).

ii *636–41.* In M.'s time there was increased trade with *Bengala* (Bengal) and *Ternate* and *Tidore* (two of the 'spice islands' or Moluccas). The spiceships would cross the *Ethiopian* sea (the ancient name for the Indian Ocean) before rounding the Cape of Good Hope. The simile is a good example of M.'s power in maintaining multiple correspondences between tenor and vehicle: 'the ships ply nightly because Satan was in the darkness visible of Hell; are far off so that they hang like a mirage and seem flying like Satan . . . and are going towards the Pole because Satan (from inside) is going towards the top of the concave wall of Hell' (Empson[2] 171). They carry *spicy drugs* because Satan is going to barter for Eve's innocence the fragrant fruit of the forbidden tree.

ii *638. Close sailing*] sailing close to the wind.

640   Their spicy drugs: they on the trading flood
       Through the wide Ethiopian to the Cape
       Ply stemming nightly toward the pole. So seemed
       Far off the flying fiend: at last appear
       Hell bounds high reaching to the horrid roof,
645   And thrice threefold the gates; three folds were brass,
       Three iron, three of adamantine rock,
       Impenetrable, impaled with circling fire,
       Yet unconsumed. Before the gates there sat
       On either side a formidable shape;
650   The one seemed woman to the waist, and fair,
       But ended foul in many a scaly fold
       Voluminous and vast, a serpent armed

ii *640. trading*] 'carrying in the way of trade' (*OED* 8); or perhaps an extension by analogy with such phrases as 'trading path' and 'trading course'. Some editors take *trading flood*='sea where the Trade Winds blow'.

ii *642. Ply*] beat up against the wind, work to windward (*OED* v.^{2} II 6). *stemming*] A pun between 'making headway against water or wind' (*OED* v.^{3} 1) and–in the tenor discourse–'mounting upwards' (*OED* v.^{4} 1). Note that the former word was often applied figuratively in the sense 'defying'.

ii *645–6.* See l. 436n.

ii *647. impaled*] enclosed.

ii *649.* 'Sin and Death are shadowy and temporary figures because they are, ultimately, unreal–figments of the "evil imagination"' (Broadbent 128f).

ii *650–66.* M.'s personified Sin incorporates several iconographical motifs, noted below. The nearest analogues are probably Spenser's Errour, who is half serpent and half woman, has a 'mortal sting', and swallows her young (*F.Q.* I i 14f), and Phineas Fletcher's Hamartia (*The Purple Island* xii 27–31), a monster who at first 'fair and lovely seems': 'A woman seem'd she in her upper part; / To which she could such lying glosse impart, / That thousands she had slain with her deceiving art. // The rest (though hid) in serpents form arayd, / With iron scales, like to a plaited mail: / Over her back her knotty tail displaid, / Along the empty aire did lofty sail: / The end was pointed with a double sting, / Which with such dreaded might she wont to fling, / That nought could help the wound, but bloud of heav'nly King.'

ii *650–3.* The serpent of sin that tempted Adam and Eve was traditionally portrayed as having a woman's head or bust: see Didron ii 139f.

ii *652. voluminous*] consisting of many convolutions (*OED* 1). Rajan^2 90 defends the word against Davie^2 78 by saying that Sin is voluminous because its 'consequences are involved'. But it is worth noting that Valeriano, discussing a not dissimilar serpent of sin in *Hieroglyphica* xiv 25, interprets the coils as 'the multiplication of pleasure by supply of variety' (Valeriano 176). M. probably only means us to notice that Sin presents three phases or

With mortal sting: about her middle round
A cry of hell hounds never ceasing barked
655   With wide Cerberian mouths full loud, and rung
A hideous peal: yet, when they list, would creep,
If aught disturbed their noise, into her womb,
And kennel there, yet there still barked and howled,
Within unseen. Far less abhorred than these
660   Vexed Scylla bathing in the sea that parts
Calabria from the hoarse Trinacrian shore:
Nor uglier follow the Night-hag, when called
In secret, riding through the air she comes
Lured with the smell of infant blood, to dance
665   With Lapland witches, while the labouring moon

aspects: the specious front of temptation, the foul involvement and the
mortal consequence.

ii 653. *mortal*] death-dealing; see *1 Cor.* xv 56: 'The sting of death is sin.'

ii 653–9. John Illo (*N & Q* ccv (1960) 425f) notes that neither Scylla nor
Errour rewhelps her young. He compares instead Du Bartas's untameable
chiurca, or opposum, who does (i 6; p. 152). More relevant, it seems, are
certain emblems of Opinion and of Error, such as Beza's *Icones* (Geneva
1580) Embl. xxxii. There is a whole *cry* (pack) of hounds, because one sin
engenders many consequences, sometimes hidden. Cerberus was the many-
headed dog who guarded Hades.

ii 655. *Cerberian*] Cerberean *Ed I*.

ii 659–61. Circe, jealous of the nymph Scylla, changed her lower parts into
a knot of 'gaping dogs' heads, such as a Cerberus might have' (Ovid. *Met.*
xiv 50–74). Later Scylla was again transformed, into a dangerous rock
between *Trinacria* (Sicily) and Calabria. Finally, in the medieval moralized
Ovid, she became a symbol of lust or of sin. See l. 746*n* and J. F. Gilliam
in *PQ* xxix (1950) 346.

ii 662. *Night-hag*] Hecate, whose charms were used by Circe in her spell
against Scylla. M. may allude here to the hellish yeth hounds which accord-
ing to popular superstition followed the queen of darkness across the sky in
pursuit of the souls of the damned. On the lore of Hecate generally, see K.
M. Briggs, *Pale Hecate's Team* (1962).   *called*] summoned by rites.

ii 664–6. Jonson cites many authorities to the effect that witches' 'killing of
infants is common, both for confection of theyr oyntment . . . as also out of
a lust to doe murder' (*The Masque of Queenes* 176*n*; ed. Herford and Simp-
son vii 291–2).

ii 665. *Lapland*] Renowned as a centre of witchcraft: see, e.g., *The Comedy of
Errors* IV iii 11 ('Lapland sorcerers'). In allowing witches power over the
moon, M. leaves the main direction of the best contemporary thought, and
follows superstition, for the sake of another poetic 'iteration of physical and
moral disorder' (Svendsen 75). The superstition was ancient; see Horace,
Epodes v 46.   *labouring*] troubled, suffering a defect; secondarily alluding

Eclipses at their charms. The other shape,
If shape it might be called that shape had none
Distinguishable in member, joint, or limb,
Or substance might be called that shadow seemed,
670 For each seemed either; black it stood as night,
Fierce as ten Furies, terrible as hell,
And shook a dreadful dart; what seemed his head
The likeness of a kingly crown had on.
Satan was now at hand, and from his seat
675 The monster moving onward came as fast
With horrid strides, hell trembled as he strode.
The undaunted fiend what this might be admired,
Admired, not feared; God and his Son except,
Created thing nought valued he nor shunned;
680 And with disdainful look thus first began.
    Whence and what art thou, execrable shape,
That darest, though grim and terrible, advance
Thy miscreated front athwart my way
To yonder gates? Through them I mean to pass,
685 That be assured, without leave asked of thee:
Retire, or taste thy folly, and learn by proof,

to Lat. *laborare*, poet., = to be eclipsed. Cp. John Wilkins, *The Discovery of a World in the Moone* (1638) 12: 'the supposed labour of the Moone in her eclipses'.
ii *666–73*. With this prosopopeia or personified description of Death, cp. Spenser's, which is similarly negative: 'Unbodied, unsoul'd, unheard, unseene' (*F.Q.* VII vii 46). The *dreadful dart* was a traditional attribute of Death, signifying his sharpness and suddenness (Hawes, *Pastime of Pleasure* 5383f: 'But whan I thoughte longest to endure / Dethe with his darte a rest me sodaynly'); see Tervarent, s.v. *Flèche*, col. 187. So was the *kingly crown*, on the basis of *Rev.* vi 2, where 'a crown was given' to the first of the riders of the apocalypse, 'and he went forth conquering'; see Didron ii 168–9. Coleridge noted the powerful indeterminateness of the phrase *what seemed his head*. Emma 41 remarks that M.'s choice of masculine gender for the personification of Death was probably guided less by linguistic considerations than by literary precedent 'from the biblical Angel of Death to the Greek cherub, twin of Sleep, and the Continental grotesque, the skeleton in the Dance of Death and the Renaissance Triumphs of Death'.
ii *677–8. admired*] wondered.   *Admired, not feared*] 'The distinction ... has all the distracting inertness of a footnote' (Davie[2] 76); 'the calm of supreme courage' (Ricks 46). But, as Rajan[2] 92 points out, 'to "value" evil is to learn to shun it'. Satan's is not the calm of admirable courage, but of nihilism: when God and his Son are *except* (past participle, *OED* A 3 b: 'excluded'), no basis for value remains.
ii *686. taste*] put to the proof.   *proof*]experience.

Hell-born, not to contend with spirits of heaven.
    To whom the goblin full of wrath replied,
Art thou that traitor angel, art thou he,
690 Who first broke peace in heaven and faith, till then
Unbroken, and in proud rebellious arms
Drew after him the third part of heaven's sons
Conjured against the highest, for which both thou
And they outcast from God, are here condemned
695 To waste eternal days in woe and pain?
And reckonest thou thyself with spirits of heaven,
Hell-doomed, and breathest defiance here and scorn
Where I reign king, and to enrage thee more,
Thy king and lord? Back to thy punishment,
700 False fugitive, and to thy speed add wings,
Lest with a whip of scorpions I pursue
Thy lingering, or with one stroke of this dart
Strange horror seize thee, and pangs unfelt before.
    So spake the grisly terror, and in shape,
705 So speaking and so threatening, grew tenfold
More dreadful and deform: on the other side
Incensed with indignation Satan stood
Unterrified, and like a comet burned,

ii *688. replied,*] The usual punctuation before direct speech in *PL* is a full stop, so that the comma is probably an error.   *goblin*] evil spirit.

ii *692.* Satan boasts that nearly half of the angels belong to his party (i 633, ix 141), but Death, Raphael (v 710) and Satan himself while in heaven (vi 156; unless this is due to Raphael's editing) reckon only a third. This estimate agrees with *Rev.* xii 4: 'And his [the dragon's] tail drew the third part of the stars of heaven, and did cast them to the earth.'

ii *693. Conjured*] sworn together in conspiracy (*OED* I 1 b; not a Latinism); secondarily 'bewitched; conveyed away by magic' (*OED* III 5 b, 7, 8). Stressed as an iamb.

ii *697. Hell-doomed*] Scornfully echoing Satan's 'Hell-born' (687).

ii *701.* The allusion to *1 Kings* xii 11 ('my father hath chastised you with whips, but I will chastise you with scorpions') implies that Satan would have done better to accept God's governance.

ii *707–11.* Cp. Tasso's description of Argantes: 'As when a comet far and wide descried, / In scorn of Phoebus midst bright heaven doth shine, / And tidings sad of death and mischief brings / To mighty lords, to monarchs, and to kings: / So shone the Pagan in bright armour clad' (*Gerus. Lib.* vii 52f, tr. Fairfax), which imitates Virgil's comparison of Aeneas to a comet, at *Aen.* x 272. For a variety of contemporary views about the significance and influence of comets, see Svendsen 91f and 266. H. H. Turner plausibly identifies the comet referred to here as the comet of 1816, a specially magnificent one with a tail of 104°, which appeared in *Ophiucus*. Evelyn in his

That fires the length of Ophiucus huge
710 In the Arctic sky, and from his horrid hair
Shakes pestilence and war. Each at the head
Levelled his deadly aim; their fatal hands
No second stroke intend, and such a frown
Each cast at the other, as when two black clouds
715 With heaven's artillery fraught, come rattling on
Over the Caspian, then stand front to front
Hovering a space, till winds the signal blow
To join their dark encounter in mid air:
So frowned the mighty combatants, that hell
720 Grew darker at their frown, so matched they stood;
For never but once more was either like
To meet so great a foe: and now great deeds
Had been achieved, whereof all hell had rung,
Had not the snaky sorceress that sat
725 Fast by hell gate, and kept the fatal key,
Risen, and with hideous outcry rushed between.

Diary held it responsible for the Thirty Years' War. See G.F. Chambers, *The Story of the Comets* (Oxford 1909) 211f. But Ophiuchus (Serpent Bearer) is also chosen to allude to Satan's later transformation into a serpent (cp. the very similar astronomical allusion at x 328f).

ii *710. Arctic*] not only because comets were traditionally associated with the north, nor because that is Satan's place (see v 689n below, and Svendsen 91) but also because the Serpent held by Ophiuchus is described by Ovid as lying 'nearest the icy pole' (*quaeque polo posita est glaciali proxima Serpens, Met.* ii 173). The relations of tenor and vehicle are multiple; the dominant suggestions, however, seem to be of transient brightness, and of ominousness, together with the identification of Satan as the cosmic serpent.   *horrid hair*] Wittily replete with aptness: 'horrid' means both 'bristling' and 'dreadful', while 'hair' alludes to the derivative meaning of comet (Greek ἀστὴρ κομήτης, 'long-haired star').

ii *714–9.* M.'s onomatopoeic lines perhaps emulate a simile of Boiardo's, which compares the shock of the encounter between Orlando and Agricane to that between two thunderclouds (*Orl. Innam.* I xvi 10). The *Caspian* of the poets was always stormy; thus Tasso's Argantes rages 'as when clouds together crushed and bruised, / Pour down a tempest by the Caspian shore' (*Gerus. Lib.* vi 38, tr. Fairfax; cp. Horace, *Odes* II ix 2 and Spenser, *F.Q.* II vii 14).

ii *718. mid air*] See i 515–16n. The middle of the three regions of air was the one in which storms arose; see Svendsen 93f.

ii *721–2.* When Christ destroys 'him that had the power of death, that is, the devil' (*Heb.* ii 14), as well as 'the last enemy . . . death' (*1 Cor.* xv 26); as Sin herself prophesies at l. 734.

O Father, what intends thy hand, she cried,
Against thy only son? What fury, O son,
Possesses thee to bend that mortal dart
730   Against thy father's head? and know'st for whom;
For him who sits above and laughs the while
At thee ordained his drudge, to execute
What e'er his wrath, which he calls justice, bids,
His wrath which one day will destroy ye both.
735   She spake, and at her words the hellish pest
Forbore, then these to her Satan returned:
       So strange thy outcry, and thy words so strange
Thou interposest, that my sudden hand
Prevented spares to tell thee yet by deeds
740   What it intends; till first I know of thee,
What thing thou art, thus double-formed, and why
In this infernal vale first met thou call'st
Me father, and that phantasm call'st my son?
I know thee not, nor ever saw till now
745   Sight more detestable than him and thee.
       To whom thus the portress of hell gate replied;
Hast thou forgot me then, and do I seem
Now in thine eye so foul, once deemed so fair
In heaven, when at the assembly, and in sight
750   Of all the seraphim with thee combined
In bold conspiracy against heaven's king,
All on a sudden miserable pain

ii *727–8.* The allegory whereby Sin is daughter of Satan and mother of Death is from St Basil's *Hexaemeron*; see John M. Steadman, 'Grosseteste on the Genealogy of Sin and Death', *N & Q* cciv (1959) 367f and 'Milton and St Basil: the Genesis of Sin and Death', *MLN* lxxiii (1958) 83f. The Scriptural authority is *James* i 15: 'Then when lust hath conceived, it bringeth forth sin: and sin, when it is finished, bringeth forth death.' Similar genealogies had been traced by Gower (*Mirour de l'Omme*); by Andreini (*Adamo caduto*); and by Phineas Fletcher, whose Hamartia is daughter of Eve by Satan (*The Purple Island* xii 29).

ii *746.* See ll. 774–7. Since Cerberus guarded the gate of Hades, Sin's 'Cerberean mouths' (l. 655) are appropriate to her function as portress. Empson 117f argues that God's choice of Sin and Death as guardians of the gate shows that he 'always intended them to let Satan out'. But Sin's office is an allegorical statement of the idea that access to hell is by sinning, so that it is difficult to think of any other guardian who could have been chosen to fill it.

ii *752–61.* See 727–8*n.* The circumstances of Sin's birth recall the ancient myth about Athene springing fully-formed from the head of Zeus. It is thus presented as a parody of God's generation of the Son, since Minerva's

Surprised thee, dim thine eyes, and dizzy swum
In darkness, while thy head flames thick and fast
755   Threw forth, till on the left side opening wide,
Likest to thee in shape and countenance bright,
Then shining heavenly fair, a goddess armed
Out of thy head I sprung: amazement seized
All the host of heaven; back they recoiled afraid
760   At first, and called me Sin, and for a sign
Portentous held me; but familiar grown,
I pleased, and with attractive graces won
The most averse, thee chiefly, who full oft
Thy self in me thy perfect image viewing
765   Becamest enamoured, and such joy thou took'st
With me in secret, that my womb conceived
A growing burden. Mean while war arose,
And fields were fought in heaven; wherein remained
(For what could else) to our almighty foe
770   Clear victory, to our part loss and rout
Through all the empyrean: down they fell
Driven headlong from the pitch of heaven, down
Into this deep, and in the general fall
I also; at which time this powerful key
775   Into my hand was given, with charge to keep
These gates for ever shut, which none can pass
Without my opening. Pensive here I sat
Alone, but long I sat not, till my womb

birth had traditionally been allegorised by theologians in that sense (see,
e.g., the *Observationum libellus*, attached to Conti's *Mythologiae*, s.v. *Pallas*).
The mention of pain (l. 752) at first seems to conflict with vi 327 and 432,
where we are told that Satan 'first knew pain' during the war in heaven (see
Empson 54). But M. is being subtle, not casual. Raphael would naturally be
ignorant of Satan's feelings during the inception of his sin at the rebel
council, while it is part of the change in Satan that he himself should have
forgotten and should not even recognize his sin for what it is. He has
certainly forgotten now (ii 744); why, then, should he not already have
forgotten at vi 432?

ii 761–7. From this passage Empson 58f concludes that, to allow time for
the gestation of Death, there must have been more than one conference of the
rebel angels; their theological opinions can thus be regarded as deeply and
rationally considered. But this is to assume that the embryology of Death
resembles that of man: an assumption hardly encouraged by the mode of his
mother's birth (following immediately on Satan's first overt act of diso-
bedience), or indeed of his own (ll. 783–5).

ii 764. Continuing the parody of divine generation: cp. iii 138ff.

ii 772. *pitch*] apex, summit, height, slope.

Pregnant by thee, and now excessive grown
780 Prodigious motion felt and rueful throes.
At last this odious offspring whom thou seest
Thine own begotten, breaking violent way
Tore through my entrails, that with fear and pain
Distorted, all my nether shape thus grew
785 Transformed: but he my inbred enemy
Forth issued, brandishing his fatal dart
Made to destroy: I fled, and cried out Death;
Hell trembled at the hideous name, and sighed
From all her caves, and back resounded Death.
790 I fled, but he pursued (though more, it seems,
Inflamed with lust than rage) and swifter far,
Me overtook his mother all dismayed,
And in embraces forcible and foul
Ingendering with me, of that rape begot
795 These yelling monsters that with ceaseless cry
Surround me, as thou sawest, hourly conceived
And hourly born, with sorrow infinite
To me, for when they list into the womb
That bred them they return, and howl and gnaw
800 My bowels, their repast; then bursting forth
Afresh with conscious terrors vex me round,
That rest or intermission none I find.
Before mine eyes in opposition sits
Grim Death my son and foe, who sets them on,
805 And me his parent would full soon devour
For want of other prey, but that he knows
His end with mine involved; and knows that I
Should prove a bitter morsel, and his bane,
When ever that shall be; so fate pronounced.
810 But thou, O Father, I forewarn thee, shun
His deadly arrow; neither vainly hope
To be invulnerable in those bright arms,
Though tempered heavenly, for that mortal dint,
Save he who reigns above, none can resist.
815   She finished, and the subtle fiend his lore

ii *799-802.* See ll. 650-66*n* and 653-9*n*. Here Sin's offspring are presented in
a new aspect, and appear to symbolize the pangs of guilt or fear.
ii *801. conscious terrors*] terrors of guilty knowledge.   *vex*] harass, irritate,
afflict, worry (in both its physical and its abstract senses).
ii *806-9.* See ll. 721-2*n*. Like all those of hell, Sin regards fate as the supreme
power; see i 116-17*n*.
ii *813. dint*] stroke given with a weapon; or thunder-clap (*OED* 1 b).
ii *815. lore*] lesson. See ix 695*n*.

Soon learned, now milder, and thus answered smooth.
Dear Daughter, since thou claim'st me for thy sire,
And my fair son here show'st me, the dear pledge
Of dalliance had with thee in heaven, and joys
820   Then sweet, now sad to mention, through dire change
Befallen us unforeseen, unthought of, know
I come no enemy, but to set free
From out this dark and dismal house of pain,
Both him and thee, and all the heavenly host
825   Of spirits that in our just pretences armed
Fell with us from on high: from them I go
This uncouth errand sole, and one for all
My self expose, with lonely steps to tread
The unfounded deep, and through the void immense
830   To search with wandering quest a place foretold
Should be, and, by concurring signs, ere now
Created vast and round, a place of bliss
In the purlieus of heaven, and therein placed
A race of upstart creatures, to supply
835   Perhaps our vacant room, though more removed,
Lest heaven surcharged with potent multitude
Might hap to move new broils: be this or aught
Than this more secret now designed, I haste
To know, and this once known, shall soon return,

ii *823. house*] Used of the place of the dead in *Job* xxx 23; cp. also Tasso, *Gerus. Lib.* ix 59, where hell is called 'the house of grief and pain' (tr. Fairfax).

ii *825. pretences*] pretensions, claims to dignity. There may be an Empsonian ambiguity, due to the modern sense, already equally well-established in M.'s time.

ii *827. uncouth*] strange, as in l. 407; here another obsolete meaning–'shocking', 'repellent'–adds a grim overtone.

ii *829. unfounded*] bottomless, uncreated.

ii *830–5.* On the implications of the prophecy, see ii 346–52*n*. Empson 57 suggests that *signs* ought perhaps to be taken very literally, since God certainly gives 'signs' at iv 997 and elsewhere.

ii *836. surcharged*] having an excess of inhabitants. Rajan draws attention to Satan's insinuation that God is a tyrant always having to be on guard against rebellion.

ii *839–44.* A promise later amply fulfilled, when Satan hands over his 'new kingdom' of earth to be administered by their 'joint power' (x 397–407). Empson 67 denies that Satan's promise to Sin and Death is evidence that he feels malice towards mankind at this stage: it is just a lie, 'the only way to make them let him pass'. But M. tells us that Beelzebub's counsel, which Empson admits to be malicious, was 'devised / By Satan' (ll. 379f). Satan's

840 And bring ye to the place where thou and Death
      Shall dwell at ease, and up and down unseen
      Wing silently the buxom air, embalmed
      With odours; there ye shall be fed and filled
      Immeasurably, all things shall be your prey.
845 He ceased, for both seemed highly pleased, and Death
      Grinned horrible a ghastly smile, to hear
      His famine should be filled, and blessed his maw
      Destined to that good hour: no less rejoiced
      His mother bad, and thus bespake her sire.
850   The key of this infernal pit by due,
      And by command of heaven's all-powerful king
      I keep, by him forbidden to unlock
      These adamantine gates; against all force
      Death ready stands to interpose his dart,
855 Fearless to be o'ermatched by living might.
      But what owe I to his commands above
      Who hates me, and hath hither thrust me down
      Into this gloom of Tartarus profound,
      To sit in hateful office here confined,
860 Inhabitant of heaven, and heavenly-born,
      Here in perpetual agony and pain,
      With terrors and with clamours compassed round
      Of mine own brood, that on my bowels feed:
      Thou art my father, thou my author, thou
865 My being gavest me; whom should I obey
      But thee, whom follow? Thou wilt bring me soon
      To that new world of light and bliss, among
      The gods who live at ease, where I shall reign
      At thy right hand voluptuous, as beseems
870 Thy daughter and thy darling, without end.

present promise is not so much a lie as an improvisation. He has just been reminded about Sin, and taught about Death; now for the first time he has an inkling of their possibilities.

ii *842. buxom*] unresisting (poet.).   *embalmed*] balmy, though the more usual meaning, 'rendered resistent to decay' is present as a sinister overtone – the whole earth is a body, fraily preserved against corruption.

ii *847. famine*] hunger.

ii *869–70*. Parodying the Nicene creed ('on the right hand of the Father . . . [Christ] whose kingdom shall have no end'). In Sin's fantasy she enjoys glory like Christ's (cp. iii 62–4); for, as Rajan (47, 50) and others have noticed, Satan, Sin and Death form a complete anti-Trinity. Even the doctrine of the procession of the Holy Ghost from the Father through the Son has its counterpart, in the begetting of Death by Satan on his own daughter. See also ll. 752–61*n*; and, on trinities of evil generally, Didron ii 21–2.

Thus saying, from her side the fatal key,
Sad instrument of all our woe, she took;
And towards the gate rolling her bestial train,
Forthwith the huge portcullis high updrew,
875   Which but her self, not all the Stygian powers
Could once have moved; then in the key-hole turns
The intricate wards, and every bolt and bar
Of massy iron or solid rock with ease
Unfastens: on a sudden open fly
880   With impetuous recoil and jarring sound
The infernal doors, and on their hinges grate
Harsh thunder, that the lowest bottom shook
Of Erebus. She opened, but to shut
Excelled her power; the gates wide open stood,
885   That with extended wings a bannered host

ii *872. instrument*] The word may stand in apposition to *she* as well as to *key*; for it could mean 'a person made use of by another, for the accomplishment of a purpose'. This possibility is important in view of Empson's theory that Satan is duping Sin (ll. 839–44*n*). Burden 25 holds that since Sin lets Satan out, she is responsible for his leaving hell, and, in the sense that she is *Satan's* disobedient sin, this must be so. But it seems simpler to take the passage as generalized allegory: by helping Satan, Sin is as usual providing the means by which man may enter the world of woe. As an image, the key is an anti-type of the key of eternal life that opens the gates of death in more conventional allegories. The fact that in *PL* it is Sin, not Christ, who opens the gates, may be yet another expression of the *felix culpa* theme. Sin's key is *fatal* because it leads not only to man's fall and death, but also to his redemption and eternal life (cp. ll. 807–9). In view of the earlier comparison with the Night-hag (l. 662), it may be of interest that the key was an attribute of Hecate.

ii *877. wards*] the incisions in a key's bit, corresponding to the wards projecting on the inside of the lock; not 'tumblers' (as Rajan).

ii *879–83*. Contrast the gates of heaven (vii 205–7), which open harmoniously, 'on golden hinges moving'. 'Both gates give access to chaos but the son makes his journey into the abyss to create, Satan in order to destroy' (Rajan[2] 100).

ii *881. grate*] great *Ed I* corr. in *Errata*. The opinion that 'the correction shows M.'s dislike of the pun inadvertently contributed by the printer' (Rajan[2] 100 following Adams 86) rests on the false assumption that the *Errata* list was authorial.

ii *883*. In *Prol i* (Yale i 223) M. cites Hesiod's line 'From Chaos sprang Erebus and black Night'. Erebus was often used to refer to hell itself–as in Virgil, *Georg.* iv 471, where the shades of the dead are 'startled from the lowest realms of Erebus' by the song of Orpheus.

Under spread ensigns marching might pass through
With horse and chariots ranked in loose array;
So wide they stood, and like a furnace mouth
Cast forth redounding smoke and ruddy flame.
890   Before their eyes in sudden view appear
The secrets of the hoary deep, a dark
Illimitable ocean without bound,
Without dimension, where length, breadth, and highth,
And time and place are lost; where eldest Night
895   And Chaos, ancestors of Nature, hold
Eternal anarchy, amidst the noise
Of endless wars, and by confusion stand.
For Hot, Cold, Moist, and Dry, four champions fierce
Strive here for mastery, and to battle bring
900   Their embryon atoms; they around the flag
Of each his faction, in their several clans,
Light-armed or heavy, sharp, smooth, swift or slow,

ii *889. redounding*] surging, issuing, overflowing.

ii *891. secrets*] 'secret places' or 'secret processes'. Suggesting also objects of
forbidden knowledge: Satan is now out of bounds.

ii *892.* On the accentuation *wìthout*, see B. A. Wright, 'Stressing of the pre-
position "without" in the verse of "Paradise Lost,"' *N & Q* cciii (1958)
202f; and cp. iv 256, iv 656, etc.

ii *894. Night*] The early edns omit italics here, by error; in general, alle-
gorical characters' names are treated as proper nouns.

ii *895–903.* In works such as Hesiod's *Theogony* and Boccaccio's *De genea-
logiis*, Chaos and Night were made *ancestors* of the more determinate
powers of nature. M.'s description of the strife between contrary qualities
that preceded the emergence of the cosmos is close to Ovid's account of the
primeval chaos where 'cold things strove with hot, moist with dry, soft
with hard, weightless with heavy' (*Met.* i 19f); though the development of
the military metaphor in *PL* is much more forceful. Backed by the authority
of Philo and the Church Fathers (e.g. St Augustine, *Conf.* XII xxix 40),
even the most orthodox Reformers managed to reconcile the Platonic and
Ovidian chaos with the doctrine of creation *e nihilo*: see, e.g., the preface
to Golding's transl. of the *Metamorphoses*; Du Bartas 8f; Spenser's creative
Garden of Adonis with its 'huge eternall Chaos' (*F.Q.* III vi 36); and the
same author's vision of Empedoclean Strife restrained by Concord (*F.Q.*
IV x 35). Sandys (² 19) thought Ovid's account of creation 'so consonant.
to the truth, as doubtlesse he had either seene the Books of Moses, or re-
ceaved that doctrine by tradition', but he balked a little at the seeming
'eternitie of his Chaos'. See Ellrodt 79 (citing St Augustine's *De Genesi*),
Svendsen 50 and Taylor 67f.

ii *899. mastery*] Spelt *Maistrie*, though this does not indicate a dissyllable
There is synaloepha with *and*.

Swarm populous, unnumbered as the sands
Of Barca or Cyrene's torrid soil,
905 Levied to side with warring winds, and poise
Their lighter wings. To whom these most adhere,
He rules a moment; Chaos umpire sits,
And by decision more embroils the fray
By which he reigns: next him high arbiter
910 Chance governs all. Into this wild abyss,
The womb of nature and perhaps her grave,
Of neither sea, nor shore, nor air, nor fire,
But all these in their pregnant causes mixed
Confusedly, and which thus must ever fight,
915 Unless the almighty maker them ordain
His dark materials to create more worlds,
Into this wild abyss the wary fiend
Stood on the brink of hell and looked a while,
Pondering his voyage; for no narrow frith
920 He had to cross. Nor was his ear less pealed

ii *904. Barca*] Well known from the mention in Virgil, *Aen.* iv 42; an ancient city of Cyrenaica, of which *Cyrene* was the capital.

ii *905–6*. The atoms are *levied*–both 'enlisted' and 'raised'–to balance, or provide ballast for, the wings of the winds. The physical raising of the army is a Latinizing pun, alluding to *levare*.

ii *906. To whom . . . adhere*] i.e., to whom most of these adhere; the one with a numerical majority.

ii *907–10*. See ll. 232–3n.

ii *911*. Cp. Spenser, *F.Q.* III vi 36, where chaos is 'the wide wombe of the world', and Lucretius, *De rerum nat.* v 259 *omniparens eadem rerum commune sepulcrum*. Lucretius refers to earth, not to the abyss; but the context, a demonstration of the material mortality of the world, is distilled into M.'s one echoing line.   *perhaps*] As usual, M. avoids committing himself to any particular cosmological theory.

ii *912–4*. Note that M.'s chaos is a confusion not of elements but of their component qualities. For the relation of this concept to the theories of the ancient atomists see Chambers 60.

ii *917–8. Stood . . . and looked*] 'standing looked', as often in *PL* (cp. v 368–9). But Bentley's stupid objection that *Into this wild abyss* cannot relate to *Stood* is a critical *felix culpa*, since it directs our attention to a fine passage of mimetic syntax. The lack of any continuation at all after the first 'Into this wild abyss' (l. 910), and the lack of the expected verb of motion after the second, render the repeated hesitations of the wary fiend: when we are fully prepared for him to leap or plunge, he stands.

ii *919. frith*] Metathetic form of 'firth'.

ii *920. pealed*] stormed, dinned.

With noises loud and ruinous (to compare
Great things with small) than when Bellona storms,
With all her battering engines bent to raze
Some capital city; or less than if this frame
925   Of heaven were falling, and these elements
In mutiny had from her axle torn
The steadfast earth. At last his sail-broad vans
He spreads for flight, and in the surging smoke
Uplifted spurns the ground, thence many a league
930   As in a cloudy chair ascending rides
Audacious, but that seat soon failing, meets
A vast vacuity: all unawares
Fluttering his pennons vain plumb down he drops
Ten thousand fathom deep, and to this hour
935   Down had been falling, had not by ill chance
The strong rebuff of some tumultuous cloud
Instinct with fire and nitre hurried him
As many miles aloft: that fury stayed,
Quenched in a boggy Syrtis, neither sea,

ii *921–2.* Here and at vi 310f, x 306, and *PR* iv 563f, M. uses a formula put in currency by Virgil (e.g. *Georg.* iv 176).   *ruinous*] falling, crashing. *Bellona*] the goddess of war, here a metonymy for war itself.

ii *924. Ed I* has comma after *city*.

ii *927. vans*] wings (poet.; lit. 'fans').   *sail-broad*] An enhancing suggestion recalling the persistent comparisons of Satan to a voyager; see ll. 410*n*, 636–41*n* above.

ii *933. pennons*] plumes, wings. In this sense a Latinism, translating *pennae*; first instance in *OED*.

ii *934. fathom*] Spelt 'fadom'.

ii *935.* Note that the temptation and Fall of man is made to depend not only on evil will, but on contingency. The threat to integrity comes *via* the realm of the chaotic and fortuitous. Although Rajan ridicules this idea, it seems to have been taken seriously by M., who frequently returns to it. See, e.g., iv 530, ix 85, 421, 423.

ii *936–8.* Thunder and lightning were commonly explained as effects of the ignition of vapours: according to one theory, of a mixture of hot sulphurous and cold nitrous vapours, as in gun-powder (cp. vi 512). See Svendsen 101, 269f, and E. H. Duncan in *PQ* xxx (1951) 442f.   *Instinct*] 'inflamed, impelled' (*OED* 2); not 'charged with' (a recent use only).

ii *939.* The Syrtes were two huge and proverbially dangerous shifting sandbanks off the North African shore. M. echoes Lucan's description: *Syrtes vel primam mundo natura figuram / Cum daret, in dubio pelagi terraeque reliquit* (*Pharsalia* ix 303f). In *Argonaut.* iv 1235ff Syrtis is elaborately described by Apollonius Rhodius as a misty featureless wasteland stretching to the dim horizon. There is a brief mention in *Acts* xxvii 17 (Greek and Vulgate).

940 Nor good dry land: nigh foundered on he fares,
    Treading the crude consistence, half on foot,
    Half flying; behoves him now both oar and sail.
    As when a gryphon through the wilderness
    With winged course o'er hill or moory dale,
945 Pursues the Arimaspian, who by stealth
    Had from his wakeful custody purloined
    The guarded gold: so eagerly the fiend
    O'er bog or steep, through straight, rough, dense, or
        rare,
    With head, hands, wings or feet pursues his way,
950 And swims or sinks, or wades, or creeps, or flies:
    At length a universal hubbub wild
    Of stunning sounds and voices all confused
    Borne through the hollow dark assaults his ear
    With loudest vehemence: thither he plies,
955 Undaunted to meet there what ever power
    Or spirit of the nethermost abyss
    Might in that noise reside, of whom to ask
    Which way the nearest coast of darkness lies

ii *941.* Spenser's dragon of evil is similarly described as 'halfe flying, and halfe footing in his hast' (*F.Q.* I xi 8).
ii *943–7.* The legend of 'gold-guarding griffins' in Scythia, from whom the one-eyed Arimaspi steal, was often retold out of Herodotus (iii 116) and Pliny (*Nat. hist.* vii 10). The griffin (a composite monster: half eagle, half lion) is appropriate here partly because it was subdued by the sun god Apollo (Valeriano 279), as Satan will be by Christ. The gold-guarding griffin is associated with Satan in an allegory of Raban Maur's (Migne cxi 342). The country of the griffin (the inhospitable Scythia) symbolizes, we are told, those who are without the warmth of the Holy Spirit, and who are Satan's subjects. The gold jealously guarded is the gold of Ophir, King David's gold, which was often allegorized as Wisdom or Righteousness (*sensus tropologicus*), or as Christ's sovereignty (*sensus allegoricus*). The gold of Ophir reappears later in the poem: see xi 396–407*n*.
ii *948–50.* Here 'verse-filling asyndeton' (see Curtius 285) imitates the hectic confusion of sense-data that a journey through chaos would occasion. The lines are also *versus rapportati*: cp. vii 502f and see Curtius 286f. For a further discussion of l. 948 see Introduction, 'Prosody', p. 22.
ii *948. straight*] The *Ed I* and *Ed II* spelling 'strait' could indicate either 'strait' or 'straight'; but only the latter will give the antithesis with *rough* that is required to match the one between *dense* and *rare*.
ii *953. borne*] the *Ed I* and *Ed II* spelling 'born', does not distinguish between 'borne' and 'born'; but the former word clearly gives the primary sense.
ii *954. vehemence*] force, intensity; perhaps also derivatively implying mindlessness (see viii 526*n*, ix Argument).

Bordering on light; when straight behold the throne
960   Of Chaos, and his dark pavilion spread
Wide on the wasteful deep; with him enthroned
Sat sable-vested Night, eldest of things,
The consort of his reign; and by them stood
Orcus and Ades, and the dreaded name
965   Of Demogorgon; Rumour next and Chance,
And Tumult and Confusion all embroiled,
And Discord with a thousand various mouths.
    To whom Satan turning boldly, thus. Ye powers
And spirits of this nethermost abyss,
970   Chaos and ancient Night, I come no spy,

ii *959–67*. In general, this court of personifications resembles Virgil's halls of Pluto (*Aen.* vi 268–81), though the only member common to both is Discord. Cp. Spenser's house of the Fates, 'Downe in the bottome of the deepe Abysse, / Where Demogorgon in dull darkenesse pent / . . . / The hideous Chaos keepes' (*F.Q.* IV ii 47). Like Spenser's, M.'s Demogorgon is from Boccaccio's *De genealogiis deorum*, where he comes first of all the dark gods. Among his brood are Night, Tartarus, Erebus, the serpent Python, Litigium (cf. M.'s Tumult and Discord) and Fama (M.'s Rumour). In *Prol i* (Yale i 222), M. supposes 'Demogorgon, the ancestor of all the gods . . . to be identical with the Chaos of the ancients'; see Fletcher ii 433–4.

ii *961. wasteful*] desolate, excessive, limitless. 'An epithet peculiarly suited to Chaos, at once an inferno of fruitlessly warring elements, and the source of all fertility, when God commands': MacCaffrey 105, where a persistent strand of imagery is shown to run through M.'s many uses of the word.

ii *962–7*. *Ed I* fails to italicize *Night*, *Rumour*, *Chance*, *Tumult*, *Confusion* and *Discord* as proper names.

ii *962. Night*] For the interesting view that M.'s Night is a personification of prime matter, see Chambers 75f. It may be because she is unformed dark and 'unapparent' that Night is not described.

ii *964–5. name / Of Demogorgon*] the divine nature of Demogorgon; alluding also to Statius' mention of 'the name whose knowing and whose speaking' the ghosts dread (*Theb.* iv 514) – identified by the scholiast as Demogorgon. *Orcus* and *Ades* are both names of the classical god of hell.

ii *965. Chance*] see 909f.

ii *966*. Broadbent 133 objects to *Confusion* being personified here, when the term has occurred as an ordinary substantive so recently (l. 897 above, cp. l. 966 below). And it is the same with *Tumult* (l. 1040). But this is to criticize not M.'s performance but a whole form of discourse: what the rhetoricians called 'mixed allegory'.

ii *967. a thousand various mouths*] Cp. Spenser, *F.Q.* IV i 27, where Ate, 'mother of debate', has a divided tongue. The presence of *Rumour* (l. 965), if not of *Tumult* (l. 966), shows that chaos gives rise to social and moral forms, as well as physical.

With purpose to explore or to disturb
The secrets of your realm, but by constraint
Wandering this darksome desert, as my way
Lies through your spacious empire up to light,
975 Alone, and without guide, half lost, I seek
What readiest path leads where your gloomy bounds
Confine with heaven; or if some other place
From your dominion won, the ethereal king
Possesses lately, thither to arrive
980 I travel this profound, direct my course;
Directed no mean recompense it brings
To your behoof, if I that region lost,
All usurpation thence expelled, reduce
To her original darkness and your sway
985 (Which is my present journey) and once more
Erect the standard there of ancient Night.
Yours be the advantage all, mine the revenge.
       Thus Satan; and him thus the anarch old
With faltering speech and visage incomposed
990 Answered. I know thee, stranger, who thou art,
That mighty leading angel, who of late
Made head against heaven's king, though overthrown.
I saw and heard, for such a numerous host

ii 972. secrets] See l. 891n: 'secret places or processes'.

ii 973. Ed II comma after way is clearly wrong.

ii 977. Confine with] border on.

ii 980. Editors generally insert a semicolon after profound; but M. may have wanted to keep the double syntax (with direct as verb or adjective) that the comma makes possible.

ii 983–5. Empson (67) is probably right in thinking that Satan here misleads Chaos and Night in order to get past them. Reduction of creation to its original darkness was only one of the alternative plans provisionally adopted at the infernal council; another was that the devils should take possession of it themselves (ii 364–6 and 397–402).

ii 988. anarch] Chaos, ruler or anti-ruler of the 'eternal anarchy' (l. 896); the word is perhaps M.'s coinage, on the analogy of 'mon-arch' from 'mon-archy', etc.

ii 989. incomposed] discomposed, disordered.

ii 990. Another contrast between Satan and Christ: these are the words addressed by a devil to Jesus in Luke iv 34.

ii 993–7. Confirmed in part by Raphael's account of the same events at vi 867–74. In his mention of bands / Pursuing, however, Chaos' account of the expulsion agrees with Satan's (see i 169–71n). One must expect Chaos to be confused. The sequence of the various reports of the expulsion, and the spatial locations of their delivery, are probably significant. In hell, Satan's

Fled not in silence through the frighted deep
995 With ruin upon ruin, rout on rout,
Confusion worse confounded; and heaven gates
Poured out by millions her victorious bands
Pursuing. I upon my frontiers here
Keep residence; if all I can will serve,
1000 That little which is left so to defend,
Encroached on still through our intestine broils
Weakening the sceptre of old Night: first hell
Your dungeon stretching far and wide beneath;
Now lately heaven and earth, another world
1005 Hung o'er my realm, linked in a golden chain
To that side heaven from whence your legions fell:
If that way be your walk, you have not far;
So much the nearer danger; go and speed;
Havoc and spoil and ruin are my gain.
1010   He ceased; and Satan stayed not to reply,
But glad that now his sea should find a shore,
With fresh alacrity and force renewed
Springs upward like a pyramid of fire

hold on the facts is inferior to Chaos'. The latter's report is merely chaotic;
Satan's is consistently perverted.
ii *1000. Ed I* omits comma after *defend.*   *so*] in this way; by keeping resi-
dence.
ii *1001. our*] Pearce's conjecture 'your' is probably right. The intestine
broils of the angels weakened Night's sceptre, because indirectly they led
to the 'encroachment' of creation. See Adams 98f.
ii *1002. Ed I* fails to italicize *Night.*
ii *1004. heaven*] the sky of earth.
ii *1005. golden chain*] See l. 1051*n.*
ii *1006. heaven*] the empyrean.
ii *1007. walk*] 'As a believer in the providence of God, Milton could not
possibly have believed in the huge success-story of Satan fighting his way to
Paradise'; thus Chaos 'jeers at the heroic piece of space-travel' (Empson
118). It is true that Satan later greatly exaggerates the difficulties of his
journey (x 477–9*n*), but the present passage hardly prepares us for that.
Far from jeering, Chaos is most respectful (see esp. 991f). *walk* may rather be
chosen for its religious overtones ('manner of behaviour', 'course of con-
duct'; cp. *Ps.* lxxxvi 11), and in any case need not imply a very easy journey.
M. explicitly states that Satan moved with difficulty, at l. 1021f.   *not
far*] the proximity of the world to chaos amplifies the fragility and delicacy
of its created order.
ii *1013. pyramid*] Often denoted an elongated spire-like or pillar-like form:
see the many examples of this use gathered in L. Hotson, *Mr W. H.* (1964)

Into the wild expanse, and through the shock
1015   Of fighting elements, on all sides round
Environed wins his way; harder beset
And more endangered, than when Argo passed
Through Bosporus, betwixt the jostling rocks:
Or when Ulysses on the larboard shunned
1020   Charybdis, and by the other whirlpool steered.
So he with difficulty and labour hard
Moved on, with difficulty and labour he;
But he once past, soon after when man fell,
Strange alteration! Sin and Death amain
1025   Following his track, such was the will of heaven
Paved after him a broad and beaten way
Over the dark abyss, whose boiling gulf
Tamely endured a bridge of wondrous length
From hell continued reaching the utmost orb
1030   Of this frail world; by which the spirits perverse
With easy intercourse pass to and fro
To tempt or punish mortals, except whom
God and good angels guard by special grace.

86. Anciently derived from πῦρ ('fire'), the root meaning was taken to be 'flame-shape', so that M.'s use of the word here constitutes a half-pun. For the symbolic meaning of the pyramid in *PL*, see v 758–9*n*.

ii *1017–8*. When Jason and the Argonauts sailed through the *Bosporus* (Straits of Constantinople) *en route* to Colchis, their boat, the *Argo*, narrowly escaped destruction between the Symplegades – the clashing or *jostling rocks*. See Apollonius Rhodius, *Argonaut*. ii 317, 552–611.   *jostling*] M.'s spelling 'justling' represents a common variant pronunciation. The comparison is said to be apt because 'The *Argo* in Greek mythology was the first ocean going ship and Satan the first to cross chaos of his own will' (Rajan[2] 108). But this is perhaps to underestimate the aptness. The Argonauts were not the first to pass through the rocks: they were preceded by a dove, just as Satan had been preceded by Messiah and by the creative spirit of God, who 'Dove-like sat'st brooding on the vast abyss'.

ii *1019–20*. Homer tells how Odysseus followed Circe's advice in avoiding *Charybdis* and sailing close by Scylla (*the other whirlpool*), in his passage through the Straits of Messina between Sicily and Italy (*Od.* xii). Sailing before a south wind, he would have Charybdis on his *larboard* (port) side – not his starboard, as Bentley had it (Pearce weakly agreeing).

ii *1024–30*. Death's construction of the bridge is described at x 293–305.

ii *1024*. *amain*] without delay.

ii *1033*. See *De doctrina* i 9 (Columbia xv 101), where M. states that the ministry of angels 'relates especially to believers'; citing *Heb.* i 14, *Ps.* xxxiv 7, etc.

                    But now at last the sacred influence
1035   Of light appears, and from the walls of heaven
                    Shoots far into the bosom of dim Night
                    A glimmering dawn; here nature first begins
                    Her farthest verge, and Chaos to retire
                    As from her outmost works a broken foe
1040   With tumult less and with less hostile din,
                    That Satan with less toil, and now with ease
                    Wafts on the calmer wave by dubious light
                    And like a weather-beaten vessel holds
                    Gladly the port, though shrouds and tackle torn;
1045   Or in the emptier waste, resembling air,
                    Weighs his spread wings, at leisure to behold
                    Far off the empyreal heaven, extended wide
                    In circuit, undetermined square or round,
                    With opal towers and battlements adorned
1050   Of living sapphire, once his native seat;
                    And fast by hanging in a golden chain

ii *1034*] *the sacred influence* / *Of light*] Cp. ix 107*n*.

ii *1037*. *nature*] the agency of creation, who begins her work with light (cp. iii 1ff).

ii *1038*. *farthest*] spelt 'fardest'.

ii *1039*. *broken*] broked *Ed II*, almost certainly an error.

ii *1042*. *dubious light*] Echoes a phrase in Seneca's account of the passage of Hercules out of hell (*Hercules furens* 668).

ii *1043*. *holds*] remains in (*OED* I 7 d, citing Gavin Douglas, 'haldand the deip see'); perhaps secondarily 'reaches' (a Latinism, cp. *tenere*, to hold, reach).

ii *1048*. So wide that it was impossible to tell whether the boundary was rectilinear or curved. See also x 381*n*.

ii *1049–50*. In *Rev.* xxi 19 one of the foundations of the wall of the heavenly city is said to be of sapphire.   *living*] native, unshaped; the city, like Jehovah's altar, is built not 'of hewn stone: for if thou lift up thy tool upon it, thou hast polluted it' (*Exod.* xx 25; see Tuve 183).

ii *1051*. Homer's Zeus asserts his transcendence by claiming that if a golden chain were lowered from Heaven, he could draw up by it all the other gods, together with the earth and the sea, and hang them from a pinnacle of Olympus (*Il.* viii 18–27). In *Prol ii* (Yale i 236) M. interprets this chain as 'the universal concord and sweet union of all things which Pythagoras poetically figures as harmony'; thus accepting a philosophical and literary tradition that runs from Plato (*Theaetetus* 153D), through Boethius (*De consolat.* iv prose 6 and metre 6: 'the bond of love'), Chaucer (*Knight's Tale* I (A) 2987–93: 'the faire cheyne of love') and Spenser (*F.Q.* II vii 46). The philosophical history of the idea is treated at length in Lovejoy 63 *et passim*, Emil Wolff, *Die goldene Kette* (Hamburg 1947) and in Ludwig Edelstein, 'The

This pendent world, in bigness as a star
Of smallest magnitude close by the moon.
Thither full fraught with mischievous revenge,
1055 Accursed, and in a cursed hour he hies.

THE END OF THE SECOND BOOK

Paradise Lost

BOOK III

The Argument

God sitting on his throne sees Satan flying towards this world, then newly created; shows him to the Son who sat at his right hand; foretells the success of Satan in perverting mankind; clears his own justice and wisdom from all imputation, having created man free and able enough to have withstood his tempter; yet declares his purpose of grace towards him, in regard he fell not of his own malice, as did Satan, but by him seduced. The Son of God renders praise to his Father for the manifestation of his gracious purpose towards man; but God again declares, that grace cannot be extended toward man without the satisfaction of divine justice; man hath offended the majesty of God by aspiring to Godhead, and therefore with all his progeny devoted to death must die, unless some one can be found sufficient to answer for his offence, and undergo his punishment. The Son of God freely offers himself a ransom for man: the Father accepts him, ordains his incarnation, pro-

Golden Chain of Homer', *Studies in Intellectual History* (Baltimore, Md. 1953) pp. 48–67. Coming as it does immediately after the poem's principal treatment of chaos, the chain of Concord (or, as it was sometimes interpreted, the chain of Necessity) has the effect of binding and ordering. It is a necessary image, as it were, before we can pass to the worlds of order that follow. According to the cabbalists and alchemical philosophers the chain was a symbol (like Jacob's ladder) of the *scala naturae*; see iii 516–17n, v 469–90n, 483n.

ii *1052-3. This pendent world*] the whole created universe, which compared with heaven seems tiny. Our own world will not be visible until Satan has penetrated the 'firm opacous globe' of iii 418. 'Pendant' may mean 'in the balance, undecided' as well as 'hanging'. The simile echoes Dante, *Par.* xxviii 19–21.

ii *1054. fraught with*] destined to produce; but continuing also the mercantile or maritime images of ll. 636–42, 1043–4, etc.

nounces his exaltation above all names in heaven and earth; commands
all the angels to adore him; they obey, and hymning to their harps in full
choir, celebrate the Father and the Son. Mean while Satan alights upon the
bare convex of this world's outermost orb; where wandering he first finds
a place since called the Limbo of Vanity; what persons and things fly up
thither; thence comes to the gate of heaven, described ascending by stairs,
and the waters above the firmament that flow about it: his passage thence
to the orb of the sun; he finds there Uriel the regent of that orb, but first
changes himself into the shape of a meaner angel; and pretending a zealous
desire to behold the new creation and man whom God had placed here,
inquires of him the place of his habitation, and is directed; alights first on
Mount Niphates.

> Hail, holy Light, offspring of heaven first-born,
> Or of the eternal co-eternal beam
> May I express thee unblamed? since God is light,

iii *1–55.* A fresh exordium, as the *mise en scène* changes from hell and chaos
to heaven (ll. 13–21; see vii 1–39*n*), and a ceremonial approach to the divine
presence is required. With the new invocation, cp. that in Bk i, to the
heavenly Muse and the Spirit, and that in Bk vii, to Urania; this is the most
personal, yet also the richest in theological, philosophical, and artistic impli-
cations, which keep the autobiographical element firmly in proportion.
There has been an extended controversy about the nature of the Light ad-
dressed in the invocation. The positions include (*a*) Sewell's, that the Light
is the Son of God, like the 'living Light' of Dante, *Par.* xiii 55; (*b*) that M.
'was speaking of light in the physical sense', as ll. 21–4 indicate (Kelley 92–
4); and (*c*) that the Light is both physical and divine: that M. followed the
Platonic system, in which Light is not only the principal image of God, but
also the divine emanation itself (cp. M.'s *effluence*), which breaks into separ-
ate beams to produce the various splendours of created things (Williams
54 and Allen 101). It is obvious from l. 2 and ll. 51–5 that more than a
merely physical light (in the modern sense) is involved. And it is difficult to
imagine that M. could have been uninfluenced by a central Christian
tradition that extended from medieval versions of pseudo-Dionysius'
mysticism of light (on which see Otto von Simson, *The Gothic Cathedral*
(New York 1956) pp. 50–5), through Renaissance Neoplatonic develop-
ments (see, e.g., Ficino's *De sole* and *De lumine*, and his commentary on
Dionysius' *De divinis nominibus*), to the philosophy of the Cambridge
Platonists. But it would appear that, in his tentative address to 'that immortall
light' which 'from th' eternall Truth . . . doth proceed' (Spenser, *An Hymne
of Heavenly Beautie* 169–75), M. has deliberately eschewed, as far as he can,
any presumptuous commitment to particular human systems of truth.
On the placement of the four invocations of *PL*, see ix 1–47*n*; also Intro-
duction, 'Numerology' (p. 24f).

iii *1–12.* The whole opening passage should be compared with Drummond
of Hawthornden's 'An Hymn of the Fairest Fair', esp. ll. 125–30 and 137–
42: 'O most holy One! / Unprocreate Father, ever-procreate Son, / Ghost

And never but in unapproached light
5   Dwelt from eternity, dwelt then in thee,
     Bright effluence of bright essence increate.

breath'd from both, you were, are, aye shall be, / Most blessed, three in one, and one in three, / Incomprehensible by reachless height, / And unperceived by excessive light. . . . so the spring, / The well-head, and the stream which they forth bring, / Are but one selfsame essence, nor in aught / Do differ, save in order, and our thought / No chime of time discerns in them to fall, / But three distinctly bide one essence all.'

iii *1–8.* M. proposes three images or forms of address, *offspring, beam,* and *stream,* each of which associates the divine Light or Wisdom with a different aspect of deity. The passage as a whole recalls the address of the Wisdom of God by 3 x 7 names in *Wisdom* vii (Charles i 547). Cp. also the opening of Tasso's *Le sette giornate del mondo creato*: 'Father of heaven, and you of the Father eternal / Eternal Son, and uncreated offspring, / Of mind unchangeable the only child: / Image divine, to your divine example / Equal; and pure light of ardent light: / And you who breathe from both, and from both shine, / Or of doubled light the Spirit kindled / Who are pure holy light, from holy flame, / Like lucid stream within a fountain clear / And true image still of image true'.

iii *1.* Either 'Light the Son of God', or, as Kelley and others interpret the line, 'Light the first creation' (cp. vii 243–4, 'Light . . . first of things'). In the New Testament Christ is several times referred to as the firstborn; see, e.g., *Col.* i 15 and 18. *Ed I* fails to give *Light* an initial capital.

iii *2.* 'Or, Light the beam of the eternal, equally eternal with him.' Sewell regards 1f as a hesitation between Arian and Trinitarian formulations–between the view that the Son, the Word or Light of God, is begotten in time, and the view that he is co-eternal with the Father. But M.'s line of thought may be quite different, and more speculative; see Broadbent 141 on Fludd's question whether 'light is increate or created by an increate light'.

iii *3.* Presumably the blame could attach only to using the second name, *co-eternal beam;* it is this name which is justified by the implicit appeal to Scriptural authority that follows (3–6).   *express*] represent symbolically, image.   *God is Light*] From 1 *John* i 5.

iii *4–5.* God 'only hath immortality, dwelling in the light which no man can approach unto' (1 *Tim.* vi 16). See vii 243–9nn for M.'s distinction between visible and invisible light.

iii *6. effluence*] effulgence, radiance; cp. *Wisdom* vii 25f, where the divine Sapience is said to be 'a clear effluence of the glory of the Almighty; / Therefore can nothing defiled find entrance into her. / For she is an effulgence from everlasting light' (Charles i 547).   *essence increate*] the uncreated divine essence. In the physics and metaphysics of M.'s time, light was regarded as an 'accident' (quality), not a body or substance; see Fletcher ii 191.

Or hear'st thou rather pure ethereal stream,
Whose fountain who shall tell? Before the sun,
Before the heavens thou wert, and at the voice
10   Of God, as with a mantle didst invest
The rising world of waters dark and deep,
Won from the void and formless infinite.
Thee I revisit now with bolder wing,
Escaped the Stygian pool, though long detained
15   In that obscure sojourn, while in my flight
Through utter and through middle darkness borne
With other notes than to the Orphean lyre
I sung of Chaos and eternal Night,
Taught by the heavenly Muse to venture down
20   The dark descent, and up to reascend,
Though hard and rare: thee I revisit safe,
And feel thy sovereign vital lamp; but thou
Revisit'st not these eyes, that roll in vain

iii *7. hear'st thou rather*] do you prefer to be called; a Latinism: first instance
in *OED*.

iii *8*. 'Where is the way where light dwelleth?' *Job* xxxviii 19; cp. Dante's
vision of a river of light, which symbolizes grace poured forth upon creation
(*Par.* xxx 61–73).

iii *9–12*. Cp. vii 233–52, and *Gen.* i 1–5.   *invest*] cover, wrap. In *Ps.* civ
2 God covers himself 'with light as with a garment'.   *void*] not of matter
(see vii 233); M. refers to chaos.

iii *13–16*. The *Stygian pool* and the *utter* (outer) darkness is hell, the *middle
darkness* chaos. The structural connections between the present ascent and the
corresponding descent in vii 12–16, 21–5, are discussed in MacCaffrey 58.
Cp. Dante's prayer in *Par.* xxxii 22–4, where he speaks of having ascended
from the 'deepest pool of the universe'.

iii *17–21*. Alluding to the 'generally-sung fable of Orpheus, whom they
faigne to have recovered his Euridice from Hell with his Musick, that is,
Truth and Equity from darkenesse of Barbarisme and Ignorance with his
profound and excellent Doctrines; but, that in the thicke caliginous way to
the upper-earth, she was lost againe' (Henry Reynolds, *Mythomystes*, in
Critical Essays of the Seventeenth Century, ed. J. E. Spingarn (Oxford, 1908)
i 158–9). The allusion is especially apt in view of the common ground be-
tween the Orphic cosmogony and the account of the court of Chaos at
the end of the last book.

iii *17. other notes*] Because M., unlike Orpheus, claims not to have lost his
Eurydice.

iii *19. the heavenly Muse*] Urania; see vii 1.

iii *20–1*. On the Virgilian echo, see ii 432–3*n*.

iii *23*. Certainly now referring to physical light. But there is no change of
address: the celestial light of Truth or Wisdom was thought of as purer and

To find thy piercing ray, and find no dawn;
25 So thick a drop serene hath quenched their orbs,
Or dim suffusion veiled. Yet not the more
Cease I to wander where the Muses haunt
Clear spring, or shady grove, or sunny hill,
Smit with the love of sacred song; but chief
30 Thee Sion and the flowery brooks beneath
That wash thy hallowed feet, and warbling flow,
Nightly I visit: nor sometimes forget
Those other two equalled with me in fate,
So were I equalled with them in renown,
35 Blind Thamyris, and blind Maeonides,
And Tiresias and Phineus prophets old.

brighter, but not categorically different from physical light. See Spenser, *An Hymne of Heavenly Beautie* 169–71, where the 'immortall light' of Truth 'is many thousand times more bright, more cleare, / More excellent, more glorious, more divine' than that of the sun.   *roll*] spelt *rowle*.

iii *25. drop serene*] Literally translating *gutta serena*, the medical term for the form of blindness from which M. suffered.

iii *26. suffusion*] cataract (medical term); *dim suffusion* perhaps translates *suffusio nigra*.

iii *29.* An allusion to Virgil's prayer that 'smitten with a great love' of the Muses (*ingenti percussus amore*), he may be shown by them the secrets of nature (*Georg.* ii 475–89).

iii *30.* Among all the 'places' of *sacred song* M. chiefly visits Sion: i.e., he loves Hebrew poetry best. See i 10–11*n*, and cp. *PR* iv 347: 'Sion's songs, to all true tastes excelling'.

iii *32.* M. was often inspired to compose during the night; see vii *29n*. *nor . . . forget*] often remember.

iii *34. So were I equalled*] would that I were similarly equalled.

iii *35–6. Thamyris*] A Thracian poet mentioned in Homer, *Il.* ii 594–600, who fell in love with the Muses and challenged them to a contest in which the loser was to give the winner whatever he wanted. The Muses having won took Thamyris' eyes and his lyre (sometimes, his ability to sing), so that it became proverbial to say of those who attempted what was beyond their talents, '*Thamyras insanit*' (*Dictionarium historicum ac poeticum* (Lyons 1579)). No prophetic compositions of Thamyris' survived, so that M. may mean that he pondered on the myth of his fate as a blinded bard. (Or perhaps M. feels a reasonable trepidation in case the portrayal of heaven may be beyond *his* talents?)   *Maeonides*] Homer's surname; 'blind Homer' would have been infelicitous, for Calepinus and others derived that name from a Greek word for eyes. The contrast between his outward blindness and inner vision was a commonplace. Pico–who like other Renaissance philosophers sought a mystical connection between blindness and initiation–cites both Homer and Tiresias as examples: 'many who were rap-

> Then feed on thoughts, that voluntary move
> Harmonious numbers; as the wakeful bird
> Sings darkling, and in shadiest covert hid
> 40   Tunes her nocturnal note. Thus with the year
> Seasons return, but not to me returns
> Day, or the sweet approach of even or morn,
> Or sight of vernal bloom, or summer's rose,
> Or flocks, or herds, or human face divine;
> 45   But cloud in stead, and ever-during dark
> Surrounds me, from the cheerful ways of men
> Cut off, and for the book of knowledge fair
> Presented with a universal blank
> Of nature's works to me expunged and razed,
> 50   And wisdom at one entrance quite shut out.

tured to the vision of spiritual beauty, were by the same cause blinded in their corporal eyes'; see Wind 61. In his Latin poem *De Idea Platonica* (p. 67), M. refers to *Tiresias* as 'the Dircaean augur, whose very blindness gave him boundless light' (*profundum lumen*). The Thracian king *Phineus* lost his sight, according to one account, because he had become too good a prophet and was publishing the counsels of the gods (Hyginus, *Fab.* xix). In the *Second Defence* M. quotes Apollonius Rhodius to similar effect, but only to refute this explanation. 'Recompensed with far more excelling gifts', Phineus' loss of sight (like M.'s own, it is implied) 'is not to be considered as the punishment for any crime' (Columbia viii 63ff).

iii *37–8*. The double syntax is noticed in Davie[2] 73. *move* seems intransitive until *Harmonious numbers* reveals it as transitive: 'This flicker of hesitation about whether the thoughts move only themselves, or something else, makes us see that the numbers aren't really "something else" but are the very thoughts themselves, seen under a new aspect.'

iii *38. numbers*] rhythmic measure.   *wakeful bird*] the nightingale. Is it coincidence that the soul of Thamyris passed into a nightingale (Plato, *Rep.* 620 A)?

iii *39. darkling*] in the dark; not yet a specially poetic word.

iii *47. the book of knowledge*] The Book of Nature; cp. viii 67, 'the book of God'. For the history of the commonplace, see Curtius 319–26; among many other examples he cites this from Quarles: 'The world's a book in folio, printed all / With God's great works in letters capital: / Each creature is a page; and each effect / A fair character, void of all defect.' The mention is appropriate here, in the invocation that begins the part of the poem in which the Book or Mirror of Nature itself will appear. See Introduction, 'Numerology'.

iii *48. blank*] spelt 'blanc' (but M. did not distinguish orthographically different senses of 'blank', as Grierson argued). The primary sense is 'blank page' (cp. *OED* 5–7), carrying on the metaphor of the previous line. But 'void' may be a secondary meaning (*OED* 6 b).

So much the rather thou celestial Light
Shine inward, and the mind through all her powers
Irradiate, there plant eyes, all mist from thence
Purge and disperse, that I may see and tell
55   Of things invisible to mortal sight.
     Now had the almighty Father from above,
From the pure empyrean where he sits
High throned above all highth, bent down his eye,
His own works and their works at once to view:
60   About him all the sanctities of heaven
Stood thick as stars, and from his sight received
Beatitude past utterance; on his right
The radiant image of his glory sat,
His only Son; on earth he first beheld
65   Our two first parents, yet the only two
Of mankind, in the happy garden placed,
Reaping immortal fruits of joy and love,
Uninterrupted joy, unrivalled love
In blissful solitude; he then surveyed

iii 51–5. On external blindness as an opportunity for inner illumination,
see 35–6n and esp. Wind 61.   *all mist . . . purge*] Cp. Beelzebub's hope
that the devils may somewhere 'purge off this gloom' at heaven's 'orient
beam' (ii 399f). See also M.'s similar prayer at i 22–6.

iii 59. Beginning the first of the poem's comprehensive panoramic views of
creation. This one has its obvious counterpart later in the book, in Satan's
'sudden view / Of all this world at once' (ll. 542f) – the view of one planning
not man's salvation but his destruction. More distantly, there is a resonance
with vi 673, where we learn that God eternally sits 'consulting on the sum
of things'.   *their works*] The works performed by creatures who are
themselves the works of God.

iii 60. *sanctities*] gods; by a metonymy they are represented by one of their
qualities, holiness.

iii 61–2. On the supreme happiness of the beatific vision of the faithful in
heaven, see i 684n and *De doctrina* i 33 (Columbia xvi 375): 'perfect
happiness, arising chiefly from the divine vision'.

iii 63. In *De doctrina* i 5 (Columbia xiv 193), M. admires the 'sublimity and
copiousness' with which 'the generation of the divine nature is described'
in *Heb.* i 2f: 'His Son . . . Who being the brightness of his glory, and the
express image of his person . . . when he had by himself purged our sins,
sat down on the right hand of the Majesty on high.'

iii 69–73. On the change in perspective, whereby Satan is now reduced in
scale to a 'small night-bird', see MacCaffrey 60.   *on this side night*]
'Translates what is for us a temporal unit into a physical area, as it would
look if we could escape the limits of earthly knowledge' (*ibid.*; but see iv
555n).   *sublime*] aloft.   *stoop*] 'descend from aloft' (esp. of bird of

70   Hell and the gulf between, and Satan there
      Coasting the wall of heaven on this side night
      In the dun air sublime, and ready now
      To stoop with wearied wings, and willing feet,
      On the bare outside of this world, that seemed
75   Firm land imbosomed without firmament,
      Uncertain which, in ocean or in air.
      Him God beholding from his prospect high,
      Wherein past, present, future he beholds,
      Thus to his only Son foreseeing spake.
80   Only begotten Son, seest thou what rage
      Transports our adversary, whom no bounds
      Prescribed, no bars of hell, nor all the chains
      Heaped on him there, nor yet the main abyss
      Wide interrupt can hold; so bent he seems
85   On desperate revenge, that shall redound
      Upon his own rebellious head. And now
      Through all restraint broke loose he wings his way
      Not far off heaven, in the precincts of light,
      Directly towards the new created world,
90   And man there placed, with purpose to assay

prey); perhaps also suggesting the human posture of weariness, as well
as metaphorical stooping or degradation. The close juxtaposition of this
bird image with that of ll. 38-40 is provocative.   dun air] perhaps imitates
the common Italian description of murkiness as *aer bruno*.

iii 74. *world*] universe, not earth; see ii 1052-3n.

iii 75. *firmament*] The firmament or atmosphere (see vii 261-7), being inside
the shell of the universe that Satan stands on, is invisible to him.

iii 76. 'It being difficult to see whether the surrounding matrix was liquid
or gaseous.' In chaos the usual categories are confused; cp. ii 939f.

iii 77. On the spatial quality of God's simultaneous vision, see MacCaffrey
53f.   *prospect*] look-out point (*OED* I 1 b).

iii 80-6. 'The only consistent view after the firm statement [at i 209f, where
Satan's release is permitted by God; cp. also the more recent statement to
the same effect, at ii 1025] is that this is the first of God's grisly jokes' (Emp-
son 119). Grisly or not, the passage is certainly sardonic—a tone set by the
opening pun on *Transports*. On the syntax Ricks 60 comments: 'The
crucial verb *can hold* flies triumphantly free, at the very end of its clause,
from the grip of the previous twenty-two words of heaped chains.'

iii 83-4. Cp. ii 405-9. *interrupt*] breached; not a Latinism.   *wide*] Formerly
as often adverbial as adjectival.

iii 88. *precincts*] Often applied to the ground immediately surrounding a
place of worship.

iii 90. *assay*] test, try. Notice that the phrase *with . . . assay* can relate not only
to *wings* (with Satan as subject) but also to *placed* (with God as subject).

> If him by force he can destroy, or worse,
> By some false guile pervert; and shall pervert
> For man will hearken to his glozing lies,
> And easily transgress the sole command,
> 95 Sole pledge of his obedience: so will fall,
> He and his faithless progeny: whose fault?
> Whose but his own? Ingrate, he had of me
> All he could have; I made him just and right,
> Sufficient to have stood, though free to fall.
> 100 Such I created all the ethereal powers
> And spirits, both them who stood and them who failed;
> Freely they stood who stood, and fell who fell.
> Not free, what proof could they have given sincere
> Of true allegiance, constant faith or love,
> 105 Where only what they needs must do, appeared,
> Not what they would? What praise could they receive?

The ambiguity expresses the character of providence: viewed in one way the purposefulness is all Satan's, in another, all God's.

iii *94–5. the sole command*] i.e. not to taste the fruit of the forbidden tree. *sole pledge*] Cp. iv 428 ('the sign of our obedience'), v 551, and viii 329; also *De doctrina* i 10 (Columbia xv 115): 'The tree of knowledge of good and evil was not a sacrament, as it is generally called; for a sacrament is a thing to be used, not abstained from: but a pledge, as it were, and memorial of obedience.' The emphasis accords with that of the main Christian tradition, as St Augustine, e.g., expresses it: the Fall was a lapse from 'obedience, the mother and guardian of all the other virtues'; the command being a single one was 'easy to observe; and so short to remember' (*Civ. Dei* xiv 12). See Lewis 67f. Burden 126 notes that the fruit is never mentioned in iii; since *sub specie aeternitatis* it is seen to exist solely as a test of obedience.

iii *96.* The epithet *faithless* is transferred from *He* to *progeny*, just as Adam's guilt and its consequences pass on to his descendants. They are involved with him in the original sin of breaking faith with God, because 'he either stood or fell for the whole human race' (*De doctrina* i 11: Columbia xv 183); cf. 209 below.

iii *98–9. Sufficient*] Referring to the doctrine of Sufficient Grace, then common ground for almost all Christians; see Corcoran 104f.

iii *100–2.* Satan later (iv 63–72) admits what is stated here and at v 525–43: that the angels, like Adam and Eve, had the power to 'persevere', to remain faithful. The equilibrium, then, was such that the fall of the rebel angels depended solely on their own free will.

iii *103–6.* See *De doctrina* i 4 (Columbia xiv 141): if free will 'be not admitted, whatever worship or love we render to God is entirely vain and of no value; the acceptableness of duties done under a law of necessity . . . is annihilated altogether, inasmuch as freedom can no longer be attributed to that will over which some fixed decree is inevitably suspended'.

What pleasure I from such obedience paid,
When will and reason (reason also is choice)
Useless and vain, of freedom both despoiled,

110 Made passive both, had served necessity,
Not me. They therefore as to right belonged,
So were created, nor can justly accuse
Their maker, or their making, or their fate,
As if predestination overruled

115 Their will, disposed by absolute decree
Or high foreknowledge; they themselves decreed
Their own revolt, not I: if I foreknew,
Foreknowledge had no influence on their fault,
Which had no less proved certain unforeknown.

120 So without least impulse or shadow of fate,
Or aught by me immutably foreseen,
They trespass, authors to themselves in all
Both what they judge and what they choose; for so
I formed them free, and free they must remain,

125 Till they enthrall themselves: I else must change

iii *108.* M. probably alludes here to Aristotle's analysis of choice in *Nic. Ethics* 1112^a (though see also *Commonplace Book* (Yale i 363)); as he does in *Areopagitica* (Yale ii 527): those are foolish who 'complain of divin Providence for suffering Adam to transgresse, foolish tongues! when God gave him reason, he gave him freedom to choose, for reason is but choosing; he had bin else a meer artificiall Adam.'

iii *110.* God disassociates himself from Necessity or Fate, which has become the devils' idea of the supreme power.

iii *113–23.* De doctrina i 4 shows that M. believed in a liberal version of the doctrine of Predestination, but that he carefully defined predestination and foreknowledge in such a way as to exclude 'necessity' or determinism. See, e.g., Columbia xiv 85: 'Future events which God has foreseen, will happen certainly . . . because the divine prescience cannot be deceived, but they will not happen necessarily, because prescience can have no influence on the object foreknown, inasmuch as it is only an intransitive action.'

iii *120.* As the use of the logical term *impulse* signalizes, M. is here explicitly allowing God to exonerate himself from responsibility for the 'more proximate' efficient causes of the Fall (Howard 158).

iii *125–8.* The predicament of God is similarly appreciated in *De doctrina* i 3 (Columbia xiv 77): 'God is not mutable, so long as he decrees nothing absolutely which could happen otherwise through the liberty assigned to man; he would indeed be mutable, neither would his counsel stand, if he were to obstruct by another decree that liberty which he had already decreed, or were to darken it with the least shadow of necessity.'

iii *125.* Apparently now referring once again to Adam and Eve, though there has been no signposting of the abandonment of 'ethereal powers' (l. 100)

Their nature, and revoke the high decree
Unchangeable, eternal, which ordained
Their freedom, they themselves ordained their fall.
The first sort by their own suggestion fell,
130   Self-tempted, self-depraved: man falls deceived
By the other first: man therefore shall find grace,
The other none: in mercy and justice both,
Through heaven and earth, so shall my glory excel,
But mercy first and last shall brightest shine.
135   Thus while God spake, ambrosial fragrance filled
All heaven, and in the blessed spirits elect
Sense of new joy ineffable diffused:
Beyond compare the Son of God was seen

as a subject. This grammatical fluidity allows the Fall (undetermined whe-
ther angelic or human) to be now future (l. 125), now present (ll. 122f and
130), now past (ll. 116, 118f, and 128); thus rendering God's single 'pros-
pect high, / Wherein past, present, future he beholds'.

iii *129. suggestion*] temptation.   *sort*] species. Some have found here a
contradiction of v 694–6 and 703–10, where Raphael implies that the rebel
angels were tempted into their Fall by Satan. But here M. simply means that
the angelic species fell by intramural temptation, from within their own
kind; whereas the human species will fall by temptation from without,
from the *other* (sort, species). The theory that a deliberate disparity is in-
tended between the two accounts of the angels' Fall leans heavily on the
existence of separate theological traditions on this point in the seventeenth
century (see E. F. Daniels, 'Milton's fallen angels–self corrupted or se-
duced?', *N & Q* ccv (1960) 447–50). Even if the theory were right, we need
not infer that God is being portrayed as harsh. *De doctrina* i 9 shows that M.
held God's more disparaging account to be true, and Raphael would natu-
rally be partial in judging his own kind.

iii *135. ambrosial*] See ii 245n.

iii *136. spirits elect*] the 'elect angels' of *1 Tim.* v 21–explained in *De doc-
trina* i 9 as angels 'who have not revolted'; for M. rejected the view that
'the good angels are now upheld, not so much by their own strength, as by
the grace of God', and that because of their own election they have a 'de-
lighted interest . . . in the mystery of man's salvation'. Instead he thought
that 'the good angels are upheld by their own strength no less than man him-
self was before his fall;–that they are called *elect*, in the sense of beloved, or
excellent;–that it is not from any interest of their own, but from their
love to mankind, that they desire to look into the mystery of our salvation'
(Columbia xv 97–9).

iii *138–42.* Ricks 140 contrasts 'the passions and pains which scar Adam and
Eve and Satan', who are 'defaced' (ix 901) by sin. In the present passage
'it is not likely to be an accident that "Grace" there so plangently echoes
"face", nor that the rhyme is proffered by the magnificent chiasmus of the

Most glorious, in him all his Father shone
140   Substantially expressed, and in his face
Divine compassion visibly appeared,
Love without end, and without measure grace,
Which uttering thus he to his Father spake.
O Father, gracious was that word which closed
145   Thy sovereign sentence, that man should find grace;
For which both heaven and earth shall high extol
Thy praises, with the innumerable sound
Of hymns and sacred songs, wherewith thy throne
Encompassed shall resound thee ever blessed.
150   For should man finally be lost, should man
Thy creature late so loved, thy youngest son

last line'. Rhyme and chiasmus were both schemes used, often, to express likeness or correspondence.

iii *139–40*. Taken by Sewell as evidence that *PL* iii represents an earlier, more orthodox, stage in the development of M.'s christological opinions than *De doctrina* i 5, which denies the Son to be co-essential with the Father (Columbia xiv 187). But *Substantially expressed* may mean only that 'God imparted to the Son as much as he pleased of the divine nature, nay of the divine substance itself, care being taken not to confound the substance with the whole essence' (*De doctrina* i 5, Columbia xiv 193, glossing *Heb.* i 2f, the same text that underlies the present passage); in which case the phrase need not conflict with M.'s later Arianism (Kelley 29f). At the same time, the emphasis laid in *all his Father* shows that M. is here avoiding theological controversy and seeking – as far as his own position will allow – a generally acceptable catholic statement of the Biblical doctrine of divine generation.

iii *140. expressed*] In one chain of discourse perhaps not a past participle but an intransitive preterite (*OED* II 8 b); then *all his Father* would be the subject of three parallel verbs – *shone, expressed* and *appeared*. The uncertainty as to the subject of *appeared* would not be a trivial ambiguity; for it would render the fulness of the Father's expression in the Son's compassion.

iii *142*. The Son of God, Adam, and Satan are all described as gloriously heroic, but each manifests heroic excess or preeminence in a characteristically different quality. With the Son it is grace 'without measure'; with Adam, 'exceeding love' (ix 961); with Satan, merit (ii 427–9) (Steadman 92).

iii *144*. Broadbent 148f thinks that 'the Son's rhetoric is more flexible'. It is true that the Father speaks more with the closed hand of logic, the Son with the open hand of rhetoric, and that the latter often gives a lyrical expansion of a theme stated by the former. But what is more striking is the faithfulness with which the Son's speeches reflect the Father's – a correlate, at the formal level, of his obedience in imaging the divine will.

iii *145. sovereign*] spelt 'sovran'.

iii *147–9. sound . . . resound*] The repetition, which Bentley disliked, is of course mimetic.

Fall circumvented thus by fraud, though joined
With his own folly? That be from thee far,
That far be from thee, Father, who art judge
155 Of all things made, and judgest only right.
Or shall the adversary thus obtain
His end, and frustrate thine, shall he fulfil
His malice, and thy goodness bring to nought,
Or proud return though to his heavier doom,
160 Yet with revenge accomplished and to hell
Draw after him the whole race of mankind,
By his corrupted? Or wilt thou thy self
Abolish thy creation, and unmake,
For him, what for thy glory thou hast made?
165 So should thy goodness and thy greatness both
Be questioned and blasphemed without defence.
    To whom the great creator thus replied.
O Son, in whom my soul hath chief delight,
Son of my bosom, Son who art alone
170 My word, my wisdom, and effectual might,
All hast thou spoken as my thoughts are, all
As my eternal purpose hath decreed:
Man shall not quite be lost, but saved who will,

iii *152–3.* 'Even if man's own folly did contribute (together with fraud) to his circumvention.'

iii *153–4.* Cp. *Gen.* xviii 25: 'That be far from thee to do after this manner, to slay the righteous with the wicked: and that the righteous should be as the wicked, that be far from thee.'

iii *156. adversary*] The literal meaning of *Satan*; see i 82*n*.

iii *163.* At ii 367–70 Beelzebub considers the possibility that if the devils seduce rather than attack mankind, God may be forced to 'abolish his own works'.

iii *166. blasphemed*] defamed.

iii *168–9.* Echoing *Mark* i 11, the words out of the heavens at Jesus' baptism: 'Thou art my beloved Son, in whom I am well pleased' (cp. *Is.* xlii 1): also *John* i 18: 'the only begotten Son, which is in the bosom of the Father'.

iii *170.* Steadman finds an echo of *Aen.* i 664 (*nate, meae vires, mea magna potentia*)—words of Venus to her son which had been transferred to the Christian God of love, speaking at the baptism of Christ, in Proba's *Centones Virgiliani ad Testimonium Veteris et Novi Testamenti* (alluded to by St Jerome: see 'Milton, Virgil, and St Jerome ("Paradise Lost", iii 168–170)', *N & Q* cciv (1959)). Cp. also, however, *1 Cor.* i 24: 'Christ the power of God'. The Son is God's *effectual* might, because he is the Word or Logos by whom God's creative will is made effective (*John* i 1–3).

iii *173–202.* In *De doctrina* i 4, M. undeniably sets out an Arminian position, explicitly opposed to the Calvinist, on such doctrines as Predestination,

Yet not of will in him, but grace in me
175 Freely vouchsafed; once more I will renew
His lapsed powers, though forfeit and enthralled
By sin to foul exorbitant desires;
Upheld by me, yet once more he shall stand
On even ground against his mortal foe,
180 By me upheld, that he may know how frail
His fallen condition is, and to me owe
All his deliverance, and to none but me.
Some I have chosen of peculiar grace
Elect above the rest; so is my will:

Election and Reprobation, and he could be regarded as doing something similar here (Kelley 15–18); e.g., his God seems to make salvation depend on man's will to avail himself of grace–or on *prayer, repentance, and obedience* (l. 191); whereas Calvinists regarded man as totally incapable of contributing in any way to his own salvation (Calvin, *Institutes* III xxii 1–3). By the logic of M.'s day, however, he would not be taken to mean that repentance was a link in a causal chain leading to salvation, but only that it was one of a set of parallel causes. In itself the notice of the 'helping cause' man's will (l. 173) as well as the 'instrumental cause' God's grace (l. 174) was uncontroversial, and might well have been acceptable to Calvinist readers (Howard 168). But, in emphasis at least, the succeeding passage is less conventional. While predestinarian theologians usually made a radical separation between the secret and the revealed wills of God, M. here asserts their unity: God's secret will is free only for good. And throughout (*pace* Empson 120) the Calvinist *impasse* of a capricious deity, at once offering redemption and predestinating reprobation, is strenuously avoided (see further Schultz 129–31). The ordonnance exemplifies this strikingly: M. makes God speak about Predestination first, long before getting round to Atonement (ll. 203–16); thus revealing his eagerness (as it were) to save man. 'The ultimate purpose of predestination is salvation . . . God could never have predestinated reprobation' (*De doctrina* i 4; Columbia xiv 99).
iii *175. vouchsafed*] spelt 'voutsafed'.
iii *176. lapsed*] decayed; fallen into sin; forfeited (like *forfeit*, legal terminology) (*OED* I 2, 1 b, 3). The theological meaning of the noun 'lapse' (='the Fall') is also relevant. The legal diction here and throughout ll. 204–24 is appropriate to the Anselmic theory of the Atonement that M. mainly relies on (see ll. 210–12*n*). The forfeit of man's powers over the passions is described in similar legal or political imagery, after it has actually taken place (ix 1127–31, xii 88–90; see Lewis 68).
iii *179. mortal*] Both 'implacable' and 'death-dealing'; cp. i 1–2*n*.
iii *180–1. Ps.* xxxix 4: 'Lord, make me to know . . . how frail I am.'
iii *184.* By the term *elect* M. usually means no more than 'whoever believes and continues in the faith' (*De doctrina* i 4; Columbia xiv 125). See also *ibid.* 117: 'Believers are the same as the elect.'

185   The rest shall hear me call, and oft be warned
Their sinful state, and to appease betimes
The incensed Deity, while offered grace
Invites; for I will clear their senses dark,
What may suffice, and soften stony hearts
190   To pray, repent, and bring obedience due.
To prayer, repentance, and obedience due,
Though but endeavoured with sincere intent,
Mine ear shall not be slow, mine eye not shut.
And I will place within them as a guide
195   My umpire conscience, whom if they will hear,
Light after light well used they shall attain,
And to the end persisting, safe arrive.
This my long sufferance and my day of grace
They who neglect and scorn, shall never taste;
200   But hard be hardened, blind be blinded more,
That they may stumble on, and deeper fall;
And none but such from mercy I exclude.
But yet all is not done; man disobeying,
Disloyal breaks his fealty, and sins
205   Against the high supremacy of heaven,
Affecting Godhead, and so losing all,
To expiate his treason hath nought left,
But to destruction sacred and devote,

iii *193*. The fulfilment of this promise begins at xi 1–47, when God receives
the prayer and repentance of Adam and Eve.

iii *194–5*. To be distinguished from the Comforter, sent to *guide* only God's
'own' (xii 486–90). The notion of conscience or reason as an arbitrator
between God and man was very important to M. In a sense the whole poem
depends on it: only if reason is the court of appeal for both, can there be any
question of justifying to man the ways of God.

iii *197–200*. Cp. *Heb*. iii 13f: 'Exhort one another daily, while it is called To
day; lest any of you be hardened through . . . sin. For we are made partakers
of Christ, if we hold the beginning of our confidence stedfast unto the
end.' M. defends God's hardening of sinners' hearts in *De doctrina* i 8 (Colum-
bia xv 81): 'As God's instigating the sinner does not render him the author
of sin, so neither does his hardening the heart or blinding the understanding
involve that consequence; inasmuch as he does not produce these effects
by infusing an evil disposition, but on the contrary by employing such just
and kind methods, as ought rather to soften the hearts of sinners than harden
them.'

iii *206*. At ix 708–17 Satan tempts Eve with the promise that she and Adam
will 'be as gods'.   *Affecting*] seeking, aiming at.

iii *208*. *sacred*] dedicated, accursed.   *devote*] consigned to destruction
(*OED* s.v. *Devoted* 3).

He with his whole posterity must die,
210   Die he or justice must; unless for him
Some other able, and as willing, pay
The rigid satisfaction, death for death.
Say heavenly powers, where shall we find such love,
Which of ye will be mortal to redeem
215   Man's mortal crime, and just the unjust to save,
Dwells in all heaven charity so dear?
He asked, but all the heavenly choir stood mute,
And silence was in heaven: on man's behalf
Patron or intercessor none appeared,
220   Much less that durst upon his own head draw
The deadly forfeiture, and ransom set.
And now without redemption all mankind
Must have been lost, adjudged to death and hell
By doom severe, had not the Son of God,
225   In whom the fulness dwells of love divine,
His dearest mediation thus renewed.

iii *210–12.* Note that the death of man is here regarded by God not as a punishment, but as a *satisfaction* for the treason. See *De doctrina* i 16 (Columbia xv 315–17): 'The satisfaction of Christ is the complete reparation made by him . . . by the fulfilment of the Law, and payment of the required price for all mankind.' In general M. takes for granted the 'Satisfaction theory' of the Atonement, which had been widely accepted ever since St Anselm first expounded it. Occasionally, however, as at ll. 221–3, he alludes to the earlier 'ransom theory' of St Irenaeus, St Augustine, and others.   *as willing*] as willing as he is able.

iii *214–15. will be mortal*] (i.e., is willing to be subject to death) corresponds to 'willing' at l. 211, as *just*– i.e., righteous, perfectly obedient within the human context, capable of offering worthy satisfaction–corresponds to 'able' in the same line. Cp. *1 Pet.* iii 18: 'Christ also hath once suffered for sins, the just for the unjust.' For the pun on 'mortal' see 179*n*; with the play on *just*, cp. l. 252, and i 642.

iii *216. charity*] compassionate love, *caritas*.

iii *217–26.* So at the hellish council (ii 418–26) 'all sat mute', since none of the devils dared undertake the expedition against man. 'Satan alone was fit to undertake the one [work], as the Son of God the other' (Newton). The passage impressed Dryden enough to inspire a sustained imitation in *The Hind and the Panther* ii 499–514.

iii *218.* Cp. *Rev.* viii 1: when the seventh seal was opened 'there was silence in heaven'.

iii *219. Patron*] advocate.

iii *221. ransom set*] put down the ransom price (i.e. by giving his own life).

iii *224. doom*] judgment.

iii *225. Col.* ii 9: 'In him dwelleth all the fulness of the Godhead bodily.'

> Father, thy word is past, man shall find grace;
> And shall Grace not find means, that finds her way,
> The speediest of thy winged messengers,
> 230 To visit all thy creatures, and to all
> Comes unprevented, unimplored, unsought,
> Happy for man, so coming; he her aid
> Can never seek, once dead in sins and lost;
> Atonement for himself or offering meet,
> 235 Indebted and undone, hath none to bring:
> Behold me then, me for him, life for life
> I offer, on me let thine anger fall;
> Account me man; I for his sake will leave
> Thy bosom, and this glory next to thee
> 240 Freely put off, and for him lastly die
> Well pleased, on me let Death wreak all his rage;
> Under his gloomy power I shall not long
> Lie vanquished; thou hast given me to possess
> Life in my self for ever, by thee I live,
> 245 Though now to Death I yield, and am his due

iii *227. thy word is past*] Not merely 'thy speech is uttered', but 'thy word of honour is pledged'.

iii *231. unprevented*] unanticipated, therefore not even prayed for. Cp. the Collect 'Prevent us, O Lord, in all our doings'; and contrast *Ps.* lxxxviii 13: 'in the morning shall my prayer prevent thee'. The line alludes to the doctrine of divine Prevenience–the priority of God's love to man's response. On the rhetorical scheme, see ii 185*n*.

iii *232–5.* Developing the idea introduced at l. 207.   *Happy*] fortunate.

iii *233. Eph.* ii 4f: 'God . . . for his great love . . . even when we were dead in sins, hath quickened us.'

iii *236–8.* The dramatic repetition of the pronoun occurs again in a related passage, vi 812–8, where the Son is an instrument, not of grace to mankind, but of revenge on the rebel angels. Cp. x 738–40, and see x 832*n*. But M. may also intend an echo of Nisus' guilt-accepting cry at *Aen.* ix 427–8: *Me, me, adsum, qui feci, in me convertit ferrum, / O Rutuli! mea fraus omnis.*

iii *240. lastly die*] As a 'description of the career of the Son' the phrase is puzzling (Empson 127). But is it intended to be such a description? Perhaps rather it mentions the third and last–in logical rather than in chronological order–of the diminishments accepted by Christ at the Incarnation.

iii *243–4.* Cp. *John* v 26: 'As the Father hath life in himself: so hath he given to the Son to have life in himself.'

iii *245–9.* Kelley thinks that M. is here 'tersely' presenting the Mortalist doctrine, according to which death is suffered not only by the body but also by the soul. Thus 'even the soul of Christ was for a short time subject unto death', and *All that of me can die* means 'the whole man . . . body, soul, and spirit' (Kelley 32). Admittedly *De doctrina* i 13 shows that M. embraced

All that of me can die, yet that debt paid,
Thou wilt not leave me in the loathsome grave
His prey, nor suffer my unspotted soul
For ever with corruption there to dwell;
250   But I shall rise victorious, and subdue
My vanquisher, spoiled of his vaunted spoil;
Death his death's wound shall then receive, and stoop
Inglorious, of his mortal sting disarmed.
I through the ample air in triumph high
255   Shall lead hell captive maugre hell, and show
The powers of darkness bound. Thou at the sight
Pleased, out of heaven shalt look down and smile,
While by thee raised I ruin all my foes,
Death last, and with his carcass glut the grave:
260   Then with the multitude of my redeemed
Shall enter heaven long absent, and return,

the so-called Mortalist 'heresy'; but the doctrine could only be extracted from the present passage by force. 'Milton is not splitting theological hairs; he is dealing with the justice of Christ's incarnation and crucifixion' (Hughes).

iii *248–59*. As is usual with the poem's divine utterances, this speech is a carefully interwoven tissue of Scriptural allusions (Sims 18–19).

iii *248–9*. Cp. *Ps.* xvi 10, where David, the type of Christ, prophesies: 'Thou wilt not leave my soul in hell; neither wilt thou suffer thine Holy One to see corruption.'

iii *251–3*. Cp. *Col.* ii 15, 'having spoiled principalities and powers'. The image of death's sting, used also by Michael in his prophecy of Christ's victory at xii 432, is from *1 Cor.* xv 55–6: 'O death, where is thy sting? O grave, where is thy victory? The sting of death is sin; and the strength of sin is the law.' *Death his death's wound* is often taken to be no more than a verbal play. But the meaning is exact: death is fatally wounded at this stage, but not 'killed' until the second coming of Christ (l. 259).

iii *255*. Cp. *Ps.* lxviii 18, applied to Christ in *Eph.* iv 8: 'When he ascended up on high, he led captivity captive.'   *maugre*] in spite of.

iii *256*. Cp. again *Col.* ii 15: 'Having spoiled principalities and powers, he made a shew of them openly, triumphing over them in it.' Also *Col.* i 13, 'power of darkness'.

iii *259. Death last*] Alludes to *1 Cor.* xv 26: 'The last enemy that shall be destroyed is death.' Cp. Sin's prophecy at ii 734.

iii *261*. A difficult line, because the Son speaks of only one absence: he conflates his first with his second coming. Since he thinks of his reentry into heaven 'with the multitude of [his] redeemed' as taking place after his final ruin of Death (ll. 259–61), it seems that he envisages being away throughout what we would call history, and perhaps also during the millenium speculated on by Michael at xii 461–5. There are at least three possible lines of interpretation: (1) The Son does not have complete foreknowledge, and

Father, to see thy face, wherein no cloud
Of anger shall remain, but peace assured,
And reconcilement; wrath shall be no more
265   Thenceforth, but in thy presence joy entire.
His words here ended, but his meek aspect
Silent yet spake, and breathed immortal love
To mortal men, above which only shone
Filial obedience: as a sacrifice
270   Glad to be offered, he attends the will
Of his great Father. Admiration seized
All heaven, what this might mean, and whither tend
Wondering; but soon the almighty thus replied:
O thou in heaven and earth the only peace
275   Found out for mankind under wrath, O thou
My sole complacence! well thou know'st how dear,
To me are all my works, nor man the least
Though last created, that for him I spare
Thee from my bosom and right hand, to save,
280   By losing thee awhile, the whole race lost.
Thou therefore whom thou only canst redeem,
Their nature also to thy nature join;
And be thy self man among men on earth,
Made flesh, when time shall be, of virgin seed,

underestimates the complexity of the task before him (Empson 127). He imagines, reasonably but mistakenly, that one mission will be enough. (2) The Son offers 'a longer mission than the Father decided to require of him' (Empson 129). Similarly the crucifixion is not mentioned for the sublime reason that it is thought a 'trivial sacrifice'. (3) M. is here presenting a supratemporal vision (like Donne's in 'At the round earths imagin'd corners, blow'), so that we should not look for detailed chronological sequence. The important thing, *sub specie aeternitatis*, is simply that heaven has to be left at all. M.'s occasional use of a timeless present is in accord with this third interpretation: see l. 301*n*.

iii *267–9.* Note that the Son's obedience is superior to his charity; as indeed it must be, according to M.'s hierarchy of the virtues. Messiah is the only heroically obedient person in the poem (see vi 820–3*n*, ix 31–2*n*, vii 602–7*n*, and Steadman 93).   *attends*] awaits.

iii *271. Admiration*] Either in its modern sense; or in its older sense, 'wonder'; or in both.

iii *276. complacence*] source of complacence, satisfaction. See ll. 210–12*n*. Comma after *dear* is almost certainly an error.

iii *277–8.* Cp. *King Lear* I i 85: to Lear, Cordelia is 'Although our last, not least'.

iii *283–4.* Echoing *John* i 14: 'The Word was made flesh.'

285 By wondrous birth: be thou in Adam's room
    The head of all mankind, though Adam's son.
    As in him perish all men, so in thee
    As from a second root shall be restored,
    As many as are restored, without thee none.
290 His crime makes guilty all his sons, thy merit
    Imputed shall absolve them who renounce
    Their own both righteous and unrighteous deeds,
    And live in thee transplanted, and from thee
    Receive new life. So man, as is most just,
295 Shall satisfy for man, be judged and die,
    And dying rise, and rising with him raise
    His brethren, ransomed with his own dear life.
    So heavenly love shall outdo hellish hate
    Giving to death, and dying to redeem,

iii 285–6. Cp. 1 Cor. xi 3: 'The head of every man is Christ.'   room]
place.

iii 287. Cp. 1 Cor. xv 22: 'As in Adam all die, even so in Christ shall all be
made alive.'

iii 290–4. The general course of the argument follows that of Rom. v 17–19.

iii 290–2. The source is ultimately Rom. iv 5–8 (e.g. 6: 'the blessedness of the
man, unto whom God imputeth righteousness without works'), but the
doctrine of Imputed Righteousness had in M.'s day come to be a very
familiar topic for theological debate. For a simple statement, see De doctrina
i 22 (Columbia xvi 27): 'As therefore our sins are imputed to Christ, so
the merits or righteousness of Christ are imputed to us through faith.'
both righteous and unrighteous] This is no pleonasm for it implies the whole
conciliatory position with respect to Justification that M. takes up in De
doctrina (see ibid.). If one simply renounced dependence on righteous deeds,
one would be justified by faith alone; but for the 'living faith'–faith issuing
in works–that M. believes necessary, one has to renounce (in a diff-
erent sense) unrighteous deeds.

iii 293. transplanted] Continues the horticultural image begun in 'seed'
(l. 284) and 'second root' (l. 288), which has its Scriptural authority in such
passages as Rom. vi 16–24. See also De doctrina i 21, 'Of being ingrafted in
Christ, and its effects': 'Believers are said to be ingrafted in Christ when they
are planted in Christ by God the Father, that is, are made partakers of
Christ' (Columbia xvi 3–5). The first of the effects of ingrafting is 'newness
of life'. The horticultural imagery (appropriate to the occupation of Adam
and Eve) runs throughout PL: see, e.g., ii 383n.

iii 295–6. Note M.'s finesse on the climax scheme.

iii 299. Giving to] Often interpreted as 'yielding to, submitting'; but it may
mean 'giving (Christ) up to'–describing the Father's part in the Atonement,
as the second half of the line describes the Son's.   redeem] Cp. Matt. xx
28, and see 210–12n.

300   So dearly to redeem what hellish hate
        So easily destroyed, and still destroys
        In those who, when they may, accept not grace.
        Nor shalt thou by descending to assume
        Man's nature, lessen or degrade thine own.
305   Because thou hast, though throned in highest bliss
        Equal to God, and equally enjoying
        Godlike fruition, quitted all to save
        A world from utter loss, and hast been found
        By merit more than birthright Son of God,
310   Found worthiest to be so by being good,
        Far more than great or high; because in thee
        Love hath abounded more than glory abounds,
        Therefore thy humiliation shall exalt
        With thee thy manhood also to this throne,
315   Here shalt thou sit incarnate, here shalt reign
        Both God and man, Son both of God and man,

iii *301.* Note the tenses: while not altogether inconsistent with the main verbs
in the prophetic future, *destroyed* and *destroys* could easily be taken to imply
that the Fall has already occurred. The overall effect is of a timeless medi-
tation, or of a comprehensive vision that enfolds many different temporal
perspectives. 'The fall is spoken of as a thing past; perhaps because all things,
even future ones, are present to the divine Mind' (Pearce). Cp. ll. 151, 181,
287, and see 261*n.*

iii *305–20.* 'The best moment of God in the poem . . . because he is envis-
aging his abdication'–the Son could not be rewarded by exaltation to the
throne he already occupies (l. 305), and must therefore be destined for the
Father's throne (Empson 137). But there is no question of reward: rather
does Christ's exaltation restore and make manifest the Godhead he already
enjoyed. See *De doctrina* i 16 (Columbia xv 315).

iii *306. Equal to God*] This seems at first a Trinitarian formulation; but as M.
shows in *De doctrina* i 5, the text to which the passage alludes –*Phil.* ii 6–can
be seen as having quite a different implication: 'Co-equality with the
Father . . . rather refutes than proves his unity of essence; since equality
cannot exist but between two or more essences' (Columbia xiv 343).
As at iii 243f, M. prefers a wording that on the one hand is Biblical, on the
other open to Arian interpretation.

iii *307.* The oddness of diction signalizes a punning allusion to Adam's
contrasting behaviour: Christ is ready to renounce *Godlike fruition* for
man, but man will not renounce the fruit that makes him Godlike (cp.,
e.g., ix 717).   *quitted*] Another pun, since it meant 'redeemed, remitted'
as well as 'left'.

iii *312.* See iii 267–9*n.*

> Anointed universal king, all power
> I give thee, reign for ever, and assume
> Thy merits; under thee as head supreme
> 320 Thrones, princedoms, powers, dominions I reduce:
> All knees to thee shall bow, of them that bide
> In heaven, or earth, or under earth in hell,
> When thou attended gloriously from heaven
> Shalt in the sky appear, and from thee send
> 325 The summoning archangels to proclaim
> Thy dread tribunal: forthwith from all winds
> The living, and forthwith the cited dead
> Of all past ages to the general doom
> Shall hasten, such a peal shall rouse their sleep.
> 330 Then all thy saints assembled, thou shalt judge
> Bad men and angels, they arraigned shall sink
> Beneath thy sentence; hell her numbers full,
> Thenceforth shall be for ever shut. Mean while
> The world shall burn, and from her ashes spring

iii *317–18.* Cp. *Matt.* xxviii 18: 'All power is given unto me'—in the *De doctrina* a proof text showing that Christ and the Father are not of the same essence (Columbia xiv 305 and 343).

iii *318–19. assume | Thy merits*] Renders even more concise Horace's valedictory to his Muse: *sume superbiam | quaesitam meritis* (*Odes* III xxx 14f. On the tense of *give*, see 301*n.* *head supreme*] See *Eph.* iv 15.

iii *320.* Alluding to *Col.* i 16. Cp. *PL* v 840, a similar roll-call by Satan in his 'rabble-rousing speech. . . . No doubt this was the standard form in Heaven, but the effect is to make the reader compare the two offers' (Empson 138). *princedoms*] principalities.

iii *321–2.* Cp. *Phil* ii 10: 'At the name of Jesus every knee should bow, of things in heaven, and things in earth, and things under the earth.' Some scent an inconsistency here; supposing that M. has fallen back to the old notion of a hell 'at the centre', discarded in Bk i Argument. There is no reason, however, why if the universe is below heaven (ii 1051) hell should not be still farther below.

iii *324–9.* The imagery of this vision of judgment is drawn from Revelation, from *Matt.* xxiv 30f, and from *1 Cor.* xv 51f. Cp. *Nativity Ode* 115f: 'To those ychained in sleep, / The wakeful trump of doom must thunder.'

iii *326–7. from all winds*] from all four points of the compass—perhaps combining the angels and winds of *Rev.* vii 1 with the resurrecting wind of *Ezek.* xxxvii 9 ('Come from the four winds, O breath, and breathe upon those slain, that they may live'). *cited*] summoned. *doom*] judgment.

iii *330. saints*] elect; a common usage in the seventeenth century.

iii *334–5.* Like xi 900f and xii 546–51, these lines are based on *2 Pet.* iii 12f, a prophecy of 'the day of God, wherein the heavens being on fire shall be dissolved, and the elements shall melt with fervent heat', but when the

335   New heaven and earth, wherein the just shall dwell,
        And after all their tribulations long
        See golden days, fruitful of golden deeds,
        With joy and love triumphing, and fair truth.
        Then thou thy regal sceptre shalt lay by,
340   For regal sceptre then no more shall need,
        God shall be all in all. But all ye gods,
        Adore him, who to compass all this dies,
        Adore the Son, and honour him as me.
           No sooner had the almighty ceased, but all

elect will 'look for new heavens and a new earth, wherein dwelleth right-
eousness'. In *De doctrina* i 33, M. dismisses as of no importance the question
whether this final conflagration means 'the destruction of the substance
of the world itself, or only a change in the nature of its constituent parts'.
In both Old and New Testament apocryphal literature, however, the oper-
ation of the destroying and refining fire was sometimes dwelt on. *Ed I*
has no comma after *dwell*.

iii *337*. A network of allusions introducing the key word 'fruit' runs through-
out the poem (MacCaffrey 83–6). The present passage refers back most
immediately to the first glimpse of Adam and Eve–'in the happy garden
placed, / Reaping immortal fruits of joy and love' (66f). But cp. also xi 20–2
and xii 550f.

iii *339–43*. Some think that M. is here expressing the view that God means to
abdicate and become an immanent or Cambridge Platonist sort of deity
(see Empson 130–5). On the frequent use of *all* in *PL*, see Empson[3] 101–4.
The present instance may be important theologically; though the frequency
is actually no more prominent than in the source, *1 Cor.* xv 28: 'When all
things shall be subdued unto him, then shall the Son also himself be subject
unto him that put all things under him, that God may be all in all.'   *need*]
be needful.   *gods*] angels; see i 116–17n and cp. *Ps.* xcvii 7: 'Worship him,
all ye gods.' In *De doctrina* i 5 (Columbia xiv 245) M. notes that 'the name
of God is not unfrequently ascribed ... even to angels and men.' But here
the deliberate–and unique–concession of the name by God himself con-
trasts with Satan's presumptuous taking of it for granted. See T. H. Banks,
'The Meaning of "Gods" in *Paradise Lost*', *MLN*, liv (1939) 450–4.

iii *343*. *John* v 23: 'All men should honour the Son, even as they honour
the Father.'

iii *344–415*. The songs of the angels occupy 72 lines because 72 was the mystic
number of Christ's disciples. There were also 72 names of angels; see Bongo
557.

iii *344–9*. The unusually sustained syntactic breath of the word group in
absolute construction (*angels ... uttering joy*) makes the main verb that
follows resoundingly emphatic. On the grammar of the sentence see
Empson[2] 160. Adams 106, however, takes *The multitude of angels* as the sub-
ject, and *heaven* as the object, of the verb *rung*.

345 The multitude of angels with a shout
Loud as from numbers without number, sweet
As from blest voices, uttering joy, heaven rung
With jubilee, and loud hosannas filled
The eternal regions: lowly reverent

350 Towards either throne they bow, and to the ground
With solemn adoration down they cast
Their crowns inwove with amarant and gold,
Immortal amarant, a flower which once
In Paradise, fast by the tree of life

355 Began to bloom, but soon for man's offence
To heaven removed where first it grew, there grows,
And flowers aloft shading the fount of life,
And where the river of bliss through midst of heaven

iii *346*. Contrasting with the 'deafening shout' with which the infernal council ends (ii 520).

iii *348*. *jubilee*] jubilation, shouting; but also 'the year of remission or emancipation'. The Hebrew jubilee–a type of the Atonement–was a ritual occasion occurring every fifty natural years, when slaves were freed and property reverted to its first owner.

iii *350–71*. Most of the details of heaven–the thrones, the crowns of gold cast down before them, the jasper (l. 363), the harps–are from Revelation. But others (like the river) combine pagan and Christian visions of bliss.

iii *350–2*. Cp. *Rev*. iv, where the twenty-four elders with 'crowns of gold' 'cast their crowns before the throne'. The crowns are *inwove with amarant* on the strength of *1 Pet*. v 4: 'Ye shall receive a crown of glory that fadeth not away' (Greek ἀμαράντινον).

iii *353–7*. *amarant*] 'unwithering'; a purple flower that, as Hume and Newton noted, was for Clement of Alexandria a 'symbol of immortality'. 'The fair crown of amaranth is laid up for those who have lived well. This flower the earth is not able to bear' (*Paedagogus* ii 8; ed. A. Roberts and J. Donaldson (Edinburgh 1867) i 237). But this is only half the story; for M. well knew–if only from the Clementine chapter just cited–that floral crowns were distinctively pagan, and the amarantine crown an ancient symbol of untroubled tranquility and health (see, e.g., Valeriano 690). Like Clement himself, M. is deliberately comparing a pagan religious symbol with a Christian one very like it. Cp. xi 78 and *Lycidas* 149.

iii *357–9*. Among many Scriptural passages that use river imagery to describe the joy of the believer, the closest is perhaps *Ps*. xxxvi 8f: 'Thou shalt make them drink of the river of thy pleasures. For with thee is the fountain of life.' Cp. also *Rev*. xxii 1. The blissful rivers of heaven contrast with the 'baleful streams' of hell at ii 575–81. The Fountain of Life emblem is developed as a symbol of heavenly bliss in Raleigh's poem 'The passionate mans Pilgrimage'.

Rolls o'er Elisian flowers her amber stream;
360 With these that never fade the spirits elect
Bind their resplendent locks inwreathed with beams,
Now in loose garlands thick thrown off, the bright
Pavement that like a sea of jasper shone
Impurpled with celestial roses smiled.
365 Then crowned again their golden harps they took,
Harps ever tuned, that glittering by their side
Like quivers hung, and with preamble sweet
Of charming symphony they introduce
Their sacred song, and waken raptures high;
370 No voice exempt, no voice but well could join
Melodious part, such concord is in heaven.
     Thee Father first they sung omnipotent,
Immutable, immortal, infinite,

iii 359. The river is probably said to roll o'er the flowers because the amarant renewed its life when it was moistened. Contrary to expectation, *Rolls* is not a Latinism, since it had been used for centuries in the sense 'undulates, flows' (*OED* II 11 b, 16). But some allusion may have been felt to Virgil, *Aen.* vi 656-9, the description of spirits chanting in chorus beside the Eridanus, in the Elysian fields. For *amber* as a standard of purity or clarity, see Callimachus, *Hymns* vi 29 and Virgil, *Georg.* iii 522.

iii 363-4. The New Jerusalem shines with light 'like a jasper stone, clear as crystal' (*Rev.* xxi 11); at *Rev.* iv 3 the throned deity himself is compared to a jasper. As so often, M.'s descriptive passages give veiled expression to a Baroque mysticism almost as intense as Crashaw's. With this beatific vision of heaven's pavement, contrast Mammon's concentration on its riches (i 679-84n) and the horror of hell's 'burning marl' (i 296).

iii 366-7. Ancient quivers designed to contain both bow and arrows were harp-shaped.

iii 367. *preamble*] prelude; *OED* gives no other example but this of the use of the word in a musical context.

iii 370. *exempt*] debarred.

iii 372. So in *Rev.* xix 6 the voice of a multitude is heard saying: 'Alleluia: for the Lord God omnipotent reigneth.' Contrast the song of the rebel angels, which is about 'their own heroic deeds' (ii 549). While the hymn is in *melodious parts*, the song is 'partial'. Note also that the mid-point of Bk. iii falls between ll. 371 and 372. Thus the second half begins with the angels' hymn to God the fountain of light, just as its first half began with the poet's. On the substantive relation between the two hymns, see ll. 410-15n.

iii 373-4. Cp. the doxology in *1 Tim.* i 17 'unto the King eternal, immortal, invisible'. But l. 373 is transplanted in its entirety from Sylvester's Du Bartas (2): 'God all in all . . . / Immutable, immortall, infinite, / Incomprehensible, all spirit, all light / All Majesty, all-self-Omnipotent / Invisible, impassive, excellent.'

Eternal king; thee author of all being,
375   Fountain of light, thy self invisible
Amidst the glorious brightness where thou sit'st
Throned inaccessible, but when thou shadest
The full blaze of thy beams, and through a cloud
Drawn round about thee like a radiant shrine,
380   Dark with excessive bright thy skirts appear,
Yet dazzle heaven, that brightest seraphim
Approach not, but with both wings veil their eyes.
Thee next they sang of all creation first,
Begotten Son, divine similitude,
385   In whose conspicuous countenance, without cloud
Made visible, the almighty Father shines,
Whom else no creature can behold; on thee

iii 375–82. Cp. v 599. In content, though not in expression, resembling *1 Tim.* vi 16 (God dwells in light that no man can approach); *Exod.* xxiv 16f (God speaks out of a cloud on Mt Sinai, yet his glory looks like fire) and xxxiii 18–23 (God promises Moses a glimpse of his 'back parts' only: to see his face would be fatal); and *Is.* vi 1f (Isaiah sees God enthroned among seraphim, who cover their faces with their wings).   *Fountain of light*] Cp. l. 8.   *but when*] i.e., except when.   *Dark with excessive bright*] Perhaps suggested by a similar oxymoron in Drummond's 'An Hymn of the Fairest Fair' (ed. Ward ii 41), where the Trinity is 'unperceived by excessive light' (l. 130) and 'angels dazzled are' (l. 144). Among other probable models are Tasso, *Gerus. Lib.* ix 57 and Spenser, *An Hymne of Heavenly Beautie,* 118f, 176–9.

iii 383. *first*] Could be regarded as theologically tendentious. In *Rev.* iii 14 Christ is 'the beginning of the creation of God', and in *Col.* i 15–17 he is 'the firstborn of every creature. For by him were all things created. . . . And he is before all things.' But *De doctrina* i 7 interprets these texts in an Arian sense. Though M. believed that Christ 'is termed first born, not only in respect of dignity, but also of time', *first* carried for him the further implication of *primus inter pares.* Christ was himself created, 'the first of the whole creation' (*De doctrina* i 5; Columbia xiv 18l). The point is a fine one, however, since M. also believed in the divinity and preexistence of Christ, and his agency in subsequent creation.

iii 384. *Begotten Son*] Cp. *John* iii 16: 'God so loved the world, that he gave his only begotten Son.'

iii 385–7. See *John* i 18 and xiv 9. For a full appreciation of the paradox, contrast ll. 387–81. In himself, the Father is invisible even when hidden (*through a cloud*); but in the Son he is visible even when not hidden (*without cloud*). *conspicuous*] clearly visible; eminent.

iii 387–9. Cp. vi 680–2.   *spirit*] There seems no reason to join Kelley (109) in doubting that the Holy Spirit is here intended. The allusion is to *John* iii 34: 'God giveth not the Spirit by measure unto him.'

Impressed the effulgence of his glory abides,
Transfused on thee his ample Spirit rests.
390   He heaven of heavens and all the powers therein
By thee created, and by thee threw down
The aspiring dominations: thou that day
Thy Father's dreadful thunder didst not spare,
Nor stop thy flaming chariot wheels, that shook
395   Heaven's everlasting frame, while o'er the necks
Thou drovest of warring angels disarrayed.
Back from pursuit thy powers with loud acclaim
Thee only extolled, Son of thy Father's might,
To execute fierce vengeance on his foes,
400   Not so on man; him through their malice fallen,
Father of mercy and grace, thou didst not doom
So strictly, but much more to pity incline:
No sooner did thy dear and only Son
Perceive thee purposed not to doom frail man
405   So strictly, but much more to pity inclined,
He to appease thy wrath, and end the strife
Of mercy and justice in thy face discerned,

iii *390.* Cp. the *Te Deum*: 'To thee all Angels cry aloud: the heavens and all the powers therein.'

iii *391. synod*] A carefully chosen term; since it could be used of the conjunction of stars as well as the meeting of councillors. We are not long allowed to forget that the devils were once 'sons of the morning'; see v 700–14*n*.

iii *392–9.* The victory briefly recalled here is narrated more fully at vi 824–92.   *dominations*] One of the orders of heavenly beings, named as having been created by Christ's agency in *Col.* i 16.

iii *397–8.* The devils would say that *back from pursuit* qualifies *powers;* since they salve their dignity by pretending that the good angels joined with Messiah in the pursuit. See i 169–71*n* and vi 880f.

iii *400.* This distinction was explained earlier, at ll. 129–32.

iii *401.* Alluding to *2 Cor.* i 3: 'Father of mercies, and the God of all comfort'. *doom*] judge.

iii *405–6.* Most editors say that *but* or *than* has to be supplied before *He*. If, however, *much more to pity inclined* refers to the Son, the *but* immediately preceding is available for the main clause. True, the repetition of l. 402 almost unchanged in l. 405 leads us to expect that the Father is again the subject. But isn't this just the point?–The syntax is miming the Son's 'divine similitude' to the Father.

iii *407. mercy and justice*] On the basis of *Ps.* lxxxv 10, God's deliberations over man's destiny had often been portrayed as a debate between four personified attributes: Mercy and Justice, Truth and Peace. See Hope Traver, *The Four Daughters of God* (Philadelphia, Pa. 1907).

Regardless of the bliss wherein he sat
Second to thee, offered himself to die
410   For man's offence. O unexampled love,
Love nowhere to be found less than divine!
Hail, Son of God, saviour of men, thy name
Shall be the copious matter of my song
Henceforth, and never shall my harp thy praise
415   Forget, nor from thy Father's praise disjoin.
    Thus they in heaven, above the starry sphere,
Their happy hours in joy and hymning spent.
Mean while upon the firm opacous globe
Of this round world, whose first convex divides
420   The luminous inferior orbs, enclosed
From Chaos and the inroad of darkness old,
Satan alighted walks: a globe far off
It seemed, now seems a boundless continent
Dark, waste, and wild, under the frown of Night
425   Starless exposed, and ever-threatening storms
Of Chaos blustering round, inclement sky;
Save on that side which from the wall of heaven
Though distant far some small reflection gains
Of glimmering air less vexed with tempest loud:
430   Here walked the fiend at large in spacious field.
As when a vulture on Imaus bred,

iii 410–15. A continuation of the hymn; though the use of the singular (*my song . . . my harp*) allows M. to add an overtone of allusion to his own art, which participates in the concord of the heavenly chorus. See 372*n.* In ancient hymns, the promise to resume the god's praises was a common feature: cp., e.g., Callimachus, *Hymns* iii 137. Broadbent (157) notices that *Hail Son of God* 'brings the episode in a circle from "Hail holy light"', the opening line of the book, also spoken by the poet in his own person.
iii 412. Echoing the concluding words of Virgil's hymn to Hercules at *Aen.* viii 301.
iii 416–21. *starry sphere*] Either, the sphere of the fixed stars; or, more loosely, the stars and planets together, as at v 620. The stars are enclosed within the *primum mobile* or *first convex* (sphere), the 'bare outside' that Satan was ready to alight on at 74. Both heaven and chaos lie outside that opaque (*opacous*) shell; see ll. 481–3*n* and ii 1052–3*n.*
iii 416–17. The preceding passage is to be contrasted with the account of how the devils 'entertain / The irksome hours' (ii 522–628).
iii 423. Cp. Astolfo's amazement at the moon's size, when he climbs onto it in *Orl. Fur.* xxxiv 71.
iii 424–6. In *Ed I* and *Ed II Chaos* is treated as a proper name, *Night* is not.
iii 429. *vexed*] tossed about.
iii 431–41. As is often the case with M.'s longer similes, many different

> Whose snowy ridge the roving Tartar bounds,
> Dislodging from a region scarce of prey
> To gorge the flesh of lambs or yeanling kids
> 435 On hills where flocks are fed, flies toward the springs
> Of Ganges or Hydaspes, Indian streams;
> But in his way lights on the barren plains
> Of Sericana, where Chineses drive
> With sails and wind their cany wagons light:
> 440 So on this windy sea of land, the fiend
> Walked up and down alone bent on his prey,

points of correspondence are involved. Thus, the *vulture* is like Satan in respect of rapacity, distant knowledge of his prey, and mode of locomotion; while the lambs and *yeanling* (new born) *kids* are like mankind in respect of innocence, and division into redeemed sheep and reprobate goats (*Matt.* xxv). One journey is from *snowy Imaus*, which notably failed to bound *the roving Tartar* Jingis Khan, to the rivers of India; the other from the 'frozen continent' (ii 587) of Tartarus, which did not keep Satan from roving, to Eden with its rivers (Huntley[2] 107f, Lerner 302). More subtly, the *barren plains of Sericana* correspond to the *primum mobile* not merely because both are stopping-places, but also because in both the elements are confused. (The Chinese use sails, the means of propulsion for ships, on their land vehicles; and the *primum mobile* is a *sea of land*.) This emphasis on confusion of the elements perhaps implies that Satan's entry into our world is an inroad of chaos (cp. 420f). Note that, as often in *PL*, evil comes here from the north; cf. v 689 and see *n*.   *Ganges*] For the identification of the Ganges with the Pison of *Gen*. ii, see e.g. Calepinus' *Dictionary*: at this point the tenor and vehicle of the simile coincide.

iii *431*. So at x 273–81, when Death scents his prey and leaves hell for earth, he is compared to a flock of vultures. Maps such as Mercator's *Tartaria* showed *Imaus* as a mountain range extending from modern Afghanistan to the Frozen (Arctic) Ocean, so that a vulture flying to the Ganges would pass Sericana (N.W. China). Some phrases of the simile can probably be traced to dictionary entries under 'Tartaria', 'Scythia' and 'Imaus' (see Starnes 322).

iii *436*. Idiosyncratic diction: cp. 36, i 469.   *Hydaspes*] the Chelum or Jhelum River in the Punjab; eastern boundary of Alexander's conquests.

iii *438–9*. The Chinese landships described by the traveller Mendoza in his *Historie of the Great and Mightie Kingdome of China* (tr. Parke, 1588) aroused great interest in Europe. Grotius himself rode in one of the copies constructed by the Dutch scientist Stevin and celebrated in De Gheyn's famous print (see Huntley).

iii *440–1*. Cp. Job i 7: 'Whence comest thou? Then Satan answered the Lord, and said, From going to and fro in the earth, and from walking up and down in it.'

Alone, for other creature in this place
Living or lifeless to be found was none,
None yet, but store hereafter from the earth
445   Up hither like aerial vapours flew
Of all things transitory and vain, when sin
With vanity had filled the works of men:
Both all things vain, and all who in vain things
Built their fond hopes of glory or lasting fame,
450   Or happiness in this or the other life;
All who have their reward on earth, the fruits
Of painful superstition and blind zeal,
Nought seeking but the praise of men, here find
Fit retribution, empty as their deeds;
455   All the unaccomplished works of nature's hand,
Abortive, monstrous, or unkindly mixed,
Dissolved on earth, fleet hither, and in vain,
Till final dissolution, wander here,

iii 444–97. In *Orl. Fur.* xxxiv 73 ff., a passage from which M. quotes in *Of Reformation*, Ariosto tells how Astolfo searches for his lost wits in a Limbo of Vanity on the moon. Ariosto's limbo is more lightly and casually portrayed than M.'s; it is filled with 'The precious time that fools misspend in play, / The vain attempts that never take effect, / The vows that sinners make and never pay, / The counsels wise that careless men neglect' (xxxiv 75; tr. Harington). But it offered a precedent for antiprelatic satire with a science fiction *mise en scène*, in its lunar mountain symbolizing the Constantine Donation, 'which once smelt sweet, now stinks as odiously' (xxxiv 80; M.'s own tr.–see Yale i 560). Addison refused to impose on himself by seeing any possibility in the passage (*Spectator* No. 297); while Bentley denied it to M. altogether. M., however, no doubt meant it to be incredible, when he based it on Ariosto's burlesque. There is also a limbo of fools in the sixteenth-century satire *Julius exclusus*; see Broadbent 163.

iii 447. Images of unnatural sexuality begin to be mingled with the images of vacuity; see, e.g., ll. 456, 463, 474. In perverse parody of God's creative generation in the void, a corrupt nature is now being conceived. See Huntley[2] 110–12, where allusions are discovered to the monstrous birth of Sin, and to the supposed hermaphroditism of vultures.

iii 452. *painful*] laborious, diligent, careful.

iii 454. The fitness of the retribution partly depends on the etymology of *vanity* (Lat. *vanus*, empty).

iii 455–8. See 447n. The *unkindly mixed* (unnaturally conceived) works correspond to the first group of fools, the Giants (ll. 463–5); the *monstrous* to the Babel-builders (ll. 466–8); and the *abortive* (prematurely born) to the embryos etc. of ll. 474–80, and the suicides of ll. 469–73, who in their 'painful superstition' begin their life after death prematurely.

Not in the neighbouring moon, as some have dreamed;
460   Those argent fields more likely habitants,
Translated saints, or middle spirits hold
Betwixt the angelical and human kind:
Hither of ill-joined sons and daughters born
First from the ancient world those Giants came
465   With many a vain exploit, though then renowned:
The builders next of Babel on the plain
Of Sennaar, and still with vain design
New Babels, had they wherewithal, would build·
Others came single; he who to be deemed
470   A god, leaped fondly into Aetna flames,
Empedocles, and he who to enjoy
Plato's Elysium, leaped into the sea,

iii *459. some*] i.e. Ariosto. Bruno, Cardan, Henry More and others specu-
latively peopled the moon, but with less abstract inhabitants. Schultz (16)
thinks it was the frivolity of such pluralist speculations that occasioned their
introduction here, as an illustration of vain curiosity. If so, then M. also
confesses the vanity of his own work; for he offers an alternative specu-
lation on his own account in ll. 460–2. See ll. 565–71*n*.

iii *461. Translated saints*] Probably such as Enoch (*Gen.* v 24) and Elijah (*2
Kings* ii). On 'Old Testament Sainthood' see C. A. Huttar, in *N & Q*
ccix (1964) 86–8.

iii *463–5*. The first group of fools are the Giants, 'mighty men . . . of re-
nown', born of the misunion of 'sons of God' with 'daughters of men'
(*Gen.* vi 4). See xi 621–2*n*.

iii *466–8*. At xii 45–7 the builders of Babel are said to have formed their
vain design out of a desire for fame. *Sennaar*, the Septuagint and Vulg. form,
is preferred to the *Shinar* of A. V. *Gen.* xi 2. *New Babels* suggests the New
Babylon of anti-Papist propaganda: see Cohn, Index s.v. *Babylon*. Schultz
(127) notes that Giants were also a common symbol of Antichrist.

iii *469–73*. *Empedocles* and *Cleombrotus* were not associated by classical
writers, but occur together in Lactantius' ch. on 'Pythagoreans and Stoics
who, Believing in the Immortality of the Soul, Foolishly Persuade a Volun-
tary Death' (*Divinae Institutiones* iii 18). Cleombrotus drowned himself after
an unwise reading of Plato's *Phaedo* (Lactantius, Migne vi 408; from
Callimachus, *Epigrams* xxv), while Empedocles' motive was to conceal his
own mortality (see, e.g., Horace, *De arte poetica* 464–6). Empedocles was
also an inhabitant of Dante's more dignified *Limbo patrum* (*Inf.* iv 138). See
Horrell 417–24, where it is argued that M. placed suicides in limbo on the
strength of Virgil's account of the regions of Hades nearest the threshold
(*Aen.* vi 426–39: 'those sad souls who in innocence wrought their own
death').   *single*: punning between 'individual' and 'celibate'.

Cleombrotus, and many more too long,
Embryos and idiots, eremites and friars
475   White, black and gray, with all their trumpery.
Here pilgrims roam, that strayed so far to seek
In Golgotha him dead, who lives in heaven;
And they who to be sure of Paradise
Dying put on the weeds of Dominic,
480   Or in Franciscan think to pass disguised;
They pass the planets seven, and pass the fixed,

iii *473. too long*] Bentley thought this 'deficiently expressed'; but it is surely a deliberate anacolouthon miming impatient negligence. Cp. *PR* ii 189.

iii *474-5*. M. here satirizes a Catholic tradition which consigned *idiots*, cretins and unbaptized infants to a much debated *limbo infantum*. The Franciscans maintained that this limbo was situated above the Earth, in a region of light.   *White*, etc.] The mendicant orders were quite usually specified by robe colour. Thus, 'white friar' meant Carmelite, 'black friar' Dominican and 'grey friar' Franciscan. The contemptuous juxtaposition of all three colours, however, ridicules the importance assigned to external trappings, and prepares for ll. 479f.   *eremites*] hermits; referring to the fourth of the four main orders: the Austin friars or Order of Friars Hermits.

iii *476-7. Golgotha*] The hill where Christ was crucified and buried (*John* xix 17 and 41). M. represents palmers as repeating the error of the disciples, before they learned of the resurrection (*Luke* xxiv 5f: 'Why seek ye the living among the dead? He is not here, but is risen').

iii *479-80*. Preparing for Satan's assumption of disguise in ll. 634 ff. Cp. *Inf.* xxvii 67-84, where Dante tells how Guido da Montefeltro hoped to get into heaven by virtue of Franciscan weeds, but found to his cost that absolution without repentance is vain. The practice was not uncommon: see Horrell 419 and Huizinga 184.

iii *481-3*. In order of proximity to earth, the spheres passed are: the seven planetary spheres; the eighth sphere, containing the *fixed* stars; the ninth, *crystalline sphere*; and the tenth sphere, the *first moved* or *primum mobile*. *balance*] A punning reference both to the sign Libra, the Scales, and to the 'libration' or balance-like movement of the Firmament in relation to the Crystalline. This trepidation of the sphere of the fixed stars, together with the Alfonsine calendrical precession, composed equinoctial precession in the modern sense. Libra measures or *weighs* trepidation, because the first point in the sign (as distinct from the constellation) Libra is the equinoctial point, the point of reference for the measurement. On the 'foolishness' of the speculative and much-discussed theory of trepidation, see Dreyer 279. The medieval state of the theory is lucidly explained in Price 104-6, while Renaissance developments are discussed in Fletcher ii 317-18 and Svendsen 54-7. Copernicus still believed that an irregular trepidation accounted for equinoctial precession (see Johnson 110f, Dreyer 329f and Rosen 45f), but the theory was exploded by Brahe, who showed the irregularities to be

And that crystalline sphere whose balance weighs
The trepidation talked, and that first moved;
And now Saint Peter at heaven's wicket seems
485   To wait them with his keys, and now at foot
Of heaven's ascent they lift their feet, when lo
A violent cross wind from either coast
Blows them transverse ten thousand leagues awry
Into the devious air; then might ye see
490   Cowls, hoods and habits with their wearers tossed
And fluttered into rags, then relics, beads,
Indulgences, dispenses, pardons, bulls,
The sport of winds: all these upwhirled aloft
Fly o'er the backside of the world far off
495   Into a limbo large and broad, since called
The Paradise of Fools, to few unknown
Long after, now unpeopled, and untrod;
All this dark globe the fiend found as he passed,
And long he wandered, till at last a gleam
500   Of dawning light turned thitherward in haste
His travelled steps; far distant he descries,
Ascending by degrees magnificent
Up to the wall of heaven a structure high,
At top whereof, but far more rich appeared

observational. On the importance of the Balance symbol in *PL*, see below,
iv 997–1004*n*.

iii *482. crystalline*] Stressed on the second syllable.

iii *484. wicket*] A 'low' word underlining the satire on the Romanist doc-
trine that St Peter controls the keys of heaven: a doctrine based on an alle-
gorization of *Matt.* xvi 19 which Protestants thought to be foolish. ll. 505–
22 is meant to show that in reality heaven's gate is not such as a man could
ever control. Cp. *Lycidas* 110f.

iii *490–3.* W. J. Grace, *SP* lii (1955), finds several echoes of *Anat. of Melan.*
III iv 1 ii, where, e.g., Burton speaks of false prophets deluding the silly
multitude who 'are apt to be carried about by the blast of every wind'.

iii *492. dispenses*] dispensations. A dispensation was an exemption from a
solemn obligation, by licence of an ecclesiastical dignitary, especially the
Pope.   *pardons*] absolutions.

iii *493.* In Virgil, *Aen.* vi 74f it is the Sibyl's pronouncements that are *ludibria
ventis*. On the association of winds with limbo, see Horrell 416.

iii *494. backside*] the dark hemisphere of the *primum mobile*, furthest from
heaven and the 'glimmering air' of ll. 428f and 499.

iii *495. limbo*] fringe region.

iii *496.* Then as now, 'fool's paradise' was a proverbial idiom.

iii *501. travelled*] experienced in travel; but cp. also Ital. *travagliato*, tired.

iii *502. degrees*] steps.

505 The work as of a kingly palace gate
    With frontispiece of diamond and gold
    Embellished, thick with sparkling orient gems
    The portal shone, inimitable on earth
    By model, or by shading pencil drawn.
510 The stairs were such as whereon Jacob saw
    Angels ascending and descending, bands
    Of guardians bright, when he from Esau fled
    To Padan-Aram in the field of Luz,
    Dreaming by night under the open sky,
515 And waking cried, *This is the gate of heaven.*

iii *506–7. frontispiece*] Either a decorated entrance or (more probably) a
pediment over the gate. Cp. the gem-studded New Jerusalem of *Tob.*
xiii 16, as well as Ovid's description of the portico of the sun's palace, carved
by Mulciber (*Met.* ii 1–19).   *orient*] 'brilliant, lustrous, resplendent'
(a term applied to gems, especially pearls); perhaps also 'like the rising sun'.
In *Rev.* xxi 21 'the twelve gates' of the New Jerusalem 'were twelve pearls'.
iii *508.* In fact Jacob's Ladder had for long been a standard subject in sacred
iconography (see Didron ii 271, 350). There is even a portrayal of it – cer-
tainly no exception to M.'s generalisation – in Fuller, *Pisgah-sight*, map to II
xii.
iii *510–15.* The unregenerate Jacob was terrified by the vision of a ladder
reaching to heaven, just after he had cheated Esau out of his father's blessing
(*Gen.* xxvii–xxviii). The experience awed him into belief and a vow to the
Lord. Jacob's ladder was often interpreted as a symbol of ascesis through
contemplation – the sense in which the image is used in *Para.* xxi. (At the
ladder's foot Dante is overwhelmed by a terrible cry of execration at the
corruption of the Church.) Here it implies that entrance to heaven is by
repentance and devotion and meditation on created nature (see 516–17n),
not by Peter's keys. The relevance of the simile to Satan's situation is usually
missed. Satan like Jacob has fled retribution and is at a parting of the ways
where he could still repent. And there is also a counterpart to Jacob's vision;
for Satan is about to contemplate 'all this world at once' (ll. 542f). The simile
is by no means one in which tenor and vehicle are dissimilar (as Ricks 127f
holds); though it is true that Satan will go on to choose deeper damnation,
Jacob to repent.
iii *511. Angels . . . descending*] The formula used in *Gen.* xxviii and *John* i 51.
iii *513.* We would put comma after *Padan-Aram*, not after *Luz*. Jacob was
fleeing to Aram (Syria); it was Bethel, where he stopped and dreamed,
that 'was called Luz at the first' (*Gen.* xxviii 19). Comma after *Luz* may be
error; but the early edns often have an apparently unnecessary comma at
the end of a line.
iii *515.* Following the punctuation of *Ed I. Ed II* omits full stop after *heaven.*
Cp. *Gen.* xxviii 17: 'And he was afraid, and said, How dreadful is this place!
this is none other but the house of God, and this is the gate of heaven.'

>   Each stair mysteriously was meant, nor stood
>   There always, but drawn up to heaven sometimes
>   Viewless, and underneath a bright sea flowed
>   Of jasper, or of liquid pearl, whereon
> 520   Who after came from earth, sailing arrived,
>   Wafted by angels, or flew o'er the lake
>   Rapt in a chariot drawn by fiery steeds.
>   The stairs were then let down, whether to dare
>   The fiend by easy ascent, or aggravate
> 525   His sad exclusion from the doors of bliss.
>   Direct against which opened from beneath,
>   Just o'er the blissful seat of Paradise,
>   A passage down to the earth, a passage wide,
>   Wider by far than that of after-times
> 530   Over Mount Sion, and, though that were large,
>   Over the Promised Land to God so dear,
>   By which, to visit oft those happy tribes,
>   On high behests his angels to and fro
>   Passed frequent, and his eye with choice regard
> 535   From Paneas the fount of Jordan's flood

iii *516–17.* Jacob's ladder had been identified with Homer's golden chain linking the universe to Jupiter (see ii 1051*n*) in Jean Bodin, *Heptaplomeres*, ed. Noack (Paris 1857) 23. Each could be interpreted as a hierarchical *scala naturae* or generative sequence, extending 'from the supreme God even to the bottomest dregs of the universe' (Macrobius, *In somn. Scip.* I xiv 15). In view of ll. 595–612 below, it is of interest that Jacob's ladder was sometimes also used as a symbol for the alchemist's ascesis of purification; see, e.g., Caron 20.   *stair*] step, degree.   *mysteriously*] as an arcane mystery; symbolically.

iii *518–19. sea*] The 'water above the firmament', outside the universe and flowing around the gate of heaven: see iii Argument; vii 271*n*, 619*n*; also *Rev.* iv 6 ('a sea of glass').   *jasper*] see 363–4*n*.

iii *521–2.* The beggar Lazarus was carried off by angels when he died (*Luke* xvi 22), and Elijah by a 'chariot of fire, and horses of fire' (2 *Kings* ii 11: cp. *PR* ii 16f); but the mention of *sailing* more specifically recalls Dante's fine image of a swift angel-powered craft, in *Purg.* ii. Cp. *Prae E* 47–50.

iii *523–5.* Or perhaps to tempt the reader to fall into the satanic point of view ironically reflected in these conjectures?

iii *530.* For Zion as a holy place, see i 10–11*nn* and 386, and iii 30f.

iii *534. eye*] An additional subject of *Passed.*   *choice*] careful, accurate.

iii *535–7. Paneas*] A later Greek name for Dan; not the city of Dan, but the spring of the same name, 'the easternmost fountain of Jordan' (Fuller, *Pisgah-sight* IV i 12).   *Beersaba*] A.V. Beersheba (for M.'s preference for Septuag. and Vulg. 's' see i 397–9*n*); the southern limit of Canaan, as Dan

To Beersaba, where the Holy Land
Borders on Aegypt and the Arabian shore;
So wide the opening seemed, where bounds were set
To darkness, such as bound the ocean wave.
540 Satan from hence now on the lower stair
That scaled by steps of gold to heaven gate
Looks down with wonder at the sudden view
Of all this world at once. As when a scout
Through dark and desert ways with peril gone
545 All night; at last by break of cheerful dawn
Obtains the brow of some high-climbing hill,
Which to his eye discovers unaware
The goodly prospect of some foreign land
First-seen, or some renowned metropolis
550 With glistering spires and pinnacles adorned,
Which now the rising sun gilds with his beams.
Such wonder seized, though after heaven seen,
The spirit malign, but much more envy seized,
At sight of all this world beheld so fair.
555 Round he surveys, and well might, where he stood

was the northern. 'From Dan even to Beersheba' is a common formula:
see, e.g., *Judges* xx 1.
iii 538–9. The darkness meant is of course that of chaos; though the many
links with the preceding line (*borders* with *bounds*, *ocean wave* with *shore*)
adumbrate a secondary, metaphorical sense: the darkness of pagan ignorance,
bounded by the borders of the Holy Land. Cp. *Job* xxviii 3: 'He setteth an
end to darkness.'
iii 542–51. 'An image that exactly conveys the effect produced by the poem
itself, a solid and intricate thing that can be seen as a whole' (MacCaffrey
50). On the moral significance of panoramic visions in *PL* as images of
order, see *ibid*. 68. The description of heaven's gate that precedes this pan-
optic vision of the universe is based on Ovid's description of the sun's
palace portico, which was itself a symbol of cosmos (see Heninger 315).
Regarded as *scala naturae*, the cosmos leads up to heaven.
iii 546. *Obtains*] reaches, occupies.
iii 552. *though . . . seen*] even after having seen heaven's wonders. The same
Latin construction that is imitated at i 573.
iii 555–61. It requires some effort to grasp the details of Satan's astronomi-
cally sophisticated vantage-point, as he stands at the passage through the
primum mobile (l. 540). Since the celestial poles mark for him points of ex-
treme separation on the interior of the shell of the universe (ll. 560f), it
follows that he is situated on the celestial equator, which before the Fall was
also the ecliptic (see x 668ff). Next, since *the fleecy star* Aries is receding
Beyond the horizon, i.e., setting behind the earth, Satan is apparently in the
portion of the ecliptic exactly opposite, namely Libra. *from . . . Libra* he

> So high above the circling canopy
> Of night's extended shade; from eastern point
> Of Libra to the fleecy star that bears

looks west to Aries along the 'length' of the universe, which is lying, as it were, on its side. (The north and south poles are the extreme points of *breadth*.) Now, it was commonly believed that the world was created at the vernal equinox (e.g. Dante, *Inf.* i 38f; for the authorities, see below, iv 268*n*; also Riccioli ii 232), so that the sun would now be in Aries. (This is explicitly confirmed at x 329: 'the sun in Aries rose'.) Hence Satan, in the opposite sign Libra, stands *above the circling canopy / Of night's extended shade* in a very precise sense. The sun is on the other side of earth, and Satan is just *above* the Earth's apparently circular shadow. Since Satan is also at the moment *just o'er* Paradise (l. 527), it follows that there it is now the critical hour of midnight – the same hour as that of his more cautious return at ix 58.

This elaborate topographia establishes an association between Satan and the portion of the firmament designated by Libra: an association that is of some importance throughout the poem. Not only is Libra opposite the sun (cp. Satan's avoidance of the sun, by keeping to the dark side of the earth, in ix 63–6), but it also contains the head of the Serpent constellation (Anguis). For the poem's most prominent piece of Serpent and Scales imagery, see iv 997–1015; for other appearances of the cosmic Serpent, ii 709, x 328. Note that Satan's entering the universe at the head of the serpent and leaving it at the tail has a correlate in the portrayal of Satan's character, which is at first alluring, then disgusting. According to a tradition that went back to Bede (see Williams 116) the serpent had the face of an attractive virgin.

iii 556–7. *canopy*] Usually an image for the whole sky; cp. *Hamlet* II ii 318–21: 'this most excellent canopy, the air . . . this brave o'erhanging firmament, this majestical roof fretted with golden fire'. Here it means the part of the heavens in the shadow of earth. It is midnight at Eden directly beneath, and from Satan's point of view earth is almost entirely dark and casts a conical shadow up towards his feet. The effect of foreshortening, however, is to flatten this long cone and make it look circular. Note, however, that the *canopy* or baldachin over a throne (*OED* s.v. *Canopy* 1) was often conical in shape.   *circling*] A pun: the shade encircles or forms a circle round Satan; but it also revolves in a circular orbit. (Note that the shade revolves irrespectively of whether the system followed is geocentric or heliocentric; in the former case the motion will be diurnal, in the latter annual.) Dramatic perspective such as this, based on a sophisticated optics, was often a feature of Baroque visual art.

iii 557–8. *Libra* is *eastern* because longitude on the celestial sphere was measured from west to east from the vernal equinoctial point in Aries. Strictly speaking this is a dramatic irony or prolepsis; for there is no vernal equinoctial point until after the Fall, when the ecliptic plane is inclined with respect to the equatorial (see x 651–706*n*, 668–80*n*). ˙

iii 558–9. Aries and Andromeda are immediately adjacent constellations,

Andromeda far off Atlantic seas
560   Beyond the horizon; then from pole to pole
He views in breadth, and without longer pause
Down right into the world's first region throws
His flight precipitant, and winds with ease
Through the pure marble air his oblique way
565   Amongst innumerable stars, that shone
Stars distant, but nigh hand seemed other worlds,
Or other worlds they seemed, or happy isles,
Like those Hesperian gardens famed of old,

which would go behind the earth together. (Note that in the prelapsarian universe constellations and signs need not be distinguished.) Qvarnström suggests that Andromeda may be singled out for mention because the mythological Andromeda was threatened by a dragon.

iii *560–1.* The poles referred to are celestial, not terrestrial (as Empson[2] 155 apparently takes them to be); just as *world's* in l. 562 refers to the universe as a whole. Turning the universe on its side, as M. does when he makes the polar axis measure *breadth*, is a tour de force of imagination. The Biblical authority is Job xxxviii 18, 'Hast thou perceived the breadth of the earth?'

iii *562–7.* Cp. Raphael's similar descent 'between worlds and worlds' in v 266–70.

iii *562. the world's first region*] Not one of the three regions of the earth's atmosphere (see i 515–16*n*) that lay below the fiery element, but a fourth layer, fatal to mortals, reaching up to the Firmament and beyond. See Svendsen 88, and cp. xii 76f below.

iii *564. marble*] 'smooth as marble' (a Latinism; cp., e.g., Virgil, *Aen.* vi 729, *marmoreo ... aequore*); perhaps also 'sparkling, glistening, gleaming' (cp. Gk μαρμάρεος). Cp. Shakespeare, Othello III iii 461, 'by yond marble heaven' (though there the image may be one of permanence).

iii *565–71.* M. introduces the idea of life on other worlds on a great many occasions: cp. ll. 459, 670; v 263; vii 621; viii 140–58 and 175. There was an extensive seventeenth-century literature concerning plurality of worlds, and most astronomers accepted the more limited idea of a plurality of inhabited globes within the solar system. See Nicolson[2]; Rajan 153; Lovejoy 108–42 *passim*; and Bernard Le Bovier de Fontenelle, *Entretiens sur la pluralité des mondes,* ed. R. Shackleton (Oxford 1955). 'Satan's voyage through Chaos is one of the great "cosmic voyages" of a period that sent imaginary mariners to the moon and planets in search of other worlds and other men' (Nicolson[3] 165). The space-travel element is complicated, however, by an allusion to the 'true earth' of *Phaedo* 114B–C, which is placed in the 'broad fields of the sky' among the *Hesperian gardens* in *Comus* 977ff.

iii *568–9.* The gardens where the Hesperides (Atlantides) unsuccessfully guarded apples entrusted to them by Jupiter were by Hesiod located beyond the ocean (cp. l. 559, 'far off Atlantic seas'). M. perhaps glances at the

Fortunate fields, and groves and flowery vales,
570 Thrice happy isles, but who dwelt happy there
He stayed not to inquire: above them all
The golden sun in splendour likest heaven
Allured his eye: thither his course he bends
Through the calm firmament; but up or down
575 By centre, or eccentric, hard to tell,
Or longitude, where the great luminary
Aloof the vulgar constellations thick,
That from his lordly eye keep distance due,
Dispenses light from far; they as they move

much-discussed question whether inhabitants of other planets were 'in-fected with Adam's sin' (John Wilkins, *cit.* Lovejoy 109); though the pro-leptic allusion to our own Fall might sufficiently account for the passage.

iii *570. happy isles*] Recalling the Isles of the Blessed of Greek myth, where favoured mortals passed without dying. Cp. viii 631f.

iii *571–3*. The sun is *above* the stars in splendour, but below many of them, of course, in space.

iii *573–6*. A difficult passage, probably because it combines cosmological alternatives with alternatives in respect of Satan's route. He can either take a collision course across the universe, travelling in a centric (*centre*) orbit such as the central meridian, or an *eccentric* orbit; or he can pursue the sun round the ecliptic, through a western *longitude*. What makes the course *hard to tell* is presumably uncertainty as to the proper terms for a description: M. scrupulously avoids accepting any single astronomical model as authoritative. For a similar avoidance, see iv 592–7. Here the sun or the earth may be at the centre of the universe; or neither. For M. would be familiar with current speculations whether the universe had any centre, or whether the stars are scattered 'without any system or common centre . . . like so many islands in an immense sea' (Bacon 683; see Lovejoy 109, and cp. 567 above).

iii *575. centre*] centric, a circle or orbit with the earth (or sun) at its centre; as distinct from an *eccentric*, a circle with the earth (sun) not at its centre. Cp. viii 83: 'the sphere / With centric and eccentric scribbled o'er'. Ec-centric orbits were postulated, to account for inequalities in the motions of the sun and planets, both by Ptolemaic and Copernican astronomers.

iii *576. longitude*] Not a line of longitude, but a distance (measured by degrees of arc) along the ecliptic (*OED* s.v. *Longitude* 4).

iii *577. Aloof*] apart from.

iii *578*. For the eye of heaven as an Orphic description of the sun, see Fowler 74; for a common symbolic interpretation of the image–God's omni-presence–see Wind 179f, 186f.

iii *579–81*. The cosmic dance is a favourite idea of M.'s; cp. v 178, vii 374, viii 125 and *Comus* 112. At v 617ff and ix 103 a correspondence between the cosmic and the celestial dance is asserted (see Rajan 151, Spaeth 43–5 and

580   Their starry dance in numbers that compute
          Days, months, and years, towards his all-cheering lamp
          Turn swift their various motions, or are turned
          By his magnetic beam, that gently warms
          The universe, and to each inward part
585   With gentle penetration, though unseen,
          Shoots invisible virtue even to the deep:
          So wondrously was set his station bright.
          There lands the fiend, a spot like which perhaps
          Astronomer in the sun's lucent orb
590   Through his glazed optic tube yet never saw.
          The place he found beyond expression bright,
          Compared with aught on earth, metal or stone;

158f). Treated elaborately in Sir John Davies's *Orchestra* (1596), the notion goes back ultimately to the 'choric dances' of the stars in Plato, *Timaeus* 40 C. The generation of the day, the month and the year is described in an earlier passage of the same dialogue: God created the planets 'for the determining and preserving of the numbers of time' (*Tim*. 38C). Cp. also *Gen*. i 14: 'And God said, Let there be lights in the firmament of the heaven to divide the day from the night; and let them be for signs, and for seasons, and for days, and years'.

iii *580. starry*] sarry *Ed I* is almost certainly an error, though the form did occur as an old variant of 'savoury' ('spiritually delightful and edifying'). *numbers*] rhythms.

iii *583–6*. The influence or *virtue* of the sun was supposed to penetrate even under the earth's surface; see v 301–3, vi 472–83n, and Svendsen 67. Kepler's theory that the planets are driven round by the sun's *magnetic* force was 'the first serious attempt to interpret the mechanism of the solar system' (Dreyer 397).

iii *586*. Probably to be scanned with *even* as a stressed monosyllable.

iii *588–90*. To appreciate the simile one needs to know that the spots on the sun were thought by some to impair its perfection and incorruptibility (see Riccioli i 97). The first descriptions of the spots had been published by Fabricius and then Galileo (*Letters on the Solar Spots* (Rome 1613)).

iii *590. optic tube*] Not poetic diction.

iii *591*. On the description of the sun that follows, Broadbent 165–8 comments that it accomplishes 'the contrast with Hell and Paradise that Heaven only suggested'. He finds M.'s sun poetry out of place, even if magnificently, in a poem where God the source of celestial light is also presented. But the Neoplatonic cult of the sun had long been assimilated to the Christian mysticism of light. Within the tradition of Christian Platonism to which *PL* belongs it is natural for dignity and splendour to be attributed to so important an image of emanation as the sun.

iii *592. metal*] medal *Eds I and II*. The case for retaining the original reading would be that the brightest stones on earth were cut precious stones, so

> Not all parts like, but all alike informed
> With radiant light, as glowing iron with fire;
> 595　If metal, part seemed gold, part silver clear;
> If stone, carbuncle most or chrysolite,
> Ruby or topaz, to the twelve that shone
> In Aaron's breastplate, and a stone besides

that the other member of the pair may be presumed an artifact too. There is also the apt resemblance between the sun's disk and a bright burnished medal. The antithesis of ll. 595f, however, seems to count decisively in favour of emending.

iii *594–605.* In Scripture, Aaron's twelve jewels simply represent the twelve tribes of Israel. M.'s numerology, however, also mimes the alchemic process. For he names one chemic stone (l. 600), two stages in the *magnum opus* (ll. 603f), three metals (ll. 594f) and four stones (ll. 596f); thus representing the 1, 2, 3, 4 of the *tetractys* in its triangular form. As the fountain of nature, the creative *tetractys* was often identified with the method and goal of the alchemist's (and the regenerate Christian's) ascesis; see, e.g., Caron 91, 138, and the title-page to Dee's *Monas hieroglyphica* (Antwerp 1564, tr. and ed. C. H. Josten in *Ambix* xii (1964) 84–221).

iii *594. With*] Which *Ed I*, wrongly.

iii *596–8.* In *Exod.* xxviii 15–20 Aaron's foursquare 'breastplate of judgment' is described as having four rows of stones, of which the first row 'shall be a sardius [marginal gloss: 'ruby'], a topaz, and a carbuncle'.   *Chrysolite*] Replaces diamond (not beryl, as Newton and Verity have it) in the fourth row, in the Vulgate version.   *to the twelve*] i.e., 'etc., until the twelve are completed'. All the stones named were associated with the sun in contemporary mineralogical theory, and were supposed to shine even in the dark; see Duncan, Svendsen 29f, Broadbent 165; also George F. Kunz, *The Curious Lore of Precious Stones* (New York 1938) 143–75, 347. Mystical interpretations gained support from the fact that the same stones occur in the walls of the New Jerusalem (see *Rev.* xxi 19f).

  Aaron was traditionally the type of the true priest, who had 'put on' Christ, and so wore 'light and perfections on the breast' (see Tuve 154): a holy disguise that contrasts ironically with Satan's disguise as a young cherub. Aaron's vestments had recently been elaborately interpreted by Henry More in his *Conjectura cabbalistica* (1662) 120f as a symbol of the universe.

iii *598–601. a stone besides*] The 'urim' contained in Aaron's breastplate (*Exod.* xxviii 30). It was *imagined . . . oft . . . elsewhere* because it was identified by many alchemical theorists (such as Joachim Tancke) with the philosopher's stone itself. The (lunar) thummim could transform base metals to silver, but the (solar) urim could transform them to gold (see Qvarnström, and cp. l. 595 above). In the Christian alchemical tradition, the philosopher's stone was regarded as a symbol of Christ's regenerating grace; see, e.g., Benlowes, *Theophila* (1652) i 90 ('grace . . . the chemic-stone') and ix 66.

Imagined rather oft than elsewhere seen,
600   That stone, or like to that which here below
Philosophers in vain so long have sought,
In vain, though by their powerful art they bind
Volatile Hermes, and call up unbound
In various shapes old Proteus from the sea,
605   Drained through a limbeck to his native form.
What wonder then if fields and regions here
Breathe forth elixir pure, and rivers run
Potable gold, when with one virtuous touch

iii *601–5.* The principal meaning is that alchemists have sought the philo-
sopher's stone in vain, however capable they may be of the intermediate
stage of making 'philosophic mercury'. The Proteus of mythology was
anciently interpreted as matter, because of his ability to assume a variety
of forms (see Wind, Index s.v. *Proteus*). Here, however, the reference is
specifically to the primal matter of creation: cp. v 472f, 'first matter . . .
Indued with various forms'. In alchemy, prime matter or philosophic
mercury was the essence or soul or ordinary *volatile* mercury, made by
binding it (removing the volatile principle air) and by freeing it from the
liquid principle. But the *native* or prime matter had then to be acted upon
by the philosopher's stone to produce the qualities desired (see *EB* i 521;
Caron 156, 162).

The passage can be applied to Satan in a variety of ways. (1) Satan is like
the alchemists, in that his deceptions fail to accomplish more than a partial
purification. Grace (the philosopher's stone) eludes him; yet without it
he can only imitate his native unfallen brightness externally (cp. Svendsen
126f). (2) Satan is like the volant deceptive Mercury, god of disguises.
In the purification of man's soul, the first step must be the binding of Satan.
(One of mercury's alchemical names was the serpent. Note, too, that some
astronomers thought sun-spots were caused by the planet Mercury.) (3) Satan
is like Proteus in that he is *unbound* from the sea of fire, suffers the meta-
morphoses of passion, and is a wily, experienced politician (Conti, *Mytho-
log.* viii 8 *ad fin.*).

iii *603. Volatile*] Spelt *Volatil*; stressed on the second syllable.   *limbeck*]
the alembic or retort in which the mercury was distilled.

iii *606. here*] Primarily, 'here in the sun'; though secondarily it may be said
of terrestrial rivers that one touch of sunshine turns them to gold. The am-
biguity runs from l. 606 to l. 610.

iii *607–8. elixir*] Any medium, such as the philosopher's stone, that would
transmute base metals to gold. The 'elixir of long life', or *potable* [liquid]
gold, was closely identified with the goal of the alchemists. According to
Bernard of Treviso it was a 'reduction of the philosopher's stone to mer-
curial water' (Caron 168; see also Svendsen 125).

iii *608–12. arch-chemic*] Because it was believed that the sun's influence
penetrated beneath the earth, and there, by an extremely slow process,

The arch-chemic sun so far from us remote
610   Produces with terrestrial humour mixed
Here in the dark so many precious things
Of colour glorious and effect so rare?
Here matter new to gaze the devil met
Undazzled, far and wide his eye commands,
615   For sight no obstacle found here, nor shade,
But all sunshine, as when his beams at noon
Culminate from the equator, as they now
Shot upward still direct, whence no way round
Shadow from body opaque can fall, and the air,
620   No where so clear, sharpened his visual ray
To objects distant far, whereby he soon
Saw within ken a glorious angel stand,
The same whom John saw also in the sun:
His back was turned, but not his brightness hid;
625   Of beaming sunny rays, a golden tiar
Circled his head, nor less his locks behind
Illustrious on his shoulders fledge with wings

generated precious stones. Cp. ll. 583–6, vi 447–81, and *Comus* 732–6; and
see Harry F. Robins, 'The Key to a Problem in Milton's *Comus*', *MLQ* xii
(1951) 422–8.   *humour*] moisture; see Dryden's note to *Annus Mirabilis*
st. 3: 'Precious Stones at first are Dew, condens'd and harden'd by the
warmth of the Sun.'

iii *613. gaze*] The transitive use was more or less confined to poetic
contexts.

iii *616–17.* A heavenly body is said to *culminate* when it reaches the highest,
meridian point of its apparent orbit. In the world as we know it, the sun
can culminate at the celestial equator only when it is at one of the equinoctial
points, where the ecliptic and the equator intersect. But before the sun went
astray from his true 'equinoctial road' at the Fall (x 668–91), equator and
ecliptic coincided; so that the disappearance of shadows was then a daily
occurrence. Elsewhere in *PL* noon symbolizes the time of divine judgment
(see ix 739*n*). Here, however, the continual noon on the solar surface also
expresses the sun's power over matter. For the Proteus of legend–unlike
the Proteus of 604 above–could not be called up at will, but had to be caught
when he emerged at noon (Homer, *Od.* iv). Thus, on the sun the prime matter
is continually available for creation.

iii *620. visual ray*] M. is probably utilizing the ancient theory of optics
according to which rays emanated from the eye onto the object seen. Cp.
SA 162f: 'inward light, alas, / Puts forth no visual beam.'

iii *623. Rev.* xix 17: 'I saw an angel standing in the sun.'

iii *625. tiar*] crown (poet.)

iii *627. illustrious*] lustrous, shining.   *fledge*] fledged, feathered.

> Lay waving round; on some great charge employed
> He seemed, or fixed in cogitation deep.
> 630 Glad was the spirit impure as now in hope
> To find who might direct his wandering flight
> To Paradise the happy seat of man,
> His journey's end and our beginning woe.
> But first he casts to change his proper shape,
> 635 Which else might work him danger or delay:
> And now a stripling cherub he appears,
> Not of the prime, yet such as in his face
> Youth smiled celestial, and to every limb
> Suitable grace diffused, so well he feigned;
> 640 Under a coronet his flowing hair
> In curls on either cheek played, wings he wore
> Of many a coloured plume sprinkled with gold,
> His habit fit for speed succinct, and held

iii *630. Ed* II and some copies of *Ed* I with uncorrected sheet have no point after *impure*; other copies of *Ed* I with corrected sheet have semicolon.

iii *634.* Discussing Satan's 'protean habit' of metamorphosis, Broadbent 106 remarks that 'all fluctuations of shape, changes of nature . . . are presented as evil, symptoms of the Fall itself.' Spenser had similarly expressed the multiplicity of evil in the metamorphoses of his Archimago; see Fowler 8. The immediate allusion is to 2 *Cor.* xi 13f: 'such are false apostles, deceitful workers, transforming themselves into the apostles of Christ. And no marvel; for Satan himself is transformed into an angel of light.'   *casts*] resolves.

iii *636–7.* Empson (59–61) finds the idea of a *stripling cherub* difficult, in view of our feeling (Satan's feeling?) that the angels are self-begot. He supposes that Satan has assumed the role of a newly promoted angel, to avoid suspicion: an ordinary angel would not be bothered to inspect the new creation 'but Uriel finds it natural for a promoted proletarian to be a busybody'. But M. more probably put 'stripling' merely because of the common iconographical representation of the cherub as a winged child. Satan's reason for preferring this particular disguise would be that the order of cherubim was supposed to excel in knowledge; so that in asking questions he is pursuing his proper vocation.   *Not of the prime*] 'not yet of the prime of life'; or, 'not one of the chief cherubim'.

iii *637–42.* Cp. Spenser's description of a young angel, in *F.Q.* II viii 5: 'a faire young man, / Of wondrous beautie, and of freshest yeares . . . / His snowy front curled with golden heares, / Like *Phoebus* face adornd with sunny rayes, / Divinely shone, and two sharpe winged sheares, / Decked with diverse plumes, like painted Jayes, / Were fixed at his backe, to cut his ayerie wayes.'

iii *643.* 'His clothing girt up' would be a possible sense. But M.'s angels are not normally clothed, so that the phrase probably means 'a uniform

Before his decent steps a silver wand.
645   He drew not nigh unheard, the angel bright,
Ere he drew nigh, his radiant visage turned,
Admonished by his ear, and straight was known
The archangel Uriel, one of the seven
Who in God's presence, nearest to his throne
650   Stand ready at command, and are his eyes
That run through all the heavens, or down to the
        earth
Bear his swift errands over moist and dry,
O'er sea and land: him Satan thus accosts.
    Uriel, for thou of those seven spirits that stand
655   In sight of God's high throne, gloriously bright,
The first art wont his great authentic will

suitable and prepared for speed'. Wings (l. 641) were a distinctive mark of the cherub order.

iii *644. decent*] graceful, as well as 'in accordance with propriety'.

iii *648–61*. In *Zech*. iv a visionary seven-branched candlestick is interpreted as 'the eyes of the Lord, which run to and fro through the whole earth' (cp. *Rev*. v 6). The seven principal angels are mentioned also in *Tob*. xii 15; *Rev*. viii 2; and *Rev*. i 4: 'Grace be unto you, and peace, from him which is, and which was, and which is to come; and from the seven Spirits which are before his throne.'

iii *648. Uriel*] 'Light of God'. The name is not Biblical, though it occurs in the apocryphal *2 Esdras*. But in Jewish and cabbalistic tradition Uriel was prominent (together with Michael, Gabriel and Raphael) as one of the great archangels who rule the four corners of the world. As the angel of the south, Uriel 'rules in the power of the Meridian Sunne' (Henry More, *cit.* West 208). While the general notion of angels or 'intelligences' guiding the spheres is a very familiar one, there has been much speculation as to M.'s authority for assigning Uriel to the sun. It has been suggested, e.g., that he drew on esoteric rabbinical lore. No doubt the system was originally esoteric; but Uriel had been assigned to Sol in a textbook as standard as Valeriano's *Hieroglyphica*: 'Greek theology calls Michael's power in God *Venus*; Gabriel it calls *Mars*; and Raphael *Jupiter*, to whom especially the throne of judgment was ascribed. Sol, the fourth, having both feminine and masculine power, the manifest origin of all generation, is named in Hebrew both *Uriel* and *Adonis*' (549). The context, an important one for the interpretation of *PL*, is an account of the cosmic chariot of God; see l. 656*n*, iv 549–50*n*, vi 749–59*n*, vii 197ff.

iii *653. Ed II* and some copies of *Ed I* with uncorrected sheet have semicolon after *accosts*, erroneously. Other copies of *Ed I* with corrected sheet have full stop.

iii *656*. Uriel was *first* of the angels in a very special sense. The chariot which Solomon constructed in *Song* iii 9f was interpreted as a type of the New

Interpreter through highest heaven to bring,
Where all his sons thy embassy attend;
And here art likeliest by supreme decree
660 Like honour to obtain, and as his eye
To visit oft this new creation round;
Unspeakable desire to see, and know
All these his wondrous works, but chiefly man,
His chief delight and favour, him for whom
665 All these his works so wondrous he ordained,
Hath brought me from the choirs of cherubim
Alone thus wandering. Brightest seraph tell
In which of all these shining orbs hath man
His fixed seat, or fixed seat hath none,
670 But all these shining orbs his choice to dwell;
That I may find him, and with secret gaze,
Or open admiration him behold
On whom the great creator hath bestowed
Worlds, and on whom hath all these graces poured;
675 That both in him and all things, as is meet,
The universal maker we may praise;
Who justly hath driven out his rebel foes
To deepest hell, and to repair that loss
Created this new happy race of men
680 To serve him better: wise are all his ways.

Covenant, which Christ established to carry believers to heaven. Now the
angels were not only related to this symbolic chariot as its parts (l. 648n),
but their names were also associated with the Heb. word for chariot,
argaman, in the following manner: *Prima litera fit Uriel, per A enim illi
scribunt. Sequenti R, Raphael. Tertia G, Gabriel. Quarta M, Michael*
(Valeriano 549). Thus Uriel, the first good angel to appear in the poem, is
also the first in the chariot of God. But the lines could also be read in simpler
senses. As the 'sharpest-sighted spirit' (l. 691), Uriel would naturally have
most insight as the interpreter of God's will; while his charge the sun had
an obvious primacy among the planets.
iii *658*. 'Satan when disguised as a good angel gets a cosy piety into his speech
chiefly by packing it with *all's*' (Empson[3] 103).   *sons*] angels; cp. *Job
ii 1.   attend*] await.
iii *664. favour*] object of favour; first post-medieval instance in *OED*, in
this sense.
iii *668–70*. As Broadbent 165 notes, Satan here echoes M.'s own antimeta-
bole of ll. 565–7.
iii *670*. The form of Satan's question shows that he would like to know
whether any of creation is out of bounds to man.
iii *671–2*. Satan echoes the words of Herod enquiring after the whereabouts
of the second Adam (*Matt.* ii 8).

So spake the false dissembler unperceived;
For neither man nor angel can discern
Hypocrisy, the only evil that walks
Invisible, except to God alone,
685   By his permissive will, through heaven and earth:
And oft though wisdom wake, suspicion sleeps
At wisdom's gate, and to simplicity
Resigns her charge, while goodness thinks no ill
Where no ill seems: which now for once beguiled
690   Uriel, though regent of the sun, and held
The sharpest sighted spirit of all in heaven;
Who to the fradulent impostor foul
In his uprightness answer thus returned.
Fair angel, thy desire which tends to know
695   The works of God, thereby to glorify
The great work-master, leads to no excess
That reaches blame, but rather merits praise
The more it seems excess, that led thee hither
From thy empyreal mansion thus alone,
700   To witness with thine eyes what some perhaps
Contented with report hear only in heaven:
For wonderful indeed are all his works,
Pleasant to know, and worthiest to be all
Had in remembrance always with delight;

iii *681. unperceived*] undetected, not seen through.

iii *682.* Cp. ll. 705–7*n* below. M. is always careful to avoid angelolatry, and perhaps for this reason he makes his good angels often unsuccessful, even unheroic.

iii *685. permissive will*] Distinguished from God's positive will, which permits only good. See i 209–13*n*.

iii *694–6.* The conditions for blamelessness in a desire for knowledge are (1) that it shall be knowledge of the right things (God's works); and (2) that it shall be sought for the right reason (to glorify God). In view of (2), the clash between Uriel's permissiveness and the prohibition of iv 515 is only apparent.

iii *696–8.* It was a doctrine of Renaissance Neoplatonism 'that no extreme in the contemplation of God and his works could violate Aristotle's principle' of the virtuous mean (Hughes). Cp. Wind 53 on Ficino's doctrine of divine love: 'Only by looking towards the Beyond as the true goal of ecstasy can man become balanced in the present.'

iii *699. empyreal*] Stressed on the second syllable.   *mansion*] dwelling place.

iii *702–4.* Cp. *Ps.* cxi 2, 4: 'The works of the Lord are great, sought out of all them that have pleasure therein. . . . He hath made his wonderful works to be remembered.'

705   But what created mind can comprehend
      Their number, or the wisdom infinite
      That brought them forth, but hid their causes deep.
      I saw when at his word the formless mass,
      This world's material mould, came to a heap:
710   Confusion heard his voice, and wild uproar
      Stood ruled, stood vast infinitude confined;
      Till at his second bidding darkness fled,
      Light shone, and order from disorder sprung:
      Swift to their several quarters hasted then
715   The cumbrous elements, earth, flood, air, fire,
      And this ethereal quintessence of heaven

iii *705–7.* As Burden 110 notes, this implies that God keeps some knowledge secret even from the angels, and so makes it more reasonable that a similar reservation should be made in the case of man. In *De doctrina* i 9 (Columbia xv 107) the limitations of the angels' knowledge are indeed emphasised: 'The good angels do not look into all the secret things of God, as the Papists pretend. . . . there is much . . . of which they are ignorant.' Even Christ 'knows not all things absolutely; there being some secret purposes, the knowledge of which the Father has reserved to himself alone' (*ibid.* i 5; Columbia xiv 317).

iii *706–7.* Cp. *Prov.* iii 19 ('The Lord by wisdom hath founded the earth'), and see *Prov.* viii, where Wisdom's part in creation as the master-workman is described at length. The present passage prepares for Raphael's account of creation by the Word of God, in *PL* vii. On the relation between the Word and the Lady Wisdom of Proverbs, see Claude Chavasse, *The Bride of Christ* (1939), 45–8.

iii *708–15.* Uriel's excited reminiscence of creation is couched in traditional Christian-Platonic terms. According to this system, creation was not from the void, but from primal matter, whose initial chaos was ordered by the separation out of the four elements in interlocking layers (see, e.g., Plato, *Timaeus* 30A and 32B–C; Ovid, *Met.* i; Macrobius, *In somn. Scip.* I vi 23–40). From the time of Philo, the Platonic cosmology had been syncretized with that of *Genesis*, as it is here (with the *second bidding* of l. 712, cp. *Gen.* i 3).

iii *708.* Like Raphael, Uriel was one of the angels who witnessed creation (vii 197–205).

iii *709. mould*] substance. Cp. vii 356.

iii *710. Confusion*] Already personified, as one of Chaos' courtiers, at ii 966.

iii *716. ethereal quintessence*] Cp. vii 243f, 'light ethereal . . . quintessence'. Unlike the four cumbrous elements, the fifth element ether had no weight, and consequently formed a heaven above the atmosphere (see Ovid, *Met.* i 23, Macrobius, *In somn. Scip.* I xxii 5). The fullest contemporary treatment of light as a quasi-element was that of Bartholomew Keckermann: see Fletcher ii 191.   *this*] The demonstrative is in order because the sun on

Flew upward, spirited with various forms,
That rolled orbicular, and turned to stars
Numberless, as thou seest, and how they move;
720   Each had his place appointed, each his course,
The rest in circuit walls this universe.
Look downward on that globe whose hither side
With light from hence, though but reflected, shines;
That place is earth the seat of man, that light
725   His day, which else as the other hemisphere
Night would invade, but there the neighbouring moon
(So call that opposite fair star) her aid
Timely interposes, and her monthly round
Still ending, still renewing, through mid heaven;
730   With borrowed light her countenance triform
Hence fills and empties to enlighten the earth,
And in her pale dominion checks the night.
That spot to which I point is Paradise,

which Uriel stands is composed of ether; see ll. 718–19n.   quintessence]
Stressed on the first and third syllables, as was usual in the seventeenth cen-
tury.

iii *717*. 'Each several soul [God] assigned to one star . . . setting them each
as it were in a chariot' (Plato, *Timaeus* 41E).

iii *718–19*. The doctrine that the ether is especially adapted to circular or
orbicular motion, and that it is the substance of the stars, is Aristotelian
(*De caelo* 270b).

iii *721*. The remaining quintessence fills the celestial spaces above the atmos-
phere, forming a sphere that encloses the universe; see Lucretius, *De rerum
nat.* v 470.

iii *724–32*. Were it not for the sun's light, this hemisphere would be invaded
like the other. But there, though Night may *invade*, the moon's dominion
prevents her from conquering–a dramatic irony on Satan's invasion. In
Mythologiae iii 15 Conti gathers a great variety of reasons why the lunar
goddess should have been described by the ancients as *triformis* (she is Luna,
Diana and Hecate; she is Juno, Diana and Proserpina; she rules in heaven,
earth and hell; etc.). The only explanation strictly relevant here, however,
is that which traces the epithet to the moon's phases. Cp. *Prae E* 56f; Jonson,
The Masque of Queenes 273f ('*three-formed Starre* . . . to Whose triple Name');
and Shakespeare, *A Midsummer Night's Dream* V ii 14 ('triple Hecate's
team').

iii *729*. Some copies of *Ed I* have comma after *heaven*, no comma after *re-
newing*; perhaps correctly.

iii *731*. *Hence*] from the sun here.

iii *733*. Since Eden is now visible from the sun, it follows that Satan's
journey from the *primum mobile* has occupied at least the latter half of Eden's

Adam's abode, those lofty shades his bower.
735 Thy way thou canst not miss, me mine requires.
          Thus said, he turned, and Satan bowing low,
     As to superior spirits is wont in heaven,
     Where honour due and reverence none neglects,
     Took leave, and toward the coast of earth beneath,
740 Down from the ecliptic, sped with hoped success,
     Throws his steep flight in many an airy wheel,
     Nor stayed, till on Niphates' top he lights.

THE END OF THE THIRD BOOK

Paradise Lost

BOOK IV

The Argument

Satan now in prospect of Eden, and nigh the place where he must now attempt
the bold enterprise which he undertook alone against God and man, falls
into many doubts with himself, and many passions, fear, envy, and despair;
but at length confirms himself in evil, journeys on to Paradise, whose outward
prospect and situation is described, overleaps the bounds, sits in the shape of
a cormorant on the tree of life, as the highest in the garden to look about
him. The garden described; Satan's first sight of Adam and Eve; his wonder
at their excellent form and happy state, but with resolution to work their

night. See ll. 556–7n. We subsequently learn that the journey took twelve
hours; see iv Argument, 564 and Introduction, 'Chronology'.
iii 739. *coast*] side.
iii 740. *ecliptic*] Not, here, the apparent orbit of the sun round the celestial
sphere, but its actual path. See ll. 616–17n.   *sped with hoped success*] Seems
to refute the theory (Empson 61) that Uriel's account of creation convinced
Satan of his own creatureliness, and so threw him into the despair he ex-
presses in his Niphates speech. Unless, of course, the shock of the discovery
was delayed.
iii 741. *in*] some copies *Ed I, Errata* and *Ed II*; other copies *Ed I* have 'with'.
iii 742. It was from the *Niphates*, a mountain on the borders of Armenia and
Assyria (see iv 126), that the Tigris took its origin; see Strabo, Geog. XI
xii 4. And at ix 71 below Tigris is the name given to the river of Paradise
before it divides. There is no evidence for the interesting speculation that
Niphates may be the same mountain from which Adam later contemplates
the world, or on which Christ is tempted (xi 376–84).

fall; overhears their discourse, thence gathers that the tree of knowledge was forbidden them to eat of, under penalty of death; and thereon intends to found his temptation, by seducing them to transgress: then leaves them a while to know farther of their state by some other means. Mean while, Uriel descending on a sunbeam warns Gabriel, who had in charge the gate of Paradise, that some evil spirit had escaped the deep, and passed at noon by his sphere in the shape of a good angel down to Paradise, discovered after by his furious gestures in the mount. Gabriel promises to find him ere morning. Night coming on, Adam and Eve, discourse of going to their rest: their bower described; their evening worship. Gabriel drawing forth his bands of night-watch to walk the round of Paradise, appoints two strong angels to Adam's bower, lest the evil spirit should be there doing some harm to Adam or Eve sleeping; there they find him at the ear of Eve, tempting her in a dream, and bring him, though unwilling, to Gabriel; by whom questioned, he scornfully answers, prepares resistance, but hindered by a sign from heaven, flies out of Paradise.

> O for that warning voice, which he who saw
> The Apocalypse, heard cry in heaven aloud,
> Then when the dragon, put to second rout,
> Came furious down to be revenged on men,
> 5   *Woe to the inhabitants on earth!* that now,
> While time was, our first parents had been warned
> The coming of their secret foe, and scaped
> Haply so scaped his mortal snare; for now
> Satan, now first inflamed with rage, came down,
> 10 The tempter ere the accuser of mankind,
> To wreak on innocent frail man his loss
> Of that first battle, and his flight to hell;

iv *1–12.* The Revelation or *Apocalypse* of St John relates a vision of a second battle in heaven between Michael and *the dragon*, Satan. Then there was 'a loud voice saying in heaven Now is come salvation, and strength, and the kingdom of our God, and the power of his Christ: for the accuser of our brethren is cast down, which accused them before our God day and night.... Woe to the inhabiters of the earth and of the sea! for the devil is come down unto you, having great wrath, because he knoweth that he hath but a short time' (*Rev.* xii 7–12). M. wishes for the voice prophesying apocalyptic afflictions 'in order to raise the horror and attention of his reader' (Newton). M.'s wishing 'that Adam and Eve could have been warned by himself... shows he felt there was something inadequate about the warning of Raphael' (Empson 61f). Empson's inference is wrong, because Raphael's warning mission has yet to take place. The present passage may be regarded as a lead-in to the warnings both of Uriel and of Raphael.
iv *6. While time was*] Echoes *Rev.* xii 12 ('but a short time'); thus implying an analogy between the end of the prelapsarian world and the end of M.'s own world.   *first-parents*] *Ed I* omits hyphen.
iv *11. wreak*] avenge.

Yet not rejoicing in his speed, though bold,
Far off and fearless, nor with cause to boast,
15   Begins his dire attempt, which nigh the birth
Now rolling, boils in his tumultuous breast,
And like a devilish engine back recoils
Upon himself; horror and doubt distract
His troubled thoughts, and from the bottom stir
20   The hell within him, for within him hell
He brings, and round about him, nor from hell
One step no more than from himself can fly
By change of place: now conscience wakes despair
That slumbered, wakes the bitter memory
25   Of what he was, what is, and what must be
Worse; of worse deeds worse sufferings must ensue.
Sometimes towards Eden which now in his view
Lay pleasant, his grieved look he fixes sad,
Sometimes towards heaven and the full-blazing sun,

iv *13–19*. Empson 61–3 attributes Satan's *horror and doubt* to the overwhelming effect of the information he received from Uriel about the creativity of God; see iii 740*n*. But M.'s own explanation is to be preferred: that the imminence of the actual aggression–*nigh the birth*–causes him to shrink in horror.   *rolling*] moving on (*OED Roll* vb.² 14: used of time, and especially of cyclic periods).   *devilish engine*] the cannon devised by Satan in the war in heaven (vi 469–500); but playing also on *engine*='plot' (*OED* 3; cp. i 750 above). Like all devilish plots this one is redounding to the confusion of the plotter.

iv *20–3*. See i 255*n*, and cp. *Doctrine and Discipline* ii 3 (Yale ii 294): 'To banish for ever into a locall hell, whether in the aire or in the center, or in that uttermost and bottomlesse gulph of Chaos, deeper from holy blisse then the worlds diameter multiply'd, [the pagan authors] thought not a punishing so proper and proportionat for God to inflict, as to punish sinne with sinne.' Also Sir Thomas Browne, *Religio Medici* i 51: 'men speake too popularly who place it in those flaming mountains, which to grosser apprehensions represent Hell. The heart of man is the place the devill dwels in; I feele sometimes a Hell within my selfe', and Marlowe, *Doctor Faustus* (1616) ed. Greg, ll. 513–5: 'Hell hath no limits, nor is circumscrib'd, / In one selfe place: but where we are is hell, / And where hell is there must we ever be.'

iv *24*. Bentley objected to the notion of remembering the future; but it is clear that M. primarily means 'recollect' (cp. *memênto mori*). The passage seems also, however, to echo St Augustine's deep meditation on time in *Confess.* xi 28, so that M. may imply that Satan *can* only remember–there is for him, as we say, no future.

iv *25*. Cp. *SA* 22: 'what once I was, and what am now'.

iv *27–8*. The etymological meaning of *Eden* was well known in the seventeenth century to be 'pleasure, delight'.

30 Which now sat high in his meridian tower:
    Then much revolving, thus in sighs began.
    O thou that with surpassing glory crowned,
    Look'st from thy sole dominion like the God
    Of this new world; at whose sight all the stars
35 Hide their diminished heads; to thee I call,

iv *30. meridian tower*] The tower image is Virgilian: *Igneus aetherias iam Sol penetrarat in arces* (*Culex* 42). Noon, when the sun crosses the *meridian*, is throughout *PL* a critical time of judgment. The basis of the association is ultimately *Mal.* iv 1f: 'The day cometh, that shall burn as an oven. . . . But unto you that fear my name shall the Sun of righteousness arise.' This *Sol iustitiae* metaphor was sometimes given an astronomical development, whereby the central position of the sun at noon was specified: 'As the sun, when in the centre of his orbit, that is to say, at the midday point, is hottest, so shall Christ be when He shall appear in the centre of heaven and earth, that is to say, in Judgment' (Pierre Bersuire, *Dictionarium seu repertorium morale* (Nuremberg 1489), iii 194ʳ, *cit.* Panofsky 262). As Panofsky notes, this analogy depends on an 'equation of the astrological notion, *medium coeli*, with the theological notion, *medium coeli et terrae*, presumed to be the seat of the Judge'. The point is of thematic importance, in view of M.'s structural positioning of Christ the Sun of righteousness at the numerological centre of the whole poem (see vi 762*n*). For other instances of a symbolic noon, see iii 616–17*n*, ix 739*n*; and for Spenser's use of the image, see Fowler 67, 70. The present moment is critical for Satan, because he is on the point of beginning his 'dire attempt'.

iv *31. revolving*] pondering; as in *PR* i 185–'Musing and much revolving in his breast, / How best the mighty work he might begin'.

iv *32–41*. According to Edward Phillips, this passage was shown to him and some others 'several Years before the Poem was begun', when M. intended to write a tragedy on the Fall. The lines were 'designed for the very beginning of the said Tragedy' (Darbishire 72f and see Introduction, 'Composition'). A resemblance to the opening of Aeschylus' *Prometheus vinctus* is sometimes discovered, but consists in little more than that both have an address to the sun. The whole speech (ll. 32–113) is intensely dramatic. It presents an interior duologue between Satan's better and worse selves, that should be compared with the repartee of good and evil angels in Marlowe's *Doctor Faustus*. At the same time, the self-dramatising of despair is for M. itself satanic. 'The characters of *Paradise Lost* do not soliloquise until they have fallen' (Broadbent 80).

iv *33*. The Orphic and Platonic doctrine that the sun is a divine image had been elaborated by Neoplatonists into a full-scale solar theology. See, e.g., Plato, *Rep.* 508; Dionysius, *De divin. nom.*; and Ficino, *De Sole* and *Epist.* vi, *Orphica comparatio Solis ad Deum* (966, 825).

But with no friendly voice, and add thy name
O sun, to tell thee how I hate thy beams
That bring to my remembrance from what state
I fell, how glorious once above thy sphere;
40 Till pride and worse ambition threw me down
Warring in heaven against heaven's matchless king:
Ah wherefore! He deserved no such return
From me, whom he created what I was
In that bright eminence, and with his good
45 Upbraided none; nor was his service hard.
What could be less than to afford him praise,
The easiest recompense, and pay him thanks,
How due! Yet all his good proved ill in me,
And wrought but malice; lifted up so high
50 I sdeigned subjection, and thought one step higher
Would set me highest, and in a moment quit
The debt immense of endless gratitude,
So burdensome still paying, still to owe;
Forgetful what from him I still received,

iv 37. 'Every one that doeth evil hateth the light' (*John* iii 20).

iv 38–9. 'Remember therefore from whence thou art fallen, and repent' (*Rev.* ii 5).

iv 41. *matchless king*] Edward Phillips gives the phrase as 'Glorious King', which may represent an earlier version. See ll. 32–41n.

iv 42–3. The *volte face* from Satan's earlier attitude to God is so complete that some have attributed it to a change in the poet's intention, others to his use of old material. Empson 64f refutes the view that this first private speech by Satan admits his earlier public ones to have been full of lies – but only to the satisfaction of those whose values are as sophisticated as Satan's own. Earlier readers seem not to have been at all surprised by the change in attitude. They would expect the first offender to be remorseful, after he had had time for solitary reflection. When remorse led not to repentance but to hardened persistence, they would recognize that a new phase in damnation had been reached: see ll. 110–12n.

iv 43. An important admission. During the rebellion in heaven Satan believed – or pretended – that the angels were 'self-begot, self-raised / By [their] own quickening power' (v 860f). See iii 740n.

iv 45. Cp. *Jas.* i 5: 'If any of you lack wisdom, let him ask of God, that giveth to all men liberally, and upbraideth not; and it shall be given him.' The context is precepts about how to behave under temptation.

iv 50. *sdeigned*] disdained (mainly poet.). Originally imitating Ital. *sdegnare*, a word with aristocratic associations: see Fowler 110.

iv 53–4. *still*] always.

55   And understood not that a grateful mind
      By owing owes not, but still pays, at once
      Indebted and discharged; what burden then?
      O had his powerful destiny ordained
      Me some inferior angel, I had stood
60   Then happy; no unbounded hope had raised
      Ambition. Yet why not? Some other power
      As great might have aspired, and me though mean
      Drawn to his part; but other powers as great
      Fell not, but stand unshaken, from within
65   Or from without, to all temptations armed.
      Hadst thou the same free will and power to stand?
      Thou hadst: whom hast thou then or what to accuse,
      But heaven's free love dealt equally to all?
      Be then his love accursed, since love or hate,
70   To me alike, it deals eternal woe.
      Nay cursed be thou; since against his thy will
      Chose freely what it now so justly rues.
      Me miserable! Which way shall I fly
      Infinite wrath, and infinite despair?
75   Which way I fly is hell; my self am hell;
      And in the lowest deep a lower deep
      Still threatening to devour me opens wide,
      To which the hell I suffer seems a heaven.
      O then at last relent: is there no place

iv 55–7. Simply by owning an obligation gratefully, one ceases to owe it;
cp. Cicero, *Pro Plancio* xxviii 68: 'In a moral debt, when a man pays he
keeps, and when he keeps, he pays by the very act of keeping.' Just as
Cicero plays on two senses of *habere*, so M. plays on owe (*OED* I 1 c,
= acknowledge as one's own; and II 2, = be under obligation to repay).

iv 59. *stood*] Combining 'remained' (*OED Stood* 15 e) with 'stood firm
and not fallen' (*OED* 9 b; cp. l. 64 below).

iv 66–70. God the Father has explained that predestination did not over-rule
the freedom of the angels' wills, and that his love desired a free response
from them (see iii 100–2n and cp. v 535–40). This divine love can be repre-
sented as ultimately responsible for Satan's fall, since it occasioned the free-
dom of his will.

iv 74. *Me miserable*] A similar exclamatory use of 'me' was common in
Elizabethan dramatic contexts (*OED* 7 a, citing also Greene, *Menaphon*:
'Ay me unhappie'. M. secondarily imitates the Lat. idiom *me miserum*,
but the primary point is that Satan's diction is theatrical.

iv 75. See ll. 20–3n and i 255n; and cp. *Comus* 384: 'Himself is his own
dungeon.'

iv 79–80. Esau having sold his birthright, 'when he would have inherited
the blessing ... was rejected: for he found no place of repentance' (*Heb.*

80   Left for repentance, none for pardon left?
      None left but by submission; and that word
      Disdain forbids me, and my dread of shame
      Among the spirits beneath, whom I seduced
      With other promises and other vaunts
85   Than to submit, boasting I could subdue
      The omnipotent. Ay me, they little know
      How dearly I abide that boast so vain,
      Under what torments inwardly I groan;
      While they adore me on the throne of hell,
90   With diadem and sceptre high advanced
      The lower still I fall, only supreme
      In misery; such joy ambition finds.
      But say I could repent and could obtain
      By act of grace my former state; how soon
95   Would highth recall high thoughts, how soon unsay
      What feigned submission swore; ease would recant
      Vows made in pain, as violent and void.
      For never can true reconcilement grow
      Where wounds of deadly hate have pierced so deep:

xii 17). The A.V. marg. gloss explains the last phrase as meaning 'way to
change his mind'.

iv 82. Not a confession by the better Satan, but a justification by the worse;
since *Disdain* carries the force of Ital. *sdegno*–'scorn, indignation; contempt
for what is base and unbecoming to the self-respect of an angel and a gentle-
man'. See l. 50n. *Disdain* is italicized as a proper name in the early edns.

iv 84. *other . . . other*] The scheme, a special form of ploce, was a favourite
with M.; cp., e.g., x 861f ('With other echo late I taught your shades / To
answer, and resound far other song'), *Comus* 612f, and *Lycidas* 174. It occurs
in Dante, *Inf.* iii 91f: *Per altra via, per altri porti | verrai a piaggia, non qui, per
passare.* ('You must pass over by other roads, by other ferries: not here.')

iv 88. Some copies *Ed I* have colon after *groan*.

iv 89. *adore*] Empson 76f imagines Satan as sneering apologetically at the
word: 'he has at times accepted for himself what he had disapproved of
giving to the Son. But this would be hard to avoid, and to worry about it
only proves that he is a deeply conscientious republican.' But 'adore' is
sufficiently explained as an amplification of the contrast between outward
supremacy and inward torment. Satan says that his advancement is made
hollow by his misery, not that it is excessive. Apparently either his remorse
or his political education is insufficient for qualms about the class structure
of hell.

iv 94. *By act of grace*] by concession of favour, not of right (*OED Grace* II 6).
The phrase was often used in political contexts, in the special sense 'free
pardon by formal act of Parliament' (*OED* II 15 b).

100   Which would but lead me to a worse relapse
        And heavier fall: so should I purchase dear
        Short intermission bought with double smart.
        This knows my punisher; therefore as far
        From granting he, as I from begging peace:
105   All hope excluded thus, behold in stead
        Of us outcast, exiled, his new delight,
        Mankind created, and for him this world.
        So farewell hope, and with hope farewell fear,
        Farewell remorse: all good to me is lost;
110   Evil be thou my good; by thee at least
        Divided empire with heaven's king I hold
        By thee, and more than half perhaps will raign;
        As man ere long, and this new world shall know.
                Thus while he spake, each passion dimmed his face
115   Thrice changed with pale, ire, envy and despair,
        Which marred his borrowed visage, and betrayed
        Him counterfeit, if any eye beheld.

iv *100*. Some copies of *Ed I* have comma after *relapse*.

iv *110–12*. The hardening of Satan's heart (see iii 200) and his despairing nihilism are analysed in Broadbent 76–8.   *by thee . . . By thee*] Curiously doubled—perhaps to render the divisive, dyadic character of the evil addressed.

iv *110*. By ix 122f the more painful converse has been experienced: 'all good to me becomes / Bane'. See i 159–68n, and cp. *Is.* v 20: 'Woe unto them that call evil good, and good evil.'

iv *111. Divided*] shared; but alluding also to the number symbolism whereby Satan's rule is dyadic and divisive.

iv *112–13*. i.e., if in addition to ruling hell Satan succeeds in conquering the world. The idea is further developed at x 372–82.   *raign*] the transitive use of 'reign' was obsolete; so that 'raign' (an aphetic form of arraign) is the word primarily indicated; 'reign', however, is clearly present as an ambiguity—indeed, most editors treat it as belonging to the primary chain of discourse.

iv *115–17*. i.e., each of the three passions named caused *pale* (paleness, pallor). Since he is disguised as a cherub (iii 636), Satan's face ought to be of the appropriate colour; and cherubim were conventionally red. See, e.g., Randle Cotgrave, *A dictionarie of the French and English tongues* (1611), s.v. *Cherubin*: '*Rouge comme un Cherubin*,' Red-faced, Cherubin-faced, having a fierie facies like a Cherubin.' M. puns visually on red the cherubic colour, and red the ordinary ruddiness of a sanguine human complexion unaffected by passion.

iv *115. ire, envy and despair*] Note that the Argument has 'fear, envy, and despair'.

For heavenly minds from such distempers foul
Are ever clear. Whereof he soon aware,
120   Each perturbation smoothed with outward calm,
Artificer of fraud; and was the first
That practised falsehood under saintly show,
Deep malice to conceal, couched with revenge:
Yet not enough had practised to deceive
125   Uriel once warned; whose eye pursued him down
The way he went, and on the Assyrian mount
Saw him disfigured, more than could befall
Spirit of happy sort: his gestures fierce
He marked and mad demeanour, then alone,
130   As he supposed, all unobserved, unseen.
So on he fares, and to the border comes,
Of Eden, where delicious Paradise,

iv *118. distempers*] disorders of the mind, due to disturbances of the proper temper or proportion of the humours.

iv *121. Artificer*] inventor; cp. the alternative formula 'father of lies'.

iv *123. couched*] hidden, laid in concealment (*OED* III 13); perhaps also—in view of l. 120—with the overtone 'quelled, suppressed' (*OED* II 10). *with* introduces a further complication, for *couched with* meant 'inlaid with, set with'.(*OED* I 4). The intricacy of the line is mimetic.

iv *124–30*. Cp. Uriel's report to Gabriel, 364–72 below.

iv *124. enough*] *Ed I* and *Ed II* have the variant form 'anough'.

iv *125. warned*] made aware; i.e., Satan had only been able to deceive Uriel temporarily, by catching him unawares (see iii 624 and 629: 'fixed in cogitation'). Or perhaps 'it only means that Uriel after being asked the way by this character felt enough curiosity to follow his later movements' (Empson 66). But Gilbert (40) finds a discrepancy here, which he puts down to inadequate assimilation of an early tragedy.

iv *126. the Assyrian mount*] Niphates; see iii 742*n*.

iv *127*. According to Henry More, *The immortality of the soul* III x 5, spirits find it quite difficult to hide their true natures: 'Nor may the various Transfiguration of their shapes conceal their persons, no more then the disguises that are used by fraudulent men.'

iv *131*. Lewis 47 comments on the gradualness of the approach to Paradise.

iv *132–59*. Starnes and Talbert (310–15) argue that M. in part built his image of Paradise out of material quarried from Stephanus' entry on the Hesperides and Conti's description of the Elysian fields. It may be misleading, however, to cite particular sources for the details of M.'s Paradise; for it really assimilates and refines upon the whole European tradition of paradises, gardens, pleasances, fortunate isles, and lands of the blessed as subjects for conventional description.

iv *132. Paradise* is the garden situated within the land of *Eden*: see ll. 209–

> Now nearer, crowns with her enclosure green,
> As with a rural mound the champaign head
> *135* Of a steep wilderness, whose hairy sides
> With thicket overgrown, grotesque and wild,
> Access denied; and over head up grew
> Insuperable highth of loftiest shade,

10*n*; also i 4–5*n*. *delicious Paradise* renders the *deliciarum paradisum* of the Fathers (see Corcoran 20*n*).

iv *134*. *champaign*] unenclosed (contrast the *enclosure*, l. 133, of Paradise itself); also open, level, free from trees.

iv *135*. *hairy sides*] Cp. 134, *head*: 'The Freudian idea that the happy garden is an image of the human body would not have frightened Milton in the least' (Lewis 47). In Spenser's Garden of Adonis there is a myrtle-clad mount with a similar anatomical significance (*F.Q.* III vi 43; see Ellrodt 88*n*, Fowler 135f). In Dante, *Purg.* xxviii 91–102 Paradise is located on the summit of the purgatorial mountain, to ensure that it will be free from the effects of atmospheric change; cp. Ariosto, *Orl. Fur.* xxxiv 48, where the hill of Paradise 'nigh touched the circle of the moon'. The elevated Paradise goes back to *Ezek.* xxviii 13f: 'Thou hast been in Eden the garden of God . . . thou wast upon the holy mountain of God'; but in its more exaggerated expression shades off into the supraterrestrial garden ridiculed by Heylyn (*Cosmographie* (1652) iii 147; see also iii 565–71*n* above, and Hanford 408f). As an *enclosed* garden it recalls the *hortus conclusus* of The Song of Solomon iv 12, which in medieval religious iconography was one of the principal symbols of Mary, the second Eve.

iv *136*. 'In most exquisite pictures they use to blaze and portraict not onely the daintie lineaments of beautye, but also rounde about it to shadow the rude thickets and craggy clifts, that by the basenesse of such parts, more excellency may accrew to the principall' (E.K., Epistle to Harvey, before Spenser's *Shepheardes Calender*).   *grotesque*] (*Ed II* gottesque) romantic, picturesque. Originally used with reference to an antique style of ornament consisting of fantastically interwoven foliage. It often took the form of extravagant, excessive, or even monstrous and diabolic forms: see André Chastel, 'La Renaissance fantaisiste' in *L'Oeil* xxi (1956) 34–41; Arnold von Salis, *Antike und Renaissance* (Bâle 1947). Curtius has labelled the pleasance within a wild wood 'the specialized Tempe motif'.

iv *138–43*. Recalling many famous *loci amoeni*–especially perhaps Spenser's Mt Acidale, which was 'plaste in an open plaine, / That round about was bordered with a wood / Of matchlesse hight, that seem'd th'earth to disdaine, / In which all trees of honour stately stood / And did all winter as in sommer bud' (*F.Q.* VI x 6); and the home of his Belphoebe, 'in a pleasant glade, / With mountaines round about environed, / And mighty woods, which did the valley shade, / And like a stately Theatre it made, / Spreading it selfe into a spatious plaine' (*F.Q.* III v 39). Cp. also the 'second paradise'

Cedar, and pine, and fir, and branching palm,
140   A sylvan scene, and as the ranks ascend
Shade above shade, a woody theatre
Of stateliest view. Yet higher than their tops
The verdurous wall of Paradise up sprung:
Which to our general sire gave prospect large
145   Into his nether empire neighbouring round.
And higher than that wall a circling row
Of goodliest trees loaden with fairest fruit,
Blossoms and fruits at once of golden hue
Appeared, with gay enamelled colours mixed:
150   On which the sun more glad impressed his beams
Than in fair evening cloud, or humid bow,

surrounding Spenser's Temple of Venus: 'No tree, that is of count, in greene-wood growes, / From lowest Juniper to Ceder tall . . . / But there was planted' (*F.Q.* IV x 22). According to a persistent tradition based on *Gen.* ii 5 ('every plant of the field') and exemplified in Dante, *Purg.* xxviii, all plant life was represented in Paradise. On the climbing serialism of the description, see Lewis 48. For the tree catalogue commonplace, cp. 693–701 and *Comus* 999ff, and see Curtius 195; the only unconventional tree in M.'s list is the palm, which is possibly to be accounted for by *Ps.* xcii 12: ' The righteous shall flourish like the palm tree: he shall grow like a cedar in Lebanon.' Cp. also Du Bartas 189, where the palm is an emblem of chastity or marital loyalty: let the adulteress, he says, 'Blush (at the least) at Palm-Trees loyaltie, / Which never bears, unless her Male be by'. *sylvan scene*] Echoes Virgil, *Aen.* i 164, *silvis scaena coruscis.*

iv *148. at once*] at the same time. The simultaneous concurrence of all stages of growth was a well-established feature of earthly paradises: cp., e.g., Ariosto, *Orl. Fur.* xxxiv 49; Tasso, *Gerus. Lib.* xvi 10f ('ere the fruit drop off, the blossom comes, / This springs, that falls, that ripeneth and this blooms. // The leaves upon the self-same bough did hide / Beside the young the old and ripened fig'); and Spenser, *F.Q.* III vi 42 ('There is continuall spring, and harvest there / Continuall, both meeting at one time'). Usually the Golden Age stasis is left unexplained, but in *PL* the absence of seasons is traced to astronomical causes, at x 651–706. For M. the motif would be associated with the exegetical controversies over *Gen.* i 12, which has God commanding the earth to bring forth simultaneously 'the bud of the herb' (Vulg. *herbam virentem*) and trees bearing fruit. Willet (9) tried to solve the problem by supposing that the first bearing of fruit was supernatural and that 'in the beginning, trees did beare fruit in the yeare more then once'– as the tree of life does in *Rev.* xxii 2.

iv *149. enamelled*] fresh, lustrous, bright; variegated. With no suggestion of hardness.

iv *151. humid bow*] rainbow; cp. *Comus* 992: 'Iris there with humid bow, / Waters the odorous banks.'

When God hath showered the earth; so lovely seemed
That landscape: and of pure now purer air
Meets his approach, and to the heart inspires
155   Vernal delight and joy, able to drive
All sadness but despair: now gentle gales
Fanning their odoriferous wings dispense
Native perfumes, and whisper whence they stole
Those balmy spoils. As when to them who sail

iv *153*. Cp. Stephanus, *Dictionarium*, s.v. *Elysium*: *Hunc locum alii inferorum
foelicitatibus plenum, alii fortunatas insulas, alii circa lunarem circulum esse
dicunt, ubi iam aer purior est*. See xii 76–8*n* below. Contrary to the common
assumption, the use of *of* to express transformation from a former con-
dition was not Latinate; see *OED* s.v. *Of* VII 20 b, where examples from
English authors as venerable as Bede are cited.   *landscape*] lantskip *Ed I*
and *Ed II*: see ii 491*n*.

iv *156–8*. Cp. Conti's description of the Elysian fields: *atque ventos plurimum
suaves et odoriferos leniter spirare*. The echo is not so clear as it may seem,
however, for *odoriferous* was a familiar word in M.'s day. The idea of per-
fumes stolen by the wind was a commonplace.

iv *156. gale*] In the eighteenth century the use of 'gale' in the sense 'gentle
breeze' was to become conventional poetic diction. But in M.'s time and
before, the ordinary (and in particular the nautical) meaning of 'gale'
was very near to Mod. Eng. 'wind'. Thus Capt. John Smith gives the
ascending series 'a calme, a brese, a fresh gaile, a pleasant gayle, a stiffe
gayle' *An accidence or the path-way to experience, necessary for all young
sea-men* (1626) 17).

iv *158. perfumes*] Stressed on the second syllable.

v *159–66*. Resuming at the end of Satan's journey to Eden the comparison
made near its beginning (see ii 636–41*n*).   *Cape of Hope*] Cape of Good
Hope. R. I. S. Jones sees an implication that Satan is now past hope. Cp.
l. 108, 'farewell hope'.   *Mozambic*] (Stressed on the second syllable.)
The Portuguese province of Mozambique, between which and Madagascar
the trade route lay.   *Sabean*] of Saba or Sheba (now Yemen). M. draws
on the description of *Arabie the blest–Arabia felix*–in Diodorus Siculus III
xlvi 4. Balsam and cassia grow along the shore, and inland thick forests of
frankincense and cinnamon: 'A divine thing and beyond the power of words
to describe seems the fragrance which greets the nostrils and stirs the senses of
everyone. Indeed, even though those who sail along this coast may be far
from the land, that does not deprive them of a portion of the enjoy-
ment . . . When the wind is blowing off shore, one finds that the sweet
odours exhaled by the myrrh-bearing and other aromatic trees penetrate to
the near-by parts of the sea.' It may be relevant that Diodorus qualifies this
impression of a country blessed with every advantage, by telling how it is
infested with poisonous serpents (III xlvii 1f). Cp.*Elegia V* 59, and *PR* ii 364.

160 Beyond the Cape of Hope, and now are past
       Mozambic, off at sea north-east winds blow
       Sabean odours from the spicy shore
       Of Arabie the blest, with such delay
       Well pleased they slack their course, and many a league
165 Cheered with the grateful smell old Ocean smiles.
       So entertained those odorous sweets the fiend
       Who came their bane, though with them better pleased
       Than Asmodeus with the fishy fume,
       That drove him, though enamoured, from the spouse

Since the mariners are sailing N.E., they must *slack their course* when they
meet N.E. winds.

iv *166–71. Tobit's son*] The apocryphal book *Tobit* relates the story of Tobit's
son Tobias, who was sent into Media on an errand, and there married
Raguel's daughter Sara. Sara had previously been given to seven men, but
all were killed by the jealous spirit *Asmodeus* before their marriages could
be consummated. By the advice of Raphael, however, Tobias succeeded
where the others had failed; for he burned the heart and liver of a fish,
and made smoke: 'the which smell when the evil spirit had smelled, he
fled into the utmost parts of Egypt, and the angel bound him' (*Tob.* viii 3).
Lewis (42) thinks that M. introduces the simile 'to make us feel the full ob-
scenity of Satan's presence in Eden by bringing a sudden stink of fish across
the sweet smell of the flowers' and finds 'the pretence of logical connection
. . . too strained'. But the connections seem close enough, once the typology
of the *Tobit* episode is recalled. Tobias directly compares himself to Adam
at *Tob.* viii 6, and like M.'s Adam is instructed by Raphael (see *Tob.* vi, and
PL v 221–3, where the parallel is drawn explicitly); while the binding of
Asmodeus foreshadows the binding of Satan by the new Adam, Christ
(see *PL* xii 454). M.'s simile is designed to amplify the inappropriateness of
the welcome Satan receives in Eden. *Though* he lacks Asmodeus' excuse
of infatuation, Satan gets no worse treatment: indeed, he is met with sweet
perfumes, even *though* they please him.   *with a vengeance*] The odd
coupling of this intensive phrase with the unemphatic *sent* alerts one to the
sardonic pun–Tobias's success was vengeance, typologically, for Adam's
failure. The story of Tobias provided several subjects that were very popu-
lar with seventeenth-century artists–e.g., Rembrandt's *The Angel Raphael
departing from Tobit and his family* (Louvre); Elsheimer's *Tobias and the
Angel* (Nat. Gall.); and Santi's *Landscape with Tobias and the Angel* (Imola,
Pinacoteca Civica).

iv *168. Asmodeus*' part in the war in heaven is related at vi 365; cp. also *PR*
ii 151f, where he is 'the fleshliest incubus'. According to a Scholastic tradi-
tion transmitted by Cornelius Agrippa, Heywood, Burton and others,
there were nine orders of devils, of which Asmodeus led the fourth, the
'malicious revenging devils' (*Anat. of Melan.* I ii I ii).

170   Of Tobit's son, and with a vengeance sent
       From Media post to Aegypt, there fast bound.
          Now to the ascent of that steep savage hill
       Satan had journeyed on, pensive and slow;
       But further way found none, so thick entwined,
175   As one continued brake, the undergrowth
       Of shrubs and tangling bushes had perplexed
       All path of man or beast that passed that way:
       One gate there only was, and that looked east
       On the other side: which when the arch-felon saw
180   Due entrance he disdained, and in contempt,
       At one slight bound high over leaped all bound
       Of hill or highest wall, and sheer within
       Lights on his feet. As when a prowling wolf,
       Whom hunger drives to seek new haunt for prey,
185   Watching where shepherds pen their flocks at eve
       In hurdled cotes amid the field secure,
       Leaps o'er the fence with ease into the fold:
       Or as a thief bent to unhoard the cash
       Of some rich burgher, whose substantial doors,
190   Cross-barred and bolted fast, fear no assault,
       In at the window climbs, or o'er the tiles;
       So clomb this first grand thief into God's fold:

iv *172. savage*] wild, rugged.

iv *176. had perplexed*] (Conditional) 'would have perplexed (tangled, inter-woven)'–i.e. would, if there had been any passing.

iv *178.* On the eastern gate, see ll. 542–50*n.*

iv *181.* The subdued pun or paronomasia is I think simply an instance of M.'s re-enlivening awareness of language–a not particularly successful instance. There is no comic implication, despite Tillyard³ 71–5.

iv *183–7.* Cp. *Lycidas* 115, and see *John* x 1: 'He that entereth not by the door into the sheepfold, but climbeth up some other way, the same is a thief and a robber.'   *cotes*] shelters.   *secure*] over-confident.

iv *188–91.* There is just possibly an allusion here to the vision of judgment in *Joel* ii 3–9: 'The land is as the garden of Eden before them . . . they shall climb up upon the houses; they shall enter in at the windows like a thief.'

iv *188. unhoard*] take out of hoard. OED gives no example earlier than this.

iv *192–3.* Returning to the simile of ll. 183–7, whose vehicle thus becomes the tenor of the intervening comparison. For the application of the Johannine parable to contemporary ecclesiastical conditions, cp. xii 507ff and *Cromwell* 11–14: 'new foes arise / Threatening to bind our souls with secular chains: / Help us to save free conscience from the paw / Of hireling wolves whose gospel is their maw.' In the debate on church government M. was against a salaried ministry and he wrote a tract in this sense, *Considerations Touching the Likeliest Means to Remove*

So since into his church lewd hirelings climb.
Thence up he flew, and on the tree of life
195   The middle tree and highest there that grew,
Sat like a cormorant; yet not true life
Thereby regained, but sat devising death
To them who lived; nor on the virtue thought
Of that life-giving plant, but only used
200   For prospect, what well used had been the pledge
Of immortality. So little knows
Any, but God alone, to value right
The good before him, but perverts best things
To worst abuse, or to their meanest use.
205   Beneath him with new wonder now he views
To all delight of human sense exposed

Hirelings out of the Church (1659) (Yale v).   *lewd*] wicked, vile; or more
probably 'untrained, ignorant'–M. thought ministers ought to support
themselves (as many Sectarians in fact did) by learning a trade or profession.
iv *195*. On the siting of the tree of life, see ll. 217–21*n*.

iv *196*. The image of the *cormorant* really continues the invective of l. 193.
Anyone guilty of greedy rapaciousness might be called a cormorant, but
the term was especially often used of 'hireling' clergy: cp. Nashe, *Anatomie
of Absurditie*: 'The cormorants of our age, who ... have alwaies their
mouthes open to aske, and ... gape after Colledge living' (ed. McKerrow
i 36). The immortal fruit of the *tree of life* is the reward promised the faith-
ful believer, in the New Jerusalem (*Rev*. ii 7, xxii 14): the cormorant is
made to sit on it, because hirelings want a corner in immortality. The image
has also, however, a broader meaning, and like other of the forms taken by
Satan foreshadows judgment. See *Is*. xxxiv 11: in the day of the Lord's
vengeance Edom will lie waste: 'The cormorant and the bittern shall
possess it.' But it should not be thought that the bird had for M. a purely
literary existence. Indeed, we know that he must often have at least heard
its cry; for just across the road from his house in Petty France the king's
cormorants were kept in St James's Park.

iv *196–201*. It is asked how Satan could ever have *used* the tree *well*. The
answer is that if he had thought on the *virtue* (secret property) of the tree,
and had been obedient, he might have *true life ... regained*. For M. consi-
dered the tree of life as 'not ... so much a sacrament, as a symbol of eternal
life, or rather perhaps the nutriment by which that life is sustained'–a
positive complement, as it were, to the tree of knowledge, which was also
'a pledge ... and memorial of obedience' (*De doctrina* i 10; Columbia xv
115). M.'s position is like that of Andrew Willet, who in his *Hexapla in
Genesin* (1608) 28 and 55 fixed in popular form the Augustinian view that
the tree of life was not effectual but significative: 'a signe of true immortali-
tie, which hee should receive of God, if he continue in obedience.' See
Gen. ii 9 and iii 22.

In narrow room nature's whole wealth, yea more,
A heaven on earth, for blissful Paradise
Of God the garden was, by him in the east
210   Of Eden planted; Eden stretched her line
From Auran eastward to the royal towers
Of great Seleucia, built by Grecian kings,
Or where the sons of Eden long before
Dwelt in Telassar: in this pleasant soil
215   His far more pleasant garden God ordained;
Out of the fertile ground he caused to grow
All trees of noblest kind for sight, smell, taste;
And all amid them stood the tree of life,
High eminent, blooming ambrosial fruit

iv 207–8. A tradition, based on *Gen.* ii 5 and 9, that creation was instanta-
neous and that Paradise comprehended the potentiality of all future life,
is traced by Ellrodt (75–81) from Augustine's *De Genesi* to Spenser's Garden
of Adonis, 'the first seminarie / Of all things, that are borne to live and die'
(*F.Q.* III vi 30). See also ll. 138–43n above. For the idea of Paradise as a
shadow of heaven, see v 574n.

iv 209–16. See *Gen.* ii 8: 'The Lord God planted a garden eastward in
Eden; and there he put the man whom he had formed.' For summary
accounts of the furious controversy about the location of Paradise, see
Willet and Heylyn iii 127. Among those who believed in a local terrestrial
Paradise, as many placed it S. of modern Persia, in Chaldea, at the fertile
confluence of the Tigris and the Euphrates, as N., at the source of these
rivers, near Mt Niphates. M. contrives to include both views. (He neatly
succeeds, also, in accommodating yet another competing theory–going
back to St Bonaventura–that Eden was 'under the Equinoctiall' (Willet
27), by making the ecliptic and the equator coincide before the Fall: see x
651–706n below.) *Auran* (Vulg. *Aran*, A.V. *Haran*), an eastern boundary of
the land of Israel in *Ezek.* xlvii 16–8, is associated with Eden at *Ezek.* xxvii
23; while in *Gen.* xi 31–xii 4 it is the town Abraham is commanded by the
Lord to leave. *Great Seleucia* was built by Alexander's general Seleucus
Nicator as a seat of government for his Syrian empire; Heylyn (iii 129)
notes that it was sometimes confused with Babylon. It is situated on the
Tigris, not E. but S.E. from Auran. The mention of *Telassar* is another
dramatic irony, for it prophesies war in Eden. The allusion is to *2 Kings*
xix 11f or *Is.* xxxvii 11f, where Telassar is an instance of lands destroyed
utterly: 'them which my fathers have destroyed, as Gozan, and Haran,
and Rezeph, and the children of Eden which were in Telassar'.

iv 217. See ll. 138–43n, and cp. Spenser's description of Mt Acidale 'in
which all trees of honour stately stood' (*F.Q.* VI x 6).

iv 217–21. See *Gen.* ii 9: 'And out of the ground made the Lord God to
grow every tree that is pleasant to the sight, and good for food; the tree of
life also in the midst of the garden, and the tree of knowledge of good and

220   Of vegetable gold; and next to life
      Our death the tree of knowledge grew fast by,
      Knowledge of good bought dear by knowing ill.
      Southward through Eden went a river large,
      Nor changed his course, but through the shaggy hill
225   Passed underneath ingulfed, for God had thrown

evil.'   *fruit of . . . gold*] Recalls the Hesperidean fruit (Ovid, *Met.* iv 637f)
which was gathered by Hercules in spite of its dragon sentinel.   *bloom-
ing*] (Trans.; rare) causing to flourish.   *ambrosial*: see ii 245n.   *vege-
table gold*] This strange phrase has more to it than the mere paradox of attri-
buting life and growth to a mineral substance. 'Vegetable stone' and
'potable gold' (see iii 608n) were both varieties of the philosophers' stone
that preserved health (*OED* s.v. *Vegetable* a. 1 d), so that M. seems here
to be imagining that there is alchemical significance in God's anxiety lest
the fruit of the tree of life prove an elixir to the fallen Adam (*Gen.* iii 22).
Both the tree of life and the Hesperian fruit gathered by Atalanta as she ran
were often used to symbolize the alchemical *Magnum Opus*; as, e.g., in
Michael Maier's emblematic *Atalanta fugiens*. For Fludd's attempt to achieve
the vegetable stone, and his partial success in producing a humor 'like
aurum potabile', see C. H. Josten, 'Robert Fludd's "Philosophical Key"
and His Alchemical Experiment on Wheat', *Ambix* xi (1963) 1–23, esp. 19.
iv *220–2*. While the other trees are splendidly described the tree of
knowledge is not, so as to avoid any suggestion of provocativeness on the
part of God (Burden 126ff).
iv *222*. Cp. *De doctrina* i 10, Columbia xv 115: 'It was called the tree of
knowledge of good and evil from the event; for since Adam tasted it, we
not only know evil, but we know good only by means of evil'; also
Areopagitica (Yale ii 514): 'It was from out the rinde of one apple tasted, that
the knowledge of good and evill as two twins cleaving together leapt forth
into the World. And perhaps this is that doom which Adam fell into of
knowing good and evill, that is to say of knowing good by evill.'
iv *223–32*. The fertility of Paradise (see ll. 215–7) is explained in *Gen.* ii
5f as not due to rain: 'But there went up a mist from the earth, and watered
the whole face of the ground.' This passage was a well-known crux (see
Willet 26f); St Jerome's Vulgate version, e.g., had a fountain instead of a
mist: *Sed fons ascendebat e terra, irrigans universam superficiem terrae.* Dante had
used the detail in his earthly paradise (*Purg.* xxviii 121ff), where it is empha-
sised that the moisture, being independent of rainfall, does not fluctuate in
abundance, 'but comes from a stable and certain source'. Dante also had
two divisions of the main stream, Lethe and Eunoe; these were allegorical
in character, however: one removed memory of sins, the other restored
memory of good deeds. The principal model for M.'s description is Philo,
Quaest. in Gen. i 12, where the difficulty of finding any location for Paradise
that meets the requirements of *Gen.* ii 10–14 is overcome by the speculation
that 'perhaps Paradise is in some distant place far from our inhabited world,

That mountain as his garden mould high raised
Upon the rapid current, which through veins
Of porous earth with kindly thirst up drawn,
Rose a fresh fountain, and with many a rill
230   Watered the garden; thence united fell
Down the steep glade, and met the nether flood,
Which from his darksome passage now appears,
And now divided into four main streams,
Runs diverse, wandering many a famous realm
235   And country whereof here needs no account,
But rather to tell how, if art could tell,

and has a river flowing under the earth, which waters many great veins so that these rising send water to other recipient veins, and so become diffused. And as these are forced by the rush of water, the force which is in them makes its way out to the surface, both in the Armenian mountains and elsewhere.' Note that M. agrees with Philo and many later exegetes in the view that the real source of the four rivers is not in Paradise, but that they have their origin in a river flowing *through Eden* and into (or under) the garden itself; cp. *Gen.* ii 10: 'A river went out of Eden to water the garden.' Lewis (49) notes the suggestion of a human body in words such as *shaggy*; *veins*; *thirst*; cf. 135n above.   *kindly thirst*] natural thirst. The phrase at first suggests capillary attraction, especially in view of *porous earth* (l. 228); but this force would be insufficient to produce the fountain and rills of ll. 229–31. Either the pressure of the head of water behind the *rapid current* l. 227) causes the fountain, or else the passage is based on a misconception. Certain branches of hydromechanics had been carried to a considerable height of sophistication in M.'s time, thanks to the work of Galileo's pupils Castelli and Torricelli, but accurate observations of capillary action were not made until 1709 (Hawksbee). The point is worth examining, because M. usually makes strenuous efforts to work out the literal implications of Genesis with all the rigour he is capable of.

iv *233–5*. *Gen.* ii 10: 'And a river went out of Eden to water the garden; and from thence it was parted, and became into four heads.' Some commentators took *Gen.* ii 5 to mean that the whole earth was watered from Paradise; and in any case the account in *Gen.* ii 11–14, of lands watered by the four distributaries Pison, Gihon, Hiddekel and Euphrates, mentioned three *famous realms*–Havilah, Ethiopia, and Assyria. According to a tradition that went back to St Ambrose and in part to Philo (see Fowler[2]) the four rivers were allegorized as the four cardinal virtues, the single source as the fountain of grace on which these depend. On M.'s use of the Tigris (Hiddekel), see ix 71n. His decision that geographical description of the four streams is unnecessary extricates him from a thorny choice between at least eight competing theories about their identity and location (see Willet 29).

How from that sapphire fount the crisped brooks,
Rolling on orient pearl and sands of gold,
With mazy error under pendant shades
240   Ran nectar, visiting each plant, and fed
Flowers worthy of Paradise which not nice art

iv *237–8. orient*] lustrous; a term specially applied to pearls. M.'s introduc-
tion of pearls into the river of Paradise has little to do with his reading of
travel books. It is authorized by *Gen.* ii 11f, the account of the first of the
four distributaries, Pison, 'which compasseth . . . Havilah, where there is
gold; And the gold of that land is good: there is bdellium and the onyx
stone.' According to Eugubinus and Oleaster, bdellium was 'a kind of
Margarite or pearle' (Willet 30). While Vulg., Tremellius and A.V. have
bdellium and onyx, Philo, who follows the Septuagint version, takes the
stones to be 'ruby and greenstone' (ὁ ἄνθραξ καὶ ὁ λίθος ὁ πράσινος: *Leg.
alleg.* i 66). Greenstone he interprets as a symbol of 'the man who exercises
good sense', and identifies with the sapphire in Aaron's breastplate (*Leg. alleg.*
i 79–81; see iii 594–605n above, also ii 1049–50n). Thus M.'s *sapphire fount*
would appear to be more than an image of natural beauty: to symbolize,
indeed, the wisdom underlying all the virtues. Delicate as it is, this touch
seems to imply a more or less moralized landscape. Cp. also *Ezek.* xxviii 13–
15: 'Thou hast been in Eden the garden of God; every precious stone was
thy covering, the sardius, topaz, and the diamond, the beryl, the onyx, and
the jasper, the sapphire, the emerald, and the carbuncle, and gold. . . . Thou
wast perfect in thy ways from the day that thou wast created, till iniquity
was found in thee.'
iv *237. crisped*] curled into short wavy folds; cp. Ben Jonson's description
of a land of perpetual spring in *The Vision of Delight* 186f: 'The Rivers runne
as smoothed by his [Zephyr's] hand; / Onely their heads are crisped by his
stroake.'
iv *239. error*] devious wandering course. One of the most resonant key words
in the poem; discussed in Stein 66f. Here 'the evil meaning is consciously
and ominously excluded. Rather than the meaning being simply "wan-
dering", it is "wandering (not error)". Certainly the word is a reminder of
the Fall, in that it takes us back to a time when there were no infected words
because there were no infected actions' (Ricks 110). Similarly the *pendant*
shades are not merely convenient hanging trees but also a proleptic sugges-
tion of the horrid shadows that impend. See viii 653n below.
iv *240.* Ovid's *saturnia regna* has rivers of nectar (*Met.* i 111). Cp. also M.'s
'river of bliss' in heaven, that 'rolls o'er Elysian flowers' (iii 358f). At this
time the amarant (iii 352–6) still grew in Paradise. See ix 70n, 71–5n; xi
278–9n.
iv *241–2.* As Burden 44ff notes, man's commission in *Gen.* i 28 is to 'sub-
due' the earth. This was a difficult notion, which in the poem is at first given
the most innocent explanation possible: namely, that the earth has to be sub-
dued only in the sense that art will be needed to put profuse nature in order.

In beds and curious knots, but nature boon
Poured forth profuse on hill and dale and plain,
Both where the morning sun first warmly smote
245 The open field, and where the unpierced shade
Embrowned the noontide bowers: thus was this place,
A happy rural seat of various view;
Groves whose rich trees wept odorous gums and balm,
Others whose fruit burnished with golden rind
250 Hung amiable, Hesperian fables true,

iv 242. *knots*] flower-beds laid out in intricate regular designs (often laby-
rinths). See e.g., Henry Peacham, *The compleat gentleman* (1634) p. 241:
'Here are the goodliest walkes in Europe, for the trees themselves are placed
in curious knots, as we use to set our herbes in gardens.' In M.'s time such
formal, artificial arrangements could already seem insipid.   *boon*]
bounteous, benign.

iv 246. *Embrowned*] darkened, made dusky (poet., probably imitating the
common Ital. use of *imbrunire* to describe any effect of shading; M.'s spelling
is 'Imbrowned'). No earlier example in *OED*. In M.'s time shadows were
in fact for some reason regularly painted brown.

iv 246–7. *thus*] such (*seat* is in apposition to *place*).   *happy rural seat*]
'is almost laughably the England of Penshurst, Cooper's Hill and Appleton
House' (Broadbent 184). M. mingles glimpses of preserved or recovered
beauty seen in many different directions: why should it be more laughable
to see them in the countryside than in books?

iv 248–9. In Diodorus' account of *Arabia felix* (see ll. 159–66n) the balsam
(balm) and other trees producing aromatic resins figure prominently.
Cp. also *Othello* V ii 349f: 'Drop tears as fast as the Arabian trees / Their
med'cinable gum.'   *rich*] Newton thought an antithesis on the basis of
commercial value was implied, between the trees producing aromatics
(which fetched a great price) and those bearing mere fruit. But Hesperian
fruit would not be cheap.   *golden rind*] With this and other particulars
of the description, cp. the deleted passage at the opening of *Comus* in *Trin.
MS*: 'fruits of golden rind, on whose fair tree / The scaly harnessed
dragon ever keeps / His unenchanted eye'. See Empson[2] 186f for the view
that the nostalgia for a lost Eden is attached here to the trees; also that 'the
same Nature produced the *balm* of healing and the fatal *fruit*; they cannot
convey to Adam either its knowledge or the knowledge that it is to be
avoided'. M. would hardly have agreed, however, that the trees 'by their
own nature foretell the necessity of the Fall'. He seems to imply quite a
different thought–that Nature's balm precedes the 'wound' of Nature
in the same way that Election to salvation precedes the Fall.

iv 250. *amiable*] desirable, lovely.   *Hesperian fables*] See ll. 217–21*n* and
iii 568–9*n*.

If true, here only, and of delicious taste:
Betwixt them lawns, or level downs, and flocks
Grazing the tender herb, were interposed,
Or palmy hillock, or the flowery lap
255 Of some irriguous valley spread her store,
Flowers of all hue, and without thorn the rose:
Another side, umbrageous grots and caves
Of cool recess, o'er which the mantling vine
Lays forth her purple grape, and gently creeps
260 Luxuriant; mean while murmuring waters fall
Down the slope hills, dispersed, or in a lake,
That to the fringed bank with myrtle crowned,
Her crystal mirror holds, unite their streams.

iv 251. *and . . . taste*] The Hesperian apples themselves were not for eating, however.

iv 255. *irriguous*] irrigated, well-watered.

iv 256. Cp. Herrick, 'The Rose': 'Before Mans fall, the Rose was born / (S. *Ambrose* sayes) without the Thorn.' Starting from the curse pronounced on Adam in *Gen.* iii 18 – 'Thorns also and thistles shall it bring forth to thee'– St Basil (*Hexaemeron* v 45) and St Ambrose (*Hexaemeron* iii 11; Migne xiv 188) went on to infer a thornless rose: *Surrexerat ante floribus immista terrenis sine spinis rosa.* See G. W. Whiting, in *RES* n.s. x (1959) 60–2. The thornless rose was used to symbolize the whole sinless state of man before the Fall; or (as Valeriano 686) the state of grace.

iv 257. *umbrageous*] shady.

iv 258. *mantling vine*] Recalls the climbing vines of Diodorus' Nysa (iii 68). Cp. *Comus* 294.

iv 262. That the *myrtle* is intended as Venus' tree is made clear by the immediately succeeding image of the mirror, another of her iconographical attributes (see Tervarent 274). Venus is present not only in her capacity as goddess of gardens, but also as the form-giver, presiding over the generative cycle unfolded in the Graces and the Hours. Paradises were commonly portrayed as gardens of Venus; see, e.g., Spenser, *F.Q.* III vi and IV x. The vine at 258–60 falls in with the same complex of associations; see Ovid, *Ars am.* i 244 (*Venus in vinis, ignis in igne fuit*), also Euripides, *Bacch.* 773, and Dodd's note there, on the theory (not confined to the Peripatetics) that wine contains *pneuma*, the stuff of life.

iv 263–6. The harmony of bird song, rustling leaves and *murmuring waters* (l. 260) was a usual feature of gardens of Venus; cp., e.g., Tasso's garden of Armida (*Gerus. Lib.* xvi 12) and Spenser's Bower of Bliss (*F.Q.* II xii 70f). Separately, the items of the description were both natural and conventional. They had their places among the 'charms of landscape' listed by the rhetoricians (see Curtius 197).   *apply*] 'join' or 'practise'.   *airs*] The primary meaning is 'breezes'; but an obvious secondary chain of discourse runs through *choir . . . airs* (melodies) *. . . attune*, as was noticed by Patrick Hume

The birds their choir apply; airs, vernal airs,
265   Breathing the smell of field and grove, attune
The trembling leaves, while universal Pan
Knit with the Graces and the Hours in dance
Led on the eternal spring. Not that fair field

in 1695, and later by Empson ([2] 157). For a full account of the needless con-
troversies the passage has occasioned, see Ricks 104–6.

iv *266–8.* The part played by the Graces in mythological poems on spring
is discussed in Wind 101ff. Ovid (*Fasti* v 193–222) tells how Chloris–Flora,
ravished by Zephyrus, brings forth the flowers of spring, which are then
gathered by the Seasons (*Hours*) and the Graces. The present passage may be
regarded as a more idealized treatment of the same subject that M. had
earlier handled in *Elegia V* (cp. also *Comus* 986).   *universal Pan*] Renais-
sance mythographers cited an Orphic Hymn as authority for interpreting
Pan as a symbol of 'universal nature' (see, e.g., Conti, *Mytholog.* v 6 and
Valeriano 730D, and cp. Gk. πᾶν, all).   *knit with the Graces*] Because the
triadic pattern of their dance was thought by Neoplatonists to express
the movement underlying all natural generation (see Wind 109).

iv *268–85.* The dismissive comparisons with other gardens recall a similar
list in Spenser, *F.Q.* II xii 52: 'More sweet and holesome, then the plea-
saunt hill / Of *Rhodope*, on which the Nimphe, that bore / A gyaunt babe,
her selfe for griefe did kill; / Or the Thessalian *Tempe*, where of yore /
Faire *Daphne Phoebus* hart with love did gore; / Or *Ida*, where the Gods
lov'd to repaire, / When ever they their heavenly bowres forlore; / Or
sweet *Parnasse*, the haunt of Muses faire; / Or *Eden* selfe, if ought with *Eden*
mote compaire.' M. mentions four streams–*Orontes; the inspired Castalian
spring; Triton;* and *Nilus*–corresponding to, and as it were replacing, the
four undescribed rivers of Paradise (235). Indeed, the two sets have a mem-
ber in common: the Nile, which was almost invariably identified with Gi-
hon, the second Biblical river (see, e.g., Valeriano 255, and the discussion
in Fowler[2] 292). Note also that the first comparison introduces a lunar
deity, the second solar and lunar deities together (ll. 272–4*n*) and the third
a solar deity; while the fourth comparison refers to the equinoctial line, and
thus to the just balancing of the domains of sun and moon, day and night.
For Adam as sun god, see l. 303*n.*

iv *268–72.* The rape of Proserpina by *Dis* (Pluto) the king of hell was lo-
cated in *Enna* by Ovid (*Fasti* iv 420ff). The search for her made the world
barren, and even when she was found she was restored to Ceres, and fruit-
fulness to the world, only for half the year. She might have been recovered
unconditionally had she not 'eaten seven graines of a Pomegrannet (a
fatall liquorishnesse, which retaines her in Hell; as the Apple thrust Evah
out of Paradice, whereunto it is held to have a relation)' (Sandys, *Ovid's
Metamorphosis* 195).

iv *268.* The view that the world was created in March had the authority of
Eusebius, Cyrillus, Athanasius, Gregory of Nazianzus, John of Damascus,

Of Enna, where Proserpine gathering flowers
270 Her self a fairer flower by gloomy Dis
Was gathered, which cost Ceres all that pain
To seek her through the world; nor that sweet grove
Of Daphne by Orontes, and the inspired
Castalian spring, might with this Paradise
275 Of Eden strive; nor that Nyseian isle
Girt with the river Triton, where old Cham,
Whom Gentiles Ammon call and Lybian Jove,
His Amalthea and her florid son
Young Bacchus from his stepdame Rhea's eye;
280 Nor where Abassin kings their issue guard,

Ambrose and Bede. It was supported by typological argument ('Christ was crucified the same day that Adam was created'); by appeal to tradition (when Moses instituted the custom of reckoning Nisan–March / April–the 'first' month, he was returning to primitive usage; see *Exod*. xii 2); and by numerical calculations based on literalistic applications of Scripture. See Willet 9f, and Riccioli ii 232; also iii 555–61*n* above.

iv 270. *Herself a fairer flower*] Cp. ix 432, describing Eve: 'Herself, though fairest unsupported flower'. See also Empson² 173: 'Proserpina, like Eve, was captured by the king of Hell, but she then became queen of it, became Sin, then, on Milton's scheme; Eve, we are to remember, becomes an ally of Satan when she tempts Adam to eat with her.'

iv 272–4. There was a beautiful grove called *Daphne* beside the River *Orontes*, near Antioch. It had an Apolline oracle (hence *inspired*) and a stream named after the famous *Castalian spring* of Parnassus.

iv 274. *Ed I* has no comma after *spring*.

iv 275–9. Diodorus' description of Nysa has been used more than once in the preceding description, and the island is now referred to directly. Diodorus relates (iii 67–70) how Ammon, King of Libya, had an illicit affair with a maiden Amaltheia, who gave birth to a marvellous son Dionysus (*Bacchus*). To protect mother and child from the jealousy of his wife Rhea (Uranus' daughter), Ammon hid them on Nysa, an island near mod. Tunis. The identifications of Ammon with the Lybian Jupiter (who appeared under the form of a ram which later became the constellation Aries) and with Noah's son Ham (Vulg. Cham) were widely accepted: see Sandys² 191, Starnes 237.   *florid*] ruddy-complexioned – a distinctive feature of Bacchus.

iv 280–5. Heylyn describes Mt *Amara* as 'a dayes journey high; the Rock so smooth and even . . . that no wall can be more evenly polished'. The summit, he says, is compassed with a high wall, within which are gardens and palaces where 'the younger sons of the *Emperour* are continually inclosed, to avoid sedition: they enjoy there whatsoever is fit for delight or *Princely* education' (iv 64). The province Amara to the west 'stretcheth towards the Nile'; and it was blessed with 'such ravishing pleasures of all

Mount Amara, though this by some supposed
True Paradise under the Ethiop line
By Nilus' head, enclosed with shining rock,
A whole day's journey high, but wide remote
285   From this Assyrian garden, where the fiend
Saw undelighted all delight, all kind
Of living creatures new to sight and strange:
Two of far nobler shape erect and tall,
Godlike erect, with native honour clad
290   In naked majesty seemed lords of all,
And worthy seemed, for in their looks divine

sorts, that some have taken (but mistaken) it for the place of *Paradise*'.
Like most of the geographers of the time, Heylyn thought Amara 'not
much distant from the *AEquator*, if not plainly under it'. M.'s emphasis on
the situation of Amara under the *Ethiop line* (equator) (l. 282) makes explicit
the notion of an equinoctial Paradise enjoying *eternal spring* (l. 268) that has
been ironically latent in the previous comparisons. Proserpina's division
of her time between the superior and inferior hemispheres was often inter-
preted as a seasonal myth. See Sandys[2] 197: 'The seede, which is Proserpina,
while the Sun is on the south of the Aequinoctiall, lies hid in the earth, which
is Pluto: but when he travells through the Northerne signes, it shouteth
[shooteth] up, and growes to maturity; and then Proserpina is said to be
above with Ceres.'

iv *285*. J. C. Maxwell points out that the present episode alludes to Homer's
account of Hermes' arrival at the isle of Calypso (*Od.* v 51–76). Common
elements include caves, vine, fourfold fountain and the comparison of the
supernatural visitor to a cormorant. Satan's reaction, however, contrasts
with Hermes', which is one of wonder and delight.

iv *288*. The notion of man's distinctive upright stance is developed at vii
506–11.

iv *289*. *Godlike*] To evoke his perfect human figure, M. appeals to 'innu-
merable remembered versions' of the pagan gods in his readers' imagina-
tions (MacCaffrey 98).   *native honour*] A striking oxymoron; for the
Golden Age was more usually portrayed as free from the restraints and
falsities of honour. See, e.g., the First Chorus of Tasso's *Aminta*. M.'s ideal
of natural honour–contrasted with fallen *honour dishonourable* (l. 314)–had
been anticipated more than once; as, e.g., in Guarini's moralization of Tasso
(*Pastor Fido* iv 9: *onor felice, verace onor*). But M. seems to go beyond Guarini,
and to entertain the conception of an honour like that of a Noble Savage–
'primitive honour', in Conrad's phrase.

iv *291–3*. See *Gen.* i 27: 'God created man in his own image.' Steadman (98)
shows that Adam and Eve here manifest the divine image in a very precise
way; for the virtues enumerated are the standard ones attributed to God,
by writers as diverse as St Gregory and Calvin. But see also MacCaffrey

The image of their glorious maker shone,
Truth, wisdom, sanctitude severe and pure,
Severe but in true filial freedom placed;
295 Whence true authority in men; though both
Not equal, as their sex not equal seemed;
For contemplation he and valour formed,
For softness she and sweet attractive grace,
He for God only, she for God in him:
300 His fair large front and eye sublime declared
Absolute rule; and hyacinthine locks
Round from his parted forelock manly hung
Clustering, but not beneath his shoulders broad:

98, on M.'s 'habit of naming qualities and attaching them to the central figures'; in the world of M.'s vision, the qualities are substantial.

iv *295. Whence*] i.e., from the divine image; the authority is symbolic. *authority*] autority *Ed I* and *Ed II*.

iv *299.* The thought corresponds to that of *1 Cor.* xi 3: 'The head of every man is Christ; and the head of the woman is the man; and the head of Christ is God.'

iv *300. front*] forehead.   *sublime*] uplifted.

iv *301–8.* The hair-length proper for each sex follows directly from the statement of their hierarchic relation; for, according to St Paul, 'a man indeed ought not to cover his head, forasmuch as he is the image and glory of God: but the woman is the glory of the man. . . . if a woman have long hair, it is a glory to her: for her hair is given her for a covering' (*1 Cor.* xi 7, 15; cp. the A.V. marginal gloss on 10, which explains that the covering is a 'sign that she is under the power of her husband').   *hyacinthine locks*] When Athene 'shed grace about his head and shoulders', Odysseus' hair flowed 'like the hyacinth flower' (Homer, *Od*, vi 231). If a colour were implied, it might be either blue, the colour of the hyacinth flower or gem (i.e., the sapphire: cp. l. 237*n*), or just possibly tawny (the hyacinth of heraldry, near to the colour of M.'s own hair), or black (Eustathius' gloss on the Homeric passage), or very dark brown (Suidas' gloss); in fact, almost any colour at all. But it is just as likely that a shape is meant (the idealized treatment accorded to hair in antique sculpture?), or an allusion to the beautiful youth Hyacinthus, beloved of Apollo but doomed to die. The elaborateness of the present passage lends some support to the theory that M. had a special sexual interest in hair. (In this connection cp. 496f, *Lycidas* 69, 175.) *wanton*] luxuriant; unrestrained.

iv *303. clustering*] So Apollo's hair is described in Apollonius Rhodius, *Argonaut.* ii 678. Adam's hair hangs clustering like bunches of grapes, Eve's like the more ancillary *vine . . . tendrils* (l. 307). The fact that Adam has been given no beard is due to the influence of visual art. Adam was usually portrayed beardless, because he had so often been represented as an Apollo. See, e.g., Panofsky 249–65 and Cartari 37.

She as a veil down to the slender waist
305   Her unadorned golden tresses wore
Dishevelled, but in wanton ringlets waved
As the vine curls her tendrils, which implied
Subjection, but required with gentle sway,
And by her yielded, by him best received,
310   Yielded with coy submission, modest pride,
And sweet reluctant amorous delay.
Nor those mysterious parts were then concealed,
Then was not guilty shame, dishonest shame
Of nature's works, honour dishonourable,
315   Sin-bred, how have ye troubled all mankind
With shows instead, mere shows of seeming pure,
And banished from man's life his happiest life,
Simplicity and spotless innocence.
So passed they naked on, nor shunned the sight
320   Of God or angel, for they thought no ill:
So hand in hand they passed, the loveliest pair
That ever since in love's embraces met,
Adam the goodliest man of men since born
His sons, the fairest of her daughters Eve.
325   Under a tuft of shade that on a green
Stood whispering soft, by a fresh fountain side
They sat them down, and after no more toil
Of their sweet gardening labour than sufficed

iv *308–11*. M. 'foreshadows the means by which Satan will manage to separate them' (Sims 25). *coy*] quiet, modest. Cp. *Ars amatoria* ii 717f: *non est veneris properanda voluptas, | Sed sensim tarda prolicienda mora.*

iv *313–15*. Cp. Tasso's and Guarini's attacks on false honour, cited in l. 289*n.*

iv *313*. *shame, dishonest shame*] Bentley's full stop after the first 'shame' obscures the gradual swell from cool appositional phrases into angry anacolouthon and apostrophe.

iv *321*. Cp. xii 648. At their entrance, as at their final exit, Adam and Eve go *hand in hand.*

iv *323–4*. 'Their children spring eternally from a syntactical union' (Broadbent 190). But M.'s syntax here is the syntax of ordinary prose, and would not have been noticed as having any special pattern. Cp., e.g., Browne, *Pseudodoxia* i 1 (ed. Keynes p. 18): 'As some affirm, [Adam] was the wisest of all men since.'

iv *328*. Burden 41ff comments on M.'s originality in achieving a variation of the usual Golden Age pastoral occupation. Instead of being shepherds his Adam and Eve are gardeners, engaged in light and pleasant, though necessary, work. Gardening had in M.'s time become a fashionable highbrow activity; as the existence of such books as Evelyn's *Sylva* testifies.

To recommend cool zephyr, and made ease
330   More easy, wholesome thirst and appetite
More grateful, to their supper fruits they fell,
Nectarine fruits which the compliant boughs
Yielded them, sidelong as they sat recline
On the soft downy bank damasked with flowers:
335   The savoury pulp they chew, and in the rind
Still as they thirsted scoop the brimming stream;
Nor gentle purpose, nor endearing smiles
Wanted, nor youthful dalliance as beseems
Fair couple, linked in happy nuptial league,
340   Alone as they. About them frisking played
All beasts of the earth, since wild, and of all chase

But, as Broadbent 177 hints, the gardening should probably be regarded as an emblem of moral or even of political activity (like the gardening in *Richard II* III iv, which symbolizes maintenance of order in the commonwealth).

iv *329. zephyr*] 'The frolic wind that breathes the spring' (*L'Allegro* 18); the west wind. In Neoplatonic mythology, the enlivening touch of Zephyr begins the initial phase in the generative progression (see Wind 103, 113). From the time of Ovid (in his account of the Golden Age, *Met.* i 107f), Zephyr had figured in most poetic visions of eternal spring; but he received particularly elaborate treatment in Jonson's masque *The Vision of Delight*. See also v 16n below.

iv *330. easy*] luxurious, comfortable.

iv *332. Nectarine*] sweet as nectar (though the variety of peach called nectarine was known at least as early as 1616).   *compliant*] pliant (by false etymology from Lat. *plicare*); *OED*'s earliest instance in this sense; perhaps a genuine Latinism.

iv *333. recline*] recumbent, reclining (Lat. *reclinis*); the only instance of this Latinising coinage listed in *OED*.

iv *334. downy*] feathery; or soft as down.

iv *335. savoury*] appetizing, fragrant. Note that the word often meant 'spiritually edifying'.

iv *337. gentle purpose*] polite (i.e., not coarse) conversation; as in Shakespeare, *Much Ado* III i 11f: 'There will she hide her, / To listen our purpose.'

iv *338. Wanted*] lacked; or were lacking.   *dalliance*] not 'conversation' (which would be pleonastic after *purpose*) but 'caressing'.

iv *340–52*. The idyllic scene of Adam and Eve surrounded by the animals was a familiar one, from countless visual representations. Among fine examples are Cranach's painting *The Garden of Eden* (Vienna, Kunsthistorisches Museum), Dürer's engraving *The Fall of Man* (Bartsch 1) and Goltzius' Windsor Castle ink drawing (No. 4758); among popular examples, the frontispiece to 'Eden' in Sylvester's 1613 Du Bartas. Contrast the scene of enmity at x 710–14.

In wood or wilderness, forest or den;
Sporting the lion ramped, and in his paw
Dandled the kid; bears, tigers, ounces, pards,
345   Gambolled before them, the unwieldly elephant
To make them mirth used all his might, and wreathed
His lithe proboscis; close the serpent sly
Insinuating, wove with Gordian twine
His braided train, and of his fatal guile
350   Gave proof unheeded; others on the grass
Couched, and now filled with pasture gazing sat,
Or bedward ruminating: for the sun
Declined was hasting now with prone career
To the Ocean Isles, and in the ascending scale
355   Of heaven the stars that usher evening rose:
When Satan still in gaze, as first he stood,
Scarce thus at length failed speech recovered sad.
       O hell! What do mine eyes with grief behold,

iv *344. ounces*] properly 'lynxes'; but in the seventeenth century applied loosely to various feline beasts.

iv *348. Insinuating*] penetrating by sinuous ways.   *Gordian twine*] coil, convolution, as difficult to undo as the Gordian knot, which it took the hero Alexander to cut (cp. ix 499, where the serpent's folds are a 'surging maze'). But 'twine' could also mean 'division, separation, disunion' (*OED* sb.²; cp. Sylvester's Du Bartas 586, 'Th'Unity dwels in God, i'th' Fiend the Twine'): an allusion, perhaps, to the division made by Satan between Adam and Eve. In *Civ. Dei* xiv 11 St Augustine says that Satan chose the serpent for his instrument because it was 'a creature slippery, pliable, wreathed in knots, and fit for his work'.

iv *350. proof unheeded*] Burden 53 argues that the serpent's guile is openly demonstrated so that man may have no excuse. But the phrase may only be meant to point the irony that no one is paying any attention to the creature who will have the most momentous importance; 'proof' need only have been chosen for the sake of the context it suggests: the serpent's very movements are dialectical.

iv *352. Bedward ruminating*] chewing the cud before going to rest.

iv *354–5. Ocean Isles*] the Azores, beneath which the sun has set in l. 592. *ascending scale*] A serious pun. Since the sun is in Aries (iii 555–61*n*, x 329*n*), the *stars that usher evening* rise in Libra, the Scales, the portion of the sky exactly opposite. But *scale of heaven* implies also the balancing of light and darkness that originally determined the visual representation of the equinoctial sign (see Eisler 100, Fowler 195*n*). For the culmination of the constellation Libra at midnight, six hours after the time of the present passage, see ll. 1014f; and for the equinoctial theme elsewhere in *PL*, see ll. 280–5*n*, ix 50f, x 651–706*n*.

Into our room of bliss thus high advanced
360   Creatures of other mould, earth-born perhaps,
Not spirits, yet to heavenly spirits bright
Little inferior; whom my thoughts pursue
With wonder, and could love, so lively shines
In them divine resemblance, and such grace
365   The hand that formed them on their shape hath
            poured.
Ah gentle pair, ye little think how nigh
Your change approaches, when all these delights
Will vanish and deliver ye to woe,
More woe, the more your taste is now of joy;
370   Happy, but for so happy ill secured
Long to continue, and this high seat your heaven
Ill fenced for heaven to keep out such a foe
As now is entered; yet no purposed foe
To you whom I could pity thus forlorn
375   Though I unpitied: league with you I seek,
And mutual amity so strait, so close,
That I with you must dwell, or you with me
Henceforth; my dwelling haply may not please
Like this fair Paradise, your sense, yet such

iv *359. room*] place. Cp. vii 189f, where God is praised by the loyal angels for bringing 'a better race' into the 'vacant room' of the rebels.

iv *361-2.* Cp. *Heb.* ii 7 and *Ps* viii 5: 'Thou hast made him a little lower than the angels, and hast crowned him with glory and honour.'

iv *370-4.* Satan's pity is by no means to his credit. He is unable to act as firmly as Michael, because he knows himself to be in the wrong. As Burden 36 notes, the implied accusation of God for making man too frail is false. Man is 'sufficient to have stood'—as indeed Satan's fear of approaching Adam shows (ix 483ff).

iv *370.* i.e., 'not so well secured as one would expect in the case of such happy creatures'. *Ed I* (catchword only) has semicolon after *Happy.*

iv *372. for heaven*] considering it is your heaven.

iv *375-7.* 'Perverting the "happy nuptial league" of Adam and Eve in the previous paragraph' (Broadbent 171).   *strait*] intimate (*OED* 14); but also with the sinister overtone 'involving privation' (*OED* 6 b). The *Ed I* and *Ed II* spelling 'streight' allows a play with *straight* = honest; but this must be considered very secondary in view of the continuation *so close.*

iv *377.* Rajan 100 finds this line characteristic, in its 'tiredness', of Satan's later speeches. It may seem differently, however, to readers who appreciate the villainous implication of the sequence *I with you* (i.e., temptation and sin, the inner hell): *you with me* (damnation, the external hell).

380   Accept your maker's work; he gave it me,
      Which I as freely give; hell shall unfold,
      To entertain you two, her widest gates,
      And send forth all her kings; there will be room,
      Not like these narrow limits, to receive
385   Your numerous offspring; if no better place,
      Thank him who puts me loth to this revenge
      On you who wrong me not for him who wronged.
      And should I at your harmless innocence
      Melt, as I do, yet public reason just,
390   Honour and empire with revenge enlarged,
      By conquering this new world, compels me now
      To do what else though damned I should abhor.
          So spake the fiend, and with necessity,
      The tyrant's plea, excused his devilish deeds.

iv *380–1*. The blasphemous echo of *Matt.* x 8 ('freely ye have received, freely give') redounds to Satan's discredit, especially in view of the more distant resonance with *Rom.* viii 32 ('He that spared not his own Son, but delivered him up for us all, how shall he not with him also freely give us all things?').

iv *381–5*. Cp. Isaiah's prophecy of the fall of Babylon (*Is.* xiv 9): 'Hell from beneath is moved for thee to meet thee at thy coming: it stirreth up the dead for thee, even all the chief ones of the earth; it hath raised up from their thrones all the kings of the nations.' Empson is deeply committed to the view that Satan is sincere in offering high honour in hell, and that 'the irony of his offer belongs only to the God who made Hell' (Empson 68f; cp. Empson[2] 168, Empson[3] 103). One may agree that Satan does not sustain the irony of 375f or of the understatement *may not please* (l. 378), and that 385f is in a certain narrow sense 'sincere'. If high honour is accompanied with woe and opposed to joy (ll. 367–9), however, it is hard to see how it could be offered other than maliciously, to harm God's image in Adam and Eve–out of *revenge*, in fact, as Satan himself admits at 386f. Besides, the offer of *room* (l. 383) is belied in advance by the sinister *so strait, so close* (l. 376).

iv *389. public reason*] 'Reason of state, a perversion of the Ciceronian principle (*Laws* III iii 8) that the good of the people is the supreme law. . . . Henry Parker approved its use by Parliament and condemned the Royalists for too frequent appeals to it. . . . In *Adamo caduto* V ii, Salandra has Satan tell the devils that they are going to corrupt mankind by inventing *ragione di stato*' (Hughes). Satan is here cast in the role of a contemporary Machiavellian politician, excusing the evil means he resorts to by appeals to such values as 'the common weal', 'the good of the state', 'policy' and *necessity* (l. 393). Cp. Dalila's excuse that she had finally been persuaded to betray Samson by 'that grounded maxim / So rife and celebrated in the mouths / Of wisest men; that to the public good / Private respects must yield' (*SA* 865–8).

395   Then from his lofty stand on that high tree
      Down he alights among the sportful herd
      Of those four-footed kinds, himself now one,
      Now other, as their shape served best his end
      Nearer to view his prey, and unespied
400   To mark what of their state he more might learn
      By word or action marked: about them round
      A lion now he stalks with fiery glare,
      Then as a tiger, who by chance hath spied
      In some purlieu two gentle fawns at play,
405   Straight couches close, then rising changes oft
      His couchant watch, as one who chose his ground
      Whence rushing he might surest seize them both
      Griped in each paw: when Adam first of men
      To first of women Eve thus moving speech,
410   Turned him all ear to hear new utterance flow.
          Sole partner and sole part of all these joys,

iv 400. Satan's overhearing the prohibition was not a common motif in hexaemeral literature; though McColley notes an instance in the *Paradise* of Moses bar Cepha, and Hughes another in Serafino della Salandra's *Adamo caduto*.

iv 401–2. In accordance with 1 *Pet*. v 8: 'Be sober, be vigilant; because your adversary the devil, as a roaring lion, walketh about, seeking whom he may devour.' Burden 49f notes that the real animals are tame and gentle before the Fall, but that Satan assumes their later, postlapsarian forms.

iv 402–8. Similarly in Du Bartas 239: 'Our freedoms felon, fountain of our sorrow, / Thinks now the beauty of a Horse to borrow; / Anon to creep into a Haifers side; / Then in a Cock, or in a Dog to hide; / Then in a nimble Hart himself to shroud; / Then in the starr'd plumes of a Peacock proud', before deciding that the serpent is best suited to his purpose. This is contrary to a strong tradition, going back to St Augustine, that Satan was not allowed to make use of any other beast but the serpent.

iv 404. *purlieu*] land on the fringe of a forest. The more specific sense–land disafforested, but still subject to the provisions of the forest laws–does not seem to apply.

iv 405. *Straight*] at once; but punning with 'Strait', 'tightly' (*OED* s.v. *Strait* adv. 1). *Ed I* and *Ed II* 'Strait' could indicate either word, and made the play more obvious.

iv 410. It soon becomes clear, from the length of the succeeding speech by Adam, that *him* must refer not to the speaker (with *Turned* reflexive), but to the eavesdropper. The momentary uncertainty, however, is enough to give the impression that Satan has insinuated himself into Adam's grammatical place.   *all ear*] Imitates a Lat. idiom, and is perhaps the earliest instance in English.

iv 411. *Sole partner and sole part*] The first *sole* means 'only', the second

Dearer thy self than all; needs must the power
That made us, and for us this ample world
Be infinitely good, and of his good
415   As liberal and free as infinite,
That raised us from the dust and placed us here
In all this happiness, who at his hand
Have nothing merited, nor can perform
Aught whereof he hath need, he who requires
420   From us no other service than to keep
This one, this easy charge, of all the trees
In Paradise that bear delicious fruit
So various, not to taste that only tree
Of knowledge, planted by the tree of life,
425   So near grows death to life, what e'er death is,
Some dreadful thing no doubt; for well thou know'st
God hath pronounced it death to taste that tree,
The only sign of our obedience left
Among so many signs of power and rule
430   Conferred upon us, and dominion given
Over all other creatures that possess
Earth, air, and sea. Then let us not think hard
One easy prohibition, who enjoy
Free leave so large to all things else, and choice
435   Unlimited of manifold delights:
But let us ever praise him, and extol
His bounty, following our delightful task
To prune these growing plants, and tend these flowers,
Which were it toilsome, yet with thee were sweet.
440   To whom thus Eve replied. O thou for whom

'unrivalled' (*OED* 5 c); Eve is the only sharer in Adam's joys, and also herself the chief part of them. Newton wanted a comma after *part*, on which to base his less obvious but more interesting interpretation – 'the only one of the joys which is a *part* of me' (cp. l. 487).

iv *421–4*. See *Gen.* ii 16f: 'The Lord God commanded the man, saying, Of every tree of the garden thou mayest freely eat: But of the tree of the knowledge of good and evil, thou shalt not eat of it: for in the day that thou eatest thereof thou shalt surely die.'

iv *428*. Cp. iii 95: 'Sole pledge of his obedience'; and see *n*.

iv *430–2*. See *Gen.* i 28: 'God said unto them . . . have dominion over the fish of the sea, and over the fowl of the air, and over every living thing that moveth upon the earth.'

iv *433. easy*] easy to keep; involving no effort; not constraining or oppressive.

iv *440. for whom*] See *1 Cor.* xi 9: 'Neither was the man created for the woman; but the woman for the man.' And cp. l. 299.

And from whom I was formed flesh of thy flesh,
And without whom am to no end, my guide
And head, what thou hast said is just and right.
For we to him indeed all praises owe,
445 And daily thanks, I chiefly who enjoy
So far the happier lot, enjoying thee
Pre-eminent by so much odds, while thou
Like consort to thyself canst nowhere find.
That day I oft remember, when from sleep
450 I first awaked, and found myself reposed
Under a shade of flowers, much wondering where
And what I was, whence thither brought, and how.
Not distant far from thence a murmuring sound
Of waters issued from a cave and spread
455 Into a liquid plain, then stood unmoved
Pure as the expanse of heaven; I thither went
With unexperienced thought, and laid me down

iv *441*. See *Gen.* ii 23: 'Adam said, This is now bone of my bones, and flesh of my flesh: she shall be called Woman, because she was taken out of Man.'

iv *443. head*] see *1 Cor.* xi 3: 'The head of every man is Christ; and the head of the woman is the man; and the head of Christ is God.'

iv *447. odds*] difference, superiority, advantage; usually construed as singular, in the seventeenth century.

iv *449–50*. At viii 253f Adam uses the same comparison to describe his experience immediately after his creation.   *reposed*] placed.

iv *449. That day*] Clearly implies that Adam and Eve have been created for two days at least, so that we must reject the theory advanced in McColley (16f *et passim*) that this is the very day of their creation. The impression that they have been in Paradise for some days is confirmed by many other passages (see, e.g., ll. 610–20, 639ff, 681ff, 710ff, v 31, v 145); though it is of course possible that M. meant us to assume that man was created with a readymade understanding of seasonal change. See Introduction, 'Chronology' (p. 444).

iv *451. of*] Preferable to *Ed I* 'on', which sounds too brisk coming so soon after *Under*.

iv *453–6*. 'Milton insists on the indistinguishable commingling [of *lake* and *sky*, l. 459] not only by the explicit comparisons, but also by the syntactical mingling in a "sound . . . spread into a liquid Plain"' (Ricks 101). Notice, though, that *issued*, *spread* and *stood* could just possibly all be transitive past participles describing *waters*. (For the trans. use of *issue*, see *OED* II 7.) The landscape is probably meant to be philosophically significant; for the water and the cave recall a Homeric image interpreted by Porphyry as a symbol of the descent of the soul (*De antro nympharum*, discussed in Henry More, *Conjectura Cabbalistica*, Defence i 6). See Homer, *Il.* v 872, 'low Hyle's [Matter's] watery plain'.

On the green bank, to look into the clear
Smooth lake, that to me seemed another sky.
460 As I bent down to look, just opposite,
A shape within the watery gleam appeared
Bending to look on me, I started back,
It started back, but pleased I soon returned,
Pleased it returned as soon with answering looks
465 Of sympathy and love; there I had fixed
Mine eyes till now, and pined with vain desire,
Had not a voice thus warned me, What thou seest,
What there thou seest fair creature is thyself,
With thee it came and goes: but follow me,
470 And I will bring thee where no shadow stays
Thy coming, and thy soft embraces, he
Whose image thou art, him thou shall enjoy
Inseparably thine, to him shalt bear
Multitudes like thyself, and thence be called
475 Mother of human race: what could I do,
But follow straight, invisibly thus led?

iv 460–71. Alluding to Ovid's story of the proud youth Narcissus, who was punished for his scornfulness by being made to fall in love with his own reflection in a pool, and to pine with vain desire (*Met.* iii 402–36). Thus the passage has considerable ironic force; for we know that Eve is to fall into precisely this error of seeking an end in herself or desiring an ideal self, until like Narcissus she 'loves an unsubstantial hope and thinks that substance which is only shadow' (*Met.* iii 417). Hence the divine warning that her true desire must be for the substantial Adam (l. 470). Bush cites a Christian tradition that 'some of the newly created angels looked up to God, others fell in love with themselves': see Donne, *Sermons*, ed. Potter and Simpson, iii 254.

iv 465. *Ed I* has comma after *love*.

iv 470. *stays*] waits for.

iv 471. *embraces*] In early edns, 'imbraces'.

iv 473. *Inseparably*] Literally true before the Fall, when Sin and Death had not yet entered the world.

iv 474–5. See *Gen.* iii 20: 'And Adam called his wife's name Eve; because she was the mother of all living.' (A.V. marginal gloss on *Eve*: 'Chavah, or, living'.) The commentators made much of the fact that this name was given only after the Fall (before, she was called simply 'woman': see *Gen.* ii 23, and Willet 54), so that M. may be deliberately correcting the conventional chronology, to enhance the status of sexuality and motherhood. See ll. 741ff for a similar piece of ideology, and on Eve's name see also xi 168f.

iv 476. *straight*] immediately; *Ed I* and *Ed II* spelling 'strait' could also indicate 'closely'.

Till I espied thee, fair indeed and tall,
Under a platan, yet methought less fair,
Less winning soft, less amiably mild,
480   Than that smooth watery image; back I turned,
Thou following cried'st aloud, Return fair Eve,
Whom fly'st thou? Whom thou fly'st, of him thou art,
His flesh, his bone; to give thee being I lent
Out of my side to thee, nearest my heart
485   Substantial life, to have thee by my side
Henceforth an individual solace dear;
Part of my soul I seek thee, and thee claim
My other half: with that thy gentle hand
Seized mine, I yielded, and from that time see
490   How beauty is excelled by manly grace
And wisdom, which alone is truly fair.
     So spake our general mother, and with eyes
Of conjugal attraction unreproved,

iv *478–80*. Burden 84f suggests that the point of the incident lies in Eve's freedom to choose. She goes with Adam not because there is no one else but because at l. 489 she freely chooses to love him rather than her own image. Similarly, her initial reluctance emphasises her freedom to have rejected him.

iv *478*. Adam is *Under a platan* (plane tree) because the plane was a symbol of Christ 'his head' (see Raban Maur, Migne cix 931; and cp. 299*n*, 443*n*). The basis of this well-known allegory was *Ecclus.* xxiv 14–16: 'I . . . grew up as a plane tree [Vulg. and Tremellius *platanus*] by the water. . . . my branches are the branches of honour and grace.' This association seems more probable than those which made the platan tree a symbol of erotic love (see Todd K. Bender, 'The Platan Tree in Donne, Horace and Theocritus', *TLS* (12 Aug. 1965) p. 704).

iv *483*. *Gen.* ii 23: 'Adam said, This is now bone of my bones, and flesh of my flesh.'

iv *484. nearest my heart*] 'It is . . . a superfluous question, out of what side of Adam Eva was taken, whether out of the right or left: it is resolved by most, out of the left, because Adams heart lay there: but these are frivolous and needelesse matters' (Willet 38, on *Gen.* ii 21f).

iv *486. individual*] inseparable; cp. Shakespeare, *Timon* I ii 6: 'Where ere thou go'st I still will folowe thee / An individuall mate.'

iv *487*. Horace consoling Maecenas in his illness calls him *meae . . . partem animae* (*Odes* II xvii 5).

iv *493. unreproved*] irreproachable, innocent. A Latin use of the past participle (e.g. *invictus*, unconquered, unconquerable) that M. was fond of imitating. Cp. 'unremoved' in l. 987, 'unreproved' in *L'Allegro* 40, 'unenchanted' in *Comus* 395, etc. Here, however, the immediate model may be Spenser, *F.Q.* II vii 16: 'The antique world, in his first flowring youth, /

And meek surrender, half embracing leaned
495 On our first father, half her swelling breast
Naked met his under the flowing gold
Of her loose tresses hid: he in delight
Both of her beauty and submissive charms
Smiled with superior love, as Jupiter
500 On Juno smiles, when he impregns the clouds
That shed May flowers; and pressed her matron lip
With kisses pure: aside the devil turned
For envy, yet with jealous leer malign
Eyed them askance, and to himself thus plained.
505   Sight hateful, sight tormenting! Thus these two
Imparadised in one another's arms
The happier Eden, shall enjoy their fill
Of bliss on bliss, while I to hell am thrust,
Where neither joy nor love, but fierce desire,
510 Among our other torments not the least,
Still unfulfilled with pain of longing pines;
Yet let me not forget what I have gained

Found no defect in his Creatours grace, / But with glad thankes, and un-reproved truth, / The gifts of soveraigne bountie did embrace: / Like Angels life was then mens happy cace.'

iv *499–501.* In the physical application of mythology, Jupiter was often the *aether* and Juno the air, source of rain-storms. And 'from the air growing ardent, animals and plants are born' (Conti, *Mytholog.* x, s.v. *Iuno*; p. 1021). Cp. also Virgil, *Georg.* ii 325–7: 'Then Heaven, the Father almighty, comes down in fruitful showers into the lap of his joyous spouse, and his might, with her mighty frame commingling, nurtures all growths.'   *impregns*] impregnates, makes pregnant.   *matron*] implying that the kisses are lawful; cp. Lucretia's 'matron cheeks' in Ovid, *Fasti* ii 828. Cp. viii 514.

iv *502. the devil*] Cp. 'the fiend' (l. 393): 'Satan's dimensions are reduced so effectively that we hardly notice how, in the process, his titles lose their lustre, how the "Archfiend" of the first book becomes "the Fiend" or the "arch-fellon" and how for the first time he begins to be "the Devil"' (Rajan 99).

iv *503.* From what Raphael tells him, Adam later imagines that conjugal love is likely to excite Satan's envy more than any other human bliss (ix 263f).

iv *506. Imparadised*] A very romantic and poetic word, here used bitterly.

iv *509–10.* Empson 68 rightly rejects Lewis's characterization of Satan as a peeping Tom, on the grounds that his jealousy is open: 'God has recently cut him off from his own corresponding pleasures.'

iv *511. pines*] torments, troubles (trans.).

From their own mouths; all is not theirs it seems:
One fatal tree there stands of knowledge called,
515 Forbidden them to taste: knowledge forbidden?
Suspicious, reasonless. Why should their Lord
Envy them that? Can it be sin to know,
Can it be death? And do they only stand
By ignorance, is that their happy state,
520 The proof of their obedience and their faith?
Of fair foundation laid whereon to build
Their ruin! Hence I will excite their minds
With more desire to know, and to reject
Envious commands, invented with design
525 To keep them low whom knowledge might exalt
Equal with gods; aspiring to be such,
They taste and die: what likelier can ensue?
But first with narrow search I must walk round
This garden, and no corner leave unspied;
530 A chance but chance may lead where I may meet
Some wandering spirit of heaven, by fountain side,

iv 513. The knowledge of devils being 'spurious, erroneous, fallacious' and limited, Satan is really dependent on eavesdropping for information. See Schultz 86, where Webster's *Displaying of Witchcraft* is cited to the effect that if a man remains silent, Satan cannot know his mind.

iv 515–22. Far from being 'genuinely indignant' (Empson 69) Satan is here exhilarated, because he has just thought of the basis of a scheme for the destruction of mankind. Enthusiastically he begins to rough out the speech with which he *will excite* (l. 522) Eve's mind. Thus *Equal with gods* (l. 526) corresponds to–though it is improved upon in–ix 547 'goddess among gods'. True, as Empson 32 rightly remarks, Satan could only invent these arguments if he half believed them. But for M. what mattered would be what was just, not what Satan contrived to half-believe. And the injustice of Satan's argument is heavily underlined: as, e.g., in the irony that God not only intended Adam and Eve to be *equal with gods*, if they were obedient (v 499–501), but even to exalt manhood to the throne of God himself, when they were disobedient, fallen and redeemed (iii 303–17). Broadbent 151 characterizes Satan's rhetoric in the present passage as 'forensic, flickering through ploce and traductio and erotema with suspicious speed; pragmatic, lacking the ceremoniousness that in places gives to what the Father (and especially Adam) says an aesthetic value.'

iv 523. Gen. iii 4f: 'The serpent said unto the woman . . . God doth know that in the day ye eat thereof, then your eyes shall be opened, and ye shall be as gods, knowing good and evil.'

iv 530. *chance but chance*] 'It is only a chance; but chance *may* lead.' Satan's jaunty jingle perhaps imitates the Lat. idiom *forte fortuna*. For a possible theological implication, see ii 935n.

>   Or in thick shade retired, from him to draw
>   What further would be learned. Live while ye may,
>   Yet happy pair; enjoy, till I return,
> 535 Short pleasures, for long woes are to succeed.
>   So saying, his proud step he scornful turned,
>   But with sly circumspection, and began
>   Through wood, through waste, o'er hill, o'er dale his
>   roam.
>   Mean while in utmost longitude, where heaven
> 540 With earth and ocean meets, the setting sun
>   Slowly descended, and with right aspect
>   Against the eastern gate of Paradise

iv 533–4. As Broadbent 190 observes, the *carpe diem* sentiment in which the more fleshly Renaissance paradises were so often bathed (e.g. Spenser, *F.Q.* II xii 74f; Tasso, *Gerus. Lib.* xvi 15) is here channelled exclusively into Satan's mouth.

iv 538. *roam*] the act of roaming. Earliest instance in *OED*.

iv 539. *utmost longitude*] the farthest west. See iii 573–6nn.

iv 541. *Slowly*] Editors have cavilled at 'Slowly' (in view, e.g., of 352f, 'the Sun / Declined was hasting now with prone career'); but M., further advanced in the study of astronomy, allowed for the refractive effect of the earth's atmosphere during the ultimate phase of the sunset. This effect produces an apparent deceleration of the sun's descent; see Riccioli ii 581, Problem 33, *Tempus Apparens Ortus et Occasus Limborum Solis definire*.

right aspect] direct view. Assuming that the gate is more or less vertical (547f), the rays of the setting sun will be at *right* angles with it.

iv 542. In *Gen.* iii 24 the guard of cherubim that excludes Adam and Eve from Paradise is placed 'at the east of the garden'. Since the gate is so high, even the setting sun's horizontal rays illuminate it, after passing over the 'insuperable height' of the western 'verdurous wall' (l. 143).

iv 542–50. A complex and highly condensed description. Among possible sources may be mentioned Purchas's and Heylyn's paradise of Mt Amara, which has smooth overhanging rock and a single 'ascending place, a faire gate' (see above, ll. 280–5n); and the marble 'crag of immense height' above the cave where Bacchus was hidden (Diodorus iii 69; see ll. 275–9n above). But earlier readers would also be quick to recognize the iconographical features of the description, in which five motifs may be distinguished. (1) The rock ascending *to the clouds* is a supraterrestrial Paradise 'in the air, under the circle of the Moon' (Heylyn iii 127; see 135n). (2) The way to its *entrance high* is an arduous Path of Virtue (see Wind 79). (3) Its *pillars* are Pillars of Virtue (see Tervarent 107). (4) The *craggy cliff* that overhangs symbolizes impending divine punishment (see Wind[2] 18), so that it proleptically foreshadows the Expulsion, in which the gate is to play a prominent part (xii 641–4). (5) the mention of *alablaster* directs attention to the receptacle in which the ointment of faith was kept uncorrupted (Vulg. *John*

Levelled his evening rays: it was a rock
Of alablaster, piled up to the clouds,
545   Conspicuous far, winding with one ascent
Accessible from earth, one entrance high;
The rest was craggy cliff, that overhung
Still as it rose, impossible to climb.
Betwixt these rocky pillars Gabriel sat
550   Chief of the angelic guards, awaiting night;
About him exercised heroic games
The unarmed youth of heaven, but nigh at hand
Celestial armoury, shields, helms, and spears,
Hung high with diamond flaming, and with gold.
555   Thither came Uriel, gliding through the even
On a sun beam, swift as a shooting star

xii 3, *nardus pisticus*; cp. *Matt.* xxvi 7, and see Raban Maur, Migne cvii 1101f).
Allegorically, then, the receptacle of Paradise must be the true Church–
as indeed M. has indicated at 193: 'So since into his Church lewd hirelings
climb.' The gate itself, however, is Christ; see *John* x 7 ('I am the door of the
sheep'), and cp. Giles Fletcher, *Christs victorie* ii 13, where Christ's legs are
'as two white marble pillars that uphold / Gods holy place'. Corcoran (20)
notes that Heylyn's description of Meroe (*Cosmographie* iv 62f) includes an
alabaster gate. Meroe was according to Josephus the capital of the Queen of
Sheba.

iv *544. alablaster*] alabaster (a common seventeenth-century spelling): a
specially white variety of marble, variegated with other colours; carbonate
of lime, used by the ancients for holding and preserving unguents.

iv *549–50. Gabriel*] 'Strength of God', one of the four archangels ruling the
corners of the world, and one of the angels of the cosmic chariot (see iii
648*n*). In the Bible (*Dan.* viii, ix; *Luke* i) he is a peaceful ambassador, rather
than a warrior. But M. followed a Jewish and cabbalistic tradition that
identified Gabriel with Mars (Valeriano 549). In making him guardian of
Paradise he followed another tradition, which presumably went back
ultimately to *Enoch* xx 7: 'Gabriel, one of the holy angels, who is over Para-
dise and the serpents and the Cherubim' (Charles ii 201). This verse does not
seem to have occurred, however, in the parts of *Enoch* accessible to M.

iv *552. unarmed*] Contrast the more aggressive games of the devils (ii 532–8).

iv *555.* Bentley objects to Satan's gliding through a period of time; Pearce
compares l. 557 (see also iii 71), interpreting *even* as the part of the celestial
hemisphere where it was evening; and at last Empson (²157f) sees the pun:
'the angle is sliding, choosing a safe gradient, down a nearly *even* sunbeam'.
For a further implication, see l. 590f below. Broadbent 87 contrasts the easy
movement of the good angels with the laboured, swarming, or zombie
movement of the devils.

iv *556–60. thwarts*] crosses (often in a nautical context, and thus appropriate
diction here); also 'obstructs'–i.e., interrupts the victory of darkness over

In autumn thwart the night, when vapours fired
Impress the air, and shows the mariner
From what point of his compass to beware
560   Impetuous winds: he thus began in haste.
     Gabriel, to thee thy course by lot hath given
Charge and strict watch that to this happy place
No evil thing approach or enter in;
This day at highth of noon came to my sphere
565   A spirit, zealous, as he seemed, to know
More of the almighty's works, and chiefly man
God's latest image: I described his way
Bent all on speed, and marked his airy gait;
But in the mount that lies from Eden north,
570   Where he first lighted, soon discerned his looks
Alien from heaven, with passions foul obscured:
Mine eye pursued him still, but under shade
Lost sight of him; one of the banished crew
I fear, hath ventured from the deep, to raise
575   New troubles; him thy care must be to find.

light. Uriel's arrival is like the *shooting star* not only in visual respects, but also because he brings a warning to the *mariner* (Gabriel) and so temporarily *thwarts* the powers of darkness. Homer (*Il.* iv 75–9) similarly compares the descent of Minerva to that of a shooting star 'portent to mariners'.

iv 556. *swift*] Yet Uriel has taken some considerable time over a journey that Satan accomplished almost instantaneously (see ll. 30 and 564). Perhaps the inference to be drawn is that Uriel had to wait until sunset, when a sun god's mythological task is completed for the day, before leaving his post.

iv 557–8. This piece of meteorology goes back at least to Seneca. Shooting stars were thought to be caused by exhalations from the earth that failed to ascend beyond a certain point, were ignited through repulsion by the surrounding air, and then slid away. Or the stars were a sign of storm because in falling they were thrust down by winds, which began earliest in the upper atmosphere. See Svendsen 89f.

iv 561. Modelled on the Hebrew temple service, in which the distribution of offices was by lot. See especially *1 Chron.* xxvi 13: 'they cast lots . . . for every gate'. Cp. v 655n.

iv 564. Note that M.'s universe is throughout on 'Paradise Time': the term *noon* can have no meaning unless a particular horizon is specified. Cp. Argument.

iv 567. God's first *image* being Christ, and the intervening images the angels, heaven and the products of the first five days of mundane creation; see iii 63, 384, etc.   *described*] descried; a common seventeenth-century confusion: see *OED* s.v *Describe* 7.

iv 572. *shade*] trees; as often in *PL* (cp. i 302-4, and see Wright 207).

To whom the winged warrior thus returned:
Uriel, no wonder if thy perfect sight,
Amid the sun's bright circle where thou sit'st,
See far and wide: in at this gate none pass
580   The vigilance here placed, but such as come
Well known from heaven; and since meridian hour
No creature thence: if spirit of other sort,
So minded, have o'erleaped these earthy bounds
On purpose, hard thou know'st it to exclude
585   Spiritual substance with corporeal bar.
But if within the circuit of these walks,
In whatsoever shape he lurk, of whom
Thou tell'st, by morrow dawning I shall know.
    So promised he, and Uriel to his charge
590   Returned on that bright beam, whose point now raised
Bore him slope downward to the sun now fallen
Beneath the Azores; whether the bright orb,

iv 577. *Uriel*] 'Light of God', one of God's 'eyes'; see iii 648–61*n*.

iv 580. *vigilance*] guard, watch; probably a metonymy, putting an attribute of the guard for the guard itself.

iv 585. See i 423–31*n*, vi 344–53.

iv 586. *Ed I* has no comma after *walks.*

iv 590–1. Since the sun has now set, its rays incline 'upwards' (regarded Ptolemaically) from the plane of the horizon. The ingenious routing, which allows Uriel to come and go without having to ascend, disgusted Addison. But the detail is no mere prettiness; for it emphasises the balancing of the hemispheres of light and dark at sunset, and so prepares for the important scales image of ll. 997ff. (Note the pun in *beam*–sunbeam, balance beam–and cp. the 'scale of heaven' at 354f, a passage linked to the present one by its mention of the 'Ocean Isles'.) Moreover, the numerological pattern demands that prominence be given to the precise moment of sunset: see l. 777*n*.

iv 592–7. Cp. iii 573–6*n*. The appearance of sunset can be regarded as caused either by orbital motion of the sun about the earth, or by the earth's rotation (a lesser movement). M.'s avoidance of the choice between the two models, Ptolemaic and post-Copernican, is rendered by a dizzying series of verbal and syntactical ambiguities: e.g., 'whether the *primum mobile* (*prime orb=* first sphere) had rolled there carrying the sun with it, or the turning earth had left him'; and 'whether the sun (*prime orb=*principal planet) had rolled there, or etc.'   *rolled*] May also be trans., with 'him' as the understood object.   *whether*] The early edns spelled 'whither', thus allowing a further chain of discourse, which does not persist, however, beyond *thither. Diurnal*] occupying one day (in the performance of the action). In the Ptolemaic system the *primum mobile* revolved about the earth, carrying the sun with it, in approximately one solar day; see Price 106.   *Incredible how*

Incredible how swift, had thither rolled
Diurnal, or this less voluble earth
595   By shorter flight to the east, had left him there
Arraying with reflected purple and gold
The clouds that on his western throne attend:
Now came still evening on, and twilight grey
Had in her sober livery all things clad;
600   Silence accompanied, for beast and bird,
They to their grassy couch, these to their nests
Were slunk, all but the wakeful nightingale;
She all night long her amorous descant sung;
Silence was pleased: now glowed the firmament
605   With living sapphires: Hesperus that led
The starry host, rode brightest, till the moon
Rising in clouded majesty, at length
Apparent queen unveiled her peerless light,

swift] An argument in favour of the Copernican system was that it avoided the enormous velocities implied by the Ptolemaic. According to Coperni-cus', Kepler's and later estimates, the velocity of the earth's diurnal motion had only to be about 0·06 German miles per second, as against 70 Ger. m.p.s. for the velocity of solar diurnal motion. And even the velocity of terrestrial annual motion was estimated at only 12.3 Ger. m.p.s. See Ric-cioli i 126f, and cp. viii 25–38 below, where Adam puts this argument to Raphael.   *voluble*] 'capable of ready rotation on its axis'; possibly stressed on the second syllable.

iv *598*. Cp. *Comus* 188f: 'the gray-hooded Even / Like a sad votarist in palmer's weed'.

iv *600–3*. *Silence accompanied*] 'Silence associated with them' (*OED* II 5, intrans., absol.); but also, possibly, 'silence accompanied musically (by the nightingale)'. The second sense is supported by *descant*, but not demanded by it; when used of a bird it could mean simply a melodious warbled song, without necessarily implying polyphony.

iv *604*. Cp. *Comus* 557–60, where Silence, surprised and captivated by the Lady's song, wishes to be forever displaced by it. Also *Il Penseroso* 51–6: 'with thee bring . . . mute silence . . . 'Less Philomel will deign a song.'

iv *605*. *sapphires*] See ll. 237–8n and ii 1049–50n.   *Hesperus*] Cp. xi 588f ('the evening star / Love's harbinger') and ix 49ff ('Hesperus, whose office is to bring / Twilight upon the earth, short arbiter / Twixt day and night').

iv *608*. *Apparent queen*] manifest queen; but also playing on 'heir-apparent' (often shortened to 'apparent'). While the moon was clouded (l. 607) her majesty was only presumptive; now, like her light, she is *peerless*, her succession unchallenged. The effect of the queen's sudden disrobing is heightened by the elaborate images of clothing at ll. 596–9.

And o'er the dark her silver mantle threw.
610   When Adam thus to Eve: Fair consort, the hour
        Of night, and all things now retired to rest
        Mind us of like repose, since God hath set
        Labour and rest, as day and night to men
        Successive, and the timely dew of sleep
615   Now falling with soft slumbrous weight inclines
        Our eyelids; other creatures all day long
        Rove idle unemployed, and less need rest;
        Man hath his daily work of body or mind
        Appointed, which declares his dignity,
620   And the regard of heaven on all his ways;
        While other animals unactive range,
        And of their doings God takes no account.
        To morrow ere fresh morning streak the east
        With first approach of light, we must be risen,
625   And at our pleasant labour, to reform
        Yon flowery arbours, yonder alleys green,
        Our walk at noon, with branches overgrown,
        That mock our scant manuring, and require
        More hands than ours to lop their wanton growth:
630   These blossoms also, and those dropping gums,
        That lie bestrewn unsightly and unsmooth,
        Ask riddance, if we mean to tread with ease;
        Mean while, as nature wills, night bids us rest.
            To whom thus Eve with perfect beauty adorned.

iv *614–15*. Cp. Spenser, *F.Q.* I i 36, 'the sad humour loading their eye liddes, /
As messenger of *Morpheus* on them cast / Sweet slombring deaw'; *Richard
III* IV i 83, 'the golden dew of sleep'; and *Julius Caesar* II i 230, 'the honey-
heavy dew of slumber'.
iv *618–19*. The Augustinian Adam, and indeed the medieval Adam generally,
lived a purely contemplative life before the Fall. But Protestants tended to
advance the prelapsarian status of the active life. See, e.g., l. 625*n*.
iv *620*. *regard*] attention, care.
iv *625*. Cp. ll. 327f. 'Though man should not have toyled or wearied him-
selfe with any labour in Paradise, for that was laid upon him as a punish-
ment afterward . . . yet it is evident that hee should have exercised himselfe
in some honest labour, even in Paradise . . . his charge was . . . to dresse
the garden . . . in which kind of husbandrie many even now doe take a
delight, and hold it rather to be a recreation, then any wearines unto them'
(Willet 33, on *Gen.* ii 15).
iv *627*. *walk*] walks *Ed I*.
iv *628*. *manuring*] cultivating, training.   *wanton*] luxuriant, unrestrained.
iv *631*. *bestrewn*] spelt 'bestrowne'.
iv *632*. *Ask*] need, call for, demand.

635   My author and disposer, what thou bid'st
       Unargued I obey; so God ordains,
       God is thy law, thou mine: to know no more
       Is woman's happiest knowledge and her praise.
       With thee conversing I forget all time,
640   All seasons and their change, all please alike.
       Sweet is the breath of morn, her rising sweet,
       With charm of earliest birds; pleasant the sun
       When first on this delightful land he spreads
       His orient beams, on herb, tree, fruit, and flower,
645   Glistering with dew; fragrant the fertile earth
       After soft showers; and sweet the coming on
       Of grateful evening mild, then silent night
       With this her solemn bird and this fair moon,
       And these gems of heaven, her starry train:

iv 635. *author*] origin (see viii 465ff); prompter, mover, initiator (*OED* 1 d). The forms of address used by Adam and Eve before the Fall have a magnificence, appropriate to their dignity, that is afterwards lost. Marjorie Barstow notices the abandonment of courteous titles after the Fall in 'Milton's use of the forms of epic address', *MLN* xxxi (1916) 120f. The prelapsarian titles are as much Biblical, however, as epic – e.g., the second Adam is called 'author of life' in *Acts* iii 15 (A.V. marg.) and 'author and finisher of faith' in *Heb.* xii 2.

iv 639–56. A rhetorically magnificent passage, exploiting to the full the possibilities of such circular or completive figures as epanalepsis (l. 641), epanodos and merismus (the division of l. 640 into the individual items of ll. 641–9) and irmus (the extreme periodicity of ll. 650–6). MacCaffrey (77) compares xii 617f ('thou to me / Art all things under heaven, all places thou'); for Eve 'Adam *is* Eden', and in their communion the constancy of Paradise reaches its culmination. The repetition of ll. 641–9 in ll. 650–6 'enacts a timeless recurrence' and renders the 'changing sameness' of time in Eden. In this connection it is particularly interesting to note the circularity of the self-subsistent 16-line passage 641–56, *Sweet is . . . is sweet*, with its large scale epanalepsis. Numerologically, 16 divided in this way, into portions of 9 and 7, symbolizes virtue harmoniously adjusting the mutable to the heavenly, *anima* to *mens*, soul to mind (see Fowler 269–88 on Spenser's use of a similar symbolism in the Castle of Alma). Note that the 9-line spiritual portion refers to Paradise with Adam, the mutable 7-line portion to Paradise without Adam. In the latter portion each item in the former suffers alteration; though this alteration is as yet hypothetical and held in check by negation.

iv 640. *seasons*] time of day; as in viii 69. Not 'seasons of the year', since it is still eternal spring.

iv 642. *charm*] song.

iv 648. *solemn bird*] Cp. 'solemn nightingale' in vii 435.

650   But neither breath of morn when she ascends
      With charm of earliest birds, nor rising sun
      On this delightful land, nor herb, fruit, flower,
      Glistering with dew, nor fragrance after showers,
      Nor grateful evening mild, nor silent night
655   With this her solemn bird, nor walk by moon,
      Or glittering starlight without thee is sweet.
      But wherefore all night long shine these, for whom
      This glorious sight, when sleep hath shut all eyes?
          To whom our general ancestor replied.
660   Daughter of God and man, accomplished Eve,
      Those have their course to finish, round the earth,
      By morrow evening, and from land to land
      In order, though to nations yet unborn,
      Ministering light prepared, they set and rise;
665   Lest total darkness should by night regain

iv 652–3. Note how *herb . . . dew*, merismus at ll. 644f, is now varied to an independent enumeratio. The passage is full of such theme-and-variation effects, which enact Eve's responsiveness to Adam, and perhaps (proleptically) the effect of her independence. See ll. 639–56n above.

iv 656. On the accentuation *without*, see ii 892n: it implies strong emphasis.

iv 675–8. A good question, in a way; for, although Adam gives partial answers in the speech that follows, his doubts have been aroused, and he himself addresses a very similar enquiry to Raphael at viii 15ff. Note, however, at what a disadvantage M. puts the question in the present context. Eve's preceding song of love is magnificent and sophisticated, but coming after it her intellectual query sounds perfunctory, casually abrupt in rhythm, shallow.

iv 660. See l. 635n. *Daughter of God* is dramatic irony, for one of the most familiar titles of Mary the second Eve is 'Mother of God' (the usual Eng. translation of the title *Theotokos*: the subject of bitter controversy in the fifth century, but a commonplace of later Marian devotion).

accomplished] An epithet of address in actual use; cp. Shakespeare, *Twelfth Night* III i 96: 'Most excellent accomplished lady'.

iv 661–73. Cp. the account of the stars' function at vii 340–52; common to both passages are the duties of illumination, and restraint of Night. Svendsen 76f traces these notions, as also that of the stars' *various influence*, to encyclopaedias such as the *De proprietatibus rerum* of Bartholomew of England. But it is misleading to give particular sources for ideas so generally held.

iv 661. *Those*] Perhaps 'These' was intended – *o* for *e* was an easy error.

iv 664. *light prepared*] Echoes *Ps.* lxxiv; see ll. 724–5n.

iv 665. Cp. iii 725–32, where Uriel explains that Night has invaded the nocturnal hemisphere, but that the moon's 'pale dominion checks the night' and prevents a return to the 'original darkness' (ii 984) of chaos.

Her old possession, and extinguish life
In nature and all things, which these soft fires
Not only enlighten, but with kindly heat
Of various influence foment and warm,
670   Temper or nourish, or in part shed down
Their stellar virtue on all kinds that grow
On earth, made hereby apter to receive
Perfection from the sun's more potent ray.
These then, though unbeheld in deep of night,
675   Shine not in vain, nor think, though men were none,
That heaven would want spectators, God want praise;
Millions of spiritual creatures walk the earth
Unseen, both when we wake, and when we sleep:
All these with ceaseless praise his works behold
680   Both day and night: how often from the steep
Of echoing hill or thicket have we heard
Celestial voices to the midnight air,
Sole, or responsive each to other's note
Singing their great creator: oft in bands
685   While they keep watch, or nightly rounding walk
With heavenly touch of instrumental sounds
In full harmonic number joined, their songs
Divide the night, and lift our thoughts to heaven.

iv 668–73. See Caxton 147f., cit. Svendsen 77: though the sun is more vir-
tuous than the other stars, 'yet somtyme they restrayne his heetes and after
they enlarge them, after that they be fer or nygh, as he otherwhile hath
nede'. In Neoplatonic astrology, Sol was said to accomplish the generation
of new life by acting through each of the other planets in turn; their function
was only to modulate his influence, or to select from his complete spectrum
of virtues. See, e.g., Ficino, In Timaeum xx (Opera omnia 1468). After the
Fall the influence of the stars becomes less kindly (benign; natural): see x
660 ff.
iv 675. The first comma may be in error for a heavier point.
iv 681–4. Cp. Lucretius, De rerum nat. iv 586ff, where the music heard is that
of Pan's pipe (often interpreted allegorically as the music of the spheres).
iv 682–3. Cp. the angels' skill in polyphony at iii 370f. Socrates Scholasticus
tells how Ignatius 'saw a vision of angels praising the Holy Trinity in
responsive hymns', and how this vision was the source of antiphonal music
in the Church (Ecclesiasticae historiae autores (Paris 1544) fol. 258ᵛ); a tradi-
tion referred to by M. in his Commonplace Book (Yale i 383).
iv 688. Divide the night] mark the watches of the night by giving the signal
for a change of guard (Lat. dividere noctem). In view of the context, perhaps
there is also a play on the musical sense of divide (OED 11 a, perform with
'divisions'—florid melodic passages or descants).

         Thus talking hand in hand alone they passed
690   On to their blissful bower; it was a place
      Chosen by the sovereign planter, when he framed
      All things to man's delightful use; the roof
      Of thickest covert was inwoven shade
      Laurel and myrtle, and what higher grew
695   Of firm and fragrant leaf; on either side
      Acanthus, and each odorous bushy shrub
      Fenced up the verdant wall; each beauteous flower,

iv *690–703.* In the description of Paradise in Bk iv Art and Nature cooper-
ate: 'The more artificial nature's works appear, the more they "illustrate"
the immanence of God. . . . When the terms of art predominate . . . the
reference is usually to the Bower of Adam and Eve which has been deliber-
ately made for them by God' (Broadbent 179f). This equilibrium of Art
and Nature is delicate and unstable, however; it is liable to slip into excess
or artificiality, 'brutalism or sophistication'.
iv *691. planter*] See *Gen.* ii 8: 'God planted a garden.'
iv *694.* Cp. the arbour of generation within the 'grove of myrtle' in the
Garden of Adonis in Spenser, *F.Q.* III vi 43–4, which is certainly sexually,
and probably even anatomically, symbolic (see Ellrodt 88*n*, Fowler 137).
laurel and myrtle] Associated in Virgil, *Ecl.* ii 54 ('You too will I pluck,
laurels, and you their neighbour myrtle, for so placed you blend sweet
fragrance'); but at this juncture M. must intend more than an elegant
allusion. Myrtle later figures prominently in an emblematic context at
a critical stage of the action, immediately before the Fall. There it is clearly
a symbol of virtue or modesty (see ix 426–31*n*). But here the trees seem
rather to symbolize the complementary roles of Apollo and Venus, male
and female, *mens* and *anima*, reason and virtue. The force of the passage
lies in the suggestion of a comprehensive polarity.
iv *696. acanthus*] Mentioned among the trees and shrubs, so that M. may
intend the Egyptian acacia, the evergreen tree that Virgil describes as
semper frondens (*Ecl.* ii 119), and not the acanthus flower. The Virgilian
context, a list of exotic fragrant trees, may account for the introduction of
the acanthus here; or perhaps the fact that since ancient times acanthus
leaves have been used as a decorative architectural motif (see ll. 690–703*n*,
and note *wall . . . mosaic . . . inlay*). Like the *hyacinth* (l. 701) the acanthus
was the result of the metamorphosis of a love of Apollo (cp. Spenser's
similar list of metamorphosed lovers in the Garden of Adonis, *F.Q.* III vi
45). *Acanthus* is treated as a proper name in *Ed I* and *Ed II*.
iv *697–701.* Combining the flowers of the Atlantic Isles, with those that
sprang up beneath Zeus and Hera to raise them from the soil of Mt Ida
(Homer, *Il.* xiv 347–9: crocus, hyacinth). See Conti, *Mytholog.* iii 19 on the
Atlantic Isles: *Hi duas esse parvas insulas referebant mari inter se divisas, atque
ventos ibi plurimum suaves et odoriferos leniter spirare, tanquam per incredibilem
florum varietatem et amoenitatem transeuntes. Nam qualis odor est multis rosis,*

Iris all hues, roses, and jessamine
Reared high their flourished heads between, and
       wrought
700   Mosaic; underfoot the violet,
Crocus, and hyacinth with rich inlay
Broidered the ground, more coloured than with stone
Of costliest emblem: other creature here
Beast, bird, insect, or worm durst enter none;
705   Such was their awe of man. In shady bower
More sacred and sequestered, though but feigned,
Pan or Silvanus never slept, nor nymph,
Nor Faunus haunted. Here in close recess
With flowers, garlands, and sweet-smelling herbs
710   Espoused Eve decked first her nuptial bed,
And heavenly choirs the hymenean sung,

violis, hyacinthis, liliis, narcissis, myrtetis, lauris, cyparissis, talis aspirantium ventorum est suavitas.'

iv *698. jessamin*] jasmine.

iv *699. flourished*] flowered, adorned with flowers.

iv *700–3. emblem*] The word could mean any ornament of inlaid work; see, e.g., the contemporary definition by the emblematist George Whitney, *cit.* Freeman 37, 'such figures, or works, as are wrought in plate, or in stones in the pavements, or on the walls, or such like, for the adorning of the place'. But it is difficult to think that the other sense of *emblem* (pictorial symbol) is not also meant to operate here, and to draw attention to the emblematic properties of the flowers (the humility of the *violet*, prudence of the *hyacinth*, amiability of the *jessamin*, etc.). More generally, the bower as a whole is an emblem of true married love. Thus its seclusion and concealment (ll. 693, 704) reflect the privacy and particular belonging of the marital relation.

iv *705–8.* Often *Pan Silvanus* and *Faunus* were confused, for all were represented as half man, half goat. For Pan as Nature, see ll. 266–8n; here he is more specifically a symbol of fecundity and a god of *sequestered* places. Silvanus, said by some to be the son of Faunus, was a god of woods, gardens and limits. Faunus himself was a more ambiguous deity. On the one hand he was the Roman Pan, a benignly priapic wood god, *nympharum fugentium amator* (Horace, *Odes* III xviii 1), who *haunted* the forest as an oracle (Virgil, *Aen.* vii 81–4); on the other, the father of satyrs, an emblem of Concupiscence (Alciati (Lyons 1600) Embl. lxxii; Ripa, *Iconologia* (Padua 1611) 315) or even of Satan, tempter of Eve (see Fowler[3] 101f).

iv *705. shady*] shadier *Ed I*.

iv *708. close*] secret.

iv *711. hymenean*] wedding hymn; Hymenaeus or Hymen being the ancient god of marriage. See *Elegia V* 105–8, where youths shout the hymenean chorus 'Io, Hymen'.

What day the genial angel to our sire
Brought her in naked beauty more adorned,
More lovely than Pandora, whom the gods
715   Endowed with all their gifts, and O too like

iv *712. genial*] nuptial, generative. The role that in poetry of a different mode would be taken by Genius, the deity presiding over generation and marriage (cp. 'Old Genius' the porter of Spenser's Garden of Adonis, *F.Q.* III vi 31f), is here instead taken by the mysterious invisible *genial angel* of ll. 467–76. Gilbert (45) finds a discrepancy between the present passage and viii 484–7, where Eve is guided by her maker; and perhaps he is right. The genial angel is not of course to be confused with Raphael, who on the day of Adam's creation was away on a mission to hell gate (viii 229).
iv *714–19.* Verbal echoes suggest that M. has followed Charles Estienne's version of the myth: 'Pandora . . . is feigned by Hesiod the first woman–made by Vulcan at Jupiter's command–*whom the gods all adorned* with their gifts. . . . hence she was called Pandora, either because she was *endowed with all their gifts*, or because she was endowed with gifts by all. The tradition is that she was afterwards sent with a closed casket to Epimetheus, since Jupiter wanted revenge on the human race for the boldness of Prometheus, who had stolen fire from heaven and taken it . . . down to earth; and that Epimetheus received her and opened the casket, which contained every kind of evil, so that it filled the world with diseases and calamaties' (*cit.* Starnes 270; my itals). Empson's queer smack at M. (Empson[2] 179: 'Not only was Eve not trying to avenge Satan but Pandora was not trying to avenge Prometheus') is beside the point, for it is not Satan who steals the authentic fire of forbidden knowledge. Man is both Prometheus and Epimetheus: so long as he has foresight and wisdom, he enjoys (as here) divine gifts; but when in the *sad event* (result) he is *unwiser*, he comes to resemble Epimetheus, and to experience the consequences of sin. M. had applied the myth in a similar manner in *Doctrine and Discipline* ii 3 (Yale ii 293): '*Plato* and *Chrysippus* with their followers the *Academics* and the *Stoics* who knew not what a consummat and most adorned *Pandora* was bestow'd upon *Adam* to be the nurse and guide of his arbitary happinesse and perseverance, I mean his native innocence and perfection, which might have kept him from being our true *Epimetheus*.' Prometheus and Epimetheus were sons of Iapetus, the Titan son of Coelus and Terra. Starnes and Talbert (260) advance the rash theory that M. invented the 'interesting identification' of Iapetus and Iaphet (Noah's son: *Gen.* ix–x) by conflating two dictionary entries. In fact the identification was an established piece of syncretism, important enough to have a chapter devoted to it in the anonymous *Observationum libellus* appended to Conti's *Mythologiae* ((Lyons 1653) Sig. Kkk iii[r]): '*De Iapeto seu Iapheto primogenito Noachi Patriarchae filio extant plurima apud Ethnicos vestigia. Is enim est, quem ipsi Hebraeam vocem ad suae linguae normam ac suavitatem inflectentes, vocant Iapetum priscum. Nam plures postea eodem hoc nomine sunt appellati. Priscus vero iste Iapetus, terrae et coeli filius.*'

In sad event, when to the unwiser son
Of Japhet brought by Hermes, she ensnared
Mankind with her fair looks, to be avenged
On him who had stole Jove's authentic fire.
720   Thus at their shady lodge arrived, both stood
Both turned, and under open sky adored
The God that made both sky, air, earth and heaven
Which they beheld, the moon's resplendent globe
And starry pole: Thou also madest the night,
725   Maker omnipotent, and thou the day,
Which we in our appointed work employed
Have finished happy in our mutual help
And mutual love, the crown of all our bliss
Ordained by thee, and this delicious place
730   For us too large, where thy abundance wants
Partakers, and uncropt falls to the ground.
But thou hast promised from us two a race
To fill the earth, who shall with us extol
Thy goodness infinite, both when we wake,
735   And when we seek, as now, thy gift of sleep.
    This said unanimous, and other rites
Observing none, but adoration pure
Which God likes best, into their inmost bower

Cp. i 507–21n above, and see Hesiod, *Theogony* 570ff. For a full history of the theological interpretation of the Pandora myth, see Dora and Erwin Panofsky, *Pandora's Box* (1956).   *authentic*] entitled to respect; original.
iv *720. stood*] See xi 1–2n. Some copies *Ed I* have comma after *stood*, others period.
iv *722.* The use of *both* to qualify more than two nouns was quite usual in prose in M.'s time (*OED* B 1 b).
iv *724–5.* Cp. *Ps.* lxxiv 16: 'The day is thine, the night also is thine: thou hast prepared the light and the sun.'   *pole*] sky (poet.).
iv *729.* Though various other syntactical connections have been proposed and are not impossible, *place* is primarily the object of *madest* (l. 724).
iv *732–3.* Referring to *Gen.* i 28, where, before the Fall, 'God said unto them, Be fruitful, and multiply, and replenish the earth'–a controversial text that could be taken as proof that marriage not only had its 'institution in mans innocencie', but was allowable to all (see Willet 21).
iv *735.* Cp. *Ps.* cxxvii 2: 'It is vain for you to rise up early, to sit up late, to eat the bread of sorrows: for so he giveth his beloved sleep.' But the idea of sleep as a divine gift is almost universal; see, e.g., Homer, *Il.* ix 713 ('they laid themselves down and took the gift of sleep'), Virgil, *Aen.* ii 268f ('rest begins, and by grace of the gods steals gratefully over them').
iv *736–7.* Cp. xii 534 on the inadequacy of 'outward rites and specious forms'.

Handed they went; and eased the putting off
740   These troublesome disguises which we wear,
Straight side by side were laid, nor turned I ween
Adam from his fair spouse, nor Eve the rites
Mysterious of connubial love refused:
Whatever hypocrites austerely talk
745   Of purity and place and innocence,
Defaming as impure what God declares
Pure, and commands to some, leaves free to all.

iv 739. *Handed*] joined hand in hand.

iv 743. *Mysterious*] In *Eph.* v St Paul describes coitus as 'mysterious' in the sense that the state of 'one flesh' is a mystery or symbol of the relations between Christ and the Church. Some think M. is guilty of the generous fault of allowing inconsistencies of plot for the sake of getting in prelapsarian sex. If Adam and Eve share the fertility of Paradise, must they not conceive before the Fall, and thus bear a child free from original sin? But the subtlety of M. and the Biblical commentators has been underestimated. Willet, e.g., was quite capable of believing both that marriage was instituted 'in mans innocencie' (21) and that 'Adam in the state of innocencie should [sc. would] not have gotten so ungratious a sonne, as Caine was' (60). It was possible, we must conclude, to hold that Adam and Eve made love in Paradise without conceiving. But in any case, traditional embryological theories allowed ample opportunity for the subsequent infection of children conceived in innocence.

iv 744-9. *1 Tim.* iv 1-3-an apocalyptic text that Protestants found it useful to apply to the church of Rome-warns that 'in the latter times some shall depart from the faith . . . Speaking lies in hypocrisy; having their consciences seared with a hot iron; Forbidding to marry'. Fervently believing that 'marriage is honourable in itself, and prohibited to no order of men' (*De doctrina* i 10, Columbia xv 155), M. leaves his reader in no doubt that the sexual act was performed in the time of man's *innocence*. To put the first intercourse of Adam and Eve before the Fall was in itself to assume a theological position-one that went back at least to Hugh of St Victor, who believed that 'if we had remained in the state of innocence we should have generated *sine carnis incentivo*' (Lewis[2] 15). Similarly, the preparatory allusion to *Gen.* i 28 (see ll. 732-3n) had ideological bearing. For Bellarmine and Pererius held that that verse contained no precept to marry, but only an 'institution of nature'; whereas Protestants found in it 'a libertie graunted to all that will marrie, that thereby mankinde may still be propagated' (Willet 21). See also Williams 88.

iv 745. *place*] Explained by l. 759.

iv 747. *commands to some*] 'It is good for a man not to touch a woman. Nevertheless, to avoid fornication, let every man have his own wife' (*I Cor.* vii 1f). 'Hence marriage is not a command binding on all, but only on those

Our maker bids increase, who bids abstain
But our destroyer, foe to God and man?
750 Hail wedded love, mysterious law, true source
Of human offspring, sole propriety
In Paradise of all things common else.
By thee adulterous lust was driven from men
Among the bestial herds to range, by thee
755 Founded in reason, loyal, just, and pure,
Relations dear, and all the charities
Of father, son, and brother first were known.
Far be it, that I should write thee sin or blame,
Or think thee unbefitting holiest place,
760 Perpetual fountain of domestic sweets,
Whose bed is undefiled and chaste pronounced,

who are unable to live with chastity out of this state' (*De doctrina* i 10; Columbia xv 155).

iv 750–65. Many Protestant hexaemeral poems had their panegyrics on married love. Cp. especially Du Bartas 172: 'O blessed Bond! o happy Marriage! / Which doost the match 'twixt Christ and us presage! / O chastest friendship, whose pure flames impart / Two Soules in one, two Hearts into one Hart! / O holy knot, in *Eden* instituted / (Not in this Earth with blood and wrongs polluted. . . .)' On the three ends of marriage (society, procreation, remedy for lust) in seventeenth-century thought, see D. Sherwin Bailey, *The Mystery of Love and Marriage* (1952) pp. 101–4. M., like Hooper, Bucer, Becon, Taylor and the majority of Anglican divines (but unlike Donne, who emphasised remedy), placed society first: 'The *form* of marriage consists in the mutual exercise of benevolence, love, help, and solace between the espoused parties. . . . The end of marriage is nearly the same with the form' (*De doctrina* i 10, Columbia xv 155). Procreation of children he regarded merely as the 'proper fruit' of marriage (*ibid.*). As for remedy, it is only 'since Adam's fall' that 'the provision of a remedy against incontinency has become in some degree a secondary end' (*ibid.*; cp. Jeremy Taylor, *cit.* Bailey 103: avoidance of fornication 'came in by the superfoetation of the evil accidents of the world'). In accordance with the same emphasis, *mutual love* comes first in the present passage (ll. 728, 750, 760), then *increase* (ll. 732, 748), while remedy, appropriately, is ignored (except perhaps in l. 753).

iv 750. *mysterious*] See l. 743n.

iv 751–2. i.e., the exclusive relationship and mutual rights of Adam and Eve were the only *propriety* (proprietorship, ownership) in Paradise. The institution of marriage was prelapsarian, but not that of property rights.

iv 756. *charities*] affections.

iv 761. Cp. *Heb.* xiii 4: 'Marriage is honourable in all, and the bed undefiled.'

Present, or past, as saints and patriarchs used.
Here Love his golden sh'afts employs, here lights
His constant lamp, and waves his purple wings,
765 Reigns here and revels; not in the bought smile
Of harlots, loveless, joyless, unendeared,
Casual fruition, nor in court amours
Mixed dance, or wanton mask, or midnight ball,
Or serenade, which the starved lover sings
770 To his proud fair, best quitted with disdain.
These lulled by nightingales embracing slept,
And on their naked limbs the flowery roof
Showered roses, which the morn repaired. Sleep on
Blest pair; and O yet happiest if ye seek

iv *763.* Cupid's *golden shafts* were sharp and gleaming, and kindled love; while those of lead were blunt, and put love to flight (Ovid, *Met.* i 468–71). The symbolism was ubiquitous in Renaissance love poetry and emblem literature (see Tervarent 186f). In the specification of golden arrows for marital love, M. had been preceded by Erasmus (*Coll.* iv).

iv *764. constant lamp*] An ironic contrast between love in Paradise and in the fallen world; for a lamp usually symbolized inconstancy of love, particularly woman's inconstancy. See Valeriano, *Hieroglyphica* xlvi 19, *Mulieris amor*: 'Among interpreters of dreams one reads that a burning lamp is the symbol of a woman who has been captivated by love; because their love is very light, inconstant and weak, and like a lamp can be extinguished by the influence of the slightest breeze' (p. 582). Since in the present passage Love himself lights the lamp, it is difficult to see how it can allude to the one Psyche used for her disastrous scrutiny of Cupid. On the other hand, the lamps of the constant virgins expecting the divine bridegroom (*Matt.* xxv 1–13) must surely constitute an allegorical overtone.   Love is probably given *purple wings* on the authority of *Rem. amor.* 701, where he has *purpureas . . . alas* (cp. also Cupid's 'winges of purple and blewe' in Spenser, *Shep. Cal.* March 33). Ovid's *purpureas*, however, meant 'shining'; whereas many of M.'s early readers would have taken the hint of *Reigns* (l. 765) and assumed that purple as an emblem of sovereignty was intended. Note also that purple was the distinctive colour of Hymen (see l. 711*n*).

iv *765. Reigns . . . revels*] Stealing from Marino's *L'Adone* (ii 114) a tune there devoted to a pagan Love: *Quivi Amor si trastulla, e quindi impera.*

iv *767–8.* Cp. the satire on the sons of Belial at i 497ff and *PR* ii 183; also the attack on the 1633 *Book of Sports* – which seemed to M. to encourage 'gaming, jigging, wassailing, and mixt dancing' – in *Of Reformation* ii (Yale i 589).   *masque*] masked ball.

iv *769.* Ironic, for the lover is both *starved* of love and perished with cold. Serenades were sung *in sereno*, on clear cold nights.   *serenade*] *Ed I* and *Ed II* have the early form 'serenate'.

iv *773. repaired*] made up for (with new roses).

775   No happier state, and know to know no more.
        Now had night measured with her shadowy cone
        Half way up hill this vast sublunar vault,
        And from their ivory port the cherubim
        Forth issuing at the accustomed hour stood armed
780   To their night watches in warlike parade,
        When Gabriel to his next in power thus spake.
        Uzziel, half these draw off, and coast the south

iv 775. Either 'know that it is best not to seek new knowledge (by eating
the forbidden fruit)' or 'know (*OED* IV 12) *how to* limit your experience
to the state of innocence'.
iv 776–80. Cp. iii 556–7. The earth's shadow is a cone that appears to circle
round it, in diametrical opposition to the sun. When the axis of the cone
reaches the meridian, it is midnight; but here it is only *Half way up*, so that
the time is nine o'clock (night and day being equal in Paradise, each is of
exactly twelve hours' duration). For the Hebrew and Roman practice of
dividing the night into four equal watches of three hours each, see, e.g.,
Riccioli i 36, and St Jerome on *Ps.* xc 4 (Vulg. lxxxix 4). Here the second
watch is just beginning. Numerologically, as the content demands, l. 777
exactly marks–'measures'–the *Half way* point between l. 539, when the
sun *in utmost longitude* begins its descent beneath the horizon at six o'clock,
and l. 1015, the last line of Bk iv, when 'the shades of night' first begin to
flee at midnight (ll. 1013–15n). The cone of the earth's shadow should be
regarded as another form of a thematic shape common in *PL*, the pyramid
of pride (see v 758–9n below). In *Reason of Church-Government* i 6, M speaks
of 'hierarchies acuminating still higher and higher in a cone of Prelaty'.
port] gate. In ancient legend deceptive dreams issued from a gate of ivory,
true dreams from a gate of horn. Since the cherubim are to interrupt a
false dream, it is the ivory gate they use.
iv 781. For Gabriel's office as keeper of Paradise and ruler of cherubim,
see l. 549–50n.
iv 782–8. Of the obscure names M. assigns to his cherub guards, *Uzziel*
(Strength of God) occurs in the Bible as an ordinary human name (e.g.
Exod. vi 18) and so does *Zephon* (Searcher of Secrets: *Num.* xxvi 15). But
the aptness goes beyond literal meaning; for in Rabbinical tradition Uzziel
was one of the seven angels before the throne of God. Though a printed
source cannot be specified, it seems very probable that M. knew of this
tradition: see West 154f and 206; also his 'The names of Milton's Angels',
SP xlvii (1950) 211–23, and Fletcher[2] 252–5. The name *Ithuriel* (Discovery
of God) is not from the Bible, but it occurs–or at least a form very like it–in
the disreputable *Key of Solomon*.
iv 782–4. Here and at ll. 797f and 974–6 the movements of the angels almost
seem to resemble the apparent nightly courses of the constellations (see also
ll. 985–7n). Uzziel's detachment are (as it were) the stars of the southern

With strictest watch; these other wheel the north,
Our circuit meets full west. As flame they part
785   Half wheeling to the shield, half to the spear.
From these, two strong and subtle spirits he called
That near him stood, and gave them thus in charge.
     Ithuriel and Zephon, with winged speed
Search through this garden, leave unsearched no nook,
790   But chiefly where those two fair creatures lodge,
Now laid perhaps asleep secure of harm.
This evening from the sun's decline arrived
Who tells of some infernal spirit seen
Hitherward bent (who could have thought?) escaped
795   The bars of hell, on errand bad no doubt:
Such where ye find, seize fast, and hither bring.
     So saying, on he led his radiant files,
Dazzling the moon; these to the bower direct
In search of whom they sought: him there they found
800   Squat like a toad, close at the ear of Eve;
Assaying by his devilish art to reach
The organs of her fancy, and with them forge
Illusions as he list, phantasms and dreams,
Or if, inspiring venom, he might taint
805   The animal spirits that from pure blood arise

hemisphere, Gabriel's those of the northern. Cp. Marvell, 'Upon Appleton House', st. 40: 'the vigilant *Patroul* / Of Stars walks round about the *Pole*'.

iv 785. *shield* for 'left' and *spear* for 'right' were ancient military terms.

iv 786. *these*] i.e., the half under his own command, who wheeled to the right.

iv 791. *secure*] unapprehensive, careless.

iv 799. Burden 93 regards the capture of Satan merely as a graphic demonstration that God could have stopped him if he had wanted to. For a partial confirmation of this view see l. 1012*n* below, and for an alternative possibility l. 996*n*.

iv 802–3. *organs*] Punning between 'instruments' and a sense nearer to the modern ('functionally adapted parts of the body').   *phantasms*] illusions, deceptive appearances; mental images.

iv 805. *Animal spirits*] Spirits in this sense were fine vapours, regarded by some as a medium between body and soul, by others as a separate soul. Natural spirits originated in the liver and circulated venously; while vital spirits were formed in the heart from the natural, and circulated arterially. Animal spirits (Lat. *anima*, soul) were formed from the vital (hence *from pure blood*), ascended to the brain and issued through the nerves to impart motion to the body. Local movement of the animal spirits could also produce imaginative apparitions, and it was through these that angels were thought to affect the human mind. The alternatives before Satan are either

Like gentle breaths from rivers pure, thence raise
At least distempered, discontented thoughts,
Vain hopes, vain aims, inordinate desires
Blown up with high conceits engendering pride.
810   Him thus intent Ithuriel with his spear
Touched lightly; for no falsehood can endure
Touch of celestial temper, but returns
Of force to its own likeness: up he starts
Discovered and surprised. As when a spark
815   Lights on a heap of nitrous powder, laid
Fit for the tun some magazine to store
Against a rumoured war, the smutty grain
With sudden blaze diffused, inflames the air:
So started up in his own shape the fiend.
820   Back stept those two fair angels half amazed

to manipulate the organ of fancy itself; or else to work on the animal spirits, the source of sense-data, which retained past experiences he could mould to his purposes. Contrary to early demonology, the doctrine of M. and his contemporaries was that devils had no access to man's reason, and could only operate through the imagination. See W. B. Hunter, 'Eve's Demonic Dream', *ELH* xiii (1946) 255–65, with extensive documentation ranging from St Thomas to Glanvill.

iv *807. distempered*] vexed, troubled; disordered.

iv *810–13. Ithuriel with his spear*] Burden (100) thinks that a magic spear has to be provided so that Ithuriel can pierce Satan's disguise more effectively than Uriel did at first. But the fact that a toad has dared to enter the nuptial bower – an unnatural occurrence; see l. 704 – is enough to alert the guard. The spear is rather an emblematic expression of their perceptiveness. It is necessary to the story in another way, however: Satan has to be got back into a presentable form for the confrontation that follows.

iv *812. temper*] tempering, temperament. The primary reference is to the spear, which has been tempered in heaven; but the odd diction allows a secondary reference to Ithuriel's own spiritual constitution.

iv *814–19.* Broadbent (110) sees this as an instance of the 'alternating inflation and deflation of the devils begun in Book i, and continued for Satan all through'; the next instance coming not far below, at ll. 986–1015.   *nitrous*] mixed with nitre (potassium nitrate or saltpetre, an ingredient in gunpowder) to form an explosive.   *Fit for the tun*] In proper condition for casking, ready for use.   *Against*] in preparation for.   *smutty grain*] Perhaps this sets up a resonance with the next simile, of corn and chaff (ll. 981–5). For earlier mentions of guns or gunpowder in connection with Satan, see ii 937, iv 17; all these passages acquire new significance with Raphael's account of the invention of gunpowder, in vi 469–500. The present simile gains aptness from the fact that gunpowder was commonly called 'serpentine powder'.

So sudden to behold the grisly king;
Yet thus, unmoved with fear, accost him soon.
    Which of those rebel spirits adjudged to hell
Comest thou, escaped thy prison, and transformed,
825   Why sat'st thou like an enemy in wait
Here watching at the head of these that sleep?
    Know ye not then said Satan, filled with scorn,
Know ye not me? Ye knew me once no mate
For you, there sitting where ye durst not soar;
830   Not to know me argues your selves unknown,
The lowest of your throng; or if ye know,
Why ask ye, and superfluous begin
Your message, like to end as much in vain?
To whom thus Zephon, answering scorn with scorn.
835   Think not, revolted spirit, thy shape the same,
Or undiminished brightness, to be known
As when thou stood'st in heaven upright and pure;
That glory then, when thou no more wast good,
Departed from thee, and thou resemblest now
840   Thy sin and place of doom obscure and foul.
But come, for thou, be sure, shalt give account
To him who sent us, whose charge is to keep
This place inviolable, and these from harm.
    So spake the cherub, and his grave rebuke
845   Severe in youthful beauty, added grace
Invincible: abashed the devil stood,
And felt how awful goodness is, and saw
Virtue in her shape how lovely, saw, and pined

iv 836. The construction makes one expect some such inverted form as
'Or [thy] brightness undiminished'; but *undiminished brightness* mimetically
resists the grammatical pressure to alter.

iv 840. *obscure*] dark, dismal; but also answering scorn with scorn by im-
plying remote, lowly.

iv 845. Cp. Virgil's description of Euryalus, *gratior et pulchro veniens in
corpore virtus*. On the significance of angelic age, see iii 636–7n. Empson (60)
thinks the 'young' angels are those recently promoted to fill the room of the
rebel third. Alternatively we may suppose that *youthful* means 'youthful':
cherubim enjoy perpetual youth iconographically.

iv 848. So at ix 457–65 Eve's innocence and 'heavenly form / Angelic'
overawe Satan. Underlying both passages is the Platonic notion that virtue
can affect a person's outward appearance; cp. Cicero, *De officiis* i 5: *Formam
quidem ipsam et quasi faciem honesti vides, quae si oculis cerneretur, mirabiles
amores (ut ait Plato) excitaret sapientiae.* The establishment of the idea as one of
the principal doctrines of Renaissance love poetry was apparently due to

His loss; but chiefly to find here observed
850   His lustre visibly impaired; yet seemed
Undaunted. If I must contend, said he,
Best with the best, the sender not the sent,
Or all at once; more glory will be won,
Or less be lost. Thy fear, said Zephon bold,
855   Will save us trial what the least can do
Single against thee wicked, and thence weak.
    The fiend replied not, overcome with rage;
But like a proud steed reined, went haughty on,
Champing his iron curb: to strive or fly
860   He held it vain; awe from above had quelled
His heart, not else dismayed. Now drew they nigh
The western point, where those half-rounding guards
Just met, and closing stood in squadron joined
Awaiting next command. To whom their chief
865   Gabriel from the front thus called aloud.
    O friends, I hear the tread of nimble feet
Hasting this way, and now by glimpse discern
Ithuriel and Zephon through the shade,
And with them comes a third of regal port,

Dante: see, e.g., *Convivio*, Ode iii 7, 'The soul whom this excellence [blessed-ness] adorns, / holds it not concealed; / for, from the first when she weds the body, / she shows it forth till death', and cp. Ode ii 4 etc.; consult also Charles Williams, *The Forgiveness of Sins* (1942) 23f. Cp. further *Reason of Church-Government* i 1: 'Discipline is . . . the very visible shape and image of vertue, whereby she is not only seene in the regular gestures and motions of her heavenly paces as she walkes, but also makes the harmony of her voice audible to mortall eares' (Yale i 751f).   *pined*] mourned.

iv *858–61*. He allows himself to be arrested by two young angels, and later is ready to fight a whole squadron, because 'it is a point of honour to refuse to fight except with his equals. This is the reason he gives, and Milton does not contradict it while adding that his feelings were more complex' (Empson 60). But doesn't M. contradict Satan's reason? The point of honour is said to be part of his seeming dauntlessness (ll. 850–2), whereas his true feeling is dismay at the visible difference between good and evil–a difference of which he has apparently repressed the full memory. We are explicitly told that Satan *to strive . . . held it vain* because he was awe-struck. Presumably this feeling has passed by the time he defies the whole squadron at l. 987: Satan would be quick to recover self-composure.

iv *862*. See ll. 782–4, where the half-circuits of the cherubim, starting from the E. gate, were arranged.   *half-rounding*] No other instance of the use as a verb is given in *OED*.

iv *868. shade*] trees; see Wright 207.

870 But faded splendour wan; who by his gait
    And fierce demeanour seems the prince of hell,
    Not likely to part hence without contest;
    Stand firm, for in his look defiance lours.
        He scarce had ended, when those two approached
875 And brief related whom they brought, where found,
    How busied, in what form and posture couched.
        To whom with stern regard thus Gabriel spake.
    Why hast thou, Satan, broke the bounds prescribed
    To thy transgressions, and disturbed the charge
880 Of others, who approve not to transgress
    By thy example, but have power and right
    To question thy bold entrance on this place;
    Employed it seems to violate sleep, and those
    Whose dwelling God hath planted here in bliss?
885   To whom thus Satan, with contemptuous brow.
    Gabriel, thou hadst in heaven the esteem of wise,
    And such I held thee; but this question asked
    Puts me in doubt. Lives there who loves his pain?
    Who would not, finding way, break loose from hell,
890 Though thither doomed? Thou wouldst thy self, no
        doubt,
    And boldly venture to whatever place
    Farthest from pain, where thou might'st hope to change
    Torment with ease, and soonest recompense
    Dole with delight, which in this place I sought;
895 To thee no reason; who know'st only good,

iv 870. Gabriel, one of the principal angels, has no difficulty in recognizing
Satan, even by his gait; so that Satan's gibe at l. 830 is evidently well-founded.
iv 872. contest] Stressed on the second syllable.
iv 879. transgressions] A pun on the etymological meaning 'transcursions'.
As usual, the pun was divided up among M.'s early editors into univocal
shares. Bentley would have only 'transcursions', Pearce only 'sins'.
charge] 'task' (OED 12); perhaps also 'ward, person entrusted to the care
of another' (OED 14)–i.e., Eve.
iv 886. esteem of wise] reputation of being wise.
iv 887. For the second time Satan attacks the question he is asked: cp. ll.
832f, also l. 930, where he again criticizes the words of his questioner.
iv 894. Dole] There is irony here; for, while Gabriel is meant to understand
'grief, distress' (From Lat. dolium: OED sb.² 1) or 'pain, suffering'
(OED sb.² 3; archaic, perhaps influenced by Lat. dolor), the word could also
mean 'guile, deceit, fraud' (from Gk δόλος: OED sb.³ 1). Cp. Hamlet I ii
13: 'In equal scale weighing delight and dole.'

But evil hast not tried: and wilt object
His will who bound us? Let him surer bar
His iron gates, if he intends our stay
In that dark durance: thus much what was asked.

900 The rest is true, they found me where they say;
But that implies not violence or harm.
      Thus he in scorn. The warlike angel moved,
Disdainfully half smiling thus replied.
O loss of one in heaven to judge of wise,

905 Since Satan fell, whom folly overthrew,
And now returns him from his prison scaped,
Gravely in doubt whether to hold them wise
Or not, who ask what boldness brought him hither
Unlicensed from his bounds in hell prescribed;

910 So wise he judges it to fly from pain
However, and to scape his punishment.
So judge thou still, presumptuous, till the wrath,
Which thou incurr'st by flying, meet thy flight
Sevenfold, and scourge that wisdom back to hell,

915 Which taught thee yet no better, that no pain
Can equal anger infinite provoked.
But wherefore thou alone? Wherefore with thee
Came not all hell broke loose? Is pain to them
Less pain, less to be fled, or thou than they

920 Less hardy to endure? Courageous chief,
The first in flight from pain, hadst thou alleged
To thy deserted host this cause of flight,
Thou surely hadst not come sole fugitive.
      To which the fiend thus answered frowning stern.

925 Not that I less endure, or shrink from pain,
Insulting angel, well thou know'st I stood
Thy fiercest, when in battle to thy aid
The blasting vollied thunder made all speed

iv *896. object*] adduce as a reason against (breaking loose from hell) (*OED*
3 and 4).

iv *899. durance*] forced confinement, imprisonment.   *thus much what*] thus
much in reply to what.

iv *904. judge of wise*] 'judge of what is wise, judge wisdom'; retorting the
rhetorical figure used by Satan at 886.

iv *906. returns*] Either transitive, with 'folly' as subject, or reflexive, with
'Satan' as subject (arch.).

iv *911. However*] howsoever, in any way he can.

iv *926. stood*] put up with, endured (*OED* V 59).

iv *928. The*] *Ed II* 'Thy' is an error, probably due to the proximity of other
instances of the word.

<blockquote>

And seconded thy else not dreaded spear.
930   But still thy words at random, as before,
Argue thy inexperience what behoves
From hard assays and ill successes past
A faithful leader, not to hazard all
Through ways of danger by himself untried,
935   I therefore, I alone first undertook
To wing the desolate abyss, and spy
This new created world, whereof in hell
Fame is not silent, here in hope to find
Better abode, and my afflicted powers
940   To settle here on earth, or in mid air;
Though for possession put to try once more
What thou and thy gay legions dare against;
Whose easier business were to serve their Lord
High up in heaven, with songs to hymn his throne,
945   And practised distances to cringe, not fight.
      To whom the warrior angel soon replied.
To say and straight unsay, pretending first
Wise to fly pain, professing next the spy,
Argues no leader but a liar traced,
950   Satan, and couldst thou faithful add? O name,
A sacred name of faithfulness profaned!
Faithful to whom? To thy rebellious crew?
Army of fiends, fit body to fit head;

</blockquote>

iv *928.* According to Raphael's account of the war in heaven, however, Messiah did not put forth all his strength, 'but checked / His thunder in mid volley, for he meant / Not to destroy' (vi 853-5).

iv *930-3.* See l. 887*n.* The sense is 'You are still talking like one ignorant of the duties of a faithful leader after hard engagements and defeats'. *assays*] attacks, efforts.

iv *938.* See i 651-4*n.*

iv *939. afflicted*] ruined, outcast. Cp. i 186.

iv *940. mid air*] See ii 275*n*; also *Eph.* ii 2: 'The prince of the power of the air, the spirit that now worketh in the children of disobedience.'

iv *942. gay*] fine; as often, used ironically (*OED* 6 b); but perhaps also with the contemptuous or envious overtone 'showily dressed' (*OED* 4), in reply to ll. 839f.

iv *945.* Zeugma; since *practised distances* goes with *fight* as well as with *cringe.* Footwork was no less important in combat than in court etiquette. *And*] Dr Johnson's emendation to 'At' is unnecessary.

iv *946.* So *Ed I. Ed II* has comma after *angel,* by error.

iv *949. traced*] discovered, searched out (*OED* v.[1] II 8). Is *traced* = 'twisted, interwoven' (*OED* v.[3] 1) a secondary implication?

Was this your discipline and faith engaged,
955 Your military obedience, to dissolve
Allegiance to the acknowledged power supreme?
And thou sly hypocrite, who now wouldst seem
Patron of liberty, who more than thou
Once fawned, and cringed, and servilely adored
960 Heaven's awful monarch? Wherefore but in hope
To dispossess him, and thy self to reign?
But mark what I aread thee now, avaunt;
Fly thither whence thou fled'st: if from this hour
Within these hallowed limits thou appear,
965 Back to the infernal pit I drag thee chained,
And seal thee so, as henceforth not to scorn
The facile gates of hell too slightly barred.
    So threatened he, but Satan to no threats
Gave heed, but waxing more in rage replied.
970   Then when I am thy captive talk of chains,
Proud limitary cherub, but ere then
Far heavier load thyself expect to feel

iv 954. *your*] Gabriel addresses the whole *Army of fiends* through their *head*
and representative Satan.
iv 957–61. 'A quaint bit of spite . . . quite enough to prove that God had
already produced a very unattractive Heaven before Satan fell' (Empson
111). If M. allowed the inference that servility was general in heaven, he
must be thought either to have blundered, or to have half-belonged to the
devil's party in the way Empson suggests. But it seems more likely that
Gabriel is simply falling in with Satan's choice of words (with *cringed*,
cp. 'cringe' l. 945, with *servilely* cp. 'serve' l. 943), as people do in the heat
of an argument. Thus he amplifies the effect of his counter-accusation of
hypocrisy – 'If it's cringing you call it you've cringed too; and without even
being sincere, either'.   *Patron*] advocate, supporter.
iv 962. *aread*] advise.
iv 965–7. As Empson (112) points out, Gabriel's being content to warn
Satan is not weakness: 'he might mean to grant Satan one hour for decision
whether to go of his own accord or be dragged in chains; it is a statesmanlike
proposal, though no use because Satan decides to fight at once.' Cp. i 45–8 and
iii 82; and see *Rev.* xx 1–3: 'An angel . . . having the key of the bottomless
pit and a great chain in his hand . . . laid hold on the dragon, that old ser-
pent . . . and bound him a thousand years, And cast him into the bottomless
pit, and shut him up, and set a seal upon him, that he should deceive the
nations no more, till the thousand years should be fulfilled: and after that
he must be loosed a little season.'   *facile*] easily moved (*OED* 5 c);
perhaps also 'working freely' (*OED* 3).
iv 971. *limitary*] stationed on the boundary; sarcastically seizing on Gabriel's
word 'limits' (l. 964). For Gabriel as a cherub see ll. 549–50n.

From my prevailing arm, though heaven's king
Ride on thy wings, and thou with thy compeers,
975 Used to the yoke, draw'st his triumphant wheels
In progress through the road of heaven star-paved.
      While thus he spake, the angelic squadron bright
Turned fiery red, sharpening in mooned horns
Their phalanx, and began to hem him round
980 With ported spears, as thick as when a field

iv *973–6*. Satan refers to the central image of the poem, the cosmic chariot
ridden by the Messiah at vi 750ff. See also iii 656n.   *the road of heaven*] the
Milky Way. See vii 577–81n.

iv *978. fiery red*] Iconographically the appropriate colour for cherubim in any
case (see ll. 115–17 above); but here indicating angry ardour.   *mooned*]
shaped like the crescent moon. Crescent-shaped formations were classic
in warfare, and still often used in M.'s time; cp. Gascoigne, *A hundreth
sundrie floures* (1572), 'The Christian crew came on in forme of battayle
pight, / And like a cressent cast themselves preparing for to fight', also
Dryden, *Annus mirabilis* st. 125. Symbolically, the description is appro-
priate not only because images of Ceres-Isis anciently had crescent horns
to indicate her lunar godhead (Plutarch, *De Iside* 372D–E), but also because
Satan is an eclipsing power of darkness, occupying as it were the shadowed
part of the imaginary lunar orb.

iv *980–5*. The comparison of an excited army to wind-stirred corn is
Homeric; see *Il*. ii 147–50. On the present passage Empson[2] (172) objects:
'If God the sower is the ploughman, then he is anxious; another hint that
he is not omnipotent. If the labouring Satan is the ploughman he is only
anxious for a moment, and he is the natural ruler or owner of the good
angels.' But the *ploughman* (peasant) cannot be Satan, since Satan has his
own simile *On the other side* (l. 985). Thus, unless with Ricks (ll. 129f) we
pay the simile off as 'beautiful but digressive', the ploughman has to be in
some sense 'like' God. This doesn't mean, of course, that he 'is' God in all
respects, or that M.'s God is anxious and less than omnipotent. Critics'
puzzlement at the simile can be traced to Bentley's introduction of an
irrelevant notion, that the ploughman is afraid of a storm. In fact M. never
specifies which of the many possible causes of poor crops the ploughman
ponders. We are only told of his fear that when threshed the crop may prove
chaff, and of his doubt whether it is time to reap. (The Virgilian lines alluded
to – *Georg*. i 192, *nequiquam pinguis palea teret area culmos* and 226, *exspectata
seges vanis elusit aristis* – refer to the consequences, not of storm damage,
but of sowing at the wrong time.) Now *threshing* was a very familiar meta-
phor for divine judgment (for the iconographical background of the meta-
phor, see Mâle 31: for its Biblical sources, see *Jer*. li 33, 'Babylon is like a
threshingfloor, it is time to thresh her: yet a little while, and the time of her
harvest shall come'; *Hab*. iii 12; etc.). Thus M. may mean that God is
careful that the final judgment, and the final reckoning with Satan, should

Of Ceres ripe for harvest waving bends
Her bearded grove of ears, which way the wind
Sways them; the careful ploughman doubting stands
Lest on the threshing floor his hopeful sheaves
985 Prove chaff. On the other side Satan alarmed
Collecting all his might dilated stood,
Like Teneriff or Atlas unremoved:
His stature reached the sky, and on his crest
Sat horror plumed; nor wanted in his grasp
990 What seemed both spear and shield: now dreadful
deeds
Might have ensued, nor only Paradise

not be premature. It might even be maintained that the simile, by opening the theme of divine judgment followed up in the Scales image of ll. 997ff, actually contributes to an impression of God's secret transcendence.

iv *980. ported*] held diagonally across the body, in both hands. A military term, denoting the arms-drill position intermediate between 'shouldered' and 'charged' (levelled). It follows that the spears are not pointing towards Satan.

iv *981. Ceres* the goddess of agriculture is by metonymy put for 'corn'; so Virgil, *Georg.* i 297: *at rubicunda Ceres medio succiditur aestu.*

iv *985-7.* On Satan's dilation, see ll. 814-19n. The impressive stance is as usual bathetically punctured–here by the grumbling retreat of ll. 1014f. Broadbent 106 compares this metamorphosis with that of the devils into dwarfs in i 777-92, noting the recurrence of the peasant as a 'mundane intensifier of the supernatural change'. He rightly emphasises that such metamorphoses would have a ludicrous mock-epic quality for early readers; see i 777-92n. The present simile is double-edged; since Satan sustains the pressure of the angels as *Atlas* sustained the weight of the stars (for the angels as stars, see ll. 782-4n), but is also, like Atlas, a rebel against the supreme deity. The comparison with the Titan Atlas has already been made at ii 306. The mountain Atlas is not the Libyan range, but the far western range of Mauretania or Morocco. Because its summit was perpetually hidden by cloud, it was regarded as one of the pillars of Hercules or pillars of the sky.   *Teneriff*] A pyramid-shaped mountain on the Canary island of the same name, estimated to be fifteen or even sixty miles high. 'With truth enough most of our *Travellers* and *Geographers* hold it to be the highest in the whole world' (Heylyn iv 88; and see v 758-9n). Notice how these Satanic sky-pillars to the west of Paradise are set over against the divine 'rocky pillars' to the east (see ll. 542-50n).   *unremoved*] perhaps 'unremovable'; see l. 493n.

iv *988.* Cp. Homer's description of Strife, sister and friend of Ares the god of war: 'her crest is lowly at first, but afterwards she holds up her head in heaven, and her feet walk on earth' (*Il.* iv 441-3).

In this commotion, but the starry cope
Of heaven perhaps, or all the elements
At least had gone to wrack, disturbed and torn
995 With violence of this conflict, had not soon
The eternal to prevent such horrid fray
Hung forth in heaven his golden scales, yet seen

iv *992. cope*] sky, firmament, as in i 345, vi 215. The primary notion was
'canopy' (cp. iii 556) or 'vault, covering of vaulted form'; but the meta-
phor had long been a dead one.

iv *996.* Empson (112f) would rather have had the fray, on the grounds that
scenery is unimportant when man's Fall is at stake. But M.'s God would have
been reckless and partial if he had ignored the risk to other species inhabiting
the *starry cope.* And besides, he is not interested in preventing the Fall by
force; he has already explained in iii 90–133 about the degree of latitude to be
allowed to Satan, in order that Adam's freedom may have real content.
When Empson concludes 'that God was determined to make man fall, and
had supplied a guard only for show' he slips into what M. himself in *De
doctrina* i 2 calls 'anthropopathy' ('It is better . . . to contemplate the Deity,
and to conceive of him, not with reference to human passions . . . forming
subtle imaginations respecting him, but after the manner of Scripture':
Columbia xiv 33). It is in one sense true that the angelic guard – like every-
thing else that is less than divine – is unnecessary and 'only for show';
Gabriel indeed admits this at l. 1009. Still, they have ambassadorial dignity.
And we are allowed to speculate that their interruption of Satan had critical
significance, if he was to get in enough suggestion to be able later to tempt
Eve, but not so much as to brainwash the freedom of choice out of her.

iv *997–1004.* A culmination in the development of the Balance image-
complex, some of whose ramifyings have already been noted (see, e.g.,
ll. 354–5*n* and iii 555–61*n*; also Fowler ch. xii where similar cosmic Balance
imagery in *The Faerie Queene* is discussed). Here the emphasis is on the
Balance as a sign of God's predestinating justice. It is not that it shows the
sequel [consequence] . . . *of fight* to be less advantageous for Satan, as Verity
suggests, but that it shows God has decided against there being any fight
at all. Homer's Zeus balances fates of death for the Trojans and Achaians
in his golden scales at *Il.* viii 68–77, and for Hector and Achilles at *Il.* xxii
208–13 (imitated by Virgil at *Aen.* xii 725–7. Note that the first of these
judgments is delivered at the critical hour of noon; see ll. 1013–15*n*). But in
Homer the loser's scale sinks down to death, while in M. the inferior con-
sequence rises, being 'found wanting' – an allusion to *Dan.* v 27, where
writing on the wall tells Belshazzar 'Thou art weighed in the balances,
and art found wanting'. The identification of God's Balance with the con-
stellation Libra is not Homeric, though the idea of Libra as a 'righteous
ballance' (Spenser, *F.Q.* V i 11) was certainly ancient; see Fowler 196. The
visual effect of the identification is startling. For Satan himself has already
been linked with the Serpent constellation, which at midnight (see 1013–5*n*)

Betwixt Astrea and the Scorpion sign,
Wherein all things created first he weighed,
1000 The pendulous round earth with balanced air
In counterpoise, now ponders all events,
Battles and realms: in these he put two weights
The sequel each of parting and of fight;
The latter quick up flew, and kicked the beam;
1005 Which Gabriel spying, thus bespake the fiend.
　　Satan, I know thy strength, and thou know'st mine,
Neither our own but given; what folly then
To boast what arms can do, since thine no more
Than heaven permits, nor mine, though doubled now
1010 To trample thee as mire: for proof look up,
And read thy lot in yon celestial sign
Where thou art weighed, and shown how light, how
　　weak,

would lie immediately beneath the beam of Libra. Thus Gabriel's words have, besides their abstract sense, a concrete astronomical reference: the Serpent is 'weighed' (1012) on a cosmic scale. On Satan's identification with the constellation Anguis, the Serpent, see iii 555–61n.

iv *998*. Libra is the seventh sign of the zodiac, coming after Virgo and before Scorpio. It is appropriate to call Virgo *Astrea* in the Fallen world, since the just Astraea lived on earth during the Golden Age, but was later driven up to heaven by human wickedness, and is there *yet seen* stellified (see, e.g., Ovid, *Met.* i 149f, Spenser, *F.Q.* V i).

iv *999–1001*. For God's use of a balance in creation, *see* Job xxviii 24f: 'He looketh to the ends of the earth, and seeth under the whole heaven; To make the weight for the winds; and he weigheth the waters by measure'; also *Job* xxxvii 16, *Is.* xl 12. For his subsequent use of it, see *Is.* xl 15 ('nations . . . are counted as the small dust of the balance') *1 Sam.* ii 3 ('by him actions are weighed') and *Prov.* xvi 2 ('the Lord weigheth the spirits'). *ponders*] A pun ('weighs' and 'weighs up') but not a Latinism, for the concrete sense of the English word was still current in M.'s time.

iv *1010*. *trample thee as mire*] Cp. *Isa.* x 6: 'I will send him against an hypocritical nation . . . to tread them down like the mire of the streets.'

iv *1012*. Cp. *Dan.* v 27, 'TEKEL; Thou art weighed in the balances, and art found wanting.' Various attempts have been made to reconcile this line with ll. 1002–4, but it would seem that the weighing is quite differently understood by God, Gabriel and Satan. God, M. tells us, is really pondering the consequences of Satan's 'parting' and of his remaining to 'fight' (l. 1003). The consequence of parting is that Satan will be able to complete the temptation of Eve, thus occasioning the Fall, the Redemption, and eventually the Last Judgment. Against this is balanced the consequence of fight—pre umably that Satan will be defeated at once, and that man's faith will remain untested Si ce the pondering of this issue may well include question

If thou resist. The fiend looked up and knew
His mounted scale aloft: nor more; but fled
1015   Murmuring, and with him fled the shades of night.

THE END OF THE FOURTH BOOK

about how many souls are to be saved at the last, it is pertinent to recall that in sacred iconography the Weighing of Souls–in a balance held by Michael and sometimes 'mounted' (l. 1014) by devils–had long been established as one of the main events of the Last Judgment (see Mâle 366, 376f). Gabriel, however, unless indeed he deliberately misapplies the omen in an exulting or gibing way, clearly fails to grasp how much it signifies; which is not surprising, in view of the strong probability that as yet he has had no news of the heavenly council on Predestination and the Fall (iii 80–343; iv 581f, 'since meridian hour / No creature thence'). For Gabriel the Balance is simply a sign of judgment upon Satan, who is being weighed and found wanting (the reference is to *Dan.* v 27: see ll. 997–1004n). As Pearce put it, 'the scale, in which lay the weight, that was the *sequel* of his *fighting*, by ascending show'd him that he was *light in arms*, and could not obtain victory', while the other scale 'was a sign that his going off quietly would be his wisest and weightiest attempt'. Satan's interpretation may not be different from Gabriel's, if we take *scale* (1014) as 'balance' (*OED* s.v. *Scale* sb.[1] II 4; cf. vi 245 below, 'long time in even scale / The battle hung'). But the more usual sense of *scale*, except in a few set phrases, was 'pan of a balance'; so that Satan may imagine that his destiny is being weighed against Gabriel's, in the Homeric (pagan) manner.

iv *1013–15*. Satan did not begin to flee at daybreak (as is usually said); for at ix 58 we are explicitly informed that he fled 'By night'. We should rather think of him as going immediately after midnight. At midnight the powers of light and darkness are for a moment in equal balance. Then the *shades of night* begin to flee, and they continue to do so during the six hours that intervene before sunrise. The state of the heavens confirms this interpretation for us, and would immediately communicate it to M.'s early readers. For Satan and the angels although on a mountain have to look *up* to see Libra (l. 1010, cp. l. 1014), so that Libra, it is to be assumed, is *hung forth* at or about the zenith. Now when the sun is in Aries, as here (see iii 555–61n and x 329n), the opposing sign Libra reaches the zenith at midnight. (At sunrise, on the other hand, Libra sets beneath the W. horizon, and Satan would not need to look up to see it.) The zenith is in any case appropriate, since it is the central position of judgment (see l. 30n, Panofsky 261f, Fowler 70–2). We recall also the tradition (traced in Mâle 368 to the *Elucidarium* of Honorius of Autun) that Christ the judge will appear at midnight, the same hour that saw the resurrection. For a discussion of M.'s numerological expression of the present midnight hour, see ll. 776–80n.

Paradise Lost

BOOK V

The Argument

Morning approached, Eve relates to Adam her troublesome dream; he likes it not, yet comforts her: they come forth to their day labours: their morning hymn at the door of their bower. God to render man inexcusable sends Raphael to admonish him of his obedience, of his free estate, of his enemy near at hand; who he is, and why his enemy, and whatever else may avail[1] Adam to know. Raphael comes down to Paradise, his appearance described, his coming discerned by Adam afar off sitting at the door of his bower; he goes out to meet him, brings him to his lodge, entertains him with the choicest fruits of Paradise got together by Eve; their discourse at table: Raphael performs his message, minds Adam of his state and of his enemy; relates at Adam's request who that enemy is, and how he came to be so, beginning from his first revolt in heaven, and the occasion thereof; how he drew his legions after him to the parts of the north, and there incited them to rebel with him, persuading all but only Abdiel a seraph, who in argument dissuades and opposes him, then forsakes him.

Now Morn her rosy steps in the eastern clime
Advancing, sowed the earth with orient pearl,
When Adam waked, so customed, for his sleep
Was airy light from pure digestion bred,

v *Argument* [1] *whatever else may avail*] It is important that Adam should be allowed the best indirect knowledge of evil, because his innocence was often regarded as one of the formal causes of the original sin (Howard 161–3). v *1–2. Now Morn*] The morning of the twenty-fourth day of the poem's action; see Introduction, 'Chronology'.   *rosy steps*] Cp. vi 2f, 'Morn . . . with rosy hand'; both passages imitate the Homeric description of Eos as ῥοδοδάκτυλος (*Il.* i 477).   *orient pearl*] 'Pearl' has been taken to mean dew, which is 'orient' because brilliant and sparkling. But the use of the singular may indicate rather a reference to the lustrous grey rising light Morn throws before her; cp. *Ps.* xcvii 11 ('Light is sown for the righteous') and Lucretius, *De rerum nat.* ii 211 (*lumine conserit arva*). A pun with *orient* = 'eastern' is secondarily operative.

v *4–7.* Contrast the 'grosser sleep' bred of the 'exhilarating vapour bland' that is developed during digestion of the forbidden fruit (ix 1046–51). After the Fall *vapours* – exhalations rising from the stomach to the brain – came to be thought of as injurious; but this is before, and *bland* has its favourable sense: 'mild, genial, balmy'. Blandness was a characteristic of the sanguine temperament, the temperament Adam and Eve were believed to have had before the Fall; see Klibansky 62, 103ff, *et passim*.

5   And temperate vapours bland, which the only sound
     Of leaves and fuming rills, Aurora's fan,
     Lightly dispersed, and the shrill matin song
     Of birds on every bough; so much the more
     His wonder was to find unwakened Eve
10   With tresses discomposed, and glowing cheek,
     As through unquiet rest: he on his side
     Leaning half-raised, with looks of cordial love
     Hung over her enamoured, and beheld
     Beauty, which whether waking or asleep,
15   Shot forth peculiar graces; then with voice
     Mild, as when Zephyrus on Flora breathes,
     Her hand soft touching, whispered thus. Awake
     My fairest, my espoused, my latest found,
     Heaven's last best gift, my ever new delight,
20   Awake, the morning shines, and the fresh field
     Calls us, we lose the prime, to mark how spring
     Our tended plants, how blows the citron grove,

v 5–7. The *only* (mere) sound of leaves, water and birds was enough to rouse Adam. The *fan* of *Aurora*, the goddess of morning, is the *leaves* not the *rills*: a word order common with M.   *dispersed*] A gentler word than 'dispelled', which Bentley substituted.

v 15–17. Ricks 91 argues that *soft* applies to *hand* as well as to *touching*; but see ix 385–6n.   *peculiar graces*] graces all its own.

v 16. Note the integration of unfallen man with his environment: Adam's vapours have had their counterparts in the *fuming rills*; now his whisper has its, in the wind. Zephyrus' sweet breath was supposed to produce flowers, as was that of his wife, the flower-goddess Flora, 'nymph of the blessed fields' (Ovid, *Fasti* v 197). For Zephyrus as the awakener of vegetation, see iv 329n; his son by Flora was Carpus (Fruit). Cp. also iv 500f, where Adam is cast in the role of Jupiter, progenitor of 'May flowers'. Eve's association with flowers is symbolic of the frailty of the flesh (see Valeriano 683 on *Imbecillitas humana*), but also of fertility. It is further developed in her Proserpina, Ceres and Pomona roles: see iv 269–71, ix 393–6, 426–32.

v 18–25. Cp. *Song of Sol.* ii 10–3 and vii 12: 'Rise up, my love, my fair one, and come away. For . . . the fig tree putteth forth her green figs, and the vines with the tender grape give a good smell. . . . Let us get up early to the vineyards; let us see if the vine flourish, whether the tender grape appear, and the pomegranates bud forth'; though M. has substituted a different catalogue of natural beauties.   *prime*, the first hour of the day, either began at six o'clock throughout the year, or else at the changing time of sunrise. In M.'s Paradise these alternative possibilities coincide, since before the Fall sunrise is always at six o'clock (see x 651–706n). In its ecclesiastical sense, prime was one of the Canonical Hours of the Divine Office. The relevance of this sense is shown by ll. 145ff.   *blow*] flourish, blossom.

What drops the myrrh, and what the balmy reed,
How nature paints her colours, how the bee
25 Sits on the bloom extracting liquid sweet.
        Such whispering waked her, but with startled eye
On Adam, whom embracing, thus she spake.
        O sole in whom my thoughts find all repose,
My glory, my perfection, glad I see
30 Thy face, and morn returned, for I this night,
Such night till this I never passed, have dreamed,
If dreamed, not as I oft am wont, of thee,
Works of day past, or morrow's next design,
But of offence and trouble, which my mind
35 Knew never till this irksome night; methought
Close at mine ear one called me forth to walk
With gentle voice, I thought it thine; it said,
Why sleep'st thou Eve? Now is the pleasant time,
The cool, the silent, save where silence yields
40 To the night-warbling bird, that now awake
Tunes sweetest his love-laboured song; now reigns
Full-orbed the moon, and with more pleasing light

v 23. *balmy reed*] For the poetic diction, cp. vii 321, 'corny reed'. The balm was a balsam-bearing tree belonging, like the *myrrh*, to the genus Balsamodendron. Both yielded aromatic resins used to soothe pain, heal wounds and prevent corruption; and from the time of Coverdale they had been associated in English translations of *Gen.* xxxvii 25: 'A company of Ishmeelites came from Gilead with their camels bearing spicery and balm and myrrh.' As the earliest balsam known, Balm of Gilead or True Balsam was an object of veneration.

v 34. *offence*] In addition to the primary sense 'transgression', this could mean 'occasion of doubt'.

v 38. Beautiful as it is, the love-song that follows appeals to unreason (notice 'ravishment' at l. 46), and may be compared with the kind of 'serenade' ridiculed by M. in iv 769f. It contrasts with the less exaggerated but more considerate true love displayed in Adam's speech in ll. 95–128 (Burden 130ff).

v 40–1. Contrary to poetic convention the nightingale is masculine; not so much because it is in fact the cock bird that sings, as because this particular nightingale is correlated with Satan. For the passage is a travesty of *Song of Sol.* ii, where the awakener is likened to a dove. Cp. ll. 18–25 above, where the same text is imitated straight; also l. 48, where the relation between Adam and Satan his supplanter is made explicit. See H. Schultz, 'Satan's Serenade', *PQ* xxvii (1948) 17–26, esp. 24. Schultz plausibly connects the language of the amorous Satan with that of the fashionable Cavalier gallantry of his time.

Shadowy sets off the face of things; in vain,
If none regard, heaven wakes with all his eyes,
45 Whom to behold but thee, nature's desire,
In whose sight all things joy, with ravishment
Attracted by thy beauty still to gaze.
I rose as at thy call, but found thee not;
To find thee I directed then my walk;
50 And on, methought, alone I passed through ways
That brought me on a sudden to the tree
Of interdicted knowledge: fair it seemed,
Much fairer to my fancy than by day:
And as I wondering looked, beside it stood
55 One shaped and winged like one of those from heaven
By us oft seen; his dewy locks distilled
Ambrosia; on that tree he also gazed;
And O fair plant, said he, with fruit surcharged,
Deigns none to ease thy load and taste thy sweet,

v *43–5*. Satan works on the doubt he heard Eve express at iv 657f: 'for whom/
This glorious sight, when sleep hath shut all eyes?'   *sets off*] makes con-
spicuous by contrast; but also 'shows to advantage, enhances'–Satan is
already appealing to Eve's vanity.

v *44*. The eyes-of-heaven image was a familiar one: cp. Ariosto, *Orl. Fur.*
xiv 99, Tasso, *Gerus. Lib.* xii 22 and Spenser, *F.Q.* III xi 45. Usually the
eyes were witnesses to clandestine love; as in Catullus, *Carm.* vii 7f: *aut
quam sidera multa, cum tacet nox, | furtivos hominum vident amores.* Here it may
also be relevant that Satan was sometimes represented as a many-eyed
Argus. *Ed I* has semicolon after *regard*.

v *45–90*. Briefly stating themes to be developed more subtly and in greater
detail in the second temptation. Thus v 45–7 corresponds to ix 532–48, and
v 67–81 to ix 679–732. Note, however, the great difference between the
concluding phases (v 86–90 and ix 782–833): Eve's aerial flight on the for-
mer occasion more closely resembles the temptation of Christ. According
to Waldock (33), Eve's dream constitutes the first phase in her fall. It is pro-
bably true (as Burden 129f suggests) that Satan needs the dream in order to
instil into Eve an evil motion. According to Aristotle (*De anima* iii 3) sleep
divests the mind of moral responsibility. But M. makes it quite explicit that
having evil motions and feeling tempted does not mean being fallen.

v *53*. The real tree, as Burden 128ff emphasises, is not provocative. In
dream, however, when judgment and reason are in abeyance, Satan can
make its image provoke the desire to taste.

v *55–7*. M. alludes to Virgil's description of Venus leaving Aeneas outside
Carthage: 'From her head her ambrosial tresses breathed celestial fragrance'
(*Aen.* i 403f.)   *Ambrosia*] Probably here referring to the fabled anointing
oil of the gods. For other senses of the word, see ii 245*n*. For Satan's disguise
as a good angel, see iii 634*n*.

60   Nor God, nor man; is knowledge so despised?
      Or envy, or what reserve forbids to taste?
      Forbid who will, none shall from me withhold
      Longer thy offered good, why else set here?
      This said he paused not, but with venturous arm
65   He plucked, he tasted; me damp horror chilled
      At such bold words vouched with a deed so bold:
      But he thus overjoyed, O fruit divine,
      Sweet of thy self, but much more sweet thus cropt,
      Forbidden here, it seems, as only fit
70   For gods, yet able to make gods of men:
      And why not gods of men, since good, the more
      Communicated, more abundant grows,
      The author not impaired, but honoured more?
      Here, happy creature, fair angelic Eve,
75   Partake thou also; happy though thou art,
      Happier thou mayst be, worthier canst not be:
      Taste this, and be henceforth among the gods
      Thy self a goddess, not to earth confined,
      But sometimes in the air, as we, sometimes

v *60. god*] spirit. See i 116–17*n* and iii 341*n*.

v *61*. Cp. ix 729.   *reserve*] limitation, restriction, or knowledge kept secret, on the part of God; but perhaps also inhibition, self-restraint on the part of man.

v *67–8*. Lewis 67f observes that the fruit has intrinsic importance only for the poem's bad characters. Satan assumes that it will communicate knowledge magically.

v *70–81*. Emotive use of the term *god* is even more fully exploited in the second temptation: cp. ix 700–32. The Scriptural authority is *Gen.* iii 5: 'God doth know that in the day ye eat thereof, then your eyes shall be opened, and ye shall be as gods, knowing good and evil.'

v *73*. Empson 155 ingeniously argues that since Satan is despised in heaven at v 665 for the grudging impulse of feeling *impaired* (injured, lowered in rank), Eve 'may naturally conclude that [this feeling] cannot also actuate God; the argument of the mysterious voice is again confirmed'. But is this not to accept the *non sequitur* concealed by Satan's audacious rhetoric? Though God cannot be impaired by the cropping of fruit (nor indeed by anything else), it does not follow that all acts honour him.

v *74. happy*] See viii 282*n* for the ironic implications.

v *79–80*. Pearce noted that 'the words *as we* are so placed between the two sentences, as equally to relate to both'.   *in the air*] So at *PR* i 39–42 and ii 117f the devils hold council in 'middle air' (see above i 515–16*n*). The idea stems from *Eph.* ii 2, where Satan is referred to as 'the prince of the powers of the air'. Cp. xii 454, where allusion to the same text is more direct. The doubt implied by the syntax 'whether he could go to Heaven himself

80   Ascend to heaven, by merit thine, and see
        What life the gods life there, and such live thou.
        So saying, he drew nigh, and to me held,
        Even to my mouth of that same fruit held part
        Which he had plucked; the pleasant savoury smell
85   So quickened appetite, that I, methought,
        Could not but taste. Forthwith up to the clouds
        With him I flew, and underneath beheld
        The earth outstretched immense, a prospect wide
        And various: wondering at my flight and change
90   To this high exaltation; suddenly
        My guide was gone, and I, me thought, sunk down,
        And fell asleep; but O how glad I waked
        To find this but a dream! Thus Eve her night
        Related, and thus Adam answered sad.
95   Best image of my self and dearer half,
        The trouble of thy thoughts this night in sleep
        Affects me equally; nor can I like
        This uncouth dream, of evil sprung I fear;
        Yet evil whence? In thee can harbour none,
100   Created pure. But know that in the soul

shows a natural embarrassment in the disguised Satan' (Empson² 163).
See further v 498–500n.
v *84–5. savoury smell*] At the second temptation the fruit again smells
'savoury' (ix 740f). This description depends on a serious pun. The primary
meaning is that the fruit has an appetizing, fragrant scent (OED s.v. *Sa-
voury*, 1). But 'savoury' could also mean 'spiritually edifying, full of
spiritual savour' (OED 2b; thus literal interpretation is described as 'some-
tyme savory, sometyme bareyne' in *The myroure of oure Ladye*, EETS (1873)
49). For ungoverned appetite as the immediate cause of the Fall, see ix 740n.
v *87*. Angels can fly, but not men; therefore the very means of locomotion
here is evil (Burden 117f). For a similar reason, knowledge about other
worlds turns out to be forbidden knowledge (viii 121).
v *88*. 'Eve is allowed for a moment to "view all things at one view", like
God' (MacCaffrey 61). Cp. iii 543 and see iii 59n.
v *89–92*. The unusual punctuation may be intended to express disturbed
abruptness in Eve's speech, incoherence in relating a strange experience, or
her dramatic rendering of the suddenness of Satan's departure.
v *94. sad*] grave, serious.
v *98. uncouth*] Perhaps 'strange' (OED 3), but in view of the continuation
more probably 'unpleasant, distasteful, unseemly' (OED 4).
v *100–13. fancy*] M. may simply mean 'imagination': Coleridge's dis-
tinction between the two faculties was not usually observed at this time.
The psychology involved here was common knowledge. Thus in Bar-

> Are many lesser faculties that serve
> Reason as chief; among these fancy next
> Her office holds; of all external things,
> Which the five watchful senses represent,
> 105 She forms imaginations, airy shapes,
> Which reason joining or disjoining, frames
> All what we affirm or what deny, and call
> Our knowledge or opinion; then retires
> Into her private cell when nature rests.

tholomew, 'the *Imaginative* vertue . . . is in the soule as the eye in the body, by beholding to receive the images that are offered unto it by the outward sences . . . Now after that the *Imagination* hath received the images . . . then doth it as it were prepare and digest them, either by joyning them together, or by separating them according as their natures require. They that distinguish *Imagination* from *Fantasie*, attribute this office to *Fantasie*' (*cit.* Svendsen 38). Cp. Burton, *Anatomy of Melancholy* I i 2 vii: 'Phantasy, or imagination . . . is an inner sense which doth more fully examine the species perceived by common sense, of things present or absent. . . . In time of sleep this faculty is free, and many times conceives strange, stupend, absurd shapes . . . it is subject and governed by reason, or at least should be.' Dr Johnson's comment on the present passage–'Adam's discourse of dreams seems not to be the speculation of a new-created being'–betrays ignorance of the Augustinian tradition that man's original righteousness included superhuman intellectual powers. See, e.g., Du Bartas, *Babilon, a part of the seconde weeke. Englished by W. L'Isle* (1595) 44f: 'Adam a man parfitly wise before he sinned . . . enriched his language with all maner of ornaments that might be required to make it parfit: So that before his fall he spake more eloquently than any mortall man since . . . from him had we first our Arts and Sciences derived.' And cp. Goulart, *A Learned Summary Upon . . . Bartas*, tr. T. Lodge (1621) 136: 'Adam . . . had a great vivacity of spirit, to meditate and comprehend the nature of things.' On the theology underlying this notion, see Williams 361f.

v *104. represent*] bring before the mind; show.

v *109*. i.e., retires from the warm and dry front ventricle or *cellula phantastica* into the warm and moist middle-brain, the *cellula logistica*. On the psychological system implied here, see Klibansky 68f. A very familiar poetic rendering of the same system is given in the turret of Spenser's Castle of Alma (*F.Q.* II ix 47–58).   *cell*] Not wholly metaphorical, for the word was regularly used for 'compartment of the brain'. Thus Burton calls the organ of the Imagination 'the middle cell of the brain' (*Anatomy of Melancholy* I i 2 vii). In Ficino's system, the topographical distribution of faculties within the brain (most usually *imaginatio, ratio* and *memoria*, in that order from front to back) is distinguished from a hierarchical division into *imaginatio, ratio* and *mens* (see Klibansky 265).

110   Oft in her absence mimic fancy wakes
       To imitate her; but misjoining shapes,
       Wild work produces oft, and most in dreams,
       Ill matching words and deeds long past or late.
       Some such resemblances methinks I find
115   Of our last evening's talk, in this thy dream,
       But with addition strange; yet be not sad.
       Evil into the mind of god or man
       May come and go, so unapproved, and leave
       No spot or blame behind: which gives me hope
120   That what in sleep thou didst abhor to dream,
       Waking thou never wilt consent to do.
       Be not disheartened then, nor cloud those looks
       That wont to be more cheerful and serene
       Than when fair morning first smiles on the world,
125   And let us to our fresh employments rise
       Among the groves, the fountains, and the flowers
       That open now their choicest bosomed smells
       Reserved from night, and kept for thee in store.
           So cheered he his fair spouse, and she was cheered,

v 115. *our last evening's talk*] their discussion of the prohibition of the Tree
of Knowledge (iv 421ff).

v 117–19. *god*] Probably 'angel', in view of ll. 59 and 70. But M. (if not
Adam) may also intend a reference to the doctrine that God's omniscience
extends to evil. Hughes cites St Thomas Aquinas, *Summa theol.* I q 14 a 10:
'God would not know good things perfectly unless he knew evil things.'
For an earlier play on different senses of *god*, see i 116f and *n*.

v 119–21. Adam's speech brings into sharp focus a problem often raised by
later books of the poem. Are we to believe, with Tillyard, that Eve, already
anxious and troubled, is no longer innocent? Or does her dream only
strengthen her resistance, and is Satan unable to do more than put ideas into
her head? See Empson 149.

v 121. Some copies *Ed I* have colon after *do*.

v 124. *Than*] spelt 'Then', but probably indicating 'than': otherwise the
rhythm would be awkward.

v 127. *bosomed*] hidden, confined in the bosom; perhaps comparing the
scent of the flowers with breath pent up, to be exhaled as Eve passes. Adam's
compliment was a gallantry common in M.'s time. Cp. Marvell, 'Upon
Appleton House' st. 38.

v 128. A grim dramatic irony, for after the Fall 'the heavens and the earth
... are kept in store, reserved unto fire against the day of judgment' (2
Pet. iii 7).

v 129. The diction is that of the A.V. Cp. *Jer.* xx 7.

130   But silently a gentle tear let fall
         From either eye, and wiped them with her hair;
         Two other precious drops that ready stood,
         Each in their crystal sluice, he ere they fell
         Kissed as the gracious signs of sweet remorse
135   And pious awe, that feared to have offended.
            So all was cleared, and to the field they haste.
         But first from under shady arborous roof,
         Soon as they forth were come to open sight
         Of day-spring, and the sun, who scarce up risen
140   With wheels yet hovering o'er the ocean brim,
         Shot parallel to the earth his dewy ray,
         Discovering in wide landscape all the east
         Of Paradise and Eden's happy plains,
         Lowly they bowed adoring, and began
145   Their orisons, each morning duly paid

v *130–1*. The allusion to the typical repentant sinner Mary Magdalene
(*Luke* vii 38: 'stood at his feet behind him weeping, and began to wash his
feet with tears, and did wipe them with the hairs of her head') need not
support the view that Eve is already partly fallen. It could imply instead a
resemblance between the unfallen and the regenerate.

v *132–3*. Cp. Marvell, 'Eyes and Tears': especially sts. 3f (the preciousness
of the tears), 8 (an allusion to the Magdalene), and 11 (the image of a 'double
sluice').

v *136*. *all was cleared*] This slightly unusual expression implies a meteoro-
logical metaphor: 'all the trouble cleared up'.

v *137*. *arborous*] consisting of trees.

v *139*. *day-spring*] daybreak, dawn. The word was too common for one to
be sure of an allusion to *Luke* i 78, 'the dayspring from on high hath visited
us'.

v *142*. See ii 491*n*.

v *144*. Contrast xi 1–2. Whereas now Adam and Eve bow *lowly*, after the
Fall they stand to pray–but in 'lowliest plight'.

v *145–52*. Often taken as a gibe at the Anglican Church's worship, on the
strength of M.'s known antipathy to set liturgical forms (See *De doctrina*
ii 4, Columbia xvii 85, and *Eikonoklastes* 16, Yale iii 503–8). But to read the
lines in this sense is to diminish them and to ignore the fact that the orisons
below are closely modelled on the liturgy. M.'s more positive meaning
appears to be that prelapsarian prayers lack neither formal elaboration
(*various style*) nor inspired spontaneity (*rapture*). Adam and Eve pray from
the heart and 'have words from thir affections' (Yale iii 505). Similarly,
it would be wrong to infer from the absence of *lute or harp* that M. dislikes
the use of instrumental music in worship: indeed, he allows it even in the
worship of the angels (e.g. vii 258 below).   *numerous*] measured, rhyth-
mic.   *tunable*] tuneful, sweet-sounding.

In various style, for neither various style
Nor holy rapture wanted they to praise
Their maker, in fit strains pronounced or sung
Unmeditated, such prompt eloquence
150   Flowed from their lips, in prose or numerous verse,
More tuneable than needed lute or harp
To add more sweetness, and they thus began.
      These are thy glorious works, parent of good,
Almighty, thine this universal frame,
155   Thus wondrous fair; thy self how wondrous then!
Unspeakable, who sit'st above these heavens
To us invisible or dimly seen
In these thy lowest works, yet these declare
Thy goodness beyond thought, and power divine:
160   Speak ye who best can tell, ye sons of light,
Angels, for ye behold him, and with songs
And choral symphonies, day without night,
Circle his throne rejoicing, ye in heaven,
On earth join all ye creatures to extol
165   Him first, him last, him midst, and without end.
Fairest of stars, last in the train of night,

v *151.* Some copies *Ed I* have comma after *harp.*

v *153–208.* The morning hymn is quasi-liturgical, being based on *Ps.* cxlviii and on the Canticle *Benedicite, omnia opera* (set for Matins in Lent in the 1549 Book of Common Prayer), in which angels, stars, light and darkness, and various meteorological entities are addressed, in the same sequence as here; see ll. 185–201n below. M. also echoes *Ps.* xix ('The heavens declare the glory of God; and the firmament sheweth his handywork'), which was set for Monday at Prime, the Office said at sunrise. According to one theory the day of the present passage is in fact Monday; see Introduction, 'Chronology'.

v *153.* Some copies *Ed I* omit comma after *works.*

v *154. frame*] Used of heaven, earth, or universe regarded as structures fabricated by God; e.g. Calvin, *Inst.* i 21, tr. T. Norton: 'The knowledge of God . . . in the frame of the world and all the creatures is . . . plainly set forth.'

v *156.* Some copies of *Ed I* have comma after *heavens.*

v *162.* M.'s heaven has twilight, but nothing darker: see ll. 642–6.   *symphonies*] concerted or harmonious music in parts.

v *165.* Cp. *Rev.* i 11; also Jonson, *Masque of Augures* 444: 'Jove is that one, whom first, midst, last, you call.'

v *166–70.* The transition from circling angels to circling stars is a smooth one: see iv 782–4n.   *Fairest of stars*] The planet Venus, which in western elongation rises in the east just before sunrise, and is known as the morning star (Lucifer, Phosphorus). Note that the astronomical events reviewed

> If better thou belong not to the dawn,
> Sure pledge of day, that crown'st the smiling morn
> With thy bright circlet, praise him in thy sphere
> 170   While day arises, that sweet hour of prime.
> Thou sun, of this great world both eye and soul,

here correspond–though in reverse order–to those of the procession of Evening (iv 593–609; here recalled by the phrase *train of night*). Newton imagined he had caught M. out, on the ground that Venus cannot be both a morning star and an evening star at the same date. But as usual M. proves a better astronomer than his critics have understood. On every occasion when Venus passes from eastern to western elongation during the hours of darkness, it will be the evening star on the evening immediately preceding the conjunction, and the morning star on the morning immediately following. (Conjunctions of Venus occur twice in each synodic period of 584 days.) This was well known in M.'s time and indeed long before. See, e.g., Riccioli i 661: 'Now we report another peculiar appearance of the same planet, most worthy of note, which occurs especially in extreme northern latitudes: namely, that on the same natural day it is seen in the evening a little after the setting of the sun, and is Hesperus, and the following morning it is seen in the morning a little before the rising of the sun, and is then Lucifer; because with the help of the northern latitude these events seem almost to coincide with the perigee of the epicycle' (citing Regiomontanus, Maurolycus *et al.*). According to Kepler, the double phenomenon could persist for as many as three days at a time. For additional evidence that Venus is at or near conjunction, see vii 366*n* below. Adam's calling on the star associated with Satan to praise God seems at first a very bitter dramatic irony. But it should be remembered that in pious tradition the identity of the Evening and Morning Stars was commonly a symbol of Christ's resurrection.

v *170. prime*] See 18–25*n* above. This reference to the first Day Hour immediately precedes the address to the sun, which traces its diurnal *course* in a way reminiscent of the psalm for Monday at Prime: *In sole posuit tabernaculum suum: et ipse tamquam sponsus procedens de thalamo suo: Exsultavit ut gigas ad currendam viam, a summo caelo egressio eius: Et occursus eius usque ad summum eius: nec est qui se abscondat a calore eius* (Ps. xix 4–6; Vulg. xviii 1).

v *171*. Renaissance writers were fond of describing the sun as an eye: cf., e.g., Spenser, *F.Q.* I iii 4, 'the great eye of heaven'; Shakespeare, Sonnet 18, 'eye of heaven'; Du Bartas, tr. Sylvester, I iv 551, 'Daies glorious Eye'. The metaphor was regarded as Orphic (Ficino, *De Sole* 6), though in fact it had a wide distribution in ancient authors: see Adams's note to Plato, *Rep.* 508B. It often implied a connection between seeing and understanding, and hence an identification of the sun with the creative word. For the eye as a symbol of divine omniscience, see Wind 186. The sun is *soul* of the world in the sense that it gives life. To many readers, the phrase would recall Orphic and Platonic solar mysticism, in which the animating power

Acknowledge him thy greater, sound his praise
In thy eternal course, both when thou climb'st,
And when high noon hast gained, and when thou
     fall'st.
175   Moon, that now meet'st the orient sun, now fly'st
With the fixed stars, fixed in their orb that flies,
And ye five other wandering fires that move
In mystic dance not without song, resound
His praise, who out of darkness called up light.
180   Air, and ye elements the eldest birth

of the sun was dwelt upon. See, e.g., Ficino's commentary on Dionysius'
De divinis nominibus: 'A single sun with a single light generates, nourishes,
vivifies, moves, distinguishes and unites the natures of all sensible things.'
v *174. noon*] On the symbolic meaning attached to noon elsewhere in *PL*,
see iv 30*n*. Here the reference is perhaps to the Church's traditional times of
prayer. But M. does not necessarily mean the Canonical Hours (Lauds or
Prime at sunrise, Sext at noon, Vespers at sunset; cp. the mention of 'prime'
at l. 170). As early as St Cyprian (*De orat. Dom.*) sunrise and sunset had been
added to the Apostolic Hours, which included noon.
v *176.* M.'s contemporaries had a reasonably good idea of stellar distances,
so that the velocity of the sphere of fixed stars in a Ptolemaic daily revolution
about the earth would have seemed to them almost incredible–a suitable
marvel to be included in the hymn of Adam and Eve. See Riccioli i 419;
also iv 592–7*n* above.
v *177.* Actually only four of the planets (Saturn, Jupiter, Mars, Mercury)
remain to be mentioned, since Venus has already appeared at ll. 166–70.
If the discrepancy is intentional, it may be designed as a correlate to the real
doubt about whether the earth should be counted as a planet: cp. viii 128f,
'six thou seest, and what if seventh to these / The planet Earth'. Alternative-
ly, the point may lie in an allusion to the correspondence between the planets
and the *quaternion* (l. 181) of elements and humours. Traditionally Saturn
was connected with earth (melancholy), Mars with fire (choler) and Jupiter
with air (sanguine), so that Venus–also connected with air–is here *de trop*.
However, the division of the planets into two chief luminaries and five
others was so routine that M.'s phrase may have slipped in in casual obedi-
ence to it.   *wandering*] Renders the etymological meaning of 'planet'
(Gk πλανήτης): poetic diction.
v *178.* On the dance of the stars, see iii 579–81*n*.   *not without*] Good
English, but possibly also felt to correspond to the Latin idiom *non sine*, a
litotes of which M. was particularly fond.   *song*] i.e., the music of the
spheres, inaudible now to fallen man's gross hearing (see *Arcades* 61–73).
v *180–2. quaternion*] The elements are not only four, but also a form of the
tetractys or 'quaternion'. Adam here shows familiarity with Macrobius'
explanation of the structure of the elements in terms of the Pythagorean
theory of symbolic numbers (*In somn. Scip.* I vi 22–41). Macrobius also held

Of nature's womb, that in quaternion run
Perpetual circle, multiform; and mix
And nourish all things, let your ceaseless change
Vary to our great maker still new praise.
185 Ye mists and exhalations that now rise
From hill or steaming lake, dusky or grey,
Till the sun paint your fleecy skirts with gold,
In honour to the world's great author rise,
Whether to deck with clouds the uncoloured sky,
190 Or wet the thirsty earth with falling showers,
Rising or falling still advance his praise.
His praise ye winds, that from four quarters blow,
Breathe soft or loud; and wave your tops, ye pines,
With every plant, in sign of worship wave.
195 Fountains and ye, that warble, as ye flow,
Melodious murmurs, warbling tune his praise.
Join voices all ye living souls, ye birds,
That singing up to heaven gate ascend,
Bear on your wings and in your notes his praise;
200 Ye that in waters glide, and ye that walk

that the seven planets can be regarded as consisting of a group of three and a group of four; the latter group corresponding to the elements' quaternion or tetrad with two mean terms. For the transformation of the elements into one another, see Cicero, *De nat. deor.* ii 33: 'As there are four sorts of bodies, the continuance of nature is caused by their reciprocal changes; for the water arises from the earth, the air from the water, and the fire from the air; and reversing this order, the air arises from fire, the water from the air, and from the water the earth, the lowest of the four elements, of which all beings are formed. Thus by their continual motions . . . the conjunction of the several parts of the universe is preserved'. Cicero, like Adam, believes that the constitution of the elements is eternal, or at least 'of very long duration' (cp. *Perpetual*).

Air is named separately from the elements either (*a*) because the upper air, above the region of the elements, is meant (cp. iii 562*n*); or (*b*) because air was the element connected with the sanguine humour, and therefore most worthy of mention (sanguine was the uncorrupted specially human humour that prevailed in man before the Fall; see Klibansky 103, 105, 110); or most likely (*c*) in allusion to an obscure passage in Ovid (*Fasti* v 11) where the 'three elements'–excluding air–are mentioned as the entities that emerged after chaos.

v *185–201.* Cp. the Canticle *Benedicite, omnia opera*: 'O ye Winds of God . . . O ye Dews and Frosts . . . O ye Lightnings and Clouds . . . O all ye Green Things upon the Earth . . . O ye Wells, bless ye the Lord: praise him, and magnify him for ever.' See ll. 153–208*n* above.

v *193. breathe*] breath *Ed I*, corr. in *Errata.*

The earth, and stately tread, or lowly creep;
Witness if I be silent, morn or even,
To hill, or valley, fountain, or fresh shade
Made vocal by my song, and taught his praise.
205   Hail universal Lord, be bounteous still
To give us only good; and if the night
Have gathered aught of evil or concealed,
Disperse it, as now light dispels the dark.
       So prayed they innocent, and to their thoughts
210   Firm peace recovered soon and wonted calm.
On to their morning's rural work they haste
Among sweet dews and flowers; where any row
Of fruit-trees over-woody reached too far
Their pampered boughs, and needed hands to check
215   Fruitless embraces: or they led the vine

v 205–19. The concluding words of the hymn recall the Collect for the
Eighth Sunday after Trinity: 'O God, whose never-failing providence
ordereth all things both in heaven and earth: We humbly beseech thee to
put away from us all hurtful things, and to give us those things which be
profitable for us. . . .' This allusion gains point when one notices that the
Gospel for the same day is *Matt.* vii 15–21, the conclusion of the Sermon on
the Mount, which develops at some length a distinction between the fruit
of 'good trees' and 'corrupt trees'. The inference would seem to be that the
rural work of Adam and Eve is of a symbolic nature.

v 206–8. Modelled, with l. *166*, on the Hymn *Somno refectis*, set in the
Breviary for Monday at Matins in summer: *Cedant tenebrae lumini,* / *Et
nox diurno sideri,* / *Ut culpa, quam nox intulit,* / *Lucis labascat munere.*

v 213. *overwoody*] Probably 'excessively bushy'.

v 214. *pampered*] Primarily 'overindulged'; but a secondary play on Fr.
pampre ('leafy vine-branch', from Latin *pampinus*), noticed by Newton,
may be Miltonic. Some authorities regarded the two words as etymologi-
cally related.

v 215–9. The idea that the elm is wedded to the vine it supports is very
ancient: Horace, *Odes* II xv 4 already takes its familiarity for granted. But
the moral allegory of mutual dependence and complementary gifts, which
ensured the popularity of the image in the Renaissance, seems to go back
principally to Ovid, *Met.* xiv 661ff, Vertumnus' persuasion of Pomona to
marry. The elm came to be an emblem of firm masculine strength, the vine
of fruitfulness and feminine softness, submission and sweetness. Here the im-
plication is that Adam and Eve are reunited after the division of Eve's dream.
'The stereotype rehearses in singularly appropriate sexual symbols an act
which has an air of ritual about it' (Svendsen 134). Cp. *Dam* 65, Horace,
Epodes ii 9, Virgil, *Georg.* ii 367, Tasso, *Gerus. Lib.* iii 75, Spenser, *F.Q.* I i 8
and instances in Bartholomew, Batman and Maplet, *cit.* Svendsen 271n.
Nowhere is the metaphor given a physically sexual application. See also

To wed her elm; she spoused about him twines
Her marriageable arms, and with her brings
Her dower the adopted clusters, to adorn
His barren leaves. Them thus employed beheld
220 With pity heaven's high king, and to him called
Raphael, the sociable spirit, that deigned
To travel with Tobias, and secured
His marriage with the seven-times-wedded maid.
  Raphael, said he, thou hear'st what stir on earth
225 Satan from hell scaped through the darksome gulf
Hath raised in Paradise, and how disturbed
This night the human pair, how he designs
In them at once to ruin all mankind.
Go therefore, half this day as friend with friend
230 Converse with Adam, in what bower or shade
Thou find'st him from the heat of noon retired,
To respite his day-labour with repast,
Or with repose; and such discourse bring on,
As may advise him of his happy state,
235 Happiness in his power left free to will,
Left to his own free will, his will though free,
Yet mutable; whence warn him to beware
He swerve not too secure: tell him withal
His danger, and from whom, what enemy
240 Late fallen himself from heaven, is plotting now
The fall of others from like state of bliss;
By violence, no, for that shall be withstood,
But by deceit and lies; this let him know,
Lest wilfully transgressing he pretend
245 Surprisal, unadmonished, unforewarned.

J. Brown, *PMLA* lxxi (1956) 16f and L. Lerner, *EC* iv (1954) 305 (one 'of the most strikingly sexual passages in *Paradise Lost*').

v *221–3*. See iv 166–71n. The name *Raphael*, 'Health of God', is Biblical (e.g. *Tob*. iii 17). Raphael was one of the four archangels who formed God's cosmic chariot (iii 648n above); in the cabbalistic fusion of planetary with angelic deities he was sometimes jovial, sometimes solar. Apparently he is the appropriate archangel to choose for a mission that involves marital relations; perhaps because his role is to effect a right psychological adjustment ('*Mixtum ex iis medicina et temperamentum Raphael*': Valeriano 549).

v *229*. So at *Exod*. xxxiii 11 'The Lord spake unto Moses face to face, as a man speaketh unto his friend.'

v *235–7*. For a fuller development of the theology underlying this portrayal of man as 'sufficient to have stood' see iii 96–125 above.

v *237–8*. i.e., 'to be careful not to err through overconfidence' (*secure*= careless).

So spake the eternal Father, and fulfilled
All justice: nor delayed the winged saint
After his charge received; but from among
Thousand celestial ardours, where he stood
250 Veiled with his gorgeous wings, up springing light
Flew through the midst of heaven; the angelic choirs
On each hand parting, to his speed gave way
Through all the empyreal road; till at the gate
Of heaven arrived, the gate self-opened wide
255 On golden hinges turning, as by work
Divine the sovereign architect had framed.
From hence, no cloud, or, to obstruct his sight,

v 246-7. *fulfilled | All justice*] Scriptural diction; cp. *Matt.* iii 15, 'thus it becometh us to fulfil all righteousness'. The application of *saint* to angel is also a Biblical usage; see *Jude* 14, and *Deut.* xxxiii 2: 'The Lord . . . shined forth from mount Paran, and he came with ten thousands of saints.' To be distinguished is *saints*='the Elect' (e.g. iii 330 above).

v 248. *After . . . received*] Imitates a Latin construction; cp. i 573.

v 249. *ardours*] Concretely 'flames', figuratively, 'zeals, fervours'. Thyer may have been right in regarding the word as a variant of 'seraphim' (see ii 512n above); but *Ps.* civ 4 suggests that any spirit could be regarded as 'a flaming fire'.

v 253. *empyreal*] M. always stresses the second syllable of the adjectival form.

v 254-6. So at *Acts* xii 10 St Peter and an angel 'came unto the iron gate that leadeth unto the city; which opened to them of his own accord'. Cp. also Homer, *Il.* v 749, where the gates of heaven open automatically for Hera. Addison, not appreciating the potential range of technological possibility, felt the need for a stiff, solemn defence of M. against the charge that he allows the marvellous 'to lose sight of the probable'. But only the squarest critics have ever objected to the science-fiction element in poetry. Poetry itself has always abounded with ingenious automata: see, e.g. Homer, *Od.* viii 555ff, Ariosto, *Orl. Fur.* xxx 10f and Spenser, *F.Q.* II vi 5 (self-propelled boats), and Homer, *Il.* xviii 376 (automatic tripods). M. probably had more centrally in view, however, the mystical machinery of *Ezek.* i, to which he makes extensive allusion in the following book. Cp. also vii 203-8.

v 257-61. The mimetically *interposed* clauses make the syntax difficult. *however . . . sees*, though it secondarily relates to *cloud* or *star*, primarily relates to *Earth*. The point of view is meant to be startling–to Raphael earth might be thought unlike *other shining globes* not because larger, but because smaller. Cp. Eve's fond hope at ix 811-3 that she is invisible from heaven; and see *Job* xxii 13: 'How doth God know? Can he judge through the dark cloud?'

v 257. Some copies *Ed I* begin a new paragraph at *From*, and omit comma after *cloud*.

Star interposed, however small he sees,
Not unconform to other shining globes,
260   Earth and the garden of God, with cedars crowned
Above all hills. As when by night the glass
Of Galileo, less assured, observes
Imagined lands and regions in the moon:
Or pilot from amidst the Cyclades
265   Delos or Samos first appearing kens
A cloudy spot. Down thither prone in flight
He speeds, and through the vast ethereal sky
Sails between worlds and worlds, with steady wing
Now on the polar winds, then with quick fan
270   Winnows the buxom air; till within soar

v 261–3. Contrast i 286–91, where there was no question of the lunar surface features being imaginary.   *glass / Of Galileo*] telescope.

v 264–6. The Cyclades, a circular group of islands in the S. Aegean (Gk κύκλος, circle), corresponds in shape to the whole *globe* of Earth.   *Delos*] 'Floating once' (x 296), was fixed among the Cyclades to provide a birth-place for Apollo and Diana; the whole island was anciently held in great reverence and elaborate precautions were taken to keep it free from pollution.   *Samos*] Not among the Cyclades. It resembles Delos only in that Juno was born there, and married there to Jupiter; so that each island is a mythic analogue to Eden. Raphael's unimpeded vision resembles the pilot's glimpse of *a cloudy spot* in the extremity of the range. Note also that whereas Satan is repeatedly compared to a trader Raphael is compared to a navigator.

v 266–70. Finely emulating the earthward plunges of Mercury in Virgil, *Aen.* iv 238–58 and of Michael in Tasso, *Gerus. Lib.* ix 60–2. Cp. also the descent of Satan between worlds at iii 562–90 above, where scale is similarly conveyed by an image of telescopic observation. 'The effect is at once to expand our attention toward the significant regions beyond Earth, and to contract it upon small, significant Paradise, as these spoke-like paths converge for their struggle' (MacCaffrey 63).   *prone*] downward sloping. *fan*] A poetic word for 'wing' (cp. ii 927 above); *winnows* adds an allusion to the apocalyptic winnowing fan of judgment at *Matt.* iii 12.   *buxom*] yielding.

v 270–4. Every 500 years the legendary *phoenix* used to build a pyre or nest of spices (cp. ll. 292f) on which it yielded up its life; whereupon a new phoenix would grow from the marrow of its bones, and would fly to Heliopolis, the City of the Sun, to deposit its *relics* (Ovid, *Met.* xv 391–407, Pliny, *Nat. hist.* x 2). Starnes and Talbert (272f) show that according to Renaissance dictionaries the names *Heliopolis* and *Egyptian* [i.e. not Boeotian] *Thebes* were interchangeable; also that the phoenix was described as *aquilae magnitudine*. It was *unica semper avis* (Ovid, *Amores* II vi 54; cf. *Dam* 187) because there was never more than one alive at a time. In Christian symbolism

Of towering eagles, to all the fowls he seems
A phoenix, gazed by all, as that sole bird
When to enshrine his relics in the sun's
Bright temple, to Aegyptian Thebes he flies.
275   At once on the eastern cliff of Paradise
He lights, and to his proper shape returns
A seraph winged; six wings he wore, to shade

the bird was an emblem of the triumph of eternal life over death, as well as of regeneration; while in secular iconography it signified uniqueness, or virtuous constancy (Tervarent 304f); or (since according to Lactantius' *De ave phoenice* it was sexless or hermaphroditic) ideal true love. See Jean Hubay and Maxime Leroy, *Le Mythe du Phénix*, Bibliothèque de la Faculté de Philosophie et Lettres de L'Université de Liège lxxxii (1939); F. J. Kermode, 'On Shakespeare's Learning', Wesleyan Univ. Centre for Advanced Studies Monday Evening Papers 2 (1965); Ripa s.v. *Resurrettione*; and Camerarius' Embl. '*Vita mihi mors est*'. Proverbially 'a faithful friend is like a phoenix' (see Whaler, *PMLA* xlvii (1932) 545). Thus Raphael resembles the phoenix in that he is a friend of man (cp. ix 2); a marriage counsellor (v 221–3); unique among eagle-sized creatures flying in that area; and bound for a consecrated solar shrine (ll. 264–6*n*; iv 268–85*nn*); but principally in that he manifests the virtue of the Elect. M. uses the phoenix myth also at *SA* 1699–1707.

v *271. towering*] The *Ed I* and *Ed II* spelling 'towring' does not distinguish between 'towering' = rising high in flight, and 'touring' = turning, wheeling. Cp. xi 185 and see *n*.

v *275*. The only gate of Paradise is on the eastern side (iv 178). Raphael's entry by the gate contrasts with Satan's climbing like a 'thief into God's fold' (iv 178–92) – a contrast for which foundation has already been laid by the introduction of the story of Tobias and Raphael at iv 170.

v *277–85*. Cp. the seraphim of *Is*. vi 2: 'Each one had six wings; with twain he covered his face, and with twain he covered his feet, and with twain he did fly.'   *regal*] Implies that the first pair of wings is purple (cp. xi 241 below); the second is *gold*; while the third is *sky-tinctured*. All these colours together with the description *downy*, seem to have been taken from the elaborate account of the plumage of the phoenix in Pliny; perhaps via Robert Estienne's dictionary (Starnes 273f).   *lineaments*] the shape of his body generally.   *starry zone*] cp. Michael's belt, which is compared to 'a glistering zodiac' at xi 247.   *mail*] A comparison between the overlapping feathers of the wing and the scales of jazerant-work armour.   *sky-tinctured grain*] tinctured sky-blue 'in grain'; fast dyed. Implying permanence, but also perhaps richness, of colour. See Cowley, *Davideis* i *n* 60: '*Sacred Blew*. Because of the use of it in the *Curtains* of the *Tabernacle*, the Curtain for the Door, the *Vail*, the *Priests Ephod, Breast-Plate*, and briefly all sacred Ornaments. The reason of chusing *Blew*, I suppose to have been in the *Tabernacle* to represent the seat of *God*, that is, the *Heavens*, of which the

His lineaments divine; the pair that clad
Each shoulder broad, came mantling o'er his breast
280 With regal ornament; the middle pair
Girt like a starry zone his waist, and round
Skirted his loins and thighs with downy gold
And colours dipped in heaven; the third his feet
Shadowed from either heel with feathered mail
285 Sky-tinctured grain. Like Maia's son he stood,
And shook his plumes, that heavenly fragrance filled
The circuit wide. Straight knew him all the bands
Of angels under watch; and to his state,
And to his message high in honour rise;
290 For on some message high they guessed him bound.
Their glittering tents he passed, and now is come
Into the blissful field, through groves of myrrh,

Tabernacle was an *Emblem*, Numb. 15.38. The Jews are commanded to make
that lace or ribband of *Blew*, wherewith their fringes are bound to their
cloaths; and they have now left off the very wearing of Fringes; because,
they say, the art is lost of dying that kind of *Blew*, which was the perfectest
sky-colour.'
v *285–7. Maia's son*] Mercury, the ambassador of the gods and giver of
grace, whose noble stance is similarly focused on in *Hamlet* III iv 58f: 'A
station like the herald Mercury / New-lighted on a heaven-kissing hill.'
See ll. 266–70n above. The shaking of the wings, but not the resultant
fragrance, had been anticipated in Fairfax's description of Gabriel's landing
on Earth (*Gerus. Lib.* i 14 – in Tasso the wings are only readjusted or smoothed).
v *288. state*] rank or degree.
v *289–90. message*] mission, errand.
v *292–4. blissful field*] Recalls the Elysian fields, home of the blessed, which
were described in Renaissance dictionaries as full of the odours of sweet
spices, and which have already provided a model for M.'s Paradise (see iv
153n, 159–66n). Cp. also the fragrant groves and mountains 'full of choice
nard and fragrant trees and cinnamon and pepper' in the Garden of Righte-
ousness visited by Enoch and Raphael (*Enoch* xxxii; not accessible to M.).
myrrh] According to Henry Hawkins (*Partheneia sacra*, 1633, *cit*. Broadbent
183) a prophylactic against devils.   *flowering odours*] Bentley, Pearce,
Richardson and Ricks (95) treat this phrase as a daring hypallage for 'odorous
flowers'; speaking of the 'beautifully [or disgustingly, as the case may be]
unexpected substantiality of the scents'. But if there is any hypallage at
all here, it is faint in the extreme; for in M.'s time 'odour' was regularly
used to mean a 'substance that emits a sweet smell . . . spice . . . odoriferous
flower' (*OED* 2). Cp. Prior, 'If wine and music': 'Thy Myrtles strow, thy
Odours burn.'   *cassia*] a cinnamon-like spice; an ingredient in the holy
oil used to anoint the Tabernacle (*Exod*. xxx 24).   *nard*] the oint-
ment poured over Jesus' head to anoint him 'to the burying' (*Mark* xiv 3,

And flowering odours, cassia, nard, and balm;
A wilderness of sweets; for nature here
295   Wantoned as in her prime, and played at will
Her virgin fancies, pouring forth more sweet,
Wild above rule or art; enormous bliss.
Him through the spicy forest onward come
Adam discerned, as in the door he sat
300   Of his cool bower, while now the mounted sun
Shot down direct his fervid rays to warm
Earth's inmost womb, more warmth than Adam needs;
And Eve within, due at her hour prepared
For dinner savoury fruits, of taste to please
305   True appetite, and not disrelish thirst
Of nectareous draughts between, from milky stream,

8; cp. iv 542–50n above). The association of the two was fairly common: cp. *Comus* l. 991 and Tasso, *Gerus. Lib.* tr. Fairfax xv 53 (Armida's isle of bliss).   *balm*] (see l. 23n above), prominent during Satan's entry of Paradise (iv 159, 248).

v *294–7. played*] represented or imitated in sport (*OED* III 16 c, citing Lamb: 'the noises of children, playing their own fancies'.   *sweet*] sweetly. *above . . . art*] Arts, though intended to repair the Fall, can never quite attain the original level of uncorrupted nature.   *enormous*] 'deviating from ordinary rule' (Lat. *norma*); but probably influenced also by the modern meaning 'immense'. Note that the punctuation makes it clear that *enormous bliss* is in apposition to the rest of the sentence, and not the object of *pouring*. *Wantoned*] An ominous word; here it is still innocent; but 'it is not long after the Fall that Adam and Eve become liable to the grimmer meaning [i.e. at ix 1015]' (Ricks 112).

v *299–300.* Adam's entertainment of Raphael is throughout modelled on Abraham's entertainment of three angels in *Gen.* xviii. Here cp. *Gen.* xviii 1: 'And the Lord appeared unto him in the plains of Mamre: and he sat in the tent door in the heat of the day.'

v *301. direct*] Since the ecliptic and equatorial planes coincided before the Fall, 'direct' implies that Paradise is situated on the line. See iv 209–16n. Some copies *Ed I* have comma after *rays*.

v *302.* For the penetration of the sun's rays beneath the surface of the earth, see iii 608–12n above.   *needs*] Some copies *Ed I* have *need* and omit semicolon after it.

v *303. due*] duly. After the Fall, by contrast, time's 'measure' falters, and Eve is late (ix 844–56).

v *304. savoury*] appetizing in odour. See ll. 84–5n above.

v *306–7. milky*, often applied to the juices of fruits, probably here qualifies *berry* and *grape* as well as *stream*. Used of water, it seems to have meant 'sweet': cp. *SA* 550. The allusion to the Promised Land 'flowing with milk and honey' (*Josh.* v 6) was not so obvious, perhaps, as it seems now.

Berry or grape: to whom thus Adam called.
      Haste hither Eve, and worth thy sight behold
Eastward among those trees, what glorious shape
310   Comes this way moving; seems another morn
Risen on mid-noon; some great behest from heaven
To us perhaps he brings, and will vouchsafe
This day to be our guest. But go with speed,
And what thy stores contain, bright forth and pour
315   Abundance, fit to honour and receive
Our heavenly stranger; well we may afford
Our givers their own gifts, and large bestow
From large bestowed, where nature multiplies
Her fertile growth, and by disburdening grows
320   More fruitful, which instructs us not to spare.
      To whom thus Eve. Adam, earth's hallowed mould,
Of God inspired, small store will serve, where store,
All seasons, ripe for use hangs on the stalk;
Save what by frugal storing firmness gains
325   To nourish, and superfluous moist consumes:
But I will haste and from each bough and brake,
Each plant and juiciest gourd will pluck such choice
To entertain our angel guest, as he
Beholding shall confess that here on earth
330   God hath dispensed his bounties as in heaven.
      So saying, with dispatchful looks in haste

v *318–20.* An argument distorted and misapplied as a justification for libertinism in *Comus* 710–29.

v *322.* Picking up Adam's inappropriate choice of word at l. 314, Eve sarcastically plays on *store*='cache' and 'abundance'.

v *321.* See *Gen.* ii 7: 'The Lord God formed man of the dust of the ground.' Eve perhaps shows herself familiar with an etymology later noted by Josephus and repeated in Renaissance dictionaries such as Calepino's, whereby Adam (Hebrew 'Red') was supposed to get his name from the red earth of which he was made.

v *324–5.* They only store food that improves in firmness or dryness by keeping. Thyer thought *superfluous moist* too philosophical for Eve, but it seems quite appropriate for an intelligent woman to have technical knowledge about food storage. Eve was in no position to leave such things to the servants.

v *326–7.* The sources of produce fall into four classes: fruit trees, bushes, small plants like the strawberry and cucurbitaceous climbers like the melon.   *gourd*] Perhaps specific enough to constitute an allusion to *Jonah* iv 6–10, where a gourd enjoyed then destroyed by a worm is a type of the corruption of mankind.

v *328. as*] that.

  She turns, on hospitable thoughts intent
  What choice to choose for delicacy best,
  What order, so contrived as not to mix
335 Tastes, not well joined, inelegant, but bring
  Taste after taste upheld with kindliest change,
  Bestirs her then, and from each tender stalk
  Whatever Earth all-bearing mother yields
  In India east or west, or middle shore
340 In Pontus or the Punic coast, or where
  Alcinous reigned, fruit of all kinds, in coat,
  Rough, or smooth rined, or bearded husk, or shell
  She gathers, tribute large, and on the board
  Heaps with unsparing hand; for drink the grape
345 She crushes, inoffensive must, and meaths

v 335. Such tastes as, if they were not well joined, would be inelegant.
But *inelegant* = 'inelegantly' gives a secondary chain of discourse. The
present passage is horribly travestied after the Fall, at ix 1017f. At least one
copy of *Ed I* has semicolon after *Tastes*.

v 336. *upheld*] sustained without impairment.   *kindliest*] most natural.
At least one copy of *Ed I* has semicolon after *change*.

v 338. Rendering the ancient titles Παμμῆτορ γῆ and *Omniparens*.

v 339–41. Eden's produce is, first, geographically comprehensive. It in-
cludes fruits later to be grown in India and the surrounding islands to the
east, in America to the west, and on the coasts of seas in between: namely
Pontus, the south shore of the Black Sea, Tunis, the *Punic* or Carthaginian
south shore of the Mediterranean and (between these north and south
limits) Scheria, the Phaeacian island paradise of *Alcinous*. (Notice the Baroque
centralised pattern: India–coast–island–coast–India.) Secondly, the places
named were anciently famous for their fruit. Thus *Pontus* gave its name to
rhubarb and to a variety of hazel-nut; Carthage was famous for its figs;
and the gardens of Alcinous are described as perpetually fruitful in Homer,
Od. vii 113–21. But the passage also contains a grim irony. For Pontus was
notorious as a source of poisons (Virgil, *Ecl.* viii 96), and the thing best
known about Punic figs was the threat to Rome they symbolized in an
anecdote of Plutarch's (*Life of M. Cato* xxvii 1 (352): the elder Cato shook an
African fig from his sleeve onto the floor of the Senate, and when it was
admired said 'The country that produced it is three days' sailing from
Rome.'). Paradise is again compared with the garden of Alcinous at ix 440f
below.

v 342. *smooth rined*] smooth-rinded.   *Rough . . . rined*] Distinguishes the
two classes of *coat*.

v 344–9. Note how the catalogue of foods is combined with a progression
through the stages of preparing a meal.

v 345. *must*] the unfermented juice of the grape. Intoxicating wine has to be
excluded because its origin was connected with rebellion against God. Thus

From many a berry, and from sweet kernels pressed
She tempers dulcet creams, nor these to hold
Wants her fit vessels pure, then strews the ground
With rose and odours from the shrub unfumed.
350   Mean while our primitive great sire, to meet
His godlike guest, walks forth, without more train
Accompanied than with his own complete
Perfections, in himself was all his state,
More solemn than the tedious pomp that waits
355   On princes, when their rich retinue long
Of horses led, and grooms besmeared with gold

the priests of Isis were forbidden to drink it 'for wine they say is blood, /
Even the bloud of Gyants, which were slaine, / By thundring Iove in the
Phlegrean plaine' and drinking it might 'stirre up old rebellious thought'
(Spenser, *F.Q.* V vii 10f, drawing on Plutarch, *De Iside* 353B–C). Moreover,
intoxication was a favourite symbol for the disturbance of rational control
caused by the Fall. See, e.g., St Bernard *Sermones in Cantica Canticorum* ix
9f on 'the pleasures of the flesh, with which we were formerly enthralled
and intoxicated as with wine'. Carnal desires are like wine because the grape
'once pressed has nothing more to yield'. A woman crushing grapes was
also a common emblem of Excess. Cp., e.g., Spenser's Dame Excess (*F.Q.*
II xii 55f); and a mural at Culross Palace, Fife, with the legend MIHI PON-
DERA LUXUS'.   *meath*] mead; here used poetically to mean simply 'a
sweet drink'. Contrast the present passage with ix 793, where the fallen
Eve is 'heightened as with wine'.
v *347. tempers*] mixes–though the word has psychological overtones, in
that it draws attention to the emblematic value of the foods (see l. 345n).
dulcet] sweet, soothing, bland.
v *348.* Even the utensils seem moralized. Cp., e.g., 1 *Thess.* iv 4: 'every
one of you should know how to possess his vessel in sanctification and
honour'; and *Is.* lxvi 20: 'The children of Israel bring an offering in a clean
vessel into the house of the Lord.' The presence of utensils in a Paradise
innocent of technological development is explained at iv 335.
v *349. unfumed*] At this holy supper there is no trace of papistical incense–
only the natural scent of the shrub. In any case the shrub could not have
been fumed, because Adam and Eve are as yet guiltless of fire. See l. 396n,
ix 387–92n, x 1078–81n.   *odours*] spices, odoriferous flowers; see ll.
292–4n.
v *353.* On an alleged absence of 'character' in Adam before the Fall, see
Broadbent 191f, where the present passage is discussed.   *state*] dignity.
v *355. retinue*] Accented on the second syllable.
v *356. besmeared with gold*] Cp. e.g. Horace, *Odes* IV ix 14f: '*aurum vestibus
illitum . . . regalisque cultus.* A note in the Columbia MS reads: 'English
Phrases derivd from the Latine tongue &c: A Coat *bedaubd* with Gold &c.
Virgil: Per Tunicam squalentem Auro. The words seem to be alike improper;

Dazzles the crowd, and sets them all agape.
Nearer his presence Adam though not awed,
Yet with submiss approach and reverence meek,
360   As to a superior nature, bowing low,
      Thus said. Native of heaven, for other place
None can than heaven such glorious shape contain;
Since by descending from the thrones above,
Those happy places thou hast deigned a while
365   To want, and honour these, vouchsafe with us
Two only, who yet by sovereign gift possess
This spacious ground, in yonder shady bower
To rest, and what the garden choicest bears
To sit and taste, till this meridian heat
370   Be over, and the sun more cool decline.
      Whom thus the angelic virtue answered mild.
Adam, I therefore came, nor art thou such
Created, or such place hast here to dwell,
As may not oft invite, though spirits of heaven
375   To visit thee; lead on then where thy bower
O'ershades; for these mid-hours, till evening rise
I have at will. So to the silvan lodge
They came, that like Pomona's arbour smiled

but the Latin is thus vindicated by Servius; and from thence our Phrase
arises *Squalens*, significat copiam densitatemque auri, in *Squammosum* spo-
lium nitenti. Quicquid igitur nimis inculcatum obsitumque aliqua re erat,
ut incuteret videntibus facie nova horrorem id squalere dicebatur. Vid:
Macrob: Lib: 6. Cap. 7.' (Columbia xviii 226).

v *358–71* Contrast the opening of the interview with Michael at xi 249ff.
With the first words of Adam here, cp. Aeneas' famous greeting of his
mother Venus: *O – quam te memorem, virgo? namque haud tibi voltus / mortalis,
nec vox hominem sonat; o dea certe!* (Virgil, *Aen.* i 327ff).

v *359. submiss*] submissive.

v *365. want*] feel the loss of, miss (*OED* 2 f).

v *366. sovreign*] spelt 'sov'ran'; see i 246n.

v *371.* Perhaps only a figurative way of saying 'the angel' (as Homer puts
'Priam's strength' for 'Priam' at *Il.* iii 105). But more likely 'as a seraph
or one of the supreme rank in the heavenly hierarchy, Raphael may have
the title of any of the inferior orders, of which the *Virtues* were one' (Hughes).
At vii 41, similarly, Raphael is an archangel.

v *374.* The ellipsis calls for some such expansion as 'invite guests, even if they
are spirits. . . .'

v *378–84.* Burden 71 draws attention to the care with which M. discriminates
between the ways in which Eve is like and unlike Pomona, her arbour and
Venus. The distinctions drawn amplify the spiritual character of Eve's

       With flowerets decked and fragrant smells; but Eve
  380   Undecked, save with her self more lovely fair
       Than wood-nymph, or the fairest goddess feigned
       Of three that in Mount Ida naked strove,
       Stood to entertain her guest from heaven; no veil
       She needed, virtue-proof, no thought infirm
  385   Altered her cheek. On whom the angel Hail
       Bestowed, the holy salutation used
       Long after to blest Marie, second Eve.
         Hail mother of mankind, whose fruitful womb

adornment (nakedness symbolized sincere virtue) and her historical reality
(not *feigned* or mythological).

v *378–81*. The Roman *wood-nymph Pomona* presided over gardens and es-
pecially fruit trees. An analogy between Eve and Pomona is drawn again
at ix 394f; but by then the goddess of fruitfulness is imminently threatened
and in flight.   *undecked ... herself*] Eve is repeatedly identified with
symbolically fair or fragile flowers; cp., e.g., iv 270, and ix 432, 'Eve though
fairest unsupported flower'.

v *381–2*. The three goddesses Juno Minerva and Venus all claimed the apple
of Strife inscribed TO THE FAIREST, and the mortal Paris, famed for his wis-
dom, was appointed arbiter. The judgment of Paris was delivered on Mount
Ida, where the goddesses appeared before him naked and without orna-
ment. But the simile has also a more ironic application. For Paris' fatal
choice of the beauty offered by Venus led to the rape of Helen and eventu-
ally to the destruction of Troy, which is for M. a mythic analogue to the
Fall of man (see i 1–94n). The inference is that, in respect of virtue, Adam is
like, but Raphael unlike, Paris. Raphael, indeed, corresponds rather to
Mercury, who is commonly present in representations of the Judgment of
Paris (see, e.g., the painting by the Paris Master in the Fogg Museum,
Harvard). For Raphael's Mercury role in *PL*, see ll. 266–70n, 285–7n.

v *384. virtue-proof*] invulnerable through her virtue. But the expected
meaning, on the analogy of other such compounds (e.g. shot-proof), is
difficult to exclude, and must have occurred to M–proof against virtue.
Proof, then, against Raphael, *the angelic virtue* (l. 371)?   *infirm*] frail;
Spenser, *Epithalamion* 236f, 'That suffers not one looke to glaunce awry, /
Which may let in a little thought unsownd.'

v *385–7*. At the Annunciation, the angel Gabriel, come to tell the Virgin
Mary she would conceive a son, to be called Jesus, addressed her with the
words 'Hail, thou that art highly favoured, the Lord is with thee: blessed art
thou among women' (*Luke* i 28).   *second Eve*] Cp. x 183. Just as Christ
is the 'last Adam' (*1 Cor.* xv 45; and see i 4–5n), so the Virgin was typologi-
cally related to Eve.

v *388*. Cp. Michael's greeting at xi 158f: 'Hail to thee, / Eve rightly called,
mother of all mankind.' Eve is mother of mankind, as Mary is *Theotokos*
or mother of God. The title is based on *Gen.* iii 20: 'Adam called his wife's

Shall fill the world more numerous with thy sons
390 Than with these various fruits the trees of God
Have heaped this table. Raised of grassy turf
Their table was, and mossy seats had round,
And on her ample square from side to side
All autumn piled, though spring and autumn here
395 Danced hand in hand. A while discourse they hold;
No fear lest dinner cool; when thus began
Our author. Heavenly stranger, please to taste
These bounties which our nourisher, from whom
All perfect good unmeasured out, descends,
400 To us for food and for delight hath caused

name Eve; because she was the mother of all living.' The juxtaposition with
the immediately preceding *Hail* is curious, in view of the prevailing opinion
of the Reformers that it was 'but a fond conceit, to derive *Ave*, the first
word of the Angels salutation to Marie of *Eva*, invented because shee re-
paired what was lost by *Eva*, for the one is a latine word, the other hebrewe'
(Willet 54).

v *391. turf*] Because the shaping of wood had not yet begun. For Renaissance
theories about the various primitive stages of technological development,
see Panofsky[2] 33–67, 'Early History of Man'.

v *393. square*] A shape emblematic of virtue and particularly of temperance.
See, e.g., Achille Bocchi, *Symbolicarum quaestionum libri quinque* (Bologna
1574), Embl. 144; also the discussions in Fowler, s.v. 'Square' and 'Quad-
rate'. The symbolism was originally Pythagorean (the square is a form of the
tetrad); but it later became generally familiar. Cp. the expressions 'four-
square'; 'square' = honest (*OED* a. II 8); and 'square' = rule (*OED* sb. I 2;
e.g. Calvin on *Ps.* i 6, tr. Golding: 'Whose duetye it is to settle the state of
the world according to the right squyre'). The moral meaning of *square*
is here reinforced by the use of the personal pronoun *her*.

v *394–5*. For the simultaneity of spring and autumn in Paradise, see iv 148*n*.
The dance of the Seasons or Horae is the same as the dance of the Graces.

v *396*. Hypersophisticated critics despise the domesticity of this line, and
even Empson seems to lack enthusiasm for fruitarian meals (Empson[2]
153). But we should give M. credit for enriching the traditional fare of primi-
tive man—acorns and water–so plausibly. Nor should we mistake his
sophistication for naivety. Fire cannot be used before the Fall, since its
discovery was one of the Fall's consequences (see l. 349*n*, ix 387–92*n*, x
1078–81*n*), but instead of accepting this as a disadvantage M. turns it to
good effect by pointing to an inconvenience of our own world.

v *397. author*] ancestor.

v *399*. 'Every good gift and every perfect gift is from above, and cometh
down from the Father of lights' (*Jas.* i 17).

> The earth to yield; unsavoury food perhaps
> To spiritual natures; only this I know,
> That one celestial Father gives to all.
>   To whom the angel. Therefore what he gives
> 405 (Whose praise be ever sung) to man in part
> Spiritual, may of purest spirits be found
> No ingrateful food: and food alike those pure
> Intelligential substances require,
> As doth your rational; and both contain
> 410 Within them every lower faculty
> Of sense, whereby they hear, see, smell, touch, taste,
> Tasting concoct, digest, assimilate,

v 401–3. Burden 112 notes that this the first of Adam's curious investiga-
tions begins (as all true knowledge began and ended) with God. Yet it verges
already on forbidden knowledge: questions about the diet of angels are in
one way not far from questions about how to become a god by eating.
In this connection it is interesting to note that Cowley actually refers to the
forbidden fruit of the tree of knowledge as 'Angels meat' (ed. Waller 45).
For the pun in *unsavoury* see ll. 84–5n above.

v 407–13. Bentley's sneer must be included, if only for its elephantine wit:
'If the Devils want *feeding*, our Author made poor Provision for them in his
Second Book; where they have nothing to eat but *Hell-fire*; and no danger
of their *Dinner cooling*.' Manna is called 'the corn of heaven' and 'angels'
food' (cp. l. 633 below) in *Ps.* lxxviii 24f; and on such authority it was be-
lieved fairly generally that angels ate *in some sense*. But many authors re-
garded the eating as merely symbolic; while most made a distinction between
merely swallowing (as the angels did) on the one hand, and on the other
really digesting (see, e.g., Willet 199 on *Gen.* xviii 8; and Vermigli, *Common-
places, cit.* Rajan 149). But M. insists on the latter sense (see esp. l. 412), and
in so doing rejects the Scholastic view that angels are immaterial. In empha-
sizing 'the reality of angelic nourishment' he adopts instead the view of
Platonic theology, according to which all created spirits are corporeal
(Lewis 105f).   No ingrateful] acceptable; but perhaps also suggesting the
recipient's gratitude.

v 408. *Intelligential substances*] intellectual beings.

v 409. Cp. *De doctrina* i 7, Columbia xv 25: 'Spirit being the more excellent
substance, virtually and essentially contains within itself the inferior one;
as the spiritual and rational faculty contains the corporeal, that is, the senti-
ent and vegetative faculty.'

v 411. The finer senses that nourish the soul (sight and hearing) take prece-
dence of the grosser senses that nourish the body. For this sequence and its
philosophical implications, see Frank Kermode, 'The Banquet of Sense',
Bulletin of the John Rylands Libr. xliv (1961) 78.

v 412. Physiological theory distinguished three stages of digestion: the
'first concoction' or digestion in the stomach (*concoct*), the 'second con-

>   And corporeal to incorporeal turn.
>   For know, whatever was created, needs
>   415   To be sustained and fed; of elements
>   The grosser feeds the purer, earth the sea,
>   Earth and the sea feed air, the air those fires
>   Ethereal, and as lowest first the moon;
>   Whence in her visage round those spots, unpurged
>   420   Vapours not yet into her substance turned.
>   Nor doth the moon no nourishment exhale
>   From her moist continent to higher orbs.
>   The sun that light imparts to all, receives
>   From all his alimental recompense
>   425   In humid exhalations, and at even

coction' or conversion to blood (*digest*) and the 'third concoction' or secretion (*assimilate*).

v *414. needs*] Ideologically an important word. Most theologians held that angels did not eat of necessity: see, e.g., Willet 199, on *Gen.* xviii 8. M. is stressing that the angels' corporeality is not assumed.

v *415–8*. On the conversion of the elements, see ll. 180–2n above.

v *418–20. lowest*] i.e., of the planetary spheres.   *round*] An exact choice of epithet; since the vapours were supposed not to be visible until the moon was full: 'So long as she appeareth by the halfe in sight, [she] never sheweth any spots, because as yet she hath not her full power of light sufficient, to draw humour unto her. For these spots be nothing els but the dregs of the earth, caught up with other moisture among the vapors' (Pliny, *Nat. Hist.*, tr. Holland (1601) ii 7). It seems odd that M. should put in Raphael's mouth an archaic theory about lunar spots that seems to us obviously inferior to Galileo's explanation of them as landscape features – an explanation already used above at i 287–91. But the subject of lunar spots was still highly controversial in M.'s time. For a survey of the different schools of opinion, see Riccioli i 206f.

v *423–6*. Older opinion about the sun's sustenance is gathered in Swan's *Speculum mundi*: 'Cleanthes . . . allowed the matter of the sunne to be fierie, and that it was nourished by humours attracted from the ocean. Also Anaximander and Diogenes, after whom Epicurus, and the Stoics' (*cit.* Svendsen 66). But this alimentary version of the Great Chain of Being was also popular in M.'s own time with mystical and alchemic Platonists such as Robert Fludd (see, e.g., the engraving to his *Utriusque cosmi historia* I v 6). Cp. also the imitation of Anacreon in Cowley 51: 'The busie *Sun* (and one would guess / By's drunken fiery face no less) / Drinks up the *Sea*, and when h'as done, / The *Moon* and *Stars* drink up the *Sun*.' And see Plato, *Tim.* 49C; Cicero, *De nat. deor.* ii 33. The cosmic generalization of eating and drinking into a universal exchange of higher and lower is indispensable to M.'s vision. For the importance of the way an apple is eaten must seem appropriate, if not organically inevitable.

Sups with the ocean: though in heaven the trees
Of life ambrosial fruitage bear, and vines
Yield nectar, though from off the boughs each morn
We brush mellifluous dews, and find the ground
430 Covered with pearly grain: yet God hath here
Varied his bounty so with new delights,
As may compare with heaven; and to taste
Think not I shall be nice. So down they sat,
And to their viands fell, nor seemingly
435 The angel, nor in mist, the common gloss
Of theologians, but with keen despatch
Of real hunger, and concoctive heat
To transubstantiate; what redounds, transpires

v 427. *ambrosial*] See ii 245n. Ambrosia was anciently the food of the gods, as *nectar* the drink. There was dominical authority for *vines* in heaven: 'I will not drink henceforth of this fruit of the vine, until that day when I drink it new with you in my Father's kingdom' (*Matt.* xxvi 29). For the perpetual *fruitage* of the tree of life, see *Rev.* xxii 2.

v 429. *mellifluous*] sweet as honey; honey-flowing.

v 430. *pearly grain*] manna, the 'corn of heaven' (see ll. 407–13n above); Cp. *Exod.* xvi 14: 'And when the dew that lay was gone up, behold, upon the face of the wilderness there lay a small round thing, as small as the hoar frost on the ground.' Iconographically, manna was represented most commonly as scattered pellets, more or less pearl-sized. See, e.g., Dirk Bouts's *The Gathering of the Manna* in St Peter's, Louvain; or Tintoretto's painting of the same subject in S. Giorgio Maggiore, Venice.

v 433. *nice*] over-refined, difficult to please.

v 434–8. See ll. 407–14nn above. *seemingly*] Refers to the Docetist theories about angelic appearances, devised to explain away the awkwardly materialistic accounts of angels in the Bible (e.g. at *Gen.* xviii 8, 'they did eat'). The Reformers on the whole rejected such mealy-mouthed evasions: 'We neither think with *Theodoret*, that these angels seemed onely [i.e., only seemed] to have bodies, and so also seemed to eate, but neither in truth' (Willet 199). It is particularly decisive that M. should make Raphael eat, because it was Raphael's explanation to Tobias (*Tob.* xii 19: 'I did neither eat nor drink, but ye did see a vision') that provided the immaterialists with their main proof text. The bases for M.'s conviction about the corporeality of spirits would include the broiled fish and honey eaten by the risen Christ (*Luke* xxiv 39–43).

v 438–9. *redounds*] remains in excess. With characteristic imaginative extremism, M. is quite prepared to envisage angels excreting, if their corporeality entails it. *transubstantiate*] The word seems to have a double function here. Most obviously it is an abstract theological term, contrasting sharply with the direct concrete simplicity of *keen . . . hunger*. More subtly,

Through spirits with ease; nor wonder; if by fire
440   Of sooty coal the empiric alchemist
Can turn, or holds it possible to turn
Metals of drossiest ore to perfect gold
As from the mine. Mean while at table Eve
Ministered naked, and their flowing cups
445   With pleasant liquors crowned: O innocence
Deserving Paradise! If ever, then,
Then had the sons of God excuse to have been
Enamoured at that sight; but in those hearts
Love unlibidinous reigned, nor jealousy
450   Was understood, the injured lover's hell.
     Thus when with meats and drinks they had sufficed,
Not burdened nature, sudden mind arose
In Adam, not to let the occasion pass
Given him by this great conference to know
455   Of things above his world, and of their being
Who dwell in heaven, whose excellence he saw
Transcend his own so far, whose radiant forms
Divine effulgence, whose high power so far
Exceeded human, and his wary speech
460   Thus to the empyreal minister he framed.

however, it makes the implicit point that Adam and Eve were already en-
joying Communion with the gods. If they had been content to wait, this
hierarchical mobility would no doubt have increased. For the themes of
ascent through eating, and of alimentary interchange between the lower
and higher stages of the scale of nature, see ll. 84–5n and 423–6n above.

v *439–43*. The analogy between physiological and alchemical processes was
regarded as very close: several terms (such as *concoction* and *digestion*) were
common to both disciplines. In both, 'heat' (l. 437) refined matter and drove
off impurities.   *empiric alchemist*] i.e., a mere 'puffer' or vulgar prac-
titioner, as distinct from the adept or grand alchemist who worked on a
theoretical and often mystical basis. See Caron 69, 78f, 89.

v *445. crowned*] filled to the brim; perhaps referring specifically to the menis-
cus. Cp. Homer, *Il.* i 470 (during a ritual meal in honour of Apollo) and
Virgil, *Georg.* ii 528 (*socii cratera coronant*, in honour of Bacchus); though the
latter passage properly refers to the wreathing of the cup with a garland.

v *446–50. sons of God*] angels; alluding to *Gen.* vi 2: 'The sons of God saw
the daughters of men that they were fair; and they took them wives of all
which they chose.' Note, however, that M. does not say that the angels
ever did take wives of the daughters of men. See xi 621–2n below.

v *451–2*. The temperance taken for granted before the Fall has to be made
the subject of explicit advice by Michael, at xi 531.

v *459*. As Burden 113 notes, Adam is *wary* because for all he knows it may
be the forbidden knowledge for which he is about to ask.

> Inhabitant with God, now know I well
> Thy favour, in this honour done to man,
> Under whose lowly roof thou hast vouchsafed
> To enter, and these earthly fruits to taste,
465 Food not of angels, yet accepted so,
> As that more willingly thou couldst not seem
> At heaven's high feasts to have fed: yet what compare?
> To whom the winged hierarch replied.
> O Adam, one almighty is, from whom
470 All things proceed, and up to him return,
> If not depraved from good, created all
> Such to perfection, one first matter all,

v 467. *compare*] comparison.

v 468. It has been said that if angelic digestion appears a far-fetched subject of instruction this may be just the point. M. may want to amplify the wideness of Adam's permitted researches by showing him at work on something really arcane. On the other hand, there is a clear thematic relevance: M. is concerned to place eating in a context of cosmic relations. Raphael changes the subject, imperceptibly but firmly, to more practical matters: how and how much to know. The transition is easy; since for M. knowledge, like eating or sex, is a moral activity which can be engaged in either obediently and in moderation, or to excess.

v 469–90. Raphael's world picture is characterised by a cyclic movement of emanation and return that marks it as Platonic; just as does the notion of successive degrees of spirituousness. It was an ancient and familiar picture; so much so that it would be pointless to list sources and models. The plant simile was a common enough way of explaining the notion of a scale of being. It is often found in a more detailed form than here, but seldom if ever so passionately expressive. Cp., e.g., Mercator's tree, whose sole trunk is chaos: 'Chaos is the onely truncke of all the Species to be created, having his roote and beginning in the Universall Idea Creatrix, which is in the mind, and divine will' (*Historia Mundi, cit.* Svendsen 115). Another common analogy for the ascent of species was the series of successive purifications of the alchemical Magnum Opus, to which M. alludes in his choice of such bivalent diction as *first matter* and *refined* and *sublimed*. The cosmic tree, identified with the Tree of Life, was itself one of the foremost symbols of theoretical alchemy; see iv 217–21n above. Note that the whole model is as dynamic as any evolutionary system of more recent times. The vision of nature as a working, striving organism could to some extent be paralleled in authors ranging from Aristotle to the Cambridge Platonists; but it is also an individual poetic vision, never fully conceptualized even in M.'s own theological work in prose. See W. C. Curry and W. B. Hunter, in *Research Studies of the Univ. of Louisiana* (1941) 173–92.

v 472. *first matter*] In *De doctrina* i 7 (Columbia xv 20–7) M. argues strongly against creation *e nihilo*. He holds that God, not nothing, is the material

Indued with various forms, various degrees
Of substance, and in things that live, of life;
475 But more refined, more spirituous, and pure,
As nearer to him placed or nearer tending
Each in their several active spheres assigned,
Till body up to spirit work, in bounds
Proportioned to each kind. So from the root
480 Springs lighter the green stalk, from thence the leaves
More airy, last the bright consummate flower
Spirits odorous breathes: flowers and their fruit
Man's nourishment, by gradual scale sublimed
To vital spirits aspire, to animal,
485 To intellectual, give both life and sense,
Fancy and understanding, whence the soul
Reason receives, and reason is her being,
Discursive, or intuitive; discourse
Is oftest yours, the latter most is ours,
490 Differing but in degree, of kind the same.
Wonder not then, what God for you saw good
If I refuse not, but convert, as you,
To proper substance, time may come when men
With angels may participate, and find

cause of the world, and that it is framed out of an 'original matter . . . in-
trinsically good, and the chief productive stock of every subsequent good'.
For primal matter as a term in alchemy, see iii 601–5n above.

v 477–9. For a moral application of this idea, see *Comus* 459–63. The Pauline
notion of change from corruptible to incorruptible (*1 Cor.* xv) had already
been combined poetically with the Aristotelian view of nature as growth
and the Platonic vision of a return or *remeatio*, in Spenser, *F.Q.* VII vii 58:
'all things . . . by their change their being doe dilate: / And turning to
themselves at length againe, / Doe worke their owne perfection so by fate'.

v 481. *consummate*] completed, perfected, final.   *airy*] A good word,
since it implies lightness and therefore a tendency upward: cp. Adam's sleep,
'airy light from pure digestion bred' (l. 4 above). Air was the element con-
nected with the sanguine temperament, generally considered the most per-
fect of the four. On sanguine as the temperament of unfallen man, see Kli-
bansky 105, 110f.

v 483. *scale*] i.e., the *scala naturae* or cosmic ladder.   *sublimed*] 'raised';
but also in its alchemic sense, 'sublimated'. For the ladder as an alchemical
symbol, see iii 516–7n. Rajan 150 n 9 gives a list of authorities on the *scala
naturae*; to which should be added Agrippa of Nettesheim (see Klibansky
352).

v 494. *vital spirits*] Extremely fine pure fluids, given off by the blood of the
heart, and sustaining life.   *animal spirits*] Had their seat in the brain, and
controlled sensation and voluntary motion. Cp. iv 805.

495   No inconvenient diet, nor too light fare:
      And from these corporal nutriments perhaps
      Your bodies may at last turn all to spirit,
      Improved by tract of time, and winged ascend

v *478–90*. The distinction between the *intuitive*, simple, undifferentiated operation of the contemplating intellect (*mens*) and the *discursive* or ratiocinative, piecemeal operation of the intellect working in conjunction with the reason (*ratio*) goes back ultimately to Plato. See, e.g., his dichotomies between pure intellect and opinion, and between understanding and knowledge of shadows, in *Rep.* 533f. It was customary to connect angels with intellect or intelligence only, and to say that they practised only the first kind of reasoning. Cp. the presupposition underlying Ficino, *De immortal. anim.* xiii 2 (*Opera omnia* 290): *Ratio interponitur, vis quaedam verarum propria animarum, per quam in universali conceptu a principiis rerum ad conclusiones temporali successione discurrunt, effectus resolvunt in causas, causas iterum in effectus deducunt, discurrunt etiam conceptu particulari ad discursionis universalis exemplar. Sed in prima ipsa et universali discursione, ratio intellectualis vocanda est, in discursione particulari, ratio cogitatrix et opinatrix. Mens autem illa quae est animae caput, et auriga, suapte natura angelos imitata, non successione, sed momento quod cupit assequitur.'* (The intellect, which is head and charioteer of the soul, by its own nature imitates the angels, and pursues what it desires not successively but in an instant). But M. describes the angels as practising both kinds of reasoning, in *De doctrina* i 9 (Columbia xv 106): the good angels know some things *per revelationem*, others *per eminentem quandam ratiocinationem*. The preoccupation of M.'s contemporaries with the ideal of intuitive knowledge has been called the 'heresy of angelism' by Jacques Maritain (see MacCaffrey 53).

v *493. proper*] distinctive, peculiar (*OED* I 2) or suitable (*OED* III 9).

v *496–500*. Cp. ll. 79–80n above. God's ambassador and the voice in Eve's dream seem to be saying the same thing, 'that God expects them to manage to get to Heaven, and that what they eat has something to do with it' (Empson 150). The resemblance is reinforced formally by the echo of 'as we'. However, there is no need to infer that this resemblance excuses Eve or convicts God of machiavellianism. On the contrary, it simplifies the issue before man into a direct choice between eating obediently and eating disobediently. Eating is shown to be in itself a neutral act. The idea that, if mankind had not fallen, it would eventually have been raised to the same spiritual level with the angels, was quite orthodox. See, e.g., St Augustine, *Civ. Dei* xiv 10, *cit.* Lewis 66. Cp. also vii 157ff, and the conclusion of *Of Reformation* with its glorious vision of the faithful being rewarded with angelic titles (Yale i 616). Burden 36f notes how important it is that the station ordained for man should be progressive rather than static. Eating the fruit must not be in any way a necessary step to man's full development. *tract*] duration, lapse; *tract of time* was ordinary prose usage (cp. Heylyn iii 127).

Ethereal, as we, or may at choice
500   Here or in heavenly paradises dwell;
If ye be found obedient, and retain
Unalterably firm his love entire
Whose progeny you are. Mean while enjoy
Your fill what happiness this happy state
505   Can comprehend, incapable of more.
      To whom the patriarch of mankind replied,
O favourable spirit, propitious guest,
Well hast thou taught the way that might direct
Our knowledge, and the scale of nature set
510   From centre to circumference, whereon
In contemplation of created things
By steps we may ascend to God. But say,
What meant that caution joined, *If ye be found
Obedient?* Can we want obedience then
515   To him, or possibly his love desert
Who formed us from the dust, and placed us here
Full to the utmost measure of what bliss
Human desires can seek or apprehend?
      To whom the angel. Son of heaven and earth,

v *501.* Cp. *Is.* i 19: 'If ye be willing and obedient, ye shall eat the good of
the land.' But the irony lies in the implied allusion to the verse following:
'But if ye refuse and rebel, ye shall be devoured with the sword: for the
mouth of the Lord hath spoken it.'

v *503.* Alluding to St Paul's Mars' Hill sermon on the Unknown God, *Acts*
xvii 28: 'For in him we live, and move, and have our being; as certain also
of your own poets have said, For we are also his offspring.' St Paul was
quoting the astronomical poet Aratus, *Phaenomena* 5. On M.'s marginal
comment on the Aratus passage (he notes another version of the idea, in
Lucretius, *De rerum nat.* ii 991f), see M. Kelley and S. D. Atkins, 'M.'s
Annotations of Aratus', *PMLA* lxx (1955) 1092.

v *504. Your fill*] Biblical diction; e.g. *Deut.* xxiii 24, 'When thou comest
into thy neighbour's vineyard, then thou mayest eat grapes thy fill at
thine own pleasure; but thou shalt not put any in thy vessel.'

v *505. incapable*] The primary meaning is that their happy state is 'unable
to hold more (happiness)' (*OED* I 1), but in a secondary dramatic irony it is
Adam and Eve who are unable to hold their happiness.

v *509–12.* Cp. the symbolic Jacob's ladder used in reverse by Satan in Bk
iii; see iii 510–5n and 516–7n. In the *scale* or ladder of nature Adam refers
to the Platonic ascesis from image to universal, up the hierarchic grades of
existence. But the alchemical language in the preceding passage (l. 469–90n
and 472n) renders probable the existence of a secondary meaning–an allu-
sion to the (presumptuous?) ladder of alchemic purification.

520   Attend: that thou art happy, owe to God;
       That thou continuest such, owe to thyself,
       That is, to thy obedience; therein stand.
       This was that caution given thee; be advised.
       God made thee perfect, not immutable;
525   And good he made thee, but to persevere
       He left it in thy power, ordained thy will
       By nature free, not over-ruled by fate
       Inextricable, or strict necessity;
       Our voluntary service he requires,
530   Not our necessitated, such with him
       Finds no acceptance, nor can find, for how
       Can hearts, not free, be tried whether they serve
       Willing or no, who will but what they must
       By destiny, and can no other choose?
535   My self and all the angelic host that stand
       In sight of God enthroned, our happy state
       Hold, as you yours, while our obedience holds;
       On other surety none; freely we serve,
       Because we freely love, as in our will
540   To love or not; in this we stand or fall:
       And some are fallen, to disobedience fallen,
       And so from heaven to deepest hell; O fall

v 520–43. Covering similar ground to that covered in God the Father's rejection of determinism and predestination at iii 93–128, but from the standpoint, now, of practical theology. The brevity of the sentences is in accordance with Horace's prescription for the style of precepts: *Quidquid praecipies esto brevis, ut cito dicta / percipiant animi dociles teneantque fideles* (*Ars poet.* 335f). ·

v 529–34. Cp. *De doctrina* i 3 (Columbia xiv 141): 'The acceptableness of duties done under a law of necessity is diminished, or rather is annihilated altogether, inasmuch as freedom can no longer be attributed to that will over which some fixed decree is inevitably suspended.' Raphael's emphasis – and the emphasis throughout *PL* – on obedience, may at first seem coldly moralistic. But a study of the passionately committed discussion of free will and predestination in *De doctrina* i 3 soon suggests that obedience is for M. bound up with the value of freedom. Only if God wishes obedience as a sign of faithful love can man's freedom of will have significance.

v 534. Satan, however, actually prefers to think in terms of destiny; see iv 58.

v 538. *Ed I* has period after *serve*.

v 540. Cp. *De doctrina* i 3 (Columbia xiv 81): 'In assigning the gift of free will God suffered both men and angels to stand or fall at their own uncontrolled choice'.

From what high state of bliss into what woe!
To whom our great progenitor. Thy words
545 Attentive, and with more delighted ear,
Divine instructor, I have heard, than when
Cherubic songs by night from neighbouring hills
Aerial music send: nor knew I not
To be both will and deed created free;
550 Yet that we never shall forget to love
Our maker, and obey him whose command
Single, is yet so just, my constant thoughts
Assured me, and still assure: though what thou tell'st
Hath passed in heaven, some doubt within me move,
555 But more desire to hear, if thou consent,
The full relation, which must needs be strange,
Worthy of sacred silence to be heard;
And we have yet large day, for scarce the sun
Hath finished half his journey, and scarce begins
560 His other half in the great zone of heaven.
Thus Adam made request, and Raphael
After short pause assenting, thus began.
High matter thou enjoinest me, O prime of men,

v 543. For the rhetorical scheme see i 91–2n.

v 547. The songs of the cherub guard, which Adam has described at iv 680–8.

v 551–2. Cp. iv 419ff and 432ff. Obey him who has given only a *single* command (and therefore easy to obey) and also (*yet*: OED I 1 a) a *just* command (and therefore right to obey).

v 553. *Ed I* has no comma after *me*.

v 556. *relation*] account.

v 557. *Worthy . . . silence*] Alluding to the songs 'worthy of sacred silence' that Sappho and Alcaeus sing to the wondering shades in Horace, *Odes* II xiii 29f: *utrumque sacro digna silentio / mirantur umbrae dicere*. But the point (as so often with M.'s allusions) lies in the passage immediately following that quoted. The fit audience would know that Horace continued: *sed magis pugnas et exactos tyrannos / densum umeris bibit aure vulgus* (but most the tale of battles and of banished tyrants the crowd, shouldering close, drinks greedily).

v 558. *large day*] ample day (OED s.v. *Large* A II 2). If the more usual sense of the phrase, 'a day and more' (OED s.v. *Large* A II 5), is present as a secondary meaning it may express M.'s formal intention. For of course Raphael's narration fills out the time until it becomes in a sense far more than a day. In fact, however, Raphael spends, as he was instructed (l. 229), just six hours with Adam and Eve: see viii 630–2.

v 563. *prime*] Already used to denote a symbolic time of freshness, perfection

Sad task and hard, for how shall I relate
565   To human sense the invisible exploits
Of warring spirits; how without remorse
The ruin of so many glorious once
And perfect while they stood; how last unfold
The secrets of another world, perhaps
570   Not lawful to reveal? Yet for thy good
This is dispensed, and what surmounts the reach
Of human sense, I shall delineate so,
By likening spiritual to corporeal forms,

and worship (ll. 18–25*n* and 170*n*); so that when it is now applied to Adam it
no longer means simply 'first' or 'best'.

v 563–4. Raphael's account of the war in heaven continues to the end of
Bk vi. It is one of the two long 'episodes' or inset narrations, that conclude
the two halves of the poem. (For the other, and its relation to this, see xi
356–8*n*; also Introduction, 'Numerology'.) Such episodes, often relating
events that happened before the time of the poem's main action, were usual
in epic; and have continued in a modified form in the flash-back of modern
fiction. Cp. Odysseus' narration to Alcinous and the Phaeacians in *Od.*
ix, a parallel drawn explicitly at l. 341 above. But the sentiment here also
recalls that of Aeneas, as he begins his long narration to Dido at *Aen.* ii 3:
infandum, regina, iubes renovare dolorem. Raphael's narration is *high matter*
in a literal as well as metaphorical sense; for he is about to rise above earth
to the high central point of the poem spatially, and to tell 'what surmounts
the reach of human sense' (ll. 571f; see MacCaffrey 57).

v 566. *how without remorse*] Burden thinks Raphael must tell the story with-
out remorse for the same reason that God was pitiless during the events
themselves. He is perfectly just, so that there is no occasion for remorse.
But Raphael may on the contrary mean that the task is going to be a *sad* one,
and that he doesn't know whether he can get through it without feeling
more remorse than he can bear. Cp. xi 99.

v 569–70. Cp. vii 120 and viii 174f. 'It occurs rather often to Raphael that
he is not sure how much God will allow him to tell' (Empson 149).

v 527–4. Hanford 416 argues on the basis of this passage that M. did not
intend his poem to be regarded as literal truth, but as a symbolic embodiment
of inspired revelation. Cp. Dante's acknowledgment at *Par.* xxiii 55–78 of
the difficulty of representing heaven (*figurando il Paradiso*). Just as Dante
plays on *figurare* (represent, symbolize), so M.'s lines apply to his own imi-
tation as much as to Raphael's, and challenge the fit reader to demytho-
logize.

v 573. *corporal*] Darbishire[2] i 298 emends to *corporeal*, on the ground that M.
observed a distinction between *corporeal* (='having a body') and *corporal*
(='relating to the body'). But if M. observed the distinction at all, he did so
erratically. See, e.g. *Treatise of Civil Power* (Columbia vi 10), 'commuting
of corporal for spiritual'; also *Art of Logic* i 7 (Columbia xi 63). *Cor-*

As may express them best, though what if earth
575   Be but the shadow of heaven, and things therein
Each to other like, more than on earth is thought?
   As yet this world was not, and Chaos wild
Reigned where these heavens now roll, where earth
            now rests
Upon her centre poised, when on a day
580   (For time, though in eternity, applied
To motion, measures all things durable
By present, past, and future) on such day
As heaven's great year brings forth, the empyreal
            host

poral='embodied, material' was common usage at the time (see *OED* s.v.
Corporal 1 c, 2).
v *574–6*. It was a fundamental doctrine of Platonism that the phenomenal
world bears to the heavenly world of Ideas the same relation as shadow to
reality. The most extensive discussion of the doctrine in Plato is *Rep.* x.
Cp. iv 207f above.
v *578–9*. For the position of earth in the creation, see vii 240–2n.   *these
heavens*] the visible, astronomical heavens.
v *579–82*. Here M. shows himself well aware of the limitations of corporeal
language, in describing spiritual and eternal actions. He has to navigate
round the Platonic doctrine (*Tim.* 37E–38E) that time, a moveable image of
eternity, is generated by the heavenly bodies 'and existed not before the
heavens came into being' (*Tim.* 37E). This he does by way of the plausible
assumption that there can be motion in eternity–a possibility excluded by
Plato himself (*Tim.* 38A). Cp. *De doctrina* i 7 (Columbia xv 35): 'It seems
even probable, that the apostasy which caused the expulsion of so many
thousands from heaven, took place before the foundations of this world were
laid. Certainly there is no sufficient foundation for the common opinion,
that motion and time (which is the measure of motion) could not, according
to the ratio of priority and subsequence, have existed before this world was
made; since Aristotle, who teaches that no ideas of motion and time can be
formed except in reference to this world, nevertheless pronounces the
world itself to be eternal.'
v *583–6*. Cp. *Job* i 6: 'Now there was a day when the sons of God [i.e.,
angels] came to present themselves before the Lord, and Satan came also
among them.'
v *583*. The *great year* or *annus magnus platonicus* is the cycle completed when
all the heavenly bodies simultaneously return to their original positions.
The period of the cycle was variously estimated (e.g. by Servius at 12,954
natural years, by Macrobius at 15,000, by Plato himself probably at 36,000),
and it was often connected with the equinoctial precessional period. The
point of the present passage lies in the fact that the Great Year was also identi-
fied with the *Politicus* Cycles of Uniformity and Dissimilarity, the latter of

Of angels by imperial summons called,
585   Innumerable before the almighty's throne
Forthwith from all the ends of heaven appeared
Under their hierarchs in orders bright
Ten thousand thousand ensigns high advanced,
Standards, and gonfalons twixt van and rear
590   Stream in the air, and for distinction serve
Of hierarchies, of orders, and degrees;
Or in their glittering tissues bear imblazed
Holy memorials, acts of zeal and love
Recorded eminent. Thus when in orbs
595   Of circuit inexpressible they stood,
Orb within orb, the Father infinite,

which was in turn identified with the process of deterioration begun with
the Fall or the loss of the Golden Age. The *day* Raphael is to describe re-
sembles the day brought forth by the Great Year because the generation
of the Son begins a new age, but also because it is the first day of the poem's
cycle. See Introduction, 'Chronology'. From another point of view, the
day may be seen as preceding the start of the angelic rebellion. The Cycle
of Uniformity is at full term, and brings forth the first day of the Cycle of
Deterioration. See Adams ii 295–302; and, for Spenser's use of the same idea,
Fowler 37f, 193–5.

v *587*. On the *orders* of the angels see i 128–9*b*; and Verity's Appendix,
680–2. A heavy point is needed after *bright*.

v *588*. Cp. Daniel's vision of the judgment of the Ancient of days: 'A fiery
stream issued and came forth from before him: thousand thousands
ministered unto him, and ten thousand times ten thousand stood before
him' (*Dan.* vii 10). The angels are multiple, and therefore unlike the divine
Monad from whom they derive their being. But before the Fall their num-
ber symbolizes a clear reflection of God; for ten and powers of ten were
held to be forms of the monad. On angelic multiplicity and unity see
Dante, *Par.* xxix 130–45; and on unity and multitude in *PL* see 610–2*n*;
vi 766*n*, 809–10*n*.

v *589. gonfalons*] banners fastened to cross-bars; unlike *Standards*, which are
fastened to the flagpoles themselves. Gonfalons were very often carried in
ecclesiastical processions.

v *593*. Contrast the ensigns of the rebel angels (i 539*n*), which naturally are
devoid of *Holy memorials* ('chronicles, commemorations', often in an
ecclesiastical sense) and instead have pagan or secular 'arms and trophies'.

v *594–6*. So Dante describes the angels as encircling God the spaceless centre
of the universe, in *Par.* xxviii. The *orbs* of the angels merge imperceptibly
both with the orbs of astronomical bodies and with 'the orbs / Of his fierce
chariot' (the Messiah's cosmic vehicle: vi 828f). For the angels, symbolically
considered, are no less than the operations of providence throughout the
universe of secondary causes.

By whom in bliss embosomed sat the Son,
Amidst as from a flaming mount, whose top
Brightness had made invisible, thus spake.
600   Hear all ye angels, progeny of light,
Thrones, dominations, princedoms, virtues, powers,
Hear my decree, which unrevoked shall stand.
This day I have begot whom I declare

v 597. For the Son in the bosom of the Father, cp. iii 168–9n; also iii 239 and 279.

v 598. whose top] whoseop Ed I, corr. in Errata.

v 599. For God's 'majesty of darkness' see ii 264–5n; and for the description of even the skirts of God as 'dark with excessive bright', iii 375–82n.

v 601. Not the mere sonorous roll-call of titles that it is usually taken to be. The Scriptural passage alluded to, Col. i 16, is a proof text for Christ's agency in the creation of the angels: 'By him were all things created, that are in heaven, and that are in earth, visible and invisible, whether they be thrones, or dominions, or principalities, or powers: all things were created by him, and for him.'

v 603–6. These lines are among the most controversial in the poem; and quite unnecessarily so. The principal allusions are to Ps. ii 6f ('Yet have I set my king upon my holy hill of Zion. I will declare the decree . . . Thou art my Son; this day have I begotten thee') and Heb. i 5 ('unto which of the angels said he at any time, Thou art my Son, this day have I begotten thee? And again, I will be to him a Father, and he shall be to me a Son?)'. Both texts are treated by M. in De doctrina i 5 as relating to the metaphorical generation of the Son (Columbia xv 182–4), and he explains 'begotten' in the first as meaning 'made him a king'. There is therefore no contradiction between the present passage and v 832 (contra Empson² 167). The Hebrews verse refers to 'the exaltation of the Son above the angels', an action by implication distinct from 'unction to the mediatorial office' (Columbia xv 183). The latter 'event' is presumably the one to be correlated with the exaltation of the Messiah (earlier in the poem but chronologically later) at PL iii 313ff. There is thus no basis for identifying the exaltations in Bks iii and v–an identification that Empson (99) rightly dislikes, since it 'lets you off attending to the story'. M. seems to have envisaged a series of 'metaphorical generations' and exaltations: see, e.g., vi 760ff and 890–2. The difficulty raised by Kelley (104), that the events of the epic belong to a far earlier era than those of De doctrina, is unimportant, since M. believed events in eternity to have sequence but no measure. Nor is there any obtrusive evidence of Arianism in the passage. Empson finds it shocking, however, because it shows arbitrariness in God: 'If the Son had inherently held this position from before the creation of all angels, why has it been officially withheld from him till this day? . . . to give no reason at all for the Exaltation makes it appear a challenge' (102). M., who was always unwilling to think of the freedom of God as conditioned, may well have intended to give just such

My only Son, and on this holy hill
605 Him have anointed, whom ye now behold
At my right hand; your head I him appoint;
And by my self have sworn to him shall bow
All knees in heaven, and shall confess him Lord:
Under his great vicegerent reign abide
610 United as one individual soul
For ever happy: him who disobeys
Me disobeys, breaks union, and that day
Cast out from God and blessed vision, falls
Into utter darkness, deep engulfed, his place
615 Ordained without redemption, without end.

an impression; for in *De doctrina* he takes *Ps.* ii to show 'that however the
generation of the Son may have taken place, it arose from no natural neces-
sity, as is generally contended, but was no less owing to the decree and will
of the Father than his priesthood or kingly power, or his resuscitation from
the dead' (i 5; Columbia xiv 185). Cp. *ibid.* 187: all God's works 'are exe-
cuted freely according to his own good pleasure'. The tradition that Christ's
exaltation was an occasion of the angelic rebellion had some vogue in the
seventeenth century; and in Valamarana's *De bello intelligentiarum* (1623)
Satan had rebelled because of God's prophecy of the Incarnation. See Mc-
Colley 33.

v *606–11.* 'The Father's delegation of His powers to the Son is paralleled
by Satan's sending Sin and Death to earth as his viceregents' (Rajan 47).

v *606. head*] Cp. *Eph.* iv 15; and *Col.* ii 9f: 'For in him dwelleth all the ful-
ness of the Godhead bodily. And ye are complete in him, which is the head
of all principality and power.'

v *607–8.* 'By myself have I sworn, saith the Lord' (*Gen.* xxii 16). Cp. also
Phil. ii 9–11: 'God also hath highly exalted him, and given him a name which
is above every name: That at the name of Jesus every knee should bow, of
things in heaven, and things in earth, and things under the earth; And that
every tongue should confess that Jesus Christ is Lord.'

v *608.* Some copies *Ed I* have comma after *Lord.*

v *609. vicegerent*] viceregent; the title was applied to kings or priests in their
capacity as representatives of God.

v *610–2.* One of the most explicit statements of the contrast between divine
unity and evil multitude that underlies so much of the poem's action and
imagery. See, e.g., ll. 588n, 898–903n, i 338ff, vi 767n and vi 809–10n.
For the evil dyad (or principle of division) as a rebellion against the monad,
see F.M. Cornford, 'Mysticism and Science in the Pythagorean Tradition',
CQ xvii (1933) 6; also Hopper 39f.   *individual*] indivisible, inseparable.

v *613. blessed vision*] Cp. the 'beatific vision' of i 684.

v *614. utter*] outer.

v *615.* For the variable positioning of stress on *without*, see B. A. Wright's
note in *N & Q* cciii (1958) 202f, and cp. ii 892n.

So spake the omnipotent, and with his words
All seemed well pleased, all seemed, but were not all.
That day, as other solemn days, they spent
In song and dance about the sacred hill,
620   Mystical dance, which yonder starry sphere
Of planets and of fixed in all her wheels
Resembles nearest, mazes intricate,
Eccentric, intervolved, yet regular
Then most, when most irregular they seem,
625   And in their motions harmony divine
So smooths her charming tones, that God's own ear

v 616. Some copies *Ed I* have no new paragraph.

v 618. *solemn days*] holy days, festivals.

v 620–4. For the notion of the universe as a dance, see l. 178*n* and iii 579–81*n*. Here M.'s intention seems to be a positive presentation of obedience, to offset the negative presentation in Satan's speech, ll. 787–99. See Rajan 63: 'That gaiety, innate yet ceremonial, those turning, pirouetting half rhymes and caesuras, reach to the heart of what discipline can give us.' In *PL* the movement of angels is frequently connected with that of astronomical bodies. See, e.g., iv 782–4*n*. The Biblical authority for the connection would be *Job* xxxviii 7: 'the morning stars sang together, and all the sons of God shouted for joy'.   *sphere*] the apparent celestial sphere.   *fixed*] fixed stars. The eccentric circles utilised in the astronomical systems of M.'s time (see iii 575*n*) were themselves instances of apparent irregularities embraced within a higher regularity. Cp. Cicero, *Tusc. disp.* V xxiv 69: *quorum vagi motus rata tamen et certa sui cursus spatia definiant*; the context is an account of the wise man's pleasure in astronomy.

v 625–8. M. devoted the whole Second Prolusion to the 'Music of the Spheres'. Originating with the Pythagoreans, the idea had attained very wide and popular distribution (see Yale i 235*n* and Svendsen 60f), but M.'s use of it here is marked by his usual precision. The Platonists believed that 'the intervals in the corporeal universe, which were filled with sesquitertians, sesquialters, superoctaves, half-tones, and a *leimma*, followed the pattern of the Soul's fabric, and that harmony was thus forthcoming, the proportional intervals of which were interwoven into the fabric of the Soul and were also injected into the corporeal universe which is quickened by the Soul' (Macrobius, *In somn. Scip.* II iii 15, quoting Porphyry). The intervals between the planetary spheres were analysed as musical proportions by astronomers as late as Kepler (see Dreyer 406–8). The *tones* of the spheres are thus not *charming* in the sense 'pleasant', but in the sense 'magical'. Cp. Macrobius, *loc. cit.* 11: 'It is natural for everything that breathes to be captivated by music since the heavenly Soul that animates the universe sprang from music.'   *now*] Added in *Ed II*. The *evening* is that of Day 2 of the poem's action, since M. reckons the days from sunset in the Hebrew manner. See Introduction, 'Chronology'. The sequence *evening . . . morn* is thus deliberate.

                    Listens delighted. Evening now approached
                    (For we have also our evening and our morn,
                    We ours for change delectable, not need)
    630   Forthwith from dance to sweet repast they turn
                    Desirous; all in circles as they stood,
                    Tables are set, and on a sudden piled
                    With angels' food, and rubied nectar flows
                    In pearl, in diamond, and massy gold,
    635   Fruit of delicious vines, the growth of heaven.
                    On flowers reposed, and with fresh flowerets crowned,
                    They eat, they drink, and in communion sweet
                    Quaff immortality and joy, secure
                    Of surfeit where full measure only bounds
    640   Excess, before the all bounteous king, who showered
                    With copious hand, rejoicing in their joy.
                    Now when ambrosial night with clouds exhaled
                    From that high mount of God, whence light and shade
                    Spring both, the face of brightest heaven had changed
    645   To grateful twilight (for night comes not there
                    In darker veil) and roseate dews disposed
                    All but the unsleeping eyes of God to rest,
                    Wide over all the plain, and wider far

v *631. Ed I* has comma after *desirous.*

v *633.* See ll. 407–13*n. Ed I* has colon after *flows.*

v *636–40. Ed I* 'They eat, they drink, and with refection sweet / Are filled,
before the all bounteous king, who showered'. One effect of the additions
is to draw closer the link with Raphael's meal with Adam and Eve (cp. ll.
451f); another is to endow the eating with a spiritual value.   *vines*] See
427*n.   *fresh flowerets*] Presumably amarant: see iii 350–7*nn.   com-
munion sweet*] Cp. the 'fellowships of joy' in which the angels sit at xi 80.
immortality] on the strength of *John* iv 10 ('living water') or *Ps.* xxxvi 8f:
'Thou shalt make them drink of the river of the pleasures. For with thee is
the fountain of life: in thy light shall we see light.'

v *642. ambrosial*] fragrant; used of night in Homer, *Il.* ii 57. But see also ii
245*n* above.

v *643.* In *De doctrina* i 7 (Columbia xv 31) M. distinguishes between the
visible heaven, and an 'invisible and highest heaven' situated in 'the heaven
of the blessed'. The latter was a 'throne and habitation of God' which per-
haps existed before creation. Cp. vi 4–12 and vii 584–6 below.

v *645.* Cp. l. 162, and see *Rev.* xxi 25: 'There shall be no night there.'

v *646.* Cp. 'the timely dews of sleep' which Adam feels inclining his eyelids
at iv 614.

v *647.* 'Behold, he that keepeth Israel shall neither slumber nor sleep'
(*Ps.* cxxi 4).

Than all this globous earth in plain out spread,
650 (Such are the courts of God) the angelic throng
Dispersed in bands and files their camp extend
By living streams among the trees of life,
Pavilions numberless, and sudden reared,
Celestial tabernacles, where they slept
655 Fanned with cool winds, save those who in their course
Melodious hymns about the sovereign throne
Alternate all night long: but not so waked
Satan, so call him now, his former name
Is heard no more in heaven; he of the first,
660 If not the first archangel, great in power,
In favour and pre-eminence, yet fraught
With envy against the Son of God, that day
Honoured by his great Father, and proclaimed
Messiah king anointed, could not bear
665 Through pride that sight, and thought himself
            impaired.
Deep malice thence conceiving and disdain,
Soon as midnight brought on the dusky hour
Friendliest to sleep and silence, he resolved
With all his legions to dislodge, and leave
670 Unworshipped, unobeyed the throne supreme

v 652. *living streams*] See ll. 636–40n. The river and the *trees of life* occur together in *Rev*. xxii 1–2.

v 655–7. Alluding to the alteration of offices in the temple-service (see iv 561n. But *course* is also an astronomical term: for the connection between angels and stars see ll. 620–4n, 700–14n and iv 782–4n.

v 656. *in*] omitted in *Ed I* (corr. in *Errata*).

v 658–9. See i 82n and 361–3: after the rebellion the names of the unfaithful were razed from the books of life and they were given the names now current. For Fludd's acceptance of the Scholastic idea that Satan's name before his fall was Lucifer, see West 76.

v 659. *in*] omitted in *Ed I* (corr. in *Errata*).

v 660. It is not certain whether Raphael means that Satan was among the first only of the *order* of archangels, or among the first angels of all orders; l. 812 favours the latter interpretation. At vi 690 we are told that Satan was created the 'equal' of Michael; and, in the first day's fighting, that he met no equal except Michael (vi 246–8).

v 664. See ll. 603–6n. Taken literally, the Hebrew title *Messiah* means 'anointed'.

v 665. *impaired*] injured, reduced in status.

v 669. *dislodge*] shift his quarters; a military term. Note the secondary transitive meaning 'displace', with *throne* as object.

Contemptuous, and his next subordinate
Awakening, thus to him in secret spake.
  Sleep'st thou companion dear, what sleep can close
Thy eyelids? And remember'st what decree
675 Of yesterday, so late hath passed the lips
Of heaven's almighty. Thou to me thy thoughts
Was wont, I mine to thee was wont to impart;
Both waking we were one; how then can now
Thy sleep dissent? New laws thou seest imposed;
680 New laws from him who reigns, new minds may raise
In us who serve, new counsels, to debate
What doubtful may ensue, more in this place
To utter is not safe. Assemble thou
Of all those myriads which we lead the chief;
685 Tell them that by command, ere yet dim night
Her shadowy cloud withdraws, I am to haste,
And all who under me their banners wave,
Homeward with flying march where we possess
The quarters of the north, there to prepare

v *671. his next subordinate*] Presumably Beelzebub; cp. ii 299f. Some critics
try to explain the fact that he is not named in the present book by recourse
to the theory that v was written before ii (see, e.g., Empson 99). It is simpler
to suppose that M. did not know the name Beelzebub had before his fall;
see ll. 658–9*n*.

v *672. in secret*] An explanation of how Raphael could know what Satan said
 in secret' is quickly given, at ll. 682f, so that there is no need to follow
Gilbert (63) in speculating whether the angelic wars may originally have
been narrated by an omniscient author. On the other hand, M. has no in-
tention of trying for naturalistic verisimilitude. Both he and his Raphael
throughout avail themselves of the antique historian's freedom to invent
speeches and probable details.

v *673.* Echoing the first words (*Il.* ii 23) of the baneful dream sent by Zeus
to Agamemnon–ostensibly to incite the Greeks to a new attack on Troy,
but with the ulterior purpose of doing honour to Achilles.

v *681.* Empson (72) thinks we can infer from this line that there had been
earlier public debate 'about the claims of God'. But the antitheses count
 gainst this inference, or at least imply that any earlier counsels–or coun-
 ils–were not disloyal.

v *685–93.* Empson (72) regards this lie, no doubt correctly, as 'an ordinary
wartime propaganda operation', but is not far from admitting that by his
deception Satan attempts to deprive his subordinates of the free option of
loyalty.

v *689. north*] See P. Salmon, 'The Site of Lucifer's Throne', *Anglia* lxxxi
(1963) 118–23; also F. N. Robinson's note to Chaucer, *Friar's Tale* 1413,

690 Fit entertainment to receive our king
     The great Messiah, and his new commands,
     Who speedily through all the hierarchies
     Intends to pass triumphant, and give laws.
       So spake the false archangel, and infused
695 Bad influence into the unwary breast
     Of his associate; he together calls,
     Or several one by one, the regent powers,
     Under him regent, tells, as he was taught,
     That the most high commanding, now ere night,
700 Now ere dim night had disencumbered heaven,
     The great hierarchal standard was to move;
     Tells the suggested cause, and casts between
     Ambiguous words and jealousies, to sound

citing Gregory's Commentary on *Job* xvii 24 (Migne lxxvi 26). The tra-
ditional association of the north with evil goes back to patristic applications
of *Is.* xiv 12–4 to the fall of Satan: 'How art thou fallen from heaven, O
Lucifer, son of the morning! . . . For thou hast said in thine heart, I will
ascend into heaven, I will exalt my throne above the stars of God: I will sit
also upon the mount of the congregation, in the sides of the north.' Cp. *Jer.*
i 14, iv 6, vi 1. The localization of Satan adds point to several other passages,
such as the simile of the multitude poured from the 'populous north' at i
351ff. Satan's rebellion was similarly placed in the north in Valamarana's
De bello intelligentiarum (1623).
v *700–14*. The revolt is described in terms of a 'sustained astronomical
metaphor', with Satan *ere dim night had disencumbered heaven* leading off a
starry flock. 'Bentley complained about the leadership of Satan that the
Morning Star disappears last of the stars in the morning, so cannot be said to
lead them; Pearce smartly replied that a shepherd walks at the back. But the
words are *drew after him*, and the inversion acts as part of the conflict of
feeling; he leads them only towards night' (Empson[2] 184f). See also ll.
620–4n. The passage partly depends on our knowledge of a long-established
symbolism whereby the morning star represented both Satan and Christ.
As evening star Christ died; as morning star he was resurrected. Satan as
morning star mimes the brightness of Christ–a point amplified here by his
role as shepherd. Cowley (244) hit on a very similar description of Lucifer,
perhaps independently, as he claims in *Davideis* i *n* 3: 'Once *General* of a
guilded *Host* of *Sprights*, / Like *Hesper*, leading forth the spangled *Nights*.'
v *701. hierarchal standard*] Cp. 591, 692, etc.; throughout this passage M.
plays on 'evocations of degree' (Rajan 63). See ll. 787–802n.
v *702. suggested*] Tends to imply 'insinuating or prompting to evil' (*OED* 1 a)
casts] machinates, schemes.
v *703. jealousies*] suspicions.
v *703–10*. Peter, Burden and others make heavy weather over a fancied

Or taint integrity; but all obeyed
705 The wonted signal, and superior voice
Of their great potentate; for great indeed
His name, and high was his degree in heaven;
His countenance, as the morning star that guides
The starry flock, allured them, and with lies
710 Drew after him the third part of heaven's host:
Mean while the eternal eye, whose sight discerns
Abstrusest thoughts, from forth his holy mount
And from within the golden lamps that burn
Nightly before him, saw without their light
715 Rebellion rising, saw in whom, how spread
Among the sons of morn, what multitudes
Were banded to oppose his high decree;
And smiling to his only Son thus said.

disparity between Raphael's and God's accounts of the Fall of the angels;
on which see iii 129*n*.

v *708-9*. Bentley questioned the propriety of Satan's *countenance* telling *lies*,
and Pearce felt it necessary to bring rhetorical analogies to M.'s defence.
But the point lies in the allusion to *Rev*. xxii 16, where Christ is the true
morning star: the bright face of 'Lucifer, son of the morning' (*Is*. xiv 12)
is itself a mendacious impersonation.

v *710*. On the size of Satan's party, see ii 692*n*.

v *711*. For the eye(s) of God, see iii 648-61*n*; also *Prov*. xv 3 ('The eyes of the
Lord are in every place, beholding the evil and the good'); *Ps*. xxxiii 18
and liv 7; etc. A single eye was a common Renaissance emblem of God's
unmoving omniscience: see Wind 179ff, 186ff.

v *713-14*. Cp. *Rev*. iv 5: 'There were seven lamps of fire burning before the
throne, which are the seven Spirits of God.' Empson[2] 184 is perhaps right
in identifying the *lamps* as planets. At least, the present passage is to be related
to iii 648ff, where the seven archangelic eyes have more or less this signifi-
cance (see iii 648*n* and 656*n*). Perhaps we should say, rather, 'intelligences
of planets'.

v *713*. Some copies *Ed I* have comma after *within*.

v *716. sons of morn*] see ll. 708-9*n*. The angels are called morning stars at
Job xxxviii 7.

v *718. smiling*] Makes us certain that the speech to follow will not be de-
livered in simple seriousness; so that it is untrue that we begin, as Empson
96 says we do, by taking God's anxiety at its face value, and hence by sharing
Satan's disbelief in his omnipotence. Empson finds the joke 'appallingly
malignant', on the grounds that God's complacent passivity will drive the
rebels 'into real evil'. But it is hard to see how God could have acted earlier
without restricting the angels' freedom of choice. For the O.T. idea that
God mocks his foes, see *Ps*. ii 4, xxxvii 13 etc. (discussed in Empson 121);
and cp. ii 190-1*n* above. Here God's laughter is specifically a manifestation

Son, thou in whom my glory I behold
720   In full resplendence, heir of all my might,
Nearly it now concerns us to be sure
Of our omnipotence, and with what arms
We mean to hold what anciently we claim
Of deity or empire, such a foe
725   Is rising, who intends to erect his throne
Equal to ours, throughout the spacious north;
Nor so content, hath in his thought to try
In battle, what our power is, or our right.
Let us advise, and to this hazard draw
730   With speed what force is left, and all employ
In our defence, lest unawares we lose
This our high place, our sanctuary, our hill.
To whom the Son with calm aspect and clear
Lightning divine, ineffable, serene,
735   Made answer. Mighty Father, thou thy foes
Justly hast in derision, and secure
Laugh'st at their vain designs and tumults vain,
Matter to me of glory, whom their hate
Illustrates, when they see all regal power
740   Given me to quell their pride, and in event
Know whether I be dextrous to subdue
Thy rebels, or be found the worst in heaven.

of his omnipotence; M.'s hope of an escape from dualism would rest in the ability of God to remain good-humoured in the face of evil. But in any case, why should God only be forbidden to smile at what is inherently absurd?

v 720. 'His Son, whom he hath appointed heir of all things, by whom also he made the worlds' (Heb. i 2).

v 726. See l. 689n for the north as the region of evil.

v 728. Some copies Ed I omit comma after battle.

v 734. Cp. the angel of the resurrection at Matt. xxviii 3, whose 'countenance was like lightning'–a description that alludes to the apocalyptic vision of Dan. x 6.

v 736-7. See l. 718n. Cp. especially Ps. ii 4: 'He that sitteth in the heavens shall laugh: the Lord shall have them in derision.'

v 739-40. Cp. Christ's words during a resurrection appearance: 'All power is given unto me in heaven and in earth' (Matt. xxviii 18).   Illustrates] renders illustrious; illumines. in event] in result.

v 741. The Son's wit matches the Father's; for Christ's 'dextrous' (OED 1) position 'at the right hand of bliss' (vi 892; cp. Mark xvi 19 etc.) is a consequence of his dextrous (skilful) defeat of Satan.

So spake the Son, but Satan with his powers
Far was advanced on winged speed, an host
745 Innumerable as the stars of night,
Or stars of morning, dewdrops, which the sun
Impearls on every leaf and every flower.
Regions they passed, the mighty regencies
Of seraphim and potentates and thrones
750 In their triple degrees, regions to which
All thy dominion, Adam, is no more
Than what this garden is to all the earth,
And all the sea, from one entire globose
Stretched into longitude; which having passed
755 At length into the limits of the north
They came, and Satan to his royal seat
High on a hill, far blazing, as a mount
Raised on a mount, with pyramids and towers

v *743. powers*] armies. Not referring to the sixth order of the celestial hier-
chies; though the vaguer sense 'celestial beings' may be a secondary mean-
ing. Cp. i 128–9*n*.

v *745.* For angels as stars, see ll. 700–14*n* and 620–4*n*.

v *746. stars of morning*] See 708–9*n*. *dew-drops*] Cp. l. 2 and see *Hos.*
vi 4–'O Judah, what shall I do unto thee? for your goodness is as a morning
cloud, and as the early dew it goeth away.' Dew as an emblem of evan-
escence was very familiar at the time from its use in Henry King's much-
imitated 'Sic vita' (1657): 'Like to the falling of a Starre; / Or as the flights
of Eagles are; / Or silver drops of morning dew; / ... / Even such is man,
whose borrowed light / Is streight call'd in, and paid to night. / ... / The
Dew dries up; the Starre is shot; / The flight is past; and Man forgot.' Some
copies *Ed I* omit comma after *morning*.

v *748. regencies*] dominions.

v *749–50. potentates*] powers; see l. 743*n*. *triple degrees*] Because from the
time of Dionysius the nine orders of the angels were divided into three
groups, or hierarchies, of three, expressing the Trinity. See, e.g., Dante,
Par. xxviii; and Spenser, *F.Q.* I xii 39: 'many an Angels voice, / Singing
before th'eternall majesty, / In their trinall triplicities on hye.'

v *753–4. globose*] sphere; the adj. (cp. vii 357) for the noun. *Stretched
into longitude*] in flat projection.

v *755. north*] See l. 689*n*.

v *756.* Empson 77 exonerates Satan from the charge of disloyalty by por-
traying him as a 'grand aristocrat' owing only loose allegiance to the central
government, like a Norman lord. But this analogy would hardly have
seemed creditable to M. Chapman's Byron plays remind us how warily the
thoughtful republican regarded the ideal of aristocratic autonomy.

v *758–9. pyramids ... From diamond quarries*] The apparent durability of
'pyramids' and 'diamond' has been undercut by the comparison of the

From diamond quarries hewn, and rocks of gold,
760 The palace of great Lucifer, (so call
That structure in the dialect of men
Interpreted) which not long after, he
Affecting all equality with God,
In imitation of that mount whereon
765 Messiah was declared in sight of heaven,
The Mountain of the Congregation called;
For thither he assembled all his train,
Pretending so commanded to consult
About the great reception of their king,
770 Thither to come, and with calumnious art
Of counterfeited truth thus held their ears.
     Thrones, dominations, princedoms, virtues, powers,
If these magnific titles yet remain

angels to dew drops; see l. 746*n*. The pyramids could be spires or obelisks
as well as the squat form the word now denotes: see ii 1013*n* (Satan himself
compared to a pyramid), iv 985–7*n*. The symbolism of the shape is clarified
by M.'s more explicit use of it in *Reason of Church-Government* i 6 (Yale i
790). There he writes that Prelaty's 'pyramid aspires and sharpens to ambition . . . it is the most dividing, and schismaticall forme that Geometricians know of'.
v *760–6*. Satan aspires in calling his mountain by the same name as God's
(see *Is.* xiv 13). But as a result he loses his own original name: *Lucifer* is his
name only before the Fall. Cp. l. 658–9*n*, vii 132.   *Affecting*] 'aspiring to'
or 'assuming a false appearance of'.   *that mount*] the 'holy hill' of l. 604.
v *772–802*. In his 1936 essay on M.'s style, T. S. Eliot chose this speech as an
example of imprecision; of complication dictated by merely musical demands. Empson 26ff shows the injustice of this attack and convincingly
proposes a Satan imprecise on purpose, bent on confusing his hearers. The
sudden changes of direction are explained in terms of the theory that the
rebels 'already hate God, or hate the recent ukase of God, so much that they
do not require completed arguments' (Empson 27f). But it seems more likely
that M. intends a brief impression of a speaker who dares not lay out any of
his points openly and fully. We need not suppose, though, that Satan's
speech was as short as Raphael makes it. It may well have seemed to him
imprudent to expose frail Adam to the full power of Satan's oratory.
v *772*. The first line (which imitates the opening of God's speech at the
anointing of the Messiah) gives the lie to what follows, since it implicitly
admits the Messiah's claim; see l. 601*n*. It is characteristic of the oversophistication of Milton criticism that several critics hold that the speech that
follows *has* to be inadequate, because if M. had let it be effective Satan would
have seemed to tempt the other angels; with the consequence that God would
have seemed unjust for not having mercy on them as on Adam. For an
escape from this impasse see iii 129*n*.

Not merely titular, since by decree
775   Another now hath to himself engrossed
All power, and us eclipsed under the name
Of king anointed, for whom all this haste
Of midnight march, and hurried meeting here,
This only to consult how we may best
780   With what may be devised of honours new
Receive him coming to receive from us
Knee-tribute yet unpaid, prostration vile,
Too much to one, but double how endured,
To one and to his image now proclaimed?
785   But what if better counsels might erect
Our minds and teach us to cast off this yoke?
Will ye submit your necks, and choose to bend
The supple knee? Ye will not, if I trust
To know ye right, or if ye know your selves
790   Natives and sons of heaven possessed before
By none, and if not equal all, yet free,
Equally free; for orders and degrees
Jar not with liberty, but well consist.
Who can in reason then or right assume
795   Monarchy over such as live by right

v *776.* For the Son's inheritance of all power, see ll. 720 and 739.

v *777. king anointed*] See l. 605.

v *783.* Cp. Gabriel's view of Satan's earlier servility (iv 959).

v *787–802.* The appeal to native freedom is 'a perfectly orthodox version of the claim that monarchy is not grounded on the law of Nature' (Rajan 63, citing an analogue in Rutherford's *Lex Rex*). But Satan omits altogether the value of obedience or discipline, which M. regarded as the essential condition of republican freedom. (The Son is exalted insofar as he is prepared to humble himself more than the angels.) See, e.g., *Reason of Church-Government* i (Yale i 751): 'The flourishing and decaying of all civill societies . . . are mov'd to and fro as upon the axle of discipline.' The angelic orders were for M. a supreme example of this discipline: 'The Angels themselves, in whom no disorder is fear'd . . . are distinguisht and quaterniond into their celestiall Princedomes, and Satrapies, according as God himselfe hath writ his imperiall decrees through the great provinces of heav'n. The state also of the blessed in Paradise, though never so perfect, is not therefore left without discipline' (*ibid.* 752). Cp. also *John* viii 33f: 'We be Abraham's seed, and were never in bondage to any man: how sayest thou, Ye shall be made free? Jesus answered them, Verily, verily, I say unto you, Whosoever committeth sin is the servant of sin.'

v *788. supple knee*] A proverbial expression. Cp., e.g. Shakespeare, *Richard II* I iv 32f: 'A brace of draymen bid God speed him well, / And had the tribute of his supple knee.'

His equals, if in power and splendour less,
In freedom equal? Or can introduce
Law and edict on us, who without law
Err not, much less for this to be our lord,
800   And look for adoration to the abuse
Of those imperial titles which assert
Our being ordained to govern, not to serve?
      Thus far his bold discourse without control
Had audience, when among the seraphim
805   Abdiel, than whom none with more zeal adored
The Deity, and divine commands obeyed,
Stood up, and in a flame of zeal severe
The current of his fury thus opposed.
      O argument blasphemous, false and proud!
810   Words which no ear ever to hear in heaven
Expected, least of all from thee, ingrate
In place thy self so high above thy peers.
Canst thou with impious obloquy condemn
The just decree of God, pronounced and sworn,
815   That to his only Son by right endued
With regal sceptre, every soul in heaven
Shall bend the knee, and in that honour due
Confess him rightful king? Unjust thou say'st

v 798. edict] Stressed on the second syllable.

v 799. for this] For this purpose of introducing law. But there may also just possibly be an allusion to Luke xix 14: 'We will not have this (man) to reign over us.'

v 802. In Satan's corrupt version of republicanism, 'every angel deserves to have some men as his slaves' (Empson 82).

v 805–7. Abdiel] 'Servant of God', occurs in the Bible only in a human genealogical context (1 Chron. v 15). But the occultists, who were short of names for angels, were accustomed to utilize any obscure names the Bible had to offer. Abdiel had been transferred in this way in the sensational Sepher Raziel. As Cornelius Agrippa remarked, 'he that is inquisitive' can discover the names of spirits from the names of notable men or places in the Bible (West 152). See Gilbert 123, West 152–4, and cp. iv 782–8n above. Abdiel opposes Satan in a flame of zeal because the seraphim were thought of as especially ardent in their devotion, and were often imagined as flames; see ii 512n.

v 809. blasphemous] Stressed on the second syllable.

v 812. For Satan's status see l. 660n.

v 817. 'God also hath highly exalted him ... That at the name of Jesus every knee should bow, of things in heaven, and things in earth, and things under the earth; And that every tongue should confess that Jesus Christ is Lord' (Phil. ii 9–11).

Flatly unjust, to bind with laws the free,
820   And equal over equals to let reign,
One over all with unsucceeded power.
Shalt thou give law to God, shalt thou dispute
With him the points of liberty, who made
Thee what thou art, and formed the powers of heaven
825   Such as he pleased, and circumscribed their being?
Yet by experience taught we know how good,
And of our good, and of our dignity
How provident he is, how far from thought
To make us less, bent rather to exalt
830   Our happy state under one head more near
United. But to grant it thee unjust,
That equal over equals monarch reign:
Thy self though great and glorious dost thou count,
Or all angelic nature joined in one,
835   Equal to him begotten Son, by whom
As by his Word the mighty Father made
All things, even thee, and all the spirits of heaven
By him created in their bright degrees,
Crowned them with glory, and to their glory named

---

v 821. *unsucceeded power*] power never to be succeeded, everlasting power; though at iii 339ff God envisaged a laying aside at least of the 'regal sceptre'.
v 822. The thought is that of *Rom.* ix 20: 'O man, who art thou that repliest against God? Shall the thing formed say to him that formed it, Why hast thou made me thus?' (Margin 'Or, answerest again, or, disputest with God?').
v 830. Cp. *Col.* ii 10: 'Ye are complete in him, which is the head of all principality and power.'   *one*] Some copies *Ed I* our.
v 832. See ll. 603–6n and 787–802n.
v 835–40. Cp. *Col.* i 16–17: 'For by him [Christ] were all things created, that are in heaven, and that are in earth, visible and invisible, whether they be thrones, or dominions, or principalities, or powers: all things were created by him, and for him: And he is before all things, and by him all things consist.' Abdiel makes explicit the doctrine that was implied in earlier allusions to the same Biblical passage, at ll. 601 and 772. Although M. was Arian to the extent that he did not believe the Son to be generated from all eternity, nevertheless he had no doubt of Christ's agency in creation as the Logos or divine Word. See *De doctrina* i 5 (Columbia xiv 180–2), and iii 170n and 383n above.
v 839. *Crowned . . . glory*] Underlines the affirmation of God's creativity, by alluding to *Ps.* viii 5: 'Thou hast made him a little lower than the angels, and hast crowned him with glory and honour.' Note also that this verse was often regarded as a prophecy of the Incarnation.

840   Thrones, dominations, princedoms, virtues, powers,
        Essential powers, nor by his reign obscured,
        But more illustrious made, since he the head
        One of our number thus reduced becomes,
        His laws our laws, all honour to him done
845   Returns our own. Cease then this impious rage,
        And tempt not these; but hasten to appease
        The incensed Father, and the incensed Son,
        While pardon may be found in time besought.
          So spake the fervent angel, but his zeal
850   None seconded, as out of season judged,
        Or singular and rash, whereat rejoiced
        The apostate, and more haughty thus replied.
        That we were formed then say'st thou? And the work
        Of secondary hands, by task transferred
855   From Father to his Son? Strange point and new!
        Doctrine which we would know whence learned: who
          saw
        When this creation was? Remember'st thou
        Thy making, while the maker gave thee being?
        We know no time when we were not as now;
860   Know none before us, self-begot, self-raised

v *842–5*. Abdiel appears to regard the Messiah's kingship over the angels as a kind of incarnation, involving the setting aside of divinity; just as his human incarnation in Jesus will, at a later stage of the divine emanation.

v *845–8*. Echoing *Ps.* ii 12 and *Is.* lv 6f.

v *853–71*. Rajan 102 draws attention to the tawdriness of Satan here, to his 'jaunty sarcasm and irrelevant puns'.

v *855*. An important line from the narrative point of view. Empson argues that the Son's agency in creation has never been mentioned in the poem before, and that it is Satan's reaction to an unfamiliar argument that brings him to deny his own creation, even his creation by the Father. God himself keeps the doctrine of creation by Christ esoteric, preferring 'to issue a bare challenge' at the coronation of the Messiah (Empson 83). However, the doctrine is known to Abdiel; so that we must conclude either that an angel who chose to be obedient could intuit it, or else that God's speech at the coronation was fuller than Raphael gives it at ll. 600–15.

v *860*. Satan commits the primal sin of wishing to exist 'on his own' (Lewis 65, citing Augustine, *Civ. Dei* xiv 13), and seeks justification in his own ignorance of the state of non-being. (Contrast viii 251, where Adam is wiser about a similar limitation of his experience.) Satan's denial of creation by God is sustained until i 116–17 (*q.v.*), but abandoned in iv 43; unless, indeed, it is all along a public profession only. The standpoint was a traditional one for the devils: see, e.g., *Par.* xxix 49–63, where Dante contrasts the angels

By our own quickening power, when fatal course
Had circled his full orb, the birth mature
Of this our native heaven, ethereal sons.
Our puissance is our own, our own right hand
865   Shall teach us highest deeds, by proof to try
Who is our equal: then thou shalt behold
Whether by supplication we intend
Address, and to begirt the almighty throne
Beseeching or besieging. This report,
870   These tidings carry to the anointed king;
And fly, ere evil intercept thy flight.
       He said, and as the sound of waters deep
Hoarse murmur echoed to his words applause
Through the infinite host, nor less for that
875   The flaming seraph fearless, though alone
Encompassed round with foes, thus answered bold.
       O alienate from God, O spirit accurst,
Forsaken of all good; I see thy fall
Determined, and thy hapless crew involved
880   In this perfidious fraud, contagion spread
Both of thy crime and punishment: henceforth
No more be troubled how to quit the yoke
Of God's Messiah; those indulgent laws
Will not be now vouchsafed; other decrees
885   Against thee are gone forth without recall;
That golden sceptre which thou didst reject
Is now an iron rod to bruise and break
Thy disobedience. Well thou didst advise,
Yet not for thy advice or threats I fly
890   These wicked tents devoted, lest the wrath

who fell with those who modestly acknowledged their status as creatures
and began the dance of the heavens.
v *861–2.* A secularised version of the Great Year that in its true version expresses the will of God: see l. 583n.
v *864–5.* Cp. *Ps.* xlv 4: 'Thy right hand shall teach thee terrible things.'
v *872.* Satan has apparently achieved his purpose, for this 'voice of many waters' is the sound of worship (*Rev.* xix 6).
v *875. flaming*] See ll. 805–7n.
v *882–3.* Cp. Christ's promise 'my yoke is easy, and my burden is light' (*Matt.* xi 30).
v *886–7.* See ii 327–8n.
v *890.* Alluding to Moses' warning to the Israelites not to support Korah's rebellion: 'Depart, I pray you, from the tents of these wicked men, and touch nothing of theirs, lest ye be consumed in all their sins' (*Num.* xvi 26).

Impendent, raging into sudden flame
Distinguish not: for soon expect to feel
His thunder on thy head, devouring fire.
Then who created thee lamenting learn,
895   When who can uncreate thee thou shalt know.
     So spake the seraph Abdiel faithful found,
Among the faithless, faithful only he;
Among innumerable false, unmoved,
Unshaken, unseduced, unterrified
900   His loyalty he kept, his love, his zeal;
Nor number, nor example with him wrought
To swerve from truth, or change his constant mind
Though single. From amidst them forth he passed,
Long way through hostile scorn, which he sustained
905   Superior, nor of violence feared aught;
And with retorted scorn his back he turned
On those proud towers to swift destruction doomed.

THE END OF THE FIFTH BOOK

Paradise Lost

BOOK VI

The Argument

Raphael continues to relate how Michael and Gabriel were sent forth to battle against Satan and his angels. The first fight described: Satan and his powers retire under night: he calls a council, invents devilish engines, which in the second day's fight put Michael and his angels to some disorder; but they at length pulling up mountains overwhelm both the force and machines of Satan: yet the tumult not so ending, God on the third day sends Messiah

devoted] doomed; just possibly felt as a Latinism, though there are many seventeenth-century instances. Before *lest*, supply 'but'.

v *893*. 'For our God is a consuming fire' (*Heb.* xii 29).

v *898–903*. Again the confrontation of one and multitude: see ll. 610–12*n*. On the Pythagorean origin of the contrast between the singleness of truth and the multiplicity of falsehood, see Fowler 5–7.

v *899*. For the rhetoric, see ii 185*n*.

v *906. retorted*] requited (*OED* I 1 a). But there is also a play between the root sense ('turned back') and *his back he turned*.

his Son, for whom he had reserved the glory of that victory: he in the
power of his Father coming to the place, and causing all his legions to
stand still on either side, with his chariot and thunder driving into the midst
of his enemies, pursues them unable to resist towards the wall of heaven;
which opening, they leap down with horror and confusion into the place
of punishment prepared for them in the deep: Messiah returns with triumph
to his Father.

> All night the dreadless angel unpursued
> Through heaven's wide champaign held his way, till
>   morn,
> Waked by the circling hours, with rosy hand
> Unbarred the gates of light. There is a cave
> 5 Within the mount of God, fast by his throne,
> Where light and darkness in perpetual round
> Lodge and dislodge by turns, which makes through
>   heaven
> Grateful vicissitude, like day and night;
> Light issues forth, and at the other door
> 10 Obsequious darkness enters, till her hour

vi *1. the dreadless angel*] Abdiel.
vi *2–4*. A very clearly defined motif. Cp. especially Ovid, *Met.* ii 112–14:
'Aurora, who keeps watch in the reddening dawn, has opened wide her
purple gates, and her courts glowing with rosy light.' The *hours* are *circling*
because they personify the spatial sidereal hours or portions of the firma-
ment that appear to revolve about the earth. Homer put them in charge of
the gates of heaven at *Il.* v 749. For their wakefulness, implied here, cp.
Spenser, *F.Q.* VII vii 45: 'Then came the *Howres*, faire daughters of high
Jove / . . . who did them Porters make / Of heavens gate (whence all the
gods issued) / Which they did dayly watch, and nightly wake / By even
turnes, ne ever did their charge forsake.' The best concise account of the
Hours is A. Kent Hieatt's Appendix in *Short Time's Endless Monument*
(New York 1960) pp. 111–13.
vi *4–11*. The thought follows on closely from l. 3, for the Hours were often
described as moving *by turns* (alternately) and as forming a set of light /
dark pairs. Hesiod's abysm, alternately inhabited by Night and by Day
(*Theog.* 736–57) is rendered more thematic by its relocation *fast by* God's
throne. Time is allowed very near to M.'s God: see v 579–82*n*. On the other
hand, God's mount clearly *contains* time in its cave; much as Venus the
form-giver keeps the boar of darkness and death and chaos imprisoned in a
cave beneath the mount in the paradise of *F.Q.* III vi 48. The breath-taking
image may, as Burden suggests, be drawn in part from *Rev.* vii 15f and xxii
5, where ordinary light and darkness are excluded from heaven.   *dis-
lodge*] move quarters; a military term; cp. v 669.   *vicissitude*] change.
obsequious] dutiful; but also in its Lat. sense 'following'.

To veil the heaven, though darkness there might well
Seem twilight here; and now went forth the morn
Such as in highest heaven, arrayed in gold
Empyreal, from before her vanished night,
15   Shot through with orient beams: when all the plain
Covered with thick embattled squadrons bright,
Chariots and flaming arms, and fiery steeds
Reflecting blaze on blaze, first met his view:
War he perceived, war in procinct, and found
20   Already known what he for news had thought
To have reported: gladly then he mixed
Among those friendly powers who him received
With joy and acclamations loud, that one
That of so many myriads fallen, yet one
25   Returned not lost: on to the sacred hill
They led him high applauded, and present
Before the seat supreme; from whence a voice
From midst a golden cloud thus mild was heard.
    Servant of God, well done, well hast thou fought
30   The better fight, who single hast maintained
Against revolted multitudes the cause
Of truth, in word mightier than they in arms;
And for the testimony of truth hast borne
Universal reproach, far worse to bear
35   Than violence: for this was all thy care
To stand approved in sight of God, though worlds
Judged thee perverse: the easier conquest now
Remains thee, aided by this host of friends,
Back on thy foes more glorious to return
40   Than scorned thou didst depart, and to subdue
By force, who reason for their law refuse,

vi *11–12.* For the absence of night in heaven, see v *645n.* The *morn* is that of
Day 2; see Introduction, 'Chronology'.

vi *16. embattled*] set in battle array.

vi *19. in procinct*] prepared; not a common phrase, it would probably be
felt as an imitation of the Latin *in procinctu.*

vi *29–34.* Cp. *Matt.* xxv 21 ('Well done, thou good and faithful servant');
1 Tim. vi 12 ('fight the good fight of faith'); and *Ps.* lxix 7 ('for thy sake
I have borne reproach').   *servant of God*] the literal meaning of Abdiel:
see v *805n.*

vi *41–3.* For M.'s sustained contrast between the devils' reliance on *force*
or strength and God's on merit or goodness, see Steadman *passim.*   *right
reason*] upright, true reason; conscience. Originally the phrase was a trans-
lation of the Stoic and Scholastic term *recta ratio.* See Robert Hoopes, *Right
Reason in the English Renaissance* (Cambridge, Mass. 1962); also xii *80–101n.*

Right reason for their law, and for their king
Messiah, who by right of merit reigns.
Go Michael of celestial armies prince,
45   And thou in military prowess next
Gabriel, lead forth to battle these my sons
Invincible, lead forth my armed saints
By thousands and by millions ranged for fight;
Equal in number to that godless crew
50   Rebellious, them with fire and hostile arms
Fearless assault, and to the brow of heaven
Pursuing drive them out from God and bliss,
Into their place of punishment, the gulf
Of Tartarus, which ready opens wide
55   His fiery chaos to receive their fall.
    So spake the sovereign voice, and clouds began
To darken all the hill, and smoke to roll
In dusky wreaths, reluctant flames, the sign

vi 44. See *Dan.* xii 1, and *Rev.* xii 7f: 'And there was war in heaven: Michael and his angels fought against the dragon; and the dragon fought and his angels, And prevailed not; neither was their place any more in heaven.' The commoner Protestant view was that Michael ('Who is like to God?') signifies Christ: see West 125. But in *De doctrina* i 9 (Columbia xv 105) M. argues at some length that 'Christ vanquished the devil, and trampled him under foot singly; Michael, the leader of the angels, is introduced in the capacity of a hostile commander waging war with the prince of the devils, the armies on both sides being drawn out in battle array, and separating after a doubtful conflict.' The same point about Christ's transcendence, and independence of angelic assistance, underlies the plot of *PL* vi.

vi 46. *Gabriel*] 'Strength of God', see iv 549–50n.

vi 49. 'From the point of view of numbers (easily) the match of the godless crew.' Actually the loyal angels are twice as numerous (see ii 692n); but Empson 41 is right to reject Peter's unnecessary speculation that God only allows half the good angels to fight.

vi 54–5. For the identification of Tartarus with hell, see ii 69n.   *fiery chaos*] An exact description, since the building of hell 'encroached' on chaos (ii 1002). Presumably hell came into existence at the moment of Satan's fall: see l. 292n .

vi 56–60. Before the issuing of the Ten Commandments, 'there were thunders and lightnings, and a thick cloud upon the mount, and the voice of the trumpet exceeding loud; so that all the people that was in the camp trembled: . . . And mount Sinai was altogether on a smoke, because the Lord descended upon it in fire: and the smoke thereof ascended as the smoke of a furnace, and the whole mount quaked greatly' (*Exod.* xix 16, 18).   *reluctant*] writhing; or in its modern sense.   *gan*] began to; not the older auxiliary verb 'gan'='did'. See xi 73–6n.

Of wrath awaked: nor with less dread the loud
60 Ethereal trumpet from on high gan blow:
At which command the powers militant,
That stood for heaven, in mighty quadrate joined
Of union irresistible, moved on
In silence their bright legions, to the sound
65 Of instrumental harmony that breathed
Heroic ardour to adventurous deeds
Under their godlike leaders, in the cause
Of God and his Messiah. On they move
Indissolubly firm; nor obvious hill,
70 Nor straitening vale, nor wood, nor stream divides
Their perfect ranks; for high above the ground
Their march was, and the passive air upbore
Their nimble tread, as when the total kind
Of birds in orderly array on wing
75 Came summoned over Eden to receive
Their names of thee; so over many a tract
Of heaven they marched, and many a province wide
Tenfold the length of this terrene: at last
Far in the horizon to the north appeared
80 From skirt to skirt a fiery region, stretched
In battailous aspect, and nearer view
Bristled with upright beams innumerable

vi *62*. Cp. the 'phalanx' of the rebels in hell, which outwardly imitates this virtuous shape; see i 550*n*.

vi *63–8*. Cp. the silent march of the rebel angels, to the music of flutes and recorders played in the Dorian mode (i 549–61).

vi *69*. *Indissolubly*] Stressed on the second syllable.   *obvious*] standing in the way.

vi *71–2*. M.'s angels move like the ancient gods, without touching the ground.

vi *73–6*. 'And Adam gave names to all cattle and to the fowl of the air, and to every beast of the field' (*Gen.* ii 20). M. overgoes the famous comparisons of gathering armies to birds in Homer *Il.* ii 459 and Virgil, *Aen.* vii 699, by achieving numerical superiority (*total kind*), but also by maintaining greater propriety. Airborne angels resemble birds more closely than earthbound human armies do; and there is the correspondence of species with orders.

vi *78–86*. Cited as an example of montage in Eisenstein 59.

vi *78. terrene*] *OED* gives no earlier instance of this absolute use of the adj. = earth.

vi *79. north*] The region of evil; see v 689*n*.

vi *81. battailous*] warlike, bellicose.   *aspect*] As usual in M., stressed on the second syllable: 'áspect' had been an alternative pronunciation for about half a century.

Of rigid spears, and helmets thronged, and shields
Various, with boastful argument portrayed,
85   The banded powers of Satan hasting on
With furious expedition; for they weened
That self same day by fight, or by surprise
To win the mount of God, and on his throne
To set the envier of his state, the proud
90   Aspirer, but their thoughts proved fond and vain
In the mid way: though strange to us it seemed
At first, that angel should with angel war,
And in fierce hosting meet, who wont to meet
So oft in festivals of joy and love
95   Unanimous, as sons of one great sire
Hymning the eternal Father: but the shout
Of battle now began, and rushing sound
Of onset ended soon each milder thought.
High in the midst exalted as a god
100   The apostate in his sun-bright chariot sat
Idol of majesty divine, enclosed
With flaming cherubim, and golden shields;
Then lighted from his gorgeous throne, for now
'Twixt host and host but narrow space was left,
105   A dreadful interval, and front to front
Presented stood in terrible array
Of hideous length: before the cloudy van,
On the rough edge of battle ere it joined,
Satan with vast and haughty strides advanced,
110   Came towering, armed in adamant and gold;

vi *83.* M.'s very corporeal angels have arms not unlike those of the comba-
tants in Homer, Ariosto, or Spenser. Contrast the conception of Heywood
in *The hierarchie of the blessed angells* (1635): 'No Lances, Swords, nor Bom-
bards they had then. . . . Onely spiritual Armes to them were lent.'
vi *84. argument*] Punning between 'motif' and 'subject for debate'. No
doubt the rebel *imprese* were provocative. M. possibly alludes to the boast-
ful arms of the Seven against Thebes (Euripides, *Phoen.* 1108–40).
vi *86. expedition*] expeditiousness, celerity.
vi *87. selfsame day*] Biblical diction; cp. *Gen.* vii 13.
vi *91. In the mid way*] See l. 762*n.*
vi *93. hosting*] hostile encounter.   *wont*] were used.
vi *100–2.* Satan is particularly an *idol* or false image of *majesty divine* when he
is mounted on his triumphal *sun-bright chariot* because Messiah himself
rides a cosmic vehicle; see ll. 749–59*n* below. The *cherubim*–always charac-
terised by their brightness–correspond to the 'four cherubic shapes' of the
divine chariot.
vi *108. edge of battle*] front line. See i 276*n.*

Abdiel that sight endured not, where he stood
Among the mightiest, bent on highest deeds,
And thus his own undaunted heart explores.
O heaven! That such resemblance of the highest
115 Should yet remain, where faith and realty
Remain not; wherefore should not strength and might
There fail where virtue fails, or weakest prove
Where boldest; though to sight unconquerable?
His puissance, trusting in the almighty's aid,
120 I mean to try, whose reason I have tried
Unsound and false; nor is it aught but just,
That he who in debate of truth hath won,
Should win in arms, in both disputes alike
Victor; though brutish that contest and foul,
125 When reason hath to deal with force, yet so
Most reason is that reason overcome.
So pondering, and from his armed peers
Forth stepping opposite, half way he met
His daring foe, at this prevention more
130 Incensed, and thus securely him defied.
Proud, art thou met? Thy hope was to have reached
The highth of thy aspiring unopposed,
The throne of God unguarded, and his side
Abandoned at the terror of thy power
135 Or potent tongue; fool, not to think how vain
Against the omnipotent to rise in arms;

vi *114–26.* A soliloquy in the manner of Homer's thoughtful combatants.
Cp. especially Hector's soliloquy, before engaging Achilles, at *Il.* xxii 99–
130. *PL* has other allusions that similarly cast Satan in the role of the proud
and jealous Achilles: see, e.g., i 286–91*n*, v 673*n*.

vi *115. realty*] reality (*OED* 1 a) or sincerity (*OED* 2) or both.

vi *120. tried*] proved, judged after trial.

vi *124. contest*] Stressed on the second syllable.

vi *122–3.* Empson (54) is right to say that M. was by no means a pacifist;
as the passage on Truth and the sword of Justice in *Eikonoklastes* makes
sufficiently clear (Yale iii 583f). On the other hand he hated war in itself
and despised it as a subject for epic (see ix 27ff below). It has been suggested
that the angelic war should be regarded as burlesque rather than serious epic.
But this is most unlikely in view of the undoubtedly serious concluding
phase, Messiah's victory. M. would not consider this ordinary war, but a
spiritual conflict like the one *milites Christiani* fight in; or at least an un-
questionably just war. In any case, it is fought solely to amplify the trans-
cendence of Christ.

vi *129. prevention*] frustration, obstruction (*OED* 4).

vi *130. securely*] confidently, without apprehension.

Who out of smallest things could without end
Have raised incessant armies to defeat
Thy folly; or with solitary hand
140 Reaching beyond all limit at one blow
Unaided could have finished thee, and whelmed
Thy legions under darkness; but thou seest
All are not of thy train; there be who faith
Prefer, and piety to God, though then
145 To thee not visible, when I alone
Seemed in thy world erroneous to dissent
From all: my sect thou seest, now learn too late
How few sometimes may know, when thousands err.
    Whom the grand foe with scornful eye askance
150 Thus answered. Ill for thee, but in wished hour
Of my revenge, first sought for thou return'st
From flight, seditious angel, to receive
Thy merited reward, the first assay
Of this right hand provoked, since first that tongue
155 Inspired with contradiction durst oppose
A third part of the gods, in synod met
Their deities to assert, who while they feel
Vigour divine within them, can allow
Omnipotence to none. But well thou com'st
160 Before thy fellows, ambitious to win
From me some plume, that thy success may show

vi *137-9.* Echoing *Matt.* xxvi 53 and iii 9: 'And think not to say within
yourselves, We have Abraham to our father: for I say unto you, that God
is able of these stones to raise up children unto Abraham.'
vi *143. there be who*] there are (those) who. Current usage in M.'s time.
faith] faithfulness.
vi *147. sect*] kind of persons. But there is probably also a reference to the
contemptuous Royalist practice of classifying all who were not in favour
of bishops as 'sectaries'. Cp. *Eikonoklastes*, Pref. (Yale iii 348): 'I never
knew that time in *England*, when men of truest Religion were not counted
Sectaries. . . . if ignorance and perversness will needs be national and uni-
versal, then they who adhere to wisdom and to truth, are not therfore to be
blam'd, for beeing so few as to seem a sect or faction.' Contrast, however,
the view expressed in *Areopagitica* (Yale ii 566).
vi *153. assay*] trial, experiment.
vi *156. third*] For the size of the rebel party, see ii 692n.   *gods*] In Satan's
mouth a presumptuous word, meaning more than 'angels': see i 116-7n.
vi *161-3.* Satan means that there will be a short pause before he destroys
Abdiel, because this is the only chance he will ever have of answering his
taunts, and he does not want Abdiel to be able to boast that they went un-
answered. The confused threat betrays a lack of confidence in his own

Destruction to the rest: this pause between
(Unanswered lest thou boast) to let thee know;
At first I thought that liberty and heaven
165 To heavenly souls had been all one; but now
I see that most through sloth had rather serve,
Ministering spirits, trained up in feast and song;
Such hast thou armed, the minstrelsy of heaven,
Servility with freedom to contend,
170 As both their deeds compared this day shall prove.
     To whom in brief thus Abdiel stern replied.
Apostate, still thou err'st, nor end wilt find
Of erring, from the path of truth remote:
Unjustly thou deprav'st it with the name
175 Of servitude to serve whom God ordains,
Or nature; God and nature bid the same,
When he who rules is worthiest, and excels
Them whom he governs. This is servitude,
To serve the unwise, or him who hath rebelled
180 Against his worthier, as thine now serve thee,
Thy self not free, but to thy self enthralled;
Yet lewdly dar'st our ministering upbraid.

ability to destroy Abdiel before he can boast again.   *plume*] 'feather in
your cap'; but there is also a dramatic irony, in which the feather is one of
pretentious display by Satan–cp. Shakespeare, *1 Hen. VI* III iii 5–7: 'Let
frantic Talbot triumph for a while, / And like a peacock sweep along his
tail; / We'll pull his plumes and take away his train.'

vi *167. ministering spirits*] The phrase is used in *Heb.* i 13f to emphasise the
low status of the angels compared with Christ: 'To which of the angels
said he at any time, Sit on my right hand? . . . Are they not all ministering
spirits, sent forth to minister for them who shall be heirs of salvation?'

vi *168. minstrelsy*] minstrels.

vi *169.* Cp. ii 255–7*n.*

vi *174. depravest*] misconstrue, vilify, defame

vi *175. Ed I* and *Ed II* italicize *servitude.*

vi *176.* Satan's vague invocation of the value of liberty at l. 164 implied an
appeal to Natural Law (see v 787–802*n*), and Abdiel makes this explicit in his
rebuttal. The agreement of Natural Law with God's Eternal Law was a
fundamental doctrine of Christian Humanism: see, e.g., Hooker, *Laws
of Eccles. Pol.* I iii 1–4, where nature is 'God's instrument'. Abdiel's argu-
ment is that when all is arranged according to 'degree' of excellence, free-
dom lies in the obedience of taking one's natural place. See Rajan 64f.

vi *181.* Cp. xii 90ff, also *PR* ii 466–9: 'Yet he who reigns within himself,
and rules / passions, desires, and fears, is more a king; / Which every wise
and vertuous man attains: / And who attains not, ill aspires to rule.'

vi *182. lewdly*] wickedly; or foolishly.

Reign thou in hell thy kingdom, let me serve
In heaven God ever blest, and his divine
185　Behests obey, worthiest to be obeyed,
Yet chains in hell, not realms expect: mean while
From me returned, as erst thou saidst, from flight,
This greeting on thy impious crest receive.
　　So saying, a noble stroke he lifted high,
190　Which hung not, but so swift with tempest fell
On the proud crest of Satan, that no sight,
Nor motion of swift thought, less could his shield
Such ruin intercept: ten paces huge
He backed recoiled; the tenth on bended knee
195　His massy spear upstayed; as if on earth
Winds under ground or waters forcing way
Sidelong, had pushed a mountain from his seat
Half sunk with all his pines. Amazement seized
The rebel thrones, but greater rage to see
200　Thus foiled their mightiest, ours joy filled, and shout,
Presage of victory and fierce desire
Of battle: whereat Michael bid sound

vi *183–6.* Remembered in hell; cp. i 263, 'Better to reign in hell, than serve in heaven', and see *n*.

vi *185.* A heavier point is needed after *obeyed*.

vi *187.* So Ascanius hurls back Numanus' gibe 'twice captured Phrygians', with the accompaniment of a blow, at *Aen*. ix 599 and 635.

vi *193–5.* Whaler 100 plausibly suggests that since ten symbolized divine power and creativity, ten reversed would symbolize destruction.　　ruin] destruction; fall. For Satan's spear see i 292–4*n*.

vi *195–8.* See i 230–7*n*. The image is not only one of destruction and chaos, but also of unnatural and proud rebellion; at least, this was most usually the meaning of the volcano as a symbol. For water as an additional cause of earthquakes and volcanoes, see Svendsen 104; but here the action of the water seems more like erosion. Cp. the fall of the Old Dragon in *F.Q.* I xi 54: 'So downe he fell, as an huge rockie clift, / Whose false foundation waves have washt away, / With dreadfull poyse is from the mayneland rift.' On the association of Satan with *pines*, see i 292–4*n*.

vi *199.* By a synecdoche, *thrones* stands for all the angelic orders. We know from v 772 and vi 102 that there were rebels of at least six different orders. Presumably M. subscribed to the medieval doctrine that 'out of all these orders some certain were lost' (Dante, *Convivio* II vi 95ff).

vi *200.* The *shout* is *Presage* of the final *victory* over Satan; when 'The Lord himself shall descend from heaven with a shout, with the voice of the archangel, and with the trump of God: and the dead in Christ shall rise' (I Thess. iv 16).

The archangel trumpet; through the vast of heaven
It sounded, and the faithful armies rung
205 Hosanna to the highest: nor stood at gaze
The adverse legions, nor less hideous joined
The horrid shock: now storming fury rose,
And clamour such as heard in heaven till now
Was never, arms on armour clashing brayed
210 Horrible discord, and the madding wheels
Of brazen chariots raged; dire was the noise
Of conflict; over head the dismal hiss
Of fiery darts in flaming volleys flew,
And flying vaulted either host with fire.
215 So under fiery cope together rushed
Both battles main, with ruinous assault
And inextinguishable rage; all heaven
Resounded, and had earth been then, all earth
Had to her centre shook. What wonder? When
220 Millions of fierce encountering angels fought
On either side, the least of whom could wield
These elements, and arm him with the force
Of all their regions: how much more of power
Army against army numberless to raise
225 Dreadful combustion warring, and disturb,
Though not destroy, their happy native seat;
Had not the eternal king omnipotent
From his strong hold of heaven high overruled
And limited their might; though numbered such
230 As each divided legion might have seemed

vi *209. brayed*] Often used of thunder, or of any jarring sound. Cp. Black-
more, *Prince Arthur* (1695) viii 375: 'Swords clash with Swords, Bucklers
on Bucklers bray.'
vi *213.* It seems that the weapons of M.'s angels are spiritual after all: cp.
Eph. vi 16, 'the shield of faith, wherewith ye shall be able to quench all the
fiery darts of the wicked', and see l. 83*n.*
vi *215. cope*] sky; see iv 992*n.*   *So under*] Sounder, *Ed I*, corr. in *Errata.*
vi *216. battles main*] the main bodies of the armies, as distinct from the van
or the wings (*OED* s.v. *Battle* II 9).
vi *221-2.* i.e., had the power to wield the four elements of which earth was
later to be created.
vi *225. combustion*] confusion, commotion, tumult; a very common seven-
teenth-century meaning.
vi *229-36.* The three features of the armies' power—numbers, strength
and skill—are probably meant to be in ascending order of importance.
numbered such] so numerous.   *yet . . . chief*] yet each single warrior seemed

A numerous host, in strength each armed hand
A legion; led in fight, yet leader seemed
Each warrior single as in chief, expert
When to advance, or stand, or turn the sway
235   Of battle, open when, and when to close
The ridges of grim war; no thought of flight,
None of retreat, no unbecoming deed
That argued fear; each on himself relied,
As only in his arm the moment lay
240   Of victory; deeds of eternal fame
Were done, but infinite: for wide was spread
That war and various; sometimes on firm ground
A standing fight, then soaring on main wing
Tormented all the air; all air seemed then
245   Conflicting fire: long time in even scale
The battle hung; till Satan, who that day
Prodigious power had shown, and met in arms
No equal, ranging through the dire attack
Of fighting seraphim confused, at length

a commander-in-chief.   *ridges of grim war*] Perhaps 'ranks'; but see Lewis
135: 'I do not think, with Verity, that Milton has Shakespeare (*Lucrece*
1438 ["To Simois' reedy banks the red blood ran, / Whose waves to imitate
the battle sought / With swelling ridges; and their ranks began / To break
upon the galled shore"]) in mind. The whole passage is full of Homeric
echoes, and the *ridges* reproduce πολέμοιο γέφυραι (*Il.* iv 371, etc.). What
they were, I do not know.'
vi *231–46*. Eisenstein 60f analyses the montage of this passage and concludes
that there is 'an identical number of lines and shots'.
vi *239. moment*] determining influence (*OED* 5); but also beginning the
balance image of l. 245–the 'moment of a balance' (*OED* 3 a, comparing
Vulg. *momentum staterae*) was a tiny increment, that might yet alter its
equilibrium. Cp. x 45–7, also Wyclif's *Is.* xl 15: 'Lo! Jentiles as a drope of a
boket, and as a moment of a balaunce ben holden.'
vi *243. on main wing*] fully airborne.
vi *245*. For the balance symbol in *PL*, see iv 999–1012*nn*.   *long time*] here
and in *De doctrina* i 9 (Columbia xv 104) M. takes the war in heaven to be
a protracted one, on slender Biblical authority. For a discussion of contem-
porary theologians who took a similar view, see Edgar F. Daniels, 'M.'s
"doubtful conflict" and the seventeenth-century tradition', *N & Q* ccvi
(1961) 430–2.
vi *248. no equal*] For Gilbert (5), evidence that Satan's encounter with Abdiel
is a late addition. But Newton may well have been right in his view that
Abdiel's advantage was only a temporary one. Of course it is *just* 'That
he who in debate of truth hath won, / Should win in arms' also (vi 122f).
Often, however, as M. knew as well as anyone, it does not happen that way.

250 Saw where the sword of Michael smote, and felled
    Squadrons at once, with huge two-handed sway
    Brandished aloft the horrid edge came down
    Wide wasting; such destruction to withstand
    He hasted, and opposed the rocky orb
255 Of tenfold adamant, his ample shield
    A vast circumference: at his approach
    The great archangel from his warlike toil
    Surceased, and glad as hoping here to end
    Intestine war in heaven, the arch foe subdued
260 Or captive dragged in chains, with hostile frown
    And visage all inflamed first thus began.
        Author of evil, unknown till thy revolt,
    Unnamed in heaven, now plenteous, as thou seest
    These acts of hateful strife, hateful to all,
265 Though heaviest by just measure on thy self
    And thy adherents: how hast thou disturbed
    Heaven's blessed peace, and into nature brought
    Misery, uncreated till the crime
    Of thy rebellion? How hast thou instilled
270 Thy malice into thousands, once upright
    And faithful, now proved false. But think not here

vi *250-1*. This passage, together with ll. 318–21, is sometimes used in explanation of the 'two-handed engine' in *Lycidas*: see Mindele C. Treip, in *N & Q* cciv (1959) 364–6, with refs. to earlier material; but also T. B. Stroup, *ibid*. 366f. Michael's sword is also referred to at ii 294 above, and xi 247f; though unauthorized by any Biblical text it was his regular iconographical attribute.

vi *254-5*. For Satan's shield, see i 286–91n. In the seventeenth century *adamant* was most often identified with diamond; and this raises something of a problem. For a shield of diamond would most obviously be an emblem either of Fortitude or of constant Faith (cp., e.g., Fido's shield 'of one pure diamond, celestiall fair' in Phineas Fletcher, *Purple Island* xii 24, or Arthur's shield used against the dragon in *F.Q.* V xi 10, or M.'s Zeal armed in complete diamond (ll. 840–1n); and see Tervarent 147f). If he means to do more than amplify the hardness of the armour, therefore, M. must intend an irony, or a deceptively pure and bright Satan.   *tenfold*] Cp. the 'sevenfold' shield of Guyon in *F.Q.* II viii 32, and the 'seven-times-folded' shield of *SA* 1122. In ancient usage the term was concrete and descriptive, but in Spenser it alluded to the protection afforded by the seven virtues against the seven deadly sins.

vi *259. Intestine war*] internal, civil war.

vi *267*. Note that for M. the angels are not supernatural, but part of (celestial) nature.

vi *269*. Perhaps question mark is in error for exclamation mark.

To trouble holy rest; heaven casts thee out
From all her confines. Heaven the seat of bliss
Brooks not the works of violence and war.
275   Hence then, and evil go with thee along
Thy offspring, to the place of evil, hell,
Thou and thy wicked crew; there mingle broils,
Ere this avenging sword begin thy doom,
Or some more sudden vengeance winged from God
280   Precipitate thee with augmented pain.
     So spake the prince of angels; to whom thus
The adversary. Nor think thou with wind
Of airy threats to awe whom yet with deeds
Thou canst not. Hast thou turned the least of these
285   To flight, or if to fall, but that they rise
Unvanquished, easier to transact with me
That thou shouldst hope, imperious, and with threats
To chase me hence? Err not that so shall end
The strife which thou call'st evil, but we style
290   The strife of glory: which we mean to win,
Or turn this heaven it self into the hell
Thou fablest, here however to dwell free,
If not to reign: mean while thy utmost force,
And join him named Almighty to thy aid,
295   I fly not, but have sought thee far and nigh.
     They ended parle, and both addressed for fight
Unspeakable; for who, though with the tongue
Of angels, can relate, or to what things
Liken on earth conspicuous, that may lift
300   Human imagination to such highth
Of Godlike power: for likest Gods they seemed,
Stood they or moved, in stature, motion, arms

vi *275–6*. For Satan's generation of Sin, see ii 743–60.

vi *282. adversary*] The literal meaning of 'Satan'; *Job* i 6, A.V. marg.; also i 82*n* above.

vi *284–8*. i.e., has your failure to defeat my followers decisively by *deeds* made you think it may be easier to deal (*transact*) with me–to negotiate at the summit and frighten me off with words?

vi *288. Err not*] do not imagine erroneously.

vi *289*. Referring to l. 262.

vi *292. fablest*] At l. 276. Hell has been in existence since ll. 54f at least, but perhaps only the loyal angels have heard about it until now. Abdiel mentions it (at l. 183) only after he has rejoined the loyalists.

vi *296. parle*] parley, truce, debate.   *addressed*] made ready.

vi *302*. For the godlike movement of the angels, see ll. 71f above.

Fit to decide the empire of great heaven.
Now waved their fiery swords, and in the air
305   Made horrid circles; two broad suns their shields
Blazed opposite, while expectation stood
In horror; from each hand with speed retired
Where erst was thickest fight, the angelic throng,
And left large field, unsafe within the wind
310   Of such commotion, such as to set forth
Great things by small, if nature's concord broke,
Among the constellations war were sprung,
Two planets rushing from aspect malign
Of fiercest opposition in mid sky,
315   Should combat, and their jarring spheres confound.
Together both with next to almighty arm,
Uplifted imminent one stroke they aimed
That might determine, and not need repeat,

vi *303*. It is curiously naive or conceited of Raphael to think that angels could even *seem* fit to decide such a matter.

vi *306–7*. Personifying the apprehension of the angels. Cp. Shakespeare, *Troilus* Prol., and *Henry V* II Prol.: 'For now sits Expectation in the air / And hides a sword from hilts unto the point / With crowns imperial.'

vi *310–11*. For the source see ii 921–2*n*; and for Raphael's metaphoric programme, v 571–6.

vi *310–15*. It is usually said that the syntax of this passage is defective, unless a copulative is added between lines 312 and 313. But no addition is necessary, if we analyse as follows: 'as planets should combat, if, concord broken (*broke*), war were sprung among the constellations.' The dramatic irony here is strong: the reader knows it will not be long before concord is in fact broken by the Fall. Already at x 657–61 the planets are taught 'aspects / . . . Of noxious efficacy'.   *aspect . . . opposition*] From the time of Ptolemy, astrologers recognized five definite geometrical relations between the heavenly bodies, called 'aspects'. Of these, two, including 'opposition' (when the bodies occupied diametrically opposite signs 'enclosing two right angles'), were disharmonious and therefore malign in their influence on man: see *Tetrabiblos* i 13.   *mid sky*] 'the zenith'; rendering *medium coeli*, a technical term in astronomy. Cp. Ulysses' famous speech on the concord of degree and sovereignty of the sun, which restrain 'the ill aspects of planets evil', as well as 'commotion in the winds', and prevent 'each thing' from meeting 'in mere oppugnancy' (*Troilus* I iii 85–111).

vi *317*. *Uplifted imminent*] For the violence and paradoxicality of diction that critics have found here, see Ricks 14f; also ll. 698–9*n*.

vi *318–20*. *determine*] settle the issue.   *repeat*] repetition.   *As . . . once*] since in any case it would be impossible to repeat it immediately.   *prevention*] anticipation.

As not of power, at once; nor odds appeared
320   In might or swift prevention; but the sword
Of Michael from the armoury of God
Was given him tempered so, that neither keen
Nor solid might resist that edge: it met
The sword of Satan with steep force to smite
325   Descending, and in half cut sheer, nor stayed,
But with swift wheel reverse, deep entering shared
All his right side; then Satan first knew pain,
And writhed him to and fro convolved; so sore
The griding sword with discontinuous wound
330   Passed through him, but the ethereal substance closed
Not long divisible, and from the gash
A stream of nectarous humour issuing flowed

vi *320-3.* Cp. *Jer.* l 25: 'The Lord hath opened his armoury, and hath
brought forth the weapons of his indignation.' Such magical accoutrements
almost always have an emblematic or symbolic value. Cp. Aeneas' god-
given armour, that breaks the mortal blade of Turnus; or the sword of
justice, stolen from Jupiter, that Astraea gives to Arthegall: 'Of most perfect
metall it was made, / Tempred with Adamant . . . there no substance was
so firme and hard, / But it would pierce or cleave, where so it came; /
Ne any armour could his dint out ward, / But wheresoever it did light, it
throughly shard' (*F.Q.* V i 10).
vi *325.* Overgoing Virgil: Turnus' sword merely shatters in fragments
(*Aen.* xii 741).
vi *326. shared*] cut into parts; cut off.
vi *327. first*] *pace* Empson (54), this need not conflict with Sin's statement
that Satan already felt pain at the assembly of v 767ff; see ii 752-61*n.*
vi *328-34.* 'Milton has here three ideas which Psellus also connects closely:
the demon's pain when his substance is cut, his quick and thorough healing,
and his "panorganic" substance' (West 146f). Cp. Ficino, *Ex Michaele Psello
de daemonibus* (Lyons 1577) vi 360f: 'The body of the demon is through its
whole self naturally sensitive in accordance with its individual parts and
without medium sees, hears, touches, suffers. It suffers with contact and divi-
sion like a solid body, but . . . when it is cut soon is recreated in itself again
and coalesces like water and air. . . . Yet meanwhile it suffers while divided,
for which cause it fears the edge of the sword.'   *convolved*] contorted.
griding] piercing, cutting, or scraping through, so as to cause intense ras-
ping pain.   *discontinuous*] The medical definition of a wound was 'dis-
solution of continuity'.
vi *331-4.* From a wound in a man there would flow blood: namely, the
sanguine humour or fluid, produced by digestion of ordinary food and
giving rise in turn to a sanguine disposition. But angels, who eat nectar
(v 633), bleed a *nectarous humour . . . / Sanguine.* For 'sanguine' as the purest
temperament, and the temperament of unfallen man, see Klibansky 103,

Sanguine, such as celestial spirits may bleed,
And all his armour stained ere while so bright.
335   Forthwith on all sides to his aid was run
By angels many and strong who interposed
Defence, while others bore him on their shields
Back to his chariot; where it stood retired
From off the files of war; there they him laid
340   Gnashing for anguish and despite and shame
To find himself not matchless, and his pride
Humbled by such rebuke, so far beneath
His confidence to equal God in power.
Yet soon he healed; for spirits that live throughout
345   Vital in every part, not as frail man
In entrails, heart or head, liver or reins,
Cannot but by annihilating die;
Nor in their liquid texture mortal wound
Receive, no more than can the fluid air:
350   All heart they live, all head, all eye, all ear,
All intellect, all sense, and as they please,
They limb themselves, and colour, shape or size
Assume, as likes them best, condense or rare.
    Mean while in other parts like deeds deserved
355   Memorial, where the might of Gabriel fought,
And with fierce ensigns pierced the deep array
Of Moloc furious king, who him defied,
And at his chariot wheels to drag him bound
Threatened, nor from the holy one of heaven
360   Refrained his tongue blasphemous; but anon

105, 110f. Cp. Homer's gods, who bleed ichor (*Il.* v 339); M. prefers to hint at a connection with the best human humour.

vi *335. was run*] In imitation of Latin syntax (*cursum est*).

vi *344–54*. Angels have no organs, since their substance is homogeneous or 'uncompounded' (i 425); see ll. 328–34*n*.

vi *355. the might of Gabriel*] Homeric diction for 'mighty Gabriel': see v 371*n*.

vi *357–62*. Gilbert suggests a resemblance with a grotesque battle between devils and saracens in Boiardo (*Italica* xx (1943) 132–4); and in a general way it is true that M.'s angelic war begins by resembling the chivalric combats of Renaissance romantic epics. But because it is more impressionistic and economical and functional, it always avoids their 'long and tedious havoc' (ix 30). See 698–9*n* below.   *furious king*] For his earlier appearances see i 392–6 and ii 43–108.

vi *359–60*. Cp. *2 Kings* xix 22: 'Whom hast thou reproached and blasphemed?... the Holy One of Israel.'   *blasphemed*] Stressed on the second syllable.

>   Down cloven to the waist, with shattered arms
>   And uncouth pain fled bellowing. On each wing
>   Uriel and Raphael his vaunting foe,
>   Though huge, and in a rock of diamond armed,
> 365 Vanquished Adramelec, and Asmadai,
>   Two potent thrones, that to be less than Gods
>   Disdained, but meaner thoughts learned in their flight,
>   Mangled with ghastly wounds through plate and mail,
>   Nor stood unmindful Abdiel to annoy
> 370 The atheist crew, but with redoubled blow
>   Ariel and Arioc, and the violence
>   Of Ramiel scorched and blasted overthrew.
>   I might relate of thousands, and their names
>   Eternize here on earth; but those elect
> 375 Angels contented with their fame in heaven

vi *362. uncouth*] strange, unknown.

vi *363–8*. With angelic objectivity, *Raphael* can refer to himself easily in the third person; Adam and Eve, it should be remembered, do not know his name. (Searching out the names of angels is a fallen kind of curiosity.) Raphael's opponent was presumably *Asmadai* (Asmodeus); a later encounter between the same two, in Biblical times, is alluded to at iv 168. It is equally appropriate that the solar intelligence *Uriel* should take on *Adramelec*, a pagan sun-god mentioned in *2 Kings* xvii 31. For the identification of the rebel angels with heathen gods, see i 364–75n. A medieval scheme, which M. does not seem to have followed regularly, made Asmodeus leader of the fourth order of an evil hierarchy. See West 157; also Burton, *Anatomy of Melancholy* I ii 1 ii.   *diamond*] See ll. 354–5n.

vi *366. gods*] See i 116–7n.

vi *370. atheist*] impious.

vi *371–2. Ariel and Arioc*] In the Bible, *Ariel* (Lion of God) is properly a name for Jerusalem (*Is.* xxix 1f); but West (152–4) traces a separate history from *1 Enoch* through the inferior O.T. translations of Aquila and Symmachus (who use it for an avatar of Mars worshipped at Arina) to the Cabbalists Agrippa, Fludd and Kircher (who apply it to the spirit of earth).   *Arioc*] originally the 'Arioch king of Ellasar' of *Gen.* xiv 1, against whom Abraham fought, he became known as the 'spirit of revenge' in Renaissance demonology (West 154). The name means 'Lion-like'. *Ramiel* is one of those angels who fall by fornication with the daughters of men, in *1 Enoch* vi 7. *violence . . . Ramiel*] For the rhetoric see l. 355n and v 371n.

vi *374–5. elect | Angels*] Biblical diction: see *1 Tim.* v 21. Gilbert scents a contradiction, here, of 363–5; since Raphael has just related his own exploit. But looked at more sympathetically, the passage can be seen as a beautiful dramatic irony. Raphael is both modest and consistent, since he never tells Adam and Eve his name. On the other hand, it is known to us—necessarily, or we should not appreciate the point.

Seek not the praise of men: the other sort
In might though wondrous and in acts of war,
Nor of renown less eager, yet by doom
Cancelled from heaven and sacred memory,
380 Nameless in dark oblivion let them dwell.
For strength from truth divided and from just,
Illaudable, naught merits but dispraise
And ignominy, yet to glory aspires
Vain glorious, and through infamy seeks fame:
385 Therefore eternal silence be their doom.
      And now their mightiest quelled, the battle swerved,
With many an inroad gored; deformed rout
Entered, and foul disorder; all the ground
With shivered armour strown, and on a heap
390 Chariot and charioteer lay overturned
And fiery foaming steeds; what stood, recoiled
O'er-wearied, through the faint Satanic host
Defensive scarce, or with pale fear surprised,
Then first with fear surprised and sense of pain
395 Fled ignominious, to such evil brought
By sin of disobedience, till that hour
Not liable to fear or flight or pain.
Far otherwise the inviolable saints
In cubic phalanx firm advanced entire,
400 Invulnerable, impenetrably armed:
Such high advantages their innocence
Gave them above their foes, not to have sinned,
Not to have disobeyed; in fight they stood
Unwearied, unobnoxious to be pained

vi *379.* See i 82*n*, 361–3*n*; v 658–9*n*.

vi *382. illaudable*] unworthy of praise.

vi *391. what*] those who.

vi *393. Defensive scarce*] scarcely capable of making any defence.

vi *394. Then first*] See 327*n*.

vi *395–7.* Unlike the obedient angels, who are *invulnerable* (l. 400), the rebels have grown 'gross' with sinning (l. 661), and are liable to pain from their wounds; see ll. 328–34*n*.

vi *398. saints*] elect (angels), as at ll. 47 and 374f; see iii 330*n*.

vi *399. cubic phalanx*] The shape of virtue and stability; see i 550*n*. It is idle to debate whether a cube proper or a square is meant here; since M. himself did not have to decide that question. Even if the angels moved as if on a single plane surface, their spears could adumbrate a tidy enough cube, after the manner of illustrations in seventeenth-century arts of war, such as Wallhausen's *Art militaire de la cavalerie*.

vi *404. unobnoxious*] not liable, not exposed (*OED* 1).

405 By wound, though from their place by violence moved.
  Now night her course began, and over heaven
  Inducing darkness, grateful truce imposed,
  And silence on the odious din of war:
  Under her cloudy covert both retired,
410 Victor and vanquished: on the foughten field
  Michael and his angels prevalent
  Encamping, placed in guard their watches round,
  Cherubic waving fires: on the other part
  Satan with his rebellious disappeared,
415 Far in the dark dislodged, and void of rest,
  His potentates to council called by night;
  And in the midst thus undismayed began.
   O now in danger tried, now known in arms
  Not to be overpowered, companions dear,
420 Found worthy not of liberty alone,
  Too mean pretence, but what we more affect,
  Honour, dominion, glory, and renown,
  Who have sustained one day in doubtful fight
  (And if one day, why not eternal days?)
425 What heaven's lord had powerfulest to send
  Against us from about his throne, and judged
  Sufficient to subdue us to his will,
  But proves not so: then fallible, it seems,

vi *406*. The evening of Day 3 of the poem's action; see Introduction, 'Chronology' (p. 26).

vi *407*. Editors compare Horace, *Sat.* I v 9: *iam nox inducere terris | umbras . . . parabat.* But *induce* = 'lead on; bring in; spread as a covering' was perfectly idiomatic Eng. See *OED* s.v. *Induce* 1, 2, 7.

vi *410. foughten field*] battle-field.

vi *411. prevalent*] victorious.

vi *413*. The cherubim, who excel in knowledge, are customarily given the role of sentinels: cp. iv 778ff, xii 590ff.

vi *415. dislodged*] moved his position (military term); cp. v 669.

vi *416*. There was Homeric precedent for this nocturnal council of war in *Il.* ix – the council called by Agamemnon after defeat by Hector.

vi *421. mean pretence*] low ambition; but also 'base false pretence'. *affect*] aspire to; but also 'assume a false appearance of'. Raphael is an excellent vessel for M.'s irony.

vi *423–4*. Empson (41) is certainly right to see this passage as a serious theological argument about the 'claims of God': if they can match God's might in battle, even to the extent of surviving unsubdued, the rebels have as much right as he to such titles as *eternal*. The fallacy is that so far the rebel party has not encountered God at all, but only angels. See i 623–4*n*.

Of future we may deem him, though till now
430   Omniscient thought. True is, less firmly armed,
Some disadvantage we endured and pain,
Till now not known, but known as soon contemned,
Since now we find this our empyreal form
Incapable of mortal injury
435   Imperishable, and though pierced with wound,
Soon closing, and by native vigour healed.
Of evil then so small as easy think
The remedy; perhaps more valid arms,
Weapons more violent, when next we meet,
440   May serve to better us, and worse our foes,
Or equal what between us made the odds,
In nature none: if other hidden cause
Left them superior, while we can preserve
Unhurt our minds, and understanding sound,
445   Due search and consultation will disclose.
    He sat; and in the assembly next upstood
Nisroc, of principalities the prime;
As one he stood escaped from cruel fight,
Sore toiled, his riven arms to havoc hewn,
450   And cloudy in aspect thus answering spake.
Deliverer from new lords, leader to free
Enjoyment of our right as gods; yet hard
For gods, and too unequal work we find
Against unequal arms to fight in pain,

vi *429. Of future*] in future (submerged idiom, building on phrases such as 'of late'); but also 'about what will happen in the future' (*OED*, s.v. *Future* sb. B 2 b).

vi *430.* Unless there is an oversight on M.'s part, Satan cannot have thought God 'omniscient' at v 682f, when he tried to keep the rebellion secret. If, that is to say, the secrecy there was genuine, and not a mere pretence to encourage the troops. But it may be futile to look for consistency in Satan.

vi *436. soon closing*] See ll. 328–34n.

vi *440. worse*] injure, make worse.

vi *444. sound*] healthy; also 'search into'.

vi *447.* One of the passages in which M. seems to think in terms of a regular antihierarchy of evil. See West 134 and 157, and cp. ll. 363–8n. The meanings of the Heb. name *Nisroc* given in Stephanus' *Dictionary*–'Flight' or 'Delicate temptation' (Starnes 268)–are in accordance with the flinching attitude portrayed here. Nisroch was the Assyrian idol which Sennacherib was worshipping when he was murdered (*2 Kings* xix 37, *Is.* xxxvii 38).

vi *452. gods*] Used vaguely and ambiguously, in a sense that varies shiftily from 'autonomous beings' to 'angels'. See i 116–17n.

455   Against unpained, impassive; from which evil
      Ruin must needs ensue; for what avails
      Valour or strength, though matchless, quelled with pain
      Which all subdues, and makes remiss the hands
      Of mightiest. Sense of pleasure we may well
460   Spare out of life perhaps, and not repine,
      But live content, which is the calmest life:
      But pain is perfect misery, the worst
      Of evils, and excessive, overturns
      All patience. He who therefore can invent
465   With what more forcible we may offend
      Our yet unwounded enemies, or arm
      Our selves with like defence, to me deserves
      No less than for deliverance what we owe.
          Whereto with look composed Satan replied.
470   Not uninvented that, which thou aright
      Believest so main to our success, I bring;
      Which of us who beholds the bright surface
      Of this ethereous mould whereon we stand,
      This continent of spacious heaven, adorned
475   With plant, fruit, flower ambrosial, gems and gold,
      Whose eye so superficially surveys
      These things, as not to mind from whence they grow
      Deep under ground, materials dark and crude,
      Of spiritous and fiery spume, till touched
480   With heaven's ray, and tempered they shoot forth

vi 455. *impassive*] not liable to suffering, impassible. *OED* gives no instance earlier than this.

vi 458. *remiss*] slack.

vi 464–8. Veiling a threat: 'Come up with something new, or we'll change our leader.'   *offend*] attack; hurt.   *to me*] Supply 'it seems'.

vi 471. *main*] highly important.

vi 472–81. Cp. the sun's generation of precious stones by its subterranean action on condensed dew at iii 608–12 above. Here minerals are formed similarly, by the action of *heaven's ray* (the celestial equivalent of sunshine) upon *spume*, the exhalation of the celestial earth. See E. H. Duncan's exposition in *Osiris* xi (1954) 388, which finds a source in Aristotle's *Meteorologica* (341ᵇ and 348ᵃ). 'Here is the scheme of chaos and cosmos, with a physical sense of the ominous minerals lying beneath the flowers and the gold. . . . The cunning choice of *toucht, temperd, shoot,* and *opening* anticipates what follows; gunpowder is invented in the images before it occurs in the narrative' (Svendsen 119f).

vi 472. *surface*] Stressed on the second syllable.

vi 475. *ambrosial*] See ii 245n.

vi 478. *crude*] raw; at an early stage of growth.

So beauteous, opening to the ambient light.
These in their dark nativity the deep
Shall yield us pregnant with infernal flame,
Which into hollow engines long and round
485   Thick-rammed, at the other bore with touch of fire
Dilated and infuriate shall send forth
From far with thundering noise among our foes
Such implements of mischief as shall dash
To pieces, and o'erwhelm whatever stands
490   Adverse, that they shall fear we have disarmed
The thunderer of his only dreaded bolt.
Nor long shall be our labour, yet ere dawn,
Effect shall end our wish. Mean while revive;
Abandon fear; to strength and counsel joined
495   Think nothing hard, much less to be despaired.
He ended, and his words their drooping cheer
Enlightened, and their languished hope revived.
The invention all admired, and each, how he

vi 483. *infernal*] Bentley objected to the word, on the grounds that Satan does not yet know his punishment; and Empson[2] 158 has Satan extrapolating from 'the previous day's hints about hell'. But only Raphael intends the allusion to hell here; Satan means simply 'flame belonging to the region below, the *deep*'.

vi 484–90. Newton found sources in Ariosto's account of the invention of firearms in *Orl. Fur.* ix 28f and 91, and (more plausibly) in Spenser's mention of 'that divelish yron Engin wrought / In deepest Hell, and framd by *Furies* skill, / With windy Nitre and quick Sulphur fraught, / And ramd with bullet round, ordaind to kill' (*F.Q.* I vii 13). Cp. also Daniel, *Civil Wars* vi 26f. But the attitude was understandably a common one. Erasmo di Valvasone had introduced the invention of cannon into his angelic war: see Kirkconnell 81. *the other bore*] the other cylindrical perforation; the touch-hole. *touch of fire*] contact with fire; but also 'touch-powder, the fine gunpowder placed over the touch-hole'. The wit of the description, which is so charged with ambiguity that it applies with equal force both to breech-loading and to muzzle-loading firearms, seems to have made little impact on critics even of the highest calibre. The two chains of discourse are: 'materials that rammed into one end of hollow engines (the breech) at the other end (the muzzle) shall send forth implements' and 'materials that rammed into (the muzzle of) hollow engines and dilated with touch-powder at the touch-hole, shall send etc.'

vi 484. *hollow*] The first three edns have 'hallow', an obsolete or dialectal form.

vi 494. *counsel*] judgment.

vi 496. *cheer*] mood, spirits.

vi 498. The zeugma is easily missed, since the second *admired*, in the sense

To be the inventor missed, so easy it seemed
500   Once found, which yet unfound most would have
            thought
      Impossible: yet haply of thy race
      In future days, if malice should abound,
      Some one intent on mischief, or inspired
      With devilish machination might devise
505   Like instrument to plague the sons of men
      For sin, on war and mutual slaughter bent.
      Forthwith from council to the work they flew;
      None arguing stood, innumerable hands
      Were ready, in a moment up they turned
510   Wide the celestial soil, and saw beneath
      The originals of nature in their crude
      Conception; sulphurous and nitrous foam
      They found, they mingled, and with subtle art,
      Concocted and adusted they reduced
515   To blackest grain, and into store conveyed:
      Part hidden veins digged up (nor hath this earth
      Entrails unlike) of mineral and stone,
      Whereof to found their engines and their balls

'marvelled' has to be supplied. Throughout this passage M. uses the most
extravagant possible figures of rhetoric, not excluding even vicious ones,
such as bomphiologia (excessively lofty diction). See ll. 698–9n.

vi 509–15. An epitome of 'mineralogical and lapidary lore' (Svendsen 121).
As Svendsen points out, it is strategically important that the materials for
gunpowder should exist in heaven. M. wishes to portray matter as morally
neutral. 'It is the fallen angels who must mingle, concoct, adust.'   *origi-
nals of nature*] original elements. Sulphur is mentioned as one of the originals
not simply because it is an ingredient of gunpowder, but also because in
alchemy it was the father of minerals and metals (mercury being the mother:
see iii 601–5n and Caron 161).   *crude*] Cp. l. 478.   *nitrous foam*] Cp. the
'nitre' that blows Satan up at ii 937; also the 'nitrous powder' (gunpowder)
to which he is compared at iv 815. Potassium nitrate (saltpetre) is an ingre-
dient of gunpowder. Cp. also 'spume' at l. 479.   *concocted*] prepared by
heating (an alchemical term; but also a physiological term denoting a phase
of digestion).   *adusted*] scorched, dried up with heat (an alchemical
term; but also a physiological term referring to a certain corruption of
humours by drying).

vi 515–16. Necessary information for Adam and Eve, since there was no
mining before the Fall. See i 684–92n.

vi 518. *found*] cast, mould.   *engines*] pieces of ordnance; the word was
quite usually applied to offensive weapons of all kinds, but especially to
those of large size.

Of missive ruin; part incentive reed
520 Provide, pernicious with one touch to fire.
So all ere day-spring, under conscious night
Secret they finished, and in order set,
With silent circumspection unespied.
Now when fair morn orient in heaven appeared
525 Up rose the victor angels, and to arms
The matin trumpet sung: in arms they stood
Of golden panoply, refulgent host,
Soon banded; others from the dawning hills
Looked round, and scouts each coast light-armed scour,
530 Each quarter, to descry the distant foe,
Where lodged, or whither fled, or if for fight,
In motion or in halt: him soon they met
Under spread ensigns moving nigh, in slow
But firm battalion; back with speediest sail
535 Zophiel, of cherubim the swiftest wing,
Came flying, and in mid air aloud thus cried.
    Arm, warriors, arm for fight, the foe at hand,
Whom fled we thought, will save us long pursuit
This day, fear not his flight; so thick a cloud

vi *519–20*. The rhetorical point of these lines is their bomphiologia or excessively inflated diction. Cannon were a mean subject, grotesquely unworthy of such high-flown learned wit. *missive*] missile (adj.). *incentive*] kindling (wrongly connected with Lat. *incendere*, to burn). The 'incentive reed' is simply the match. *pernicious*] quick; also 'destructive' (the pun is between separate words, from different Lat. roots). *touch*] The same bad pun as at l. 485.

vi *521. dayspring*] early dawn. *conscious*] Perhaps 'aware and interested', but certainly 'guilty' (*OED* 4 b). Night is personified as an accessory sharing the guilty knowledge.

vi *524*. The morning of Day 3 of the poem's action; see Introduction, 'Chronology' (p. 26).

vi *532. halt*] Ed I and Ed II have 'alt', a common seventeenth-century spelling that possibly allows a secondary sense depending on the idiom *in alt*='in an excited frame of mind' (*OED* s.v. *Alt*² b).

vi *533–4*. Apparently courageous stoicism; but the slow pace turns out to be a necessary camouflage: see l. 555.

vi *535*. West (155) in disgust gives up the search for a definite source for *Zophiel* (Spy of God) among a tangle of misprints, mistranslations and mistransliterations in Agrippa and Fludd.

vi *539. cloud*] Incidentally imitates Virgil's *nubes belli* (*Aen.* x 809), but the main allusion is to the 'clouds . . . to whom the mist of darkness is reserved for ever' of 2 Pet. ii 17: namely, false teachers who 'speak great swelling words of vanity'.

540   He comes, and settled in his face I see
      Sad resolution and secure: let each
      His adamantine coat gird well, and each
      Fit well his helm, gripe fast his orbed shield,
      Borne even or high, for this day will pour down,
545   If I conjecture aught, no drizzling shower,
      But rattling storm of arrows barbed with fire.
      So warned he them aware themselves, and soon
      In order, quit of all impediment;
      Instant without disturb they took alarm,
550   And onward move embattled; when behold
      Not distant far with heavy pace the foe
      Approaching gross and huge; in hollow cube
      Training his devilish enginery, impaled
      On every side with shadowing squadrons deep,
555   To hide the fraud. At interview both stood
      A while, but suddenly at head appeared
      Satan: and thus was heard commanding loud.
         Vanguard, to right and left the front unfold;
      That all may see who hate us, how we seek
560   Peace and composure, and with open breast
      Stand ready to receive them, if they like
      Our overture, and turn not back perverse;
      But that I doubt, however witness heaven,

vi 541. sad] sober, serious.   secure] confident, free from apprehension.
vi 542-6. See Eph. vi 14-17 for this spiritual armour against 'fiery darts',
and cp. l. 213n.
vi 543. gripe] seize, grip.
vi 545. conjecture] prognosticate, interpret the signs. Fenton's proposed
emendation of aught to 'right' is unnecessary.
vi 548. impediment] hindrance, obstruction; also 'baggage'.
vi 549. instant] pressing, urgent (adj.); though in a secondary chain of dis-
course it is used adverbially=instantly.   disturb] disturbance.   took
alarm] responded to the call to arms; took up action stations.
vi 550. embattled] formed in order of battle.
vi 552. hollow cube] the outward form of virtue (see l. 399n and i 550n)
emblematically conceals a hollow and devilishly aggressive interior.
vi 553. Training] pulling.   enginery] artillery; see 518n.   impaled]
enclosed for defence (military term).
vi 555. at interview] in mutual view (OED s.v. Interview 2). A rare usage.
vi 560. composure] settlement.   breast] heart (OED I 5 a); broad front of a
moving company (OED I 7).
vi 562. overture] A pun between 'opening of negotiations for a settlement'
(OED 3) and 'aperture, hole' (OED 1)–the 'bore' (485) or 'hideous orifice'
(577) of the cannon.

Heaven witness thou anon, while we discharge
565   Freely our part; ye who appointed stand
Do as you have in charge, and briefly touch
What we propound, and loud that all may hear.
    So scoffing in ambiguous words he scarce
Had ended; when to right and left the front
570   Divided, and to either flank retired.
Which to our eyes discovered new and strange,
A triple mounted row of pillars laid
On wheels (for like to pillars most they seemed
Or hollowed bodies made of oak or fir,
575   With branches lopped, in wood or mountain felled)
Brass, iron, stony mould, had not their mouths
With hideous orifice gaped on us wide,
Portending hollow truce; at each behind

vi 566. The pun on *touch* has been made so often (ll. 479, 484–90n, 520) that it now seems as laboured as the ones on 'discharge' (l. 564) and 'loud'. Since frequent puns are quickly felt to be extravagant and excessive, the figure is highly appropriate in the present context. See ll. 698–9n. This strategic purpose behind the puns was missed by Landor when he cleverly said that 'the first overt crime of the refractory angels was *punning*' (*Works*, ed. T. E. Welby (1927–36) v 258).

vi 568. Following the punctuation of *Ed I*. *Ed II* wrongly moves the comma to the end of the line.

vi 569–70. A recognized stratagem in the warfare of the time; see H. H. Scudder in *N & Q* cxcv (1590) 335.

vi 572. *triple-mounted*] The ordnance the rebel angels have made are 'organs' or *orgues*–weapons consisting of several barrels fired simultaneously. In the seventeenth century these were chiefly used in siege war; see *EB* xvii 238. There have to be *three* barrels to underline the antithesis with Messiah's 'three-bolted thunder' (l. 764).

vi 572–8. Just as the cubic battle formation of the devils is deceptive and hollow (ll. 552–5), so also are the *pillars* of their ordnance. The column, like the cube, was an emblem of virtue; see Tervarent 107. Scudder (*art. cit.* 569–70n) cites a contemporary historical instance of the use of fake cannon as a tactical stratagem.

vi 576. *Brass . . . mould*] made of brass, etc.

vi 578–94. The sustained physiological imagery (e.g. *belched, embowelled, entrails, disgorging, glut;* cp. *concocted* and *adusted* at 514) amounts almost to a Freudian allegory about alimentary and anal aggression. Devils were often portrayed defecating or vomiting. See, e.g., the mural of the Campo Santo at Pisa (flames issuing from mouth, belly and anus) and Lorch's engraving, illus. Cohn, Fig. 2 (vomiting, in accordance with *Rev.* xvi 13). The passage abounds in diction that is indecorously low.   *hollow*] insincere, false;

A seraph stood, and in his hand a reed
580   Stood waving tipped with fire; while we suspense,
Collected stood within our thoughts amused,
Not long, for sudden all at once their reeds
Put forth, and to a narrow vent applied
With nicest touch. Immediate in a flame,
585   But soon obscured with smoke, all heaven appeared,
From those deep throated engines belched, whose roar
Embowelled with outrageous noise the air,
And all her entrails tore, disgorging foul
Their devilish glut, chained thunderbolts and hail
590   Or iron globes, which on the victor host
Levelled, with such impetuous fury smote,
That whom they hit, none on their feet might stand,
Though standing else as rocks, but down they fell
By thousands, angel on archangel rolled;
595   The sooner for their arms, unarmed they might
Have easily as spirits evaded swift
By quick contraction or remove; but now
Foul dissipation followed and forced rout;
Nor served it to relax their serried files.
600   What should they do? If on they rushed, repulse
Repeated, and indecent overthrow
Doubled, would render them yet more despised,
And to their foes a laughter; for in view
Stood ranked of seraphim another row
605   In posture to displode their second tire
Of thunder: back defeated to return
They worse abhorred. Satan beheld their plight,

and concave; see l. 566n.   *suspense*] in a state of mental suspense; unde-
cided.   *amused*] puzzled, absorbed; deceived as to the enemy's real
designs (military: *OED* 5)   *narrow vent*] at one level, the touch-hole.
embowelled] disembowelled (*OED* I 2); or filled the bowels of (*OED* II 3).
glut] surfeit, excessive flow of bile.

vi 594. The only line in *PL* 'that might be read to signify an archangelic
order' (West 133f). Usually M. uses the term *archangel* to connote personal
rank rather than membership of an order.

vi 597. For the ability of angels to change their size and shape, see i 423–31n.

vi 598. *dissipation*] dispersal, scattering.

vi 601. *indecent*] unbecoming, uncomely.

vi 605. *posture*] A military term denoting any one of the particular positions
in weapon drill–cp. Gervase Markham, *The souldiers accidence* (1625) 24:
'The three Postures or words of Command, which are used for the Musquet
in the face of the enemie . . . are these–1. Make readie. 2. Present. 3. Give
fire.'   *tire*] volley, broadside.

And to his mates thus in derision called.
           O friends, why come not on these victors proud?
610   Ere while they fierce were coming, and when we,
           To entertain them fair with open front
           And breast, (what could we more?) propounded terms
           Of composition, straight they changed their minds,
           Flew off, and into strange vagaries fell,
615   As they would dance, yet for a dance they seemed
           Somewhat extravagant and wild, perhaps
           For joy of offered peace: but I suppose
           If our proposals once again were heard
           We should compel them to a quick result.
620   To whom thus Belial in like gamesome mood,
           Leader, the terms we sent were terms of weight,
           Of hard contents, and full of force urged home,
           Such as we might perceive amused them all,
           And stumbled many, who receives them right,
625   Had need from head to foot well understand;
           Not understood, this gift they have besides,
           They show us when our foes walk not upright.
               So they among themselves in pleasant vein
           Stood scoffing, highthened in their thoughts beyond
630   All doubt of victory, eternal might
           To match with their inventions they presumed
           So easy, and of his thunder made a scorn,
           And all his host derided, while they stood
           A while in trouble; but they stood not long,
635   Rage prompted them at length, and found them arms
           Against such hellish mischief fit to oppose.
           Forthwith (behold the excellence, the power
           Which God hath in his mighty angels placed)
           Their arms away they threw, and to the hills

vi *611–12. open front*] candid face (*OED* s.v. *Front* I 2); also 'front line': 'Divi-
ded, and to either flank retired' (l. 570). For the pun on *breast*, see l. 560n.
propound] propose.
vi *614. vagaries*] frolics; fantastic or capricious actions. So Aeneas taunts
Meriones with dancing to avoid his spear-throw at *Il.* xvi 617f.
vi *620–7. Belial*, who was described as 'timorous' at ii 117, is in the angelic
war 'celebrated for nothing but that scoffing speech' (Addison). The
puns are all obvious, except perhaps for that in *understand* = comprehend, also
'prop up, support' (*OED* I 9).   *amused them*] engaged their whole
attention; cp. 581.   *stumbled*] puzzled; tripped up.
vi *635.* Cp. Virgil, *Aen.* i 150: *furor arma ministrat.*
vi *639–66.* Cp. the simile of the hill 'torn from Pelorus, or the shattered
side / Of thundering Aetna' at i 230ff, or the comparison of Satan to a

640   (For earth hath this variety from heaven
          Of pleasure situate in hill and dale)
          Light as the lightning glimpse they ran, they flew,
          From their foundations loosening to and fro
          They plucked the seated hills with all their load,
645   Rocks, waters, woods, and by the shaggy tops
          Up lifting bore them in their hands: amaze,
          Be sure, and terror seized the rebel host,
          When coming towards them so dread they saw
          The bottom of the mountains upward turned,
650   Till on those cursed engines' triple-row
          They saw them whelmed, and all their confidence
          Under the weight of mountains buried deep,
          Themselves invaded next, and on their heads
          Main promontories flung, which in the air
655   Came shadowing, and oppressed whole legions armed,
          Their armour helped their harm, crushed in and bruised
          Into their substance pent, which wrought them pain
          Implacable, and many a dolorous groan,
          Long struggling underneath, ere they could wind
660   Out of such prison, though spirits of purest light,
          Purest at first, now gross by sinning grown.
          The rest in imitation to like arms
          Betook them, and the neighbouring hills uptore;
          So hills amid the air encountered hills

displaced mountain at vi 195ff. MacCaffrey 88–90 rightly treats these and
similar passages as images of the chaos, tamed in creation, into which cosmos
is always liable to relapse. M. here makes the most direct of his many allu-
sions to the war of the Giants against Jupiter – the chief pagan analogue of the
angelic rebellion. In the Giant War hills were used as missiles, and at the end
several Giants remained buried to form the volcanoes of later time (see i
197–200n, 230–7n). Among M.'s closest models is Claudian: with ll. 644–7
cp. the wonderfully detailed account of hill throwing in *Gigantomachia*
70f: 'Enipeus, gathered up with its beetling crags, scatters its waters over
yon giant's shoulders.' Claudian, too, presents the war as a return to the
confusion of chaos.

vi *650. triple-row*] the 'triple-mounted pillars'; see l. 572n.

vi *653. invaded*] attacked.

vi *654. main*] whole, solid (*OED* 4 b).

vi *655. oppressed*] weighed down.

vi *664–7.* The anthropomorphic scene is hard to imagine because of the
difficulties of scale. That this effect is intended as an alienation device seems
clear from *Be sure*, with its recall from the second-order fictive sequence to
Adam and Eve in the first-order sequence.   *amaze*] bewilderment;
stupefaction, panic.

665   Hurled to and fro with jaculation dire,
        That under ground they fought in dismal shade;
        Infernal noise; war seemed a civil game
        To this uproar; horrid confusion heaped
        Upon confusion rose: and now all heaven
670   Had gone to wrack, with ruin overspread,
        Had not the almighty Father where he sits
        Shrined in his sanctuary of heaven secure,
        Consulting on the sum of things, foreseen
        This tumult, and permitted all, advised:
675   That his great purpose he might so fulfil,
        To honour his anointed Son avenged
        Upon his enemies, and to declare
        All power on him transferred: whence to his Son
        The assessor of his throne he thus began.
680   Effulgence of my glory, Son beloved,
        Son in whose face invisible is beheld
        Visibly, what by deity I am,
        And in whose hand what by decree I do,
        Second omnipotence, two days are past,
685   Two days, as we compute the days of heaven,
        Since Michael and his powers went forth to tame
        These disobedient; sore hath been their fight,

vi 665. *jaculation*] hurling.

vi 666. Following the punctuation of *Ed I*. *Ed II* wrongly adds comma after *ground*.

vi 670. Surpassing the effect of the first day's fighting. Cp. 218 above.

vi 673. *sum of things*] 'Universe' is the usual explanation, by analogy with Lucretius' phrase *summarum summa* (v 362); but a closer Latin original (if such be desired) is *summa rerum*, 'highest public interest', and in any case 675 makes it clear that M. also intends 'goal of things' (*OED* s.v. *Sum* 13). Cp. *Natur* 35, and Ovid, *Met*. ii 300, *rerum consule summae*.

vi 674. *advised*] after consideration, deliberately.

vi 679. *assessor*] sharer. The term is used of one who sits beside another, participating in his status and position.

vi 680–2. Cp. *Heb*. i 3, 'the brightness of his glory, and the express image of his person'; also *Col*. i 15, 'the image of the invisible God'.

vi 684. *Second omnipotence*] No less an oxymoron than 'invisible . . . Visibly' at l. 681f.

vi 685. For the nature of time in heaven, see v 579–82*n*. In spite of the difficult theology involved M. is bound to continue computing the days of the action, even when it does not take place on earth, for the sake of his numerological structure. See ll. 4–11*n*, 698–9*n*, v 579–82*n*; also Introduction, 'Chronology'.

As likeliest was, when two such foes met armed;
For to themselves I left them, and thou know'st,
690 Equal in their creation they were formed,
Save what sin hath impaired, which yet hath wrought
Insensibly, for I suspend their doom;
Whence in perpetual fight they needs must last
Endless, and no solution will be found:
695 War wearied hath performed what war can do,
And to disordered rage let loose the reins,
With mountains as with weapons armed, which makes
Wild work in heaven, and dangerous to the main.
Two days are therefore past, the third is thine;
700 For thee I have ordained it, and thus far

vi *689. thou know'st*] This has been ridiculed, on the ground that the Son is omniscient (see Peter 13, Ricks 19). But if the tone of the phrase is rightly imagined–'*thou* knowest, thou of all beings, thou by whose agency I created them, thou who sharest with me the secrets of creation'–it will be seen to have the right sublime intimacy. Of course, the more general objection stands: that any attempt to verbalize God must fail. Only, the degree of unsuccess seems to count for something.

vi *690–1.* For the status of Satan and Michael see v 660n. Their equality continues, because sin has so far affected Satan only *insensibly* (imperceptibly).

vi *698–9.* Christ is now to put an end to the confusion and chaos of the first two days' fighting. Note the answering change to a steadier and more exalted style: the *wild work* was portrayed in an appropriately grotesque manner. See ll. 357–62n, 498n and 566n. The delay of Messiah's entry into the war, which so offends Empson, could scarcely have been avoided by M.; for it was Scriptural (see *De doctrina* i 7, Columbia xv 105, on Rev. xii 7f) and in any case it was necessary if there was to be any angelic war. There was also an arithmological reason: namely, that the dyad of the two days' fighting symbolized rebellion and excess and division, whereas the triad of the third day symbolizes virtue and limitation and order and a return to the principle of unity (Bongo 95ff; Fowler 5f). Typologically, the reference would be to Christ's rising on the third day (e.g. *Luke* xiii 32, 'the third day I shall be perfected'): Messiah's defeat of Satan here foreshadows the later victory of the resurrection.   *main*] whole, universe.

vi *700–9.* Empson's thesis (e.g. *Milton's God* 41f) is largely built on the argument that God's delay in finishing the war amounted to intentional deception of Satan about his omnipotence. Here precisely the opposite reason is given for the delay: namely, that it will make possible a manifest distinction between the power of angels and the power of Christ. The distinction turns out to be so clear that to keep his rebellion intellectually respectable Satan has to forget about the third day's fighting altogether: see, e.g., i 169–71n.

Have suffered, that the glory may be thine
Of ending this great war, since none but thou
Can end it. Into thee such virtue and grace
Immense I have transfused, that all may know
705   In heaven and hell thy power above compare,
And this perverse commotion governed thus,
To manifest thee worthiest to be heir
Of all things, to be heir and to be king
By sacred unction, thy deserved right.
710   Go then thou mightiest in thy Father's might,
Ascend my chariot, guide the rapid wheels
That shake heaven's basis, bring forth all my war,
My bow and thunder, my almighty arms
Gird on, and sword upon thy puissant thigh;
715   Pursue these sons of darkness, drive them out
From all heaven's bounds into the utter deep:
There let them learn, as likes them, to despise
God and Messiah his anointed king.
      He said, and on his Son with rays direct
720   Shone full, he all his Father full expressed
Ineffably into his face received,
And thus the filial Godhead answering spake.

vi *701. suffered*] In the sense 'allowed', followed by a clause introduced by
'that', was a common construction (*OED* s.v. *Suffer* II 14 a). But *suffered
that*='waited patiently, endured, so that' leads to a possible secondary
chain of discourse.
vi *706.* 'And that all may know this insurrection (controlled thus by your
power alone) to manifest. . . .'
vi *708. heir*] Cp. v 720 ('heir of all my might'), and see *Heb.* i 2: 'His
Son, whome he hath appointed heir of all things, by whom also he made
the worlds.'
vi *709.* For the anointing of the Messiah, see v 603–6*n*, 664*n*.
vi *712. war*] A synecdoche for 'weapons of war'. Whether or not M.
invented the figure, it was soon after a popular one; cp. Dryden (*Aen.* viii
572: 'His broken Axeltrees, and blunted War'); Addison, *Cato* i 4 ('th'em-
battled Elephant, / Loaden with war'); etc.
vi *715. sons of darkness*] Contrast v 716, where the angels generally were
'sons of morn'.
vi *716. utter*] outer.
vi *718.* The literal meaning of *Messiah* is *anointed king*.
vi *720–1.* Cp. x 63–7, and see *2 Cor.* iv 6: 'God, who commanded the light
to shine out of darkness, hath shined in our hearts, to give the light of the
knowledge of the glory of God in the face of Jesus Christ.'

O Father, O supreme of heavenly thrones,
First, highest, holiest, best, thou always seek'st
725 To glorify thy Son, I always thee,
As is most just; this I my glory account,
My exaltation, and my whole delight,
That thou in me well pleased, declar'st thy will
Fulfilled, which to fulfil is all my bliss.
730 Sceptre and power, thy giving, I assume,
And gladlier shall resign, when in the end
Thou shalt be all in all, and I in thee
For ever, and in me all whom thou lovest:
But whom thou hatest, I hate, and can put on
735 Thy terrors, as I put thy mildness on,
Image of thee in all things; and shall soon,
Armed with thy might, rid heaven of these rebelled,
To their prepared ill mansion driven down
To chains of darkness, and the undying worm,
740 That from thy just obedience could revolt,
Whom to obey is happiness entire.
Then shall thy saints unmixed, and from the impure

vi 724–34. Following the thought, and to some extent the diction, of *John* xvii 1–23, Jesus' prayer at the last supper: 'Thou hast given him power. . . . I have glorified thee on the earth. . . . And now, O Father, glorify thou me . . . that they might have my joy fulfilled in themselves . . . I in them, and thou in me.' Cp. also *Matt.* iii 17 ('my beloved Son, in whom I am well pleased'). The argument whether this passage is Arian or Trinitarian (Kelley 120, etc.) seems both endless and pointless. Even if every single text used here were interpreted to Arian effect in *De doctrina* i 5, M. could hardly have expected readers of *PL* to know this. The texts were comparatively uncontroversial ones and they are not provided here with any context of dogmatic theology.

vi 731–2. See iii 339–43n, and cp. *1 Cor.* xv 24, 28: 'Then cometh the end, when he shall have delivered up the kingdom to God, even the Father; when he shall have put down all rule and all authority and power. . . . And when all things shall be subdued unto him, then shall the Son also himself be subject unto him that put all things under him, that God may be all in all.'

vi 734. 'Do not I hate them, O Lord, that hate thee? and am not I grieved with those that rise up against thee?' (*Ps.* cxxxix 21).

vi 738. The grim obverse of Christ's promise, 'In my Father's house are many mansions: if it were not so, I would have told you. I go to prepare a place for you' (*John* xiv 2).   mansion] dwelling. Cp. *Nativity Ode* 140.

vi 739. See i 48n, and cp. *Jude* 6: 'And the angels which kept not their first estate, but left their own habitation, he hath reserved in everlasting chains under darkness unto the judgment of the great day.' At *Mark* ix 44 hell is 'where their worm dieth not'.

>   Far separate, circling thy holy mount
>   Unfeigned hallelujahs to thee sing,
> 745 Hymns of high praise, and I among them chief.
>   So said, he o'er his sceptre bowing, rose
>   From the right hand of glory where he sat,
>   And the third sacred morn began to shine
>   Dawning through heaven: forth rushed with
>   whirlwind sound

vi 744. At ii 243 submission means to Mammon a prospect of singing 'forced hallelujahs'.

vi 748. Day 4 of the poem's action, though only the third *morn*; see Introduction, 'Chronology'. M. has so arranged the action that the number 4, which is a form of the holy *tetractys*, denoted the sacred day when the triumph of Messiah is celebrated.

vi 749–59. The principal image of the poem, which has been prepared for by many partial anticipations. See, e.g., Satan's counterfeit chariot at ll. 100–3 and 338; the seven archangels of the cosmic chariot (see iii 656n); and the many mentions of this and other chariots (i 311, ii 887, iii 394, 522, vi 211, 358, 390, 711). Messiah's chariot is a 'triumphal chariot' (l. 881), so that his ascent of it constitutes a factitive claim to sovereignty. The triumph of a god or allegorical abstraction was one of the principal motifs of Renaissance and Baroque art, and it generally included as one of its most prominent features a chariot or mobile throne; see the relevant ch. in E. Van Marle, *Iconographie de l'art profane* ii (The Hague 1932); É. Mâle, 'Les triomphes' in *Revue de l'art ancien et moderne* (1906); and C. Lorgues-Lapouge, 'Triomphes renaissants' in *L'Oeil* xxxv (1957) 27–35. The Triumph of Christ was a distinct subject, an example of which is illustrated *ibid*. 32. M.'s chariot of sovereignty, however, is unusually mysterious and mystical, even if the distinct detail of the portrayal may mislead us into thinking otherwise. His principal source is Ezekiel's apocalyptic vision of God in a machine (i 4–6, 16, 26–8, x 12, 16): 'Behold, a whirlwind . . . a great cloud, and a fire infolding itself, and a brightness was about it, and out of the midst thereof as the colour of amber . . . four living creatures. . . . And every one had four faces and every one had four wings. . . . The appearance of the wheels and their work was like unto the colour of a beryl: and they four had one likeness: and their appearance and their work was as it were a wheel in the middle of a wheel. . . . the firmament that was over their heads was the likeness of a throne, as the appearance of a sapphire stone. . . . the appearance of a man above upon it. And I saw as the colour of amber . . . as the appearance of the bow that is in the cloud in the day of rain. . . . And their whole body, and their backs, and their hands, and their wings, and the wheels, were full of eyes round about, even the wheels that they four had. . . . And when the cherubims went, the wheels went by them.' These verses had generally been interpreted in a cosmic sense, its various tetrads being identified with the four elements, the four seasons, etc., but also with the four cardinal

750   The chariot of paternal deity,
      Flashing thick flames, wheel within wheel undrawn,
      It self instinct with spirit, but convoyed
      By four cherubic shapes, four faces each
      Had wondrous, as with stars their bodies all
755   And wings were set with eyes, with eyes the wheels
      Of beryl, and careering fires between;
      Over their heads a crystal firmament,
      Whereon a sapphire throne, inlaid with pure
      Amber, and colours of the showery arch.
760   He in celestial panoply all armed
      Of radiant urim, work divinely wrought,

virtues, after the usual manner of expansion of the *tetractys* (see, e.g., Jerome, *Comm. in Ezech.*, Migne xxv 22ff; Valeriano 549; Bongo 243). But M. underlines the cosmic aspect by adding *stars* (l. 754) to the Biblical *firmament*. Here, no less than in the overtly hexaemeral parts of *PL*, M. presents his distinctive vision of a nature that is a vehicle for divinity. Messiah's chariot is nothing less than the cosmic chariot of *Timaeus* 41E and *Laws* 899A. A less obvious source is the golden chariot of the king in *Song of Sol.* iii 9f, which seems to have been a prominent subject of meditation in the mystical thought of the time. See, e.g., G. Foliot, *Expositio in Canticum Canticorum* (1643) 174f, where, however, the chariot is interpreted as a symbol of the Church, or the New Covenant. For other allusions to King Solomon and his gold in *PL* see i 403*n*.

     The throne on the 'firmament' is with a special appropriateness placed at the sovereign centre of the heavens, by its placement at the numerical centre of the whole poem (by line-count, *Ed I* only; see l. 761*n*, iv 30*n*; also Qvarnström, *passim*, and Fowler, Index s.v. *Central Position of Sovereignty*). In his description of the ideal Christian poet in *Reason of Church-Government*, M. singles out the power 'to celebrate in glorious and lofty Hymns the throne and equipage of Gods Almightinesse' (Yale i 817). Rupert of Deutz had anticipated M. in combining the divine chariot with the angelic rebellion (McColley 36–8). (The theology underlying this use of an apocalyptic vision to portray the earliest events of the redemptive history has still to be worked out.) In view of the alchemical implications of *radiant urim* (see l. 761*n*) it is interesting to compare a stanza in one of Cowley's *Pindarique Odes* (1668), describing Elijah's chariot: ' 'Twas gawdy all, and rich in every part, / Of *Essences* of *Gems*, and *Spirit* of *Gold* / Was its *substantial mold*; / Drawn forth by *Chymique Angels* art. . . .' (ed. Waller p. 205).

vi *752. instinct*] animated, impelled.

vi *761. urim*] see *Exod.* xxviii 30: 'And thou shalt put in the breastplate of judgment the Urim and the Thummim; and they shall be upon Aaron's heart, when he goeth in before the Lord.' For the symbolism of Aaron's breastplate of priesthood, see iii 594–605*nn* above. As Qvarnström explains, *urim* was not only a sacerdotal emblem and a symbol of virtue, but was also

Ascended, at his right hand Victory
Sat, eagle-winged, beside him hung his bow
And quiver with three-bolted thunder stored,
765   And from about him fierce effusion rolled
Of smoke and bickering flame, and sparkles dire;
Attended with ten thousand thousand saints,

identified with the Philosopher's Stone; Tancke called it 'the right, true sun itself . . . the right *Urim* and fiery Carbuncle'. Thus, Messiah's armour carries on the cosmic image of the preceding lines and again asserts his sovereign claim as creator. The one true alchemist, he wears the stone that in Fludd's philosophy mediates between God and the material world. Note that in the arrangement of *Ed I* the stone of judgment justly divides the poem's central paragraph–a pattern that Qvarnström shows to have a precedent in Benlowes's *Theophila*. The centralization is emphasized structurally by such features as the speeches of equal length on either side of the midpoint. Messiah's speeches at ll. 723-45 and 801-23 are both of 23 lines, 23 being a number that symbolized both divine vengeance upon sinners (on the basis of Vulg. *Num.* xxv 9) and the consummation of the salvation of man (the 3 of perfect faith in the Trinity + the 10 of the Old Covenant or Decalogue + the 10 of the New Covenant); see Bongo 441-3. For the idea that Christ's judgment is delivered from a central position in the cosmos, see Panofsky's discussion of 'the equation of the astrological notion, *medium coeli*, with the theological notion, *medium coeli et terrae*, presumed to be the seat of the Judge' (Panofsky 262); and cp. iv 30*n* and 1013-15*n*. The centricity of Christ was an idea current in seventeenth-century mystical theology. In Fludd's system, e.g., the divine Word is the centre of *mens*; see C. H. Josten, 'Robert Fludd's Theory of Geomancy', *JWI* xxvii (1964) 329.

vi *762-3*. The eagle, bird of Jupiter, and therefore a symbol of imperial majesty (Valeriano 228f), was sometimes placed at the feet of Victory, who normally had wings (Ripa 516). M. condenses these two attributes into a single image.

vi *764*. The Jehovah of the Bible has his thunder; but there is a secondary allusion to the thunderbolt of the Jupiter of the Giant War.   *three-bolted*] See l. 572*n*.

vi *765*. Cp. *Ps.* xviii 8: 'There went up a smoke out of his nostrils, and fire out of his mouth devoured: coals were kindled by it.'

vi *766*. *bickering*] darting, flashing.

vi *767*. Cp. *Rev.* v 11: 'And I beheld, and I heard the voice of many angels round about the throne and the beasts and the elders: and the number of them was ten thousand times ten thousand, and thousands of thousands.' Note that while the rebels are indeterminate 'multitudes' (l. 31), the elect are numbered in multiples of ten. See v 588, 610-12*n*, 898-903*n*; also Bongo 659f and 667, where large numbers generated by ten are treated as virtuous and unsearchable, whereas innumerable multitudes are evil and opposed to unity. For the elect angels as 'saints', see l. 398*n*.

He onward came, far off his coming shone,
And twenty thousand (I their number heard)
770   Chariots of God, half on each hand were seen:
He on the wings of cherub rode sublime
On the crystalline sky, in sapphire throned.
Illustrious far and wide, but by his own
First seen, them unexpected joy surprised,
775   When the great ensign of Messiah blazed
Aloft by angels borne, his sign in heaven:
Under whose conduct Michael soon reduced
His army, circumfused on either wing,
Under their head embodied all in one.
780   Before him power divine his way prepared;
At his command the uprooted hills retired
Each to his place, they heard his voice and went

vi *769*. Cp. *Ps*. lxviii 17: 'The chariots of God are twenty thousand, even thousands of angels: the Lord is among them, as in Sinai, in the holy place.' M.'s disposition of the chariots in two wings not only puts Messiah in the sovereign central position, but arrives at the number ten thousand, which expresses philosophically the supreme perfection of the angels (Bongo 658; cp. previous note).

vi *771*. So in *Ps*. xviii 10 'He rode upon a cherub, and did fly: yea, he did fly upon the wings of the wind' (cp. *2 Sam*. xxii 11).   *sublime*] set aloft, high up.

vi *772*. 'And above the firmament that was over their heads was the likeness of a throne, as the appearance of a sapphire stone' (*Ezek*. i 26). The *crystálline sky* or heaven was the sphere next to the firmament; see vii *271n*.

vi *773–4*. Though Messiah was clearly visible from a distance, his own army were the first to see him.

vi *776*. Alluding to the prophecy of *Matt*. xxiv 30: 'And then shall appear the sign of the Son of man in heaven: and then shall all the tribes of the earth mourn, and they shall see the Son of man coming in the clouds of heaven with power and great glory.'

vi *777*. *reduced*] led back (*OED* I 2 b); but there may also be a secondary sense, 'took back to their origin' (*OED* I 4 a, citing the *De Imitatione* iii 59, 'Grace reducith all thinges to god, of whom thei wellith oute groundely and originally').

vi *779*. For Messiah as 'the head of the body, the Church', see *Col*. i 18, and cp. v *606n*.

vi *780–4*. In a general way these lines are to be related to Isaiah's prophecy (xl 3f) of a divine advent, which is similarly expressed in terms of moralized landscape: 'Prepare ye the way of the Lord, make straight in the desert a highway for our God. Every valley shall be exalted, and every mountain and hill shall be made low: and the crooked shall be made straight, and the rough places plain.'

Obsequious, heaven his wonted face renewed,
And with fresh flowerets hill and valley smiled.
785 This saw his hapless foes but stood obdured,
And to rebellious fight rallied their powers
Insensate, hope conceiving from despair.
In heavenly spirits could such perverseness dwell?
But to convince the proud what signs avail,
790 Or wonders move the obdurate to relent?
They hardened more by what might most reclaim,
Grieving to see his glory, at the sight
Took envy, and aspiring to his highth,
Stood re-embattled fierce, by force or fraud
795 Weening to prosper, and at length prevail
Against God and Messiah, or to fall
In universal ruin last, and now
To final battle drew, disdaining flight,
Or faint retreat; when the great Son of God
800 To all his host on either hand thus spake.
    Stand still in bright array ye saints, here stand
Ye angels armed, this day from battle rest;
Faithful hath been your warfare, and of God
Accepted, fearless in his righteous cause,
805 And as ye have received, so have ye done
Invincibly; but of this cursed crew
The punishment to other hand belongs,
Vengeance is his, or whose he sole appoints;
Number to this day's work is not ordained

vi *785. obdured*] hardened. On God's hardening of the heart of sinners, see iii 197–200*n*.

vi *788*. Imitating Virgil's famous apostrophe at Juno's malevolence: *tantaene animis caelestibus irae?' (Aen.* i 11).

vi *789–91*. So Pharaoh's heart was hardened (*Exod.* xiv 4), in spite of the miraculous plagues.   *by . . . reclaim*] Theologically exact; sinners were supposed to be hardened by precisely the kind and just treatment that 'ought rather to soften the hearts of sinners' (*De doctrina* i 8; Columbia xv 81).

vi *801*. So at *Exod.* xiv 13 Moses tells the children of Israel to stand and watch the destruction of the Egyptians.

vi *808*. The belief that vengeance on sinners was a divine prerogative, not delegated lightly, expressed often in the Bible (*Deut.* xxxii 35, *Ps.* xciv 1, *Rom.* xii 19, *Heb.* x 30), was one of the finest elements in Hebrew religion.

vi *809–10*. The rebels are to be confronted, not by the numerous multitude of the faithful, but by Messiah alone (l. 820). One is not a number, because as the divine monad it is 'itself not a number, but the source and origin of numbers' (Macrobius, *In somn. Scip.* I vi 7f). See Bongo 13–61 *passim*, where the idea is developed at quite unusual length; significantly, it is

810   Nor multitude, stand only and behold
       God's indignation on these godless poured
       By me, not you but me they have despised,
       Yet envied; against me is all their rage,
       Because the Father, to whom in heaven supreme
815   Kingdom and power and glory appertains,
       Hath honoured me according to his will.
       Therefore to me their doom he hath assigned;
       That they may have their wish, to try with me
       In battle which the stronger proves, they all,
820   Or I alone against them, since by strength
       They measure all, of other excellence
       Not emulous, nor care who them excels;
       Nor other strife with them do I vouchsafe.
       So spake the Son, and into terror changed
825   His countenance too severe to be beheld
       And full of wrath bent on his enemies.
       At once the four spread out their starry wings
       With dreadful shade contiguous, and the orbs
       Of his fierce chariot rolled, as with the sound
830   Of torrent floods, or of a numerous host.
       He on his impious foes right onward drove,

applied (15) to Lucifer's illusion of autonomy. For the opposition of unity and multitude in *PL* see i 338ff, v 610–2*n*, vi 767*n*, etc. In another sense, *number . . . is not ordained* to Day 4 of the poem's action because the tetrad is a form of the *tetractys*, which is *omnium numerorum radix et exordium* (Giorgio 50ᵛ, cit. Fowler 276).

vi *815*. 'And lead us not into temptation, but deliver us from evil: For thine is the kingdom, and the power, and the glory, for ever' (*Matt.* vi 13).

vi *820–3*. This censure of the rebel angels for their narrow conception of excellence is one of the main supports for Steadman's theory that *PL* sets out a definite hierarchy of virtues. Cp. i 144, 273, ii 232, etc.; and see Steadman 93.

vi *827. four*] The 'four cherubic shapes' of l. 753. At l. 755 they had wings set with eyes, the regular iconographical attribute of cherubim, authorized by *Ezek.* x 12.   *starry wings*] These are less usual; they may be intended to emphasize the cosmic nature of Messiah's equipage (see ll. 749–59*n*).

vi *828. contiguous*] Explained by *Ezek.* i 9, where the wings of the cherubim moving the chariot are said to be 'joined one to another'.

vi *830*. 'I heard the noise of their wings, like the noise of great waters' (*Ezek.* i 24).

vi *831*. In *Ezekiel* (i 12) the steadiness of the cherubim's progress is repeatedly emphasized: 'And they went every one straight forward: whither the spirit was to go, they went; and they turned not when they went.' Cp. i 9, x 22.

Gloomy as night; under his burning wheels
The steadfast empyrean shook throughout,
All but the throne it self of God. Full soon
835   Among them he arrived; in his right hand
Grasping ten thousand thunders, which he sent
Before him, such as in their souls infixed
Plagues; they astonished all resistance lost,
All courage; down their idle weapons dropt;
840   O'er shields and helms, and helmed heads he rode
Of thrones and mighty seraphim prostrate,

vi *832. burning wheels*] Cp. the 'fervid wheels' of the chariot in which the Son
rides to the creation, at vii 218; and see l. 846n.

vi *833–4.* Conflicting with Satan's claim at i 105, to have shaken the throne
itself. The allusion is to *Is.* xiii 12f: 'I will make a man more precious than
fine gold; even a man than the golden wedge of Ophir. Therefore I will shake
the heavens, and the earth shall remove out of her place, in the wrath of the
Lord of hosts, and in the day of his fierce anger' – verses that have resonance
time and again in distant parts of the poem. See, e.g., the allusion to Solo-
mon's golden triumphal chariot (ll. 749–59n); and the sovereign position of
Ophir at xi 400.

vi *836. ten thousand*] See l. 767n.   *thunders*] see l. 764n.

vi *838. plagues*] Probably in the Latinizing sense 'blow, stroke, wound'
(*OED* 1), though the more general current meaning 'afflicting visitation
of divine anger' might be adequate. A secondary allusion to the Egyptian
plagues has been rendered obvious by such earlier allusions as l. 801.   *aston-
ished*] bewildered, stupefied.

vi *840–1.* As Verity pointed out, the imagery of these lines, like that of the
supplementary account at iii 393–6, closely resembles M.'s description in
An Apology Against a Pamphlet of the zeal that is sometimes needed to 'as-
tonish the proud resistance of carnall, and false Doctors'. Against new
heresies and old corruptions, 'Zeale whose substance is ethereal, arming in
compleat diamond ascends his fiery Chariot drawn with two blazing Mete-
ors figur'd like beasts, but of a higher breed then any the Zodiack yields,
resembling two of those four which *Ezechiel* and S. *John* saw, the one visag'd
like a Lion to expresse power, high autority and indignation, the other
of count'nance like a man to cast derision and scorne upon perverse and
fraudulent seducers; with these the invincible warriour Zeale shaking loosely
the slack reins drives over the heads of Scarlet Prelats, and such as are insolent
to maintaine traditions, brusing their stiffe necks under his flaming wheels.
Thus did the true Prophets of old combat with the false; thus Christ himselfe
the fountaine of meeknesse found acrimony anough to be still galling and
vexing the Prelaticall Pharisees' (Yale i 900f).   *prostrate*] Stressed on the
second syllable.

That wished the mountains now might be again
Thrown on them as a shelter from his ire.
Nor less on either side tempestuous fell
845 His arrows, from the fourfold-visaged four,
Distinct with eyes, and from the living wheels
Distinct alike with multitude of eyes,
One spirit in them ruled, and every eye
Glared lightning, and shot forth pernicious fire
850 Among the accursed, that withered all their strength,
And of their wonted vigour left them drained,
Exhausted, spiritless, afflicted, fallen.
Yet half his strength he put not forth, but checked
His thunder in mid volley, for he meant
855 Not to destroy, but root them out of heaven:
The overthrown he raised, and as a herd
Of goats or timorous flock together thronged

vi *842*. What before had caused them 'many a dolorous groan' (l. 658) now seems preferable to the wrath of Messiah. Cp. *Rev*. vi 16, where the damned at the Last Judgment cry 'to the mountains and rocks, Fall on us, and hide us from the face of him that sitteth on the throne, and from the wrath of the Lamb'.

vi *845*. Cp. Ezekiel's vision of the wheels (x 14): 'every one had four faces: the first face was the face of a cherub, and the second face was the face of a man, and the third the face of a lion, and the fourth the face of an eagle.'

vi *846*. In Ezekiel's vision the wheels set with eyes (x 12) are living creatures, though not necessarily members of an order of angels. In cabbalistic literature, however, wheels constituted the second of the angelic orders. West (157f) finds significance in M.'s regular association of wheels with cherubim, the second order of the Dionysian hierarchies (see vii 218 and 224 below), especially in view of the fact that Agrippa actually identified cherubim and wheels. But the association in *PL* is perhaps accounted for by the assignment of wheels to cherubim in *Ezek*. x 9. Nor should one forget the quite unesoteric iconographical tradition in which wheels were the attributes of the order of thrones (see Didron ii 92, 98, 103).   *Distinct*] adorned (poetic).

vi *847*. A heavier point is required after *eyes*.

vi *849*. *pernicious*] destructive, fatal; but perhaps also 'swift'–in *Ezek*. i 13 the living creatures shoot forth lightning.

vi *856–7*. Earlier editors should not be ridiculed for trying to justify the baseness of the simile with Homeric precedent: M. might at least have agreed that it lowers the rebels drastically.   *goats*] Alludes to the parable of the sheep and the goats in *Matt*. xv, especially 33 and 41. At the Last Judgment the goats are to be banished 'into everlasting fire, prepared for the devil and his angels'.

Drove them before him thunderstruck, pursued
With terrors and with furies to the bounds
860   And crystal wall of heaven, which opening wide,
Rolled inward, and a spacious gap disclosed
Into the wasteful deep; the monstrous sight
Strook them with horror backward, but far worse
Urged them behind; headlong themselves they threw
865   Down from the verge of heaven, eternal wrath
Burnt after them to the bottomless pit.
      Hell heard the unsufferable noise, hell saw
Heaven ruining from heaven and would have fled
Affrighted; but strict fate had cast too deep
870   Her dark foundations, and too fast had bound.
Nine days they fell; confounded Chaos roared,
And felt tenfold confusion in their fall
Through his wild anarchy, so huge a rout
Encumbered him with ruin: hell at last
875   Yawning received them whole, and on them closed,

vi *858. thunderstruck*] Used both literally and figuratively. It may also be relevant that the word was specifically applied to ecclesiastical censure (*OED* 2 b; cp., e.g., Henry More, *Apocalypsis apocalypseos* (1680) 132: 'Gregory the seventh, when he had excommunicated the Emperor Henry the fourth, said, he was *fulmine afflatus* thunder-struck by him'); particularly in view of ll. 840–1n.

vi *859.* Combining *Job* vi 4 ('the terrors of God do set themselves in array against me') with *Is.* li 20 ('thy sons have fainted . . . they are full of the fury of the Lord, the rebuke of thy God').   *furies*] Has also, however, a classical overtone, suggesting the avenging deities sent from Tartarus to punish wrong.

vi *861. rolled*] turned on its axis. Cp. the automated gate of heaven, v 254–6 and *n.*

vi *862. wasteful*] desolate, uninhabited, void.

vi *866.* Continuity is here established with the events of the flashback of i 44–9, which are there said to have come to their conclusion nine days before the first-order time of Bk i. See Introduction, 'Chronology'.

vi *868. ruining*] falling headlong.

vi *871.* An important line for the poem's chronology; see Introduction. On the meaning of this time interval, see i 50–83n.

vi *873. rout*] disreputable crowd; or defeat.

vi *874. Encumbered*] burdened; blocked up; involved; harassed.   *ruin*] fall, destruction; or failure. Cp. ii 995f where Chaos tells Satan how at the fall of the angels he heard 'ruin upon ruin, rout on rout, / Confusion worse confounded'.

vi *875.* 'Therefore hell hath enlarged herself, and opened her mouth without

Hell their fit habitation fraught with fire
Unquenchable, the house of woe and pain.
Disburdened heaven rejoiced, and soon repaired
Her mural breach, returning whence it rolled.
880 Sole victor from the expulsion of his foes
Messiah his triumphal chariot turned:
To meet him all his saints, who silent stood
Eye witnesses of his almighty acts,
With jubilee advanced; and as they went,
885 Shaded with branching palm, each order bright,
Sung triumph, and him sung victorious king,
Son, heir, and Lord, to him dominion given,
Worthiest to reign: he celebrated rode
Triumphant through mid heaven, into the courts
890 And temple of his mighty Father throned
On high: who into glory him received,
Where now he sits at the right hand of bliss.
  Thus measuring things in heaven by things on earth
At thy request, and that thou mayst beware
895 By what is past, to thee I have revealed
What might have else to human race been hid;

measure: and their glory, and their multitude, and their pomp, and he that rejoiceth, shall descend into it.' (*Is.* v 14).

vi *876–7.* 'It is better for thee to enter into life maimed, than having two hands to go into hell, into the fire that never shall be quenched (*Mark* ix 43).

vi *877. house . . . pain*] For the diction, see ii 823n.

vi *880–3.* See i 169–71n and ii 993–7n for Satan's and Chaos' versions of the expulsion. Only now does the extent of Messiah's triumph emerge.

vi *882–92.* The whole scene is apocalyptic in conception and even in imagery. Thus the *palm* (emblematic of victory) resembles that carried by the servants of God in *Rev.* vii 9 and the triumph song is like the one in *Rev.* v 12, while the reception into glory at *the right hand of bliss* recalls the Ascension after the Atonement (*Heb.* i 3). In other words, at the mid-point of *PL* M. not only loops back to the first point of the action, but also forwards to subsequent stages of the redemptive history (see MacCaffrey 57, where a similar point is made).   *Sung triumph*] at a Roman triumph, the soldiers returning with the victorious general shouted '*Io triumphe*' as they entered the Capitol. The Renaissance tradition of festival triumphs was of course based on Roman precedent; see C. Lorgues-Lapouge in *L'Oeil* xxxv (1957) 27–35, also ll. 749–59n.

vi *884–8.* In *Rev.* xii 9f, immediately after the 'old serpent' Satan is cast out from heaven a loud voice is heard celebrating Christ's victory.   *jubilee*] joyful shouting, sound of jubilation.

The discord which befell, and war in heaven
Among the angelic powers, and the deep fall
Of those too high aspiring, who rebelled
900   With Satan, he who envies now thy state,
Who now is plotting how he may seduce
Thee also from obedience, that with him
Bereaved of happiness thou mayst partake
His punishment, eternal misery;
905   Which would be all his solace and revenge,
As a despite done against the most high,
Thee once to gain companion of his woe.
But listen not to his temptations, warn
Thy weaker; let it profit thee to have heard
910   By terrible example the reward
Of disobedience; firm they might have stood,
Yet fell; remember, and fear to transgress.

THE END OF THE SIXTH BOOK

Paradise Lost

BOOK VII

The Argument

Raphael at the request of Adam relates how and wherefore this world was
first created; that God, after the expelling of Satan and his angels out of

vi 900–7. Raphael is evidently a good enough judge of Satan's character to
recognize at least two of the passions, envy and despite, that we know–on
M.'s authority–to actuate him; see iv 115 and ix 126–8. The Lat. proverb
Solamen miseris socios habuisse doloris had been the devils' motive for cor-
rupting man in Marlowe, Faustus 480. These lines contain the warning re-
ferred to in v Argument, which according to many critics Raphael never
delivered. Empson 151 complains that the terms of the warning are insuf-
ficiently specific. But perhaps we should rather admire the delicacy with
which Raphael refrains from usurping Adam's prerogatives in any way.
A hint should be enough: to give detailed information or instructions would
mean limiting Adam's independent role.
vi 909. weaker] supply 'vessel'. The allusion is to 1 Pet. iii 7: 'Likewise, ye
husbands, dwell with them according to knowledge, giving honour
unto the wife, as unto the weaker vessel, and as being heirs together of the

heaven, declared his pleasure to create another world and other creatures to
dwell therein; sends his son with glory and attendance of angels to perform
the work of creation in six days: the angels celebrate with hymns the perfor-
mance thereof, and his re-ascension into heaven.

> Descend from heaven Urania, by that name
> If rightly thou art called, whose voice divine
> Following, above the Olympian hill I soar,
> Above the flight of Pegasean wing.
> 5   The meaning, not the name I call: for thou
> Nor of the Muses nine, nor on the top
> Of old Olympus dwell'st, but heavenly born,

grace of life; that your prayers be not hindered.' Ironically, the verse occurs
in a homily on duties of wives and husbands, which, if they were performed,
would unquestionably counteract any tendency to uxoriousness.

vii *1–50*. The third of the four invocations in *PL*, the others being i 1–49,
iii 1–55, and ix 1–47. For their rhetoric, see Condee; for their structural
disposition, ix 1–47*n*.

vii *1–7*. Only in this invocation is M.'s Muse ever named; the departure
here being apparently for the sake of a decorum. For *Urania* (Celestial) was
anciently the Muse of Astronomy, and as such she has an obvious right to
preside over the part of the poem primarily concerned with the macro-
cosm, Bks vii–viii (*Ed II*; *Ed I* Bk vii). M.'s denial that his Urania is one *of
the Muses nine*, however, directs attention to a more recent, single Muse.
Since Du Bartas's *L'Uranie*, the name had been used for the specifically
Christian Muse of the divine poetry movement; see L. B. Campbell, 'The
Christian Muse', *HLB* viii (1935), and cp. Drummond's *Urania, or Spiritual
Poems*. M.'s hesitation about using the name is unusual, and conveys the
seriousness of his determination to transcend pagan forms of thought. The
classical Muse was only *named* Urania; but M. wants to call upon a truly
celestial being. Cp. Tasso's invocation, *Gerus. Lib.* i 2: 'O heavenly Muse,
that not with fading bays / Deckest thy brow by the Heliconian spring, /
But sittest crowned with stars' immortal rays / In Heaven, where legions of
bright angels sing' (tr. Fairfax).   *Descend*] Because from this point on-
ward the course of the poem is steadily downwards; see ll. 12–25*n*.   *the
Olympian hill*] Mt Olympus, a resort of the classical Muses, like Helicon, the
'Aonian mount' of i 15; M. has therefore to diminish it by calling it a mere
hill. (The distinction between hill and mountain, though comparatively
recent, was quite clear in M.'s time.)

vii *1*. Some copies *Ed I* omit comma after *Urania*.

vii *3*. Some copies *Ed I* omit comma after *Following*.

vii *4*. The winged horse Pegasus was regularly an emblem for the inspired
poet. Consult R. J. Clements, '*Picta Poesis*,' Temi e testi vi (Rome 1960)
51f, 55f, 229f; and for a typical example see Lebey-Batilly, *Emblemata*
(Frankfurt 1596), Emblem 49. After striking the Muses' spring from Heli-
con, Pegasus flew up to the heavens; hence he could symbolize the poet

Before the hills appeared, or fountain flowed,
Thou with eternal Wisdom didst converse,
10   Wisdom thy sister, and with her didst play
In presence of the almighty Father, pleased
With thy celestial song. Up led by thee
Into the heaven of heavens I have presumed,
An earthly guest, and drawn empyreal air,

soaring above ordinary sources of inspiration. To aspire to top Pegasus is
thus a sublime piece of overgoing. More usually, Pegasus was itself the
Christian aspiration; cp. *Mirror for Magistrates*, 'Tragedy of the Poet Colling-
bourn', 176–8: 'Like Pegasus a Poet must have wynges, / To flye to heaven,
thereto to feede and rest: / He must have knoweledge of eternal thynges.'
vii *8–12*. In the tremendous eighth chapter of *Proverbs*, Wisdom the daughter
of God is said to have been brought forth 'when there were no fountains . . .
Before the mountains were settled': 'Then I was by him, as one brought up
with him: and I was daily his delight, rejoicing (Vulgate *ludens*) always
before him' (*Prov*. viii 24–5, 30). The Wisdom of *Proverbs* claims to have
been present when the Lord 'prepared the heavens . . . when he set a com-
pass upon the face of the depth' (viii 27); and in *Wisdom of Solomon* vii–viii
a Wisdom 'conversant with God', and privy to all the mysteries of natural
philosophy, is conceived almost as a Muse–'in all ages entering into holy
souls, she maketh them . . . prophets' (vii 27). The idea of Wisdom as a
divine consort proved amenable to Platonic development and was popular
in the Renaissance. But we should note that Wisdom is not M.'s Muse but the
sister of his Muse. Fletcher[2] 112 draws an explanation from a rabbinical
source, Ben Gerson, according to whom two spirits, Wisdom and Under-
standing, accompanied God at the creation. His theory, that M.'s Muse is an
aspect of the Holy Spirit, is convincingly demolished by Kelley (115–18),
who in turn proposes a theory almost equally untenable–that M. invokes
some unspecified attribute of God the Father. It seems far more likely that
M.'s Muse is the Logos, the agency of creation and the Son of God. For we
know that M. rejected the usual identification of the Wisdom of *Prov*. viii
with Christ (see *De doctrina* i 7, Columbia xv 13) and that he believed both
Wisdom and Christ to have been present at the Creation with their Father.
A similar conclusion is arrived at in Robins 157–75.
vii *11*. Some copies *Ed I* omit comma after *Father*.
vii *12–25*. Matching the ascending movement in the invocation of iii 13–22,
we have here a descent; the central eminence of Messiah's triumph is past.
For the downward course of the last part of the poem, see MacCaffrey 58f.
vii *14–15*. The air of the 'first region' (iii 562–4) was normally fatal to
mortals: see Svendsen 88 and *n*. It was well known in M.'s time that at high
altitudes men could suffer from the thinness of the air. Cp. xii 76–8, where
Adam expects the presumptuous builders of the Tower of Babel to be

15 Thy tempering; with like safety guided down
      Return me to my native element:
      Lest from this flying steed unreined, (as once
      Bellerophon, though from a lower clime)
      Dismounted, on the Aleian field I fall
20 Erroneous there to wander and forlorn.
      Half yet remains unsung, but narrower bound
      Within the visible diurnal sphere;
      Standing on earth, not rapt above the pole,
      More safe I sing with mortal voice, unchanged
25 To hoarse or mute, though fallen on evil days,
      On evil days though fallen, and evil tongues;
      In darkness, and with dangers compassed round,

famished of breath.   *Thy tempering*] air tempered by you; but also im-
plying that the Muse had been tempering, attuning, raising the poet himself
to a high pitch.

vii *16. native element*] earth.

vii *17–20*. When Bellerophon tried to fly to heaven upon Pegasus, Jupiter
sent an insect to sting the horse and throw the rider. According to Conti,
Bellerophon fell on the Aleian plain, the 'field of error', and wandered blind
and lonely till his death (*Mythologiae* ix 4, p. 953; following a tradition
traceable only in part to Calepinus' and Stephanus' Dictionaries: see Starnes
240f). Among many interpretations of the myth listed by Conti, the most
relevant is a euhemeristic one–that Bellerophon was an astronomer, who
ascended into the heavens in the sense that he explored the stars.   *clime*]
region: note the pun.   *erroneous*] Both 'wandering' and 'straying from
the ways of wisdom'. In the former sense, probably rare enough to be felt
as a Latinism.

vii *19*. Some copies *Ed I* omit comma after *Dismounted*.

vii *20*. *Ed I* wrongly has comma after *Erroneous*.

vii *21*. *Half . . . unsung*] A clear indication that M. means us to see the poem's
invocations as disposed structurally according to a two–part division.
See ix 1–47n. But Richardson and Newton were perhaps also right in taking
the line to refer to the bisection of Raphael's episode.

vii *22*. That is, within the astronomical universe, which appears to revolve
around the earth with a *diurnal* motion or period of about a day.

vii *23*. *rapt*] entranced, enraptured.   *pole*] Either the celestial pole or
(more probably) synecdoche for the sky.

vii *25–8*. The obfuscated syntax conceals a topical allusion to M.'s dangerous
situation during the persecutions that immediately followed the Restor-
ation. See John Toland's early biography (reprinted in Darbishire 175–7)
for M.'s leaving his house near St James's Park and going into temporary
retirement.

vii *25*. *days*] Some copies *Ed I* have 'tongues'.

vii *27*. *In darkness*] Refers to M.'s blindness; cp. iii 45.

And solitude; yet not alone, while thou
Visit'st my slumbers nightly, or when morn
30   Purples the east: still govern thou my song,
Urania, and fit audience find, though few.
But drive far off the barbarous dissonance
Of Bacchus and his revellers, the race
Of that wild rout that tore the Thracian bard
35   In Rhodope, where woods and rocks had ears
To rapture, till the savage clamour drowned
Both harp and voice; nor could the Muse defend
Her son. So fail not thou, who thee implores:
For thou art heavenly, she an empty dream.
40   Say goddess, what ensued when Raphael,

vii *29. nightly*] So iii 31f and ix 21–4. See Jonathan Richardon's *Life*, re-
printed Darbishire 291: 'that he frequently Compos'd lying in Bed in a
Morning . . . I have been Well inform'd, that when he could not Sleep, but
lay Awake whole Nights, he Try'd; not One Verse could he make; at Other
times flow'd *Easy his Unpremeditated Verse*, with a certain *Impetus* and
Aestro, as Himself seem'd to Believe. Then, at what Hour soever, he rung
for his Daughter to Secure what Came.' For the diction cp. *Ps.* xvii 3: 'Thou
hast proved mine heart; thou hast visited me in the night.'
vii *31.* Not necessarily implying an esoteric intention. Any serious writer
might similarly have adapted Horace's advice (*Sat.* I x 73f): *neque te ut
miretur turba labores, / contentus paucis lectoribus*, which in context was an
encouragement to write bluntly and with integrity. In *Eikonoklastes*, Pref.,
Yale iii 339f, M. speaks of 'readers; few perhaps, but those few, such of
value and substantial worth, as truth and wisdom, not respecting numbers
and bigg names, have bin ever wont in all ages to be contented with.'
Some copies *Ed I* have colon after *few*.
vii *32–8.* Orpheus was generally a type of the inspired poet; but also par-
ticularly appropriate to the present context because of his life of isolation.
The myth of his dismemberment by Thracian women during orgies of
Bacchus seems to have focused some of M.'s deepest fears: cp. the even
more intense application in *Lycidas* 58–63.   *Rhodope*] A mountain range
in Thrace.   *woods and rocks*] Because in Ovid's account of the myth these
were enthralled by the *Threicius vates* and mourned his loss–though they
also provided the instruments for his murder (*Met.* xi 1–60).   *drowned*]
The word has a secondary overtone, since Orpheus' head was thrown into
the Hebrus river.   *harp*] The lyre given to Orpheus by Apollo or Mer-
cury.
vii *36.* Some copies of *Ed I* omit comma after *rapture*.
vii *39.* Some copies *Ed I* omit comma after *heavenly*.   *she*] The heroic
Muse Calliope, Orpheus' mother.
vii *40.* Some copies *Ed I* omit comma after *goddess*.

The affable archangel, had forewarned
Adam by dire example to beware
Apostasy, by what befell in heaven
To those apostates, lest the like befall
45 In Paradise to Adam or his race,
Charged not to touch the interdicted tree,
If they transgress, and slight that sole command,
So easily obeyed amid the choice
Of all tastes else to please their appetite,
50 Though wandering. He with his consorted Eve
The story heard attentive, and was filled
With admiration, and deep muse to hear
Of things so high and strange, things to their thought
So unimaginable as hate in heaven,
55 And war so near the peace of God in bliss
With such confusion: but the evil soon
Driven back redounded as a flood on those
From whom it sprung, impossible to mix
With blessedness. Whence Adam soon repealed
60 The doubts that in his heart arose: and now
Led on, yet sinless, with desire to know
What nearer might concern him, how this world
Of heaven and earth conspicuous first began,
When, and whereof created, for what cause,
65 What within Eden or without was done

vii *41*. A variant of the formula is 'sociable spirit' (v 221). Adam thanks Raphael for his affability at viii 648–50. Some copies *Ed I* omit comma after *archangel.*

vii *47*. *that sole command*] i.e. 'not to taste that only tree / Of knowledge'; see iv 421–4*n.*

vii *50*. *consorted*] associated, espoused, united as consorts.

vii *52*. *admiration*] amazement. Some copies *Ed I* omit the comma immediately following.

vii *56*. Some copies *Ed I* have comma after *confusion.*

vii *57–9*. Cp. Belial on 'the ethereal mould / Incapable of stain' (ii 138–41). *redounded*] flowed back.

vii *59*. *repealed*] abandoned (*OED* 2); cp. Henry More, *Psychathanasia* (1647), II ii 23: 'Therefore repeal / This grosse conceit, and hold as reason doth reveal.'

vii *61*. In view of the common opinion that the M. was antiscientific, it is worth noting that he here explicitly judges Adam's cosmological enquiry to be blameless.

vii *63*. *conspicuous*] visible; implying the distinction between the astronomical 'visible diurnal sphere' (l. 22) and the empyreal 'heaven of heavens' (l. 13).

Before his memory, as one whose drouth
Yet scarce allayed still eyes the current stream,
Whose liquid murmur heard new thirst excites,
Proceeded thus to ask his heavenly guest.
70   Great things, and full of wonder in our ears,
Far differing from this world, thou hast revealed
Divine interpreter, by favour sent
Down from the empyrean to forewarn
Us timely of what might else have been our loss,
75   Unknown, which human knowledge could not reach:
For which to the infinitely good we owe
Immortal thanks, and his admonishment
Receive with solemn purpose to observe
Immutably his sovereign will, the end
80   Of what we are. But since thou hast vouchsafed
Gently for our instruction to impart
Things above earthly thought, which yet concerned
Our knowing, as to highest wisdom seemed,
Deign to descend now lower, and relate
85   What may no less perhaps avail us known,
How first began this heaven which we behold
Distant so high, with moving fires adorned
Innumerable, and this which yields or fills
All space, the ambient air wide interfused

vii *66–9*. So Dante thirsts for further information from Virgil at *Purg.* xviii 4.
The conception of the epistemological desire as thirst for a *fons sapientiae*
goes back at least to patristic commentaries on *Ps.* xlii 1f ('As the hart pan-
teth after the water brooks ... My soul thirsteth for God').   *drouth*]
thirst.   *current*] flowing.

vii *72*. Cp. Virgil, *Aen.* iv 378, where Mercury is *interpres divum*, coming
from Jupiter with a dread command. In the Jewish Cabala Mercury was
often identified with Raphael; see Cirlot 271.

vii *79*. See *Eccles.* xii 13: 'Fear God, and keep his commandments: for this
is the whole duty of man.' But many of M.'s readers would appreciate the
irony that in Calvin's Catechism the first question and answer were: 'What
is the principal and Chiefe Ende of Man's Life?–To know God' (see Fletcher
ii 95).

vii *83. seemed*] seemed good (*OED* II 7 e)–a usage rare enough for us to
notice secondary chains of discourse, e.g. 'as to highest seemed wise'. Note
also seemed = 'was suitable' (*OED* I 1 b). Some copies *Ed I* omit comma after
knowing.

vii *88–9*. Cp. ii 842, 'buxom air'. The air *yields* to solid bodies or *fills* the
space they leave vacant.

90   Embracing round this florid earth, what cause
      Moved the creator in his holy rest
      Through all eternity so late to build
      In chaos, and the work begun, how soon
      Absolved, if unforbid thou mayst unfold
95   What we, not to explore the secrets ask
      Of his eternal empire, but the more
      To magnify his works, the more we know.
      And the great light of day yet wants to run
      Much of his race though steep, suspense in heaven
100 Held by thy voice, thy potent voice he hears,

vii *90–2*. It is curious that M. should put Adam's question so absurdly – as if he were to ask, like a child, what moved the prime mover. In *De Doctrina* i 7 (Columbia xv 3) M. calls it 'the height of folly' to enquire into 'the actions of God before the foundation of the world'. He rejects even the usual assumption that God 'was occupied with election and reprobation, and with decreeing other things relative to these subjects'. For 'it is not imaginable that God should have been wholly occupied from eternity in decreeing that which was to be created in a period of six days'. The Occasional Cause commonly assigned for creation – the dispeopling of heaven – is explicitly rejected at ll. 145–9.   *florid*] flowery; or perhaps in a broader sense, 'resplendent'.

vii *93–4*. Note the interest in the exact duration of the work.   *Absolved*] accomplished, finished; not a Latinism.

vii *93*. Some copies *Ed I* omit comma after *begun*.

vii *97*. Job. xxxvi 24: 'Remember that thou magnify his work.' Adam knows that he may be asking for the forbidden knowledge, so that he has to tread circumspectly, making clear his motive. On the other hand, M. minimises the limitation on knowledge to which *Genesis* commits him, by showing that the permissible ration is far from meagre (Burden 114f). Some copies *Ed I* omit comma after *works*.

vii *98–100*. The appeal to continue a narration was an epic commonplace, going back to Homer, *Od.* xi 372–6. Since the sun's course is *steep* it must be near the end of its race; but Adam is no doubt mindful of the apparent deceleration produced by atmospheric refraction (see iv 541*n*). In a secondary chain of discourse the same phenomenon becomes by a pathetic fallacy the sun's reluctance to end Raphael's narration.   *suspense*] certainly both 'attentive' (*OED* 1) and 'hanging' (*OED* 4); perhaps also 'undecided (whether to set)' (*OED* 2). Underlying these meanings is a philosophical allusion to the anakuklesis or change in the course of the sun that was anciently supposed to accompany entry into a new World Cycle (here a cycle of decay); see Plato, *Politicus* 268E, *Rep.* ed. Adams ii 298, and, for Spenser's similar use of *Josh.* x 12–14, Fowler 42. M. had explicitly mentioned the transition to a new Cycle at v 583 above. Cp. also x 687ff below, where the sun turns aside in disgust at man's sin.

And longer will delay to hear thee tell
His generation, and the rising birth
Of nature from the unapparent deep:
Or if the star of evening and the moon
105 Haste to thy audience, night with her will bring
Silence, and sleep listening to thee will watch,
Or we can bid his absence, till thy song
End, and dismiss thee ere the morning shine.
     Thus Adam his illustrious guest besought:
110 And thus the godlike angel answered mild.
This also thy request with caution asked
Obtain: though to recount almighty works
What words or tongue of seraph can suffice,
Or heart of man suffice to comprehend?
115 Yet what thou canst attain, which best may serve
To glorify the maker, and infer
Thee also happier, shall not be withheld
Thy hearing, such commission from above
I have received, to answer thy desire
120 Of knowledge within bounds; beyond abstain

vii *103*. The deep was *unapparent* (invisible, secret) before creation not only because it was dark, but also because chaos was without form.

vii *105*. *audience*] assembly of listeners. But Adam is also courteously acknowledging Raphael's position, since the formal interviews held by an ambassador were *audiences* in another sense.

vii *106*. *watch*] remain awake.

vii *108*. Adam's majesty is carried so modestly that he avoids saying outright that he will dismiss Raphael. Just as the antecedent of *we* could be Adam *and* Eve, so *dismiss* could = 'release', with *song* as subject.

vii *112–14*. *words or tongue*] Bentley wanted this to read 'words from tongue', but as Empson[2] 161 points out this would lose 'the completeness of the statement; "How can any stage in the production of the speech of seraphs be adequate; how can they find words, and if they could how could their tongues pronounce them?" But besides this, the merit of *or* is its fluidity; the way it allows "words from tongue" to be suggested without pausing for analysis, without holding up the single movement of the line.' Cp. *1 Cor.* ii 9: 'Eye hath not seen, nor ear heard, neither have entered into the heart of man, the things which God hath prepared for them that love him.'

vii *113*. In Isaiah's vision of the Lord's glory it was a seraph who purified his mouth with fire (*Is.* vi 6).

vii *116*. *infer*] render, induce, procure (*OED* 1).   *the*] thy *Ed I*, some copies.

To ask, nor let thine own inventions hope
Things not revealed, which the invisible king,
Only omniscient, hath suppressed in night,
To none communicable in earth or heaven:
125   Enough is left besides to search and know.
But knowledge is as food, and needs no less
Her temperance over appetite, to know
In measure what the mind may well contain,
Oppresses else with surfeit, and soon turns
130   Wisdom to folly, as nourishment to wind.
   Know then, that after Lucifer from heaven
(So call him, brighter once amidst the host
Of angels, than that star the stars among)
Fell with his flaming legions through the deep
135   Into his place, and the great Son returned
Victorious with his saints, the omnipotent
Eternal Father from his throne beheld
Their multitude, and to his Son thus spake.
   At least our envious foe hath failed, who thought

vii *121. inventions*] reasonings; cp. *Eccles.* vii 29: 'God hath made man up-right; but they have sought out many inventions.' An allusion to scientific inventions (discoveries) is possible; cp. in this connection viii 76.   *hope*] hope for.

vii *122–3.* Cp. *1 Tim.* i 17, 'the King eternal, immortal, invisible, the only wise God'; also Horace, *Odes* III xxix 29–32: *prudens futuri temporis exitum / caliginosa nocte premit deus, / ridetque si mortalis ultra / fas trepidat.*

vii *124. none*] Cp. *Matt.* xxiv 36: 'But of that day and hour knoweth no man, no, not the angels of heaven, but my Father only.' For the bounds set to man's knowledge of the astronomical universe, see viii 70ff below.

vii *126–30.* The metaphor implicit in earlier uses of savoury (see, e.g., v 84–5*n*) is now made an explicit simile. Cp. Davenant, *Gondibert* (1651) II viii 22: 'For though Books serve as Diet of the Minde; / If knowledg, early got, self vallew breeds, / By false digestion it is turn'd to winde; / And what should nourish, on the Eater feeds.'

vii *126. as*] a *Ed I*, some copies.

vii *132.* Cp. v 658f, and see i 82*n* and 361–3 on Satan's loss of his original name. In ancient times Lucifer was a name for the planet Venus when it appeared as a morning star. The symbolic possibilities of the connection between Satan and the morning star were well worked at the outset of Raphael's narration: see v 700–14*n*.

vii *135. his place*] Biblical diction; cp. *Acts* i 25: 'This ministry and apostleship, from which Judas by transgression fell, that he might go to his own place.'

vii *136. saints*] angels; cp. vi 398*n*, 767.

vii *139. least*] Perhaps to be amended to 'last', though the case for this is not so clear-cut as Adams 94 suggests.

140   All like himself rebellious, by whose aid
      This inaccessible high strength, the seat
      Of deity supreme, us dispossessed,
      He trusted to have seized, and into fraud
      Drew many, whom their place knows here no more;
145   Yet far the greater part have kept, I see,
      Their station, heaven yet populous retains
      Number sufficient to possess her realms
      Though wide, and this high temple to frequent
      With ministeries due and solemn rites:
150   But lest his heart exalt him in the harm
      Already done, to have dispeopled heaven
      My damage fondly deemed, I can repair
      That detriment, if such it be to lose

vii *141.* For the inaccessible highest heaven, see v 643*n*.

vii *142. us dispossessed*] The absolute construction when not in the nominative case would perhaps be felt as a Latinism; though there were many precedents in Middle English usage. Cp., e.g., Wyclif's *Matt.* xxviii 13, 'they han stolen him us slepinge'.

vii *143. fraud*] faithlessness.

vii *144.* 'He that goeth down to the grave shall come up no more. He shall return no more to his house, neither shall his place know him any more' (*Job* vii 9f). Some copies *Ed I* omit comma after *many*.

vii *145. greater part*] On different estimates of the proportion of loyal to disloyal angels see ii 692*n*.

vii *145–56.* See ll. 90–2*n*. The repeopling of heaven is a 'convenient' feature of the creation of man, but M. goes out of his way to insist that that does not make creation 'necessary'. God's works are all 'executed freely according to his own good pleasure' (*De doctrina* i 5; Columbia xiv 187). Thus it would be wrong to speak of *repair* of *detriment*. Note that Raphael does not make God say 'I will create *so that* Satan's heart may not exalt him'; thus Empson (56, 87) is wrong to interpret the passage as meaning that God creates us 'to spite the devils'. Raphael nowhere advances any theory about the cause of man's creation. Being an angel, however, he would no doubt be interested in the idea, afterwards patristic, that men supply the places of the fallen angels. See St Augustine, *Civ. Dei* xxii 1: 'Gathering so many unto this grace as should supply the places of the fallen angels, and so preserve (and perhaps augment) the number of the heavenly inhabitants.' For Augustine this is an instance of God's ability to turn apparent evil into eventual good. Dr Johnson and A. H. Gilbert (132–4) see a discrepancy between the present passage and others that speak of a rumour of man's creation having been 'rife' before the fall of the angels (e.g. ii 345–53). But this can be explained as an attempt to render God's foreknowledge and providence. See ix 136–8*n*.

vii *151.* Some copies *Ed I* omit comma after *done*.

> Self-lost, and in a moment will create
> 155   Another world, out of one man a race
> Of men innumerable, there to dwell,
> Not here, till by degrees of merit raised
> They open to themselves at length the way
> Up hither, under long obedience tried,
> 160   And earth be changed to heaven, and heaven to
>   earth,
> One kingdom, joy and union without end.
> Mean while inhabit lax, ye powers of heaven,
> And thou my Word, begotten Son, by thee
> This I perform, speak thou, and be it done:
> 165   My overshadowing spirit and might with thee
> I send along, ride forth, and bid the deep
> Within appointed bounds be heaven and earth,
> Boundless the deep, because I am who fill

vii *154. Self-lost*] Cp. St Augustine, *Civ. Dei* xxii 1: 'Nor had there been any evil at all, but that those spirits . . . procured such evil unto themselves by sin.'   *moment*] The theory that creation was instantaneous, and that all living creatures not immediately developed were nevertheless present from the first as *rationes seminales*, was Augustinian. See the *De Genesi* i 1–3, and consult the useful account in Ellrodt 77ff. Here 155f looks almost like a rationalisation of Augustine's doctrine in protogenetic terms.

vii *156–60.* See v 496–500*n*. Some copies *Ed I* omit comma after *innumerable*.

vii *161. without*] For accentuation on the first syllable indicating emphasis, see B. A. Wright in *N & Q* cciii (1958) 202f.

vii *162. inhabit lax*] spread out; live spaciously; annex the principalities of the rebel third. The phrase imitates Cicero, *De domo sua* xliv 115: *habitare laxe et magnifice voluit.*

vii *162.* Some copies of *Ed I* have semicolon after *heaven*.

vii *163–4.* M.'s Arianism did not lead him to question Christ's role as the Neoplatonic Logos (Word), the agency of creation, nor his special generation before the rest of creation. See iii 170*n*, v 601*n*; *John* i 1–3; and *De doctrina* i 7, Columbia xv 5: 'Creation is that act whereby God the Father produced every thing that exists by his Word and Spirit.' In the same ch. M. argues at some length that Christ was the instrumental, though not the principal, cause of creation (*ibid.* xv 6–10).

vii *165–6. spirit*] M. would privately mean God's 'will' or his 'divine power, rather than any person' of the Trinity (*De doctrina* i 7, Columbia xv 5, 13). *overshadowing*] The angel Gabriel said to Mary 'the power of the Highest shall overshadow thee' (*Luke* i 35). Cp. also *Gen.* i 2: 'And the Spirit of God moved upon the face of the waters.'

vii *168.* Set in a metrically prominent place, *fill* 'aligns the plenitude of God against the emptiness of opposing forces' (MacCaffrey 105, contrasting ii 932).

Infinitude, nor vacuous the space.
170   Though I uncircumscribed my self retire,
And put not forth my goodness, which is free
To act or not, necessity and chance
Approach not me, and what I will is fate.
    So spake the almighty, and to what he spake
175   His Word, the filial Godhead, gave effect.
Immediate are the acts of God, more swift
Than time or motion, but to human ears
Cannot without process of speech be told,
So told as earthly notion can receive.
180   Great triumph and rejoicing was in heaven
When such was heard declared the almighty's will;

vii *168–73*. The basis for Saurat's hypothesis that M. held a 'retraction theo-
ry' of creation, and believed God to have produced the universe by a simple
act of withdrawal. Saurat's theory is dismantled by R. J. Z. Werblowski in
JWI xviii (1955) 90–113 and in Kelley 209–11. The *De Doctrina* has nothing
about creation by retraction, while the present passage seems to imply a
theory almost diametrically opposed. It says that space is not void; and that
it is infinite because God, who fills it, is. It also asserts that the chaotic
character of the deep (where Chance governs; see ii 909f) does not show God
being circumscribed by randomness–only choosing not to extend his
creative form-giving goodness. According to Fletcher ii 173 all the ideas in
the passage could have been derived from Magirus' standard school textbook
of natural philosophy. See also Howard 169f, Robins 47f. In 'Milton and
the Creation,' *JEGP* lxi (1962), J. H. Adamson suggests that the corollary
of an *ex Deo* theory of Creation is a deiform nature, and a theological justi-
fication for the appreciation of beauty.
vii *173*. In hell Satan attempted in Stoic fashion to assert the supremacy of
Fate; see i 116–7*n*. God here explains, however, that there is no Fate other
than his own decree. The devils sometimes admitted this–especially Belial
(ii 197–9). In *De doctrina* i 2 (Columbia xiv 27) M. as usual insists on the
subordination of all laws to God's untrammelled decree: 'There are some
who pretend that nature or fate is this supreme Power: but the very name
of nature implies that it must owe its birth to some prior agent, or, to speak
properly, signifies in itself nothing; but means either the essence of a thing,
or that general law which is the origin of every thing, and under which every
thing acts; on the other hand, fate can be nothing but a divine decree ema-
nating from some almighty power.'
vii *176–9*. Raphael here implies that his account of creation will be a myth,
like his narration of the angelic war (cp. v 571–6). On instantaneous creation
see l. 154*n* above. The topic was one that invited speculation, then as now.
Augustinian commentators on *Genesis* explained the six days of creation as a
manifestation of what had really been performed instantaneously. Cp.
Bacon's distinction between two emanations of virtue from God in creation:

Glory they sung to the most high, good will
To future men, and in their dwellings peace:
Glory to him whose just avenging ire
185   Had driven out the ungodly from his sight
And the habitations of the just; to him
Glory and praise, whose wisdom had ordained
Good out of evil to create, in stead
Of spirits malign a better race to bring
190   Into their vacant room, and thence diffuse
His good to worlds and ages infinite.
So sang the hierarchies: mean while the Son
On his great expedition now appeared,
Girt with omnipotence, with radiance crowned
195   Of majesty divine, sapience and love
Immense, and all his Father in him shone.
About his chariot numberless were poured
Cherub and seraph, potentates and thrones,
And virtues, winged spirits, and chariots winged,
200   From the armoury of God, where stand of old
Myriads between two brazen mountains lodged
Against a solemn day, harnessed at hand,
Celestial equipage; and now come forth

by power he instantaneously created the confused matter of the universe;
by wisdom he disposed it in the orderly works of the six days (*Advancement
of Learning* I vi 2).   *process*] Stressed on the second syllable.   *notion*]
understanding.

vii *182–3*. Modelled on the angels' song in *Luke* ii 14; because that accom-
panied the beginning of the New Creation, as this does the old. Cp. also
Job xxxviii 7, where 'the morning stars sang together, and all the sons of
God shouted for joy' at the creation.

vii *183*. Some copies *Ed I* have semicolon after *peace*.

vii *191. worlds*] world *Ed I*, some copies.

vii *194. Girt with omnipotence*] Presumably refers to 'thunders' such as those
of vi 836. Cp. *Ps.* xviii 39: 'thou hast girded me with strength'.

vii *195*. For the particular association of Christ with *Sapience*, see ll. 8–12*n*;
also Ellrodt 166ff.

vii *196*. See iii 139–40*n*.

vii *197. poured*] Cp. vi 830.

vii *200*. Cp. *Jer.* l 25: 'The Lord hath opened his armoury.'

vii *201*. Cp. Zechariah's vision (vi 5, 1) of chariots that were 'spirits of the
heavens, which go forth from standing before the Lord of all the earth':
'behold, there came four chariots out from between two mountains; and the
mountains were mountains of brass.'

vii *203. equipage*] retinue, apparatus for the expedition. But there may also
be a sombre overtone; since 'equipage' often meant apparatus of war, and

Spontaneous, for within them spirit lived,
205 Attendant on'their Lord: heaven opened wide
Her ever during gates, harmonious sound
On golden hinges moving, to let forth
The king of glory in his powerful Word
And Spirit coming to create new worlds.
210 On heavenly ground they stood, and from the shore
They viewed the vast immeasurable abyss
Outrageous as a sea, dark, wasteful, wild,
Up from the bottom turned by furious winds
And surging waves, as mountains to assault
215 Heaven's highth, and with the centre mix the pole.
     Silence, ye troubled waves, and thou deep, peace,
Said then the omnific Word, your discord end:
     Nor stayed, but on the wings of cherubim
Uplifted, in paternal glory rode
220 Far into chaos, and the world unborn;
For chaos heard his voice: him all his train
Followed in bright procession to behold
Creation, and the wonders of his might.
Then stayed the fervid wheels, and in his hand

the *solemn day* (l. 202) is left so indeterminate that it could refer to the day of judgment.

vii *204*. For the animated chariots, cp. *Ezek.* i 20, and see vi 846*n*.

vii *205–8*. Cp. *Ps.* xxiv 7: 'Lift up your heads, O ye gates; and be ye lift up, ye everlasting doors; and the King of glory shall come in.' There is an obvious contrast with the gates of hell, which opened with a 'jarring sound' to give Satan his very different view of the *abyss*, at ii 879ff. The syntax of these lines is discussed by Lewis (46). On the self-opening gates see v 254–6*n*.

vii *208–9*. Cp. ll. 163–5. Notice how *word* and *spirit* are made subordinate to God.

vii *210–15*. 'The earth is the Lord's, and the fulness thereof; the world, and they that dwell therein. For he hath founded it upon the seas, and established it upon the floods' (*Ps.* xxiv 1f).   *Outrageous*] excessive, unrestrained.   *wasteful*] desolate, excessive. See ii 961*n*.   *Up . . . bottom*] Probably alludes to the sea upheaved *a sedibus imis* by the winds, but calmed by Neptune, in Virgil, *Aen.* i 84ff, 106ff, 124ff; if so, there is a contrast with Death's Neptune role in the pseudo-creation at x 295. Like *mountains*, *centre* and *pole* belong to the vehicle of the simile; chaos itself is without place (ii 894).

vii *217*. *omnific*] all-creating. *OED* gives no instance earlier than this.

vii *218*. *cherubim*] Those of Messiah's triumphal chariot; see ll. 197–9 and vi 846*n*.

vii *224*. *fervid*] burning. Cp. the 'burning wheels' of the chariot, at vi 832.

225   He took the golden compasses, prepared
      In God's eternal store, to circumscribe
      This universe, and all created things:
      One foot he centred, and the other turned
      Round through the vast profundity obscure,
230   And said, Thus far extend, thus far thy bounds,
      This be thy just circumference, O world.
      Thus God the heaven created, thus the earth,
      Matter unformed and void: darkness profound
      Covered the abyss: but on the watery calm
235   His brooding wings the spirit of God outspread,

In Ezekiel's vision the mystical chariot is repeatedly described as burning.
the] his *Ed I*, some copies.

vii *225–30*. Cf. l. 170, where by contrast God calls himself 'uncircum-
scribed'. The notion of a divine geometrical construction stems originally
from *Prov.* viii 27 ('When he prepared the heavens, I was there: when he set
a compass upon the face of the depth'), where an abstract circle–Vulgate
gyrus–is meant. Biblical commentators, however, made the compass a
concrete one (see Fletcher[2] 108), so that in *Par.* xix 40f Dante could speak of
God as him 'who turned his compass (*sesto*) round the confines of the uni-
verse'. For visual art, the history of the motif of God circumscribing the
world with compasses is summarised and traced back to the *Bible moralisée*
in Klibansky 339*n*. In view of the variant in which God holds both compasses
and scales, it is of interest to recall that in *PL* the divine scales have already
appeared, at iv 997ff. The image implied an anthropomorphic conception of
God as an architect, planning the universe according to the principles of
number and proportion (see Wittkower 15, 101). Cp. also *Job* xxxviii 11:
'Hitherto shalt thou come, but no further: and here shall thy proud waves
be stayed.' For a list of articles containing speculations about how M. could
have known the familiar compass image, see Svendsen 258f.

vii *227*. Empson[2] 167 builds a great deal on the assumption that this line
implies that the angels are not created. But M. is here speaking of the visible
universe, and even specifically of *things*. From *De doctrina* i 7 (Columbia xv
32f) we know that he believed the angels to have been created long before
the material world.

vii *233*. *Matter unformed*] The 'first matter' of v 472. Plato's account of crea-
tion from formless substance (*Tim.* 50ff) had from patristic times been
synthesized with that given in *Genesis*. The authoritative work, which in-
fluenced M. a good deal, was Philo's *De opificio mundi*. In *De doctrina* i 7
(Columbia xv 19) M. explicitly rejects the doctrine of creation *ex nihilo*.
darkness] Cp. ii 962, where Night is Chaos' consort.

vii *235*. Gen. i 2: 'And the earth was without form, and void; and darkness
was upon the face of the deep. And the Spirit of God moved upon the face
of the waters.' See i 17–22*n* above for M.'s use of *brooding* to translate the
Heb. word wrongly rendered in A.V. 'moved'; and cp. *De doctrina* i 7

And vital virtue infused, and vital warmth
Throughout the fluid mass, but downward purged
The black tartareous cold infernal dregs
Adverse to life: then founded, then conglobed
240   Like things to like, the rest to several place
Disparted, and between spun out the air.
And earth self balanced on her centre hung.
    Let there be light, said God, and forthwith light
Ethereal, first of things, quintessence pure
245   Sprung from the deep, and from her native east
To journey through the airy gloom began,
Sphered in a radiant cloud, for yet the sun
Was not; she in a cloudy tabernacle

(Columbia xv 13), *Spiritus Dei incubabat.* In the same place M. argues that by *spirit* is meant God's 'divine power, rather than any person'; or that, if a person is meant, it can have been 'only a subordinate minister: God is first described as creating the heaven and the earth; the Spirit is only represented as moving upon the face of the waters already created'.

vii *236–42. virtue*] influence, power.   *vital warmth*] Perhaps building on Plato's myth about God making the body of the cosmos from fire and earth (*Tim.* 31B–C), Neoplatonists had come to speak of a 'primal heat' of creation (see, e.g., Ficino 1468). In the interest of stability and amity, fire and earth required the bond of two intermediate elements, for reasons explained in *Tim.* 31f; cp. Macrobius, *In somn. Scip.* I vi 22–41. The present passage recalls Ovid's account of the separation of four elements, in *Met.* i 21–31, or Lucretius' in *De rerum nat.* v 438ff; but M. has added psychological overtones. Thus, the *infernal dregs* are *black* and *Adverse to life* because earth was associated with melancholy. M. here accepts the common Christian evaluation of that temperament as evil (see Klibansky *passim*).   *conglobed*] formed (the earth) into a ball; placing the other elements in order about it.

vii *242.* 'He stretcheth out the north over the empty place, and hangeth the earth upon nothing' (*Job* xxvi 7). Cp. Ovid, *Met.* i 12f: *circumfuso pendebat in aere tellus / ponderibus librata suis*; *Nativity Ode* 117–24; also iv 1000 and v 578f ('earth now rests / Upon her centre poised') above.

vii *243–9.* Developing the passage on the primogeniture of light at iii 8–12. See *Gen.* i 3: 'And God said, Let there be light: and there was light.' 'Patristic theory had by Milton's time pretty much accounted for the difficulty implicit in the delayed creation of the heavenly bodies by calling the first light "informed", though real, and by assigning its perfection in form to the fourth day' (Svendsen 64). Light was 'not one of the four warring elements of chaos but a fifth element (quintessence)' (Fletcher ii 191). See iii 1–55*n*, 6*n*, and 716*n* above.   *Ethereal*] of the nature of ether, the highest purest and subtlest element; celestial. Cp. iii 7, 'pure ethereal stream'.

vii *248–9.* Negotiating the difficulty that light is mentioned on the first day of creation, but the heavenly bodies not till the fourth (*Gen.* i 16–19 and

Sojourned the while. God saw the light was good;
250   And light from darkness by the hemisphere
Divided: light the day, and darkness night
He named. Thus was the first day even and morn:
Nor passed uncelebrated, nor unsung
By the celestial choirs, when orient light
255   Exhaling first from darkness they beheld;
Birth-day of heaven and earth; with joy and shout
The hollow universal orb they filled,
And touched their golden harps, and hymning praised
God and his works, creator him they sung,
260   Both when first evening was, and when first morn.
Again, God said, Let there be firmament

see previous note). In *De doctrina* i 7 (Columbia xv 29–31) M. admits the impossibility of our conceiving 'light independent of a luminary', but attempts to distinguish between visible light and the perpetual invisible light of the heaven of heavens. See John Swan, *Speculum mundi* (*cit.* Svendsen 64), where the controversy about presolar light is summarized. Swan believed the light to be 'no spirituall Light', but shared St Thomas Aquinas' view that it was 'an informed light, which on the fourth day had its perfect form'. Swan refers to an idea utilized by M. (at ll. 245f above) when he writes that 'this first Light was made in motion, and was created in the Eastern part of that Hemisphere in which Man was made.'   *tabernacle*] in *Ps.* xix 4 God sets 'a tabernacle for the sun' in the sequence of days and nights.

vii *249–52*. 'And God saw the light, that it was good: and God divided the light from the darkness. And God called the light Day, and the darkness he called Night. And the evening and the morning were the first day' (*Gen.* i 4f).   *even and morn*] An important phrase from the point of view of the poem's chronology, since it indicates that M. is to follow the Hebrew system and 'to account the naturall day from evening to evening' (Willet 4). The interpretation of the phrase as it occurs in *Gen.* i 5 had been so controversial that M. could not have used it casually; and indeed it later becomes clear that he has systematically followed St Jerome's exegesis. For he consistently takes 'evening' to stand for 'night' (and not for 'day', as Sts Ambrose and Chrysostom held); see ll. 255 and 582f, also Introduction, 'Chronology'.
vii *256–60*. When God 'laid the foundations of the earth ... the morning stars sang together, and all the sons of God shouted for joy' (Job xxxviii 4, 7). The *first* evening of creation is the evening that begins Day 14 of the poem's action. See Introduction, 'Chronology' (p. 26).
vii *261–9*. 'And God said, Let there be a firmament in the midst of the waters ... And God made the firmament, and divided the waters which were under the firmament from the waters which were above the firmament ... And God called the firmament Heaven' (*Gen.* i 6–8). The 'waters ... above the

Amid the waters, and let it divide
The waters from the waters: and God made
The firmament, expanse of liquid, pure,
265   Transparent, elemental air, diffused
In circuit to the uttermost convex
Of this great round: partition firm and sure,
The waters underneath from those above
Dividing: for as earth, so he the world
270   Built on circumfluous waters calm, in wide
Crystalline ocean, and the loud misrule
Of Chaos far removed, lest fierce extremes
Contiguous might distemper the whole frame:
And Heaven he named the firmament: so even
275   And morning chorus sung the second day.
        The earth was formed, but in the womb as yet
Of waters, embryon immature involved,

firmament' were the subject of one of the greatest controversies of pre-
Newtonian cosmology. See Svendsen 56–60, where M.'s model is shown to
be a highly eclectic one. In his interpretation of the firmament as a penetrable
atmosphere (cp. iii 574) rather than a hard shell, M. agrees with the sceptical
Raleigh, Petavius and Thomas Vaughan. On the other hand, he will not
join them in explaining away the *circumfluous waters* as clouds; and he
retains an outer 'firm opacous globe' at iii 418. The diction of the passage
has many technical overtones: e.g., *expanse* implies Lat. *expansum*, the
correct rendering–as various cosmologists had explained; see Svendsen
59–of the Hebrew word translated as 'firmament' in A.V. (though A.V.
marg. has 'expansion').   *liquid*] Often a poetical Latinism, but here more
technical in flavour. Cp. Burton, *Anatomy of Melancholy* II ii 3, on Tycho's
view that the spheres are not 'hard, impenetrable, subtile, transparent, etc.,
or making music, as Pythagoras maintained of old, and Robert Constantine
of late, but still, quiet, liquid, open'.   *round* and *world*] universe.
vii *271. Crystalline ocean*] Cp. iii Arg. and 518–19n; and see H. F. Robins in
PMLA lxix (1954) 904. Robins distinguishes the crystalline ocean from the
crystalline sphere; Svendsen does not. This uncertainty seems a faithful
rendering of seventeenth-century confusions.
vii *272–3.* In chaos, opposed qualities war directly, since they are not
attached to elements and separated out.   *distemper*] The primary sense is
'disturb the order and mixture of the elements' (*OED* v[1]); but there is a
secondary overtone of 'mix with water; impair by dilution' (*OED* v[2]).
vii *274. heaven*] the atmosphere. The Hebrew world picture also included a
starry heaven, and a 'third heaven' inhabited by the angels.
vii *275. chorus*] The early edns treat as a proper name.   *second day*] Day
15 of the poem's action.
vii *277. embryon*] embryo.   *involved*] enfolded, enveloped.

Appeared not: over all the face of earth
Main ocean flowed, not idle, but with warm
280   Prolific humour softening all her globe,
Fermented the great mother to conceive,
Satiate with genial moisture, when God said
Be gathered now ye waters under heaven
Into one place, and let dry land appear.
285   Immediately the mountains huge appear
Emergent, and their broad bare backs upheave
Into the clouds, their tops ascend the sky:
So high as heaved the tumid hills, so low
Down sunk a hollow bottom broad and deep,
290   Capacious bed of waters: thither they
Hasted with glad precipitance, uprolled
As drops on dust conglobing from the dry;
Part rise in crystal wall, or ridge direct,
For haste; such flight the great command impressed
295   On the swift floods: as armies at the call
Of trumpet (for of armies thou hast heard)
Troop to their standard, so the watery throng,

vii *279–82*. At l. 236 we had 'vital warmth', the *primus calor* of the Neo-
platonic cosmogony; now is added the genial moisture of creation, the
primus humor. On the conception of a generative ocean in Renaissance
Neoplatonism, see Wind (117n), who cites Boyle's *The Sceptical Chymist*.
Main] uninterrupted.   *prolific*] generative; fertilizing.   *genial*] gener-
ative.

vii *283–91*. Cp. Gen. i 9f: 'And God said, Let the waters under the heaven
be gathered together unto one place, and let the dry land appear . . . And
God called the dry land Earth; and the gathering together of the waters
called he Seas.' Cp. also *Ps*. civ 6–8: 'The waters stood above the mountains.
At thy rebuke they fled; at the voice of thy thunder they hasted away. They
go up by the mountains; they go down by the valleys unto the place which
thou hast founded for them.'   *Immediately*] Cp. 243 ('forthwith'), and
see ll. 176ff on the instantaneousness of God's acts.   *So high*] For a tra-
dition that the seas' depths and the mountains' heights exactly correspond,
see Nicolson[3] 20.   *tumid*] swollen.

vii *292. conglobing*] Cp. l. 239. The repetition of the rare word clarifies the
parallel between the separation of the elements at large and the separation
of terrestrial earth and water.

vii *293*. Repeated in the division of the Red Sea into 'two crystal walls'
at xii 197–itself a type of the power of God's grace.

vii *296*. Anticipating the charge of anachronism: the simile would not have
made Raphael's narration any more intelligible to Adam and Eve, if he had
not already recounted the angelic war in Bk vi. By such alienations M.
encourages us to scrutinize what his Paradise includes and excludes.

Wave rolling after wave, where way they found,
If steep, with torrent rapture, if through plain,
300 Soft ebbing; nor withstood them rock or hill,
But they, or under ground, or circuit wide
With serpent error wandering, found their way,
And on the washy ooze deep channels wore;
Easy, ere God had bid the ground be dry,
305 All but within those banks, where rivers now
Stream, and perpetual draw their humid train.
The dry land, earth, and the great receptacle
Of congregated waters he called seas:
And saw that it was good, and said Let the earth
310 Put forth the verdant grass, herb yielding seed,
And fruit tree yielding fruit after her kind;
Whose seed is in her self upon the earth.
He scarce had said, when the bare earth, till then
Desert and bare, unsightly, unadorned,
315 Brought forth the tender grass whose verdure clad
Her universal face with pleasant green,
Then herbs of every leaf, that sudden flowered
Opening their various colours, and made gay
Her bosom smelling sweet: and these scarce blown,
320 Forth flourished thick the clustering vine, forth crept
The swelling gourd, up stood the corny reed

vii *299. rapture*] force of movement (*OED* 2). Cp. Chapman, *Od.* xiv 427f:
'That 'gainst a rock, or flat, her keel did dash / With headlong rapture.'
vii *297–306.* The first falling of the rivers to the sea is with Du Bartas an
elaborate set piece; see 'The Third Day of the First Week', ll. 135ff.   *train*]
The metaphor of a trailed robe was old enough to be unemphatic. Cp. e.g.,
Countess of Pembroke, *Psalms* (1586) lxxviii 20f: 'All that rich land, where
over Nilus trailes / Of his wett robe the slymy seedy train.'
vii *302.* By itself, *error* might just be a simple Latinism ('winding course'),
but with *serpent* it unmistakably belongs to the large class of instances of the
word used as reminders of the Fall (Ricks 110 following Stein 66f).
vii *307–12.* 'And God called the dry land Earth; and the gathering together
of the waters called he Seas: and God saw that it was good. And God said,
Let the earth bring forth grass, the herb yielding seed, and the fruit tree
yielding fruit after his kind, whose seed is in itself, upon the earth: and it was
so' (*Gen.* i 10f).   *congregated waters*] Cp. Vulgate *Gen.* i 10, *congregation-
esque aquarum.*
vii *317–18.* The odours are from the account of the third day's creation in
2 *Esdras* vi 44.
vii *321. swelling*] The *Ed I* and *Ed II* reading 'smelling' is clearly a misprint;
for once an emendation of Bentley's is acceptable.   *corny reed*] Cp. v 23,
'balmy reed'. But also perhaps corny = Latin *corneus*, horny. 'The horn

Embattled in her field: and the humble shrub,
And bush with frizzled hair implicit: last
Rose as in dance the stately trees, and spread
325   Their branches hung with copious fruit; or gemmed
Their blossoms: with high woods the hills were
      crowned,
With tufts the valleys and each fountain side,
With borders long the rivers. That earth now
Seemed like to heaven, a seat where gods might dwell,
330   Or wander with delight, and love to haunt
Her sacred shades: though God had yet not rained
Upon the earth, and man to till the ground
None was, but from the earth a dewy mist
Went up and watered all the ground, and each
335   Plant of the field, which ere it was in the earth
God made, and every herb, before it grew
On the green stem; God saw that it was good.
So even and morn recorded the third day.
    Again the almighty spake: Let there be lights

reed stood upright among the undergrowth of nature, like a grove of spears
or a battalion with its spikes aloft' (Hume, comparing Virgil, *Aen.* iii 22f:
tumulus, quo cornea summo / virgulta et densis hastilibus horrida myrtus.

vii *322. Embattled*] Cp. iv 980-2, where the 'ported spears' of the angelic
guard are compared with heads of corn blown in the wind.   *and*] con-
siderations of diction and scansion suggest that *Ed I* 'add' may be preferable;
see Adams 102f.   *humble*] low-growing.

vii *323.* A characteristically Bartasian or Sylvestrian conceit. Cp. the famous
line 'And perriwig with wooll the bald-pate woods'.   *frizzled*] curled
crisply.   *implicit*] entangled, interwoven.

vii *325. gemmed*] budded, put forth (*OED* 1). Possibly rare enough to be felt
as a Latinism (*gemmare*=to bud).

vii *331-4.* 'The Lord God had not caused it to rain upon the earth, and there
was not a man to till the ground. But there went up a mist from the earth,
and watered the whole face of the ground' (*Gen.* ii 5f). Note however that
after man was put in Paradise at least *showers* of rain fell, even before the Fall;
see iv 646.

vii *335-7.* Cp. Gen. ii 4f: 'The Lord God made . . . every plant of the field
before it was in the earth, and every herb of the field before it grew.'   *ere*]
some commentators, notably Philo and St Augustine, took this passage
to mean that creation was instantaneous, but comprised in the first instance
generic forms or *rationes seminales.* See, e.g., Philo, *Legum allegoria* i 22-4.

vii *338. recorded*] bore witness to (*OED* III 10) or rendered in song (*OED* I 2
b).   *third day*] Day 16 of the poem's action.

vii *339-45.* 'And God said, Let there be lights in the firmament of the heaven
to divide the day from the night; and let them be for signs, and for seasons,

340 High in the expanse of heaven to divide
       The day from night; and let them be for signs,
       For seasons, and for days, and circling years,
       And let them be for lights as I ordain
       Their office in the firmament of heaven
345 To give light on the earth; and it was so.
       And God made two great lights, great for their use
       To man, the greater to have rule by day,
       The less by night altern: and made the stars,
       And set them in the firmament of heaven
350 To illuminate the earth, and rule the day
       In their vicissitude, and rule the night,
       And light from darkness to divide. God saw,
       Surveying his great work, that it was good:
       For of celestial bodies first the sun
355 A mighty sphere he framed, unlightsome first,
       Though of ethereal mould: then formed the moon
       Globose, and every magnitude of stars,
       And sowed with stars the heaven thick as a field:
       Of light by far the greater part he took,
360 Transplanted from her cloudy shrine, and placed
       In the sun's orb, made porous to receive
       And drink the liquid light, firm to retain
       Her gathered beams, great palace now of light.

and for days, and years: And let them be for lights in the firmament of the heaven to give light upon the earth' (*Gen.* i 14f). For the determining of time by the lights, see iii 579–81 above.   *expanse*] More accurate than A.V. 'firmament'; see ll. 261–9*n*. For the use of the stars see iv 661–73*n*.

vii *346–52.* 'And God made two great lights; the greater light to rule the day, and the lesser light to rule the night: he made the stars also. And God set them in the firmament of the heaven to give light upon the earth. And to rule over the day and over the night, and to divide the light from the darkness' (*Gen.* i 16–18).   *altern*] in turns, alternately.   *vicissitude*] reciprocal succession.

vii *355. unlightsome*] dark. A rare word, which had been used is a similar context by Chapman in *Hymnus in Noctem*, 30–2: 'When unlightsome, vast, and indigest / The formelesse matter of this world did lye' Night 'fildst every place with [her] Divinitie.'

vii *356. ethereal mould*] aether, regarded as the material of the sun's body. Cp. *Nativity Ode* 138, 'earthly mould'.

vii *360. cloudy shrine*] the 'cloudy tabernacle' (l. 248) in which light moved before the sources of light were created.

vii *361–3.* Controversy about the sun's density and permeability, opacity and diaphanousness, was rife in M.'s day; see e.g. Riccioli i 93.

Hither as to their fountain other stars
365   Repairing, in their golden urns draw light,
And hence the morning planet gilds her horns;
By tincture or reflection they augment
Their small peculiar, though from human sight
So far remote, with diminution seen.
370   First in his east the glorious lamp was seen,
Regent of day, and all the horizon round
Invested with bright rays, jocund to run
His longitude through heaven's high road: the grey
Dawn, and the Pleiades before him danced

vii *364–9*. Svendsen 68f draws attention to M.'s deliberate accumulation here of alternative views about the origin of stellar light. She cites the *Speculum mundi*: 'The sunne . . . is indeed the chief fountain from whence the whole world receiveth lustre . . . some Philosophers and Astronomers have been of opinion that the fixed starres shine not but with borrowed light from the sunne. . . . But according to the minds of the best Authours . . . the starres are called lights, as well as the sunne. . . . For if they had not their proper and peculiar light (being so farre distant from inferiour bodies) it is thought they could not alter them in such sort as they sometimes do.' It was believed as late as Kepler that the planets were self-luminous; see Dreyer 411.   *tincture*] infusion of a quality; imbuing with an active principle emanating from elsewhere (*OED* 5 b, 6 b), but also secondarily referring to the alchemical elixir or 'universal tincture' (*OED* 6 a) – see iii 607 above for the sun's exhalation of 'elixir'.   *peculiar*] A semi-technical term for inherent or 'proper' light, as opposed to light 'strange' or borrowed.
vii *366. her*] Venus'. *Ed I* has 'his', with Lucifer as the implied antecedent, introducing an inappropriate association that M. did well to remove. *horns*] Alludes to the horned appearance of Venus (*cornuta*] when near to conjunction – as we know her to be at present, from various astronomical data given in Bks iv and v above; see v 166–70*n*. An added aptness lies in the fact that Venus' House Taurus was often represented with gilded horns. Note that it is just possible for Venus to be at conjunction in Taurus, when Sol is in Aries (as here: see iii 555–61*n*). In the *thema coeli* or state of the heavens at creation, the planets were supposed to have occupied their own houses. But Venus was more usually placed in Libra than in Taurus. For a list of contemporary published observations of the phases of Venus, including Galileo's, see Riccioli i 484.
vii *372–3*. Cp. *Ps.* xix 5, where the sun 'rejoiceth as a strong man to run a race'.   *longitude*] course round the ecliptic–equatorial circle. For the identity of the ecliptic and the equator in the prelapsarian cosmos, see x 651–706*n*.
vii *374–5*. 'Canst thou bind the sweet influences of Pleiades, or loose the bands of Orion ?'(*Job* xxxviii 31). Note that while *Dawn* goes before the sun

375 Shedding sweet influence: less bright the moon,
     But opposite in levelled west was set
     His mirror, with full face borrowing her light
     From him, for other light she needed none
     In that aspect, and still that distance keeps
380 Till night, then in the east her turn she shines,
     Revolved on heaven's great axle, and her reign
     With thousand lesser lights dividual holds,
     With thousand thousand stars, that then appeared
     Spangling the hemisphere: then first adorned
385 With their bright luminaries that set and rose,
     Glad evening and glad morn crowned the fourth day.

in his diurnal motion, the *Pleiades* do not. For they are situated in the con-
stellation Taurus, which before the Fall was also the sign Taurus; and the
sun is here still in Aries, the preceding sign (see x 329 and iii 555–61*n*;
creation was at the vernal equinox). Thus the Pleiades dance *before* the sun
only in the sense that they occupy his next position in the *annual* motion
round the ecliptic. Almost imperceptibly, the seasonal movement is gather-
ing way.

Hughes, following Newton, compares Guido Reni's painting *Aurora*,
which he describes as showing nymphs who represent the Pleiades alongside
the sun's chariot. Unfortunately, Reni's nymphs are not the Pleiades but the
Hours–as their spaced-out arrangement shows: cp. Ovid, *Met.* ii 26:
positae spatiis aequalibus Horae. They number seven because the four Hours
or Seasons were commonly accompanied by the three Graces (see Hieatt
111). The painting bears some relation, however, to another Ovidian pas-
sage, *Met.* ii 112ff, that was used by M. at vi 2–4 above. See Cesare Gnudi
and Gian Carlo Cavalli, *Guido Reni* (Florence 1955) 66.

vii 375–9. Svendsen 72f finds a contradiction between the moon of this
passage and the self-luminous moons of viii 150 (see ll. 364–9*n*). But M.
says only that 'proper light' is unnecessary in this one *aspect* of opposition.
The point of the passage lies in an allusion to a theory of Anastasius Synai-
ta's, that 'when God made these two luminaries, the greater–namely the
sun–he placed immediately at the east of the firmament; but the moon at the
west' (*In hexaemeron* iv; Migne *P.G.* lxxix 890–914). Hence it was full moon
at creation, and the sun and the moon were in an aspect of opposition (180°
apart). Bede and many other theologians held that since the moon was
created perfect, it must have been full on the fourth day of creation. For a
synthesis of this theory with the placement of the sun in Aries at creation,
see Riccioli ii 232.   *aspect*] Stressed on the second syllable.

vii *382. dividual*] divided, shared.

vii *385. set and rose*] In that order; since the Biblical day begins with evening.
See Introduction, 'Chronology' (p. 26).

vii *386.* The fourth day is crowned in a formal or ceremonial sense in that it
occupies the sovereign central place among the days of creation, and also

And God said, Let the waters generate
Reptile with spawn abundant, living soul:
And let fowl fly above the earth, with wings
390   Displayed on the open firmament of heaven.
And God created the great whales, and each
Soul living, each that crept, which plenteously
The waters generated by their kinds,
And every bird of wing after his kind;
395   And saw that it was good, and blessed them, saying,
Be fruitful, multiply, and in the seas
And lakes and running streams the waters fill;
And let the fowl be multiplied on the earth.
Forthwith the sounds and seas, each creek and bay
400   With fry innumerable swarm, and shoals
Of fish that with their fins and shining scales
Glide under the green wave, in schools that oft
Bank the mid sea: part single or with mate
Graze the sea weed their pasture, and through groves
405   Of coral stray, or sporting with quick glance

the central 17th place among the 33 days of the poem's action (see Intro-
duction, 'Chronology'; and, for numerological precedents, Fowler, Index,
s.v. *Central position of sovereignty*). The reason for so dignifying the fourth
day is that the luminaries created then are 'regent' (371 above). Commen-
tators often gave *Gen.* i 18 an elaborate mystical treatment. See, e.g.,
Anastasius' anagogies, in which sun and moon are not only Adam and Eve
but also *Sol iustitiae* and Holy Church (Migne *P.G.* lxxix 890–914); also
Henry More, *Conjectura Cabbalistica*.

vii *387–98*. Cp. *Gen.* i 20–2: 'Let the waters bring forth abundantly the
moving creature that hath life, and fowl that may fly above the earth in the
open firmament of heaven. And God created great whales, and every living
creature that moveth, which the waters brought forth abundantly, after
their kind, and every winged fowl after his kind: and God saw that it was
good. And God blessed them, saying, Be fruitful, and multiply, and fill the
waters in the seas, and let fowl multiply in the earth.'   *Reptile*] crawling
animal. Vulgate *Gen.* i 20 has *producant aquae reptile animae viventis, Tremellius
reptilia animantia.*   *soul*] animate existence.   *crept*] Takes in *Gen.* i 20
A.V. marg., or *Ps.* civ 24f: 'The earth is full of thy riches. So is this great
and wide sea, wherein are things creeping innumerable.'

vii *402. schools*] sculles *Ed I* and *Ed II*.

vii *403. Bank*] form a shelving elevation rising almost to the surface of the
sea (a verbal use of *OED* sb[1] I 5).

vii *404.* Not merely a piscatory modulation of the pastoral mode: the
fishes' diet has an ideological bearing. See x 710–14*n*.

Show to the sun their waved coats dropped with gold,
Or in their pearly shells at ease, attend
Moist nutriment, or under rocks their food
In jointed armour watch: on smooth the seal,
410   And bended dolphins play: part huge of bulk
Wallowing unwieldy, enormous in their gait
Tempest the ocean: there leviathan
Hugest of living creatures, on the deep
Stretched like a promontory sleeps or swims,
415   And seems a moving land, and at his gills
Draws in, and at his trunk spouts out a sea.
Mean while the tepid caves, and fens and shores

vii *406–10*. A subdued allegoria in which the colour-patterns of the fish are
likened to various heraldic patterns or *coats*. Thus *waved*, though it may also
directly express the appearance of fish glimpsed through the waves, at the
level of the vehicle means 'divided undy or wavy'; see Sir G. Mackenzie,
The Science of Herauldry (Edinburgh 1680) 26: '*Waved* is so call'd, from the
waves of the Sea, which it represents, and is therefore called *undê*, and is used for
signifying that the Bearer got his Arms for service done at sea.'   *dropped*
(spotted) *with gold*] The whole phrase was heraldically possible; the Grayn-
dores, e.g., bore 'Party ermine and vert, the vert dropped with gold'.
Similarly *bended* means not only 'striped, banded' but also 'bendy,
having a bend': e.g. John Bossewell, *Workes of armorie* (1572) ii 85: 'One
greate difference betwene Armes Bended, and these Armes . . . In Armes
Bendee the colours contained in the shielde are equally divided.   *attend*]
wait for. Bended (*curvus*) was the ancient stock epithet for *delphinus*,
especially for the Dolphin constellation; see R. H. Allen, *Star Names*
(New York 1963) p. 199.   *smooth*] smooth water. Probably this sub-
stantive use had a nautical tang: cp. *OED* s.v. *Smooth*, sb. 1 c, 'a stretch
of comparatively smooth or calm water in a rough sea'. Although the
earliest *OED* instance in this sense is 1840, it would make the dolphins'
habitat so much more appropriate that coincidence seems unlikely.
vii *415. seems . . . land*] This reminds the reader of the deceptiveness of
leviathan in the simile of i 200–8. Here, however, the illusion is not dan-
gerous.   *tempest*] disturb violently.
vii *417–21*. Just possibly alluding to the ancient question whether the egg
came before the bird or vice versa, which had been debated by Plutarch
(*Symposiacs*), by Macrobius (*Saturnalia*) and more recently by Hendrik Van
der Putte (*Ovi encomium*); see D. C. Allen in *MLN* lxiii (1948) 264. The
account of creation given by the mystical alchemists has too prominent a
place in *PL* for M. to decide the question otherwise than in favour of the
Orphic primal egg. See, however, i 17–22 above.   *kindly*] natural.
disclosed] set free; hatched.   *callow*] unfeathered.   *fledge*] fledged,
fit to fly.   *summed their pens*] brought their plumage to completion.
The past participle 'summed' (as at *PR* i 14) was a technical term in falconry;

Their brood as numerous hatch, from the egg that
   soon
Bursting with kindly rupture forth disclosed
420   Their callow young, but feathered soon and fledge
They summed their pens, and soaring the air sublime
With clang despised the ground, under a cloud
In prospect; there the eagle and the stork
On cliffs and cedar tops their eyries build:

cp. George Turberville, *The Booke of Faulconrie* (1575) p. 117: 'When . . .
hir principal feathers be ful sommed.' M.'s use of 'summed' as an active
verb in this sense, however, may be a departure from prose usage.   *soaring*]
reaching, flying up through.   *sublime*] aloft, high up.
vii *422–3. clang*] harsh scream; resonant cry. Probably poetic, in imitation
of Latin *clangor* or Greek κλαγγή; cp. Chapman, *Il.* x 244: 'By her clange
they knew . . . it was a hern.'   *ground . . . prospect*] The ground seemed
under a cloud of birds. Perhaps, however, there is a secondary prolepsis:
in future prospect earth is under a cloud, metaphorically.
vii *423–46.* The seven birds named all symbolized virtues. It will be observed
that M. repeatedly draws attention to these emblematic qualities; so that
the passage is as far as possible from being a simple catalogue.
vii *423–30.* The eagle is named first as the sovereign of birds. It could sym-
bolize divine grace, or human generosity, majesty, or elevation of thought–
even spiritual illumination (see, e.g., Valeriano 234, and consult Tervarent 6,
Cirlot 87–9). 'Doth the eagle mount up at thy command, and make her nest
on high? She dwelleth and abideth on the rock, upon the crag of the rock,
and the strong place' (*Job* xxxix 27f). The stork, on the other hand, was an
emblem of impartial justice (cp. Arnold Freitag's emblem, illustrated
Scoular Plate 9), of gratitude, of filial piety and of enmity to the snake
(Valeriano 203–6, Tervarent 97). Its habit of building its *eyrie* in the towering
fir (*Ps.* civ 17) signified *animus divinis intentus* (Valeriano 207). Eagle and
stork are respectively notable examples of the sub-classes of those that
wing *loosely* (separately) and those that fly in formation. Thus the eagle
was proverbially solitary (Valeriano 231), while the stork was an emblem of
military discipline because of its unanimity of movement (Valeriano 206,
with woodcut illustrating the wedge formation).   *Intelligent* (cognizant)
of seasons] see *Jer.* viii 7: 'The stork in the heaven knoweth her appointed
times; and the turtle and the crane and the swallow observe the time of their
coming; but my people know not the judgment of the Lord.'   *caravan*]
company travelling together for security. *mutual wing* probably refers to
St Basil's belief that storks use their wings to support their aged parents
(Robin 63f). But cp. a similar tradition about migrating birds originating
in Pliny and attached by the encyclopedists either to the *crane* or the wild-
goose: namely, that they take it in turns to head the flight wedge, and fly
each with his beak resting on the bird in front (Svendsen 158). Strictly

425   Part loosely wing the region, part more wise
       In common, ranged in figure wedge their way,
       Intelligent of seasons, and set forth
       Their airy caravan high over seas
       Flying, and over lands with mutual wing
430   Easing their flight; so steers the prudent crane
       Her annual voyage, borne on winds; the air
       Floats, as they pass, fanned with unnumbered plumes:
       From branch to branch the smaller birds with song
       Solaced the woods, and spread their painted wings
435   Till even, nor then the solemn nightingale
       Ceased warbling, but all night tuned her soft lays:
       Others on silver lakes and rivers bathed
       Their downy breast; the swan with arched neck
       Between her white wings mantling proudly, rows
440   Her state with oary feet: yet oft they quit
       The dank, and rising on stiff pennons, tower
       The mid aerial sky: others on ground
       Walked firm; the crested cock whose clarion sounds

speaking, all these references to migration are prolepses or dramatic ironies, since earth has no seasons until after the Fall. Cp. l. 374f above for a similar prolepsis.

vii *430–2. The prudent crane*] An emblem of diligence and vigilance, the crane belonged like the stork to the sub-class of formation-fliers. Its military propensities have already been mentioned at i 576; cp. also *Prol vii* (Yale i 304). *floats*] undulates.

vii *434. painted wings*] Imitates Virgil, *Aen. iv* 525, *pictae volucres*, in a passage immediately preceding Dido's suicide.

vii *435–6.* The nightingale, to which the central place among the seven named birds is given, is also prominent elsewhere in *PL*: see iii 38–40, iv 602–4, 648, v 40, and viii 518–20. It was the bird 'most musical, most melancholy' (*Il Penseroso* 62). Perhaps because it signified music, poetry and nocturnal meditation (Valeriano 275f), perhaps too because it sang in the dark, M. seems to have made of it a highly personal symbol. But it should also be recalled that in the seventeenth century there was an extensive poetic cult of the nightingale. On this, see L. C. Martin's note to Crashaw's 'Musicks Duell', *The Poems* (Oxford 1927) p. 439f.

vii *438.* The *swan*, like the nightingale, was a symbol of music and poetry, and often signified purity of soul. *mantling*] forming a mantle. Note also, however, that in falconry mantling was a technical term for the perched bird's practice of stretching alternate wings over the corresponding leg for exercise.

vii *441. dank*] pool, mere. *tower* soar aloft into (*OED* I 5).

The silent hours, and the other whose gay train
445   Adorns him, coloured with the florid hue
Of rainbows and starry eyes. The waters thus
With fish replenished, and the air with fowl,
Evening and morn solemnised the fifth day
   The sixth, and of creation last arose
450   With evening harps and matin, when God said,
Let the earth bring forth soul living in her kind,
Cattle and creeping things, and beast of the earth,
Each in their kind. The earth obeyed, and straight
Opening her fertile womb teemed at a birth
455   Innumerous living creatures, perfect forms,
Limbed and full grown: out of the ground up rose
As from his lair the wild beast where he wons
In forest wild, in thicket, brake, or den;
Among the trees in pairs they rose, they walked:
460   The cattle in the fields and meadows green:
Those rare and solitary, these in flocks

vii *444–5. other*] i.e., the peacock.   *starry eyes*] Clearly indicates that
the peacock is here a symbol of night, to offset the *cock*, herald of day (see
Ripa 210f, Klibansky 313*n*). Morally, the cock was often an emblem of
vigilance, the peacock of marital concord.

vii *448. fifth day*] Day 18 of the poem's action.

vii *449*. The account of the sixth day of creation (Day 19) is not an eye-
witness report, for according to viii 229 Raphael was on that day absent on a
mission to the gates of hell.

vii *450–8*. 'And God said, Let the earth bring forth the living creature after
his kind, cattle, and creeping thing, and beast of the earth after his kind:
and it was so' (*Gen.* i 24).

vii *450. matin*] morning (*OED* II 3 and III 5 b); but with a secondary allusion
to the Office of Matins, which was said either early in the morning or on the
preceding evening. The latter practice was based on the *Genesis* formula
'evening and morning were one day'.

vii *451. soul*] foul *Ed I* and *Ed II*; the emendation is Bentley's. With *soul
living* cp. 'living soul' (l. 388); in any case, the fowl were created on the
fifth day, not the sixth. Adams 94f ingeniously suggests retaining 'foul'
as a common variant spelling of 'foal'=young quadruped. But foal would
not have the requisite generality of meaning; and besides, the creatures are
'full grown' (l. 456).

vii *454. teemed*] produced, bore.

vii *457. wons*] lives, stays.

vii *461–2. Those* presumably refers to the *wild* beasts, *these* to the *cattle* or
domestic livestock (*OED*, *Cattle* II 4), which in turn are divided between
those in *flocks* (sheep, goats) and those in *herds* (cows).   *rare*] keeping far

Pasturing at once, and in broad herds upsprung.
The grassy clods now calved, now half appeared
The tawny lion, pawing to get free
465 His hinder parts, then springs as broke from bonds,
And rampant shakes his brinded mane; the ounce,
The libbard, and the tiger, as the mole
Rising, the crumbled earth above them threw
In hillocks; the swift stag from underground
470 Bore up his branching head: scarce from his mould
Behemoth biggest born of earth upheaved
His vastness: fleeced the flocks and bleating rose,
As plants: ambiguous between sea and land
The river horse and scaly crocodile.
475 At once came forth whatever creeps the ground,
Insect or worm; those waved their limber fans
For wings, and smallest lineaments exact
In all the liveries decked of summer's pride
With spots of gold and purple, azure and green:
480 These as a line their long dimension drew,
Streaking the ground with sinuous trace; not all

apart, spread out at wide intervals (*OED* 2 a, 3 a).   *broad herds*] Homeric
diction; cp. *Il*. xi 679, αἰπόλια πλατέ' αἰγῶν.

vii *463-70*. The parallel with Lucretius ii 991-8 suggested by Hughes is not
close. Coleridge following Newton compared Raphael's paintings of the
Creation in the Loggie of the Vatican, but thought the motif unworthy
of poetic expression. There may be more than pictorial naivety, however,
in the lion's imprisoned hindquarters. Expounding an image of Adargatis–
the earth goddess from whom all life emerges when she is quickened by the
rays of the sun, Valeriano 14 remarks: *Sed enim ipsa Leonis effigies utrumque
referre videtur hieroglyphicum: quippe quae anterioribus partibus Solem exscribit,
posterioribus vero Terram.* Note that the animal named first is the sovereign
of beasts; cp. l. 423, where the eagle was the first-named of the birds.
brinded] brindled, brownish, marked with streaks of a different colour.
ounce] In M.'s time the term was applied to various feline beasts of moderate
size, but principally to the lynx; cp. iv 344.   *libbard*] leopard.

vii *471*. 'Behold now behemoth, which I made with thee' (*Job* xl 15). The
Hebrew word 'behemoth' is interpreted in A.V. margin as 'either the
elephant or the hippopotamus'; l. 474 shows that M. opted for the former.

vii *473*. *ambiguous*] of doubtful classification; or hesitating.

vii *474*. *river horse* for 'hippopotamus' would not be felt as etymological
word-play; the usage was current until the nineteenth century.

vii *475*. *creeps*] The first instance given in *OED* of this rare transitive use.

vii *476*. *worm*] Includes serpents, and the grubs, maggots and caterpillars that
after the Fall became pests.

Minims of nature; some of serpent kind
Wondrous in length and corpulence involved
Their snaky folds, and added wings. First crept
485   The parsimonious emmet, provident
Of future, in small room large heart enclosed,
Pattern of just equality perhaps
Hereafter, joined in her popular tribes
Of commonalty: swarming next appeared
490   The female bee that feeds her husband drone

vii *482. minim*] A form of life of the least importance or size. Usually con-
temptuous, as in Lancelot Andrewes, *Sermons* (1629) p. 279: 'They be the
base people, the minims of the world.' The source of the expression, which
is alluded to here, is Vulg. *Prov.* xxx 24: *Quattuor sunt minima terrae, et ipsa
sunt sapientiora sapientibus.* On the interest taken in small animals and insects
in the seventeenth century, see Scoular 81–117, 'Much in Little'.

vii *483. corpulence*] bulk; not to be taken with *involved*, as Hughes.   *in-
volved*] coiled: a past tense, not a participle.

vii *484.* The notion of winged serpents is traced by D. C. Allen, *MLN* lix
(1944) 538, through the natural historians back to *Is.* xxx 6 ('fiery flying
serpent') and Herodotus ii 75. Belief in the existence of dragons, which it
must have been very hard to distinguish from winged serpents, was almost
universal; but Allen may be right to refer the passage to a more scientific
context. The pterodactyl of more recent zoology is a winged reptile.

vii *485. parsimonious*] careful (a neutral, not a dyslogistic term). Cp. *Prol vii*
(Yale i 304), where we are told that our 'domestic economy owes much to
the ants'.   *emmet*] ant. 'The ants are a people not strong, yet they prepare
their meat in the summer' (*Prov.* xxx 25); therefore 'Goe to the emmote o
sluggard' (Douay version *Prov.* vi 6).

vii *486. large heart*] This phrase does not quite translate Virgil's description
of bees as having *ingentis animos angusto in pectore* (*Georg.* iv 83). As at i 444
above and Coverdale and A.V. *1 Kings* iv 29, it meant 'capacious intellect;
wisdom' (see *OED* s.v. *Large* A II 3 c).

vii *487–9.* As Svendsen 150–2 shows, both the prudence and the 'commonal-
ty' (democracy) of ants were common information among the encyclo-
pedists; while the idea that ants have no kings went back to Aristotle. Since
this lack manifestly did not lead to anarchy, the ants were used as examples of
successful republicanism.   *perhaps*] Either because Raphael cannot be
certain about future events, or because he is unconvinced about the justice
(rightness) of republicanism.

vii *490–2.* The bee pairs with the ant in exemplifying civil merits. It need not
serve, however, as a complementary example of the alternative, monarchic
virtues, as is sometimes said. Indeed, in his controversy with Salmasius (who
had used the example of the bee to defend monarchy), M. presses the argu-
ment that most bees 'have republics'; see Svendsen 152f. The belief that
worker bees were female and drones male was general.

Deliciously, and builds her waxen cells
With honey stored: the rest are numberless,
And thou their natures know'st, and gavest them
    names,
Needless to thee repeated; nor unknown
495 The serpent subtlest beast of all the field,
Of huge extent sometimes, with brazen eyes
And hairy mane terrific, though to thee
Not noxious, but obedient at thy call.
Now heaven in all her glory shone, and rolled
500 Her motions, as the great first mover's hand
First wheeled their course; earth in her rich attire
Consummate lovely smiled; air, water, earth,
By fowl, fish, beast, was flown, was swam, was walked
Frequent; and of the sixth day yet remained;
505 There wanted yet the master work, the end

vii *493.* For the naming of the animals see vi 73–6 and viii 342–54.
vii *495–8.* Note how the serpent is singled out for special mention last of all the beasts, and next to man: coincidence, presumably, as far as Raphael is concerned, though design on M.'s part. Cp. *Gen.* iii 1: 'Now the serpent was more subtil than any beast of the field which the Lord God had made.' *mane*] Virgil describing the serpent that killed Laocoon has *iubaeque sanguineae superant undas*; *iuba* can mean either 'mane' or 'crest'. The destruction of Troy, in which Virgil's maned serpents played a crucial part, is in *PL* often used as a mythic analogue of the Fall; see, e.g., i 1–49n. Cp. also the description of the serpent animated by Satan at ix 496ff.
vii *500. motions*] movements of the heavenly bodies.
vii *502–3.* For the rhetoric, cp. Shakespeare, *Hamlet* III i 160: 'The courtier's, soldier's, scholar's, eye, tongue, sword'. Curtius 286f traces this scheme from the medieval Latin *versus rapportati* to German Baroque. See also *ibid.* 285, on the piling up of words by 'verse-filling asyndeton': M.'s present intention is to render the teeming abundance of life.   *consummate*] completed, perfect.   *was ... walked*] Not an impersonal Latin construction (*pace* Hughes), but an ordinary English passive; see, e.g., *OED* s.v. *Walk* III 17, 15.
vii *504. frequent*] crowded; abundantly. Not a Latinism.
vii *505–11.* The idea that man's upright posture distinguishes him from other animals, and indicates his special destiny, was a commonplace of hexaemeral literature. It had the authority of various classical authors (Plato, *Tim.* 90A; Cicero, *De nat. deor.* ii 56; etc.); but Ovid's version (*Met.* i 76–86) is closest to M.'s: 'A living creature of finer stuff than these, more capable of lofty thought, one who could have dominion over all the rest, was lacking yet.... And, though all other animals are prone, and fix their gaze upon the earth, he gave to man an uplifted face and bade him stand erect and turn his

Of all yet done; a creature who not prone
And brute as other creatures, but endued
With sanctity of reason, might erect
His stature, and upright with front serene
510   Govern the rest, self-knowing, and from thence
Magnanimous to correspond with heaven,
But grateful to acknowledge whence his good
Descends, thither with heart and voice and eyes
Directed in devotion, to adore
515   And worship God supreme, who made him chief
Of all his works: therefore the omnipotent
Eternal Father (for where is not he
Present) thus to his Son audibly spake.
        Let us make now man in our image, man
520   In our similitude, and let them rule
Over the fish and fowl of sea and air,
Beast of the field, and over all the earth,
And every creeping thing that creeps the ground.
This said, he formed thee, Adam, thee O man
525   Dust of the ground, and in thy nostrils breathed
The breath of life; in his own image he

eyes to heaven.' Cp. also iv 288 above.   *front*] forehead, face; or com-
posure.   *magnanimous*] great-souled, nobly ambitious, lofty of purpose;
for the Aristotelian and medieval background of this elusive term, see R. A.
Gauthier, *Magnanimité: l'ideal de la grandeur dans la philosophie païenne et
dans la théologie chrétienne*, Bibliothèque Thomiste xxviii (Paris 1951).
vii *518*. 'Previously, however, to the creation of man, as if to intimate the
superior importance of the work, the Deity speaks like to a man deliberating:
Gen. i.26. "God said, Let us make man in our own image, after our own
likeness"' (*De doctrina* i 7, Columbia xv 37).
vii *519–23*. 'Let us make man in our image, after our likeness: and let them
have dominion over the fish of the sea, and over the fowl of the air, and over
the cattle, and over all the earth, and over every creeping thing that creepeth
upon the earth' (*Gen.* i 26). Broadbent 198*n* notices M.'s avoidance of the
distinction between *Imago* and *Similitudo Dei*.
vii *524–8*. 'And the Lord God formed man of the dust of the ground, and
breathed into his nostrils the breath of life; and man became a living soul'
(*Gen.* ii 7). M.'s formulation suggests that he here sides with St Chrysostom,
who thought that man's soul was created *after* his body, against Origen
(who thought it *earlier* created) and St Thomas Aquinas (*simultaneously*).
Note the three degrees–as Willet 32 calls them–of man's creation: 'The
forming of his bodie, the giving of it life, the endewing of him with a
reasonable soule.'   *image ... Express*] Cp. *Heb.* i 3: 'Who being the
brightness of his glory, and the express image of his person, and upholding
all things by the word of his power . . . purged our sins.'

Created thee, in the image of God
Express, and thou becamest a living soul.
Male he created thee, but thy consort
530   Female for race; then blessed mankind, and said,
Be fruitful, multiply, and fill the earth,
Subdue it, and throughout dominion hold
Over fish of the sea, and fowl of the air,
And every living thing that moves on the earth.
535   Wherever thus created, for no place
Is yet distinct by name, thence, as thou know'st
He brought thee into this delicious grove,
This garden, planted with the trees of God,
Delectable both to behold and taste;
540   And freely all their pleasant fruit for food
Gave thee, all sorts are here that all the earth yields,
Variety without end; but of the tree
Which tasted works knowledge of good and evil,
Thou mayst not; in the day thou eat'st, thou diest;
545   Death is the penalty imposed, beware,
And govern well thy appetite, lest Sin
Surprise thee, and her black attendant Death.
Here finished he, and all that he had made

vii *529–30*. 'So God created man in his own image, in the image of God created he him; male and female created he them' (*Gen.* i 27).   consort] Stressed on the second syllable.

vii *530–4*. Cp. *Gen.* i 28: 'And God blessed them, and God said unto them, Be fruitful, and multiply, and replenish the earth, and subdue it: and have dominion over the fish of the sea', etc.

vii *535–8*. See *Gen.* ii 8, 15: 'And the Lord God planted a garden eastward in Eden; and there he put the man whom he had formed. . . . And the Lord God took the man, and put him into the garden of Eden to dress it and to keep it'; also *2 Esdras* iii 6: 'And thou leddest him into paradise, which thy right hand had planted, before ever the earth came forward.' M. follows the literal interpretation of Josephus (*Antiq.* i 1), that Adam was created outside Paradise; rather than the figurative interpretation, that Adam was put in Paradise merely in the sense of being stationed there. Cp. viii 296ff.   de-licious] delightful.

vii *539–41*. 'And out of the ground made the Lord God to grow every tree that is pleasant to the sight, and good for food' (*Gen.* ii 9). For the notion that Paradise contained every species of tree, cp. iv 138–43*n* and v 339–41*n*.

vii *542–5*. Cp. *Gen.* ii 16f, and contrast x 210 below, where the penalty is mitigated. See viii 323–33*n*.

vii *547. attendant*] Does this imply that Raphael is not privy to the guilty secret of Death's true relation with Sin?

vii *548–50*. Cp. *Gen.* i 31.

Viewed, and behold all was entirely good;
550   So even and morn accomplished the sixth day:
Yet not till the creator from his work
Desisting, though unwearied, up returned
Up to the heaven of heavens his high abode,
Thence to behold this new created world
555   The addition of his empire, how it showed
In prospect from his throne, how good, how fair,
Answering his great idea. Up he rode
Followed with acclamation and the sound
Symphonious of ten thousand harps that tuned
560   Angelic harmonies: the earth, the air
Resounded, (thou remember'st, for thou heard'st)
The heavens and all the constellations rung,
The planets in their station listening stood,
While the bright pomp ascended jubilant.
565   Open, ye everlasting gates, they sung,
Open, ye heavens, your living doors; let in
The great creator from his work returned
Magnificent, his six days' work, a world;
Open, and henceforth oft; for God will deign
570   To visit oft the dwellings of just men

vii *552. unwearied*] This carefully obviates any false conclusion from *Gen.*
ii 2, where God is said to have rested on the seventh day (Burden 9).
vii *553. heaven of heavens*] the empyrean; cp. l. 13.
vii *557–81.* Messiah's triumphal return from creation is closely corres-
pondent to his return from the expulsion of the rebels at vi 880–92.
vii *557.* The thought is Platonic, and M. may have in mind *Timaeus* 37C–D,
where God rejoices in the life of the newly-created universe and its resem-
blance to the perfect paradeigma.
vii *559. symphonious*] harmonious; sounding in concert.   *ten thousand*]
See vi 767n.   *tuned*] uttered, gave vent to.
vii *561–3.* Cp. iv 680–8. But after the Fall the sound of the heavens will
become inaudible: see *Nativity Ode* 125f and *Solemn Music* 19–21. Cp. *Job*
xxxviii 7: 'The morning stars sang together, and all the sons of God shouted
for joy.' The word texture of the present passage is discussed in Rajan 114.
station] stations *Ed I*. A technical term in astronomy for the apparent arrest
of a planet at its apogee or perigee; but here applied to quite a different set of
limiting positions—the places of the planets in the *thema coeli* or disposition
of the heavens at creation.
vii *564. pomp*] triumphal procession.
vii *565–7.* 'Lift up your heads, O ye gates; and be ye lift up, ye everlasting
doors; and the King of glory shall come in' (*Ps.* xxiv 7). For the *living doors*
of M.'s heaven, see v 254–6n, vi 861, and 205–8 above.

Delighted, and with frequent intercourse
Thither will send his winged messengers
On errands of supernal grace. So sung
The glorious train ascending: he through heaven,
575 That opened wide her blazing portals, led
To God's eternal house direct the way,
Abroad and ample road, whose dust is gold
And pavement stars, as stars to thee appear,
Seen in the galaxy, that Milky Way
580 Which nightly as a circling zone thou seest
Powdered with stars. And now on earth the seventh
Evening arose in Eden, for the sun
Was set, and twilight from the east came on,
Forerunning night; when at the holy mount

vii 571. Cp. iii 528–37.
vii 575–81. blazing portals] The immediate connection with the Milky Way
shows that these can only be the 'Portals of the Sun', the tropical signs
Capricorn and Cancer that mark the limits of the solar path. See Porphyry,
De antro nymph. 28; Helpericus of Auxerre, De computo 2 (Migne, cxxxvii
25); and Macrobius, In Somn. Scip. I xii 1f: 'The Milky Way girdles the
zodiac, its great circle meeting it obliquely so that it crosses it at the two
tropical signs, Capricorn and Cancer. Natural philosophers named these the
'portals of the sun' because the solstices lie athwart the sun's path on either
side, checking farther progress and causing it to retrace its course across the
belt beyond whose limits it never trespasses. Souls are believed to pass through
these portals when going from the sky to the earth and returning from the
earth to the sky. For this reason one is called the portal of men and the other
the portal of gods: Cancer, the portal of men, because through it descent is
made to the lower regions; Capricorn, the portal of gods, because through
it souls return to their rightful abode of immortality, to be reckoned among
the gods.' Thus the route taken by the returning creator continues the solar
symbolism associated throughout PL with the triumphant Messiah. Mar-
jorie Nicolson (ELH ii (1935) 12, 24) classes this description of the Milky
Way with other pieces of 'Galilean' astronomy; but in itself the theory of
stellar composition was as old as Democritus: see Macrobius, ibid. I xv 6.
Cp. Ovid, Met. i 170, where the Milky Way is the route by which 'the
gods fare to the halls and royal dwelling of the mighty Thunderer'; also
iv 976 above, where Satan refers contemptuously to triumphs on the 'road
of heaven star-paved'.   galaxy] Specifically the Milky Way.   zone]
belt, band; region of the sky.
vii 581–4. Chronologically a crucial passage, since it clearly indicates that the
'evenings' of PL are to be reckoned from sunset. See ll. 249–52n and Intro-
duction, 'Chronology' (p. 26).   seventh / Evening] The evening that
begins Day 20 of the poem's action.

585 Of heaven's high-seated top, the imperial throne
Of Godhead, fixed for ever firm and sure,
The filial power arrived, and sat him down
With his great Father (for he also went
Invisible, yet stayed [:] such privilege
590 Hath omnipresence) and the work ordained,
Author and end of all things, and from work
Now resting, blessed and hallowed the seventh day,
As resting on that day from all his work,
But not in silence holy kept; the harp
595 Had work and rested not, the solemn pipe,
And dulcimer, all organs of sweet stop,
All sounds on fret by string or golden wire
Tempered soft tunings; intermixed with voice
Choral or unison: of incense clouds
600 Fuming from golden censers hid the mount.

vii *584–5. holy mount*] See v 643n.

vii *588–90.* The early edns begin parentheses with opening brackets both after *Father* (l. 588) and after *stayed* (l. 589); and have comma after *ordained* (l. 590). Editors usually remove the first of these opening brackets, with the result that the subject changes, so that it is the Father who *rests*, and is the *Author and end.* The allusion to *Heb.* xii 2, however, strongly suggests that *The filial power* is at least jointly in apposition to *Author and end.* I conclude that the parenthesis more probably runs from *for* (l. 588) to *omnipresence* (l. 590), and that opening bracket after *stayed* is an error for colon or comma. For the Father's universal presence, cp. l. 517f.

vii *592.* 'And God blessed the seventh day, and sanctified it: because that in it he had rested from all his work which God created and made' (*Gen.* ii 3). *hallowed*] Introduced from the variant account in A.V.*Exod.* xx 11.

vii *594–9.* Even by the standards of the time, M.'s portrayal of the music of heaven is unusually concrete and specific. A defence of music on the Sabbath is incidentally implied. Note the comprehensiveness of the classification of instruments. The *harp* takes precedence because it was played by David the type of Christ. As the context indicates, the *dulcimer* is here not the stringed instrument usually called by that name, but the Hebrew 'bagpipe' (Gk. συμφωνία). Consult Spaeth 40n and *OED* s.v. *Dulcimer* 1 b; and see *Dan.* iii 5: 'At what time ye hear the sound of the cornet, flute, harp, sackbut, psaltery, dulcimer, and all kinds of musick, ye fall down and worship the golden image that Nebuchadnezzar the king hath set up' (A.V. margin 'symphony'). *frets*] The ridges dividing the finger-board of guitar-like stringed instruments, so as to regulate the fingering. *string . . . wire*] both the gut strings of instruments such as the lute, and the wire strings of such as the cittern. *tunings*] musical sounds.

vii *600. censers*] In no way Papist in association, but taken direct from the Jewish Temple (Broadbent 157), or rather from *Rev.* viii 3. 'It would appear

Creation and the six days' acts they sung,
Great are thy works, Jehovah, infinite
Thy power; what thought can measure thee or tongue
Relate thee; greater now in thy return
605 Than from the giant angels; thee that day
Thy thunders magnified; but to create
Is greater than created to destroy.
Who can impair thee, mighty king, or bound
Thy empire? Easily the proud attempt
610 Of spirits apostate and their counsels vain
Thou hast repelled, while impiously they thought
Thee to diminish, and from thee withdraw
The number of thy worshippers. Who seeks
To lessen thee, against his purpose serves
615 To manifest the more thy might: his evil
Thou usest, and from thence createst more good.
Witness this new-made world, another heaven
From heaven gate not far, founded in view
On the clear hyaline, the glassy sea;
620 Of amplitude almost immense, with stars
Numerous, and every star perhaps a world

that all allegories whatever are likely to seem Catholic to the general reader. . . . Catholicism is allegorical' (Lewis[2] 322).

vii *601–32*. A 'hymn of the creation' is included in Act i of Draft iii of M.'s outline for a tragedy on Paradise Lost; see Introduction, 'Composition' (p. 4).

vii *601*. The angels' praise harmonizes with M.'s own, just as on the chronologically later occasion described in Bk iii. See iii 410–15*n*.

vii *604–7*. Implying a hierarchy of virtues in which creativity takes precedence over strength or power or fortitude. Cp. iii 267–9*n*, vi 820–3*n*, and see Steadman 93.   *giant angels*] Throughout *PL*, but especially in Bks i and vi, the war against the rebel angels is compared with its mythic analogue, Jupiter's war against the Giants.

vii *613–6*. That God's creativity manifests itself in the power to use evil for good is a central theme of *PL*: cp, e.g., i 216–9 and xii 469–73; and·see Lewis 66 and Rajan 45f. Contrast Satan's determination to pervert good to evil (i 164f).

vii *619. hyaline*] The θάλασσα ὑαλίνη of *Rev.* iv 6, the 'sea of glass like unto crystal' before the throne of God. It is the same as the waters above the firmament: see l. 271*n* and iii 518–9*n*; also Svendsen 55f. 'Hyaline' is wrongly treated as a proper name in the early edns.

vii *620–2*. For the idea of other inhabited worlds see iii 565–71*n*. Here the possibility is presented as an expression of God's continued and unsearchable creativity.   *immense*] infinite; immeasurable.

> Of destined habitation; but thou know'st
> Their seasons: among these the seat of men,
> Earth with her nether ocean circumfused,
> 625   Their pleasant dwelling place. Thrice happy men,
> And sons of men, whom God hath thus advanced,
> Created in his image, there to dwell
> And worship him, and in reward to rule
> Over his works, on earth, in sea, or air,
> 630   And multiply a race of worshippers
> Holy and just: thrice happy if they know
> Their happiness, and persevere upright.
>   So sung they, and the empyrean rung,
> With hallelujahs: thus was Sabbath kept.
> 635   And thy request think now fulfilled, that asked
> How first this world and face of things began,
> And what before thy memory was done
> From the beginning, that posterity
> Informed by thee might know; if else thou seek'st
> 640   Aught, not surpassing human measure, say.

THE END OF THE SEVENTH BOOK

---

vii *622–3*. Either 'you know whether their seasons are compatible with habitation' or 'you know the seasons when they are destined for habitation'. The latter meaning seems the primary one, in view of the probable allusion to *Acts* i 7: 'It is not for you to know the times or the seasons, which the Father hath put in his own power.'

vii *624. nether ocean*] the ocean of the nether world earth, in antithesis to the waters above the firmament. In ancient geography, Oceanus was a great river encompassing the disc of the earth.

vii *629*. 'Thou madest him to have dominion over the works of thy hands; thou hast put all things under his feet' (*Ps.* viii 6).

vii *631–2*. Alluding to Virgil's exclamation over the happiness of simple peasants: 'O happy husbandmen! too happy, should they come to know their blessings! for whom, far from the clash of arms, most righteous Earth, unbidden, pours forth from her soil an easy sustenance' (*Georg.* ii 458–60). *persevere*] continue in a state of grace (a technical term in theology). In M.'s time the main stress in *persevere* was moving from the second to the third syllable; he consistently used the more modern form. Cp. the elaboration of this warning at viii 639ff.

vii *634. halleluiah*] 'praise ye the Lord' (*Ps.* cxlvi: A.V. margin 'Halleluiah'); italicized in the early edns.

vii *636. face*] outward form.

vii *639*. The belief that the *artes* had their origin in the relics of Adam's

Paradise Lost

BOOK VIII

The Argument

Adam inquires[1] concerning celestial motions, is doubtfully answered, and exhorted to search rather things more worthy of knowledge: Adam assents, and still desirous to detain Raphael, relates to him what he remembered since his own creation, his placing in Paradise, his talk with God concerning solitude and fit society, his first meeting and nuptials with Eve, his discourse with the angel thereupon; who after admonitions repeated departs.

The angel ended, and in Adam's ear
So charming left his voice, that he awhile
Thought him still speaking, still stood fixed to hear;
Then as new waked thus gratefully replied.
5   What thanks sufficient, or what recompense
Equal have I to render thee, divine
Historian, who thus largely hast allayed
The thirst I had of knowledge, and vouchsafed
This friendly condescension to relate
10 Things else by me unsearchable, now heard
With wonder, but delight, and, as is due,
With glory attributed to the high
Creator; something yet of doubt remains,

prelapsarian wisdom was a common tenet of seventeenth-century theological art-theory. See Curtius, *Excursus* xxii, especially p. 556. There is a good deal about this topic in Goulart's Commentary on Du Bartas. See, e.g., Lodge's translation, p. 138: 'From him it is as from a living source, that this current of celestiall science floweth unto us'; and cp. L'Isle's version (1595), p. 45: 'From him had we first our Arts and Sciences derived.'
viii *Argument*[1]. *Adam inquires*] Adam then inquires *Ed I*.
viii 1–4. Bks vii and viii of *Ed II* form a single book in *Ed I*. *Ed I* vii 641, which corresponds to *Ed II* viii 4, reads *To whom thus Adam gratefully replied*. The three opening lines of *Ed II* viii may have been added to provide in terms of action for the inevitable pause between books.   *charming*] enchanting, spell-binding.   *still stood fixed*] After digressions in classical epics, audiences often remain similarly rapt. Cp. e.g., Homer, *Od.* xiii 1; Apollonius, *Argonaut.* i 512–16. The latter passage is the more immediate model; for there the silence ensues after Orpheus has sung the story of creation, to dispel thoughts of strife.
viii *12*. The accentuation *attribùted* continued to be possible, at least in verse, as late as the nineteenth century.

Which only thy solution can resolve.
15   When I behold this goodly frame, this world
Of heaven and earth consisting, and compute
Their magnitudes, this earth a spot, a grain,
An atom, with the firmament compared

viii *14. solution*] explanation.

viii *15. frame*] universe; see v 154*n*.

viii *15–38*. Adam proposes to Raphael essentially the same problem proposed
to him by Eve at iv 657f; though he carries it to a higher level of abstraction.
It was a topic of the schools, which M. had already touched in *Prol vii*
(Yale i 292). There he maintains that the heavens cannot exist simply for the
material convenience of man, but that they call for meditation and study
and reverence: 'Can we indeed believe, my hearers, that the vast spaces of
boundless air are illuminated and adorned with everlasting lights, that these
are endowed with such rapidity of motion and pass through such intricate
revolutions, merely to serve as a lantern for base and slothful men, and to
light the path of the idle and the sluggard here below?' Here, however, the
question is given a new precision; so that the problem of the wastefulness
of an anthropocentric universe is focused in the problem of the incom-
prehensible distribution of kinetic energy entailed by the geocentric system.
Cp. M.'s own doubt at iv 592–5, 'whether the prime orb, / Incredible how
swift, had thither rolled / Diurnal, or this less voluble earth / By shorter
flight to the east. . . .' For the velocities thought to be involved and their
bearing on the Copernican hypothesis, which had been taken up by Kepler,
Gilbert, Galileo and others, see iv 592–7*n*. Burton's discussion of 'that main
paradox, of the earth's motion, now so much in question' at *Anat. of Mel.*
II ii 3 covers very similar ground; dwelling on the impossible velocities
with which the heavens must move in a geocentric system, and quoting
Gilbert's exclamation 'what fury is that . . . that shall drive the heavens about
with such incomprehensible celerity in twenty-four hours'.

Burden (116) comments that Adam is here almost a sceptical astronomer
reasoning falsely about final causes. Far from concentrating on the glorifica-
tion of God Adam in effect indicts providence; showing that this sphere of
knowledge is beyond his capacity. It seems that at least part of astronomy (or
a certain kind of astronomical speculation) may come within the category
of forbidden knowledge; not because M. is against science, but because
some knowledge is of 'no avail' for man. Raphael's volte face at l. 122 will
indicate that what avails is not the intricate choice of one particular cosmo-
logical model but the enjoyment of our own station in the universe (cp. ll.
160–87).

viii *15. goodly frame*] Cp. *Hamlet* II ii 317: 'It goes so heavily with my dispo-
sition that this goodly frame, the earth, seems to me a sterile promontory.'

viii *16. Ed I* and *Ed II* wrongly have comma after *compute*.

And all her numbered stars, that seem to roll
20   Spaces incomprehensible (for such
      Their distance argues and their swift return
      Diurnal) merely to officiate light
      Round this opacous earth, this punctual spot,
      One day and night; in all their vast survey
25   Useless besides, reasoning I oft admire,
      How nature wise and frugal could commit
      Such disproportions, with superfluous hand
      So many nobler bodies to create,
      Greater so manifold to this one use,
30   For aught appears, and on their orbs impose
      Such restless revolution day by day
      Repeated, while the sedentary earth,
      That better might with far less compass move,
      Served by more noble than her self, attains
35   Her end without least motion, and receives,
      As tribute such a sumless journey brought

viii 19. *numbered*] numerous (the same rare usage as at vi 229: cp. Shakespeare, *Cymbeline* I vi 36, 'the number'd beach'); but perhaps also alluding to *Ps.* cxlvii 4: 'He telleth the number of the stars; he calleth them all by their names.'

viii 22. *officiate*] supply, minister. Implying that the stars are ordained (like the angels) to minister to men.

viii 23. *opacous*] opaque.   *punctual*] point-like, minute (*OED* II 3 a). The idea that the earth is a mere point compared with the heavens is perennial. It was constantly reiterated in encyclopedias and astronomical works from the late Middle Ages onwards (e.g., Alexander Neckham: *tanta est firmamenti quantitas ut ipsi totalis terra collata quasi punctum esse videatur*), but, as Svendsen 40 shows, some scholars are reluctant to admit that it was not a Copernican discovery. In M.'s time the commonplace was given, however, an almost novel turn: the question became 'How big would earth seem, viewed from the heavens?' See Riccioli i 57, where the answer of Cleomedes (*c.* 50 A.D.) is quoted: from the sun, the earth would seem a point; from the stars, it would be invisible. The question of size was now related, moreover, to the question of plurality of worlds. Thus, Tycho Brahe would never believe that the huge stars 'were made to no other use than this that we perceive, to illuminate the earth, a point insensible in respect of the whole' (Burton, *Anat. of Mel.* II ii 3). Note also that Adam introduces the traditional encyclopedia paradox about little earth's centrality as matter for *doubt* (l. 13) rather than for wonder.

viii 25. *admire*] wonder, marvel.

viii 32. *sedentary*] Not only 'motionless' but also 'slothful': cp. *Prol. vii, loc. cit.* ll. 15–38*n*.

Of incorporeal speed, her warmth and light;
Speed, to describe whose swiftness number fails.
    So spake our sire, and by his countenance seemed
40 Entering on studious thoughts abstruse, which Eve
Perceiving where she sat retired in sight,
With lowliness majestic from her seat,
And grace that won who saw to wish her stay,
Rose, and went forth among her fruits and flowers,
45 To visit how they prospered, bud and bloom,
Her nursery; they at her coming sprung
And touched by her fair tendance gladlier grew.
Yet went she not, as not with such discourse
Delighted, or not capable her ear
50 Of what was high: such pleasure she reserved,
Adam relating, she sole auditress;
Her husband the relater she preferred
Before the angel, and of him to ask
Chose rather; he, she knew would intermix
55 Grateful digressions, and solve high dispute
With conjugal caresses, from his lip
Not words alone pleased her. O when meet now
Such pairs, in love and mutual honour joined?
With goddess-like demeanour forth she went;
60 Not unattended, for on her as queen

viii 37. *incorporeal speed*] Cp. l. 110, 'Speed almost spiritual'.   *warmth*]
Not merely heat, but also the fomenting 'influence' of iv 669.

viii 45–7. By making the flowers respond so to Eve's coming, M. is in
effect casting her in the role of a Venus. Cp. Marino, *Adone* iii 65: 'Plants
bleached and yellowed by the sun became all green, and every flower
opened and lifted its head.' Eve's Venus role is further developed at ll.
59–63.   *visit*] inspect (OED II 9).   *Her nursery*] her nursing; objects
of her care.   *tendance*] attention, care.

viii 48–56. Eve has to be absent for the discussion of marital relations that
follows later in the book, but M. is anxious that her departure should not
be taken to imply that women are by nature unsuited to intellectual pur-
suits. He may also have felt a need to square his account with *1 Cor.* xiv 35:
'And if they will learn any thing, let them ask their husbands at home: for
it is a shame for women to speak in the church.'

viii 59–63. *pomp*] train, procession. The Graces were attendants upon Venus,
with whom M. more than once identifies Eve. Cp. l. 46f and v 381. *shot*
is intransitive, with *darts* as its subject; since darts were an attribute, not of the
Graces, but of Venus herself, or of Cupid (Tervarent 186f; an alleged ex-
ception in Titian's *The Blinding of Amor* is dismissed by Wind at 76f). On the
potential danger of the *darts of desire*, which for the first half of l. 63 remain
unspecified and ambiguous, see Stein 91 and Ricks 98.

A pomp of winning graces waited still,
And from about her shot darts of desire
Into all eyes to wish her still in sight.
And Raphael now to Adam's doubt proposed
65   Benevolent and facile thus replied.
      To ask or search I blame thee not, for heaven
Is as the book of God before thee set,
Wherein to read his wondrous works, and learn
His seasons, hours, or days, or months, or years:
70   This to attain, whether heaven move or earth,
Imports not, if thou reckon right, the rest
From man or angel the great architect
Did wisely to conceal, and not divulge
His secrets to be scanned by them who ought
75   Rather admire; or if they list to try
Conjecture, he his fabric of the heavens

viii 65. *facile*] easy of converse; mild.

viii 67–9. For the traditional and at first theological metaphor of the cosmos as the *book of God* or 'book of nature' setting forth the wisdom of the creator, see Curtius 320f, 339, 344, etc. By M.'s time it was commonly secularized; but it still often occurred in its original mystical form, as here. Note that many of the creatures mentioned in Bk vii (e.g. bees, ants, behemoth, leviathan) were the same with those singled out as important pages of the book of nature (Curtius 222f).

viii 69. Cp. vii 340–52; and *Gen.* i 14, where the 'lights in the firmament' are 'for signs, and for seasons, and for days, and years'.

viii 71–84. McColley, 'Milton's Dialogue on Astronomy: the Principal Immediate Sources', *PMLA* lii (1937) 759f, thinks that this passage expresses radical opposition to the scientific movement of the time. But Svendsen 77f and Schultz convincingly show that M.'s true targets are dubious speculation and corrupted learning. In *First Defence* i (Columbia vii 67), indeed, M. defends astronomers 'who should be trusted in their own faculties' against the attack of Salmasius. The relativity of the centre of the universe, and of the motion of heavenly bodies, including the earth, had been asserted by Nicholas of Cusa (*De docta ignorantia* ii 11; tr. Heron (1954) 107ff); by taking up some such position it would not be difficult for an intelligent theologian of M.'s time to remain detached from the cosmological controversy.

viii 74. *scanned*] criticized, passed judgment on; discussed minutely. So Calvin on *Deut.* xiii 76, tr. Golding (1583): 'When men will needs scanne of Gods workes and providence according to their owne reason: they shall finde thinges to grudge at.'

viii 75. *admire*] wonder.

viii 76. Cp. Vulg. *Eccles.* iii 11: *Cuncta fecit bona in tempore suo, et mundum tradidit disputationi eorum, ut non inveniat homo opus, quod operatus est Deus ab initio usque ad finem.*

Hath left to their disputes, perhaps to move
His laughter at their quaint opinions wide
Hereafter, when they come to model heaven
80   And calculate the stars, how they will wield
The mighty frame, how build, unbuild, contrive
To save appearances, how gird the sphere
With centric and eccentric scribbled o'er,
Cycle and epicycle, orb in orb:
85   Already by thy reasoning this I guess,
Who art to lead thy offspring, and supposest
That bodies bright and greater should not serve
The less not bright, nor heaven such journeys run,
Earth sitting still, when she alone receives
90   The benefit: consider first, that great
Or bright infers not excellence: the earth

viii *78. wide*] astray, mistaken; not an ellipsis.

viii *80. calculate*] compute the number of (*OED* 1); predict the motions of (*OED* 2); arrange, frame (*OED* 4, 5).

viii *82. To save appearances*] Or 'to save the phenomena', a term of the Schools, meaning 'to reconcile the observed facts with some theory they appear to disagree with'. Cp. Bacon, *Essays* (1625), 'Of Superstition': 'Astronomers, which did faigne Eccentricks and Epicycles, and such Engines of Orbs, to save the Phenomena; though they knew, there were no such Things.' For the history of the term see Karl Hammerle, '*To Save Appearances* (*Par. L.*, VIII 82), ein Problem der Scholastick', *Anglia* lxii (1938) 368–72.

viii *83. centric and eccentric*] See iii 573–6n. Note that the terms *eccentric* and *epicycle* come in a logical expository sequence. In the Ptolemaic system, observed irregularities in the motion of the heavenly bodies were accounted for first by hypothesizing slight displacements from the earth of the centres of orbit (hence the eccentric circles); secondly – since this was insufficient for planets other than the sun – by adding epicycles, smaller circles whose centres ride on the circumferences of the main eccentric circles and carry the planets. 'In the case of the outer planets (Mars, Jupiter, Saturn) the epicycle corresponds to the motion of the Earth, and the eccentric main circle to that of the planet concerned. For the inner planets (Mercury, Venus) this situation is reversed, and it is the main circle that contains the annual revolution' (Price 99). Copernicus still required as many as thirty-four auxiliary circles, to account for the varying velocities of the planets; see Dreyer 331, 343.

viii *90–1. excellence*] Raphael's dissociation of size and brightness from excellence is perhaps to be related to the underlying hierarchy of virtues and qualities in *PL*, discussed by Steadman. Cp. vi 820–3, where a distinction between modes of excellence is developed.   *infers*] implies, entails.

viii *91–9.* Raphael's argument is doubly *a fortiori*: 'even if the sun (the chief luminary) ministers, and even if he ministers merely to Earth, it is not

Though, in comparison of heaven, so small,
Nor glistering, may of solid good contain
More plenty than the sun that barren shines,
95 Whose virtue on it self works no effect,
But in the fruitful earth; there first received
His beams, unactive else, their vigour find.
Yet not to earth are those bright luminaries
Officious, but to thee earth's habitant.
100 And for the heaven's wide circuit, let it speak
The maker's high magnificence, who built
So spacious, and his line stretched out so far;
That man may know he dwells not in his own;
An edifice too large for him to fill,
105 Lodged in a small partition, and the rest
Ordained for uses to his Lord best known.
The swiftness of those circles attribute,
Though numberless, to his omnipotence,
That to corporeal substances could add
110 Speed almost spiritual; me thou think'st not slow,
Who since the morning hour set out from heaven
Where God resides, and ere mid-day arrived
In Eden, distance inexpressible
By numbers that have name. But this I urge,

unfitting'. Cp. Marlowe, *Doctor Faustus* 620: the heavens were 'made for man, therefore is man more excellent'.   *barren*] W. B. Hunter (*MLR* xliv (1949) 89) compares Proclus' description of the sun as 'shadowless and unreceptive of generation'. Because the sun already contains a plenitude of life, it requires no addition from its own virtuous beams.

viii *99. officious*] dutiful; attentive; efficacious in performing its function.

viii *102.* Cp. *Job* xxxviii 5, where God asks, concerning the earth, 'Who hath laid the measures thereof, if thou knowest? or who hath stretched the line upon it?'

viii *107. circles*] orbital courses.   *attribute*] Stressed on the first syllable.

viii *108. numberless*] Probably qualifies swiftness (cp. ll. 36–8, 'a sumless journey . . . to describe whose swiftness number fails'); though the number of stars that have to move in a geocentric universe, and therefore the great number of *circles*, is conceivably also alluded to (cp. ll. 28, 80).

viii *110. Speed almost spiritual*] Cp. l.37. The notion that speed is spiritual depends on the ancient and medieval belief that the spheres were moved by intelligences or spirits. See especially Ficino's Commentary on Plotinus' *Enneads* ii 1–3, where an extended analogy is traced between the movement of the heavens and the movement of the soul in thought.

viii *114–18.* With an unexpected change of direction Raphael disengages himself from the Ptolemaic position. The contrast between conversation with M.'s angels and with, say, Marlowe's, is very striking. Marlowe's

115   Admitting motion in the heavens, to show
        Invalid that which thee to doubt it moved;
        Not that I so affirm, though so it seem
        To thee who hast thy dwelling here on earth.
        God to remove his ways from human sense,
120   Placed heaven from earth so far, that earthly sight,
        If it presume, might err in things too high,
        And no advantage gain. What if the sun
        Be centre to the world, and other stars
        By his attractive virtue and their own
125   Incited, dance about him various rounds?

Mephistophilis glumly casts his vote for the traditional world picture
(*Doctor Faustus* 653–87), whereas Raphael is detached, provocative, agile,
intellectually stimulating.

viii *117–22*. The elusiveness of Raphael's position reflects the difficulty M.
must have felt in making a final decision in favour of any one of the many
alternative planetary systems available. He had little enthusiasm for the Ptole-
maic system, but, as Rajan 152f rightly stresses, the main struggle was
between the Copernican system and the Tychonic or geoheliocentric.
Throughout the present dialogue the diction is often ingeniously designed
to allow simultaneous reference to more than one of these alternative sys-
tems; e.g., the first part of Raphael's speech (ll. 85–114) refers to the Tychonic
system as well as to the Ptolemaic, so that Rajan regrets M.'s omission of the
Tychonic system needlessly. Grant McColley, 'Milton's Dialogue on
Astronomy', *PMLA* lii (1937) 728–62, is useful for its reference of *PL* to the
context of contemporary scientific controversy, and particularly for its
demonstration of a close relation with Bishop Wilkin's *Discourse that the
Earth May be a Planet* (1640) and Ross's *The New Planet no Planet*. McColley
is not at all convincing, however, in his view that M.'s purpose was to re-
primand the Royal Society by criticizing the speculations of one of its
secretaries. On the contrary, the opinions of Wilkins seem fairly evenly
distributed between Adam and Raphael, while on the main issue of helio-
centricity we find Wilkins on the 'right' side.

viii *122–3. What if the sun / Be centre*] Appropriately the word *sun* is placed
in the centre of the 113–line paragraph. But this is no evidence of numer-
ology in the pattern of stressed syllables (as Whaler takes it to be); only of
line-count numerology. See Introduction, 'Numerology'; also Fowler,
Index, s.v. *Central Position of Sovereignty.   world*] universe.

viii *124*. For the theory that the planets are impelled by the magnetic in-
fluence of the sun, see iii 583–6*n*.   *attractive virtue*] influence or power of
attraction.

viii *125*. For the image of a cosmic dance, see iii 579–81*n*.   *rounds*] A
pun between 'circles' (*OED* II 6) and 'dances in which the performers move
in a ring' (*OED* III 11). Cp. *Comus* 114.

Their wandering course now high, now low, then hid,
Progressive, retrograde, or standing still,
In six thou seest, and what if seventh to these
The planet earth, so steadfast though she seem,
130   Insensibly three different motions move?
Which else to several spheres thou must ascribe,

viii *126. wandering*] Literally translates Gk πλανήτης, from which *planet*
is derived. Common poetic diction.

viii *127. retrograde*] Apparently moving from east to west, that is, in a direc-
tion contrary to the order of the zodiacal signs.

viii *128. six*] Saturnus, Jupiter, Mars, Venus, Mercurius and Luna. Since
Copernicus, the main subject debated by astronomers was whether the
earth or the sun constituted the seventh planet.

viii *130. three different motions*] The three motions attributed to the earth by
Copernicus: namely, diurnal rotation, annual orbital revolution about the
sun and a 'third motion' or 'motion in declination'. The last of these,
'whereby the axis of the earth describes the surface of a cone in [about]
a year, moving in the opposite direction to that of the earth's centre', was
unnecessarily introduced to account for 'the fact, that the axis of the earth,
notwithstanding the annual motion, always points to the same spot on the
celestial sphere' (Dreyer 329, 328). Later, Tycho Brahe was able to dispense
with this third motion (*ibid.* 361). It is important not to join Hughes in
confusing 'motion in declination' with the much slower resultant of axial
and orbital annual revolutions, which in the fallen world causes precession
of the equinoxes (a motion with a period, in Copernicus' estimation, of
some 25,798 years). For Raphael is speaking in a prelapsarian world in which
ecliptic and equator coincide, so that there is no equinoctial point to precess.
(Contrast iii 483 above, where M. can refer to 'trepidation', because the
digression is in 'real' or seventeenth-century time.) Before the Fall, the
period of 'motion in declination' was presumably exactly equal to the
period of annual orbital revolution. On the beginning of the distinction
between ecliptic and equator, see x 651-706n; also Introduction, 'M.'s
Universe'.

viii *131-2.* Meaning 'if you don't ascribe motion to the earth, then to
account for the observed phenomena you will have to posit a number of
spheres moving in contrary directions'. In the ancient and medieval planetary
systems the motion of each planet was explained as the resultant of the cir-
cular motions of several concentric spheres (for a simple account, consult
Crombie i 80f).   *thwart obliquities*] The zodiac was frequently referred to
as the 'thwart circle'; see, e.g., Robert Recorde, *The castle of knowledge*
(1556) 30: 'The Zodiak (whiche many doo call the Thwarte circle).' It
seems very probable, therefore, that M. intends an allusion to the inclination
of the ecliptic circle; though from Raphael's point of view there is as yet
no obliquity in this sense. The allusion is thus a dramatic irony: Adam would
take the phrase to refer to the obliquity of the equator–ecliptic with respect

> Moved contrary with thwart obliquities,
> Or save the sun his labour, and that swift
> Nocturnal and diurnal rhomb supposed,
> *135*   Invisible else above all stars, the wheel
> Of day and night; which needs not thy belief,
> If earth industrious of her self fetch day
> Travelling east, and with her part averse
> From the sun's beam meet night, her other part
> *140*   Still luminous by his ray. What if that light
> Sent from her through the wide transpicuous air,
> To the terrestrial moon be as a star

to the horizon (which in the Ptolemaic system was a fixed frame of reference), or to mean simply 'awkward indirections'. For the inclining of the ecliptic to the equator after the Fall, see x 651–706*n*, 668–80*n*.

viii *134*. The accuracy and subtlety of this line is generally missed. *rhomb* is from Gk. ῥόμβος, a magic wheel, and refers to the imaginary *primum mobile* or tenth sphere, which in the medieval planetary system revolved diurnally about the earth with incredible swiftness, carrying the interior spheres of the stars and planets with it. But 'rhomb' more obviously means 'rhombus, lozenge-shape'; a sense that has precise though secondary relevance here. In diagrams illustrating the Ptolemaic system, the triangle of the sun's rays, together with the triangle of the umbra or darkest central part of the earth's shadow, formed an elongated rhombus (well described as *Nocturnal and diurnal*), which was to be thought of as rotating about its own centroid or the earth's centre, like a pair of spokes of a parti-coloured wheel. Based on such illustrations were certain more mystical diagrams showing the intersection of 'the pyramid of light' with 'the pyramid of shadows'. A particularly interesting example is the geometrical development of the *tetractys* in Kircher, *Musurgia* ii 450, where the rhombus of intersection of the two 'pyramids' extends beyond the heavens to the *circulus universorum*. Cp. iii 556f above, and see v 758–9*n*.

viii *137*. *industrious*] Contrast the 'sedentary earth' of the Ptolemaic system, l. 32.

viii *140–5*. *that light*] the light from the earth's *other part . . . luminous* by the rays of the sun. Cp. Burton, *Anat. of Mel*. II ii 3: 'If the earth move, it is a planet, and shines to them in the moon, and to the other planetary inhabitants, as the moon and they do to us upon the earth: but shine she doth, as Galileo, Kepler, and others prove, and then *per consequens*, the rest of the planets are inhabited, as well as the moon.' This curious argument, in which Burton follows Kepler more or less faithfully, is based on the anthropocentric assumption that there is no point in having planets or satellites that shine, unless they shine for creatures similar to men. Kepler shares this assumption with Adam and Eve (see ll. 24f and iv 568) and with Raphael himself (ll. 153–8). For seventeenth-century speculations about the plurality of worlds, see iii 565–71*n*.

Enlightening her by day, as she by night
This earth? Reciprocal, if land be there,
145   Fields and inhabitants: her spots thou seest
As clouds, and clouds may rain, and rain produce
Fruits in her softened soil, for some to eat
Allotted there; and other suns perhaps
With their attendant moons thou wilt descry
150   Communicating male and female light,
Which two great sexes animate the world,
Stored in each orb perhaps with some that live.
For such vast room in nature unpossessed
By living soul, desert and desolate,
155   Only to shine, yet scarce to contribute
Each orb a glimpse of light, conveyed so far
Down to this habitable, which returns
Light back to them, is obvious to dispute.

viii *144–5.* Cp. i 290f, where Galileo can 'descry new lands, / Rivers or mountains in her spotty globe'.

viii *145–6.* In M.'s time, reported changes or movements of the spots of the moon were often ascribed to the effects of a lunar atmosphere; see Riccioli i 207½ [*sic*], 'De Novis Maculis Lunae, eiusque Asperitatibus, Vallibus, Cavernis, Montibus, Collibus etc.', where, however, the movements are attributed to lunar libration or to faulty observation. The theory that the spots were clouds, rather than surface features revealed by gaps in the clouds, was held, e.g., by Julius Caesar Lagalla. Raphael seemed to commit himself to that view at v 418–20 more definitely than he does here.

viii *148.* The idea that the fixed stars are suns with their attendant planets went back to Nicholas of Cusa. It was accepted by, e.g., Bruno, and rejected by Kepler; and in M.'s time was a topic of much speculation and controversy.

viii *150.* In Pliny, *Nat. hist.* i 129f the sun is 'a masculine star, burning up and absorbing everything' while the moon is 'a feminine and delicate planet': a sexual differentiation that was taken over from mythology. But the context makes it clear that Raphael refers to the fact that while the light of suns is 'peculiar', that of moons or planets is mostly reflected; cp. vii 368. The passage thus has a bearing on Raphael's teaching about relations between the sexes at ll. 561ff. It is also possible that M. may intend a more covert allusion to a Gnostic polarity in which 'male light' was mental light and 'female light' physical.

viii *151–2.* i.e., animate the universe, each orb of which is perhaps inhabited.

viii *154. desert*] Stressed on the second syllable.

viii *155. contribute*] Stressed on the first syllable.

viii *157. this habitable*] Probably imitates the Gk idiom ἡ οἰκουμένη, 'the inhabited (world), the Greek world'.

viii *158. obvious to dispute*] open to dispute. M. had himself formally disputed it at Cambridge; see the passage from *Prol vii* quoted in ll. 15–38n.

But whether thus these things, or whether not,
160 Whether the sun predominant in heaven
Rise on the earth, or earth rise on the sun,
He from the east his flaming road begin,
Or she from west her silent course advance
With inoffensive pace that spinning sleeps
165 On her soft axle, while she paces even,
And bears thee soft with the smooth air along,
Solicit not thy thoughts with matters hid,
Leave them to God above, him serve and fear;
Of other creatures, as him pleases best,
170 Wherever placed, let him dispose: joy thou
In what he gives to thee, this Paradise
And thy fair Eve; heaven is for thee too high
To know what passes there; be lowly wise:
Think only what concerns thee and thy being;
175 Dream not of other worlds, what creatures there
Live, in what state, condition or degree,
Contented that thus far hath been revealed
Not of earth only but of highest heaven.
    To whom thus Adam cleared of doubt, replied.
180 How fully hast thou satisfied me, pure
Intelligence of heaven, angel serene,
And freed from intricacies, taught to live,

viii 162–6. Raphael's personification of sun and earth has the effect of setting up a large-scale metaphor in which the issues of astronomical and of social sexual hierarchy are subtly related.   *inoffensive*] harmless; also in the Latin sense 'unobstructed'.

viii 166. M. provides for the stock anti-Copernican argument that rotation of the earth would cause violent winds, by having the atmosphere move with the earth. Cp. Riccioli i 51.

viii 167. The extent and the tenor of Raphael's conversation with Adam shows that the forbidden fruit is not scientific knowledge *per se*, but that scientific knowledge like any other kind may come within the forbidden category (Burden 121f).   *solicit*] disturb, make anxious (*OED* I 1).

viii 168. 'Let us hear the conclusion of the whole matter: Fear God, and keep his commandments: for this is the whole duty of man' (*Eccles* xii 13).

viii 176. Speculation about the nature of the inhabitants of other planets was rife in M.'s day, and covered a range of topics that have since become the province of science fiction. Kepler, e.g., at one time wondered whether aliens were rational, whether they had souls to be saved and whether they or men were lords of creation.

viii 181. Some copies of *Ed I* wrongly have full stop after *serene*.   *Intelligence*] spirit; intellectual being.

The easiest way, nor with perplexing thoughts
To interrupt the sweet of life, from which
185   God hath bid dwell far off all anxious cares,
And not molest us, unless we our selves
Seek them with wandering thoughts, and notions vain.
But apt the mind or fancy is to rove
Unchecked, and of her roving is no end;
190   Till warned, or by experience taught, she learn,
That not to know at large of things remote
From use, obscure and subtle, but to know
That which before us lies in daily life,
Is the prime wisdom, what is more, is fume,
195   Or emptiness, or fond impertinence,
And renders us in things that most concern
Unpractised, unprepared, and still to seek.
Therefore from this high pitch let us descend
A lower flight, and speak of things at hand
200   Useful, whence haply mention may arise
Of something not unseasonable to ask
By sufferance, and thy wonted favour deigned.
Thee I have heard relating what was done

viii *183–97*. M. has far more than scientific curiosity in mind here. Like the Cambridge Platonists, he is concerned that the understanding should be kept clear of all the phantasms of the imagination (*fancy*) as well as all the idle speculations of the intellect (*mind*). Cp. John Smith, *Discourses* (1673) 4 and 21: 'The reasons why, notwithstanding all our acute reasons and subtile disputes, Truth prevails no more in the world, is, we so often disjoyn *Truth* and true Goodness, which in themselves can never be disunited. . . . Our own *Imaginative Powers*, which are perpetually attending the highest acts of our Souls, will be breathing a gross dew upon the pure Glass of our Understandings.' For the fancy as a source of evil, cp. v 102–19 above. Restored to its context of seventeenth-century speculative thought, the present speech might well appear not an attack on science but a plea for science of a more practical and sensible kind. Bush cites Ralph Cudworth's sermon to the House of Commons, 31 March 1647: 'We think it a gallant thing to be fluttering up to heaven with our wings of knowledge and speculation: whereas the highest mystery of a divine life here, and of perfect happiness hereafter, consisteth in nothing but mere obedience to the divine will.'

viii *194. fume*] something unsubstantial, transient, imaginary (*OED* II 5); something which goes to the head and clouds the reason (*OED* II 6). Some copies *Ed I* have semicolon after *wisdom*.

viii *195. fond impertinence*] foolish irrelevance.

viii *197. to seek*] deficient; as at *Comus* 366.

viii *202. By sufferance*] by permission; probably implying 'by divine permission'.

Ere my remembrance: now hear me relate
205 My story, which perhaps thou hast not heard;
And day is yet not spent; till then thou seest
How subtly to detain thee I devise,
Inviting thee to hear while I relate,
Fond, were it not in hope of thy reply:
210 For while I sit with thee, I seem in heaven,
And sweeter thy discourse is to my ear
Than fruits of palm-tree pleasantest to thirst
And hunger both, from labour, at the hour
Of sweet repast; they satiate, and soon fill,
215 Though pleasant, but thy words with grace divine
Imbued, bring to their sweetness no satiety.
    To whom thus Raphael answered heavenly meek,
Nor are thy lips ungraceful, sire of men,
Nor tongue ineloquent; for God on thee
220 Abundantly his gifts hath also poured
Inward and outward both, his image fair:
Speaking or mute all comeliness and grace
Attends thee, and each word, each motion forms.
Nor less think we in heaven of thee on earth
225 Than of our fellow servant, and inquire
Gladly into the ways of God with man:
For God we see hath honoured thee, and set
On man his equal love: say therefore on;
For I that day was absent, as befell,

viii *211–16.* So Virgil's Menalcas compliments Mopsus by comparing his song to the slaking of thirst in summer heat, at *Ecl.* v 45–7. But M.'s introduction of the notion of satiety develops the alimentary / epistemological analogy of *PL* v 84, 400–500, etc.; so that ix 248, with its implication that Adam's converse is in danger of satiating Eve, acquires an ominous resonance. Cp. *Ps.* xix 103: 'How sweet are thy words unto my taste!'

viii *213. from*] Either 'when I come from' or 'caused by'.

viii *218.* Cp. *Ps.* xlv 2: 'Grace is poured into thy lips: therefore God hath blessed thee for ever.'

viii *221.* The doctrine of man's *outward* imaging of God was developed in the first description of Adam and Eve, at iv 289–95; though 'it was chiefly with respect to the soul that Adam was made in the divine image' (*De doctrina* i 7, Columbia xv 45). It is difficult to see how the present passage could be thought to make M. an anthropomorphite (Warburton's sneer).

viii *225.* When the author of *Revelation* tried to worship the angel who interpreted his vision, the latter prevented him: 'for I am thy fellowservant, and of thy brethren the prophets' (*Rev.* xxii 9).

viii *229.* The sixth day of creation, and Day 19 of the poem's action. See ll. 242–4*n*, and Introduction, 'Chronology', p. 26 above.

230   Bound on a voyage uncouth and obscure,
       Far on excursion toward the gates of hell;
       Squared in full legion (such command we had)
       To see that none thence issued forth a spy,
       Or enemy, while God was in his work,
235   Lest he incensed at such eruption bold,
       Destruction with creation might have mixed.
       Not that they durst without his leave attempt,
       But us he sends upon his high behests
       For state, as sovereign king, and to inure
240   Our prompt obedience. Fast we found, fast shut
       The dismal gates, and barricadoed strong;
       But long ere our approaching heard within
       Noise, other than the sound of dance or song,

viii *230. uncouth*] unfamiliar, unaccustomed.

viii *232.* For other instances of the angels' practice of adopting square formations, see i 758 and vi 62; and for the significance of the shape see i 550*n*.

viii *233–40.* Apparently an unsatisfactory passage, betraying the poet's difficulties and afterthoughts. No sooner has a reason been given for the expedition than M. seems to think it makes God look less than omnipotent, so that a qualification is hurried in: 'Not that. . . .' But the new formulation is if possible worse; as Empson 110 puts it, 'Raphael . . . assumes God gave him a job at the time merely to disappoint him.' We should remember, however, that Raphael is supposed to be concerned to give Adam just the right impression about things he is unable to understand. It may be, too, that M. means to portray Raphael as expressing a very strong wish that he had been present at man's creation. One way to do that would be to exaggerate the tediousness of the obedience that took him elsewhere. The main reason for Raphael's absence–to provide an occasion for the present episode–must of course remain unmentioned.

viii *238–40. state*] ceremony. That there is no point to the angel's errands is precisely their point; for they are tests of obedience. Burden 124f compares St Augustine's view that God is insulted when a higher reason than his will is required–a view with which Calvin (*Inst.* I xiv 1) agreed.

viii *241. barricadoed*] barred securely. Sin later (ii 877–84) unbarred the gates; but to close them again excelled her power, so that she had to leave them open. The point of this detail, as well as of the chronological array discussed in the following note, is evidently to express the total absence of evil from the original state of creation. When Satan begins his mission, however, evil is already admitted (though not yet sin).

viii *242–4.* M. assimilates Virgil's famous image of Aeneas terrified outside the gate of Tartarus, listening to 'groans and the sound of the savage lash, then the clank of iron and dragging of chains' (*Aen.* vi 557–9). Cp. Ariosto, *Orl. Fur.* xxxiv 4, where Astolfo hears the air 'torn with sobs and howls and everlasting mourning, sure sign that it was hell'. The present passage

>   Torment, and loud lament, and furious rage.
> 245 Glad we returned up to the coasts of light
>   Ere Sabbath evening: so we had in charge.
>   But thy relation now; for I attend,
>   Pleased with thy words no less than thou with mine.
>   So spake the godlike power, and thus our sire.
> 250 For man to tell how human life began
>   Is hard; for who himself beginning knew?
>   Desire with thee still longer to converse
>   Induced me. As new waked from soundest sleep
>   Soft on the flowery herb I found me laid
> 255 In balmy sweat, which with his beams the sun
>   Soon dried, and on the reeking moisture fed.
>   Straight toward heaven my wondering eyes I turned,
>   And gazed a while the ample sky, till raised

helps to date the week of creation with respect to the infernal events with which the poem opens. Thus the fact that the gate is barred is evidence that the 6th day of creation lies letween Days 13 and 22 of the poem's action. Some assume that the *furious rage* Raphael heard must be the raging of the assembled host of rebels at i 666, since the devils prostrate on the lake were silent (i 83) and stupefied (i 281) before Satan spoke to Beelzebub. This would put the creation of man on the 22nd day of the poem's action (see Introduction, 'Chronology', p. 27): a timing that would have some numerological fitness in view of the microcosmic properties of 22 (Bongo 439f, Fowler 285*n*), and some dramatic fitness in view of the fact that the poem begins *in medias res* on that day. On the other hand, we would expect the devils to be tormented during their stupor, so that there is no real obstacle to the more probable supposition that the 6th day of creation, and Raphael's excursion, took place on Day 19. Henry More tells us that demons begin their punishment by falling into 'an unquiet sleep, full of furious tormenting Dreams' (*The Immortality of the Soul* III xviii 10).

viii *246. sabbath-evening*] the evening that began the sabbath, the seventh day of rest after the creation of man. M., like the Hebrews, reckoned the day from sunset. See Introduction, 'Chronology' (p. 26).

viii *247. relation*] narration.

viii *249.* In *Ed I* the episode that follows was symmetrically placed with respect to Eve's narration of *her* origin. For it occurred as vii 886–1157, being followed by three complete books; just as Eve's narration was preceded by three books. For other instances of symmetry about the centre of *PL*, see vi 761*n*.

viii *256. reeking*] steaming. On the sun's sustenance from vapours, see v 423–6. But there the vapours of the whole earth were meant, so that the present line becomes a magnificent piece of microcosmic grandiloquence.

viii *258. gazed*] The transitive use was poetic.

By quick instinctive motion up I sprung,
260 As thitherward endeavouring, and upright
Stood on my feet; about me round I saw
Hill, dale, and shady woods, and sunny plains,
And liquid lapse of murmuring streams; by these,
Creatures that lived, and moved, and walked, or flew,
265 Birds on the branches warbling; all things smiled,
With fragrance and with joy my heart o'erflowed.
My self I then perused, and limb by limb
Surveyed, and sometimes went, and sometimes ran
With supple joints, and lively vigour led:
270 But who I was, or where, or from what cause,
Knew not; to speak I tried, and forthwith spake,
My tongue obeyed and readily could name
What e'er I saw. Thou sun, said I, fair light,
And thou enlightened earth, so fresh and gay,
275 Ye hills and dales, ye rivers, woods, and plains,
And ye that live and move, fair creatures, tell,
Tell, if ye saw, how came I thus, how here?
Not of my self; by some great maker then,
In goodness and in power pre-eminent;
280 Tell me, how may I know him, how adore,

viii 260. On Adam's upright posture, see vii 505–11n.

viii 263. lapse] gliding flow. Probably a Latinism: the present instance is the earliest cited in OED for this sense.

viii 265. warbling] singing sweetly.

viii 266. Richardson and Ricks speculate about what this line would mean if the comma before it had been put at various places in the middle. But we may rest content with the deliberately naïf zeugma of the line as it stands; the syntax is not, here, particularly fluid.

viii 268. went] walked.

viii 269. and] as Ed I.

viii 272. Whereas Gen. ii 19 says only 'whatsoever Adam called every living creature, that was the name thereof', M. agreed with most commentators in an Augustinian assumption of Adam's ability to administer the true names of things. M.'s version, however, is relatively simple and literal; see ll. 343–56n. Note that the sun is the first entity addressed by Adam. Cf. the hymn to the sun at v 171ff, and see Broadbent 166f, where the importance of the sun as a divine symbol in PL is rightly stressed.

viii 277. Willet 36 gives it as the first purpose of the naming of the beasts 'that man seeing his excellent creation farre surpassing all other, might thereby be stirred up to praise his Creator'.

viii 280–2. Smith 162 draws attention to the manner in which 'the Latinized elliptical construction' of ll. 280–1 'suddenly resolves itself with ease and grace' in l. 282.

From whom I have that thus I move and live,
And feel that I am happier than I know.
While thus I called, and strayed I knew not whither,
From where I first drew air, and first beheld
285   This happy light, when answer none returned,
On a green shady bank profuse of flowers
Pensive I sat me down; there gentle sleep
First found me, and with soft oppression seized
My drowsed sense, untroubled, though I thought
290   I then was passing to my former state
Insensible, and forthwith to dissolve:
When suddenly stood at my head a dream,
Whose inward apparition gently moved
My fancy to believe I yet had being,
295   And lived: one came, methought, of shape divine,
And said, Thy mansion wants thee, Adam, rise,
First man, of men innumerable ordained
First father, called by thee I come thy guide
To the garden of bliss, thy seat prepared.
300   So saying, by the hand he took me raised,
And over fields and waters, as in air

viii *281*. Cp. St Paul's Mars' hill sermon on the Unknown God, *Acts* xvii 28: 'For in him we live, and move, and have our being, as certain also of your own poets have said, For we are also his offspring.'

viii *282*. A dramatic irony, in view of vii 631f, 'thrice happy if they know / Their happiness'. Throughout *PL* happiness is a resonant and often ironic term. Cp. especially v 74, where Satan tempting Eve uses the word three times, yet tells her she may be 'Happier'.

viii *287*. *oppression*] the action of weighing down; gentle pressure. Normally the word had a much more violent sense–as it has in the description of Adam's satiety after the Fall, at ix 1044; see Ricks 115.

viii *291*. Lewis 46 suggests that the ambiguous syntax here renders the 'crumbling of consciousness'.

viii *292–5*. For the dream psychology implied, see v 100–13 above, where fancy forms imaginations of external things represented by the senses; and cp. ll. 460–1.   *dream*] Not merely a synecdoche for 'figure seen in a dream'; M. is imitating Homer, *Il.* ii 8, 16, etc., where *Oneiros* is a dream personified.   *stood . . . head*] An allusion to the position taken up by the false dream sent by Zeus to Agamemnon, *ibid*. 20.

viii *296–9*. According to *Gen.* ii 8 and 15, Adam was created outside Paradise and only afterwards placed in it. See vii 535–8*n* above.   *mansion*] dwelling-place, home. An allusion to *John* xiv 2 ('In my Father's house are many mansions. . . . I go to prepare a place for you') is possible.   *wants*] lacks.
seat] residence; or throne.

Smooth sliding without step, last led me up
A woody mountain; whose high top was plain,
A circuit wide, enclosed, with goodliest trees
305   Planted, with walks, and bowers, that what I saw
Of earth before scarce pleasant seemed. Each tree
Loaden with fairest fruit that hung to the eye
Tempting, stirred in me sudden appetite
To pluck and eat; whereat I waked, and found
310   Before mine eyes all real, as the dream
Had lively shadowed: here had new begun
My wandering, had not he who was my guide
Up hither, from among the trees appeared
Presence divine. Rejoicing, but with awe
315   In adoration at his feet I fell
Submiss: he reared me, and Whom thou sought'st
     I am,
Said mildly, author of all this thou seest
Above, or round about thee or beneath.
This Paradise I give thee, count it thine
320   To till and keep, and of the fruit to eat:
Of every tree that in the garden grows
Eat freely with glad heart; fear here no dearth;
But of the tree whose operation brings

viii *302.* For the accentuation *withòut*, implying emphasis, see ii 892*n* above.
viii *303–5.* For a fuller account of the geography of Paradise, cp. iv 132ff.
viii *308. tempting*] Here an innocent word, which takes on in the course of
the poem an increasingly moral significance. Cp. esp. ix 595, where the
dramatic irony is emphatic. All the trees are made provocative here, so that
the forbidden tree may not seem specially so (Burden 127).
viii *311. lively*] realistically, to the life.
viii *316. Submiss*] submissive. Those who wish to will of course find a
Latinism (*submissus*=cast down); unnecessarily.   *whom . . . am*] The
inversion throws enough stress on *I am* to make an allusion to *Exod.* iii 14.
There God answers Moses' enquiry about his name with the words 'I AM
THAT I AM. . . . Thus shalt thou say unto the children of Israel, I AM
hath sent me unto you.'
viii *320–2.* 'And the Lord God took the man, and put him into the garden of
Eden to dress it and to keep it. And the Lord God commanded the man,
saying, Of every tree of the garden thou mayest freely eat' (*Gen.* ii 15f).
till] A.V. has 'dress', and does not introduce the idea of tilling until after the
Fall, at iii 23; but M., who refuses to consider work as a punishment, follows
the Heb., Septuagint and Vulg. versions, where the same word is used in
both places.
viii *323–33.* Cp. *Gen.* ii 17: 'But of the tree of the knowledge of good and
evil, thou shalt not eat of it: for in the day that thou eatest thereof thou

Knowledge of good and ill, which I have set
325   The pledge of thy obedience and thy faith,
Amid the garden by the tree of life,
Remember what I warn thee, shun to taste,
And shun the bitter consequence: for know,
The day thou eat'st thereof, my sole command
330   Transgressed, inevitably thou shalt die;
From that day mortal, and this happy state
Shalt loose, expelled from hence into a world
Of woe and sorrow. Sternly he pronounced
The rigid interdiction, which resounds
335   Yet dreadful in mine ear, though in my choice
Not to incur; but soon his clear aspect
Returned and gracious purpose thus renewed.
Not only these fair bounds, but all the earth
To thee and to thy race I give; as lords
340   Possess it, and all things that therein live,

shalt surely die.' *From that day mortal* is more careful diction than may at
first appear. Since patristic times, Biblical commentators had puzzled over an
apparent discrepancy in the Genesis account of the Fall, in that 'mere bodily
death, as it is called, did not follow the sin of Adam on the self-same day,
as God had threatened' (*De doctrina* i 12, Columbia xv 203). One way out of
the difficulty was to distinguish between different 'degrees of death',
namely guiltiness, spiritual death, bodily death and eternal death (*De doctrina*
i 12–14, Columbia xv 202–50; see Willet 35 for a similar classification). The
first two of these followed Adam's transgression immediately, as M. shows
in his description of the results of eating the fruit, ix 1010ff below. Willet
like M. follows St Jerome's interpretation 'that Adam began in the same day
to die, not actually, but because then he became mortall and subject to death
. . . So Symmachus readeth, thou shalt be mortall. Many of the Fathers
speculated that if Adam had not sinned he would have been immortal (see,
e.g., Augustine, *Civ. Dei* xiv 1. Cp. M.'s speculation in *PL* v 497; and see
De doctrina i 8 (Columbia xv 91): 'God, at least after the fall of man (*post
lapsum saltem hominis*), limited human life to a certain term.'   operation]
effect. The warning is recalled by the echo of this word at ix 1012.
viii *329.* Cp. iii 95 above. As Lewis 68 stresses, the fruit has for M.'s good
characters no intrinsic magic: it is important only as a pledge of obedience.
viii *332. loose*] break up, do away with (*OED* 7); violate (*OED* 8); also
'lose', which previous editors have assumed to be the only word indicated,
in spite of the awkwardness of its accord with *state*. *Ed I* and *Ed II* have the
form 'loose', which could indicate either word.
viii *334. interdiction*] prohibition.
viii *336. incur*] (Intrans.) become liable (*OED* I 2).
viii *337. purpose*] discourse.
viii *338–41.* Cp. *Gen.* i 28; see vii 530–4*n*.

Or live in sea, or air, beast, fish, and fowl.
In sign whereof each bird and beast behold
After their kinds; I bring them to receive
From thee their names, and pay thee fealty
345 With low subjection; understand the same
Of fish within their watery residence,
Not hither summoned, since they cannot change
Their element to draw the thinner air.
As thus he spake, each bird and beast behold
350 Approaching two and two, these cowering low
With blandishment, each bird stooped on his wing.

viii *343–56*. For other references to the naming of the beasts, cp. l. 276; also vi 73–6, vii 493. The present account illustrates most of the five causes of the ceremony assigned by Willet (36): '1. that man seeing his excellent creation farre surpassing all other, might thereby be stirred up to praise his Creator. 2. that their might be a triall of Adams wisdome: *he brought them to see how he would call them.* 3. that by this meanes the Hebrewe language, wherein those names were given, might be founded. 4. that mans authoritie and dominion over the creatures might appeare: *for howsoever man named every living creature, so was the name thereof.* 5. that man finding among all the creatures no helpe or comfort meete for him: v. 20. might have a greater desire thereunto, and more lovingly embrace his helper, which should be brought to him.' Adam's wisdom was shown particularly in the effortless suddenness of his perceptions: cp. *De doctrina* i 7, Columbia xv 53: 'Certainly without extraordinary wisdom he could not have given names to the whole animal creation with such sudden intelligence, *Gen.* ii 20.' St Thomas Aquinas had held that Adam had an angelic understanding, capable of moving through objects to concepts instantly (*Summa Theol.* I xciv 2–4; see MacCaffrey 36–8).

The naming of the creatures had a strong topical interest, for in M.'s time, after such 'natural' classifications of species as Cesalpino's and Jung's, the movement towards morphological systematisation gathered momentum and was soon to culminate in the work of Linnaeus. In 1682 John Ray could list as many as 18,000 species of plants alone. On Adam's endowment with science, see vii 639*n*, The ability to name implied great knowledge, for 'names were given at the first according to the severall properties and nature of creatures' (Willet 37)–a doctrine that seems to have owed as much to Plato, *Crat.* 422, as to *Genesis*. Names could still be regarded magically; thus Bacon prophesied that when man 'shall be able to call the creatures by their true names he shall again command them' (*Of the Interpretation of Nature*).

viii *350. two and two*] A grim reminder of the next mythic gathering of the beasts, 'two and two unto Noah into the ark' (*Gen.* vii 9).

viii *351. stooped*] caused to bow down; brought to the ground (*OED* II 7); but with a secondary allusion to the intrans. sense, common of birds of

I named them, as they passed, and understood
Their nature, with such knowledge God endued
My sudden apprehension: but in these
355   I found not what me thought I wanted still;
And to the heavenly vision thus presumed.
O by what name, for thou above all these,
Above mankind, or aught than mankind higher,
Surpassest far my naming, how may I
360   Adore thee, author of this universe,
And all this good to man, for whose well being
So amply, and with hands so liberal
Thou hast provided all things: but with me
I see not who partakes. In solitude
365   What happiness, who can enjoy alone,
Or all enjoying, what contentment find?
Thus I presumptuous; and the vision bright,
As with a smile more brightened, thus replied.
What call'st thou solitude, is not the earth
370   With various living creatures, and the air
Replenished, and all these at thy command
To come and play before thee, know'st thou not
Their language and their ways, they also know,
And reason not contemptibly; with these
375   Find pastime, and bear rule; thy realm is large.
So spake the universal Lord, and seemed
So ordering. I with leave of speech implored,
And humble deprecation thus replied.
Let not my words offend thee, heavenly power,
380   My maker, be propitious while I speak.

prey: 'descend swiftly upon, swoop down on' (*OED* I 6)–foreshadowing
postlapsarian carnivorousness. See xi 182–90*nn*.
viii *357*. Adam follows the order of natural theology, in proceeding from
the names of the creatures to the name of their creator–an order to which the
contentious Warburton took needless exception.
viii *371*. *Replenished*] abundantly stocked (*OED* I 1).
viii *373*. For evidence that M. read Lactantius on the relation between
human and animal nature, see *Commonplace Book*, Yale i 373. It was a wide-
spread Jewish belief that before the Fall Adam understood the language of the
beasts: see Josephus, *Antiq.* I i 4 ('all the living creatures had one language');
Philo, *Quaest. in Gen.* i 32; *Jubilees* iii 28. The original language was usually
supposed, understandably enough, to have been Hebrew; but sometimes
Syriac or Greek or Aramaic. See Charles ii 17.   *know*] have understanding
or knowledge.
viii *379*. Cp. Abraham's apprehensive preface to a bold request, at *Gen.*
xviii 30: 'Oh let not the Lord be angry, and I will speak'.

Hast thou not made me here thy substitute,
And these inferior far beneath me set?
Among unequals what society
Can sort, what harmony or true delight?
385   Which must be mutual, in proportion due
Given and received; but in disparity
The one intense, the other still remiss
Cannot well suit with either, but soon prove
Tedious alike: of fellowship I speak
390   Such as I seek, fit to participate
All rational delight, wherein the brute
Cannot be human consort; they rejoice
Each with their kind, lion with lioness;
So fitly them in pairs thou hast combined;
395   Much less can bird with beast, or fish with fowl
So well converse, nor with the ox the ape;
Worse then can man with beast, and least of all.
Whereto the almighty answered, not displeased.
A nice and subtle happiness I see
400   Thou to thy self proposest, in the choice

viii *384–9*. An extended musical allegoria. For true harmony, there has to be the right mathematical proportion–a proportion that is here punningly described as reciprocal. Thus, in a stringed instrument the strings should bear a due ratio of length and frequency. But the human string is too strained (*intense*) and therefore high in pitch; while the animal string is too *remiss*, i.e., low in pitch. The moral or psychological meanings of *intense* and *remiss*, which give the allegoria its force, are perhaps to be considered as a dramatic irony (it is not the animals who prove remiss, in the event).   *sort*] fit, be in harmony.

viii *390. participate*] impart, share out (*OED* I 2).

viii *392–7*. i.e., 'Animals rejoice with their own species. Less converse is possible across the major divisions between kinds; indeed, even with more closely related species it is difficult. How much less converse is possible, therefore, between man and beast.' Intercourse would certainly be difficult between the emasculated ox, which drew Diana's car, and the ape, proverbially lascivious (Carroll 19, 92). Note how the choice of examples introduces notions of moral restraint and psychological adjustment; cp. Adam's phrase *rational delight* (l. 391).

viii *396. converse*] consort, associate familiarly.

viii *398*. Burden 31f notices how God plays out the scene with Adam as if he did not know he was going to create Eve. Providence must never be allowed to appear deterministic; though from the point of view of a human character he may seem to improvise.

viii *399. nice*] fastidious; but with 'over-refined, luxurious', even 'wanton', as overtones.

Of thy associates, Adam, and wilt taste
No pleasure, though in pleasure, solitary.
What think'st thou then of me, and this my state,
Seem I to thee sufficiently possessed
405 Of happiness, or not? Who am alone
From all eternity, for none I know
Second to me or like, equal much less.
How have I then with whom to hold converse
Save with the creatures which I made, and those
410 To me inferior, infinite descents
Beneath what other creatures are to thee?
    He ceased, I lowly answered. To attain
The highth and depth of thy eternal ways
All human thoughts come short, supreme of things;
415 Thou in thy self art perfect, and in thee
Is no deficience found; not so is man,
But in degree, the cause of his desire
By conversation with his like to help,
Or solace his defects. No need that thou
420 Shouldst propagate, already infinite;
And through all numbers absolute, though one;

viii 402. *in pleasure*] in a state of pleasure. Eden was often explained as
meaning 'pleasure'.
viii 406–7. Cp. Horace, *Odes* I xii 17f: *unde nil maius generatur ipso*, / *nec
viget quicquam simile aut secundum*. Hughes compares Aristotle, *Nic. Ethics*
1154[b], on God's 'single and simple pleasure' in unchanging immobile
activity.
viii 413. 'O the depth of the riches both of the wisdom and knowledge of
God! how unsearchable are his judgments, and his ways past finding out!'
(*Rom.* xi 33).
viii 416–19. As Howard 160 shows, Adam's awareness of this *deficience*
makes him the proegumenic or impulsive helping cause of the Fall. For his
need for companionship leads to the creation of Eve, who in turn will pro-
vide the procatarctic cause, or occasion. See iii 120*n* above. At *Eud. Ethics*
1244[b] Aristotle says that a god 'needing nothing . . . will not need a friend,
nor have one, supposing that he does not need one'; at 1245[b] he argues
against the position that a virtuous man should imitate the divine by dis-
pensing with his friends.   *But*] except.
viii 420. Ridiculously taken as evidence of Arianism by Kelley 121–as ll.
405–7 above were taken by Verity. There was no necessary connection be-
tween the theology of the monad and rejection of the doctrine of the Trinity.
viii 421. Editors have seen this line as a 'quibble' between *numbers* in anti-
thesis to *one*, and *numbers* in the Latin sense 'parts', as in such idiomatic
phrases as *perfectum . . . omnibus numeris* (Cicero, *De nat. deor.* ii 13) or *liber
numeris omnibus absolutus* (Pliny, *Epistles* ix 38). But the primary meaning

But man by number is to manifest
His single imperfection, and beget
Like of his like, his image multiplied,
425   In unity defective, which requires
Collateral love, and dearest amity.
Thou in thy secrecy although alone,
Best with thy self accompanied, seek'st not
Social communication, yet so pleased,
430   Canst raise thy creature to what highth thou wilt
Of union or communion, deified;
I by conversing cannot these erect
From prone, nor in their ways complacence find.
Thus I emboldened spake, and freedom used
435   Permissive, and acceptance found, which gained
This answer from the gracious voice divine.
    Thus far to try thee, Adam, I was pleased,
And find thee knowing not of beasts alone,
Which thou hast rightly named, but of thy self,
440   Expressing well the spirit within thee free,
My image, not imparted to the brute,
Whose fellowship therefore unmeet for thee

is that the divine monad contains all other numbers, and is therefore complete and perfect (*absolute*, *OED* II 4, 5) through them all. Bongo 13f explains that the monad is like God because it is the fountain and origin of all numbers, as God is the origin of created being. His extended analogy opens with a distinction between divine and created singleness that closely resembles M.'s. Whereas creaturely singleness (*single imperfection*) means the absence of a second member of the species, God's oneness means universality: *Unus si dicatur, non numeri, sed universitatis est nomen.* See vi 809–10n.

viii *426. collateral*] parallel, ranking side by side with, accompanying.

viii *427–8.* The paradox perhaps imitates Cato's famous description of Scipio Africanus: *Numquam minus solum esse, quam cum solus esset'* (Cicero, *De re pub.* I xvii 27, cp. *De offic.* III i 1).

viii *431. deified*] absorbed in the divine nature. A theological term for 'the elevation of the human soul to a supernatural state' by sanctifying grace; see Corcoran 103. Although *union* and *communion* could be taken as general terms distinguishing degrees of separateness or plurality in the relationship, it is difficult not to see references to mystical union and Holy Communion (Eucharist). See v 438–9n, on similar use of *transubstantiate*.

viii *432.* For the symbolic significance of the human posture, see vii 505–11.

viii *433. complacence*] object or source of pleasure; cp. iii 276, where the Father's 'sole complacence' is Messiah. The original accentuation *còmplacence* occurred certainly as late as 1675: as in many cases, M. prefers the newer pronunciation.

viii *435. permissive*] allowed.

Good reason was thou freely shouldst dislike,
And be so minded still; I, ere thou spakest,
445   Knew it not good for man to be alone,
And no such company as then thou saw'st
Intended thee, for trial only brought,
To see how thou couldst judge of fit and meet:
What next I bring shall please thee, be assured,
450   Thy likeness, thy fit help, thy other self,
Thy wish exactly to thy heart's desire.
    He ended, or I heard no more, for now
My earthly by his heavenly overpowered,
Which it had long stood under, strained to the highth
455   In that celestial colloquy sublime,
As with an object that excels the sense,
Dazzled and spent, sunk down, and sought repair
Of sleep, which instantly fell on me, called
By nature as in aid, and closed mine eyes.
460   Mine eyes he closed, but open left the cell
Of fancy my internal sight, by which

viii *445*. 'And the Lord God said, It is not good that the man should be alone' (*Gen.* ii 18).

viii *448*. God's motive is Scriptural: see ll. 343–56*n*, and cp. *Prov.* xvii 3, *John* vi 6.

viii *450. fit help*] Recalls *Gen.* ii 18, 'I will make him an help meet for him'. *other self*, however, is a classical term for a close friend (Lat. *alter ego*, Gk ἕτερος αὐτός); cp. x 128. In *De doctrina* i 10 (Columbia xv 163) M. gives the reasons for Eve's creation in the same order: 'God gave a wife to man at the beginning to the intent that she should be his help and solace and delight.' If she ceases to be such, he argues, then the husband should have no hesitation in divorcing her. Ever the Biblical theologian, M. invariably stressed the relational aspect of marriage.

viii *452–86*. 'And the Lord God caused a deep sleep to fall upon Adam, and he slept: and he took one of his ribs, and closed up the flesh instead thereof; And the rib, which the Lord God had taken from man, made he a woman, and brought her unto the man' (*Gen.* ii 21f).

viii *453. earthly*] Supply 'nature'. For the difficulty of sustaining conversation with God, see *Dan.* x 17: 'How can the servant of this my lord talk with this my lord? for as for me, straightway there remained no strength in me, neither is there breath left in me.'

viii *460–1. cell* / *Of fancy*] The *cellula phantastica*; see v 109*n*. For the action of fancy in producing dreams, see v 100–13*n*, and cp. viii 294. The present passage perhaps rationalizes the open-eyed trance of *Num.* xxiv 4: 'He hath said, which heard the words of God, which saw the vision of the Almighty, falling into a trance, but having his eyes open.'

Abstract as in a trance methought I saw,
Though sleeping, where I lay, and saw the shape
Still glorious before whom awake I stood,
465 Who stooping opened my left side, and took
From thence a rib, with cordial spirits warm,
And life-blood streaming fresh; wide was the wound,
But suddenly with flesh filled up and healed:
The rib he formed and fashioned with his hands;
470 Under his forming hands a creature grew,
Manlike, but different sex, so lovely fair,
That what seemed fair in all the world, seemed now
Mean, or in her summed up, in her contained
And in her looks, which from that time infused
475 Sweetness into my heart, unfelt before,
And into all things from her air inspired

viii *462. Abstract*] withdrawn, separated. The soul was believed to become separated from the body in the state of 'ecstasy', when meditating on divine truths.   *trance*] Follows Septuagint *Gen.* ii 21, ἔκστασιν, where A.V. has only 'deep sleep'.

viii *465–6.* Cp. iv 484. *Gen.* ii 21 does not specify from which side the rib was taken; but most commentators thought the left, since that was nearer Adam's heart. M. clinches the allusion to this pathetic theory by his use of the term *cordial* [i.e. cardiac] *spirits*, a rather old-fashioned synonym for 'vital spirits' (on which see v 484*n*). Willet (37), who thinks it needless to specify the left side, considers it more important to note that Eve was formed 'not out of his head, that shee should not be proud'. Perhaps the birth of Sin, described in *PL* ii, is meant to contrast in this respect with the birth of Eve. See, however, ii 752–61*n*.

viii *469. fashioned*] The early edns have 'fashoned', a spelling introduced, and abandoned, in the seventeenth century (cp. Fr. *façonner*).

viii *471–4.* So Marino, of the beautiful but fatally destructive Helen: 'So well does beauty's aggregate / In that fair face summed up unite, / Whatever is fair in all the world / Flowers in her' (*Adone* ii 173).

viii *471.* Poetic and difficult syntax. M. probably means to imply that Eve is the archetype of a whole sex; so that *sex* is in apposition to *creature*: 'a sex like man, yet also distinct'. But it may well be that both syntax and rhythm were beautifully complicated by the presence of a contemporary (and shortlived) predicative quasi-adj. use of sex='feminine' (*OED* 1 f); cp. Dryden, *Cymon and Iphigeneia* 367f (ed. Kinsley iv 1750): 'She hugg'd th'Offender, and forgave th'Offence, / Sex to the last!'

viii *476. air*] Radically ambiguous, two main possibilities being separable: (1) mien, look; (2) breath, *OED* I 9, as in Shakespeare, *Winter's Tale* V iii 77f: 'Still me thinkes / There is an ayre comes from her.' (2) gains support from the fact that in M.'s time the physical sense of *inspired* ('breathed') was still current.

The spirit of love and amorous delight.
She disappeared, and left me dark, I waked
To find her, or for ever to deplore
480 Her loss, and other pleasures all abjure:
When out of hope, behold her, not far off,
Such as I saw her in my dream, adorned
With what all earth or heaven could bestow
To make her amiable: on she came,
485 Led by her heavenly maker, though unseen,
And guided by his voice, nor uninformed
Of nuptial sanctity and marriage rites:
Grace was in all her steps, heaven in her eye,
In every gesture dignity and love.
490 I overjoyed could not forbear aloud.
     This turn hath made amends; thou hast fulfilled
Thy words, creator bounteous and benign,
Giver of all things fair, but fairest this
Of all thy gifts, nor enviest. I now see
495 Bone of my bone, flesh of my flesh, my self
Before me; woman is her name, of man
Extracted; for this cause he shall forego
Father and mother, and to his wife adhere;
And they shall be one flesh, one heart, one soul.

viii 478. Editors compare Sonnet XXIII, but the motif was not a rare one.
viii 481. out of hope] beyond hope.
viii 488. Cp. Shakespeare, Troilus IV iv 118, 'The lustre in your eye, heaven
in your cheek', of Cressida. Again an ominous analogue for Eve.
viii 490. aloud] Supply 'saying'.
viii 494. enviest] grudge, give reluctantly. Continuing the thought of
'thou hast fulfilled'.
viii 495-9. See Gen. iii 23f: 'And Adam said, This is now bone of my bones
and flesh of my flesh: she shall be called Woman, because she was taken out
of Man. Therefore shall a man leave his father and his mother, and shall
cleave unto his wife: and they shall be one flesh.' In Matt. xix 4-6 and Mark
x 6-8 these verses are made the basis of Jesus' doctrine of marriage as henosis
or union in one flesh.   my self] See l. 450n.   adhere] A.V. has 'cleave'
but Vulg. adhaerebit.
viii 499. The Biblical expression 'one flesh' is replaced by the familiar
Platonic tripartite division into parts, in order to preclude any misunder-
standing. Cp. Willet 39: 'They shall be one flesh, not onely in respect of
carnall copulation . . . for so bruit beasts may bee said to be one flesh: but
is respect of their perpetuall societie, the conjunction both of their bodies
and minds.'   flesh] Corresponds to the Platonic concupiscible part, as
heart to the irascible and soul to the rational.

500   She heard me thus, and though divinely brought,
         Yet innocence and virgin modesty,
         Her virtue and the conscience of her worth,
         That would be wooed, and not unsought be won,
         Not obvious, not obtrusive, but retired,
505   The more desirable, or to say all,
         Nature her self, though pure of sinful thought,
         Wrought in her so, that seeing me, she turned;
         I followed her, she what was honour knew,
         And with obsequious majesty approved
510   My pleaded reason. To the nuptial bower
         I led her blushing like the morn: all heaven,

viii 500. *divinely brought*] Cp. l. 485 and see *Gen.* ii 22.

viii 501. *modesty*] As Burden 46f points out, the modesty has nothing to do with guilt but springs from a sense of the exclusiveness of the relationship. M.'s difficulty is that many of the passions he wishes to write about only have an imaginable existence in fallen communities larger than two.

viii 502. *conscience*] consciousness; inward knowledge.

viii 504. *obvious*] open to influence. So H. Brooke, *Fool of Quality* iii 13, as late as 1809: 'She was artless and obvious to seduction.'

viii 508. Alluding to *Heb.* xiii 4: 'Marriage is honourable in all, and the bed undefiled: but whoremongers and adulterers God will judge.' The source of Eve's knowledge about honour was explained at l. 487 above. In expressing the notion that honour antedated the Fall, M. must have recalled Guarini's famous distinction between the *verace onor* of the Golden Age and the false honour of later times (*Pastor Fido* iv 10) – itself a correction of the First Chorus of Tasso's *Aminta*, which had declared the Golden Age free from honour altogether. Lewis (119f) agrees with Tasso, disliking the suggestion here of sexual shame in the unfallen Eve; though he grants that a spiritual modesty may be entirely appropriate. Empson 104f, 107 wonders if it is possible to make a distinction between a blameless sexual pleasure at the blushes of others, and an offensive sense of mastery. While the answer in respect of our fallen world must clearly be negative, I suspect that M. is trying to sustain some such distinction in respect of the world before the Fall. He would naturally wish all imaginable desires to have their innocent counterparts: in particular, perhaps, a desire for 'sweet reluctant amorous delay' (iv 311).

viii 509. *obsequious*] compliant; without any suggestion of undue servility. The oxymoron was not so violent as it has become. Cp. Spenser, *Epithalamion* 306f: 'In proud humility; / Like unto Maia, when as Jove her tooke.'

viii 511. *blushing*] Here we have to make allowance for what seems a general change in sensibility since the seventeenth century. Englishmen of that time had a strong taste for disdain or denial on the lady's part, so that however much M. was on the side of fruition, he was bound to share a little in the

> And happy constellations on that hour
> Shed their selectest influence; the earth
> Gave sign of gratulation, and each hill;
> 515 Joyous the birds; fresh gales and gentle airs
> Whispered it to the woods, and from their wings
> Flung rose, flung odours from the spicy shrub,
> Disporting, till the amorous bird of night
> Sung spousal, and bid haste the evening star
> 520 On his hill top, to light the bridal lamp.
> Thus I have told thee all my state, and brought
> My story to the sum of earthly bliss
> Which I enjoy, and must confess to find
> In all things else delight indeed, but such
> 525 As used or not, works in the mind no change,

feeling that 'willing kisses yield no joy' (Stanley, *Poems and Translations*, ed. G. M. Crump (Oxford 1962) 55). Burden's view (47) is that the 'sole propriety' of wedded love, its exclusive privacy, must give rise to a modesty that had nothing to do with guilt.

viii 513. The happy *influence* of the constellations is introduced not only to clarify the analogy between generation of a universe and generation of its microcosm (cp. the 'sweet influence' of the Pleiades at the creation, vii 375), but also to stress that until the Fall Adam and Eve enjoyed every benefit of astral influence. Their natures and sexual adjustment being perfect, they lack any excuse for error. The evil influence of stars and planets begins at x 657–64, when the macrocosm is altered as a result of the Fall.

viii 514. So in Homer, *Il.* xiv 347ff, earth gives signs of joy at the coition of Zeus and Hera. See iv 499–501n above.   *gratulation*] joy; congratulation.

viii 515. *gales*] Simply 'winds'; see iv 156n. The play on *airs*=melodies, which is underlined by *sung* in l. 519, was noticed by M.'s first commentator, Patrick Hume; see Ricks 106.

viii 516. For the *wings* of the personified *airs*, cp. iv 156ff; also *Comus* 989, 'And west winds with musky wing'.

viii 518. *amorous bird of night*] the nightingale; cp. v 40f.

viii 519. *evening star*] The planet Venus, here mythologized as Hesperus; cp. iv 605 above. The *hill top* recalls Virgil, *Ecl.* viii 30, or Catullus, *Carm.* lxii 1–4: *Vesper adest, iuvenes, consurgite: Vesper Olympo | expectata diu vix tandem lumina tollit. | surgere iam tempus, iam pingues linquere mensas, | iam veniet virgo, iam dicetur Hymenaeus.* In epithalamial tradition, the rising of Venus was the occasion for lighting the *bridal lamp* and conducting the bride to the bridegroom. In view of the considerable epithalamic element in *PL* (cf. iv 710–18, 741–70, xi 588–95) it is interesting that a marriage song is included in M.'s second draft of a tragedy on Paradise Lost. The tragedy was to have 'Evening Star' among its dramatis personae (see Introduction, 'Composition'; also Gilbert 19).

Nor vehement desire, these delicacies
I mean of taste, sight, smell, herbs, fruits, and flowers,
Walks, and the melody of birds; but here
Far otherwise, transported I behold,
530   Transported touch; here passion first I felt,
Commotion strange, in all enjoyments else
Superior and unmoved, here only weak
Against the charm of beauty's powerful glance.
Or nature failed in me, and left some part
535   Not proof enough such object to sustain,
Or from my side subducting, took perhaps
More than enough; at least on her bestowed
Too much of ornament, in outward show
Elaborate, of inward less exact.
540   For well I understand in the prime end
Of nature her the inferior, in the mind
And inward faculties, which most excel,
In outward also her resembling less
His image who made both, and less expressing
545   The character of that dominion given
O'er other creatures; yet when I approach
Her loveliness, so absolute she seems
And in her self complete, so well to know
Her own, that what she wills to do or say,
550   Seems wisest, virtuousest, discreetest, best;

viii 526. *vehement*] A highly significant word here, in view of its derivation from *vehe-mens* 'lacking in mind'. Cp. ii 954 and Argument to Bk ix.

viii 527–8. Note the absence of any mention of touch, in Renaissance thought the lowest and most physical of the five senses (see Kermode[2] *passim*). In the nuptials, on the contrary, touch is prominent (l. 530). See ll. 579–85*n*.

viii 530–1. *Transported*] put in an ecstasy. But there may be an ominous overtone ('banished'), in view of the contiguity of *passion*, not usually an innocent word. *Commotion*] mental perturbation; strong excitement.

viii 535. *proof*] of tried power of resistance, impervious.

viii 536. *subducting*] taking away from its place, subtracting.

viii 539–44. *exact*] perfect, consummate, finished, refined (*OED* I 1, 2). As soon as Adam has taken the forbidden fruit, however, he tells Eve 'now I see thou art exact of taste, / And elegant, of sapience no small part' (ix 1017f). Cp. also the question of the Chorus at *SA* 1025–30: 'Is it for that such outward ornament / Was lavished on their sex, that inward gifts / Were left for haste unfinished, judgment scant, / Capacity not raised to apprehend / Or value what is best / In choice, but oftest to affect the wrong?' Most of the commentators on *Genesis* agreed that Eve was a less perfect image of God than Adam was; see Williams 87.

viii 547. *absolute*] entire, perfect, independent.

All higher knowledge in her presence falls
Degraded, wisdom in discourse with her
Looses discountenanced, and like folly shows;
Authority and reason on her wait,
555   As one intended first, not after made
Occasionally; and to consummate all,
Greatness of mind and nobleness their seat
Build in her loveliest, and create an awe
About her, as a guard angelic placed.
560   To whom the angel with contracted brow.
        Accuse not nature, she hath done her part;
Do thou but thine, and be not diffident
Of wisdom, she deserts thee not, if thou
Dismiss not her, when most thou need'st her nigh,
565   By attributing overmuch to things
Less excellent, as thou thy self perceiv'st.
For what admir'st thou, what transports thee so,
An outside? Fair no doubt, and worthy well
Thy cherishing, thy honouring, and thy love,

viii 551–2. The dramatic irony is strong: Adam is betraying a tendency to mistake the appointed hierarchy of relationships that we know will prove fatal. 'The higher falls, and other falls inevitably follow' (MacCaffrey 69). Note, however, that Adam's continuation makes it clear that the tendency is meanwhile held in check, so that it does not yet constitute a defect. All we can say is that the 'balanced perfection' of life before the Fall 'becomes less stable: the knife-edge between man's "disposition to do good" and his "liability to fall", as Milton puts it in De doctrina, is sharpened through Books v, vii and viii' (Broadbent 197).

viii 553. Proleptic of the argument between Adam and Eve at ix 205–385. Looses] 'goes to pieces; comes unstuck' (OED 5). Or perhaps 'loses' is intended. The Ed I and Ed II spelling 'Looses' could indicate either word.

viii 556. Occasionally] accidentally–i.e., as a result of the contingency of Adam's need for companionship.   consùmmate] complete.

viii 557. Greatness of mind] magnanimity, on which see vii 505–11n.

viii 561–70. We are reminded of this warning, after the Fall, by Christ's censure at x 145–56.   nature] Here 'God' or 'God's work in forming your nature'. Adam might conceivably–even after Raphael's account of the creation–have thought of nature as responsible for a fault in his constitution (l. 534); but he certainly knew that it was specifically God who subducted from his side (ll. 398 and 536). We have already, therefore, reached a point at which there can be talk of accusing God.   diffident] mistrustful. wisdom] Not simply Adam's own wisdom, but also the eternal Wisdom of vii 9f etc.; thus Raphael is in effect saying 'Have faith in God'.   attributing] Stressed on the third syllable.

viii 569. Cp. the verses used in the Prayer Book marriage service, Eph. v

570 Not thy subjection: weigh with her thy self;
     Then value: oft times nothing profits more
     Than self esteem, grounded on just and right
     Well managed; of that skill the more thou know'st,
     The more she will acknowledge thee her head,
575 And to realities yield all her shows:
     Made so adorn for thy delight the more,
     So awful, that with honour thou mayst love
     Thy mate, who sees when thou art seen least wise.
     But if the sense of touch whereby mankind
580 Is propagated seem such dear delight
     Beyond all other, think the same vouchsafed
     To cattle and each beast; which would not be
     To them made common and divulged, if aught

28f ('So ought men to love their wives as their own bodies. He that loveth his wife loveth himself. For no man ever yet hated his own flesh; but nourisheth and cherisheth it, even as the Lord the church') and *1 Pet.* iii 7 ('Likewise, ye husbands, dwell with them according to knowledge, giving honour unto the wife, as unto the weaker vessel, and as being heirs together of the grace of life; that your prayers be not hindered').

viii 570. *Not thy subjection*] Cp. the similar sentiment expressed in M.'s own voice at ix 1182–6.

viii 573. *that skill*] Not 'self-esteem', as Verity and Hughes, but 'the skill of managing well just and right'.

viii 574. *head*] Alludes to *1 Cor.* xi 3: 'The head of every man is Christ; and the head of the woman is the man; and the head of Christ is God.' A similar hierarchic conception underlies the Scriptural passages alluded to at l. 569.

viii 575. *Ed I* has semicolon after *shows*.

viii 576. *adorn*] Apparently M.'s coinage, on the analogy of Italian *adorno*, the contracted form of *adornato* (adorned).

viii 577. *honour*] Raphael carefully distinguishes between different senses of the term. Here the sense is not that of l. 569, but is related rather to that of l. 508 (on which see *n*).

viii 579–85. See ll. 527–8*n*. Throughout the exchange between Raphael and Adam, M. assumes familiarity with the Neoplatonic ordering of different kinds of love and with the related ordering of the five senses in the Banquet of Sense tradition. Cp., e.g., Chapman, *Ovids banquet of sence* St. 92: 'Pure love (said she) the purest grace pursues, / And there is contact, not by application / Of lips or bodies, but of bodies vertues.' Touch, which Chapman's Ovid calls 'the sences Emperor', was the fifth course of the Banquet, often associated – as it is here – with coitus; see *Commonplace Book* (Yale i 369*n*), also Kermode[2] 97f. Not far in the background, too, is the *quinque linea amoris* scheme of erotic poetry; on which see Hutton in *MLN* lvii (1942) 657–61.

Therein enjoyed were worthy to subdue
585   The soul of man, or passion in him move.
What higher in her society thou find'st
Attractive, human, rational, love still;
In loving thou dost well, in passion not,
Wherein true love love consists not; love refines
590   The thoughts, and heart enlarges, hath his seat
In reason, and is judicious, is the scale
By which to heavenly love thou mayst ascend,
Not sunk in carnal pleasure, for which cause
Among the beasts no mate for thee was found.
595   To whom thus half abashed Adam replied.

viii *588. passion*] This must be wrong, because it entails the overthrow of the reason. On the medieval Christian condemnation of passionate sexual love, even within marriage, see Lewis[2] 15f. Although this attitude had changed by M.'s time, it had by no means been replaced by formal approval of passion. According to generally received doctrine, passion was never experienced until after the Fall. Raphael's frown, therefore, is entirely understandable: for a horrified moment, indeed, he may even have thought that the Fall was already under way. And though Adam's answer reassures him, clearly the 'liability to fall' is now in fact considerable. See Broadbent 197f, on the inadequacy of M.'s psychology to the task of rendering the metaphysical transition from innocence to guilt.

viii *589–94*. Raphael here expounds the very familiar Neoplatonic distinction between divine or celestial love; human or terrestrial love; and bestial love. The first (M.'s *heavenly love*) is the love of the contemplative, belonging to mind alone. The second (*true love*) is the force that drives a man to propagate the earthly image of divine beauty, but may also, in its ideal form, lead him to the first—as Spenser describes in his first *Hymn*. The third (*sunk . . . pleasure*) is experienced by him who 'stoops to debauchery, or, even worse, abandons for sensual pleasures a contemplative state already attained' (Panofsky[2] 143). Cp. *Comus* 1003–11; also the conclusion of *Dam*.

viii *590. heart enlarges*] Probably 'makes wise'; see vii 486n.

viii *591. scale*] Not the scale or ladder of nature (v 509), but the Neoplatonic ladder of love. The proximity of *judicious*, however, and the fairly recent 'weigh with her thyself' (l. 570), support the suspicion of an ambiguity in which the scale is a balance and Adam's soul is weighed against Eve's. For the importance of the balance symbol in *PL*, see iv 997–1004n.

viii *595*. Adam is only *half abashed*, for he goes on to give a spirited defence of his love. One is presumably to conclude that it is still rational and unfallen; so that Raphael's unsympathetic sharpness has been occasioned by an anxiety without present foundation. The occasion can hardly, in view of ll. 624–9, have been angelic bias against the mystery of human marriage with its involvement of physical sex. Nevertheless, the conversation of

Neither her outside formed so fair, nor aught
In procreation common to all kinds
(Though higher of the genial bed by far,
And with mysterious reverence I deem)
600 So much delights me as those graceful acts,
Those thousand decencies that daily flow
From all her words and actions mixed with love
And sweet compliance, which declare unfeigned
Union of mind, or in us both one soul;
605 Harmony to behold in wedded pair
More grateful than harmonious sound to the ear.
Yet these subject not; I to thee disclose
What inward thence I feel, not therefore foiled,
Who meet with various objects, from the sense
610 Variously representing; yet still free
Approve the best, and follow what I approve.
To love thou blamest me not, for love thou say'st
Leads up to heaven, is both the way and guide;

Raphael and Adam does in some respects resemble a debate between Hea-
venly Love and Human Love, in which the angel / man distinction is inten-
sified into an antithesis. In this connection it is interesting that in the first
three drafts of M.'s projected drama on the Fall, there is a character called
'Heavenly Love'. See Introduction, 'Composition'.

viii 598. genial] 'nuptial'; see iv 712n. i.e., 'I value marital sex higher than
animal coition'–also, perhaps, 'I value marital sex higher than you do'.

viii 599. mysterious] such as is due to a mystery; the only instance of this
sense given by OED. The relation of one flesh is described as a 'great mys-
tery' in Eph. v 32. Eph. v sets out a theology of sex, based on an analogy be-
tween the love of a husband for his wife, and the love of Christ for the
Church.

viii 600. Ed I has comma after me.

viii 601. decencies] instances of comeliness or of propriety.

viii 604. Cp. l. 499. In stressing the union of souls, Adam is appealing to the
value of friendship, which was regarded as superior to sexual love.

viii 607. i.e., 'These (the thousand decencies, etc.) do not put me in subjection
to her.'

viii 608. foiled] overcome; also defiled, polluted; dishonoured. Adam ad-
mits to feeling passion, but not to yielding to it. The distinction is fine
enough for the precariousness of his position to be felt.

viii 609–11. i.e., 'Though my senses present me with a variety of objects, and
these under a variety of forms, I am not committed to approve any of them
unless I choose.' But the speech is ominous if the echo of Ovid, Met. vii 20 is
caught: 'I see the better, I approve it too: / The worse I follow' (tr. Sandys).
See Douglas Bush in JEGP lx (1961) 639. Cp. v 117–9: 'Evil into the mind
of god or man / May come and go, so unapproved, and leave / No spot

Bear with me then, if lawful what I ask;
615   Love not the heavenly spirits, and how their love
Express they, by looks only, or do they mix
Irradiance, virtual or immediate touch?
    To whom the angel with a smile that glowed
Celestial rosy red, love's proper hue,
620   Answered. Let it suffice thee that thou know'st
Us happy, and without love no happiness.
Whatever pure thou in the body enjoy'st
(And pure thou wert created) we enjoy
In eminence, and obstacle find none
625   Of membrane, joint, or limb, exclusive bars:
Easier than air with air, if spirits embrace,
Total they mix, union of pure with pure

or blame behind.' The interplay between *subject* (l. 607) and *objects* (l. 609) is thematic; cp. Jonson's antithesis in *Hymenaei* (ed. Herford and Simpson vii 209): 'It is a noble and just advantage, that the things subjected to understanding have of those which are objected to sense. . . .'

viii *617*. Expression of love by looks would be essential or *virtual* contact; expression by irradiance, *immediate*. A division was made logically between 'real' and 'virtual' causes.

viii *618–20*. Raphael may be blushing at a successful riposte of Adam's ('"Come now, what do you know about this? Have you got any sex?"' as Empson 105 paraphrases); but it seems more likely that the riposte is unsuccessful, and that the angel's smile glows red because that is the colour of angelic ardour (cp. iv 977f). Certainly M. and Raphael go on to insist proudly on the closeness and totality of angelic coitus, much as angelic digestion was flaunted at v 433ff. The tone of 'In eminence' (l. 624, q.v.) is not modest but superior; it is a point of honour with the servants of Love that their several modes of expression should fall short neither in fulness nor in pureness.

viii *624–9*. Cp. Henry More, *The immortality of the soul* (1659) III ix 4, p. 421, where the angels are imagined as 'reaping the lawful pleasures of the very *Animal* life, in a far higher degree than we are capable of in this World. . . . Wherefore they cannot but enravish one anothers Souls, while they are mutual Spectators of the perfect pulchritude of one anothers persons, and comely carriage, of their graceful dancing, their melodious singing and playing.' On the fluidity and penetrability of angelic bodies, see i 423–31*n* and vi 328–34*n*.   *In eminence*] superlatively, in a superior way. As Burden 158f remarks, M.'s tactic in introducing angelic sexuality was to establish the innocence of sexuality in general, and to relate it to the theme of the transmutation of flesh to spirit. One might add that he was specifically countering the disparagement of sex as a merely animal activity. Cp. Donne's approach in 'Air and Angels'.

Desiring; nor restrained conveyance need
As flesh to mix with flesh, or soul with soul.
630   But I can now no more; the parting sun
Beyond the earth's green cape and verdant isles
Hesperean sets, my signal to depart.
Be strong, life happy, and love, but first of all
Him whom to love is to obey, and keep
635   His great command; take heed lest passion sway
Thy judgment to do aught, which else free will
Would not admit; thine and of all thy sons
The weal or woe in thee is placed; beware.
·I in thy persevering shall rejoice,

viii *628. restrained conveyance*] restricting, confined, limited mode of ex-
pression or communication (*OED*, s.v. *Conveyance* I 5, 9, 14). Angelic
natures exhibit no differentiation into flesh and soul, so that their love is
simple and complete. 'The angels which are in heaven' 'neither marry, nor
are given in marriage' (*Mark* xii 25), because they have no need of an insti-
tutionalised or organic channel of expression. For the use of *conveyance* in a
sacramental sense, cp. Hooker, *Eccles. Pol.* V lxvii 4: 'those mysteries should
serve as conducts of life and conveyances of his body and blood unto them'.
Cp. also Donne, 'The Ecstasy', where the souls acknowledge that their
bodies 'Did us, to us, at first convey'.
viii *631–2.* Cp. iv 354 and 592, where the sun sets 'Beneath the Azores'.
Here the *green cape* is Cape Verde and the *verdant isles* the Cape Verde Islands.
Stephanus' entry runs: 'Hesperium ceras . . . Africae extremum promon-
torium . . . Hodie vocant Caput viride. vulgo, *Le cap verd*' (*cit.* Starnes 314).
Hesperian should be grouped with *sets*; it is impossible to imagine a rhythm
and juncture that would allow it to be taken with *isles* as Hughes proposes.
Thus its primary meaning must be 'western' (*OED* A 1). At the same time,
the context exerts a strong pull in the direction of a secondary allusion to the
Hesperian Isles; cp. iii 567f above. Perhaps at a tertiary level the sun is even
a Hesperian fruit; vegetable as well as potable gold (iii 607–8*n*, iv 217–21*n*).
Signal] see v 229 and 376 for the term set to Raphael's mission.
viii *633. Be strong*] Recalls the exhortation of *Josh.* i 6.
viii *634–5.* Cp. *1 John* v 3: 'For this is the love of God, that we keep his
commandments.'
viii *637–8.* Note how Adam's posterity and its destiny, *of . . . woe*, is carried
within the personal pronoun of which he is the antecedent, *thine . . . thee.*
admit] allow.
viii *639–40.* However, 'joy shall be in heaven over one sinner that repenteth,
more than over ninety and nine just persons' that persevere (*Luke* xv 7).
persevering] A theological term, meaning 'continuance in a state of grace';
cp. vii 632.

640 And all the blest: stand fast; to stand or fall
     Free in thine own arbitrament it lies.
     Perfect within, no outward aid require;
     And all temptation to transgress repel.
        So saying, he arose; whom Adam thus
645 Followed with benediction. Since to part,
     Go heavenly guest, ethereal messenger,
     Sent from whose sovereign goodness I adore.
     Gentle to me and affable hath been
     Thy condescension, and shall be honoured ever
650 With grateful memory: thou to mankind
     Be good and friendly still, and oft return.
        So parted they, the angel up to heaven
     From the thick shade, and Adam to his bower.

THE END OF THE EIGHTH BOOK

---

viii *640–1.* Cp. *1 Cor.* vii 37: 'Nevertheless he that standeth stedfast in his
heart, having no necessity, but hath power over his own will, and hath so
decreed in his heart that he will keep his virgin, doeth well.' Raphael echoes
the drift of his commission at v 235, which in turn echoes the words of God
the Father at iii 99.   *arbitrament*] free choice; absolute decision.

viii *642. require*] look for (*OED* III 9); ask (*OED* I 2; II 5, 6).

viii *646. ethereal*] celestial, heavenly.

viii *648.* Cp. vii 41, 'affable archangel'.

viii *651. oft return*] But Raphael will not return in the poem (except in the
sense that v 222, e.g., referred to a chronologically later visit); instead, the
less affable archangel, Michael, will come to expel Adam and Eve from
Paradise. For the diction, cp. Virgil, *Ecl.* v 65, addressing the dead Daphnis:
sis bonus o felixque tuis; also *Lycidas* 183f: 'thou art the genius of the shore /
. . . and shalt be good / To all that wander in that perilous flood.'

viii *653.* Since Adam's bower has been described as 'of thickest covert . . .
inwoven shade' (iv 693, cp. v 367), the line is heavy with overtones. The
angel leaves the thick shade of the lower world for the light of heaven; but
Adam is bound for ever darker shade. Within a few lines we shall come to a
mention of Sin's 'shadow Death' (ix 12). 'Shade' and 'shadow' are among
the poem's most resonant words: they are gradually transformed from in-
nocence (iv 138, 141, 245, 325, 532), through evil associations (iv 1015, ix
185, x 249), back to hope of salvation (xii 233, 291, 303).

Paradise Lost

BOOK IX

The Argument

Satan having compassed the earth, with meditated guile returns as a mist by night into Paradise, enters into the serpent sleeping. Adam and Eve in the morning go forth to their labours, which Eve proposes to divide in several places, each labouring apart: Adam consents not, alleging the danger, lest that enemy, of whom they were forewarned, should attempt her found alone: Eve loth to be thought not circumspect or firm enough, urges her going apart, the rather desirous to make trial of her strength; Adam at last yields: the serpent finds her alone; his subtle approach, first gazing, then speaking, with much flattery extolling Eve above all other creatures. Eve wondering to hear the serpent speak, asks how he attained to human speech and such understanding not till now; the serpent answers, that by tasting of a certain tree in the garden he attained both to speech and reason, till then void of both: Eve requires him to bring her to that tree, and finds it to be the tree of knowledge forbidden: the serpent now grown bolder, with many wiles and arguments induces her at length to eat; she pleased with the taste deliberates a while whether to impart thereof to Adam or not, at last brings him of the fruit, relates what persuaded her to eat thereof: Adam at first amazed, but perceiving her lost, resolves through vehemence of love[1] to perish with her; and extenuating the trespass eats also of the fruit: the effects thereof in them both; they seek to cover their nakedness; then fall to variance and accusation of one another.

No more of talk where God or angel guest
With man, as with his friend, familiar used

ix *Argument*[1] *vehemence of love*] Note the root meaning of Lat. *vehementia*, 'mindlessness'; see viii 526n, and cp. 431 below.

ix *1–47*. The fourth and last of the poem's invocations, the others being i 1–49, iii 1–55 and vii 1–50. This, unlike the others, avoids direct address to the divine Muse; possibly in response to the increased *distance* (l. 9) of heaven in the part of the poem it introduces. In *Ed II*, the placing of the invocations draws attention to the poem's two-part structure. Thus, if **i** denotes a book with an invocation, we have the following array:

i 2 **i** 4 5 6 ‖ **i** 8 **i** 10 11 12

(*Ed II*). The first part, broadly speaking, deals with the fall of the angels, the second with the fall of man. For other indications of a binary structure, with simple balance about the mid-point at the end of vi, see vii 20n and vi 761n. But the positions of the invocations were originally determined by the subtler, four-part structure of *Ed I*; and it is only in terms of that structure that they can be fully understood: **i** 2 | **i** 4 5 6 ‖ **i** | **i** 9 10 (*Ed I*). If invocations are taken to be inceptions of new parts of the poem, as, strictly speaking, they

To sit indulgent, and with him partake
Rural repast, permitting him the while
5   Venial discourse unblamed: I now must change
Those notes to tragic; foul distrust, and breach

ought to be, then the total numbers of books composing the four parts run:
2 | 4 ‖ 1 | 3. Now this arrangement makes good sense numerologically.
For, first, it divides the ten books of *Ed I* into the four numbers composing
the creative number principle, the divine *tetractys* (1, 2, 3, 4). Secondly, it
reorders the number of the *tetractys* to give a sequence running from the evil
and rebellious *dyad*, through the *tetrad* of the ordered world (4 elements,
4 humours, 4 virtues, etc.; see Bongo 193f), through the *monad* fountain
of creation, to the *triad* of mediation between God and the fallen world.
(For these number symbolisms, see Hopper, Fowler.). Properly considered,
the content of the books will be seen to be appropriate to their numerologi-
cal arrangement: e.g., the origin of creation is related in vii (monad); while
i–ii (*dyad*) are given over to the portrayal of evil and disorder.

ix *1–9*. See Ricks 69–72 on the meanings underlying the alliterative cre-
scendo *discourse . . . distrust . . . disloyal . . . disobedience . . . distance and dis-
taste*. *heaven* is put where we would expect *God*, to introduce the notion of
space and physical distance. Before the Fall it was no matter that heaven was
far from earth; 'but the distance is now moral and spiritual, and not merely
material'. The force of *distaste* depends on the frequency with which 'the
Fall is described as the *tasting* of the apple. The real structure of the phrase
is of a brilliantly unspoken pun. On the part of man, *taste*; on the part of
Heaven, *distaste*.' See also l. 9*n*.

ix *1–4*. See viii 651*n*. God talked with Adam after putting him in Paradise
(viii 316–51). There was no mention in Bk viii of any common meal be-
tween man and God; nevertheless, it seems illegitimate to escape, by
supplying 'spoke' after *God* (Verity) or by arguing that God was present in
his angel (Richardson, more plausibly), from M.'s obscure implication that
before the Fall there could be some meal with God less tragic than Holy
Communion. The implication is that the subject of the present book is to be
a feast of a different kind: namely, Adam's disloyal feast with Eve and
Satan. See l. 9*n*.   *Rural*] pastoral, in contrast to the *tragic* melody about
to be played; but alluding also to the alfresco character of the meal partaken
by Adam and his *angel guest* Raphael in v. *Exod.* xxxiii 11 authorized the
notion of God speaking to man 'face to face, as a man speaketh unto his
friend'.

ix *2. familiar*] Carries, in addition to its modern meaning, the sense 'on a
family footing'.   Its use here is also enriched by the overtone 'familiar
angel'='guardian angel' (*OED* A 2 d).

ix *5. Venial*] allowable, permissible (*OED* A 3; a rare usage).

ix *6*. In the medieval tradition that regarded tragedies as stories *de casibus
virorum illustrium*, the fall of Adam had an important place. It comes second,
e.g., with the fall of Lucifer first, in Chaucer's *Monk's Tale*. Newton

Disloyal on the part of man, revolt,
And disobedience: on the part of heaven
Now alienated, distance and distaste,
10   Anger and just rebuke, and judgment given,
That brought into this world a world of woe,
Sin and her shadow Death, and Misery
Death's harbinger: sad task, yet argument

thought that M. intended here to announce a change to a less lofty style:
'what follows is more of the *tragic* strain than of the *epic*'. But all *PL* is epic;
and there is no lowering of diction in the part of the poem that follows.
Scaliger praised the epic genre for containing all genres within itself. Thus,
the earlier portrayal of Paradise was pastoral (see, e.g., iv 328*n*), while in the
part to follow, which takes us out of the Golden Age into a world of woe,
there is an appropriate move from the pastoral to the tragic mode. Yet the
poem remains epic and (as ll. 13f below explicitly affirm) there is no drop
in heroic elevation.   *distrust*] Recalls Raphael's warning at viii 562: 'be
not diffident / Of wisdom'.   *breach*] Primarily 'break-up of friendly
relations' (*OED* I 5 b); but also, elliptically, 'violation (of God's command-
ment)'.

ix *9. distaste*] dislike, aversion. A secondary meaning, 'disrelish, dislike of
food', keeps up the feast theme, which recurs throughout the book and is
given a very prominent place in the present invocation (cp. ll. 3f, 37–9).
After the Fall, M. returns to the theme with a clinching statement at x 687f:
'At that tasted fruit / The sun, as from Thyestean banquet, turned'. See also
ll. 1–9*n*.

ix *10–19*. Burden (11f), developing a point made by Newton, calls this passage
'a characteristic exercise in close discrimination, turning on anger'. Achilles
is *stern* in his *wrath* because he refused any covenant with Hector; whereas
Messiah, more heroically, is not implacable in his anger. He issued his sole
commandment 'sternly' (viii 333); but when it is disobeyed, he works for
reconciliation. Similarly, God's anger is distinguished from *Neptune's
ire* and *Juno's* (which merely 'perplexed' Odysseus and Aeneas) in that
it is expressed in justice rather than in victimisation. The Christian epic,
by contrast with the pagan, unravels perplexity; cf. xii 275f: 'Erewhile
perplexed . . . but now I see'.   *Perplexed*] tormented, plagued; also
confused, bewildered.   *Cytherea's son*] The periphrasis is to emphasise
that Juno's persecution of Aeneas had a petty motive in her envy of Venus,
as a result of Paris' fatal judgment.

ix *11*. Cp. xi 627 for a very similar play on *world*. Cp. *Rom*. v 12, 'by one
man sin entered into the world'.

ix *12–13*. Bentley objected to the image of *Misery* as *Death's harbinger*, on the
ground that misery often invokes death in vain. But, as Burden 6f points out,
the image springs naturally from the idea of different stages of death, which
was developed to explain the apparent non-fulfilment of Gen. ii 17. See viii
323–33*n* above. *Sin and her shadow Death* do not enter the world, at least in

Not less but more heroic than the wrath
15   Of stern Achilles on his foe pursued
Thrice fugitive about Troy wall; or rage
Of Turnus for Lavinia disespoused,
Or Neptun's ire or Juno's, that so long
Perplexed the Greek and Cytherea's son;
20   If answerable style I can obtain
Of my celestial patroness, who deigns
Her nightly visitation unimplored,
And dictates to me slumbering, or inspires
Easy my unpremeditated verse:
25   Since first this subject for heroic song
Pleased me long choosing, and beginning late;
Not sedulous by nature to indite

the fable, until x 230ff, but the present invocation refers to the whole of
the fourth part of *PL*; see ll. 1–47n.

ix *16*. M.'s selection of the pursuit of Achilles as an episode representative
of the *Iliad* is by no means casual. It works, in a way, to Homer's disadvantage;
in the *Poetics* Aristotle selects this very episode as an example of epic's ad-
mitting what would be ridiculous in another genre. M.'s implication is that
his Christian epic need have no recourse to such dubious material.

ix *17. disespoused*] Makes Turnus' claim to Lavinia as strong as possible, so
that Virgil's hero Aeneas is presented in a somewhat discreditable light.

ix *20. answerable*] equal, equivalent; corresponding (*OED* II 3, 5); but with
the secondary sense 'accountable' (*OED* I 1) continuing the theme of re-
sponsibility from the preceding contrast between God's accountable anger
and the mere passions of pagan epic.

ix *21–4. celestial patroness*] The heavenly Muse, Urania; see vii 1–7n. Hanford
(415) finds M.'s emphasis here on the unconsciousness of his inspiration sig-
nificant, and believes that he thought himself actually possessed.   *nightly*]
on the nocturnal composition of *PL*, see vii 29n.   *dictates*] Stressed on the
first syllable.

ix *26*. For an account of the genesis of *PL*, see Introduction, 'Composition'
(pp. 3–7).

ix *27–41*. Cp. i 16, where M. parodies Ariosto's claim to originality. It
was true that both ancient and modern epics had always had war, or at least
fighting, as a principal ingredient. (So has *PL*, in the first half of the poem;
but in the second this subject is transcended.) M. now glances unfavourably
at the typical matter of the romantic epic, whereas ll. 10–19 were solely
concerned with classical epic. The claim to originality is expressed in a form
itself unusual in epic (though there were precedents, such as Spenser's
Faerie Queene). Thus Johnson felt that M.'s 'extrinsick paragraphs' of auto-
biographical digression were incorrect; though he was prepared to defend
them on the ground of their popularity: 'Since the end of poetry is pleasure,

Wars, hitherto the only argument
Heroic deemed, chief mastery to dissect
30   With long and tedious havoc fabled knights
In battles feigned; the better fortitude
Of patience and heroic martyrdom
Unsung; or to describe races and games,
Or tilting furniture, emblazoned shields,

that cannot be unpoetical with which all are pleased.'   *argument*] matter, subject.

ix *29. mastery*] (Spelled 'maistrie') art, skill.   *dissect*] Both ancient and Italian epic poets were given to describing wounds with a minuteness and technicality that would have been more appropriate in text books of anatomy.

ix *30–1.* M. frequently insists on the authenticity of his matter, implying its superiority in this respect to legendary or mythical subjects. Cp., e.g., i 746f and iv 706. Yet at one time he seriously considered writing an Arthurian epic (see, e.g., *Dam* 162–78), so that he evidently did not hold–or did not always hold–feigned matter in contempt. The extent and continuance of his interest in early British history is shown by the *History of Britain*, as well as by the British subjects for epic projected in *Trin. MS.*   *feigned*] fictional.

ix *31–2.* Clearly implying a hierarchy of heroic virtues, in which patience is to be regarded as occupying a superior place to that of fortitude. See Steadman 94, and cf. iii 267–9n, vi 820–3n and vii 604–7n above. These are tragic rather than heroic values (Burden 59).

ix *33. describe . . . games*] Games were de rigueur in classical epic; see Homer, *Od.* viii 83ff and *Il.* xxiii 262ff, Apollonius Rhodius ii 1ff, Virgil, *Aen.* v 104ff, Statius, *Theb.* vi 255ff, Quintus Smyrnaeus iv 171ff and Nonnus xxxvii 103ff, and consult H. A. Harris, *Greek Athletes and Athletics* (1964), Ch. 3. Such passages perhaps seemed objectionable to M. as much for their irrelevance as for their triviality. Johnson, commenting on the spareness of *PL*, says: 'Here are no funeral games, nor is there any long description of a shield' (*Lives*). M. does touch on games, at ii 528ff and iv 551f; but in both instances briefly, not sedulously. By such means he achieved a real advantage of compression over most earlier epic poets.

ix *34–7.* Referring to chivalric epics such as those of Boiardo, Ariosto, Tasso and Spenser. Sidney's *Arcadia* has particularly elaborate descriptions of *Impreses* (heraldic devices, often with accompanying mottos), as has Trissino's *La Italia liberata* (Rome 1547). See, e.g., *Arc.* (1590) I xvii 1: '*Phalantus* was all in white, having in his bases, and caparison imbroidered a waving water: at each side whereof he had nettings cast over, in which were divers fishes naturally made, and so pretily, that as the horse stirred, the fishes seemed to strive, and leape in thê nette. But the other knight . . . was all in black, with fire burning both upon his armour, and horse. His *impresa* in his shield, was a fire made of Juniper, with this word, *More easie, and more*

35   Impreses quaint, caparisons and steeds;
      Bases and tinsel trappings, gorgeous knights
      At joust and tournament; then marshalled feast
      Served up in hall with sewers, and seneschals;
      The skill of artifice or office mean,
40   Not that which justly gives heroic name
      To person or to poem. Me of these
      Nor skilled nor studious, higher argument
      Remains, sufficient of it self to raise
      That name, unless an age too late, or cold

sweete.'   Bases] cloth housings of horses.   *tinsel trappings*] Cp. the description of Florimell in *F.Q.* III i 15: 'All her steed with tinsell trappings shone.'   *tournament*] The spelling in the early edns, 'torneament', may possibly be Miltonic, and intended to give an Italian flavour.

ix 37–9. The *sewer* superintended the seating of guests and the tasting and serving of the dishes; while the *seneschal* was a steward with wider responsibilities.   *artifice*] mechanic art, applied art. M. means that it is beneath the dignity of epic to teach etiquette and social ceremony and heraldry. Yet he did not dislike chivalric epics; or, if he did, he made an exception in the case of Tasso, whom he quite often echoes (see, e.g., 147–51n), and of Spenser—as we know from *Areopagitica* (Yale ii 516). The mention of the *feast* as a subject has strong overtones here, since M. himself is at the moment in transition from the feast with Raphael to the forbidden Thyestean feast; see 1–4n, 9n.

ix 41. *Me . . . remains*] Imitates Latin *me manet*.

ix 44. *That name*] i.e., of epic. M.'s argument is not only high enough for epic, but high enough to raise the very name of epic and set a new standard.

ix 44–7. M. mentions three defects of nature that might prevent his success. First, the decline of culture, and the general progressive corruption of nature. Cp. *Reason of Church-Government* ii Pref. (Yale i 814), where M. thinks of something 'adverse' in 'the fate of this age' as a possible obstacle to epic-writing. In the poem *Naturam non pati senium* and in *Prol vii*, however, he had opposed the view that the earth is decaying. A cosmic pessimism that drew its strength both from apocalyptic theories of history and from recent astronomical thought was current in M.'s time, and in the generation preceding had been even commoner. See J. L. Lievesay in *MLN* lix (1944). The theory went that change in the declination of the sun, since Ptolemy's measurements, marked a deterioration in nature (cp. *F.Q.* V Proem 7) which would eventually bring the end of the world. Secondly, *cold / Climate* might be an obstacle. Cp. *Reason of Church-Government, ibid.*, 'that there be nothing advers in our climate'; also *Mans* 24–9, where M. modestly asks indulgence for his poetry, on the ground that he has been 'poorly nourished under the frozen Bear'. On the wide distribution and scientific basis for this theory of the inferiority of the north, see Z. S. Fink in *MLQ* ii (1941) 67–80 and T. B. Stroup in *MLQ* iv (1943) 185–9. Burton, e.g.,

45 Climate, or years damp my intended wing
Depressed, and much they may, if all be mine,
Not hers who brings it nightly to my ear.
  The sun was sunk, and after him the star
Of Hesperus, whose office is to bring
50 Twilight upon the earth, short arbiter
Twixt day and night, and now from end to end
Night's hemisphere had veiled the horizon round:
When Satan who late fled before the threats
Of Gabriel out of Eden, now improved
55 In meditated fraud and malice, bent
On man's destruction, maugre what might hap
Of heavier on himself, fearless returned.
  By night he fled, and at midnight returned
From compassing the earth, cautious of day,
60 Since Uriel regent of the sun descried
His entrance, and forewarned the cherubim

believed that 'cold air in the other extreme is almost as bad as hot. . . . In those northern countries, the people are therefore generally dull, heavy. . . . these cold climes are more subject to natural melancholy' (*Anatomy of Melancholy* I ii 2 v). Thirdly, M.'s own age (*years*). *Ed I* did not appear in print until M. was fifty-eight years old.

While the present passage is certainly autobiographical, it should be noticed that it also relates to x 651ff, where such phenomena as climate and variable declination are shown to have their origin in the Fall. Not even a personal aside is allowed to be entirely digressive. *climate*] Both in the sense 'region' (the place, as *age* is the time, of his life) and in the modern sense. *wing*] Cp. iii 13, vii 4.

ix 48–9. *star* / *Of Hesperus*] the planet Venus; cp. iv 605. *office*] contrast 'office mean' at l. 39. The offices described in M.'s epic are cosmic ones, not mere domestic duties or political places.

ix 50–1. Twilight maintains an even balance between light and darkness; but only briefly. So also the precarious stasis of prelapsarian life cannot long be sustained. For twilight as an expression of the balance theme that runs throughout *PL*, see iv 354–5n and 998–1015nn.

ix 53. *late*] i.e., at the end of Bk iv, a week earlier.

ix 54. *improved*] intensified, made worse (*OED* 4).

ix 58. *midnight*] On the eighth night (l. 67), after his journey of ll. 63–6.

ix 59. Cp. iii 440–1, and see *Job* i 7: 'And the Lord said unto Satan, Whence comest thou? Then Satan answered the Lord, and said, From going to and fro in the earth, and from walking up and down in it.'

ix 60. For Uriel's regency of the sun, see iii 648 above; for his report of having seen Satan's entrance, iv 564–75.

That kept their watch; thence full of anguish driven,
The space of seven continued nights he rode
With darkness, thrice the equinoctial line

ix 62. *thence . . . driven*] As recounted at the end of Bk iv. There seems to be
no support in the text for taking this phrase to refer to a separate attempt by
Satan to return on the first night following his expulsion.

ix 63. *seven continued nights*] From the night of the first temptation (iv 800ff),
the night preceding Day 24, to the night preceding Day 31. (For the reckon-
ing of the days of *PL* from sunset, see Introduction, 'Chronology' (p. 26
above); also vii 249–52n). Thus Satan accomplishes the preliminaries of his
successful second temptation in a week, which travesties the divine week of
creation. This symmetry not only renders the contrast between good and
evil, but also the dyadic doubling of the singleness of creation that makes
moral choice necessary. Spenser's formal application of a similar idea is
discussed in Fowler 7f. Cp. ll. 136–8, where Satan draws attention to (but
falsely denies) the correspondence between the times of creation and de-
struction.   *continued*] by keeping to earth's shadow Satan contrives to
experience a whole week of darkness. The first of these continued nights
runs midnight 24–midnight 25; the second, midnight 25–midnight 26 . . .
and the seventh, midnight 30–midnight 31.

ix 64–6. Satan's repeated girdling of the earth, which is scarcely authorized
by Job i 7 (see l. 59n), is essentially an astronomical modulation of a motif
found in religious iconography, particularly in certain types of the Virgin
of the Immaculate Conception. In these, the infernal serpent is shown
wrapped round a lunar or terrestrial globe and spurned by the Virgin. See
Manuel Trens, *María. Iconografía de la Virgen en el arte español* (Madrid 1946)
144–6 and 173, Figs 83f, 99. Each day of the unnatural week of uncreation
has to be turned into night by a journey that keeps Satan in the shadow of the
earth. On three occasions, this is achieved simply by going round the equator
(*equinoctial line*) from east to west, always keeping ahead of the sun. On the
other four, Satan is supposed to follow great circles or colures, taking in the
poles. These lines are usually taken at their face value; but a moment's
reflection will show that the journey is strictly speaking impossible. For,
before the Fall, ecliptic and equator coincided, so that the earth's axis was
always perpendicular to the direction of the sun. Since the sun is larger than
the earth, it follows, therefore, that the poles were never in darkness. We
must choose one of two possibilities: (1) oversight on M.'s part–unlikely,
in view of his accuracy elsewhere in astronomical matters; (2) deliberate
prolepsis and dramatic irony, looking forward to the tilting of the poles at
x 669. Satan is as it were describing a fallen world; in contrast to Christ's
describing of the universe at vii 226–32.   *each colure*] The two colures
were great circles, intersecting at right angles at the poles and dividing the
equinoctial circle into four equal parts. One colure passed through the
solstitial points of the ecliptic, the other through the equinoctial points. Since
the solstitial and equinoctial points did not exist before the Fall, M.'s mention

65 He circled, four times crossed the car of Night
From pole to pole, traversing each colure;
On the eighth returned, and on the coast averse
From entrance or cherubic watch, by stealth
Found unsuspected way. There was a place,
70 Now not, though sin, not time, first wrought the
change,
Where Tigris at the foot of Paradise

of colures must again be either oversight or prolepsis. The division of the
nights into three and four continues the parody of the week of creation;
for it symbolizes the body-forming power of seven. See Macrobius, *In
somn. Scip.* I vi 22–44, where the division is discussed at length.   *car of
night*] Simply the dark part of earth or the shadow of earth. But there is a dis-
torted echo, in the vehicle earth provides for Night, of the bright cosmic
vehicle of Messiah (vi 749–59n).
ix 67–8. The midnight before Day 32; see Introduction, 'Chronology' (p.
26). On the *eighth* night Satan is to descend into a serpent; whereas on the
eighth day of Passion Week Christ rose. The association of eight with re-
surrection, and consequently with baptism, was very familiar: see Simson
21, 40, 48, 144; Hopper 114; and Fowler 53. The symbolism can be observed
in the octagonal design of many Gothic columns and baptismal fonts.
coast averse] side turned away.   *entrance . . . watch*] To the east of Paradise
(iv 542); the river enters from the north (iv 223). For the north as the direction
from which evil comes, see v 689n.
ix 70. At first sight this line seems to have an allegorical meaning only: the
change is a moral or spiritual one. xi 829–38, however, will show that there
is also a literal and historical sense. As in many other instances the effect of the
Fall is to reduce the significant to the merely factual. Conversely, the line
indicates that the geography of Paradise is not only physical. Sin bars
natural access to the fountain of life, but Christ will reopen it to believers:
see xi 278–9n.
ix 71–5. For a fuller account of the landscape, see iv 223–232 and *nn*.   *mist*]
Probably not a mist in the ordinary sense, but a fountain rising by capillary
attraction. M. obeys *Gen.* ii 10 to the letter in making the undivided foun-
tain of Paradise come, not from a source, but from a river. On the other
hand, he takes an unusual step in calling the undivided river *Tigris*. In *Gen.*
ii 14, Tigris (Hiddekel) is the name of one of the four distributaries, and in
M.'s time, though nomenclatures and geographical identifications of the
rivers abounded in great profusion (Willet 29ff summarizes a dozen schemes),
Tigris does not seem to have been singled out as the source river. Hughes
says that M. had the authority of Josephus, *Antiq.* I i 3; but this is not so.
(St Ambrose, however, attributes to Josephus a theory that the *Euphrates*
was the source.) The undivided river was usually allegorized as Grace, or
the Water of Life; whereas the Tigris was either Self-mastery (being over
against the Assyria of pleasure) or Courage. See, e.g., Philo, *Quaest. in Gen.*

Into a gulf shot under ground, till part
Rose up a fountain by the tree of life;
In with the river sunk, and with it rose
75   Satan involved in rising mist, then sought
Where to lie hid; sea he had searched and land
From Eden over Pontus, and the pool
Maeotis, up beyond the river Ob;
Downward as far antarctic; and in length
80   West from Orontes to the ocean barred
At Darien, thence to the land where flows
Ganges and Indus: thus the orb he roamed
With narrow search; and with inspection deep
Considered every creature, which of all
85   Most opportune might serve his wiles, and found

i 12f. The main drift of the present passage, however, is clear enough:
the mode of Satan's entry indicates that evil enters life at its very origin, and
that even Baptism does not free us from its taint. The point is further made at
x 20 that not even the caution of angels could exclude evil and temptation.
The angelic guard is there described as 'wondering' at Satan's successful
entry: perhaps they do not grasp how primordially the choice of good and
evil is instilled into the very stream of life. On the Tigris' source on Mt
Niphates, see iii 742n above. Its subterranean course is from Lucan's *Phar-
salia*: '*Tigris*, soon swallowed by the thirsty earth, / Finds there a buriall
where it had its birth' (tr. Heylyn iii 143).
ix *76–82*. Satan's journey, already described in astronomical terms, is now
retraced geographically. In his north–south circles he passed *Pontus* (Pontus
Euxinus, the Black Sea), the *pool / Maeotis* (Palus Maeotis, the Sea of Azov)
and the Siberian *River Ob*, which flows north into the Gulf of Ob and from
there into the Arctic Ocean; in his westward circling of the equinoctial line,
he crossed the Syrian River *Orontes*, then the Pacific ('peaceful') *Ocean
barred* by the Isthmus of *Darien* (Panama). Note that every landscape feature
mentioned is a sea or river; probably in order to suggest Satan's gradual in-
sinuation into the water of life. In this connection it is significant that St
Jerome, St Ambrose, St Epiphanius and others identified the *Ganges* with
Pison, one of the four rivers of Paradise of *Gen.* ii 10. The seven features are
divided four and three, just as the circlings of the globe were (see ll. 64–6n
above); only here the north–south features number three, the east–west
features four. The geographical journey is thus an anti-creation, just as the
astronomical journey was.   *barred*] Alludes to the creation-myth at *Job*
xxxviii 10f: at the separation of land and sea God 'set bars and doors' to the
ocean.
ix *84*. Roughly corresponding to the forming and naming of the species in
the week of creation. See l. 63n above.

The serpent subtlest beast of all the field.
Him after long debate, irresolute
Of thoughts revolved, his final sentence chose
Fit vessel, fittest imp of fraud, in whom
90   To enter, and his dark suggestions hide
From sharpest sight: for in the wily snake,
Whatever sleights none would suspicious mark,
As from his wit and native subtlety
Proceeding, which in other beasts observed
95   Doubt might beget of diabolic power
Active within beyond the sense of brute.
Thus he resolved, but first from inward grief
His bursting passion into plaints thus poured:
      O earth, how like to heaven, if not preferred

ix *86*. In *Gen.* iii 1 the serpent's subtlety is directly connected with the temptation: 'Now the serpent was more subtil than any beast of the field which the Lord God had made. And he said unto the woman, Yea, hath God said, Ye shall not eat of every tree of the garden?'
ix *87. irresolute*] undecided.
ix *88. sentence*] judgment, decision.
ix *88–9. chose | Fit vessel*] Highly ironic, for it is only the divine potter who chooses vessels, 'one vessel unto honour, and another unto dishonour' (*Rom.* ix 20–4; cp. *Acts* ix 15, *2 Tim.* ii 21). The implication is that the final sentence on the serpent and on Satan will be that they are 'vessels of wrath fitted to destruction' (*Rom.* ix 22). See also v 348*n* above on 'fit vessels pure'.
ix *89*. Patrick Hume rightly perceived that M. is using a horticultural image here, but wrongly interpreted *imp* as the serpent stock on which *fraud* is grafted. In reality an imp is a shoot or slip, so that the serpent is fraud's scion or extension. The image implies that from the little slip represented by the serpent the Fall will grow and a whole new tree (world) of evil. There is possibly an allusion to St Paul's use of grafting as a symbol of Incorporation in Christ in *Rom.* xi.
ix *90. suggestions*] temptations.
ix *95. Doubt*] suspicion.
ix *99*. Raphael too thought the earth *like to heaven*. cp. viii 329.
ix *99–178*. Rajan 103f compares Satan's earlier plaints at iv 32ff: 'This time he addresses the earth instead of the sun and, just as the sun once reminded him of the glory he had lost, the earth now suggests to him the glory he is to recover.' (Satan must convince himself that earth is superior, in order to enhance the glory he wins by destroying it.) A consistent offsetting against the earlier soliloquy works to amplify Satan's decline. The contrast is even underlined structurally; the present soliloquy is succeeded by a serpent metamorphosis, whereas the earlier was preceded by metamorphosis to a cherub. The two soliloquies correspond almost exactly in length.

100   More justly, seat worthier of gods, as built
        With second thoughts, reforming what was old!
        For what god after better worse would build?
        Terrestrial heaven, danced round by other heavens
        That shine, yet bear their bright officious lamps,
105   Light above light, for thee alone, as seems,
        In thee concentring all their precious beams
        Of sacred influence: as God in heaven
        Is centre, yet extends to all, so thou
        Centring receivest from all those orbs; in thee,
110   Not in themselves, all their known virtue appears
        Productive in herb, plant, and nobler birth
        Of creatures animate with gradual life
        Of growth, sense, reason, all summed up in man.

ix *101–2. second thoughts*] Satan's bad theology; an omniscient and provident God cannot be said to make mistakes or to correct them.

ix *103–13.* The case for a geocentric hypothesis, put at viii 86–114 by Raphael in the role of *advocatus diaboli*, is now put in a perverse form by Satan. Man's microcosmic nature no longer speaks 'the maker's high magnificence', but becomes instead an occasion for pride.   *bright officious lamps*] Echoes Raphael's 'bright luminaries / Officious' (viii 98f; see ix 48–9n). Satan's use of *officious* may, however, be edged with contempt, for a reason suggested at 154f below.   *as seems*] Avoids any suggestion of diabolic confirmation of anthropocentricity, such as Marlowe's Mephistophilis had accorded the conservative cosmology of an earlier generation. *in thee, / Not in themselves*] Corresponds to Raphael's 'the sun that barren shines, / Whose virtue on itself works no effect, / But in the fruitful earth' (viii 94–6); though the application is very different. Satan makes use of the same point at the height of the temptation, ll. 721f. For the productive effect of stellar influence, see also iii 608–12n; and for the sacredness of light iii 1–55n.

ix *103.* On the stellar motions as a dance, see iii 579–81n. *Terrestrial heaven* means 'heaven on earth', whereas *heavens* means 'spheres'. Such rapid semantic transitions, concealed by surface harmonies and fluent unbroken syntax, are characteristic of Satan's sophistical style.

ix *108–9.* Again a confusion of thought: receiving is not really like extending. The idea that 'God is an infinite sphere, whose centre is everywhere, whose circumference nowhere' was widespread among Renaissance Neoplatonists. For a particularly fine expression of it, see Nicholas of Cusa, *De docta ignorantia* ed. E. Hoffmann and R. Klibansky (1932) 104.

ix *112–13. gradual*] arranged in grades or steps; *growth*, *sense* and *reason* are the activities of the vegetable, animal and rational souls in man respectively. Plant life exhibited the first, and animal life the first and second; but only man and a few of the higher animals combined all three.

> With what delight could I have walked thee round,
> 115   If I could joy in aught, sweet interchange
> Of hill, and valley, rivers, woods and plains,
> Now land, now sea, and shores with forest crowned,
> Rocks, dens, and caves; but I in none of these
> Find place or refuge; and the more I see
> 120   Pleasures about me, so much more I feel
> Torment within me, as from the hateful siege
> Of contraries; all good to me becomes
> Bane, and in heaven much worse would be my state.
> But neither here seek I, no nor in heaven
> 125   To dwell, unless by mastering heaven's supreme;
> Nor hope to be my self less miserable
> By what I seek, but others to make such
> As I, though thereby worse to me redound:
> For only in destroying I find ease

ix *114. Ed I* has no comma after *round*.

ix *115*. Satan's one remaining joy lies in destruction: see ll. 477-9. For the pleasure demons take in landscape, see Henry More, *The immortality of the soul* (1659) III iv 7.

ix *116-18*. The landscape features include several pairs of *contraries*–which, however, are pleasant, unlike those in Satan's mind (ll. 121f). Thus *hill* opposes *valley, woods plains* and *land sea*. The patterning of the items, which is complex, includes yet another use of the sovereign central position. Thus the *forest crowned* is physically above the *shore* in the central position, between *land* and *sea*, in the central line of the three composing the list. Note that the first line repeats exactly the centralized pattern of viii 275: 'Ye hills and dales, ye rivers, woods, and plains'.

ix *119. place or refuge*] Bentley wanted 'place of refuge', but M. obviously means to depart from this idiom just far enough to add a further meaning. Newton rightly paraphrases: '*I in none of these find place* to dwell in *or refuge* from divine vengeance.'

ix *120-2*. Since Satan is surrounded by *pleasures*, and carries *torment* within him, the *siege | Of contraries* is the 'beleaguering' of pain by its contrary; a novel version of the allegorical siege, in which it was usually Satan, with pleasure as his ally, who beleaguered the human soul. But siege could also mean 'throne', so that there may be a punning allusion to Satan's having brought *torment* (cp. iv 75) from his hellish kingdom of opposites, where he rules over all that is contrary to Paradise.

ix *122-3*. Closely corresponding to iv 109f. Satan's state would be worse in heaven, presumably, because the contraries there would be more intense.

ix *126-8*. Confirming Raphael's interpretation of Satan's motives, at vi 900-7.

ix *129-30*. Cp. ll. 115 and 477-9.

130   To my relentless thoughts; and him destroyed,
         Or won to what may work his utter loss,
         For whom all this was made, all this will soon
         Follow, as to him linked in weal or woe,
         In woe then; that destruction wide may range:
135   To me shall be the glory sole among
         The infernal powers, in one day to have marred
         What he almighty styled, six nights and days
         Continued making, and who knows how long
         Before had been contriving, though perhaps
140   Not longer than since I in one night freed
         From servitude inglorious well-nigh half
         The angelic name, and thinner left the throng
         Of his adorers: he to be avenged,
         And to repair his numbers thus impaired,
145   Whether such virtue spent of old now failed
         More angels to create, if they at least
         Are his created, or to spite us more,

ix *133. Follow*] i.e., follow man to destruction; a shrewd prediction, which is fulfilled at x 651ff. See also ix 782–4n. A heavier stop is needed after *woe*.

ix *136–8*. Satan here anticipates a difficulty felt by many commentators in the *Genesis* account of creation: namely, that an omnipotent God should require time to create; see vii 154n and 176–9n above. For the structural symmetry between the periods of creation and destruction, see ix 63n above. How Satan learned the time required for creation is not clear: perhaps this piece of information formed part of the rumour mentioned at ii 346, perhaps Uriel told him, perhaps it is evident to any angelic intelligence that such a work must take six days, perhaps M. nodded.

ix *138–9. Who . . . contriving*] For M.'s opinion of the folly of speculating that God spent an eternity predestining election and reprobation, see vii 90–2n. The flaw in that line of thought is exploited here by Satan, whose insinuation is that God's creative efforts were laborious.

ix *139–43*. Implying lack of providence on God's part, as well as the contingency of creation on Satan's initiative. This suggestion is flatly contradicted not only by the one immediately before it, but also by the fact of the existence of an ancient rumour of creation, referred to, e.g., by Beelzebub at ii 346. (*Pace* Gilbert, 132f, who sees the inconsistency as M.'s, not Satan's.)   *well nigh half*] An exaggeration; see ii 692n.

ix *144–7*. Contemplation of nature, which even to Satan is clear evidence of God's creativity, again leads him inexorably to the awkward matter of his own creatureliness; see iv 43n and iii 740n. He has to resist the implication of his own words by adding the hasty proviso *if . . . created.   virtue*] power.

ix *147. Ed I* omits comma after *created*.

ix *147–51*. See iv 359n. Satan means only to be contemptuous that the

Determined to advance into our room
A creature formed of earth, and him endow,
150 Exalted from so base original,
With heavenly spoils, our spoils: what he decreed
He effected; man he made, and for him built
Magnificent this world, and earth his seat,
Him lord pronounced, and, O indignity!
155 Subjected to his service angel wings,
And flaming ministers to watch and tend
Their earthly charge: of these the vigilance
I dread, and to elude, thus wrapped in mist
Of midnight vapour glide obscure, and pry
160 In every bush and brake, where hap may find
The serpent sleeping, in whose mazy folds
To hide me, and the dark intent I bring.
O foul descent! That I who erst contended
With gods to sit the highest, am now constrained
165 Into a beast, and mixed with bestial slime,
This essence to incarnate and imbrute,

human race, vile and dust-born as it is, should be favoured by God (cp. ii 350) and given the rebels' possessions or offices (*OED* s.v. *Spoils* I 1-4). But unwittingly he prophesies also the exaltation of human nature through the Incarnation and Christ's second victory over Satan, in which human nature was very often referred to as 'spoil' ('the armour or body of the slain': *OED* II 5-6). Cp. iii 250f, where Christ himself prophesies: 'I shall rise victorious, and subdue/My vanquisher, spoiled of his vaunted spoil'. Both the contempt for man's material origin and the prophecy of Christ's victory have analogues in a speech of Tasso's Satan, *Gerus. lib.* iv 10f. *original*] origin.

ix *154-7*. Cp. *Ps.* xci 11 ('he shall give his angels charge over thee') and *Heb.* i 14 ('ministering spirits, sent forth to minister for them who shall be heirs of salvation'). *flaming ministers*] Cp. xi 101, where the cherubim are 'flaming warriors'; and see *Ps.* civ 4.

ix *158*. *wrapped*] spelt 'wrapt', which could conceivably also indicate rapt='carried' (*OED* 6).

ix *164*. *constrained*] compressed, contracted (*OED* 7); forced (*OED* 1) But the image of l. 89 above might be taken to support a third meaning: forced out; produced by effort; produced in opposition to nature (*OED* 3).

ix *166*. With Satan's reluctance to *incarnate* his essence, however briefly, contrast Christ's willingness to undertake the permanent incarnation of his incomparably purer essence (iii 227ff; see Ricks 73). For the angels' 'ethereal' or 'empyreal' *essence* or substance, cp. i 117, 138, and v 499, and see vi 328-34*nn*. Gilbert 93 argues that there is an internal inconsistency at this point, since no indication is given that this is not the first time Satan has taken the form of a beast. But perhaps he has to become *incarnate* in a way

That to the highth of deity aspired;
But what will not ambition and revenge
Descend to? Who aspires must down as low
170   As high he soared, obnoxious first or last
To basest things. Revenge, at first though sweet,
Bitter ere long back on it self recoils;
Let it; I reck not, so it light well aimed,
Since higher I fall short, on him who next
175   Provokes my envy, this new favourite
Of heaven, this man of clay, son of despite,
Whom us the more to spite his maker raised
From dust: spite then with spite is best repaid.
     So saying, through each thicket dank or dry,
180   Like a black mist low creeping, he held on
His midnight search, where soonest he might find
The serpent: him fast sleeping soon he found
In labyrinth of many a round self rolled,
His head the midst, well stored with subtle wiles:
185   Not yet in horrid shade or dismal den,
Nor nocent yet, but on the grassy herb

he never was before, in order to be able actually to speak through the serpent. The lion, tiger and toad were mute.

ix *170. obnoxious . . . to*] open to the influence of; exposed to (*OED* 4).

ix *172–4. recoils* and *well aimed* and *fall short* belong to an allegoria that recalls the cannon simile used by Satan in his first soliloquy; see iv 13–19*n*. Throughout Satan's speeches his aggressiveness is indirectly suggested in this way by his choice of imagery.   *higher*] i.e., when I aim higher, at God, I fall short.

ix *175*. For spite and envy as Satan's motives, see ii 379–85, iv 358–92 and 381–5*n*. St Augustine explained Satan's motives similarly, in *Civ. Dei* xiv 11: 'that proud, and therefore envious angel . . . envying man's constancy'.

ix *180*. The analogue usually cited, Homer, *Il.* i 359, is not very close. Perhaps M. had in mind *Gen.* ii 6, 'there went up a mist from the earth'; which would make Satan's disguise particularly effective. But the loyal cherubim also move like mist: cp. xii 629–32. Hughes cites Sylvester's *Du Bartas*: 'As in liquid clouds (exhaled thickly), / Water and Ayr (as moist) do mingle quickly, / The evill Angells slide too easily, / As subtle spirits into our fantasie.'

ix *185. horrid*] bristling; frightful, dreadful. Not a Latinism.   *dismal*] sinister; dark, gloomy.

ix *186. Nor nocent*] Not nocent *Ed I*, a possible but uneuphonious reading: both 'nor harmful' (*OED* A 1) and 'nor guilty; innocent' (*OED* A 2). The phrase is heavily charged, for it refers not only to the serpent's becoming morally harmful when Satan possesses it, but also to its 'guilty' part in the

Fearless unfeared he slept: in at his mouth
The devil entered, and his brutal sense,
In heart or head, possessing soon inspired
190   With act intelligential; but his sleep
Disturbed not, waiting close the approach of morn.
Now when as sacred light began to dawn
In Eden on the humid flowers, that breathed
Their morning incense, when all things that breathe,
195   From the earth's great altar send up silent praise
To the creator, and his nostrils fill
With grateful smell, forth came the human pair
And joined their vocal worship to the choir
Of creatures wanting voice, that done, partake
200   The season, prime for sweetest scents and airs:
Then commune how that day they best may ply
Their growing work: for much their work outgrew

Fall, and to its change of habit and habitat (as a result of the curse of x 163–81), when it becomes physically harmful.   *grassy herb*] cp. Virgil, *Ecl.* v 26, *graminis . . . herbam.*

ix *187. at his mouth*] Because the soul was often said to enter and leave the body by that orifice. See Didron ii 173f.

ix *188. brutal*] animal.

ix *190. act intelligential*] (the power of) intelligent action. A precise phrase, since in Aristotelian thought the term 'act' was reserved for rational agents, and denied to both animals and children; see *Eud. Ethics* 1224ᵃ.

ix *191. close*] concealed.

ix *192.* The morning of Day 32; see Introduction, 'Chronology' (p. 26). For the sacredness of light, see iii 1–6nn.   *whenas*] when.

ix *195–7.* Closely considered, *altar* might be thought to constitute a dramatic irony; for it can have no purpose other than sacrifice. Cp. *Gen.* viii 21 and *Lev.* i 9, where God is said to enjoy the 'sweet savour' of burnt offerings. However, one should also remember, in this connection, the Penitential Psalm, li 17: 'The sacrifices of God are a broken spirit.' Of the latter, *praise* might be the prelapsarian equivalent.

ix *198–200. choir . . . wanting voice*] Less paradoxical than it has come to seem: 'choir' commonly meant any orderly band or group of people or even of objects (*OED* 6). However, the modern meaning is probably present in a secondary way, just as *airs* suggests 'melodies' (see Ricks 106); both the voiceless *creatures* and the *season* almost succeed in uttering audible praise. *prime*, in this ecclesiastical context, must have something of its force at v 170 ('the first canonical Hour': see v 18–25n and 170n).

ix *199.* A heavier stop is needed after *voice*.

ix *201. commune*] Stressed on the first syllable. Both distributions of stress were common, and both were used by M. In view of ll. 195–7n, it may be relevant that *commune* could mean 'take communion'.

The hands' dispatch of two, gardening so wide.
And Eve first to her husband thus began.
205   Adam, well may we labour still to dress
This garden, still to tend plant, herb and flower,
Our pleasant task enjoined, but till more hands
Aid us, the work under our labour grows,
Luxurious by restraint; what we by day
210   Lop overgrown, or prune, or prop, or bind,
One night or two with wanton growth derides
Tending to wild. Thou therefore now advise
Or hear what to my mind first thoughts present,
Let us divide our labours, thou where choice

ix *204*. Note that Eve speaks *first*, something she has not previously done. The point is underlined by *first thoughts* (l. 213). Contrast v 17ff and esp. iv 408–10, where Adam's right to the initiative seems insisted on.

ix *205–384*. As Burden 86ff points out, the main lines of this debate are determined by the logical requirements of M.'s matter. Eve has to be alone intentionally, and Adam has to condone her being alone, in order that both may be fully responsible for their Fall. There must be nothing accidental about the events: man's own actions must constitute at each stage the 'cause'.

ix *206*. *Ed I* misprints full stop after *flower*.

ix *207–8*. *till . . . us*] Forestalls any accusation of improvidence on God's part. The work may be too great for Adam and Eve; but this has been foreseen and provided for by the command to 'be fruitful, and multiply' (*Gen.* i 22, 28; *PL* vii 531).

ix *209–12*. M. was committed by *Gen.* i 28 to the view that even prelapsarian nature had to be 'subdued'.   *luxurious*] luxuriant (*OED* 4). *wanton*] profuse (*OED* 7); unmanageable. But both words are also meant to suggest their less innocent moral meanings. Nature has a continual tendency to wildness that Eve is perhaps already beginning to experience almost as a moral temptation.   *wild*] (Vb.) grow wild, or make wild.

ix *213*. *hear*] bear *Ed II*: probably a misprint; though it is by no means an impossible reading (bear = tolerate). Having given Adam the choice between considering for himself or listening to her, Eve chooses for him by immediately going on to present her own scheme.

ix *214*. *Pace* John Crowe Ransom, *God without Thunder* (1931) 133f, the division of labour referred to here has little directly to do with that of the political economist or the efficiency expert. (Though it is true that, in so far as she argues about means without considering ends, Eve resembles, in a general way, the modern technocrat. Note that Adam (l. 241) soon brings the debate back to the 'end of human life'.) The division should rather be seen as an expression of the *dyad*, the divisive principle, moral or cosmic, in the Pythagorean system. Cp. the separation of Redcrosse and Una in *F.Q.* I ii 9, and see Fowler 7f.

215 Leads thee, or where most needs, whether to wind
     The woodbine round this arbour, or direct
     The clasping ivy where to climb, while I
     In yonder spring of roses intermixed
     With myrtle, find what to redress till noon:
220 For while so near each other thus all day
     Our task we choose, what wonder if so near
     Looks intervene and smiles, or object new
     Casual discourse draw on, which intermits
     Our day's work brought to little, though begun
225 Early, and the hour of supper comes unearned.
          To whom mild answer Adam thus returned.
     Sole Eve, associate sole, to me beyond
     Compare above all living creatures dear,
     Well hast thou motioned, well thy thoughts employed
230 How we might best fulfil the work which here

ix *216–19.* Eve 'doesn't care what he does, and she knows very well what she will do' (Ricks 144). After the argument we see her exactly where she had first insisted she was going–in the *spring of roses intermixed | With myrtle* (cp. ll. 426–31). Note also, however, the contrast between the two pairs of plants mentioned. The *ivy* need only be directed to climb the 'married elm', for it to make an emblem of true love like that used above at v 215f. *Woodbine*-honeysuckle has a similar meaning, which M. further specifies by locating the plant at the nuptial bower (*arbour*). Cp. Vaughan, 'Upon the Priorie Grove', 13f: 'Only the Woodbine here may twine, / As th'Embleme of her Love, and mine'; also Stanley, *Poems and Translations*, ed. Crump (1962) 26, 'Love's innocence'. Shakespeare combined both emblems at *Midsummer Night's Dream* IV i 48–51: Titania embracing her lover says: 'So doth the woodbine the sweet honeysuckle / Gently entwist; the female ivy so / Enrings the barky fingers of the elm. / O! how I love thee; how I dote on thee!' Eve, on the other hand, is determined to leave the bower for a pair of plants associated by Ovid with a goddess' defence of her virtue; see ll. 426–33*nn* below. Emblematically, she is abandoning the interdependence of true love for the independence of a dangerous adventure.   *spring*] grove of young trees.   *redress*] raise again to an erect position (horticultural: *OED* 1 a). In the event, however, Eve '"her self, though fairest unsupported Flour" will be "drooping unsustained"' (Ricks 146).

ix *222–5.* On the irony here, that after separation an *object new* (the snake) will draw on far from *Casual discourse* and bring to nothing much more than their day's work, see Ricks *ibid*.

ix *225.* The irony is very exact. Not only will their *supper* be *unearned*, as things turn out, but even *the hour of supper*; since their crime carries sentence of death 'that day' (viii 331).

ix *227. Sole Eve*: i.e., sole mother; see *Gen.* iii 20.

ix *229. motioned*] proposed.

God hath assigned us, nor of me shalt pass
Unpraised: for nothing lovelier can be found
In woman, than to study household good,
And good works in her husband to promote.
235   Yet not so strictly hath our Lord imposed
Labour, as to debar us when we need
Refreshment, whether food, or talk between,
Food of the mind, or this sweet intercourse
Of looks and smiles, for smiles from reason flow,
240   To brute denied, and are of love the food,
Love not the lowest end of human life.
For not to irksome toil, but to delight
He made us, and delight to reason joined.
These paths and bowers doubt not but our joint hands
245   Will keep from wilderness with ease, as wide
As we need walk, till younger hands ere long
Assist us: but if much converse perhaps
Thee satiate, to short absence I could yield.
For solitude sometimes is best society,
250   And short retirement urges sweet return.
But other doubt possesses me, lest harm
Befall thee severed from me; for thou know'st
What hath been warned us, what malicious foe
Envying our happiness, and of his own
255   Despairing, seeks to work us woe and shame
By sly assault; and somewhere nigh at hand
Watches no doubt, with greedy hope to find
His wish and best advantage, us asunder,
Hopeless to circumvent us joined, where each
260   To other speedy aid might lend at need;
Whether his first design be to withdraw
Our fealty from God, or to disturb

ix *245. wilderness*] uncultivated condition. On the progressive increase of
wildness in *PL*, see ll. 209–12*n* and MacCaffrey 131f.

ix *247. converse*] Stressed on the second syllable.

ix *249.* Cp. *PR* i 302. Cicero's aphorism, *numquam minus solus quam cum
solus* (*De rep.* I xvii 27 and *De off.* III i 1); was said by Cowley to have be-
come 'a very vulgar saying' ('Of Solitude'). Defended by Sir George
MacKenzie in *A moral essay, preferring solitude to publick employment* (Edin-
burgh 1665), Cicero's position was an antique strong-point of some strategic
importance in the long campaign fought through the seventeenth and
eighteenth centuries between the devotees of retirement and of public life.

ix *250.* Poetic syntax: Adam cannot bear to think of a long *retirement*, and
so, touchingly, he adds *short*, though it works against the logical prose
meaning of the rest of the line.

ix *262. fealty*] The feudal obligation of vassal to lord; fidelity.

Conjugal love, than which perhaps no bliss
Enjoyed by us excites his envy more;
265   Or this, or worse, leave not the faithful side
That gave thee being, still shades thee and protects.
The wife, where danger or dishonour lurks,
Safest and seemliest by her husband stays,
Who guards her, or with her the worst endures.
270   To whom the virgin majesty of Eve,
As one who loves, and some unkindness meets,
With sweet austere composure thus replied.
      Offspring of heaven and earth, and all earth's lord,
That such an enemy we have, who seeks
275   Our ruin, both by thee informed I learn,
And from the parting angel overheard
As in a shady nook I stood behind,
Just then returned at shut of evening flowers.
But that thou shouldst my firmness therefore doubt
280   To God or thee, because we have a foe
May tempt it, I expected not to hear.
His violence thou fear'st not, being such,
As we, not capable of death or pain,
Can either not receive, or can repel.
285   His fraud is then thy fear, which plain infers
Thy equal fear that my firm faith and love

ix 265. *Or this, or worse*] whether this, or worse (be his first design). The creation of Eve from Adam's side is described at viii 465ff: she was taken from the side nearer his heart, and so from the *faithful* side.

ix 267–9. In accordance with the adoption of a tragic mode (see l. 6 above), the style has become noticeably sententious; cp. ll. 232–4, etc. Adam's abstract generalizations not only demonstrate his full moral responsibility, but also conceal bitter ironies. In the present case, we know that Adam will endure the worst with Eve in a sense very different from that he intends–not faithfully, but desperately.

ix 270. *virgin*] chaste, innocent; *virgin majesty* is a formula, but not only a formula. As the Fall nears, Eve's innocence and integrity are expressed more and more in sexual terms. Cp. ll. 216–19 above, and 396, 466–31, etc. below. For the tradition that Satan tempted Eve sexually, see Svendsen 277.

ix 272. *Ed II* erroneously has comma after *replied*.

ix 273. Contrast the informality of l. 205: Eve is now standing on her dignity.

ix 276. Eve's knowledge of the prohibition was often stressed by commentators; see Williams 114. The warning referred to here is viii 633–43; though Eve was also present when Raphael gave his more specific warning at vi 900ff.   *overheard*] Taken by some to imply eavesdropping, a sign of moral deterioration in Eve; but this is perhaps a forced interpretation.

ix 278. *shut*] the time of shutting (poetic).

Can by his fraud be shaken or seduced;
Thoughts, which how found they harbour in thy breast
Adam, misthought of her to thee so dear?
290   To whom with healing words Adam replied.
Daughter of God and man, immortal Eve,
For such thou art, from sin and blame entire:
Not diffident of thee do I dissuade
Thy absence from my sight, but to avoid
295   The attempt it self, intended by our foe.
For he who tempts, though in vain, at least asperses
The tempted with dishonour foul, supposed
Not incorruptible of faith, not proof
Against temptation: thou thy self with scorn
300   And anger wouldst resent the offered wrong,
Though ineffectual found: misdeem not then,
If such affront I labour to avert
From thee alone, which on us both at once
The enemy, though bold, will hardly dare,
305   Or daring, first on me the assault shall light.
Nor thou his malice and false guile contemn;
Subtle he needs must be, who could seduce
Angels, nor think superfluous others' aid.
I from the influence of thy looks receive

ix *287. seduced*] See l. 270n.

ix *288–9.* The syntax is defended against Peter by Ricks (34f), who is surely right in treating it as a rendering of the disjointedness of actual speech. Thus there is a shift of construction between *Thoughts, which* and the more direct *how found they.* . . . The indignant, sharp word-play in *misthought* – 'not thoughts, *mis*-thoughts rather' – confirms this interpretation. *Ed I* has comma after *breast.*

ix *291.* The formula used by Adam exactly balances the formula Eve used at 273; for she was created out of *man*, as Adam was out of 'earth'. But it is a *healing word*, in that it implies that for him to mistrust her would be to mistrust his own substance. *Eve* implies 'mother of all living' (Gen. iii 20); so that the line has an internal symmetry. But the primary sense depends on another Hebrew meaning of *Eve*: 'subject unto thee': it is to this, as much as to *immortal*, that *such* in the following line refers. The point that Eve is in a way Adam's daughter makes unexpected sense of M.'s puzzling statement in the *De doctrina* that the first sin included parricide (see ll. 1003–4n); for Eve killed Adam by persuading him to eat the forbidden fruit.

ix *292. entire*] unblemished, blameless; not a Latinism.

ix *293. diffident*] mistrustful. One of the preoccupations of Bk ix is mistrust, with its various forms and objects; cp. e.g., ll. 6, 355, 357.

ix *296. asperses*] spatters; falsely charges (*OED* 4).

ix *298. faith*] fidelity.

310 Access in every virtue, in thy sight
    More wise, more watchful, stronger, if need were
    Of outward strength; while shame, thou looking on,
    Shame to be overcome or over-reached
    Would utmost vigour raise, and raised unite.
315 Why shouldst not thou like sense within thee feel
    When I am present, and thy trial choose
    With me, best witness of thy virtue tried.
      So spake domestic Adam in his care
    And matrimonial love; but Eve, who thought
320 Less attributed to her faith sincere,
    Thus her reply with accent sweet renewed.
      If this be our condition, thus to dwell
    In narrow circuit straitened by a foe,
    Subtle or violent, we not endued
325 Single with like defence, wherever met,
    How are we happy, still in fear of harm?
    But harm precedes not sin: only our foe
    Tempting affronts us with his foul esteem

ix *310. Access*] addition, increase. It was a fundamental doctrine of Renaissance Neoplatonism that love inspires the lover to virtue: 'Such is the powre of that sweet passion, / That it all sordid basenesse doth expell, / And the refyned mynd doth newly fashion / Unto a fairer forme, which now doth dwell / in his high thought, that would it selfe excell; which he beholding still with constant sight, / Admires the mirrour of so heavenly light' (Spenser, *An Hymne of Love* 190–6). Especially in Petrarchan poetry, this effect was above all ascribed to the glance of the beloved; Sidney's Astrophil, e.g., exclaims: 'O eyes... / Whose beames be joyes, whose joyes all vertues be' (*Astrophil and Stella* xlii). Thus Adam should be regarded as wooing Eve, at this point, with the arguments of a love poet.

ix *312–14*. Just as the influence of love would increase Adam's *virtue* or power, so shame also would increase his *vigour* (rigorous force) and join it to his virtue. Love and shame were thought of as contrary passions.

ix *318. domestic*] concerned about the wellbeing of the family.

ix *319*. *Ed I* has comma after *love*.

ix *320. Less*] too little; a Latinism.   *attributed*] Stressed on the third syllable.   *sincere*] pure, morally uncorrupted, or true. *Fides sincera* was a watchword or semitechnical theological term among the Reformers.

ix *322–41*. Unless Eve is right here, M. appears to be contradicting the rejection of cloistered virtue in *Areopagitica* (Waldock 22). But the point of the present speech is that Eve is already being tested: since her dream she has been drawn in the direction of excessive strength and curiosity.

is *328–30*. *affronts*] The primary meaning is 'insults' or 'causes to feel ashamed, put to the blush'; but a secondary meaning, 'sets face to face' is played on by *front* = face. In this connection, see l. 358*n* below.

          Of our integrity: his foul esteem
    330 Sticks no dishonour on our front, but turns
          Foul on himself; then wherefore shunned or feared
          By us? Who rather double honour gain
          From his surmise proved false, find peace within,
          Favour from heaven, our witness from the event.
    335 And what is faith, love, virtue unassayed
          Alone, without exterior help sustained?
          Let us not then suspect our happy state
          Left so imperfect by the maker wise,
          As not secure to single or combined;
    340 Frail is our happiness, if this be so,
          And Eden were no Eden thus exposed.

ix *329. integrity*] Like 'entire' (l. 292) and 'unite' (l. 314), emphasises the completeness, unity and wholesomeness–in short, the monadic quality–of innocent virtue. See l. *214n.*

ix *334.* But it is not from the *event* (result) that the true believer ought to expect *witness*, for that would be justification by works. Rather 'the Spirit itself beareth witness . . . that we are the children of God' (*Rom.* viii 16). With modern punctuation there would be a comma after *witness.*

ix *335.* Cp. *Areopagitica* (Yale ii 527): in the absence of freedom to encounter temptation 'what were vertue but a name?'   *faith, love, virtue*] Alluding to the Neoplatonic Triad of Fidius, Alciati's *Fidei symbolum* (Embl. ix, p. 55–7); on which see P. L. Williams in *JWI* iv (1941). In the Triad of Fidius, Veritas and Virtus appear with linked hands, united by a third, Amor. Thus the answer to Eve's rhetorical question is, They are an emblem of integrity and faithfulness, if only they stay together with linked hands. In view of Miss Williams's demonstration that the Triad of Fidius is related to Pico's triad of human nature (*intellectus, ratio* and *voluntas* or the passionate part), it is significant that many passages in *PL* suggest that Adam allegorically represents *intellectus* or *mens*, Eve *ratio* or *anima.* See ll. 358*n*, 360–1*n*, and 385–6*n*. One suspects that the present scene is intended in part as a tableau, in which Intellectus and Ratio adopt appropriate roles and exhibit even the physical arrangement (see ll. 385f) of the Triad of Fidius emblem.

    We should not assume that because in *Areopagitica* M. rejects 'cloistered virtue' he therefore approves Eve's sentiments here, in the very different context of an unfallen world. At least before the Fall it hardly has the same force to say 'how much we . . . expell of sin, so much we expell of virtue' (*Areopagitica*, Yale ii 527). At the same time, M. would naturally want to involve his own cherished convictions and aspirations in Eve's dangerous individualism; both for the sake of idealizing her, and in the interests of self-discovery.

ix *339.* Some copies of *Ed II* have an illegible point (not semicolon) after *combined. Ed I* has full stop.

ix *341. no Eden*] i.e., no pleasure, the literal Hebrew meaning of 'Eden'.

To whom thus Adam fervently replied.
O woman, best are all things as the will
Of God ordained them, his creating hand
345 Nothing imperfect or deficient left
Of all that he created, much less man,
Or aught that might his happy state secure,
Secure from outward force; within himself
The danger lies, yet lies within his power:
350 Against his will he can receive no harm.
But God left free the will, for what obeys
Reason, is free, and reason he made right,
But bid her well beware, and still erect,
Lest by some fair appearing good surprised
355 She dictate false, and misinform the will
To do what God expressly hath forbid.
Not then mistrust, but tender love enjoins,
That I should mind thee oft, and mind thou me.

ix 342. *fervently*] Often taken as a euphemism for 'angrily', but Adam is 'first incensed' only at l. 1162.

ix 343. *O woman*] Not a cold form of address but a reminder of the ontological relation instituted between man and wo-man. The implication is that Eve has been pressing for an unsuitable form of liberty (Burden 88).

ix 347–8. *secure, / Secure*] The repetition has a certain ironic force. By the second *secure*, Adam means only 'safe, carefree' (*OED* A II 3 c); but Eve is being conspicuously *secure* in another sense: 'over-confident' (*OED* A I 1 a). It is a key word in *PL*, related to the faith / distrust complex. Cp. e.g., l. 371 below, and 339, iv 791 above; and see l. 293*n* above.

ix 351–6. Cp. *Areopagitica*: 'Many there be that complain of divin Providence for suffering *Adam* to transgresse, foolish tongues! when God gave him reason, he gave him freedom to choose, for reason is but choosing; he had bin else a meer artificiall *Adam*, such an Adam as he is in the motions [puppet-shows]' (Yale ii 527); where however, the application is almost exactly contrary.   *still erect*] always attentive; but also with a glance at *right* = upright.

ix 354. So Eve is in the event *surprised* by Satan: see l. 551.

ix 358. *mind thee . . . mind thou me*] The repetition of *mind* ('admonish' and 'pay heed to') punningly brings into play the third of the divisions of human nature that provide the psychological scheme of the present passage. We have already had Reason and Will, and now we get a hint that Adam himself stands for Mind. The same threefold division was alluded to more obliquely in the Triad of Fidius at l. 335. Note that in the Triad, Mind (Veritas) and Reason (Virtus) are opposed face to face, because it is the function of Reason to reflect obediently, and to translate into practical terms, the truth contemplated by Mind. (See Williams, *art. cit.* l. 335*n*.) This reflexive relation seems to be rendered in the symmetry of the present

> Firm we subsist, yet possible to swerve,
> 360 Since reason not impossibly may meet
> Some specious object by the foe suborned,
> And fall into deception unaware,
> Not keeping strictest watch, as she was warned.
> Seek not temptation then, which to avoid
> 365 Were better, and most likely if from me
> Thou sever not: trial will come unsought.
> Wouldst thou approve thy constancy, approve
> First thy obedience; the other who can know,
> Not seeing thee attempted, who attest?
> 370 But if thou think, trial unsought may find

line: *I . . . thee . . . thou me.* Throughout *PL* repetitive figures, especially those developed on a large scale, are used to express a responsive relation of obedient love. See, e.g., iv 639–56n (Adam and Eve); iii 131, 145, 227 (God and Messiah); and x 1098–1104n (God and man).

ix *360–1.* Since it is Eve who meets the *specious object* (in the shape of the serpent), these lines give the clearest possible indication that Eve is allegorically cast in the role of Reason, *ratio*, the faculty that chooses and directs the will. Cp. ll. 351f, and see *Areopagitica* (Yale ii 527): 'reason is but choosing'. This symbolism was by no means peculiar to M.; on the contrary, in a cruder form it was so commonplace as to be the subject of a chapter in a school textbook, Valeriano's *Hieroglyphica* (xiv 26, p. 176 *Sensus a Voluptate, Mens a Sensu Decepta*; also 27, p. 177). It goes back to St Augustine (*Enarr. in Ps.* xlviii), for whom, whoever, *caro nostra Eva est, quae seducit virum, id est, rationem.* Valeriano's version of the allegory, in which Eve represents *sensus* and Adam *intellectus*, may be regarded as logically intermediate between St Augustine's and M.'s. The ultimate source of the tradition is probably Philo, *De opificio* 165 (Loeb i 131).

ix *361.* Ordinary reasoning on *a priori* grounds would let Adam see that it would take an *object* to tempt them. See ll. 413n below.

ix *367. approve*] demonstrate; make proof of; test.

ix *370–5.* One of the most critical passages in the whole poem. Waldock 34 goes as far as to attribute the Fall to Adam's failure to assume full responsibility here – an interpretation that comes very close to Eve's accusation in ll. 1155–61. With more penetration, Burden 89ff suggests that M. has a theological difficulty: If Adam was not deceived (*1 Tim.* ii 14) how could his judgment at this point fail, unless God had been improvident in creating him? The answer may be that Adam, the image of God, here experiences the same kind of dilemma as God himself in iii 100ff. He sees the risk of letting Eve go perfectly well, as l. 361 shows; so that his judgment does not fail. But to keep Eve in passive obedience would be to lose her (with l. 372 cp. iii 110). Eve, already in the grip of temptation, has put Adam in an impossible position, transmitting to him the pressure, the excessive motion, put

Us both securer than thus warned thou seem'st,
Go; for thy stay, not free, absents thee more;
Go in thy native innocence, rely
On what thou hast of virtue, summon all,
375   For God towards thee hath done his part, do thine.
      So spake the patriarch of mankind, but Eve
Persisted, yet submiss, though last, replied.
      With thy permission then, and thus forwarned
Chiefly by what thy own last reasoning words
380   Touched only, that our trial, when least sought,
May find us both perhaps far less prepared,
The willinger I go, nor much expect
A foe so proud will first the weaker seek;
So bent, the more shall shame him his repulse.
385   Thus saying, from her husband's hand her hand
Soft she withdrew, and like a wood-nymph light
Oread or dryad, or of Delia's train,

on her by Satan. Perhaps, however, more emphasis should be laid on symbolic meanings of the separation. If Adam symbolizes intellect or *mens*, and Eve *ratio* (or perhaps *voluntas*), then the separation may be a loss of integration. Man fails to inform and support his moral choices with intellect and wisdom.

ix *371. securer*] more careless, more over-confident. Cp. ll. 347–8.

ix *377. submiss*] submissive. 'Eve persisted; yet she replied submissively (even if she insisted on having the last word).' The balanced words and phrases, and the successive qualifications, render the contradictions entering human nature, as well as miming Eve's persistence. Burden 92 comments that Eve, being unfallen, is submissive even when having the last word.

ix *383*. Whether or not the dramatic irony here is intentional, it is certainly difficult at this point to regard Eve as altogether the weaker of the two.

ix *385–6*. Clasped hands are an emblem of faith, troth, or concord, so that Eve withdrawing hers is symbolically breaking trust. The bond thus so broken will not be fully restored until xii 648. See l. 335*n* on the Triad of Fidius or *Fidei symbolum*, in which Veritas (*mens*) and Virtus (*ratio*) clasp hands. Ricks (90) thought that *Soft* may go with *hand*, secondarily, as a enhancing suggestion; but this is unlikely, since a monosyllabic adjective hardly ever follows a monosyllabic noun in English.   *light*] Not merely 'nimble' (*OED* IV 15), but in the context clearly also 'unsteady, fickle' (*OED* IV 16). A true ambiguity; for the moral condition of Eve is at this point uncertain and in process of alteration.

ix *387. Oreads*] mountain nymphs, such as attended on Diana.   *dryads*] wood nymphs. Neither class of nymphs were immortal; the dryads perished with the trees over which they presided.

ix *387–92*. The simile is so discriminating that it consists mainly of qualifications. Eve is like the immortal Diana (called *Delia* from Delos, her

Betook her to the groves, but Delia's self
In gait surpassed and goddess-like deport,
390   Though not as she with bow and quiver armed,
But with such gardening tools as art yet rude,
Guiltless of fire had formed, or angels brought.
To Pales, or Pomona thus adorned,

secluded island birthplace and refuge–see x 293–6n) in outward bearing
(*deport*), but lacks the *quiver* of counsel (on which see Valeriano 525f). In-
stead she has gardening tools; but only *rude* ones, since before the Fall mech-
anical arts dependent on the invention of fire were unknown (see v 396n).
Guiltless of] inexperienced in, unskilled in (*OED*'s first instance in this sense);
but with a secondary allusion to the association of fire with man's guilt.
Only as a result of the Fall did it become necessary for him to have some
means of warming himself: see x 1078–81n. There may also be an allusion to
the fire stolen from heaven by Prometheus, in a myth which was regarded
as one of the main pagan distortions of the history of the Fall.
ix *393–6.* The previous simile was based on *gait*, this on equipment. In
respect of the *gardening tools* she carries, Eve resembles *Pales*, the Roman
goddess of pastures; *Pomona*, the nymph or goddess of fruit-trees (often
represented sitting on a basket of flowers and fruit, holding in her hand
apples); and *Ceres*, the goddess of corn and agriculture. The qualifications
are again very precise. Pomona might be thought a morally favourable
analogue, since Ovid described her as shutting herself in her orchard to
escape male attentions, and as carrying 'no javelin, but the curved pruning-
hook with which now she repressed the too luxuriant growth' (*Met.* xiv
628–36). M., however, specifically refers to her seduction by the disguised
Vertumnus (*ibid.* 654ff).   *fled*] Used ironically, for Pomona only fled
Vertumnus until his guileful persuasions awakened 'answering passion'
(*ibid.* 771). Ceres was occasionally represented with a plough, but far more
usually with a lighted torch–the fire explicitly excluded at l. 392 above.
The torch was the one she used to search for her daughter Proserpina, after
Proserpina had been abducted by Pluto, in what was another of the main
mythic analogues to the Fall. *Jove* is brought in not merely to shift the time
back before the Fall to Ceres' virginity and its loss, but also to allude to his
incestuous seduction of Proserpina, in the form of a serpent. For an inverted
use of the same myths, in which Proserpina is the prelapsarian Eve and Ceres
the postlapsarian, see iv 268–72 above; the inversion serves to render the
deterioration taking place in Eve, or perhaps to move the action on to an
atemporal plane altogether.
    The present simile, like that immediately preceding, is three-fold;
and refers, like it, to two sub-deities and one major goddess. But the simile
of ll. 387–92 compared Eve to deities who preside over wild places, while
observing that she nevertheless carried the tools of cultivation; this compares
her to deities who preside over domesticated nature, while alluding to the

Likeliest she seemed, Pomona when she fled
395   Vertumnus, or to Ceres in her prime,
Yet virgin of Proserpina from Jove.
Her long with ardent look his eye pursued
Delighted, but desiring more her stay.
Oft he to her his charge of quick return
400   Repeated, she to him as oft engaged
To be returned by noon amid the bower,
And all things in best order to invite
Noontide repast, or afternoon's repose.
O much deceived, much failing, hapless Eve,
405   Of thy presumed return! Event perverse!
Thou never from that hour in Paradise
Found'st either sweet repast, or sound repose;
Such ambush hid among sweet flowers and shades
Waited with hellish rancour imminent
410   To intercept thy way, or send thee back

loss of virginity and sexual restraint. On wildness as a category in *PL*, see l. 245n above.

ix *394. Likeliest*] Likest *Ed I*, a paler word preferred by Newton and subsequent editors. But according to the principle whereby, other things being equal, the reading with the less usual word is favoured, one should prefer *Likeliest*, 'portraying most accurately' (*OED* s.v. *Likely* A 1). As a term of art criticism it is specially appropriate in the context of an iconographical simile. For comparable elision or synaloepha, see, e.g., l. 505 below.

ix *395.* Apart from the secondary reference to the time of day (see ll. 200n and *401n*), *prime* means simply 'in her best time; before the loss of Proserpina brought cares and suffering upon her'. There is no need to join Bentley and Empson in asking whether goddesses experience old age; though one must admire the latter's comment: 'the very richness of the garden makes it heavy with autumn. Ceres when virgin of the queen of Hell was already in her full fruitfulness upon the world; Eve is virgin of sin from Satan and of Cain, who in the Talmud was his child' (Empson[2] 185f).

ix *401.* For *noon* as the critical time of judgment in *PL*, see iv 30n; also ll. 739–40n.

ix *404–5.* 'Adam was not deceived, but the woman being deceived was in the transgression' (*1 Tim.* ii 14). Ricks 97 notices that at first we take *failing* absolutely, as part of a general apostrophe about Eve. 'But then the next line–"Of thy presum'd return!"–declares that she is *deceived in* the one present circumstance: her presumed return. So the lines are both tragically prophetic and dramatically momentary.'   *event perverse*] adverse event, outcome.   *hapless*] By parting from Adam Eve makes herself more exposed to the effects of chance. But the present exclamation is something of a trap for the unwary reader: Eve's fall will not just be bad luck. See l. 421n.

Despoiled of innocence, of faith, of bliss.
For now, and since first break of dawn the fiend,
Mere serpent in appearance, forth was come,
And on his quest, where likeliest he might find
415   The only two of mankind, but in them
The whole included race, his purposed prey.
In bower and field he sought, where any tuft
Of grove or garden-plot more pleasant lay,
Their tendance or plantation for delight,
420   By fountain or by shady rivulet
He sought them both, but wished his hap might find
Eve separate, he wished, but not with hope
Of what so seldom chanced, when to his wish,

ix 411. *innocence . . . faith . . . bliss*] A triad of qualities that would be felt to correspond with the more ontological triad given at l. 335, 'faith, love, virtue'. Innocence is a condition of the virtuous part, as bliss or joy of the appetitive.

ix 413. *Mere serpent*] plain serpent; i.e., he seemed just an ordinary serpent. M. is not specially concerned to exclude the half-humanized serpent common in Gothic paintings of the temptation (e.g. Hugo van der Goes' *Fall of Man*); though he would no doubt have agreed with Willet (48) that in human form Satan could never have deceived Eve, since she 'knewe well enough, that her selfe and Adam, were all mankind.' The point is a subtler one, to which commentators on Genesis iii devoted a good deal of space: namely, whether the serpent was a true serpent possessed, or only the appearance of a serpent. Thus Willet, like M., rejects the theory of Thomas Cajetan, 'who by a continued allegorie, by the serpent, would have the devill understood: that there was neither serpent in trueth nor in shew that appeared to Eva, but this tentation was altogether internall and spirituall: for by this meanes, the whole storie of the creation may as well be allegorized, and so the truth of the narration called in question, and beside, whereas the divell internally tempteth onley two wayes, either by alluring the sense by some object, or else by mooving and working the phantasie, our parents before their fall could not be so tempted, having no inordinate motion.' He also rejects St Cyril's opinion, 'that it was not a true serpent, but a shewe onely and apparition' (ll. 45f). M.'s phrase is very carefully drafted; 'serpent in appearance', e.g., without the *mere*, might have been taken to imply that he agreed with St Cyril.

ix 418–19. The *garden plot* would be a *tendance* (object of care), the *grove* a *plantation*.

ix 421–5. *wished . . . hap / wished . . . hope / wish . . . hope*] The sinuous verbal pattern here seems to Adams (89) 'verbal frippery', to Ricks (38), more subtly, a net woven by Satan.

ix 421. In Satan's world picture, events usually occur either by necessity or by chance (*hap*). Cp. iv 530 and vii 172.

Beyond his hope, Eve separate he spies,
425 Veiled in a cloud of fragrance, where she stood,
Half spied, so thick the roses bushing round
About her glowed, oft stooping to support
Each flower of slender stalk, whose head though gay
Carnation, purple, azure, or specked with gold,
430 Hung drooping unsustained, them she upstays
Gently with myrtle band, mindless the while,
Her self, though fairest unsupported flower,
From her best prop so far, and storm so nigh.
Nearer he drew, and many a walk traversed
435 Of stateliest covert, cedar, pine, or palm,
Then voluble and bold, now hid, now seen
Among thick-woven arborets and flowers

ix *426–31*. See ll. 216–9*n*, and cp.ll. 628f.   *roses . . . myrtle*] The two were
associated in the festival of Venus; myrtle, to commemorate an occasion
when wanton satyrs surprised Venus bathing, and the naked goddess hid
behind a myrtle tree (Ovid, *Fasti* iv 138ff; for the Renaissance use of Faunus
and satyr to symbolise Excess or Concupiscence or even Satan, see Fowler[3]
101). The rose, particularly when the focus is on the head as distinct from the
leaves, as here, was a symbol of human frailty and of the mutability of mortal
happiness (see Valeriano lv 1, *Imbecillitas humana*, 638f; also Ripa, s.v. *Amici-
tia*, where the rose signifies 'the pleasures of friendship, so long as a union of
will is maintained'). Thus Eve's supporting the rose with myrtle should be
read as an emblem of the dependence of unfallen bliss upon conjugal virtue.
Her activity is the moral one of keeping up the marriage. For an icono-
graphical use of the *myrtus coniugalis* in a similar sense, see Panofsky[2] 161f.
Specifically sexual interpretations of the present passage (virginity supported
by virtue, passion restrained by modesty, etc.) are not ruled out, but must
clearly be subordinate.   *Half spied*] for a moment we are allowed to think
Eve concealed by the fragrance: see Ricks 95f.   *purple, azure . . . gold*]
the colours of Minerva, the virgin goddess. Cp. *Comus* 448 where in a
similar situation the Lady carries a Minerva-shield of 'chaste austerity'.
mindless] heedless; see l. 358*n*.
ix *432–3*. The syntax and the images of the preceding lines have worked to
identify Eve very closely with the roses (note the ambiguous agreements,
and such echoes as *stooping / drooping*); and now the identification is made
explicit. Cp. iv 270, where Proserpina (and by implication Eve) was 'Her-
self a fairer flower' when she was carried off by the king of hell.   *though
fairest*] This implies condemnation of Adam: was it not his duty to prop this
flower above all? Adam as Eve's prop returns to the emblems of ll. 216–19.
ix *435*. For the trees, cp. iv 139.
ix *436. voluble*] Punning between 'gliding easily with an undulating move-
ment' (*OED* I 3) and 'glib, fluent' (*OED* II 5 a). Neither meaning is a
Latinism.

Embordered on each bank, the hand of Eve:
Spot more delicious than those gardens feigned
440   Or of revived Adonis, or renowned
Alcinous, host of old Laertes' son,
Or that, not mystic, where the sapient king
Held dalliance with his fair Egyptian spouse.

ix *438. Embordered*] (Spelled 'Imborderd') set as a border. But the aptness
of the image depends on some degree of fusion with 'Imbordured', a
heraldic term meaning 'furnished with a bordure (a bearing all round the
escutcheon, in the shape of a hem) of the same tincture as the rest of the
field'.   *hand*] handiwork; as one might say with respect to a painting-
or an embroidery.

ix *439–43.* 'The Circumstances of these Gardens of *Adonis* being to Last but a
very little while, which even became a Proverb among the Ancients, adds
a very Pathetick propriety to the Simile: Still More, as that 'tis not the
Whole Garden of *Eden* which is Now spoken of, but that One *Delicious
Spot* where *Eve* was, This *Flowrie Plat* and This was of her Own Hand, as
those Gardens of *Adonis* were always of the Hands of those *Lovely Damsels,
Less Lovely yet than She*' (Richardson 416). Ricks 133–5 convincingly
argues that the relevance of the comparison to the Garden of Solomon
(*Song of Sol.* vi 2) depends on an analogy between the *sapient king* and Adam:
both were wise, both uxorious and both beguiled by 'fair idolatresses'
(i 444–6). Only the analogy was not M.'s. It goes back at least to St Augustine;
see *Civ. Dei* xiv 11: 'As . . . Solomon . . . yielded worship to idols [not] of his
own erroneous belief, but was brought unto that sacrilege by his wives'
persuasions: so is it to be thought, that the first man did not yield to his
wife in this transgression of God's precept, as if he thought she spoke the
truth; but only being compelled to it by this social love to her.'   *sapient*]
A heavily thematic word in *PL*; at x 1015–8 it again occurs associated with
'dalliance', and used in a way that brings out its root meaning in Latin,
'knowledge gained by tasting'. The Garden of Adonis and the Garden of
Alcinoüs (cp. v 341) were *feigned* because only mythical (*mystical*) and pagan.
These comparisons belong to a line of thought that in part went back to
Lactantius; see Williams 108. For a late and popular mythographic expres-
sion, see the anonymous *Observationum libellus* (attached to Conti's *Mytho-
logiae*), s.v. *Adonidis horti: Imo vox ipsa Graeca* ἡδονή *quae voluptatem signifi-
cat, ab Hebraea Eden deducta videtur. Unde et* Adonis *fictitius poetarum, et
Adonis sive Edonis regio (quae Edene est) sed vitiose a peregrinis Graecis pro-
nuntiata, pro Edenis vel Edene*' ((Lyons 1653) Sig. Iii 1ʳ).   *revived*] Because
after being killed by a boar Adonis was restored to life every year during the
season of growth. It is just possible that M. alludes specifically to Spenser's
addition to the myth: namely, that Venus keeps Adonis hidden in a secret
garden (*F.Q.* III vi). Cp. *Comus* 998–1002.   *Laertes' son*] The sapient king
Odysseus; much-travelled as he was, when he saw the Garden of Alcinoüs
he marvelled (Homer, *Od.* vii 112–35). The periphrasis is to bring in *Laertes,*

> Much he the place admired, the person more.
445   As one who long in populous city pent,
>   Where houses thick and sewers annoy the air,
>   Forth issuing on a summer's morn to breathe
>   Among the pleasant villages and farms
>   Adjoined, from each thing met conceives delight,
450   The smell of grain, or tedded grass, or kine,
>   Or dairy, each rural sight, each rural sound;
>   If chance with nymph-like step fair virgin pass,
>   What pleasing seemed, for her now pleases more,
>   She most, and in her look sums all delight.
455   Such pleasure took the serpent to behold
>   This flowery plat, the sweet recess of Eve
>   Thus early, thus alone; her heavenly form

who resigned his kingship to take up gardening; unlike Satan, who keeps his crown and destroys the Garden.

Note that, like several other similes in ix, this consists of three parts arranged AAB (i.e., two pagan analogues, one sacred). See ll. 393–6n above. The pattern may only be for climax, or it may be intended to express the opposition of Monad and Dyad. It may also be worth noting that according to Pico della Mirandola the 1 : 2 ratio symbolizes the relation of the reason to the concupiscible faculty (see i 73–43n, Fowler 281n).

ix *444.* Ricks 135–8 points out that while this single-line sentence applies to Satan, it is also very apt for Solomon–and for Adam, whose tendency was to admire Eve too much (viii 567f, ix 1178f). Here, as at v 40–8, a passage also based on *Song of Solomon*, Satan takes Adam's place syntactically.

ix *445–54.* There seems at first little need to connect this simile with the autobiographical event reflected in *Elegia VII*. It is common sense to suppose that M. sometimes took walks in inhabited country places. But the girl in *Elegia VII* affected him deeply; and when he never saw her again his grief was like 'the grief of Hephaestus for his lost heaven'. Note that the simile is based on pastoral assumptions: hell is like a city, Paradise like the country. One has to be a very devoted member of the devil's party to stop short at sympathy with the townsman's need for a holiday and his appreciation of beauty–without reflecting how mean it would be for him to take advantage of the country girl's innocence. The contrast of smells recalls that made on the occasion of Satan's entry into Paradise (iv 168).   *annoy*] affect injuriously.
tedded] spread out to dry.   *kine*] cows; Emma 34 notes that archaic plurals are uncommon in M.   *nymphlike*] Keeps in play the comparison of l. 387 above.   *for*] because of.

ix *456. plat*] patch, piece of ground.

ix *457–8.* Bentley sneered at *soft*, on the ground that if Eve's form were softer than *angelic*, she would be altogether fluid and 'no fit Mate for her Husband'; and Empson[2] 153f also finds the word 'vague' and conflicting 'with concrete details already settled'. But it is ingenuous to suppose that

Angelic, but more soft, and feminine,
Her graceful innocence, her every air
460   Of gesture or least action overawed
His malice, and with rapine sweet bereaved
His fierceness of the fierce intent it brought:
That space the evil one abstracted stood
From his own evil, and for the time remained
465   Stupidly good, of enmity disarmed,
Of guile, of hate, of envy, of revenge;
But the hot hell that always in him burns,
Though in mid heaven, soon ended his delight,
And tortures him now more, the more he sees
470   Of pleasure not for him ordained: then soon
Fierce hate he recollects, and all his thoughts
Of mischief, gratulating, thus excites.

soft must always mean 'physically yielding and flexible'. Much more appropriate in the present context is the sense 'gentle; free from severity or rigour' (*OED* II 8). 'Emotionally impressionable' (*OED* III 13) is just possible as an overtone.   *form*] beauty; or simply 'appearance' (*OED* I 1 a).
ix *459–66*. The resemblance to the Elder Brother's account of the power of chastity and its effect on outward form (*Comus* 450ff) is very marked; see G. D. Hildebrand in *N & Q* cxcvii (1952) 246. The idea in common is that while virtue makes corporeality immortal, lust 'lets in defilement to the inward parts', so that 'the soul grows clotted by contagion, / Imbodies and imbrutes' (*Comus* 466–8; cp. l. 166 above, where Satan was constrained to *imbrute* himself in the serpent). Thus Satan is *abstracted* not only in the sense 'absent in mind' but also 'separated, removed from matter'–turned momentarily, in fact, 'to the soul's essence' (*Comus* 462). This line of thought is reinforced by the play *evil one . . . own evil*, which in the pronunciation of M.'s time would be a fully-fledged pun (see Dobson ii 676 and 694). For a moment Satan's evil becomes a separate thing, rather than a quality of himself. Conversely, even Eve's outward *form* is heavenly.   *air*] manner; mien. For M.'s concrete embodiment of such abstract qualities as have the power to affect the mind, see MacCaffrey 67.
ix *467*. See i 255*n* and iv 20–3*n*.
ix *468*. No mere hyperbole: M. had it on the authority of Job i 6 and ii 1 that Satan is sometimes summoned to heaven.
ix *470–9*. Cp. ll. 129f. This passage seems at first to contain a very damaging admission, for at ii 365f and 400ff Beelzebub, speaking for Satan, had held out hope that the devils might possess earth and enjoy its 'soft delicious air'. But perhaps Satan did not deceive his followers; he may only now be discovering how far pleasure is bound up with goodness, and hence *not for him ordained*.
ix *472. gratulating*] expressing joy at the event (of meeting Eve).

>   Thoughts, whither have ye led me, with what sweet
>   Compulsion thus transported to forget
> 475   What hither brought us, hate, not love, nor hope
>   Of Paradise for hell, hope here to taste
>   Of pleasure, but all pleasure to destroy,
>   Save what is in destroying, other joy
>   To me is lost. Then let me not let pass
> 480   Occasion which now smiles, behold alone
>   The woman, opportune to all attempts,
>   Her husband, for I view far round, not nigh,
>   Whose higher intellectual more I shun,
>   And strength, of courage haughty, and of limb
> 485   Heroic built, though of terrestrial mould,
>   Foe not informidable, exempt from wound,
>   I not; so much hath hell debased, and pain
>   Enfeebled me, to what I was in heaven.
>   She fair, divinely fair, fit love for gods,

ix 480. See l. 421n, and cp. l. 160, 'where hap may find'. As Burden 93f points out, *occasion* (opportunity) is a key word in Satan's ideology of chance and necessity. For a general account of the concept *Occasio* and its relation to *Fortuna*, see Panofsky[2] 72 and H. R. Patch, *The Goddess Fortuna in Mediaeval Literature* (Cambridge, Mass. 1927) pp. 115ff.

ix 481. *opportune*] liable, exposed (rare in this sense: a genuine Latinism; cp. *opportunus*); secondarily, 'convenient as to time and place'.

ix 482–8. An important passage, since it provides evidence that Satan would have avoided Adam and Eve if they had stayed together. The point of separation is thus seen to have been critical. See ll. 404–5n above, and cp. l. 1145 below.   *intellectual*] mind (OED B 1).   *higher*] Because allegorically Adam corresponds to *Mens*, Eve to *Ratio*; see ll. 358n, 360–1n. Adam is no doubt also to be thought of as a man having (as it happens) higher intellectual powers than Eve; cp. in this connection viii 541. But M. was perfectly capable of noticing that a woman sometimes has a better intellect than her husband, and he held that in such cases the man should submit to the woman (*Tetrachordon*; Yale ii 589). He thought the differentiation of sexual roles less fundamental than the 'superior and more naturall law . . . that the wiser should govern the lesse wise'. Thus it is quite possible that he intended the tragedy of Eve's fall to typify (among other things) the tragedy of a people betrayed by its intellectuals and leaders.   *courage*] spirit.

ix 485. *terrestrial mould*] Cp. 'formed of earth' (l. 149) and 'man of clay' (l. 176); Satan despises man's material substance.

ix 486. Cp. l. 283 and see vi 327 for Satan's discovery that his own exemption had expired.

ix 489–93. As with the first temptation, M. comes very near to presenting the second as a seduction. See v 40–1n and cp. v 48. For a poetic precedent for sexual union between Satan and Eve, see ii 727–8n. Sylvester's Du Bartas

490   Not terrible, though terror be in love
       And beauty, not approached by stronger hate,
       Hate stronger, under show of love well feigned,
       The way which to her ruin now I tend.
          So spake the enemy of mankind, enclosed
495   In serpent, inmate bad, and toward Eve
       Addressed his way, not with indented wave,
       Prone on the ground, as since, but on his rear,
       Circular base of rising folds, that towered
       Fold above fold a surging maze, his head
500   Crested aloft, and carbuncle his eyes;
       With burnished neck of verdant gold, erect
       Amidst his circling spires, that on the grass

244 similarly describes the serpent 'as a false Lover that thick snares hath laid. / T'intrap the honour of a fair young Maid'.   *tend*] turn my energies, apply myself.

ix *496–504*. *Gen.* iii 14 makes it clear only that the serpent has gone on its belly since the curse after the Fall; Biblical commentators disagreed as to the serpent's earlier gait. Three principal theories may be distinguished: (1) the serpent always went on his belly, but after the Fall this became a curse; (2) the serpent previously went upright, and began to go on its belly after the curse; (3) the serpent assumed an upright posture only while being used as an instrument by Satan (see the summary of these theories in Willet 47, 52). M. rejects (1) but does not decide between (2) and (3), for his account of the curse at x 175ff does not touch this point; while his description of the un-possessed serpent at iv 347–9 is ambiguous.   *indented*] zigzagged.   *maze*] The train of error is labyrinthine and elusive; cp. ii 651, where Sin has 'many a scaly fold'. M. here fuses two traditional images of Error (monster and labyrinth), which were merely juxtaposed by Spenser (*F.Q.* I i 11–15). *carbuncle* or reddish eyes denoted rage; cp. Shakespeare, *Coriolanus* V i 64f. But a precious stone in a *crested* serpent's head may also allude to Philostratus, *Life of Apollonius* iii 8, where we are told that there was just such a stone, from just such a serpent, in Gyges' ring. The Gyges legend has a grim relevance, for Eve, like Candaules' wife, has been shown naked by her husband; will be angry at his weakness in allowing her to be dishonoured (1155–61 below); and will arrange his death. The carbuncle in particular may be specified in the interest of having a chthonic antitype to the arch-chemic stone of the sun (see iii 596–601*nn*). More certain is the allusion to *Ezek.* xxviii 13: 'Thou hast been in Eden the garden of God; every precious stone was thy cover-ing, the sardius, topaz, and the diamond, the beryl, the onyx, and the jasper, the sapphire, the emerald, and the carbuncle, and gold', a verse that is applied to Satan by St Augustine in *Civ. Dei* xi 15.   *spires*] coils, spirals (not a Latinism).   *redundant*] copious overflowing (perhaps a Latinism in this sense); possibly also 'wavelike' (which would certainly be a Lati-nism), and 'abundant to excess'.

> Floated redundant: pleasing was his shape,
> And lovely, never since of serpent kind
> 505 Lovelier, not those that in Illyria changed
> Hermione and Cadmus, or the god
> In Epidaurus; nor to which transformed
> Ammonian Jove, or Capitoline was seen,
> He with Olympias, this with her who bore
> 510 Scipio the height of Rome. With tract oblique

ix 505–10. No doubt M. was aware of the tradition that Eve was charmed by the serpent's beauty (see John Salkeld, *A treatise of paradise* (1617), 218, *cit.* Hughes); and Empson[2] 175 is probably right in taking the simile to imply in some sense 'that Eve turned into a snake and became Satan's consort.' Or, at least, that she is tempted to imbrute herself like him. But another application of the simile is possible. Cadmus was metamorphosed into a serpent first; and only after he had embraced his wife Hermione (Harmonia) in his new form – an act that filled all who watched with horror – did she too change (Ovid, *Met.* iv 572–603). In the same way (though less innocently) Eve is the cause of a change in her spouse Adam.   *changed*] Modern punctuation would introduce a comma, but this would resolve an ambiguity. As it stands the line can be an inversion of 'Hermione and Cadmus changed (i.e. became) serpents'; cp. x 540f. *Hermione,* not an Ovidian form, occurs in Stephanus; see Starnes 243f. M. almost certainly intends an allusion to Vulcan's fatal gift to Hermione, which made all her children impious and wicked.   *the god | In Epidaurus*] Aesculapius, the god of healing, who restored so many to life that he aroused the anger of Pluto the king of hell. Once when an embassy from Rome came to Epidaurus to ask help, Aesculapius changed into a serpent 'raised breast-high', and accompanied the Romans in that form (Ovid, *Met.* xv 626–744).

ix 508. *Ammonian Jove*] Jupiter Ammon, the 'Lybian Jove' of iv 277. In his account of the parentage of Alexander the Great, Plutarch relates that his ostensible father Philip of Macedonia withdrew his love from *Olympias* because she was given to sleeping with a serpent; only to be told by the Delphic oracle that the serpent was a form of Jupiter Ammon.   *Capitoline*] Jupiter Capitolinus, so called from his temple at Rome, the capitol.

ix 510. *Scipio*] Scipio Africanus, the height of Rome because the greatest Roman.   *tract*] course. Svendsen 169f cites Camerarius' *The Living Librarie*: 'Philo and the Hebrewes say, That the Serpent signifieth allegorically, Lecherie. *Alexander* the Great held for certaine, That his mother *Olympias* was gotten with child of him by a Serpent, which the superstitious Pagans called *Jupiters* Genius. Wherefore having upon a time written to his mother thus; King *Alexander* the sonne of *Jupiter Ammon*, saluteth his mother *Olympias.* . . . The like is reported of *Scipio Africanus*; *C.Oppius* that hath written his life, *Titus Livius, Gellius,* and *Julius Higinus* doe say, That a great Serpent lay with *Scipios* mother, and was seene often in her chamber, and when any bodie came in, he would vanish away. *Valerius*

At first, as one who sought access, but feared
To interrupt, sidelong he works his way.
As when a ship by skilful steersman wrought
Nigh river's mouth or foreland, where the wind
515 Veers oft, as oft so steers, and shifts her sail;
So varied he, and of his tortuous train
Curled many a wanton wreath in sight of Eve,
To lure her eye; she busied heard the sound
Of rustling leaves, but minded not, as used
520 To such disport before her through the field,
From every beast, more duteous at her call,
Than at Circean call the herd disguised.
He bolder now, uncalled before her stood;
But as in gaze admiring: oft he bowed
525 His turret crest, and sleek enamelled neck,
Fawning, and licked the ground whereon she trod.
His gentle dumb expression turned at length
The eye of Eve to mark his play; he glad
Of her attention gained, with serpent tongue
530 Organic, or impulse of vocal air,
His fraudulent temptation thus began.
        Wonder not, sovereign mistress, if perhaps

Maximus also speaketh of it.' So also E. Topsell, *The historie of serpents*
(1608) 5.

ix *521–6.* The intention of this passage is not to bait Eve by making her
a sorceress, as Empson[2] ·176 suggests. Circe was in M.'s time regarded alle-
gorically as a type of the Excess that leads to the imbruting of man; see
M. Y. Hughes, 'Spenser's Acrasia and the Renaissance Circe', *JHI* iv (1943)
381–99. Homer's Circe changed men into wolves and lions who surprised
Odysseus' company by *fawning* on them like dogs (*Od.* x 212–19).

ix *523. bolder*] A difference is made in the serpent's behaviour so that there
may be a clue for Eve, if only she chooses to pay attention to it.

ix *525. enamelled*] of variegated colour (*OED* 3).

ix *530. organic*] instrumental, serving as an instrument (*OED* 1, rare). The
serpent lacks the organs that ordinarily produce human speech, so that
Satan has to use its tongue as an instrument, or else pulses of air.   *im-
pulse*] A pun: both 'motion, thrust' (*OED* 1) and 'strong suggestion from a
spirit' *OED* 3 a; cp. Roger Coke, *Elements of power and subjection* (1660)
177: 'If he by chance offend by the impulse of the Devil, let him make
amends therefore.' The means by which the serpent spoke were much dis-
cussed by the Biblical commentators; see Williams 116f.

ix *532–48.* Cp. v 38ff, the dream temptation, whose themes the present
speech develops. The flattery of Eve as a goddess, however, is an addition.
Such flattery was common in Renaissance poems on the Fall; but M. gives
it a contemporary immediacy: see D. S. Berkeley, 'Précieuse Gallantry and the

Thou canst, who art sole wonder, much less arm
Thy looks, the heaven of mildness, with disdain,
535 Displeased that I approach thee thus, and gaze
Insatiate, I thus single, nor have feared
Thy awful brow, more awful thus retired.
Fairest resemblance of thy maker fair,
Thee all things living gaze on, all things thine
540 By gift, and thy celestial beauty adore
With ravishment beheld, there best beheld
Where universally admired; but here
In this enclosure wild, these beasts among,
Beholders rude, and shallow to discern
545 Half what in thee is fair, one man except,
Who sees thee? (And what is one?) Who shouldst
        be seen
A goddess among gods, adored and served
By angels numberless, thy daily train.
        So glozed the tempter, and his proem tuned;
550 Into the heart of Eve his words made way,
Though at the voice much marvelling; at length
Not unamazed she thus in answer spake.
What may this mean? Language of man pronounced

Seduction of Eve', *N & Q* cxcvi (1951) 337-9. The contemptuous references
to Eve's *retired . . . rude* environment flout the pastoral values M. insisted on
in a recent simile; see ll. 445-54*n*. The offer of a *numberless* multitude of
admirers in exchange for Adam's single admiration makes explicit a fun-
damental opposition underlying much of the poem's number symbolism.
See vi 809-10*n*. Satan's appeal to Eve's pride is in accordance with the central
Christian tradition concerning the causes of the Fall; see Lewis 68, citing St
Augustine on the desire for independent selfhood. By l. 790, Eve is lost in
thoughts of her own 'godhead'. Burden 141 comments on Satan's use of
sovereign, a word that calls up the whole hierarchical cosmic order, in which
Eve's role is in fact quite a different one.

ix *549. glozed*] fawned, flattered, spoke smoothly and speciously.   *proem*]
prelude.

ix *553-66.* Eve's speech touches on one of the puzzles of the Genesis account
for seventeenth-century commentators: namely, 'how without fear or
doubt she could discourse with such a creature, or hear a serpent speak,
without suspicion of imposture' (Sir Thomas Browne, *Pseudodoxia epidemica*
i 1). M. has already provided partial answers, by making the prelapsarian
serpent harmless (ll. 185f) and beautiful (ll. 504ff), and by arranging for Eve
to be aware of the existence and powers of angels. All these explanations had
been resorted to by the commentators: see Willet 47. M. is unusually favour-
able to Eve, however, in making her ask the serpent (shrewdly enough) how
it came by its voice. The Eve of Scriptural exegesis, on the contrary, is

By tongue of brute, and human sense expressed?
555   The first at least of these I thought denied
To beasts, whom God on their creation-day
Created mute to all articulate sound;
The latter I demur, for in their looks
Much reason, and in their actions oft appears.
560   Thee, serpent, subtlest beast of all the field
I knew, but not with human voice endued;
Redouble then this miracle, and say,
How camest thou speakable of mute, and how
To me so friendly grown above the rest
565   Of brutal kind, that daily are in sight?
Say, for such wonder claims attention due.
    To whom the guileful tempter thus replied.
Empress of this fair world, resplendent Eve,
Easy to me it is to tell thee all
570   What thou command'st, and right thou shouldst be
      obeyed:
I was at first as other beasts that graze
The trodden herb, of abject thoughts and low,
As was my food, nor aught but food discerned
Or sex, and apprehended nothing high:
575   Till on a day roving the field, I chanced
A goodly tree far distant to behold
Loaden with fruit of fairest colours mixed,
Ruddy and gold: I nearer drew to gaze;
When from the boughs a savoury odour blown,
580   Grateful to appetite, more pleased my sense

carried away by the words, and makes no enquiry into their source, whether a good or a bad spirit.

ix 558. demur] hesitate about. Cp. vii 485ff on the emmet's wisdom; or viii 374, where Adam's God says that the beasts 'reason not contemptibly'.

ix 563. speakable] capable of speech; OED's earliest instance of this rare usage.   of] from being.

ix 560. For the serpent's subtlety, see Gen. iii 1, 2 Cor. xi 3. I knew establishes Eve's responsibility (Burden 101). She has been put on her guard against subtlety by Raphael's narration; cp. l. 307.

ix 572. abject] mean-spirited (OED A 3). There is some irony here; since, after the Fall and the curse, the serpent will be literally 'cast down' and subject like the herb to being trodden.

ix 578–88. Cp. ll. 740–2, where Eve experiences similar sensations.

ix 579. savoury] appetizing; edifying; see v 84–5n on a very similar pun in Eve's account of the first temptation. Note that Satan has already connected thought and eating by a piece of casual syntax at ll. 572f.

Than smell of sweetest fennel or the teats
Of ewe or goat dropping with milk at even,
Unsucked of lamb or kid, that tend their play.
To satisfy the sharp desire I had
585   Of tasting those fair apples, I resolved
Not to defer; hunger and thirst at once,
Powerful persuaders, quickened at the scent
Of that alluring fruit, urged me so keen.
About the mossy trunk I wound me soon,
590   For high from ground the branches would require
Thy utmost reach or Adam's: round the tree
All other beasts that saw, with like desire
Longing and envying stood, but could not reach.
Amid the tree now got, where plenty hung
595   Tempting so nigh, to pluck and eat my fill
I spared not, for such pleasure till that hour
At feed or fountain never had I found.
Sated at length, ere long I might perceive
Strange alteration in me, to degree
600   Of reason in my inward powers, and speech

ix *581–3.* Again a simile with an AAB pattern (see ll. 439–43*n*): the comparison is with one plant, and the teats of two species of animals. Milk from the teat and *fennel* were supposed to be favourite foods of serpents. Fennel was said to renew the serpent in spring, either by inducing it to cast its skin, or by sharpening its sight. See Pliny, *Nat. hist.* viii 99, xx 254; and cp. M.'s *An Apology against a Pamphlet* (Yale i 909): 'to see clearer then any fenell rub'd Serpent'. Note also, however, that fennel was an emblem of flattery; see *OED* 3, citing, e.g., Robert Greene: 'Woman's weeds, fennel I mean for flatterers' (*A quip for an upstart courtier* (1592)).

ix *585.* The identification of the forbidden fruit as an apple may have been drawn from the Ursinian (Heidelberg) Catechism; see Fletcher ii 96. But it was also a popular belief.

ix *587. defer*] delay.

ix *588.* As Burden 133 points out, Satan is lying when he describes the forbidden fruit as specially *alluring*. See iv 221–2*n* and v 53*n*.

ix *590–1.* Even when giving a simple estimate of height, Satan manages to insinuate an image of man's disobedience. But M., more subtle still, simultaneously makes the point in favour of divine providence, that if the fruit was so difficult of access there was no chance of its being plucked without a firm decision.

ix *595–601.* See v 45–90*n*. In this second temptation, the appearances of the first are traced back to their causes. How did the dream tempter know the effect of the fruit? Because, it turns out, he had once been an abject serpent.

ix *599. to degree*] to a certain amount; the idea of a degree as a step or stage in an ascent is secondarily present.

Wanted not long, though to this shape retained.
Thenceforth to speculations high or deep
I turned my thoughts, and with capacious mind
Considered all things visible in heaven,
605   Or earth, or middle, all things fair and good;
But all that fair and good in thy divine
Semblance, and in thy beauty's heavenly ray
United I beheld; no fair to thine
Equivalent or second, which compelled
610   Me thus, though importune perhaps, to come
And gaze, and worship thee of right declared
Sovereign of creatures, universal dame.
        So talked the spirited sly snake; and Eve
Yet more amazed unwary thus replied.
615   Serpent, thy overpraising leaves in doubt
The virtue of that fruit, in thee first proved:
But say, where grows the tree, from hence how far?
For many are the trees of God that grow
In Paradise, and various, yet unknown
620   To us, in such abundance lies our choice,
As leaves a greater store of fruit untouched,
Still hanging incorruptible, till men
Grow up to their provision, and more hands

ix *602.* The use the serpent makes of his newly acquired reason is not to glorify God, but to engage in *speculations high*–no doubt of the kind dismissed by Raphael as unprofitable at viii 173–8; *deep* speculations recalls the 'causes deep' of creation that Uriel said were hid by God as his secrets (iii 707).

ix *605. middle*] the space between.

ix *609.* Echoing Horace *Odes* I xii 18, *nec viget quicquam simile aut secundum*: praise appropriate only to God. Cp. viii 406f, where God in fact described himself in precisely these terms.

ix *612. dame*] mistress (*OED* I 1).

ix *613. spirited*] indued with an animating spirit, stirred up (*OED* s.v. *Spirit*, vb. I 2 d and 3); also energetic, enterprising (*OED* s.v. *Spirited*, a. 2 b). The sense 'possessed by a spirit', if it is operative, may be an extension original with M.

ix *616. virtue*] power. Eve is flirting: 'If you pay silly compliments like that, the tree can't have done much for your reason.'   *proved*] tested by experiment.

ix *618–24.* There is no single and complete syntactic line: *in such . . . choice* must be attached in turn to the word group before and the one after. *trees of God*] Biblical diction; cp. *Ps.* civ 16.

ix *623. to their provision*] to what is already (providentially) provided for them.

Help to disburden nature of her birth.
625   To whom the wily adder, blithe and glad.
Empress, the way is ready, and not long,
Beyond a row of myrtles, on a flat,
Fast by a fountain, one small thicket past
Of blowing myrrh and balm; if thou accept
630   My conduct, I can bring thee thither soon.
Lead then, said Eve. He leading swiftly rolled
In tangles, and made intricate seem straight,
To mischief swift. Hope elevates, and joy
Brightens his crest, as when a wandering fire,
635   Compact of unctuous vapour, which the night
Condenses, and the cold environs round,
Kindled through agitation to a flame,
Which oft, they say, some evil spirit attends
Hovering and blazing with delusive light,
640   Misleads the amazed night-wanderer from his way
To bogs and mires, and oft through pond or pool,
There swallowed up and lost, from succour far.

ix *624. birth*] the early edns have the unusual spelling 'bearth'.

ix *627. myrtles*. See 426–31*n* above. Read emblematically, the *row of myrtles* is the obstacle of Eve's virtue. In view of the strong element of sexual seduction in M.'s presentation of the temptation, however, it may be that the myrtles (not to speak of the *fountain, thicket* and *balm*) also have an anatomical sexual symbolism. For this see Valeriano 639 or Liceti 377 (myrtle as female *pudenda*).

ix *629. blowing*] blooming.

ix *630. conduct*] Ostensibly 'guidance' (*OED* I 1); but in reality, as we know, 'management' (*OED* II 5, 6).

ix *632. made*] *Ed I* misprints 'make'.

ix *634–42*. Cp. *Com* 433. See Svendsen (108) who explains that Renaissance meteorologists 'regularly treated *ignis fatuus* and *ignis lambens* together, and nearly always as emblems of self-deception'. She quotes Swan's *Speculum mundi*: 'These kinds of lights are often seen in Fennes and Moores, because there is always great store of unctuous matter fit for such purposes. . . . Wherefore the much terrified, ignorant, and superstitious people may see their own errours in that they have deemed these lights to be walking spirits. . . . They are no spirits, and yet lead out of the way, because those who see them are amazed, and look so earnestly after them that they forget their way' (*ibid.* 109). See also Lerner 306, with the correction of Ricks 126. The implication of the simile is that Eve is led astray because she lacks the guidance of intellect, which would have obviated her amazement.   *amazed*] Recalls Eve's amazement at l. 614 above.

ix *635. compact of*] composed of.

So glistered the dire snake, and into fraud
Led Eve our credulous mother, to the tree
645   Of prohibition, root of all our woe;
Which when she saw, thus to her guide she spake.
    Serpent, we might have spared our coming hither,
Fruitless to me, though fruit be here to excess,
The credit of whose virtue rest with thee,
650   Wondrous indeed, if cause of such effects.
But of this tree we may not taste nor touch;
God so commanded, and left that command
Sole daughter of his voice; the rest, we live
Law to our selves, our reason is our law.

ix *643–5*. Discussed persuasively by Ricks (75f), who notices the silent pun in *root*; the oxymoron *credulous mother*; the accuracy of *tree / Of prohibition* (not Latinism, but literal truth: 'of all prohibitions'); and the 'calculated brutality' of *snake*, in *PL* an unusual variant for serpent. Burden points out that the forbidden tree is never described by M. as attractive or provocative except when appetite is perversely aroused; hence the present description is flat and bare. The passive use of *fraud* – 'the state of being deceived; error' or 'injury, detriment' – is an extension perhaps original with M.; cp. Latin *fraus*.

ix *647–50*. On the dramatic irony or unspoken puns, see Ricks 73f. To Eve the words are mere jaunty levity, to us they are truer than she knows – *excess* in a darker sense is not far off.   *virtue*] Another pun, between 'power' and 'virtuousness'.

ix *651*. Cp. l. 663, where Eve, as in *Gen.* iii 3, refers to a prohibition against even touching the fruit. The Prohibition itself, however, was only against eating: see *Gen.* ii 17. Some Biblical commentators held that Eve was unwarrantably adding to God's precept, but M. evidently agreed with Willet 49 that Eve 'faithfully expoundeth the meaning of the precept', for he harmonizes the two formulas and uses them almost indifferently. Thus at l. 925 Adam speaks of the 'ban to touch'; and at vii 46 so does M., *in persona auctoris*.

ix *653*. *daughter of his voice*] Perhaps a Hebraism for 'voice sent from heaven' (a revelation of less weight than God's own voice), and Eve is perhaps palliating the prohibition; see W. Hunter in *MLQ* ix (1948) 279f. But a more salient feature of the passage is that Eve has omitted one of God's daughters. vii 8–12 made it clear that God has *two* daughters, Wisdom and Urania (perhaps Logos), so that *Sole daughter* is a dramatic irony. Eve slights an obedience she ought to acknowledge. She is not as independent as she claims, for she owes allegiance to Wisdom, and hence to Adam.

ix *654*. Cp. *Rom.* ii 14: 'When the Gentiles, which have not the law, do by nature the things contained in the law, these, having not the law, are a law unto themselves.'

655   To whom the tempter guilefully replied.
       Indeed? Hath God then said that of the fruit
       Of all these garden trees ye shall not eat,
       Yet lords declared of all in earth or air?
       To whom thus Eve yet sinless. Of the fruit
660   Of each tree in the garden we may eat,
       But of the fruit of this fair tree amidst
       The garden, God hath said, Ye shall not eat
       Thereof, nor shall ye touch it, lest ye die.
       She scarce had said, though brief, when now more
         bold
665   The tempter, but with show of zeal and love
       To man, and indignation at his wrong,
       New part puts on, and as to passion moved,
       Fluctuates disturbed, yet comely and in act
       Raised, as of some great matter to begin.
670   As when of old some orator renowned

ix 655–8. Closely following *Gen.* iii 1; but with a very different effect, since we know that Satan is well aware of the terms of the prohibition. Hence *guilefully*.

ix 659. *yet sinless*] Important, not only for its indication that (at least as far as M.'s intention is concerned) we are not to think of Eve as corrupted by the first temptation in any way that involves guilt, but also for its more elusive implication that there are different degrees of corruption or proximity to the place of sin. If an Eve who has accepted Satan's 'conduct . . . into fraud' (ll. 630, 643) is still sinless, then presumably an Eve who presses her will on Adam and separates from him, while certainly also sinless, might similarly, though to a lesser degree, be led by an evil proclivity.

ix 663. See l. 651n. Commentators generally agreed that in saying 'lest ye die' (*Gen.* iii 3; Vulgate, even more strikingly, *ne forte moriamini*) Eve was hedging: what God actually said was 'thou shalt surely die' (*Gen.* ii 17; see Willet 48). Similarly *this fair tree amidst | The garden* (l. 661; *Gen.* iii 3) is a vague evasion of the morally definitive 'tree of the knowledge of good and evil'.

ix 668. *Fluctuates*] undergoes changes of form; is unstable (*OED* 2 a); but perhaps with the additional overtone 'undulates' (Latinism).

ix 670–6. A very intricate simile; since three strands of meaning – oratorical, theatrical and theological – are kept going simultaneously, in addition to the one being illustrated. Thus *part* means 'part of the body', 'dramatic role' and 'moral act' (*OED* II 11); *motion* means 'gesture', 'mime' (or 'puppet-show') and 'instigation, persuasive force, inclination' (*OED* 7, 9); while *act* means 'action', 'performance of a play' and 'the accomplished deed itself, as distinct from the mere motion' (*OED* 2). The implication is that Satan, besides talking persuasively, is acting a part; and that each feature of his performance could be given an unattractive definition, if only Eve

In Athens or free Rome, where eloquence
Flourished, since mute, to some great cause addressed,
Stood in himself collected, while each part,
Motion, each act won audience ere the tongue,
675   Sometimes in highth began, as no delay
Of preface brooking through his zeal of right.
So standing, moving, or to highth upgrown
The tempter all impassioned thus began.
    O sacred, wise, and wisdom-giving plant,
680   Mother of science, now I feel thy power
Within me clear, not only to discern
Things in their causes, but to trace the ways
Of highest agents, deemed however wise.
Queen of this universe, do not believe
685   Those rigid threats of death; ye shall not die:
How should ye? By the fruit? It gives you life
To knowledge. By the threatener? Look on me,
Me who have touched and tasted, yet both live,
And life more perfect have attained than fate

cared to use the terms of moral theology.   *since mute*] Because eloquence
has declined; but also (literally, not hyperbolically) because the serpent now
no longer speaks.   *in himself collected*] completely in control of himself.
The phrase imitates the Ital. idiom *in se raccolto*, but also precisely defines the
inwardness of the serpent's self-command: *in himself* being in mild antithesis
to *while each* (outward serpentine) *part*. Cicero's first oration against Catiline
is an instance of the beginning without preface (*in highth*).   *audience*]
attention.

ix *679–80*. Having endowed the tree with power ('virtue': ll. 616, 649),
Satan now animates it: the step to Eve's worship at ll. 835f is a short one.
Contrast the many earlier presentations of the tree as no more than a pledge
of obedience (iii 95*n*, iv 428, viii 325, etc.).   *science*] knowledge.

ix *682*. See l. 602*n* above. The knowledge and wisdom Satan offers con-
sists in exploration of God's forbidden secrets (cp. iii 707), and in scepti-
cism about the wisdom of *highest agents* (Burden 105).

ix *685*. Cp. *Gen.* iii 4f: 'The serpent said unto the woman, Ye shall not
surely die: For God doth know that in the day ye eat thereof, then your
eyes shall be opened, and ye shall be as gods, knowing good and evil.'

ix *687–90*. The early edns have a question mark after *knowledge* and a comma
after *threatener*, but this is evidently an error. The antithesis between fruit
and *threatener* requires that the latter, like the former, shall be interrogative.
threatener is a metrical dissyllable, spelled 'threatner'.   *To*] in addition
to.

ix *689–90*. Satan has to invoke in one sentence both Necessity and Chance
(the two powers acknowledged in his ideology), to escape using such awk-
ward terms as commandment, obedience and natural law. Throughout

690 Meant me, by venturing higher than my lot.
     Shall that be shut to man, which to the beast
     Is open? Or will God incense his ire
     For such a petty trespass, and not praise
     Rather your dauntless virtue, whom the pain
695 Of death denounced, whatever thing death be,
     Deterred not from achieving what might lead
     To happier life, knowledge of good and evil;
     Of good, how just? Of evil, if what is evil
     Be real, why not known, since easier shunned?
700 God therefore cannot hurt ye, and be just;
     Not just, not God; not feared then, nor obeyed:
     Your fear it self of death removes the fear.

the temptation he encourages Eve to wish for an absolute freedom, uncon-
ditioned by the organic limitations of human nature. To this end, he repre-
sents the differentiation of species as a chance affair–a matter of *lot*; en-
forced, however, by Fate, to produce the bondage from which Eve is to be
liberated. Burden 143 compares Grotius, *Adamus exul* 1075–80, where Satan
uses a necessitarian argument, though a much cruder one.

ix *692. incense*] kindle, excite.

ix *694.* Satan's deceptions are here concentrated on a single word. He
renders the concept of *virtue* so uncertain that the word comes to mean no
more than 'courage, manliness': a possible significance (see *OED* i 7), but
here a narrow and perverse one. Empson (159), rightly wishing to give the
most sublime explanation of Eve's motives, thinks she is moved by this
argument of Satan's above the others: 'She feels the answer to this elaborate
puzzle must be that God wants her to eat the apple, since what he is really
testing is not her obedience but her courage.' This is plausible; especially
since virtue (though in a wider sense) is after all the specific concern of Eve
as *ratio* (see l. 335*n*). Adam, however, would have known that the virtue of
obedience takes precedence.

ix *695.* Again Satan acts the part of innocence. At ii 781–816 Sin explained
the nature of Death to him in some detail, and we were told that 'the subtle
fiend his lore / Soon learned'.

ix *698–9.* If the knowledge is of good, how is it just to prohibit it? The matter
of the prohibition is dangerous ground for Satan, so that he has to argue even
more quickly and elliptically than usual. Here occurs the most egregious
logical fallacy in the speech: the alteration of the meaning of *knowledge*
in the middle of a sorites. (In order that evil may be *shunned*, it is not at all
necessary that it should be *known* in the sense of the prohibition.) The dis-
tinction between theoretical knowledge and knowledge in the sense of
'miserable experience' (Willet 50) was a standard one in commentaries on
Gen. iii.

Why then was this forbid? Why but to awe,
Why but to keep ye low and ignorant,
705   His worshippers; he knows that in the day
Ye eat thereof, your eyes that seem so clear,
Yet are but dim, shall perfectly be then
Opened and cleared, and ye shall be as gods,
Knowing both good and evil as they know.
710   That ye should be as gods, since I as man,
Internal man, is but proportion meet,
I of brute human, ye of human gods.
So ye shall die perhaps, by putting off
Human, to put on gods, death to be wished,
715   Though threatened, which no worse than this can
          bring.

ix *703–9*. 'For God doth know that in the day ye eat thereof, then your eyes shall be opened, and ye shall be as gods, knowing good and evil' (*Gen.* iii 5). The argument that God's prohibition was made out of envy and a desire to protect his own vested interest had often been assigned to the serpent. M. Nicolson (*PQ* vi (1927) 17) usefully compares Henry More's *Conjectura Cabbalistica*: 'God indeed loves to keep his creatures in awe ... but he knows very well that if you take your liberty with us, and satiate yourselves freely with your own will, your eyes will be wonderfully opened ... so that you will ... like God know all things whatsoever whether good or evil.' Her conclusion, however, that 'the ethical import of the fall is that man followed his instincts and will, not his reason' is too simple. M. is unambiguous that to Eve Satan's words seem *impregned / With reason* (l. 737f). In other words, Eve follows what she thinks is reason: she is not shown, in the first instance, as giving way to instinct or will, but rather as being *deceived* (cf. 404 above, and see 1 *Tim.* ii 14). Her error, more subtly, lies in her failure to reflect or respond faithfully to wisdom or intellect (mind); for the duty of *ratio* is to translate the mind's contemplations of truth into practical terms. Thus Eve is not abandoning reason, exactly, but the 'higher intellect' (l. 483).

ix *710–12*. Cp. ll. 932–7, where Adam reasons similarly. In the event, however, God turns out to have ordained a different *proportion*; not *Change from serpent: Change from man :: Man : Angel*, but rather *Angel : Man :: Change to serpent : Change to fallen man*. For Satan's punitive metamorphosis see x 507ff.   *internal man*] see l. 600; the serpent's pretence is that his 'inward powers' are human.

ix *713–15*. Satan offers a travesty of Christian mortification and death to sin; cp. 1 *Cor.* xv 53, or *Col.* iii 1–15, esp. 2f and 9f: 'Set your affection on things above ... For ye are dead, and your life is hid with Christ in God.... ye have put off the old man with his deeds; And have put on the new man, which is renewed in knowledge after the image of him that created him.'

And what are gods that man may not become
As they, participating godlike food?
The gods are first, and that advantage use
On our belief, that all from them proceeds;
720 I question it, for this fair earth I see,
Warmed by the sun, producing every kind,
Them nothing: if they all things, who enclosed
Knowledge of good and evil in this tree,
That whoso eats thereof, forthwith attains
725 Wisdom without their leave? And wherein lies
The offence, that man should thus attain to know?
What can your knowledge hurt him, or this tree
Impart against his will if all be his?
Or is it envy, and can envy dwell
730 In heavenly breasts? These, these and many more
Causes import your need of this fair fruit.
Goddess humane, reach then, and freely taste.
      He ended, and his words replete with guile
Into her heart too easy entrance won:
735 Fixed on the fruit she gazed, which to behold

ix 716–17. *participating*] sharing; partaking of. Both language and thought
echo v 493–500, where Raphael holds out hope of a permissible evolution,
until eventually 'men / With angels may participate'. Thus the choice
before Eve is not made to lie between aspiration and stasis, but between the
right aspiration and the wrong (Burden 144).

ix 720–2. A perverse form of the argument advanced by Raphael – at viii
93ff; after Eve had left the table – about the fruitfulness of the earth compared
with the sun (not with God). See Rajan 161.   *they*] 'produce' understood.

ix 722–5. The dualistic implication of these lines completely contradicts the
earlier monotheistic arguments; throughout, Satan's speech lacks any
steady metaphysical orientation. Satan here assumes the magical operation
of the tree; see Lewis 68.

ix 728. *impart*] communicate; bestow, give a share in.

ix 729–32. See ll. 10–19n and 703–9n, and cp. Virgil, *Aen.* i 11, *tantaene
animis caelestibus irae?* Burden 142ff comments that Satan presents the choice
to Eve as one between Fate and 'free virtue' (ii 551 above); he is inviting her
to participate in a Satanic or pagan epic – complete with machinery of
jealous gods – about her 'own heroic deeds' (ii 549).   *import*] occasion
(*OED* I 4).

ix 732. *goddess humane*] human goddess. Satan must now be very sure to risk
so wild an oxymoron. The paradox is only partially softened by a secondary
sense 'gracious goddess'.

ix 735–43. Cp. *Gen.* iii 6: 'When the woman saw that the tree was good for
food, and that it was pleasant to the eyes, and a tree to be desired to make
one wise, she took of the fruit thereof, and did eat.' The forbidden fruit is

> Might tempt alone, and in her ears the sound
> Yet rung of his persuasive words, impregned
> With reason, to her seeming, and with truth;
> Mean while the hour of noon drew on, and waked
> 740 An eager appetite, raised by the smell
> So savoury of that fruit, which with desire,
> Inclinable now grown to touch or taste,
> Solicited her longing eye; yet first
> Pausing a while, thus to her self she mused.
> 745   Great are thy virtues, doubtless, best of fruits,

now for the first time described as specially attractive and tempting to man (Burden 134). It would have been improvident or provoking of God to have allowed it to seem so before; but now Eve's heart is corrupted. Note that Eve is deceived into following what seems to her the *truth*: she does not follow her appetite in the first instance; see ll. 703–9*n*. Burden cites the Puritan divine Thomas Cartwright (1535–1603) on the precedence of the heart's corruption before the abuse of sight and taste (which he regarded as outward causes of the Fall).   *impregned*] impregnated.   *savoury*] Not only 'appetizing' but also, secondarily, 'edifying'. For earlier uses of the word in similar contexts, see l. 579*n* above; also v 84–5*n*.   *inclinable*] disposed. This can only describe Eve's *desire*, hardly the fruit; in the sense 'amenable' it seems not to have been applied to inanimate objects.   *now*] Implies that Eve never before desired to touch or taste the fruit. We have thus reached the second of the three phases of sin recognized in the moral theology of M.'s day: *Suggestio, Delectatio* and *Consensus*.

ix *739–40*. Burden (134ff) has it that the fact that Eve would always be hungry at *noon* contributes to the crisis. The increased appetitive urge is not, of course, evil in itself–even Raphael got hungry at this time (v 301 and 436ff); but M. means to rùn excitingly close to a tragedy of necessity. It seems likely, however, that M. intends noon, as such an apparently temporal specification is often intended in Scripture, 'not as an indication of time, but for the sake of its ethical significance' (Auerbach 7; cp. MacCaffrey 52). This significance is to be found in the common symbolism whereby noon was the critical time of judgment; see iv 30*n*. There was also a tradition, going back at least to Hugh of St-Victor, that the Fall actually occurred, like the Expulsion and the death of Christ, at the Biblical sixth hour (see Bongo 280, also xii 1*n*).

ix *743–4*. The pause is indispensable: Eve must have time to resolve deliberately before acting (Burden 136, citing Hobbes's analysis of the conversion of appetite into will).

ix *745*. *Ed II* wrongly has full stop after *fruits*.   *virtues*] powers.   *doubtless*] without question; certainly.

ix *745–79*. The resemblances between Eve's speech and earlier speeches of

Though kept from man, and worthy to be admired,
Whose taste, too long forborne, at first assay
Gave elocution to the mute, and taught
The tongue not made for speech to speak thy praise:
750 Thy praise he also who forbids thy use,
Conceals not from us, naming thee the tree
Of knowledge, knowledge both of good and evil;
Forbids us then to taste, but his forbidding
Commends thee more, while it infers the good
755 By thee communicated, and our want:
For good unknown, sure is not had, or had
And yet unknown, is as not had at all.
In plain then, what forbids he but to know,
Forbids us good, forbids us to be wise?
760 Such prohibitions bind not. But if death
Bind us with after-bands, what profits then
Our inward freedom? In the day we eat
Of this fair fruit, our doom is, we shall die.
How dies the serpent? He hath eaten and lives,
765 And knows, and speaks, and reasons, and discerns,
Irrational till then. For us alone
Was death invented? Or to us denied
This intellectual food, for beasts reserved?
For beasts it seems: yet that one beast which first
770 Hath tasted, envies not, but brings with joy
The good befallen him, author unsuspect,
Friendly to man, far from deceit or guile.
What fear I then, rather what know to fear
Under this ignorance of good and evil,
775 Of God or death, of law or penalty?

Satan's are too obvious to list separately. She has trusted Satan's account of
the fruit, and consequently argues from false premises—such as its magical
power.

ix 748. elocution] utterance (OED 3); eloquence, oratory (OED 2).

ix 758. In plain] in plain terms, plainly (OED s.v. Plain a.¹ A V 19 a).

ix 761. after-bands] subsequent bonds (possibly a coinage: only instance in
OED).

ix 766–7. The irony here is strong, for we know from the divine colloquy
of Bk iii that death was invented for man.

ix 771. author unsuspect] Eve means 'informant not subject to suspicion';
it may be an irony that author could also mean 'inventor' or 'instigator,
prompter'.

ix 773. 'What fear I, then—or rather (since I'm not allowed to know any-
thing) what do I know that is to be feared?'

> Here grows the cure of all, this fruit divine,
> Fair to the eye, inviting to the taste,
> Of virtue to make wise: what hinders then
> To reach, and feed at once both body and mind?
> 780   So saying, her rash hand in evil hour
> Forth reaching to the fruit, she plucked, she ate:
> Earth felt the wound, and nature from her seat
> Sighing through all her works gave signs of woe,
> That all was lost. Back to the thicket slunk
> 785   The guilty serpent, and well might, for Eve
> Intent now wholly on her taste, naught else
> Regarded, such delight till then, as seemed,
> In fruit she never tasted, whether true
> Or fancied so, through expectation high
> 790   Of knowledge, nor was godhead from her thought.
> Greedily she engorged without restraint,

x776 . *cure of all*] The primary meaning is 'remedy of all (this ignorance, etc.)', the ironic secondary meaning 'charge, duty, of all (men)'. Whether an older meaning of *cure* (care, trouble) is also operative, is more difficult to say. See *OED* s.v. *Cure* I 2, 3 and II 7, and cp. Latin *cura*=grief.

ix 777. The fruit is now *inviting*, and therefore a provocation; see ll. 735–43*n*.

ix 778. *Of virtue to make wise*] Primarily 'having power to make wise'; secondarily and ironically 'to make experienced, wise after the event, instead of virtuous'.

ix 781. *ate*] spelt 'eat' in the early edns, and possibly pronounced 'et' (still a correct alternative to 'ate' in unstressed positions).

ix 782–4. Cp. ll. 1000–4 below, where nature gives a 'second groan' at Adam's fall; also x 651–719, where the changes in nature occasioned by the Fall are described in more detail. The effect was anticipated by Satan at ll. 132f above: 'all this will soon / Follow, as to him linked in weal or woe'. The thought, which goes back to *Rom.* viii 22 ('the whole creation groaneth and travaileth in pain') was common in poetry: Hughes cites instances as far apart as Gower, *Mirrour* 26,810ff and Joseph Beaumont, *Psyche* vi 254. Nature's sigh is only a *sign* (portent) of mutability, because the changes themselves will not take place until man's case has been heard and judged. Sylvester's Du Bartas 254–75 ('The Furies'), one of the most elaborate and interesting accounts of the changes in nature at the Fall, puts them after the Expulsion.

ix 789. *fancied*] See ll. 735–43*n*.

ix 790. *god-head*] See ll. 532–48*n*.

ix 791–2. Svendsen (128) cites Sebastian Franck, *The Forbidden Fruit, or a Treatise of the Tree of Knowledge of Good and Evil which Adam at First, and as yet All Mankind doe eate death* (1640): like Eve, all men 'doe eate death, and yet . . . thinke themselves to eate life, and hope to be Gods'. She offers

And knew not eating death: satiate at length,
And heightened as with wine, jocund and boon,
Thus to her self she pleasingly began.
795   O sovereign, virtuous, precious of all trees
In Paradise, of operation blest
To sapience, hitherto obscured, infamed,
And thy fair fruit let hang, as to no end
Created; but henceforth my early care,
800   Not without song, each morning, and due praise
Shall tend thee, and the fertile burden ease
Of thy full branches offered free to all;
Till dieted by thee I grow mature
In knowledge, as the gods who all things know;
805   Though others envy what they cannot give;

the interesting suggestion that Eve here devours in a manner reminiscent of Death himself: 'the release of inordinate appetite into the world brings on the insatiable devourer of all men'.   *knew . . . death*] knew not that she was eating death; imitating a Greek construction in which verbs of knowing or perceiving are followed by a participle. But also 'she was unaware, while she ate death' or even 'she *knew*; not eating (immediate) death'.   *satiate*] contrast the temperate eating of v 451f.

ix *793*. The only 'heightening' effect achieved is inebriation (Burden 145). It should be recalled that fermented wine was unknown before the Fall; see v 345*n*. At least since the time of St Bernard, drunkenness has always been a convenient symbol of the loss of rationality resulting from the Fall. Bersuire in one of his allegorizations specifies that 'by wine can be understood the human will; for . . . the human will burns with desire' (*Reductorium morale* VIII iii 33).   *boon*] jolly, convivial. Eve's new state is characterized by a gaiety shockingly trivial and inappropriate.

ix *795. virtuous, precious*] the positive for the superlative; a classicism. Richardson instances Homer, *Il.* v 381 (δῖα θεάων), Virgil *Aen.* iv 576 (*sancte deorum*).

ix *796–7. operation*] agency; efficacy (*OED* 2, 3). 'Of efficacy in producing sapience'. As l. 1018 will show more clearly, *sapience* contains a word-play similar to that in 'savour' at l. 579 and v 84f; though here the wit is appropriately even more learned and laborious. 'Sapience' is derived from Latin *sapientia* (discernment, taste), and ultimately from *sapere* (to taste).   *infamed*] defamed.

ix *800*. Eve proposes to offer the tree the morning orisons she has till now kept for God; cp. e.g., v 145.

ix *804–7*. Eve parrots Satan's argument at ll. 722–5 (that God cannot have put knowledge in the tree if he forbids its use), and gets it wrong.   *gods*] God; Eve has learned from Satan to use the vaguer pagan form (cp. l. 718 above).   *others*] i.e., God. Eve's language is now full of lapses in logic and evasions in theology.

For had the gift been theirs, it had not here
Thus grown. Experience, next to thee I owe,
Best guide; not following thee, I had remained
In ignorance, thou open'st wisdom's way,
810 And giv'st access, though secret she retire.
And I perhaps am secret; heaven is high,
High and remote to see from thence distinct
Each thing on earth; and other care perhaps
May have diverted from continual watch
815 Our great forbidder, safe with all his spies
About him. But to Adam in what sort
Shall I appear? Shall I to him make known
As yet my change, and give him to partake
Full happiness with me, or rather not,
820 But keep the odds of knowledge in my power
Without copartner? So to add what wants
In female sex, the more to draw his love,
And render me more equal, and perhaps,
A thing not undesirable, sometime
825 Superior; for inferior who is free?
This may be well: but what if God have seen,
And death ensue? Then I shall be no more,
And Adam wedded to another Eve,
Shall live with her enjoying, I extinct;
830 A death to think. Confirmed then I resolve,
Adam shall share with me in bliss or woe:

ix *810. access*] Stressed on the second syllable.   *secret*] uncommunicative,
not given to revelation (*OED* A 2 a); secluded from observation (*OED* A 1
c); abstruse, mystical (*OED* A 1 g).
ix *811–13. secret*] hidden. See *Job* xxii 13f, *Is.* xlvii 10 and *Ps.* x 11 ('He hath
said in his heart, God hath forgotten: he hideth his face; he will never see it').
ix *815. safe*] safely remote; a usage that Pearce felt to have only colloquial
warrant.
ix *821–30.* Eve's decision now lies only between one selfish purpose and
another: the motive of desire for sexual domination is ranged against fear
and jealousy. The idea of Eve's jealousy is traced to rabbinical sources by
D.C. Allen in *MLN* lxiii (1948) 262f; and to Christian commentators in
Williams 123.
ix *821–2.* The first suggestion we have had that Eve feels any inadequacy.
ix *824. A thing not undesirable*] The parenthesis is probably to be taken as
a piece of solemn self-deception: Eve really thinks it very desirable indeed
that she should be almost always superior. Contrast the first description of
Adam and Eve, 'not equal, as their sex not equal seemed' (iv 296).

So dear I love him, that with him all deaths
I could endure, without him live no life.
    So saying, from the tree her step she turned,
835   But first low reverence done, as to the power
That dwelt within, whose presence had infused
Into the plant sciential sap, derived
From nectar, drink of gods. Adam the while
Waiting desirous her return, had wove
840   Of choicest flowers a garland to adorn
Her tresses, and her rural labours crown,
As reapers oft are wont their harvest queen.
Great joy he promised to his thoughts, and new
Solace in her return, so long delayed;
845   Yet oft his heart, divine of something ill,
Misgave him; he the faltering measure felt;

ix *832–3*. The first explicit expression of love from Eve–and the first false
expression. For in effect she is planning to kill Adam to ease her own mind.
Note the confusion of her thought: in reality there is no question of Eve's
living without Adam, since if she loses him it will be because she is dead.
The lines perhaps echo Horace, *Odes* III ix 24: *tecum vivere amem, tecum obeam
libens*. If so, the point would not just be that Horace's poem is a dialogue,
and Eve is having a dialogue with herself. There would be an allusion to the
contrast between Lydia's professed willingness to die *for* Calais, if only he can
survive her (ll. 15f), and her less noble readiness to die *with* her old flame.
Eve's attitude lies all on the latter side of this contrast; the former has not
even occurred to her as a possibility. The allusion would have some chance
of being recognized by M.'s earlier readers, as Horace's poem was extremely
popular in the seventeenth century. There were translations or imitations by
Jonson, Herrick, Stanley, Ashmore (three), Hannay, John Hall, Collop and
Flatman; see Marianne Mays, 'Some Themes and Conventions in Caroline
Lyrics' (Oxford B. Litt. thesis).
ix *835–6*. 'She who thought it beneath her dignity to bow to Adam or to
God, now worships a vegetable. She has at last become "primitive" in the
popular sense' (Lewis 122). Empson 155 argues that Eve really prays to the
power, not the tree; but the same could be said of primitive man.
ix *837*. *sciential*] endowed with knowledge.
ix *842*. This simile returns us to earlier comparisons of Eve with the
agricultural goddesses Pales, Pomona and Ceres (ll. 393–6). The irony is
powerful; for when Eve comes she bears no natural crop in her hand.
ix *845*. Eve had previously been 'due at her hour'; see v 303.   *divine*]
prophet, diviner, soothsayer (*OED* 1); perhaps secondarily a Latinism
(*divinus*, prophetic).
ix *846*. Primarily the rhythm of his own heart, the *faltering measure* may also
be nature's 'signs of woe' (l. 783). Cp. Sin's attraction by a feeling of
sympathy at x 245–7.

And forth to meet her went, the way she took
That morn when first they parted; by the tree
Of knowledge he must pass, there he her met,
850   Scarce from the tree returning; in her hand
A bough of fairest fruit that downy smiled,
New gathered, and ambrosial smell diffused.
To him she hasted, in her face excuse
Came prologue, and apology to prompt,
855   Which with bland words at will she thus addressed.
          Hast thou not wondered, Adam, at my stay?
Thee I have missed, and thought it long, deprived
Thy presence, agony of love till now
Not felt, nor shall be twice, for never more
860   Mean I to try, what rash untried I sought,
The pain of absence from thy sight. But strange
Hath been the cause, and wonderful to hear:
This tree is not as we are told, a tree
Of danger tasted, nor to evil unknown
865   Opening the way, but of divine effect
To open eyes, and make them gods who taste;
And hath been tasted such: the serpent wise,

ix *851. smiled*] Ricks (59) thinks that M. is here enlivening the metaphor:
the smile is one of heartless indifference. But Burden 138 remarks that the
bough is fair and smiling to Adam because from his point of view it is a
nondescript bough like any other. It is attractive until he knows it to be from
the forbidden tree; see ll. 735–43n.

ix *852. ambrosial*] A dramatic irony: to Adam the bough is 'fragrant',
but to Eve the sap of the forbidden tree has seemed literally 'drink of gods'
(l. 838).

ix *853–4*. The expression on Eve's face is visible in advance as she approaches,
and so is like the *prologue* (i.e., prologue-speaker) of a play. But it also re-
mains on her face as she speaks, to help out her words, and so is like the
prompter of the play. The actor prompted is apology: i.e., justification
or defence personified (not 'expression of regret'). The simile has an exact
counterpart in the theatrical simile of ll. 670–6, during the temptation of
Eve.

ix *856–85*. In view of this subtly persuasive speech, which leaves hardly any
stop unpulled, it is strange that both Tillyard (263) and Waldock (46, 48)
found it possible to advance the thesis that Adam decides to eat the fruit
without being tempted by Eve. It is less surprising that they were unde-
terred by l. 999 ('fondly overcome with female charm'): that is only M.'s
conscious and deliberate statement of his intention with respect to Adam's
fall.

ix *864*. 'If' is to be understood after *danger*.

Or not restrained as we, or not obeying,
Hath eaten of the fruit, and is become,
870 Not dead, as we are threatened, but thenceforth
Endued with human voice and human sense,
Reasoning to admiration, and with me
Persuasively hath so prevailed, that I
Have also tasted, and have also found
875 The effects to correspond, opener mine eyes,
Dim erst, dilated spirits, ampler heart,
And growing up to godhead; which for thee
Chiefly I sought, without thee can despise.
For bliss, as thou hast part, to me is bliss,
880 Tedious, unshared with thee, and odious soon.
Thou therefore also taste, that equal lot
May join us, equal joy, as equal love;
Lest thou not tasting, different degree
Disjoin us, and I then too late renounce
885 Deity for thee, when fate will not permit.
    Thus Eve with countenance blithe her story told;
But in her cheek distemper flushing glowed.
On the other side, Adam, soon as he heard
The fatal trespass done by Eve, amazed,
890 Astonied stood and blank, while horror chill
Ran through his veins, and all his joints relaxed;
From his slack hand the garland wreathed for Eve

ix 868. Or . . . or] either . . . or.

ix 874. tasted] experienced, tested (OED I 2, 3).

ix 881. lot] A word redolent of Satanic ideology; cp. l. 690. Eve is inviting
Adam to subject himself to fortune and necessity.

ix 883. An implicit admission that she has offended against the principle of
degree.

ix 885. Eve pretends readiness to renounce a deity she does not have; but,
as we know from l. 830, she is in reality not even prepared to renounce her
claim on Adam after she dies.

ix 886. blithe] Cp. the description of the serpent as 'spirited' (l. 613).

ix 887. distemper] Either 'intoxication' (OED 4 d; cp. l. 793 above) or 'a dis-
ordered condition, due to disturbance of the temperament of the bodily
humours'.

ix 890. Cp. Job xvii 8: 'Upright men shall be astonied at this'; also Virgilian
passages such as Aen. ii 120f: obstipuere animi, gelidusque per ima cucurrit / ossa
tremor.   astonied] bewildered; stunned, benumbed, paralysed.   blank]
resourceless; discomfited; deprived of speech (OED 5); pale (OED 1): these
two senses are separated at l. 894.

Down dropped, and all the faded roses shed:
Speechless he stood and pale, till thus at length
895   First to himself he inward silence broke.
        O fairest of creation, last and best
        Of all God's works, creature in whom excelled
        Whatever can to sight or thought be formed,
        Holy, divine, good, amiable or sweet!
900   How art thou lost, how on a sudden lost,
        Defaced, deflowered, and now to death devote?
        Rather how hast thou yielded to transgress
        The strict forbiddance, how to violate
        The sacred fruit forbidden! Some cursed fraud
905   Of enemy hath beguiled thee, yet unknown,
        And me with thee hath ruined, for with thee

ix *893. faded*] The first instance of decay in Paradise. There may be an allusion
to Statius, *Theb.* vii 149f, where Bacchus, frightened by the impending
destruction of Thebes, drops his thyrsus, and 'unimpaired grapes' fall from
his head. Adam has earlier been cast as Bacchus (iv 279 above); and M. may
mean to contrast the unimpaired grapes and the faded roses. See E. M. W.
Tillyard, *TLS* (1 July 1949) 429. The image derives iconographical precision
from the fact that roses were a symbol of human frailty, or of the mutability
of happiness. (Contrast the innocent Eve's support of roses with myrtle
bands, and see ll. 426–31*n*.) Thus, the fall of the garland conveys the idea that
Adam is losing his hold on happiness; perhaps, in part, through a slackness
of grip not entirely caused by the relaxation of horror.
ix *899. amiable*] kind; lovable, lovely.
ix *901. Defaced*] Stein 8 cites a definition of sin in *De doctrina* i 12: 'a diminu-
tion of the majesty of the human countenance, and a conscious degradation
of mind'.   *deflowered*] Primarily metaphorical, though in a literal sense
it would apply to the suggested seduction of Eve by Satan (see l. 270*n*).
The word has many other resonances; for Eve has been carefully portrayed
as 'the gatherer and guardian of flowers, "her self, though fairest unsupported
Flour"' (Ricks 140).   *devote*] cursed, consigned to destruction.
ix *905*. Adam as yet only suspects some connection between Satan and the
serpent Eve told him about at ll. 867ff. As Burden 160 notes, the shrewd-
ness of his guess and his grasp of the implications show the superiority
of his intellect.
ix *906–7.* The principal strands of meaning are: 'firm my resolution is to
die with thee', 'assuredly my resolution is to die with thee' and '(if I stay)
with thee my resolution [in the theological sense] is certain to die away'.
Adam's 'vehemence' of love is excessive, but M. means it to be moving too.
It is precisely the comparative goodness of Adam's motives in acting wrongly
that amplifies the extent of our own fall. Waldock's thesis testifies to the
success of at least one phase of this tactic.

Certain my resolution is to die;
How can I live without thee, how forgo
Thy sweet converse and love so dearly joined,
910 To live again in these wild woods forlorn?
Should God create another Eve, and I
Another rib afford, yet loss of thee
Would never from my heart; no no, I feel
The link of nature draw me: flesh of flesh,

ix 908–9. Adam is not deceived (1 Tim. ii 14). 'He did not believe what his wife said to him to be true, but yielded because of the social bond (socialis necessitudo) between them' (Lewis 67, citing Augustine, Civ. Dei xiv 11); an interpretation confirmed by 998 below. Because Adam is not prepared to make an independent stand he consciously surrenders to the false assumption underlying Eve's speech at ll. 879–85: namely, that separation is unthinkable. As before, Eve is pressing for what Adam cannot refuse her, except by opting for a love and a purpose larger than human. He now fails to choose separation, just as at ll. 342–75 he failed to resist it. Burden 163ff connects this passage with the prose expression of M.'s views on marriage and divorce in Tetrachordon. In a sense Adam becomes corrupt because he refuses to divorce Eve: because he wants solace at any price. Williams 123 notes the important fact that the commentators agreed that 'since Original Sin is an effect of Adam's sin, the human race would not have been involved if only Eve had sinned'.   sweet converse] Ironic in view of the recriminations that are to close the book.

ix 910. Verity, Brooks 273f, and Margaret Giovannini in Explicator xii (Oct. 1953), take the wildness of the woods to be subjective; G. Koretz retorts in Explicator (June 1954) that Paradise was already a 'wilderness of sweets' (v 294) 'wild above rule or art' (v 297) before the Fall. Only, the wilderness that was sweet before now becomes desolate and forlorn.

ix 911–13. Waldock 47 argues that these lines show Adam to be acting out of love for this Eve in particular. This need not be denied; but it is also very likely that M. introduces the possibility of another Eve to avoid the appearance of improvidence on the part of his God. Adam must not be forced to fall by an awareness that there can never be anyone but Eve to solace his loneliness and be a help meet for him.

ix 914–15. See viii 495–9n. By making Adam use the Dominical institution of the married state of one flesh to counter the prohibition, M. has fined down the choice to the point of sublimity. Adam's disobedience surpasses the virtue of most fallen men. On the other hand, M. would certainly have thought it wrong to interpret the Biblical terms as Adam does. In Tetrachordon (Yale ii 599ff) M. rejects the view that the expression 'flesh of my flesh' (Gen. ii 23) refers to a natural and indissoluble bond of marriage. It has rather to be taken metaphorically, he argues, as meaning a state of love, solace and mutual fitness. Significantly, Adam in the present passage refers only to the bond of flesh and of heart (l. 913), not to that of soul (contrast

915   Bone of my bone thou art, and from thy state
        Mine never shall be parted, bliss or woe.
          So having said, as one from sad dismay
        Recomforted, and after thoughts disturbed
        Submitting to what seemed remediless,
920   Thus in calm mood his words to Eve he turned.
          Bold deed thou hast presumed, adventurous Eve,
        And peril great provoked, who thus hath dared
        Had it been only coveting to eye
        That sacred fruit, sacred to abstinence,
925   Much more to taste it under ban to touch.
        But past who can recall, or done undo?
        Not God omnipotent, nor fate, yet so
        Perhaps thou shalt not die, perhaps the fact
        Is not so heinous now, foretasted fruit,
930   Profaned first by the serpent, by him first
        Made common and unhallowed ere our taste;
        Nor yet on him found deadly, he yet lives,

viii 499). In any case, Burden 167 remarks, the power of nature is only an excuse if no power above nature's is acknowledged. See also l. 1044n.

ix *919. seemed*] M. does not endorse Adam's decision. Since Eve is an unbeliever, there was the remedy of divorce (Burden 168ff).

ix *920. calm*] There is nothing excited or inadvertent about Adam's entry into sin, for he was 'not deceived' (see ll. 998f and *n*). Here he seems to have fallen into the stoicism or 'apathy' earlier characterized as devilish; cp. ii 564.

ix *921*. Adam responds to Eve's presentation of her deed as epic, and therefore worthy of admiration (Burden 146). Contrast Eve's correct response (tragic horror) to the 'venturous' act of the tempter, when he tasted the forbidden fruit in her dream, v 65.   *adventurous*] Spelled 'adventrous': prosodically a trisyllable.

ix *922. hath*] hast *Ed I.* The *Ed II* reading makes the thought more general; see B. A. Wright in *RES* n.s. v (1954) 170. Adams 92 gives good reasons for preferring 'hast'.

ix *924*. As in l. 902, the fruit is described quite flatly: it has lost its attraction. See l. 851n above.

ix *925. ban to touch*] See l. 651n.

ix *927. yet so*] even so. Burden 172f notes the close alternation of God and fate. Adam has adopted the satanic ideology.

ix *928. Perhaps*] Adam joins Eve in evasiveness about the terms of God's commandment: see l. 663n above.   *fact*] crime (*OED* 1 c: in the seventeenth century the commonest sense).

ix *930*. Instead of exploring the enemy's 'fraud', as ll. 904f held out hope he might, Adam now uncritically accepts Eve's recension of the serpent's story.

Lives, as thou saidst, and gains to live as man
Higher degree of life, inducement strong
935   To us, as likely tasting to attain
Proportional ascent, which cannot be
But to be gods, or angels demi-gods.
Nor can I think that God, creator wise,
Though threatening, will in earnest so destroy
940   Us his prime creatures, dignified so high,
Set over all his works, which in our fall,
For us created, needs with us must fail,
Dependent made; so God shall uncreate,
Be frustrate, do, undo, and labour loose,
945   Not well conceived of God, who though his power
Creation could repeat, yet would be loth
Us to abolish, lest the adversary
Triumph and say; Fickle their state whom God
Most favours, who can please him long; me first
950   He ruined, now mankind; whom will he next?
Matter of scorn, not to be given the foe,
However I with thee have fixed my lot,
Certain to undergo like doom, if death
Consort with thee, death is to me as life;

ix 936. *Proportional ascent*] on Adam's Satanic reasoning here, see ll. 710–12n above. Note that Adam does not merely comply with Eve's wishes, but displays a definite ambition of his own.

ix 941–2. On the involvement of nature in the Fall, see ll. 782–4n. Adam's theology disintegrates as fast as Eve's: he is already attributing to God an unjust compunction.

ix 944. *loose*, the spelling in the early edns, could indicate either 'loose'– 'undo' (*OED* 2); 'break up, do away with' (*OED* 7)–or 'lose'. In the first case *labour* would have its common seventeenth-century meaning 'work performed' (*OED* 3, 4).

ix 947–8. Cp. *Deut.* xxxii 27. For *adversary*=Satan, see vi 282n. Scan *Tri-úmph*.

ix 949. Adversary or not, Adam is working himself into the Satanic role.

ix 952. *lot*] On the ideological implications, see l. 881n.

ix 953. *Certain*] resolved. Perhaps a Latinism on the analogy of *certus*, but the word was sometimes used in the sense 'resolved' in prose (see *OED* I 5 b) and there is also a possibility that *Certain* may have the commoner meaning 'sure' (*OED* I 6).   *doom*] Three separate meanings are possible: judgment, sentence of punishment (*OED* 2); irrevocable destiny, adverse fate (*OED* 4 a); ruin, death (*OED* 4 b). Burden 173 holds that Adam uses the word in the second, the fallen angels' sense; cp. ii 550, 'doom of battle'.

ix 954. Whereas Satan asserts his resolution in terms such as 'evil be thou my good' (iv 110), Adam's antinomies are less abstract and fundamental.

955   So forcible within my heart I feel
      The bond of nature draw me to my own,
      My own in thee, for what thou art is mine;
      Our state cannot be severed, we are one,
      One flesh; to lose thee were to lose my self.
960   So Adam, and thus Eve to him replied.
      O glorious trial of exceeding love,
      Illustrious evidence, example high!
      Engaging me to emulate, but short
      Of thy perfection, how shall I attain,
965   Adam, from whose dear side I boast me sprung,
      And gladly of our union hear thee speak,
      One heart, one soul in both; whereof good proof
      This day affords, declaring thee resolved,
      Rather than death or aught than death more dread
970   Shall separate us, linked in love so dear,
      To undergo with me one guilt, one crime,
      If any be, of tasting this fair fruit,
      Whose virtue, for of good still good proceeds,
      Direct, or by occasion hath presented
975   This happy trial of thy love, which else
      So eminently never had been known.

ix *956. bond of nature*] Cp. 'link of nature' (l. 914), and see ll. 908–9*n* and 914–15*n*.

ix *956.* The 'link of nature' (l. 914) has now become a *bond*–in allusion to the 'bondage' of marriage with an unbeliever in *1 Cor.* vii 15 (Burden 172f).

ix *959.* The *Ed I* and *Ed II* spelling 'loose' could indicate either 'lose' or 'loose'.

ix *961. exceeding*] Ostensibly 'extremely great', but 'excessive' is present as a dramatic irony. Steadman 92 holds that Satan, Eve and Adam all display certain moral virtues in excess.

ix *962. evidence*] manifestation (*OED* I 2, II 3); but in view of *trial*, probably complicated by the legal connotation 'proof; witness'.

ix *967. One heart, one soul*] Contrast the relationship as it was before the Fall–'Union of mind, or in us both one soul' (viii 604). Intellect (*mens*) has been displaced by the more passionate *heart*.

ix *974. Direct . . . occasion*] i.e. directly or indirectly.

ix *975. trial*] Cp. l. 961. Eve's insistence on a test of love was common in literary treatments of the Fall. Hughes compares Grotius, *Adamus exul* ll. 1398–1468, and Andreini, *L'Adamo caduto* III i (Kirkconnell 180–4, 254–7).

ix *976. eminently*] conspicuously, notably (*OED* 2, 3). There is also a blasphemous play on the theological sense of the word (*OED* 4). God was said to possess the excellences of human character not *formally* (in the ordinary, creaturely sense of their formal definition) but *eminently* (in a higher sense). At first there may indeed seem to be a true analogy between Adam's offer to

Were it I thought death menaced would ensue
This my attempt, I would sustain alone
The worst, and not persuade thee rather die
980 Deserted, than oblige thee with a fact
Pernicious to thy peace, chiefly assured
Remarkably so late of thy so true,
So faithful love unequalled; but I feel
Far otherwise the event, not death, but life
985 Augmented, opened eyes, new hopes, new joys,
Taste so divine, that what of sweet before
Hath touched my sense, flat seems to this, and harsh.
On my experience, Adam, freely taste,
And fear of death deliver to the winds.
990   So saying, she embraced him, and for joy
Tenderly wept, much won that he his love
Had so ennobled, as of choice to incur
Divine displeasure for her sake, or death.
In recompense (for such compliance bad
995 Such recompense best merits) from the bough
She gave him of that fair enticing fruit
With liberal hand: he scrupled not to eat
Against his better knowledge, not deceived,
But fondly overcome with female charm.
1000 Earth trembled from her entrails, as again
In pangs, and nature gave a second groan,
Sky loured and muttering thunder, some sad drops

undergo death, and Christ's. But the analogy is really a contrast. M. has
carefully indicated that love was not with Christ the dominating motive:
'above . . . shone / Filial obedience' (iii 268–9).

ix *980. oblige*] make liable to a penalty (*OED* II 5 a).   *fact*] crime, deed.

ix *981. chiefly assured*] i.e., especially since I have been assured.

ix *984. event*] result, outcome.

ix *989.* Primarily 'cast away your fear of death'; but there is a horrible
dramatic irony if the line is connected with the image of Death sniffing
from far away 'the smell / Of mortal change on earth' (x 267–81).

ix *994. compliance*] unworthy submission, conformity (*OED* II 6); see ll.
908–9n, and cp. *Gen.* iii 17: 'Because thou hast hearkened unto the voice of
thy wife, and hast eaten of the tree . . . cursed is the ground.'

ix *996.* The fruit is now again *enticing* to Adam, because his heart, and con-
sequently also his appetite, are now corrupt; see ll. 735–43n, 851n, 924n.

ix *998–9.* In accordance with *1 Tim.* ii 14. For the implications of this sum-
mary author-comment, see ll. 856–85n and 908–9n.

ix *1000–1.* For nature's first groan, see ll. 782–4 and *n*.

ix *1002.* The first thunderstorm. Until now there have only been gentle
showers in Paradise (iv 646).

Wept at completing of the mortal sin
Original; while Adam took no thought,
1005 Eating his fill, nor Eve to iterate
Her former trespass feared, the more to soothe
Him with her loved society, that now
As with new wine intoxicated both
They swim in mirth, and fancy that they feel
1010 Divinity within them breeding wings
Wherewith to scorn the earth: but that false fruit
Far other operation first displayed,
Carnal desire inflaming, he on Eve
Began to cast lascivious eyes, she him

ix 1003–4. The only occurrence in PL of the term Original Sin. The doctrine
denoted is discussed in De doctrina i 11 (Columbia xv 180ff). There Original
Sin, 'the sin which is common to all men', is defined as 'that which our first
parents, and in them all their posterity committed, when, casting off their
obedience to God, they tasted the fruit of the forbidden tree' (ibid. 181). The
comprehensiveness of the first sin is next defined, in terms that have had
some interest for critics of PL: 'If the circumstances of this crime are duly
considered, it will be acknowledged to have been a most heinous offence, and
a transgression of the whole law. For what sin can be named, which was not
included in this one act? It comprehended at once distrust in the divine
veracity, and a proportionate credulity in the assurances of Satan; unbelief;
ingratitude; disobedience; gluttony; in the man excessive uxoriousness, in
the woman a want of proper regard for her husband, in both an insensibility
to the welfare of their offspring, and that offspring the whole human race;
parricide, theft, invasion of the rights of others, sacrilege, deceit, presumption
in aspiring to divine attributes, fraud in the means employed to attain the
object, pride, and arrogance' (ibid. 181–3). The sin was original in the sense
that 'all sinned in Adam'–the Pauline doctrine, for which M. cites the autho-
rity of Rom. v 12–21 and offers the explanation that it is the 'principle' or
'method' of God's justice to visit penalties 'incurred by the violation of
things sacred' on the whole of the sinner's posterity (ibid. 185). M. thought
this principle to be entirely just, and to be acknowledged as such in a multi-
tude of pagan testimonies (ibid. 191).

ix 1008. On the intoxication consequent on the Fall, see l. 793n.

ix 1010. The illusion of divinity breeds the wings appropriate to a god or
angel. Cp. Eve's dream, in which she actually takes flight with her angel
tempter (v 86–90).

ix 1012. operation] Either the 'influence, action' of the fruit, or a 'vital pro-
cess' in Adam and Eve (OED 3, 4).

ix 1013. Beginning the account of the 'formal cause' of the Fall, the cause
through which the Fall is what it is. The 'form' of man's disobedience is the
change in his nature that accompanies sin: it can be illustrated only by its
effects. See Howard 163f.

1015   As wantonly repaid; in lust they burn:
      Till Adam thus gan Eve to dalliance move.
        Eve, now I see thou art exact of taste,
      And elegant, of sapience no small part,
      Since to each meaning savour we apply,
1020   And palate call judicious; I the praise
      Yield thee, so well this day thou hast purveyed.
      Much pleasure we have lost, while we abstained
      From this delightful fruit, nor known till now
      True relish, tasting; if such pleasure be
1025   In things to us forbidden, it might be wished,
      For this one tree had been forbidden ten.
      But come, so well refreshed, now let us play,

ix *1017–20*. The fullest development of one of the poem's most central thematic word-play complexes, that on tasting and discerning: *exact of taste, | And elegant* is a grotesque travesty of Eve's discriminating avoidance of 'inelegant' mixtures of tastes in her preparation of supper for Raphael (v 332–6). At the same time, *exact of taste* has also a more figurative sense: before the Fall Adam remarked that nature had perhaps bestowed on Eve 'too much of ornament, in outward show / Elaborate, of inward less exact [perfect, refined]' (see v 539–44*n*); whereas now he calls her discernment perfect. It seems that mind can no longer be distinguished from lower faculties of perception.   *elegant*] refined, delicate – a word that would normally be applied to literary taste; so that Adam implies that Eve has made cookery a fine art, and by doing so betrays his confusion of values. For the play in *sapience*, see ll. 796–7*n*; Schultz 10 traces it to St Bernard, who writes that Eve 'transgressed, with the fruit of ill-savour, the Apostle's rule *sapere ad sobrietatem*'.   *savour*] tastiness (*OED* 1 b); understanding (*OED* 5); see v 84*n*.

ix *1019. we*] *Ed II* misprints 'me'.

ix *1021. purveyed*] provided, made provision.

ix *1023. known*] i.e., have known.

ix *1026. For*] instead of. The wish will come true when under the Covenant there are ten commandments.

ix *1027*. Cp. *Exod.* xxxii 6f: 'The people sat down to eat and to drink, and rose up to play [taken at *1 Cor.* x 7 to mean *fornicate*]. And the Lord said unto Moses, Go, get thee down; for thy people, which thou broughtest out of the land of Egypt, have corrupted themselves.'

ix *1027–45*. Lewis (69) thinks that the contrast between this indulgence and earlier pictures of unfallen sexual activity is a failure: 'He has made the un-fallen already so voluptuous and kept the fallen still so poetical that the contrast is not so sharp as it ought to have been.' But M. may have wanted to steal one of the devil's best tunes, and so deliberately made sex before the Fall as exciting as possible. Here, by contrast, the foreplay is perfunctory, even crude: 'now let us play'.   *seized*] (l. 1037) is a word that would have been

As meet is, after such delicious fare;
For never did thy beauty since the day
1030 I saw thee first and wedded thee, adorned
With all perfections, so inflame my sense
With ardour to enjoy thee, fairer now
Than ever, bounty of this virtuous tree.
So said he, and forbore not glance or toy
1035 Of amorous intent, well understood
Of Eve, whose eye darted contagious fire.
Her hand he seized, and to a shady bank,
Thick overhead with verdant roof embowered
He led her nothing loth; flowers were the couch,
1040 Pansies, and violets, and asphodel,
And hyacinth, earth's freshest softest lap.
There they their fill of love and love's disport
Took largely, of their mutual guilt the seal,
The solace of their sin, till dewy sleep
1045 Oppressed them, wearied with their amorous play.

unthinkable in the earlier passages; contrast, e.g., viii 508–11. Williams 125 notes that a Jewish idea that the first effect of the fruit was to stimulate lust was taken over by certain Christian commentators on *Genesis*.

ix *1029–41.* Addison compares Homer, *Il.* xiv, where Hera, bent on deceiving Zeus, comes to him with Aphrodite's zone, and seems more charming to him than ever before. Lines 1029f correspond closely to *Il.* xiv 327f, while the flowers of the present passage have *hyacinth* in common with those of the couch prepared by Earth for Zeus and Hera (cp. also the flowers of the nuptial bower, iv 697–703 above). In view of the comparison of Eve to 'Ceres in her prime, / Yet virgin of Proserpina from Jove' at ll. 395f above, it is possible that M. also means to recall an adjacent line in the Homeric passage (xiv 326) comparing Hera favourably with Demeter (Ceres).

ix *1029–33.* Echoing the pagan sensuality of the similarly fatal Paris in Homer, *Il.* iii 442ff, xiv 313ff. See Douglas Bush in *JEGP* lx (1961) 640.

ix *1033.* Before the Fall Eve was adorned with virtues; now it is the tree that is virtuous. See l. 778n on a similar transfer; and cp. ll. 616, 649, 745 and 795.

ix *1038. embowered*] Recalls, but by no means implies, the nuptial bower of iv 690–711 etc. The indefinite article in the preceding line indicates that Adam and Eve now copulate casually, wherever they happen to be.

ix *1042–4.* The impudent woman of *Prov.* vii entices a youth to adultery with similar words: 'Come, let us take our fill of love until the morning: let us solace ourselves with loves.' As Burden 166 notes, *solace* is here debased in meaning. It is for the first time applied to mere physical sex; the deeper solace of relationship in true love having disappeared. See ll. 914–15n above.

Soon as the force of that fallacious fruit,
That with exhilarating vapour bland
About their spirits had played, and inmost powers
Made err, was now exhaled, and grosser sleep
1050   Bred of unkindly fumes, with conscious dreams
Encumbered, now had left them, up they rose
As from unrest, and each the other viewing,
Soon found their eyes how opened, and their minds
How darkened; innocence, that as a veil
1055   Had shadowed them from knowing ill, was gone,

ix *1046–51*. Contrast the 'airy light' sleep of unfallen man, bred of 'temperate vapours bland' (v 3–7).   *bland*] Here means 'pleasing to the senses', whereas at v 5 it meant 'genial'.   *unkindly*] unnatural.   *fumes*] vapours or exhalations rising from the stomach to the brain; especially often used of the vapours that result from drinking alcohol. Fumes are to some degree inevitable, but their quality is critical. It is the grosser fumes that produce sleep. See Vives, *De anima et vita* (Basel 1538) 109f: *Non potest quidem tolli omnino ea effumigatio, quae a ventriculo ascendit ad caput: sed eius densitas ad certum aliquem modum efficit somnum, subtilitas vigiliam, hoc est solutionem sensuum.* Vives goes on to treat sleep as an image of death: an idea that may well be relevant to the present passage (see 1052–9n on the degrees of death).   *conscious*] guilty.

ix *1052–9*. Cp. *Gen.* iii 7: 'The eyes of them both were opened, and they knew that they were naked.' Before the Fall Eve needed no veil even when a third was present, for she was 'virtue-proof' (see v 384 and *n*). Iconographically, nudity in most cases signified simplicity, integrity and virtue. This was also the usual emphasis in ancient authors; cp., e.g., Horace, *Odes* I xxiv 6f: *Pudor et Iustitiae soror, / incorrupta Fides, nudaque Veritas.* In the terms of traditional moral theology, this *nuditas virtualis* (symbol of innocence) has been replaced by *nuditas criminalis*. See Panofsky[2] 156.   *shame*] For Horace a good quality, for M. a bad one, shame was the first of the four degrees of death distinguished by theologians; see *De doctrina* i 12 (Columbia xv 202f), and viii 323–33n above. Note that the number of virtues lost, four, was itself a number that symbolised virtue (the *tetractys*; the four cardinal virtues; etc.): see ll. 1074–6n.   *he covered*] Perhaps cp. *Ps.* cix 29: 'Let mine adversaries be clothed with shame, and let them cover themselves with their own confusion, as with a mantle.' Editors usually let in heavy punctuation between *shame* and *he*, but the absence of punctuation in the early edns is essential to M.'s ambiguity. He wants to leave us in doubt whether honour or shame is doing the covering; because prelapsarian honour did not cover, but the honour we know does. Cp. the discrimination between true and false honour in Guarini's *Pastor Fido* iv 9, and see iv 289n above, on 'with native honour clad'. Cp. also x 216ff, where Christ clothes man both inwardly and outwardly. In a lesser ambiguity, Adam covers in response to Eve's guilty shame.

Just confidence, and native righteousness
And honour from about them, naked left
To guilty shame he covered, but his robe
Uncovered more, so rose the Danite strong
1060   Herculean Samson from the harlot-lap
Of Philistean Dalilah, and waked
Shorn of his strength, they destitute and bare
Of all their virtue: silent, and in face
Confounded long they sat, as strucken mute,
1065   Till Adam, though not less than Eve abashed,
At length gave utterance to these words constrained.
     O Eve, in evil hour thou didst give ear
To that false worm, of whomsoever taught
To counterfeit man's voice, true in our fall,
1070   False in our promised rising; since our eyes
Opened we find indeed, and find we know
Both good and evil, good lost, and evil got,
Bad fruit of knowledge, if this be to know,
Which leaves us naked thus, of honour void,
1075   Of innocence, of faith, of purity,
Our wonted ornaments now soiled and stained,
And in our faces evident the signs
Of foul concupiscence; whence evil store;

ix *1059–63.* See *Judges* xvi for the story of Samson's betrayal by Delilah.
Danite] Samson's father Manoah is said to be of the tribe of Dan, at *Judges*
xiii 2. Dalilah is in its first syllable nearer to the Greek form. The comparison
between Adam and Samson was traditional; cp., e.g., Willet 48.
ix *1059. more. So*] *Ed I. Ed II* misprints 'more, so'.
ix *1067.* See ll. 1029–41n. When Zeus woke after Hera had seduced him, he
was similarly resentful. See Ricks 103: Adam's 'cry proclaims that the word
evil is derived from Eve, and that evil derives from her.' The name *Eve*
was in the Bible only given after the Fall (*Gen.* iii 20). There was a great deal
of speculation as to its significance; see Willet 54; also l. *291n* above.
ix *1070–4.* Cp. *De doctrina* i 10 (Columbia xv 115): 'It was called the tree
of knowledge of good and evil from the result; for since Adam tasted it, we
not only know evil, but we know good only by means of evil.' The point
that Adam by his transgression got no wisdom, but only the miserable
experience or 'experimental knowledge' of evil, was often made by com-
mentators; see, e.g., Willet 43, where it is ascribed to St Augustine.
ix *1074–6.* Again the quadrate of virtue. The four ornaments are essentially
the same as those of ll. 1054–7: *honour* and *innocence* are repeated, and *faith*
corresponds to 'confidence', *purity* to 'righteousness'. Cp. Willet 38 on a
different arithmological treatment of the *ornaments* of Eve: a Hebrew
'curiosity' in which they were reckoned twenty-four in number.

Even shame, the last of evils; of the first
1080 Be sure then. How shall I behold the face
Henceforth of God or angel, erst with joy
And rapture so oft beheld? Those heavenly shapes
Will dazzle now this earthly, with their blaze
Insufferably bright. O might I here
1085 In solitude live savage, in some glade
Obscured, where highest woods impenetrable
To star or sunlight, spread their umbrage broad
And brown as evening: cover me ye pines,
Ye cedars, with innumerable boughs
1090 Hide me, where I may never see them more.
But let us now, as in bad plight, devise
What best may for the present serve to hide
The parts of each from other, that seem most
To shame obnoxious, and unseemliest seen,
1095 Some tree whose broad smooth leaves together sewed,
And girded on our loins, may cover round

ix *1079. last*] least.

ix *1083. earthly*] earthly nature; cp. viii 453.

ix *1085–90.* The archetypal poem of retirement. Revulsion from vice was of course an obvious motive in the literature of retirement and solitude. See Henry Vaughan, 'Retirement' (*Works*, ed. Martin (1914) ii 642); Thomson, 'Hymn on Solitude'; Grainger, 'Ode on Solitude'; etc. Often this motive took a specifically sexual turn; as, e.g., in Marvell's 'The Garden' 25f: 'When we have run our Passions heat, / Love hither makes his best retreat.' At the same time, the *woods impenetrable / To star or sun-light* distinctly recall Statius' dark grove of Sleep, *nulli penetrabilis astro, / lucus iners* (*Theb.* x 85f) and Spenser's labyrinthine wood of Error, 'Whose loftie trees . . . / Did spred so broad, that heavens light did hide, / Not perceable with power of any starre' (I i 7). Adam's guilty impulse to retirement is by no means approved of by M.   *umbrage*] shade (*OED* 1); foliage (*OED* 2 c).   *brown*] See iv 246n on 'Embrowned'.   *them*] i.e., the *shapes* of l. 1090.

ix *1091–8.* 'And the eyes of them both were opened, and they knew that they were naked; and they sewed fig leaves together, and made themselves aprons' (*Gen.* iii 7; marg. 'things to gird about'). M. took the shame mentioned in this verse to have arisen from the pollution of the 'whole man': ' "their mind and conscience is defiled" : whence arises shame' (*De doctrina* i 12; Columbia xv 205).   *obnoxious*] exposed (*OED* 1 a); objectionable (*OED* 6).   *sewed*] Taken to mean plaited, so that the simile of the Indian *cincture* at l. 1117 is exact.

ix *1092–3.* So *Ed I. Ed II* wrongly transposes *for* and *from*.

Those middle parts, that this new comer, shame,
There sit not, and reproach us as unclean.
So counselled he, and both together went
1100   Into the thickest wood, there soon they chose
The fig-tree, not that kind for fruit renowned,
But such as at this day to Indians known
In Malabar or Decan spreads her arms
Branching so broad and long, that in the ground
1105   The bended twigs take root, and daughters grow
About the mother tree, a pillared shade
High overarched, and echoing walks between;
There oft the Indian herdsman shunning heat
Shelters in cool, and tends his pasturing herds

ix *1097*. In view of the context it may be relevant to note that *comer* was a horticultural term, = 'springer'.

ix *1100–10*. The banyan or Indian fig had been described at length by Pliny, Raleigh and encyclopedists such as Bartholomew, so that a source is hard to assign (see Svendsen 31f). But Gerard's description is probably as close as any to the present passage: 'The ends thereof hang downe, and touch the ground, where they take roote and grow in such sort that those twigs become great trees; and these being growen up to the like greatnes, do cast their branches and twiggie tendrels unto the earth, where they likewise take hold and roote. . . . Of one tree is made a great wood, or desart of trees, which the Indians do use for coverture against the extreme heate of the sunne. . . . Some likewise use them for pleasure, cutting downe by a direct line a long walke, or as it were a vault, through the thickest part, from which also they cut certaine loope holes or windowes in some places, to the end to receive thereby the fresh coole aire that entereth therat; as also for light, that they may see their cattle. . . . The first or mother of this wood or desart of trees, is hard to be knowne from the children' (*Herball* (1597) 1330f). Svendsen 135 treats this fig-bower as a 'deep interior sanctuary'. But it seems more probable that M. intends a contrast with the prelapsarian nuptial bower of iv 690–708. The Indian herdsman is put in because he is primitive and pagan, and perhaps also because his work is connected with fallen man's non-vegetarian diet. Similarly the Amazonian targe is carried over from Gerard because before the Fall man never thought of fighting, let alone woman. The proliferating tree is a tree of error: it is an objective correlative of the proliferating sin that will ramify through Adam's and Eve's descendants. In this connection, cp. Thomas Becon's allegorization of the fig-tree: 'As this Tree (saith he) so did Man grow straight and upright towards God, untill such time as he had transgressed and broken the Commandment of his Creatour; and then like unto the boughes of this tree, he beganne to bend downeward, and stouped toward the earth, which all the rest of *Adam's* posteritie have done, rooting themselves therein and fastening themselves to this corrupt world' (*cit.* Svendsen 136 from Raleigh).

1110   At loop-holes cut through thickest shade: those leaves
        They gathered, broad as Amazonian targe,
        And with what skill they had, together sewed,
        To gird their waist, vain covering if to hide
        Their guilt and dreaded shame; O how unlike
1115   To that first naked glory. Such of late
        Columbus found the American so girt
        With feathered cincture, naked else and wild
        Among the trees on isles and woody shores.
        Thus fenced, and as they thought, their shame in part
1120   Covered, but not at rest or ease of mind,
        They sat them down to weep, nor only tears
        Rained at their eyes, but high winds worse within
        Began to rise, high passions, anger, hate,
        Mistrust, suspicion, discord, and shook sore
1125   Their inward state of mind, calm region once
        And full of peace, now tossed and turbulent:
        For understanding ruled not, and the will
        Heard not her lore, both in subjection now
        To sensual appetite, who from beneath
1130   Usurping over sovereign reason claimed
        Superior sway: from thus distempered breast,
        Adam, estranged in look and altered style,
        Speech intermitted thus to Eve renewed.
           Would thou hadst hearkened to my words, and
             stayed
1135   With me, as I besought thee, when that strange
        Desire of wandering this unhappy morn,

ix *1117. cincture*] A wittily exact word. Besides meaning 'belt' (*OED* 3 a),
it is the term applied in architecture to the fillet that divides the shaft of a
column from the capital and base (*OED* 3 b); thus the comparison of Eve's
savage posterity to pillars is carried on from ll. 1105f.

ix *1112.* The microcosm–macrocosm analogy not only universalizes the
change in human nature, but also prepares for the meteorological disturbances
to be treated in the next book. With the stormy tears which here *rain* down,
contrast Eve's gentle tears before the Fall (v 130). For a corresponding con-
trast in the macrocosm, see 1002*n* above.   *high winds*] Cp., in the external
world, the violent winds of x 695ff and the 'gentle gales' before the Fall
(e.g. iv 156).

ix *1127–31.* Cp. 351–6. This model, too, has a universalizing effect – man's
fall means the corruption of the state as well as of the individual psyche. For
a similar politico-legal *allegoria* of the Fall, see iii 176*n* and 204ff.

ix *1132–3. estranged*] changed, rendered remote from his normal condition,
made unlike himself (*OED* 4).   *style*] tone; but see also Introduction,
'Prosody' (p. 21 above).

I know not whence possessed thee; we had then
Remained still happy, not as now, despoiled
Of all our good, shamed, naked, miserable.
1140   Let none henceforth seek needless cause to approve
The faith they owe; when earnestly they seek
Such proof, conclude, they then begin to fail.
      To whom soon moved with touch of blame thus Eve.
What words have passed thy lips, Adam severe,
1145   Imput'st thou that to my default, or will
Of wandering, as thou call'st it, which who knows
But might as ill have happened thou being by,
Or to thy self perhaps: hadst thou been there,
Or here the attempt, thou couldst not have discerned
1150   Fraud in the serpent, speaking as he spake;
No ground of enmity between us known,
Why he should mean me ill, or seek to harm.
Was I to have never parted from thy side?
As good have grown there still a lifeless rib.
1155   Being as I am, why didst not thou the head
Command me absolutely not to go,
Going into such danger as thou saidst?
Too facile then thou didst not much gainsay,

ix 1140–2. Referring to Eve's argument of ll. 332–6 above.   *approve*]
demonstrate practically, give proof of (*OED* 3). The rhythm mimes the
sense; for *Let . . . owe* can be read as the first half of a common metre stanza
(alternate iambic tetrameters and trimeters); but if *when . . . fail* is read as the
second half of the stanza, it tails away into ineffectual sententiousness.
owe] 'be under obligation to render' (*OED* I 2) or 'possess' (*OED* I 1 a).

ix 1144. *What . . . lips*] Echoes Odysseus' disapproval of a speech of Aga-
memnon's, *Il.* xiv 83.

ix 1146–50. Belied by Satan's admission at l. 483 that he shuns Adam's
'higher intellectual'. M. is enforcing the point that temptation should be
dealt with by intellectual discernment, nor merely by emotional resistance
or exertion of the will. Burden 81 notices Eve's use of *happened*, redolent of
the Satanic ideology of mischance.

ix 1155. *head*] Alludes to *1 Cor.* xi 3: 'The head of every man is Christ;
and the head of the woman is the man; and the head of Christ is God.'
Eve, having implied in ll. 1146–50 that Adam is no wiser than she is, now
blames him nevertheless for not guiding her. Thus she empties headship of
its true meaning, and makes it mere status in a hierarchy of power and com-
mand. Contrast iv 442f.

ix 1158–61. It is true that Adam permitted her to go: see ll. 372 and 378
above. But then, to command her 'absolutely not to go' (l. 1156) would have
made her stay 'not free' (l. 372). Whether Adam was *Too facile* is harder
to say: *facile* in the sense 'courteous, mild, gentle' (*OED* 4) he certainly

Nay didst permit, approve, and fair dismiss.
1160 Hadst thou been firm and fixed in thy dissent,
Neither had I transgressed, nor thou with me.
  To whom then first incensed Adam replied,
Is this the love, is this the recompense
Of mine to thee, ingrateful Eve, expressed
1165 Immutable when thou wert lost, not I,
Who might have lived and joyed immortal bliss,
Yet willingly chose rather death with thee:
And am I now upbraided, as the cause
Of thy transgressing? Not enough severe,
1170 It seems, in thy restraint: what could I more?
I warned thee, I admonished thee, foretold
The danger, and the lurking enemy
That lay in wait; beyond this had been force,
And force upon free will hath here no place.
1175 But confidence then bore thee on, secure
Either to meet no danger, or to find
Matter of glorious trial; and perhaps
I also erred in overmuch admiring
What seemed in thee so perfect, that I thought
1180 No evil durst attempt thee, but I rue
That error now, which is become my crime,
And thou the accuser. Thus it shall befall

was: whether he was 'easily led, compliant' (*OED* 5) is controversial;
see ll. 370–5n above. In view of the falsity of the rest of Eve's arguments, it
seems that this accusation is also unjust, and that Adam's culpable errors
begin only at l. 906.

ix *1164. ingrateful*] ungrateful.   *expressed*] revealed by external actions
(*OED* II 7).

ix *1166. joy*] enjoy.

ix *1175. confidence*] unfounded assurance, overboldness, presumption
(*OED* 4, citing Hooker: 'Their confidence, for the most part, riseth from
too much credit given to their own wits').   *secure*] over-confident
(*OED* I 1).

ix *1177. matter*] pretext, occasion (*OED* 13).

ix *1178–86*. The admiration confessed by Adam at viii 540–59. There he
spoke–to Raphael's displeasure–of 'greatness of mind and nobleness'
creating 'an awe / About her, as a guard angelic placed'. The passage
clearly indicates a psychological interpretation of the Fall. Marjorie Nicolson
compares Henry More's interpretation of Adam and Eve as Intellect and
Will. This is a useful comparison, but M.'s scheme may not have been identi-
cal. Indeed, if his Eve were human will, the phrase *her will* (l. 1184) would be
a type fallacy. See further in ll. 703–9n above.

> Him who to worth in women overtrusting
> Lets her will rule; restraint she will not brook,
> 1185 And left to her self, if evil thence ensue,
> She first his weak indulgence will accuse.
>   Thus they in mutual accusation spent
> The fruitless hours, but neither self-condemning,
> And of their vain contest appeared no end.

THE END OF THE NINTH BOOK

Paradise Lost

BOOK X

The Argument

Man's transgression known, the guardian angels forsake Paradise, and return up to heaven to approve their vigilance, and are approved, God declaring that the entrance of Satan could not be by them prevented. He sends his Son to judge the transgressors, who descends and gives sentence accordingly; then in pity clothes them both, and re-ascends. Sin and Death sitting till then at the gates of hell, by wondrous sympathy feeling the success of Satan in this new world, and the sin by man there committed, resolve to sit no longer confined in hell, but to follow Satan their sire up to the place of man: to make the way easier from hell to this world to and fro, they pave a broad highway or bridge over chaos, according to the track that Satan first made; then preparing for earth, they meet him proud of his success returning to hell; their mutual gratulation. Satan arrives at Pandemonium, in full assembly relates with boasting his success against man; instead of applause is entertained with a general hiss by all his audience, transformed with himself also suddenly into serpents, according to his doom given in Paradise; then deluded with a show of the forbidden tree springing up before them, they greedily reaching to take of the fruit, chew dust and bitter ashes. The proceedings of Sin and Death; God foretells the final victory of his Son over them, and the renewing of all things; but for the present commands his angels to

ix *1183. women*] Bentley emended to 'woman', but the transition from plural to singular can be defended, either as artful imitation on M.'s part (for a Latin precedent see Terence, *Eun.* II i 10) or as artless impatience on Adam's.
ix *1188. fruitless*] Enlivened by the thematic pun made explicit at l. 648.
neither self-condemning] Cp. the Fourth Draft of M.'s projected Paradise Lost tragedy, where 'Adam then and Eve return accuse one another but especially Adam lays the blame to his wife, is stubborn in his offence'.
ix *1189. contest*] Stressed on the second syllable.

make several alterations in the heavens and elements. Adam more and more perceiving his fallen condition heavily bewails, rejects the condolement of Eve; she persists and at length appeases him: then to evade the curse likely to fall on their offspring, proposes to Adam violent ways which he approves not, but conceiving better hope, puts her in mind of the late promise made them, that her seed should be revenged on the serpent, and exhorts her with him to seek peace of the offended Deity, by repentance and supplication.

> Mcanwhile the heinous and despiteful act
> Of Satan done in Paradise, and how
> He in the serpent, had perverted Eve,
> Her husband she, to taste the fatal fruit,
> 5 Was known in heaven; for what can scape the eye
> Of God all-seeing, or deceive his heart
> Omniscient, who in all things wise and just,
> Hindered not Satan to attempt the mind
> Of man, with strength entire, and free will armed,
> 10 Complete to have discovered and repulsed
> Whatever wiles of foe or seeming friend.
> For still they knew, and ought to have still remembered
> The high injunction not to taste that fruit,
> Whoever tempted; which they not obeying,

x 1–16. Rhetorically, these lines function both as *principium*, stating the subject of the book, and as *initium*, introducing the first scene. They also sum up the theological content of Bk iii, which will receive specific application in the present book, in the exchanges between the Father and the Son (ll. 34–84 below) and between the Son and Adam (ll. 124ff). Note the structural symmetry whereby the divine decrees of the third book are balanced by those of the third last. Addison remarks that the book 'has a greater variety of Persons in it than any other in the whole Poem. The Author upon the winding up of his Action introduces all those who had any Concern in it, and shews with great Beauty the influence which it had upon each of them. It is like the last Act of a well written Tragedy, in which all who had a part in it are generally drawn up before the Audience, and represented under those Circumstances in which the determination of the Action places them' (*Spectator*, No. 357; ed. Bond iii 329f).

x 5–7. Showing the impossibility of Eve's illusory hope of concealment at ix 811–16. For the all-seeing eye of God, cp. iii 534 and 578, with *n*. On the eye as an ancient and Renaissance hieroglyph of Justice, see Wind (186f), who discusses the application of it in Alberti's emblem, with its threatening allusion to the Day of Judgment, which will come 'in the twinkling of an eye' (*1 Cor.* xv 52).

x 10. *Complete*] fully equipped or endowed (qualifying *mind*).

x 12. *still*] always, ever.

x 14. Scan by stressing *which* and *not*, with *obeying* a dissyllable by synaloepha.

15 Incurred, what could they less, the penalty,
     And manifold in sin, deserved to fall.
     Up into heaven from Paradise in haste
     The angelic guards ascended, mute and sad
     For man, for of his state by this they knew,
20 Much wondering how the subtle fiend had stolen
     Entrance unseen. Soon as the unwelcome news
     From earth arrived at heaven gate, displeased
     All were who heard, dim sadness did not spare
     That time celestial visages, yet mixed
25 With pity, violated not their bliss.
     About the new-arrived, in multitudes
     The ethereal people ran, to hear and know
     How all befell: they towards the throne supreme
     Accountable made haste to make appear
30 With righteous plea, their utmost vigilance,
     And easily approved; when the most high
     Eternal Father from his secret cloud,
     Amidst in thunder uttered thus his voice.
          Assembled angels, and ye powers returned
35 From unsuccessful charge, be not dismayed,
     Nor troubled at these tidings from the earth,
     Which your sincerest care could not prevent,
     Foretold so lately what would come to pass,
     When first this tempter crossed the gulf from hell.

x *16. manifold*] multiplied; alluding to *Ps.* xxxviii 19: 'they that hate me wrongfully are multiplied'; and perhaps also to *Ps.* xvi 4: 'their sorrows shall be multiplied that hasten after another god'. In both cases, early English versions used 'manifolded' to translate Vulg. *multiplicati*. The epithet should be connected with the fundamental opposition in the number symbolism of *PL* between good unity and evil multiplicity; see vi 767*n* and 809–10*n*. It is now apparent why (from a philosophical point of view) so much emphasis was laid on the separation or *division* of Adam and Eve: it was to enact their 'manifolding'. For M.'s analysis of the manifold character of the first sin itself, see ix 1003–4*n*.

x *18. angelic guards*] the cherubim of iv 550ff and ix 61f.

x *28–31*. Double syntax: either 'liable to be called to answer for their responsibilities (*OED* s.v. *Accountable* 1) they hastened . . . to make appear their vigilance', or 'they hastened . . . to make their vigilance appear explicable (*OED* s.v. *Accountable* 5)'.   *approved*] confirmed (qualifying *vigilance*).

x *32–3*. For the imagery, cp. *Rev.* iv 5, and see ii 264–5*n* and iii 375–82*n*.

x *34–62*. Burden 40 notes that, like all the divine speeches, this initiates action; eliciting an immediate response from the Son (l. 85 below).

x *39. gulf*] From *Luke* xvi 26.

40 I told ye then he should prevail and speed
     On his bad errand, man should be seduced
     And flattered out of all, believing lies
     Against his maker; no decree of mine
     Concurring to necessitate his fall,
45 Or touch with lightest moment of impulse
     His free will, to her own inclining left
     In even scale. But fallen he is, and now
     What rests but that the mortal sentence pass
     On his transgression, death denounced that day,
50 Which he presumes already vain and void,
     Because not yet inflicted, as he feared,
     By some immediate stroke; but soon shall find

x *40. then*] i.e., at iii 92f.   *speed*] be successful.

x *43-4*. See iii 113–23n on God's rejection of any Predestinarian account of his decrees that would lay him open to the charge of necessitating evil. *concurring*] cooperating (with man's free will).

x *45-7*. On the balance image, which is one of the most fully developed in the poem, see iv 997–1004n; *moment* belongs to the figure, for it was a term specifically applied to the smallest increment that could affect the equilibrium of a balance; see vi 239n.   *impulse*] Cp. iii 120, 'without least impulse . . . of fate', and see n.   *inclining*] Cp. ix 740, where Eve's desire is 'inclinable'. The metaphor of the true balance gains point from the iconographical tradition whereby in the weighing of souls at the last judgement the devils tried to cheat by leaning on one of the scales. Empson 116f rightly finds it noteworthy that we should here be reminded of the incident at the end of Bk iv, when God moved the Balance 'to expose mankind to the tempter'. But the discrepancy is only apparent. If man had been protected from the tempter, then there would have been real interference with the free action of the scales of justice.

x *48. rests*] remains.

x *49-53*. See viii 323–33n on the literalistic interpretation of *Gen.* ii 17, 'in the day that thou eatest thereof', which necessitated an allegorical interpretation of 'thou shalt surely die'. Cp. Adam's wishful argument of ix 927–37.   *ere day end*] The fact that Christ descends to judge man at sunset (l. 92ff) seems to imply that in one sense the day of the Fall is to be regarded as ending at that hour. This accords with the reckoning of the Hebrew day from sunset to sunset (see Introduction, 'Chronology', p. 26). Later, however, Adam can refer to the night as still belonging to the day of the Fall (see l. 773n), and a midnight-to-midnight reckoning–even a sunrise-to-sunrise reckoning–appears to be followed. It would seem that Adam fearfully holds back the *terminus ad quem* of the day of reckoning, until at last he realizes the figurative meaning of the prohibition, at l. 1050.

Forbearance no acquittance ere day end.
Justice shall not return as bounty scorned.

55 But whom send I to judge them? Whom but thee
Vicegerent Son, to thee I have transferred
All judgment, whether in heaven, or earth, or hell.
Easy it might be seen that I intend
Mercy colleague with justice, sending thee

60 Man's friend, his mediator, his designed
Both ransom and redeemer voluntary,
And destined man himself to judge man fallen.
So spake the Father, and unfolding bright
Toward the right hand his glory, on the Son

65 Blazed forth unclouded deity; he full
Resplendent all his Father manifest
Expressed, and thus divinely answered mild.
Father Eternal, thine is to decree,
Mine both in heaven and earth to do thy will

70 Supreme, that thou in me thy Son beloved
Mayst ever rest well pleased. I go to judge

x *53. acquittance*] satisfaction or settlement of a debt. 'Omittance is not quittance' was a proverb; cp. *As You Like It* III v 133.

x *54.* 'My just dealing must not meet a return of generosity scorned' – i.e. not without further satisfaction. There is some difficulty in the diction, as a result of M.'s wish to continue the commercial metaphor with *return*.

x *56–7.* Cp. *John* v 22: 'The Father judgeth no man, but hath committed all judgment unto the Son'; and see *De doctrina* i 5 (Columbia xiv 251): 'The Son . . . was entitled to the name of God both in the capacity of a messenger and of a judge.'

x *58. might*] may *Ed I.*

x *59–62. colleague*] allied, united for a common purpose. For the alliance of mercy with justice cp. iii 131–4 and 407; also *Nativity Ode* 141–6. *Ps.* lxxxv 10 is usually cited, but that verse concerns four qualities (mercy and truth, righteousness and peace), not two. Justice and mercy as a pair recall rather the imperial virtues, Iustitia and Clementia; on which see Frances A. Yates, 'Queen Elizabeth as Astraea', *JWI* x (1947) 67. The double syntax–l. 62 can be read either 'himself a man, destined to judge man' (primary) or 'destined to judge man himself, man fallen'–mimes the close identification of Christ with man; for the pronoun has now Christ, now mankind, as its antecedent. See also *De doctrina* i 15 (Columbia xv 285): 'The mediatorial office of Christ is that whereby . . . he voluntarily performed, and continues to perform, on behalf of man, whatever is requisite for obtaining reconciliation with God, and eternal salvation.'

x *64–7.* Cp. the similar passages, all based on *Heb.* i 3, at iii 138–42, 384–9; vi 680–4, 719–21 above; and see *nn.*

x *70–1.* Echoing *Matt.* iii 17.

On earth these thy transgressors, but thou know'st,
Whoever judged, the worst on me must light,
When time shall be, for so I undertook
75   Before thee; and not repenting, this obtain
Of right, that I may mitigate their doom
On me derived, yet I shall temper so
Justice with mercy, as may illustrate most
Them fully satisfied, and thee appease.
80   Attendance none shall need, nor train, where none
Are to behold the judgment, but the judged,
Those two; the third best absent is condemned,
Convict by flight, and rebel to all law
Conviction to the serpent none belongs.
85   Thus saying, from his radiant seat he rose
Of high collateral glory: him thrones and powers,
Princedoms, and dominations ministrant
Accompanied to heaven gate, from whence
Eden and all the coast in prospect lay.
90   Down he descended straight; the speed of gods
Time counts not, though with swiftest minutes winged.

x 74. Alluding, like iii 284, to *Gal.* iv 4: 'When the fulness of the time was come, God sent forth his Son, made of a woman, made under the law.' The Son's undertaking was made at iii 227–65.

x 75–9. Burden (39f) sees this part of the speech as apologetics, laying a theoretical foundation for the incident of Christ's clothing of Adam and Eve (ll. 211–21) that *Genesis* lacks.   *derived*] channelled (*OED* I 1); diverted (*OED* I 2); imparted, passed on by descent (*OED* I 4); not a Latinism. *illustrate*] (Stressed on the second syllable) make clear; display to advantage (*OED* 3, 6). *Them* primarily refers to *Justice* and *mercy*, whose demands are satisfied; but in a secondary chain of discourse it could refer to Adam and Eve, who constitute a debt to God (*thee*) that is 'paid off' (*OED* s.v. *Satisfy* I 1, debt as object).

x 82–4. *the third*] Satan. On the distribution of guilt between Satan and the serpent, see ll. 164–74n.   *Convict*] convicted.   *Conviction*] Has both the legal sense (proof of guilt: *OED* I) and the theological (the condition of being convinced of sin: *OED* 8). As an animal lacking reason, the serpent can have no heightened awareness of sin.

x 85–9. Cp. the departure of Messiah to the Creation, vii 192–215.

x 86. *collateral*] side by side (*OED* A 1); or conceivably 'subordinate' (*OED* A 3).

x 86–7. On the roll-call of titles, see v 601n.

x 89. *coast*] region; or perhaps 'side (of the world)'; cp. iii 739, vi 529.

x 90–1. Either 'however swift he may be, Time cannot count the speed of gods' or 'though their speed is winged with minutes–takes place in time– Time cannot count it'. Cp. viii 110, 'Speed almost spiritual'.   *with . . .*

Now was the sun in western cadence low
From noon, and gentle airs due at their hour
To fan the earth now waked, and usher in
95   The evening cool when he from wrath more cool
Came the mild judge and intercessor both
To sentence man: the voice of God they heard
Now walking in the garden, by soft winds
Brought to their ears, while day declined, they heard,
100   And from his presence hid themselves among
The thickest trees, both man and wife, till God
Approaching, thus to Adam called aloud.
Where art thou Adam, wont with joy to meet

minutes winged] Iconographically precise, for there was a type of Time–here deliberately overgone–which showed him with four wings to represent the seasons, and twelve feathers the months. See Panofsky[2] 79 and Fig. 50. Cowley 252 describes the descent of an angel similarly: 'Slow *Time* admires, and knows not what to call / The *Motion*, having no *Account* so small.' Cp. also vii 176f: 'Immediate are the acts of God, more swift / Than time or motion.' The parallel between the two descents of Christ is of the first importance; for it gives formal expression to the idea that the new creation is now beginning; the second task of Christ the second Adam.

x *92–102*. See *Gen.* iii 8: 'They heard the voice of the Lord God walking in the garden in the cool of the day: and Adam and his wife hid themselves from the presence of the Lord God amongst the trees of the garden.' Christ did not come at *noon*, the hour of the Fall, because symbolically that was the time of destructive judgment (see iv 30*n*); but neither may he wait until the sun has quite gone down on his wrath, in view of *Eph.* iv 26.   *cadence*] falling; sinking; probably a Latinism, though there are prose instances. *gentle airs*] Picks up 'wind', the A.V. marginal alternative to 'cool', in *Gen.* iii 8. Ricks 107 traces a secondary musical chain of discourse in *airs* and *cadence.   evening*] Day 33.

x *101. God*] Christ assumes the divine title while on earth, since there he is 'Vicegerent' (l. 56). Cp. *De doctrina* i 5, (Columbia xiv 251): 'The name of God is ascribed to judges, because they occupy the place of God to a certain degree in the administration of judgment.'

x *102–8*. Following *Gen.* iii 9, but greatly developing God's pretence of ignorance. No doubt this is to give Adam and Eve every chance to be candid.   *obvious*] 'standing in the way' (*OED* 1) or 'plain, palpable' (*OED* 4).   *change*] Followed so closely by *chance* this strongly recalls the First Collect after the Offertory: 'the changes and chances of this mortal life'. *chance* is a very deliberate and pointed choice of word: God knows perfectly well that Adam and Eve are absent by design, and that they have become subject to chance in a sense much graver than is ostensibly intended here. He is giving them an opening for confession. See ix 404–5*n*, 421*n*, 480–1*nn*.

My coming seen far off? I miss thee here,
105 Not pleased, thus entertained with solitude,
Where obvious duty erewhile appeared unsought:
Or come I less conspicuous, or what change
Absents thee, or what chance detains? Come forth.
He came, and with him Eve, more loath, though first
110 To offend, discountenanced both, and discomposed;
Love was not in their looks, either to God
Or to each other, but apparent guilt,
And shame, and perturbation, and despair,
Anger, and obstinacy, and hate, and guile.
115 Whence Adam faltering long, thus answered brief.
    I heard thee in the garden, and of thy voice
Afraid, being naked, hid myself. To whom
The gracious judge without revile replied.
    My voice thou oft hast heard, and hast not feared,
120 But still rejoiced, how is it now become
So dreadful to thee? That thou art naked, who
Hath told thee? Hast thou eaten of the tree
Whereof I gave thee charge thou shouldst not eat?
    To whom thus Adam sore beset replied.
125 O heaven! In evil strait this day I stand
Before my judge, either to undergo
My self the total crime, or to accuse
My other self, the partner of my life;
Whose failing, while her faith to me remains,
130 I should conceal, and not expose to blame
By my complaint; but strict necessity
Subdues me, and calamitous constraint
Lest on my head both sin and punishment,
However insupportable, be all
135 Devolved; though should I hold my peace, yet thou
Wouldst easily detect what I conceal.
This woman whom thou madest to be my help,
And gavest me as thy perfect gift, so good,
So fit, so acceptable, so divine,

x *112. apparent*] evident.
x *116–8.* Closely following *Gen.* iii 10.   *revile*] reviling.
x *119–23.* See *Gen.* iii 11: 'And he said, Who told thee that thou wast naked?
Hast thou eaten of the tree, whereof I commanded thee that thou shouldest
not eat?'   *still*] always.
x *128. other self*] Cp. viii 450.
x *135. devolved*] caused to fall upon (*OED* I 3 c); also 'caused to pass to ano-
ther, by legal succession, especially through the deficiency of one previously
responsible' (*OED* I 3 a, b).

140   That from her hand I could suspect no ill,
      And what she did, whatever in it self,
      Her doing seemed to justify the deed;
      She gave me of the tree, and I did eat.
         To whom the sovereign presence thus replied.
145   Was she thy God, that her thou didst obey
      Before his voice, or was she made thy guide,
      Superior, or but equal, that to her
      Thou didst resign thy manhood, and the place
      Wherein God set thee above her made of thee,
150   And for thee, whose perfection far excelled
      Hers in all real dignity: adorned
      She was indeed, and lovely to attract
      Thy love, not thy subjection, and her gifts
      Were such as under government well seemed,
155   Unseemly to bear rule, which was thy part
      And person, hadst thou known thy self aright.

x *141–3.* A less reputable version of Adam's enthusiastic speech to Raphael at viii 548–50: 'So well to know / Her own, that what she wills to do or say, / Seems wisest, virtuousest, discreetest, best.' Similarly Raphael's rebuke, with its insistence on headship, has its parallel in Christ's, ll. 144–56.

x *143. She*] Carries very heavy stress from its position in the line–appropriately to its rhetorical force as the summation of ll. 137–42. The verse closely follows *Gen.* iii 12 : 'The woman whom thou gavest to be with me, she gave me of the tree, and I did eat.'

x *144.* Burden (90f) will not allow Waldock's sneer that the speech which follows presents a false official version of the facts. He argues that M. started (at least in order of logical priority) with this summary synoptic view, and then expanded it into the series of actions that have just ensued.

x *147. equal*] Cp. ix 823–5, where fallen Eve wondered if she would keep the fruit to herself, to make her 'more equal, and perhaps ... sometime / Superior'.

x *149–50.* See *1 Cor.* xi 8f: 'For the man is not of the woman; but the woman of the man. Neither was the man created for the woman; but the woman for the man.'

x *151. real*] royal, regal (*OED* s.v. *Real* a.¹); perhaps secondarily 'true, actual' (*OED* s.v. *Real* a.²).

x *154–5.* See *1 Tim.* ii 12.

x *155–6.* Christ analyses the error as a wrong choice of role.   *part*] dramatic part, role. If the allegorical interpretation advanced at ix 360–1*n* above is accepted, then *thy part* will be seen to mean also 'your part of human nature, i.e., the intellect'.   *person*] character (in a play). Cp. *PR* ii 240, 'some active scene / Of various persons, each to know his part', or Jeremy Taylor, *A course of sermons* (1653), 'put on a person and act a part'. Not a Latinism.

So having said, he thus to Eve in few:
Say woman, what is this which thou hast done?
To whom sad Eve with shame nigh overwhelmed,
160   Confessing soon, yet not before her judge
Bold or loquacious, thus abashed replied.
The serpent me beguiled and I did eat.
Which when the Lord God heard, without delay
To judgment he proceeded on the accused

x *157. in few*] in few words; not a Latinism. Cp. Shakespeare, *Hamlet* I iii
126; *II Henry IV* I i 112.

x *159–61.* M. carefully gives a lead as to how we should imagine the brief
answer spoken. He does this sympathetically, making Eve immediately
responsive to Christ. She experiences certain of the emotions of contrition,
or at least of attrition, much more readily than Adam. See ix 1188*n* but also
ll. 989–1008 below.

x *162.* Repeating A.V. *Gen.* iii 13, with only a slight alteration of word
order.

x *164–74.* See ix 186*n*. Burden (54f) thinks that M. is in difficulty here, and
that he betrays uneasiness at Christ's seeming injustice to the helpless serpent.
The mysteriousness of the curse is not enough to remove its injustice; so that
Satan too must be made to grovel on his belly, in the entirely invented epi-
sode of ll. 508ff. This is possible; though it is hardly to be supposed that M.
would consciously have dissented from the view of, say, Mercerus (Willet
52), that 'God curseth the serpent because he was Sathans organe and instru-
ment: and this standeth with Gods justice to punish the instrument with the
principall [the authority cited is *Lev.* xx 15, 'if a man lie with a beast, he
shall surely be put to death: and ye shall slay the beast']. . . . And though
the serpent had no understanding, yet God curseth him for mans instruction,
that he might see how much this their action in seducing him, was displeasing
to God.' There was more difference of opinion as to the exact meaning of the
curse (for which see following *n*). Some referred the whole curse to the ser-
pent, others to Satan 'by way of allegorie', while others again understood it
literally of the serpent and mystically of Satan, and a fourth group (to which
Calvin belonged) gave the first part of the curse to the serpent and the last
part to Satan. M.'s lines embrace the views of almost all these groups.
For *at last* seems at l. 171 to refer to the last part of the curse, though at l. 190
it turns out to refer also to the 'last things', the final reckoning with Satan.
Similarly, ll. 182–9 applies the curse allegorically or 'mysteriously' to Satan,
and ll. 176–81 can be taken to apply literally to the serpent (particularly since
at ix 496ff we saw it upright and 'not . . . / Prone on the ground, as since');
yet the curse seems to be applied literally to Satan at ll. 508ff, where he and the
other devils actually fall prone and eat dust.   *unable*] Probably qualifies
serpent.   *no further*] At this stage Adam and Eve have no knowledge of the
verification of the oracle, in the redemptive history (see ll. 182–9); that the
serpent is an instrument, Adam has already a shrewd idea (see ix 904f).

165   Serpent though brute, unable to transfer
       The guilt on him who made him instrument
       Of mischief, and polluted from the end
       Of his creation; justly then accursed,
       As vitiated in nature: more to know
170   Concerned not man (since he no further knew)
       Nor altered his offence; yet God at last
       To Satan first in sin his doom applied,
       Though in mysterious terms, judged as then best:
       And on the serpent thus his curse let fall.
175   Because thou hast done this, thou art accursed
       Above all cattle, each beast of the field;
       Upon thy belly grovelling thou shalt go,
       And dust shalt eat all the days of thy life.
       Between thee and the woman I will put
180   Enmity, and between thine and her seed;
       Her seed shall bruise thy head, thou bruise his heel.
          So spake this oracle, then verified
       When Jesus son of Mary second Eve,
       Saw Satan fall like lightning down from heaven,
185   Prince of the air; then rising from his grave
       Spoiled principalities and powers, triumphed
       In open show, and with ascension bright
       Captivity led captive through the air,
       The realm it self of Satan long usurped,

mysterious] mystical. Adam's still formidable intellect will have given him an inkling of the inner meaning of the curse by ll. 1030ff.

x *175–81.* See *Gen.* iii 14f: 'And the Lord God said unto the serpent, Because thou hast done this, thou art cursed above all cattle, and above every beast of the field; upon thy belly shalt thou go, and dust shalt thou eat all the days of thy life: And I will put enmity between thee and the woman, and between thy seed and her seed; it shall bruise thy head, and thou shalt bruise his heel.'

x *183. second Eve*] Cp. v 386f.

x *184.* When the disciples returned from preaching and reported that they had subjected devils through Jesus' name, he said 'I beheld Satan as lightning fall from heaven' (*Luke* x 18).

x *185.* Cp. *Eph.* ii 2: 'In time past ye walked . . . according to the prince of the power of the air.'

x *186.* Cp. *Col.* ii 14f, where Christ is said to have put the condemnation of the Law out of the way, 'nailing it to his cross; And having spoiled principalities and powers, he made a shew of them openly, triumphing over them in it.'

x *188.* Cp. *Ps.* lxviii 18: 'Thou hast ascended on high, thou hast led captivity captive'; applied to Christ at *Eph.* iv 8.

190 Whom he shall tread at last under our feet;
Even he who now foretold his fatal bruise,
And to the woman thus his sentence turned.
        Thy sorrow I will greatly multiply
By thy conception; children thou shalt bring
195 In sorrow forth, and to thy husband's will
Thine shall submit, he over thee shall rule.
        On Adam last thus judgment he pronounced.
Because thou hast hearkened to the voice of thy wife,
And eaten of the tree concerning which
200 I charged thee, saying: Thou shalt not eat thereof,
Cursed is the ground for thy sake, thou in sorrow
Shalt eat thereof all the days of thy life;
Thorns also and thistles it shall bring thee forth
Unbid, and thou shalt eat the herb of the field,
205 In the sweat of thy face shalt thou eat bread,
Till thou return unto the ground, for thou
Out of the ground wast taken, know thy birth,
For dust thou art, and shalt to dust return.
        So judged he man, both judge and saviour sent,
210 And the instant stroke of death denounced that day

x *190*. See *Rom.* xvi 20, a proof text for the mystical interpretation of the curse on the serpent: 'And the God of peace shall bruise [margin 'tread'] Satan under your feet shortly.'

x *192*. The order of the curses is of vital importance. See *De doctrina* i 14, (Columbia xv 253): 'In pronouncing the punishment of the serpent, previously to passing sentence on man, [God] promised that he would raise up from the seed of the woman one who should bruise the serpent's head, Gen. iii 15. and thus anticipated the condemnation of mankind by a gratuitous redemption.' Cp. the analogous order of subjects in the divine conversation in Bk iii; see iii 173–202n.

x *197–202*. Cp. *Gen.* iii 17: 'And unto Adam he said, Because thou hast hearkened unto the voice of thy wife, and hast eaten of the tree, of which I commanded thee, saying, Thou shalt not eat of it; cursed is the ground for thy sake; in sorrow shalt thou eat of it all the days of thy life'.

x *203–8*. Cp. *Gen.* iii 18–9: 'Thorns also and thistles shall it bring forth to thee; and thou shalt eat the herb of the field; In the sweat of thy face shalt thou eat bread, till thou return unto the ground; for out of it wast thou taken: for dust thou art, and unto dust shalt thou return.'   *know thy birth*] This is puzzling, since Adam has already been told by Raphael that he was formed of 'dust of the ground' (vii 525).

x *210–1*. On the terms of the prohibition, see viii 323–33n. Christ removes the fear that physical death will follow the eating of the fruit on the same day, by his mention of 'all the days' of Adam's life (l. 202).   *denounced*] proclaimed, implying a warning.

Removed far off; then pitying how they stood
Before him naked to the air, that now
Must suffer change, disdained not to begin
Thenceforth the form of servant to assume,
215 As when he washed his servants' feet so now
As father of his family he clad
Their nakedness with skins of beasts, or slain,
Or as the snake with youthful coat repaid;
And thought not much to clothe his enemies:
220 Nor he their outward only with the skins
Of beasts, but inward nakedness, much more
Opprobrious, with his robe of righteousness,
Arraying covered from his Father's sight.
To him with swift ascent he up returned,
225 Into his blissful bosom reassumed

x *211–19.* Burden 39 notes how Christ's pity is immediately active.

x *213.* The *change* in the air is at ll. 692–706.

x *214.* Cp. *Phil.* ii 7: 'made himself of no reputation, and took upon him the form of a servant, and was made in the likeness of men'.

x *215. Ed I* has comma after *feet.*

x *216. father]* See *Heb.* ii 13: 'the children which God hath given me'.

x *216–23.* See *Gen.* iii 21. Willet 54f mentions, only to reject, the view that God slew beasts and clothed Adam and Eve 'to betoken . . . the cloathing of the nakednesse of the soule by repentance'. Reasons he accepts include: to show man how to care for his body; to cover his nakedness with what the Chaldee paraphrase calls *vestimenta honoris*; to teach man he may kill for clothing; and to remind him of mortality. If the animals are *slain*, then in this the first instance of actual death, Christ is the immediate cause (see *ere thus was . . . judged,* l. 229). The mention of the *snake's* slough probably alludes to a neat theory in the *Targum*, ascribed to Jonathan ben Uzziel, that man's needs were by a poetic justice met from the skin of the serpent that had occasioned them. Christ's clothing man with a robe of righteousness was a commonplace of religious poetry; cp., e.g., George Herbert, 'Sunday': 'The brightnesse of that day / We sullied by our foul offence: / Wherefore that robe we cast away, / Having a new at his expence, / Whose drops of bloud paid the full price, / That was requir'd to make us gay, / And fit for Paradise.' The Biblical source is *Is.* lxi 10: 'My soul shall be joyful in my God; for he hath clothed me with the garments of salvation, he hath covered me with the robe of righteousness, as a bridegroom decketh himself with ornaments, and as a bride adorneth herself with her jewels.' Cp. ix 1054–9, where Adam and Eve discover themselves to have lost the veils of innocence, confidence, righteousness and honour.

x *219. enemies]* See *Rom.* v 10: 'If, when we were enemies, we were reconciled to God by the death of his Son, much more, being reconciled, we shall be saved by his life.'

In glory as of old, to him appeased
All, though all-knowing, what had passed with man
Recounted, mixing intercession sweet.
Meanwhile ere thus was sinned and judged on earth,
230   Within the gates of hell sat Sin and Death,
In counterview within the gates, that now
Stood open wide, belching outrageous flame
Far into chaos, since the fiend passed through,
Sin opening, who thus now to Death began.
235   O son, why sit we here each other viewing
Idly, while Satan our great author thrives
In other worlds, and happier seat provides
For us his offspring dear? It cannot be
But that success attends him; if mishap,
240   Ere this he had returned, with fury driven
By his avengers, since no place like this
Can fit his punishment, or their revenge.
Methinks I feel new strength within me rise,
Wings growing, and dominion given me large
245   Beyond this deep; whatever draws me on,
Or sympathy, or some connatural force

x 230. Addison disapproved of the long allegory that follows, thinking it
improper for epic. But Newton illuminatingly remarks that much of M.'s
poem 'lies in the invisible world. . . . The actions of Sin and Death are at
least as probable as those ascribed to the good or evil Angels.' Such allegories
were fairly common in literary treatments of the Fall. Hughes cites Samuel
Pordage; and there is a very elaborate example indeed in Sylvester's Du
Bartas II i 3, 'The Furies', where Dearth, War and Sickness, all with their
attendant abstractions, come in procession with their 'steely Cars' across
'th'ever-shaking nine-fold steely bars / Of Stygian Bridge'.
x 231. See ii 649, where Sin and Death sit 'before the gates' of hell, 'on
either side'.
x 232. The gates have been open since Sin's failure to shut them, at ii 883f.
outrageous] fierce; enormous; immoderate.
x 236. author] parent; inventor.
x 241. avengers] avenger Ed I.   like] i.e., so well as.
x 244. Cp. ix 1009f, where Adam and Eve, newly intoxicated by their fall,
'fancy that they feel / Divinity within them breeding wings'. The three sets
of wings are bred simultaneously, for the sub-plot concerning Sin is not a
separate action, but a treatment of the main action in a different mode and
from a different point of view. M. discreetly indicates this at l. 229, by
noticing the simultaneity of Sin's rise and man's fall.
x 246-9. or . . . or] either . . . or.   sympathy] affinity by virtue of which
two entities might influence one another, regardless of distance. Philemon
Holland defined the term as meaning 'a fellow-feeling, used in Pliny, for the

Powerful at greatest distance to unite
With secret amity things of like kind
By secretest conveyance. Thou my shade
250   Inseparable must with me along:
For Death from Sin no power can separate.
But lest the difficulty of passing back
Stay his return perhaps over this gulf
Impassable, impervious, let us try
255   Adventurous work, yet to thy power and mine
Not unagreeable, to found a path
Over this main from hell to that new world
Where Satan now prevails, a monument
Of merit high to all the infernal host,
260   Easing their passage hence, for intercourse,
Or transmigration, as their lot shall lead.
Nor can I miss the way, so strongly drawn
By this new felt attraction and instinct.

agreement or amitie naturall in divers sencelesse things, as betweene yron
and the loadstone' (Pliny's *Historie of the world* (1634) tom. ii, A 6ᵛ). Lewis
(66) thinks that Sin here shows her deluded ignorance, by mistaking for sym-
pathy with Satan what is really God's summons of his hell-hounds 'to
lick up the draff and filth' made by the Fall (see ll. 616–40). From another
point of view, the feeling of sympathy is to be related to Adam's feeling of
sympathy with Eve, which gave him a premonition of her Fall (Burden 167f;
see ix 845f).   *conveyance*] communication.

x *252–323.* A great work of building was traditionally an ingredient of
epic; the building of Carthage in Virgil *Aen.* i 423ff is probably the most
famous instance. *PL* has several such works. God performs a single work of
creation in vii, and this is doubled in the two devilish works, Pandaemonium
(i) and the bridge over chaos. The latter forms a close antitype to God's
creation out of chaos, as Tillyard notes in *SP* xxxviii (1941) 269.

x *253–4.* See *Luke* xvi 26 on the 'great gulf' fixed between the elect and the
reprobate 'so that they which would pass from hence to you cannot; neither
can they pass to us, that would come from thence'.   *impervious*] affording
no passage (*OED* 1).

x *255. Adventurous*] Spelt 'Adventrous', and scanned as a trisyllable.

x *256. found*] build; establish. Not a Latinism.

x *257. main*] ocean, expanse; i.e., chaos.

x *260–1.* Sin inevitably uses the terms of the satanic ideology; speaking of
lot as the determining factor. Cp. Eve at ix 881 and Adam at ix 952.   *inter-*
course] communication to and fro between two places.   *transmigration*]
permanent migration from one place to another.

x *263. instinct*] Stressed on the second syllable.

Whom thus the meagre shadow answered soon.
265 Go whither fate and inclination strong
Leads thee, I shall not lag behind, nor err
The way, thou leading, such a scent I draw
Of carnage, prey innumerable, and taste
The savour of death from all things there that live:
270 Nor shall I to the work thou enterprisest
Be wanting, but afford thee equal aid.
        So saying, with delight he snuffed the smell
Of mortal change on earth. As when a flock
Of ravenous fowl, though many a league remote,
275 Against the day of battle, to a field,
Where armies lie encamped, come flying, lured
With scent of living carcasses designed
For death, the following day, in bloody fight.
So scented the grim feature, and upturned
280 His nostril wide into the murky air,
Sagacious of his quarry from so far.
Then both from out hell gates into the waste
Wide anarchy of chaos damp and dark
Flew diverse, and with power (their power was great)
285 Hovering upon the waters; what they met

x *264. meagre*] emaciated (*OED* 1); Death was usually represented as an almost fleshless skeleton.

x *266. err*] mistake.

x *267. draw*] inhale (*OED* II 23).

x *268–70. savour of death*] For the word play see ix 1017–20n, and for a resemblance between Death and Eve, ix 791–2n.

x *271. Ed II* wrongly has comma after *aid*.

x *273–8*. Satan is similarly compared to a vulture at iii 431ff. The prolepsis here (*living carcasses*) may have been suggested by Pliny, *Nat. hist.* x 7: *triduo antea volare eos ubi cadavera futura sunt*, or by one of several passages based on this in encyclopedists such as Aldrovandus. As in the simile at ll. 307–11, an implied correspondence between tenor and vehicle is the numerousness, in each case, of those who are to die.

x *279. feature*] form, shape (*OED* 1 c); cp. *Areopagitica* (Yale ii 549), 'an immortall feature of loveliness and perfection'.

x *281. Sagacious*] acute of perception (especially by smell). Cp. Eve, who is 'exact of taste', ix 1017.

x *283. anarchy*] Cp. ii 988, vi 873.

x *284. diverse*] turning in opposite directions. The parenthesis discriminates between God's creation and that of Sin and Death: the latter have power, but not goodness.

x *285–8*. Contrast vii 235–40, where the spirit of God hovered over the same deep, but made it a 'watery calm', and 'purged / The black tartareous cold

Solid or slimy, as in raging sea
Tossed up and down, together crowded drove
From each side shoaling towards the mouth of hell.
As when two polar winds blowing adverse
290   Upon the Cronian sea, together drive
Mountains of ice, that stop the imagined way
Beyond Petsora eastward, to the rich
Cathaian coast. The aggregated soil
Death with his mace petrific, cold and dry,
295   As with a trident smote, and fixed as firm
As Delos floating once; the rest his look

infernal dregs'.   *shoaling*] crowding together, assembling in swarms
(*OED* v.³ 2).

x *289–93. Cronian Sea*] the Arctic Ocean, better known as the *mare concretum* –
an apt choice, therefore, in view of the solidifying work Death is soon to
engage in.   *the imagined way*] A north east passage to Cathay had been
searched for by Hudson in 1608; but he was unable to find an opening
through the ice. *Petsora* or Pechora is a river in Siberia, mentioned by M.
in his *Brief History of Muscovia.* Cathay (see xi 388) was regarded as a separate
empire from China, to the north.   *rich*] Makes the point of the simile
clear: Cathay is so desirable that it stands for the objective of human effort,
Paradise. Nevertheless, the simile is an intricate one, whose logical structure
includes the unusual feature of double tenors carried on a single vehicle
(due to the fact that Sin's actions are allegorical). Thus Cathay in the vehicle
corresponds in one tenor to Paradise on earth, in the other to paradise in
heaven. The Cronian ice – i.e., the structure of fallen human nature – is like
the *bridge* built to make access from the earthly Paradise to hell easy; but it
also constitutes a *barrier* making man's ascent to paradise above difficult.
See ll. 321–4*n.*

x *293–6. mace petrific*] Cp. Marlowe, *Dido,* II i 115, 'pale Death's stony mace'.
The mace conveys utter destruction, yet at the same time travesties the
creative sovereignty of Christ; see Cirlot 186. Whereas the spirit of God
infused 'vital warmth' into the 'fluid mass' of chaos (vii 236f), Death chooses
cold and dry – the qualities inimical to life – for his work.   *Delos*] An
island raised by the trident of Neptune, to provide a refuge where Latona
might give birth to Apollo and Diana; a floating island, until Jupiter fastened
it with chains to the bottom of the sea. Delos has already been connected
with Paradise, the refuge of Adam and Eve, at v 265 and ix 387, so that the
implication is that Death's effect is as irrevocable as Jupiter's chains of neces-
sity.   *As with a trident*] Highly ambivalent: on the one hand the implied
comparison with Neptune the controller of waves suggests peace, on the
other, the trident was an attribute of Satan (its triple form symbolizing the
infernal trinity).

x *296–8.* The Gorgons turned to stone all whom they looked at; see ii 611*n.*
But it is not clear why Death treats some of the material of chaos with his

Bound with Gorgonian rigor not to move,
And with asphaltic slime; broad as the gate,
Deep to the roots of hell the gathered beach
300   They fastened, and the mole immense wrought on
Over the foaming deep high arched, a bridge
Of length prodigious joining to the wall
Immovable of this now fenceless world
Forfeit to Death; from hence a passage broad,
305   Smooth, easy, inoffensive down to hell.
So, if great things to small may be compared,
Xerxes, the liberty of Greece to yoke,

mace, and the rest with his look. Bentley and Empson[2] 154 have some elusive
objection to M.'s mixture of concrete and abstract in this zeugma: a mixture
which is of course the staple of allegory.   *asphaltic slime*] asphaltus, jew's
pitch; used by the devils at i 729. M. no doubt selected this particular cement
less for its black colour and connection with the Dead Sea (l. 562) than for
the association of *Ecclus.* xiii 1: 'He that toucheth pitch shall be defiled
therewith' (a verse that had become proverbial; cp. Spenser, *Shepheardes
Calender*, May 74).   *slime*] In A.V. *Gen.* xi 3 'slime' translates the Hebrew
word for pitch (Vulgate *bitumen*).   *rigor*] numbness, stiffness. OED cites
no instance of the form *rigor mortis* earlier than 1839. On a possible source
(which however does not help with the interpretation of the passage) see
Tillyard in *SP* xxxviii (1941) 267.

x *300.* The bridge is fastened to hell, as God's work, the universe, is fastened
to heaven (ii 1051).

x *302–3.* The *wall* is 'the utmost orb / Of this frail world', the firm opaque
outer shell to which we were told at ii 1024–31 the bridge was fastened.
In spite of the wall, the world is without defence(*fenceless*) against Death.

x *305. inoffensive*] not giving offence (i.e., to society: the passage is designed
for conformists), and 'not causing stumbling; free from obstacles' (Lat.
inoffensus). The word also continues the play on *fence*. Cp. *Matt.* vii 13:
'Enter ye in at the strait gate: for wide is the gate, and broad is the way, that
leadeth to destruction, and many there be which go in thereat.'

x *306.* See ii 921–2n.

x *307–11.* Starnes and Talbert (285) show the source to be not Herodotus
vii 33 but Stephanus: *Xerxes, Persarum rex fuit filius Darii . . . Graeciae bellum
intulit . . . tantum autem habuit navium apparatum, ut totum Hellespontum ope-
riret, et Asiam Europae ponte coniungeret.* Susa was the winter seat of the Persian
kings; it was sometimes called *Memnonia*, after Memnon, son of Tithonus
and Aurora, who lived there. The comparison has many points of similarity,
widely varying in degree of subtlety. Death and Xerxes both build bridges,
both intend to subdue whole nations, are both proud and both strike the
deep (295 above; Zerxes had the Hellespont scourged because his first
bridge was destroyed by a storm). Less obviously, both are doomed to fail

From Susa his Memnonian palace high
· Came to the sea, and over Hellespont
310   Bridging his way, Europe with Asia joined,
And scourged with many a stroke the indignant waves.
Now had they brought the work by wondrous art
Pontifical, a ridge of pendent rock
Over the vexed abyss, following the track
315   Of Satan, to the self same place where he
First lighted from his wing, and landed safe
From out of chaos to the outside bare
Of this round world: with pins of adamant
And chains they made all fast, too fast they made
320   And durable; and now in little space
The confines met of empyrean heaven
And of this world, and on the left hand hell
With long reach interposed; three several ways
In sight, to each of these three places led.
325   And now their way to earth they had descried,
To Paradise first tending, when behold
Satan in likeness of an angel bright
Betwixt the Centaur and the Scorpion steering

in spite of initial successes. But the simile gains most force from a silent allu-
sion to the well-known story that Xerxes wept while reviewing his army,
at the thought that within a century such multitudes would all be dead.
Note how much of the imagery is drawn from military contexts, in passages
concerned with evil agents.

x *313. Pontifical*] bridge-making. A learned pun on Lat. *pons* and *facere*;
but the usual sense of the word, 'episcopal', must obviously be intended too.
The implication that the priesthood are as good at making the way easy to
hell as Sin and Death draws ironic force from the fact that the Pope's title
pontifex was interpreted as meaning that his role was one of bridge-builder
between the present world and the world to come (Cirlot 31, citing St
Bernard).

x *314. vexed*] disturbed by storms; see vii 212-5.

x *316. First lighted*] See iii 418-22.

x *321-4.* Previously, the *confines* (common boundaries) of heaven and the
world (universe) met without interruption; but now the way to hell is
interposed; see ll. 289-93*n*. The three ways are: the stair to heaven (iii 510ff),
the passage through the opaque outer sphere of the universe down to earth
(iii 526ff) and the new bridge.   *left*] the sinister evil side, to which the
reprobate are put, in the parable of the sheep and the goats (*Matt*. xxv 33).

x *327.* On Satan's disguise, see iii 634*n*.

x *328-9.* Verity and Hughes repeat Newton's canard that Satan, to avoid
discovery by Uriel, keeps at as great a distance as possible from him, so that,
since the sun is in Aries, Satan steers between 'two constellations which lay

His zenith, while the sun in Aries rose:
330   Disguised he came, but those his children dear
Their parent soon discerned, though in disguise.
He after Eve seduced, unminded slunk
Into the wood fast by, and changing shape
To observe the sequel, saw his guileful act
335   By Eve, though all unweeting, seconded
Upon her husband, saw their shame that sought

in a quite different part of the Heavens'. But if Satan were hiding from Uriel
in Aries, he would steer in Libra, the sign in opposition to Aries. And besides,
if he were invisible to Uriel he would need no disguise. The real reason for
steering *betwixt the Centaur* (Sagittarius) *and the Scorpion* is rather that the
only constellation noticeably spread over these two signs is Anguis, the
serpent held by Ophiuchus. (This can easily be verified by a glance at any
celestial globe, or at a figured star map such as Dürer's.) Anguis has its
head in Libra, and extends through Scorpio into Sagittarius. Accordingly,
Satan enters the world in Libra (see iii 551–61n), but leaves it between Scor-
pio and Sagittarius. Cp. ii 707–11nn on a similar allusion to Ophiuchus.
The sun is in *Aries* not because it had strong astrological influence in the sign
of its exaltation (Svendsen 83), but because it was situated in that sign in the
thema coeli that prevailed from the creation to the Fall (see iii 555–61n). The
present verse is the most explicit indication M. has given us that the state
of his universe before the Fall corresponds to the traditional vernal schema.
It is therefore of crucial importance to the interpretation of such passages as
iii 555ff and iv 267f, 354f. The information that a point between Scorpio and
Sagittarius is at Satan's zenith clearly indicates that the time in Paradise is
between 2.00 a.m. and 4.00 a.m. (or, assuming Sol to be in the centre of
Aries, 3.00 a.m.) on Day 33, the day after the Fall. It should be noted that
Sin and Death are not observing Satan from Paradise, so that the present
passage must not be taken to imply that the sun is rising there. Satan, flying
straight up from Paradise (*steering / His zenith*), is between Scorpio and
Sagittarius, i.e., at an aspect of 120°–150° to the sun in Aries; hence the
horizon of reference cannot possibly be that of Paradise (where his aspect
to a rising sun would be 90°). See further l. 773n. The emendation of *rose*
to *rode* proposed by Bentley is quite unnecessary. From the vantage-point
of Sin and Death, the sun might well seem to rise from beyond the earth;
just as at iii 558–60 Aries seemed to Satan (in a similar position) to bear
Andromeda 'Beyond the horizon'. Sin and Death, we are told, follow 'the
track that Satan first made' (x Argument).

x 332. *after Eve seduced*] For the Lat. construction cp. i 573, 'since created
man'.   *unminded*] unnoticed; perhaps secondarily expressing the removal
of mind from the serpent when Satan changes his shape.

x 334. *sequel*] consequence.

x 335. *unweeting*] unconsciously.   *seconded*] repeated; or supported,
followed up.

Vain covertures; but when he saw descend
The Son of God to judge them terrified
He fled, not hoping to escape, but shun
340　The present, fearing guilty what his wrath
Might suddenly inflict; that past, returned
By night, and listening where the hapless pair
Sat in their sad discourse, and various plaint,
Thence gathered his own doom, which understood
345　Not instant, but of future time. With joy
And tidings fraught, to hell he now returned,
And at the brink of chaos, near the foot
Of this new wondrous pontifice, unhoped
Met who to meet him came, his offspring dear.
350　Great joy was at their meeting, and at sight
Of that stupendous bridge his joy increased.
Long he admiring stood, till Sin, his fair
Enchanting daughter, thus the silence broke.
　　O parent, these are thy magnific deeds,
355　Thy trophies, which thou view'st as not thine own,
Thou art their author and prime architect:
For I no sooner in my heart divined,
My heart, which by a secret harmony
Still moves with thine, joined in connection sweet,
360　That thou on earth hadst prospered, which thy looks
Now also evidence, but straight I felt
Though distant from thee worlds between, yet felt
That I must after thee with this thy son;

x 337. *covertures*] Both the garments of ix 1110–14 and the dissimulations and excuses of x 116ff (see *OED* s.v. *Coverture* 3 and 7f).

x 342. *night*] Evidently the night during which Adam's complaint is uttered; see ll. 716ff.

x 344–5. Referring to Adam's recollection and interpretation of the curse, at ll. 1030ff. The full stop after *time* in the early edns makes *understood* a verb in the past tense, with its subject omitted. If there were a comma only, *understood* could be a participle, and the passage would flow more easily.

x 347. *foot*] the end of the slope or hump of the bridge. See *OED*, s.v. *Foot* V 18 b.

x 348. *pontifice*] bridge (*OED* 2) or priest (*OED* 1); see l. 313n. The ambiguity is accentuated rather than resolved by *foot* in the preceding line.

x 331. *stupendous*] The early edns have 'stupendious', the accepted form until the latter seventeenth century.

x 352. The double-cross juncture after *increased*, followed by a spondee, mimes Satan's admiring pause.

x 358. *secret harmony*] The 'sympathy' or 'connatural force' of ll. 346–9; see *n* there.

Such fatal consequence unites us three:
365 Hell could no longer hold us in her bounds,
Nor this unvoyageable gulf obscure
Detain from following thy illustrious track.
Thou hast achieved our liberty, confined
Within hell gates till now, thou us empowered
370 To fortify thus far, and overlay
With this portentous bridge the dark abyss.
Thine now is all this world, thy virtue hath won
What thy hands builded not, thy wisdom gained
With odds what war hath lost, and fully avenged
375 Our foil in heaven; here thou shalt monarch reign,
There didst not; there let him still victor sway,
As battle hath adjudged, from this new world
Retiring, by his own doom alienated,
And henceforth monarchy with thee divide
380 Of all things parted by the empyreal bounds,
His quadrature, from thy orbicular world,

x *364. consequence*] cause-effect relationship.

x *365.* For the falsity of this boast, see i 209–13*n* and iii 80–6*n*. The trinity Satan-Sin-Death is an antitype of the divine Trinity, so that l. 365 may be seen as a parody of *Matt.* xvi 18 ('the gates of hell shall not prevail') and of similar Biblical texts applied to Christ's resurrection.

x *370. fortify*] grow strong (intrans.: *OED* I 6); strengthen structurally (trans., *OED* I 1), referring to the bridge, is perhaps secondarily operative.

x *371. portentous*] prodigious (*OED* 2); but also 'portending a calamity (to man)' (*OED* 1).

x *372–3.* A parody of Justification.

x *372. virtue*] power; courage – the commonest senses when the word is used by evil agents. See i 320, ix 616*n*, 647–50*n*, 778*n* and 694*n*.

x *374. odds*] advantage.

x *375. foil*] defeat.

x *378. doom*] judgment.

x *379.* See *n* on iv 111: 'Divided empire with heaven's king I hold.'

x *381.* Cp. ii 1048, and see *Rev.* xxi 16, on the New Jerusalem: 'The city lieth foursquare, and the length is as large as the breadth: and he measured the city with the reed, twelve thousand furlongs. The length and the breadth and the height of it are equal.' The *world* (universe) is repeatedly referred to in *PL* as *orbicular*: cp., e.g., iii 718 (Uriel on the creation). Sin's subtle sneer depends on the notion that the sphere is a more perfect form than the cube, since more capacious, and on the fact that the square and the circle are incommensurate. But there is probably also a dramatic irony, depending on a common development of the same arithmological doctrine. The mysterious integration of spirit and matter in man's nature was often symbolized by the squaring of the circle (see Fowler 267), so that the present passage may allude

Or try thee now more dangerous to his throne.
    Whom thus the prince of darkness answered glad.
Fair daughter, and thou son and grandchild both,
385   High proof ye now have given to be the race
Of Satan (for I glory in the name,
Antagonist of heaven's almighty king)
Amply have merited of me, of all
The infernal empire, that so near heaven's door
390   Triumphal with triumphal act have met,
Mine with this glorious work, and made one realm
Hell and this world, one realm, one continent
Of easy thorough-fare. Therefore while I
Descend through darkness, on your road with ease
395   To my associate powers, them to acquaint
With these successes, and with them rejoice,
You two this way, among these numerous orbs
All yours, right down to Paradise descend;
There dwell and reign in bliss, thence on the earth
400   Dominion exercise and in the air,
Chiefly on man, sole lord of all declared,
Him first make sure your thrall, and lastly kill.
My substitutes I send ye, and create
Plenipotent on earth, of matchless might

to the Incarnation, when a perfect man will combine sovereignty over both
the square and the orbicular worlds.

x *382. try*] find by experience to be (*OED* 13); 'extract by refining with fire'
(*OED* 3) may be operative as a secondary irony.

x *384. son and grandchild*] Because he is the offspring of Satan's incestuous
relations with his daughter Sin.

x *386–7. Satan* literally means 'adversary'.

x *390.* The work of Sin and Death is probably to be regarded as a triumphal
work in the specific sense that the bridge constitutes a triumphal arch.

x *397. these*] those *Ed I.*

x *397–8.* Not so much a parallel with Satan's descent 'amongst innumerable
stars' (iii 565) as a contrast with Christ's triumphal and creative descent into
chaos at vii 180ff; see MacCaffrey 61.

x *399–402.* Cp. ii 839–44, and see *Rom.* v 14, 17, 21: 'death reigned from
Adam to Moses'; 'by one man's offence death reigned by one'; 'as sin hath
reigned unto death, even so might grace reign through righteousness unto
eternal life by Jesus Christ our Lord.'   *thrall*] See *John* viii 34: 'Whoso-
ever committeth sin is the servant of sin.' But we should also note the echo of
man's commission at *Pl.* viii 338ff, which implies that Sin and Death are now
to institute a whole new estate of subjugated man.

x *404. Plenipotent*] possessing full authority. Cp. God's commission of
Messiah, iii 317ff.

405   Issuing from me: on your joint vigour now
       My hold of this new kingdom all depends,
       Through Sin to Death exposed by my exploit.
       If your joint power prevails, the affairs of hell
       No detriment need fear, go and be strong.
410   So saying he dismissed them, they with speed
       Their course through thickest constellations held
       Spreading their bane; the blasted stars looked wan,
       And planets, planet-strook, real eclipse
       Then suffered. The other way Satan went down
415   The causey to hell gate; on either side
       Disparted chaos over built exclaimed,
       And with rebounding surge the bars assailed,
       That scorned his indignation: through the gate,
       Wide open and unguarded, Satan passed,
420   And all about found desolate; for those
       Appointed to sit there, had left their charge,

x 407. Cp. *Rom.* v 12: 'By one man sin entered into the world, and death by sin; and so death passed upon all men, for that all have sinned.'

x 408. *prevails*] prevail *Ed I*–a reading that Adams prefers because the subjunctive is more Latinate.

x 409. So Moses gives Joshua his commission to lead the people of Israel to take possession of the Promised Land, at *Deut.* xxxi 7f (cp. xi 8). But the joke is on Satan; for, after the redemption, death will indeed for man be the way to a promised paradise. The whole triumph tradition was based on Roman models. Appropriately, therefore, *detriment* alludes to the charge given to the two consuls at Rome, when supreme power was conferred on them in times of crisis: *Videant consules ne quid respublica detrimenti capiat.* Note that this commission, temporary like Satan's, conferred no powers *de iure.* Thus, if the consuls put anyone to death, they could later plead the commission; but they would still have to justify their action legally.

x 412–13. The wild figures here approach the chaotic bomphiologia of Bk vi (on which see vi 698–9*n*).   *blasted*] breathed on balefully–specifically applied to the influence of a malignant planet (see *OED* s.v. *Blast* II 7 and *Blasted* 1), so that the inverted application here, to the effect *on* stars, would be felt as a radical dislocation of meaning. Similarly with *planets, planet-strook* (planet-struck, 'stricken by the malign influence of an adverse planet'); though here a preposterous pun may also be intended (planets struck by planets).   *real eclipse*] Usually an eclipse is only an observational phenomenon, but in this case the obscuration is real.

x 415. *causey*] causeway, raised way over wet ground; sometimes applied to an arched viaduct; see ll. 300f.

x 418. i.e., the bars scorned Chaos' indignation. Cp. Virgil, *Georg.* ii 161f, where the ocean is *indignatum* at the Lucrine breakwater.

x 420. i.e., Sin and Death.

Flown to the upper world; the rest were all
Far to the inland retired, about the walls
Of Pandaemonium, city and proud seat
425   Of Lucifer, so by allusion called,
Of that bright star to Satan paragoned.
There kept their watch the legions, while the grand
In council sat, solicitous what chance
Might intercept their emperor sent, so he
430   Departing gave command, and they observed.
As when the Tartar from his Russian foe
By Astracan over the snowy plains
Retires, or Bactrian sophy from the horns
Of Turkish crescent, leaves all waste beyond
435   The realm of Aladule, in his retreat
To Tauris or Casbeen. So these the late
Heaven-banished host, left desert utmost hell
Many a dark league, reduced in careful watch
Round their metropolis, and now expecting
440   Each hour their great adventurer from the search
Of foreign worlds: he through the midst unmarked,
In show plebeian angel militant
Of lowest order, passed; and from the door

x *423. inland*] Two words in *Ed I.*

x *425-6. paragoned*] compared, placed side by side. On the comparison of
Satan to the morning star, see v 700-14*n* and vii 132*n*.

x *427. the grand*] The 'great seraphic lords and cherubim' of the secret
conclave at i 794ff.

x *428. solicitous*] anxious, concerned.

x *431-9. Astracan*] A Tartar kingdom and capital city near the mouth of the
Volga, often referred to in M.'s *Brief History of Muscovia.*   *Bactrian*]
Persian.   *sophy*] shah, Persian king.   *horns . . . crescent*] Refers not only
to the Turkish ensign, but also to their battle formations; cp. the similar
play in Dryden, *Annus Mirabilis* (1667), St. 125: 'Their huge unwieldy Navy
wasts away: / So sicken waning Moons too neer the Sun, / And blunt their
crescents on the edge of day.'   *Aladule*] greater Armenia. *Tauris* (mod.
Tabriz) is in the extreme north-west of Persia;   *Casbeen*] Kazvin, north
of Teheran. The simile is a complex one. Physically, the *snowy plains* re-
mind us of the 'frozen continent' of hell at ii 587, where the devils are haled
for punishment 'at certain revolutions', and so prepares us for the punitive
metamorphosis soon to follow. Morally, the grand devils are being com-
pared to Saracens (cp. i 348, ii 1-4, etc.): either barbarians (Tartars) or proud
but ineffective rulers (sophies). The last point is underlined with a sarcastic
pun; for *sophy* meant 'sage' (*OED* 3) as well as 'shah' (*OED* 2).   *Many a*]
Requires synaloepha.   *reduced*] led back.

Of that Plutonian hall, invisible
445 Ascended his high throne, which under state
Of richest texture spread, at the upper end
Was placed in regal lustre. Down a while
He sat, and round about him saw unseen:
At last as from a cloud his fulgent head
450 And shape star bright appeared, or brighter, clad
With what permissive glory since his fall
Was left him, or false glitter: all amazed
At that so sudden blaze the Stygian throng
Bent their aspect, and whom they wished beheld,
455 Their mighty chief returned: loud was the acclaim:
Forth rushed in haste the great consulting peers,
Raised from their dark divan, and with like joy
Congratulant approached him, who with hand
Silence, and with these words attention won.
460   Thrones, dominations, princedoms, virtues, powers,
For in possession such, not only of right,
I call ye and declare ye now, returned
Successful beyond hope, to lead ye forth
Triumphant out of this infernal pit
465 Abominable, accursed, the house of woe,

x 444. *Plutonian*] pertaining to Pluto, ruler of the classical underworld. First instance in *OED*.

x 445. *state*] canopy (*OED* II 20 b). For an earlier description of Satan's glittering throne, see ii 1–4.

x 448. *saw unseen*] One motive of Satan's invisible entry is evidently to check on the loyalty of his followers.

x 450–2. Satan's original form is recalled, so that his metamorphosis to a serpent (ll. 511ff) will have maximum effect. On the 'process of alternating inflation and deflation of the devils' see Broadbent 110.   *permissive*] permissible; permitted (by God). Cp. i 591ff.

x 450. *star bright*] Hyphenated in *Ed I*.

x 453. *Stygian throng*] Cp. 'Stygian council', ii 506.

x 454. *aspect*] Stressed on the second syllable.

x 457. *divan*] oriental council of state; continuing the Saracen implication of ll. 431–9.

x 458. *Congratulant*] expressing congratulation (Latinism; cp. *congratulantes*).

x 460. Cp. ii 11–14, v 772, and see v 601n. Empson 79 suggests that M.'s repetition of the roll-call of titles is sardonic: that Satan is no longer morally conscious enough to see the irony of this claim to have provided victims for them to rule.

x 465. *house of woe*] For the diction see ii 823n.

And dungeon of our tyrant: now possess,
As lords, a spacious world, to our native heaven
Little inferior, by my adventure hard
With peril great achieved. Long were to tell
470 What I have done, what suffered, with what pain
Voyaged the unreal, vast, unbounded deep
Of horrible confusion, over which
By Sin and Death a broad way now is paved
To expedite your glorious march; but I
475 Toiled out my uncouth passage, forced to ride
The untractable abyss, plunged in the womb
Of unoriginal Night and Chaos wild,
That jealous of their secrets fiercely opposed
My journey strange, with clamorous uproar
480 Protesting fate supreme; thence how I found
The new created world, which fame in heaven
Long had foretold, a fabric wonderful
Of absolute perfection, therein man
Placed in a paradise, by our exile
485 Made happy: him by fraud I have seduced
From his creator, and the more to increase
Your wonder, with an apple; he thereat
Offended, worth your laughter, hath given up
Both his beloved man and all this world,
490 To Sin and Death a prey, and so to us,
Without our hazard, labour, or alarm,

x 466. The angelic dignities need no longer be merely titular, as Satan suggested they were at v 773f.

x 469–502. This summary of the action to date is one of the strongest pieces of evidence in support of Burden's contention that there is a 'satanic epic' running parallel to M.'s. Satan is inviting the devils (and the reader) to think of him as the hero of a falsely heroic epic in which they too may participate.

x 471. unreal] Because formless, and therefore not fully material.

x 475. uncouth] unfamiliar, strange; solitary (OED 2b, 5).

x 477–9. unoriginal] uncreated (only instance in OED). See ii 962 where Night is 'eldest of things'. Neither Night nor Chaos in fact opposed Satan; and Chaos even helped him. See especially ii 1004–9.

x 481–2. For the rumour, see i 651–4n, ii 346–52n, vii 145–56n.

x 484. exile] Stressed on the second syllable.

x 485. On the Satanic view that because 'the apple has no intrinsic magic . . . the breach of the prohibition becomes a small matter' see Lewis 68.

x 485–90. Gilbert 20 compares M.'s Fourth Draft of a tragedy on Paradise Lost (see Introduction, 'Composition', p. 5 above): 'Here again may appear Lucifer relating, and insulting in what he had done to the destruction of man.'

To range in, and to dwell, and over man
To rule, as over all he should have ruled.
True is, me also he hath judged, or rather
495   Me not, but the brute serpent in whose shape
Man I deceived: that which to me belongs,
Is enmity, which he will put between
Me and mankind; I am to bruise his heel;
His seed, when is not set, shall bruise my head:
500   A world who would not purchase with a bruise,
Or much more grievous pain? Ye have the account
Of my performance: what remains, ye gods,
But up and enter now into full bliss.
    So having said, a while he stood, expecting
505   Their universal shout and high applause
To fill his ear, when contrary he hears
On all sides, from innumerable tongues
A dismal universal hiss, the sound
Of public scorn; he wondered, but not long
510   Had leisure, wondering at himself now more;
His visage drawn he felt to sharp and spare,
His arms clung to his ribs, his legs entwining
Each other, till supplanted down he fell
A monstrous serpent on his belly prone,
515   Reluctant, but in vain, a greater power
Now ruled him, punished in the shape he sinned,
According to his doom: he would have spoke,

x 496. *that*] i.e., that part of the curse; see ll. 164–74*n*.

x 508. *dismal*] dreadful, sinister, gloomy. See i 60*n*.

x 511–14. Cp. the metamorphosis of Cadmus in Ovid, *Met.* iv 572–603, already alluded to at ix 506 above; Lucan, *Phars.* ix 700ff; and P. Fletcher, *Purple Island* vii 11. Dante had carried the evocation of horror through serpentine metamorphoses to considerable lengths in *Inf.* xxiv and xxv. *clung*] drawn together, shrunk, shrivelled (participle; *OED* s.v. *Clung* 2).

x 513. *supplanted*] tripped up, made to stumble (*OED* 1); caused to fall from a position of power or virtue (*OED* 2). See Ricks 64f: 'The applied moral meaning is in the background, and provides the grim irony with which Satan is always seen–Satan, on whom always evil "recoils". . . . Satan is the great supplanter: "He set upon our fyrst parentes in paradyse, and by pride supplanted them" (More, 1522).'

x 517. The *doom* (judgment) referred to is the curse on the serpent (see ll. 164–74*n*), which is now accomplished literally. Nevertheless, the metamorphosis should not be seen merely as a punishment, but also as a divine judgment of Satan's character, and a repudiation of the false ideal of heroism that has just been set forth. At the moment of acclaim Satan is revealed in his true brutishness as the monstrous opponent of heroic virtue; see

> But hiss for hiss returned with forked tongue
> To forked tongue, for now were all transformed
> 520   Alike, to serpents all as accessories
> To his bold riot: dreadful was the din
> Of hissing through the hall, thick swarming now
> With complicated monsters head and tail,
> Scorpion and asp, and amphisbaena dire,
> 525   Cerastes horned, hydrus, and ellops drear,

Steadman 101f. As a peripeteia, the episode is highly dramatic: just when the devils seem about to become heroes in Satan's epic (see ll. 469–502*n*) they turn out instead to be monsters in God's. Hughes cites Boehme: after 'the divine light went out of the Devils, they lost their beauteous forme and Image, and became like Serpents, Dragons, Wormes, and evill Beasts: as may be seen by *Adam's* Serpent.'

x *523. complicated*] compound, composite (*OED* 4); tangled (*OED* 2).

x *524–6.* The *amphisbaena* is a serpent with a head at either end, according to Lucan (*Phars.* ix 719) with eyes like lamps; it is the subject of a paper by G. C. Druce in *Arch. Journ.* lxvii, No. 268; 2nd ser. xvii, No. 4, pp. 285–317. The *cerastes* has four horns on its head, shaped like a ram's. The *hydrus* (not to be confused with the many-head hydra) is a water-snake, enemy of the crocodile; its venom causes dropsy. The *ellops*, though sometimes identified as the swordfish, is mentioned as a serpent in Pliny, *Nat. hist.* xxxii 5, while the *dipsas* causes raging thirst by its bite. On all these serpents, see Robin; White 174–85; and Svendsen (35f), who gives illustrations from popular authorities such as Bartholomew, Batman, Topsell (*The historie of serpents* (1608)) and Swan. Hughes, drawing on the more high-powered natural history of Aldrovandus (which carried over a good deal of moralization from the bestiaries and medieval encyclopedias) assigns complex emblematic significances to the serpents: e.g., the amphisbaena could stand for inconstancy and adultery. Seven serpents are named, with cerastes (symbolic of power-lust) in the central position of sovereignty, so that it would be tempting to correlate them with the deadly sins. But M. has given far too little descriptive differentiation of the serpents for this approach to be made with any confidence. More likely he intended the passage simply as a counterpart to ix 185ff. Cp. in this connection Sylvester's Du Bartas I vi: 'O wert thou pleas'd to form / Th'innammel'd *Scorpion*, and the *Viperworm*, / Th'horned *Cerastes*, th' *Alexandrian Skink*, / Th'*Adder*, and *Drynas* (full of odious stink) / Th'*Eft*, *Snake*, and *Dipsas* (causing deadly Thirst): / Why hast thou arm'd them with a rage so curst? / Pardon, good God, pardon me; 't was our pride, / Not thou, that troubled our first happy tyde, / And in the Childehood of the World, did bring / Th' *Amphisbena* her double banefull sting'; with side-note: 'Why God created such noysom and dangerous creatures: Sin the occasion of the hurt they can do us.' The serpents are actual species, and M. is grappling with the problem how Providence

And dipsas (not so thick swarmed once the soil
Bedropped with blood of Gorgon, or the isle
Ophiusa) but still greatest he the midst,
Now dragon grown, larger than whom the sun
530   Ingendered in the Pythian vale on slime,
Huge Python, and his power no less he seemed
Above the rest still to retain; they all
Him followed issuing forth to the open field,
Where all yet left of that revolted rout
535   Heaven-fallen, in station stood or just array,
Sublime with expectation when to see
In triumph issuing forth their glorious chief;
They saw, but other sight instead, a crowd
Of ugly serpents; horror on them fell,
540   And horrid sympathy; for what they saw,
They felt themselves now changing; down their arms,
Down fell both spear and shield, down they as fast,
And the dire hiss renewed, and the dire form
Catched by contagion, like in punishment,
545   As in their crime. Thus was the applause they meant,
Turned to exploding hiss, triumph to shame
Cast on themselves from their own mouths. There stood
A grove hard by, sprung up with this their change,
His will who reigns above, to aggravate
550   Their penance, laden with fair fruit, like that

can allow them to exist. The early edns italicize the names of the serpents as technical terms.

x *526–7.* When Perseus was bringing back the severed head of Medusa, drops of blood fell to earth, and that is why Libya is full of serpents. See Ovid, *Met.* iv 617–20; also Lucan, *Phars.* ix 699ff, where the asp, cerastes, dipsas and amphisbaena are all mentioned as having been produced in this way.

x *528. Ophiusa*] Literally 'full of serpents'; a name anciently given to several islands, including Rhodes and one of the Balearic group.

x *529–32.* Cp. *Elegia VII*, and for the birth of *Python* from the *slime* remaining after the flood see Ovid, *Met.* i 438–40. M. cannot allude to Python without introducing also the slaying of Python by Apollo. Similarly, Satan's *dragon* shape is that of the 'old dragon' of Christian apocalypse; see *Rev.* xii 9: 'the great dragon was cast out, that old serpent, called the Devil, and Satan'.

x *535.* i.e., either on guard or drawn up for review.

x *536. Sublime*] uplifted.

x *546. exploding*] Used both in its modern sense and 'driving off the stage'.

x *546.* 'As they were increased, so they sinned against me: therefore will I change their glory into shame' (*Hos.* iv 7).

x *550. penance*] punishment (*OED* 5).   *fair*] so in *Ed I*; erroneously omitted in *Ed II*.

Which grew in Paradise, the bait of Eve
Used by the tempter: on that prospect strange
Their earnest eyes they fixed, imagining
For one forbidden tree a multitude
555 Now risen, to work them further woe or shame;
Yet parched with scalding thirst and hunger fierce,
Though to delude them sent, could not abstain,
But on they rolled in heaps, and up the trees
Climbing, sat thicker than the snaky locks
560 That curled Megaera: greedily they plucked
The fruitage fair to sight, like that which grew
Near that bituminous lake where Sodom flamed;
This more delusive, not the touch, but taste
Deceived; they fondly thinking to allay
565 Their appetite with gust, instead of fruit

x 555. *furder*] further.

x 556. The Tantalus-like thirst of the devils, together with other echoes at ll. 432, 537 and 560, suggests that the present passage bears some close relation to that describing the punishment of the devils at ii 596ff. The punishment by metamorphosis, like the others, is administered periodically; see ll. 575ff, and i 193–5n. For a similar view see John M. Steadman, 'Tantalus and the Dead Sea Apples' in *JEGP* lxiv (1965) 35–40. Steadman shows that 'the apples of the Tantalus myth are cross grafted with those of the Dead Sea and the tree of knowledge'. In this grafting operation M. had possibly been anticipated by Edward Browne. Tantalus' doom, it should be noted, is like that of the devils a talion punishment.

x 560. *Megaera*] one of the Furies or Eumenides who punish sin; thus at ii 596 it is 'harpy-footed Furies' who hale the devils off for their periodic punishments. The Furies are often described as snaky-haired.

x 562. *bituminous lake*] The Dead Sea, beside which lies Sodom. The allusion is to Josephus, *Wars* IV viii 4, where it is said that traces still remain of the divine fire that burnt Sodom; such as 'ashes growing in their fruits, which fruits have a colour as if they were fit to be eaten; but if you pluck them with your hands, they dissolve into smoke and ashes'. Svendsen 28f shows that this passage was widely drawn on by the encyclopedists. M. himself refers to the tradition as if it were a commonplace, in *Eikonoklastes* (Yale iii 552). At a more fundamental level, however, the present passage depends on *Deut.* xxxii 32f: 'Their vine is of the vine of Sodom, and of the fields of Gomorrah: their grapes are grapes of gall, their clusters are bitter: Their wine is the poison of dragons, and the cruel venom of asps.' By the 'vine of Sodom' (which was identified with the fruit described by Josephus) Moses was taken to mean that the people of Israel had become corrupt and rotten at the core.

x 565. *gust*] relish.

Chewed bitter ashes, which the offended taste
With spattering noise rejected: oft they assayed,
Hunger and thirst constraining, drugged as oft,
With hatefulest disrelish writhed their jaws
570   With soot and cinders filled; so oft they fell
Into the same illusion, not as man
Whom they triumphed once lapsed. Thus were they
      plagued
And worn with famine, long and ceaseless hiss,
Till their lost shape, permitted, they resumed,
575   Yearly enjoined, some say, to undergo
This annual humbling certain numbered days,
To dash their pride, and joy for man seduced.
However some tradition they dispersed

x 566–70. In literal enactment of the curse of l. 178, that the serpent 'dust shalt eat'. See ll. 164–74n. Topsell 16 discusses a popular fallacy that serpents eat nothing but dust.

x 568. drugged] nauseated (first instance in OED in this sense). Richardson explains the word as 'a metaphor taken from the general nauseousness of drugs'.

x 571–2. i.e., 'did not as man (whom they conquered) fall once'; secondarily, 'not like man, whom they triumphed over, once he was fallen'. See OED s.v. Triumph 2 c.

x 574. See l. 451 and n.

x 578–84. See Apollonius Rhodius, Argonaut. i 503–9, where Orpheus sings how Ophion and Eurynome daughter of Ocean ruled Olympus until the one yielded to Cronos (Saturn), the other to Rhea (Ops). Their two successors then ruled the Titans 'while Zeus still . . . dwelt in the Dictaean cave'. Starnes and Talbert (269), correcting Verity and Hughes, argue that M. is fusing Apollonius' Ophion with another, a friend of Cadmus, one of those born from the serpent's teeth, ideoque et nomen habet a serpente, qui Graece ὄφις dicitur (Stephanus, Thesaurus). But the identification of Apollonius' Ophion as a serpent is better explained simply as an allusion to De raptu Proserpinae iii 332–56. Claudian there describes a dreadful grove hung with Jupiter's spoils from the Giant War: 'Here hang the gaping jaws and monstrous skins of the Giants; affixed to trees their faces still threaten horribly, and heaped up on all sides bleach the huge bones of slaughtered serpents. Their stiffening sloughs smoke with the blow of many a thunderbolt, and every tree boasts some illustrious name.' Among them 'spoiled Ophion weighs down those branches' (348). Not only does this allusion follow naturally after the punitive grove of 547ff (indeed, M.'s 'There stood / A grove hard by' directly translates Claudian's lucus erat prope), but it satisfactorily deflates the triumph of the devils by recalling their defeat under the type of Giants. (For the casting of the devils in the role of rebel Giants, see i 50–83n, 197–200n.) Thus, while the devil-inspired tradition

Among the heathen of their purchase got,
580   And fabled how the serpent, whom they called
Ophion with Eurynome, the wide-
Encroaching Eve perhaps, had first the rule
Of high Olympus, thence by Saturn driven
And Ops, ere yet Dictaean Jove was born.
585   Mean while in Paradise the hellish pair
Too soon arrived, Sin there in power before,
Once actual, now in body, and to dwell
Habitual habitant; behind her Death
Close following pace for pace, not mounted yet
590   On his pale horse: to whom Sin thus began.
        Second of Satan sprung, all conquering Death,
        What think'st thou of our empire now, though earned

claims precedence over Jupiter, M.'s allusion shows Jupiter supreme. The
association of Ophion with Satan was traditional; see Sandys[2] 27: 'Phere-
cides the Syrian writes how the Divels were throwne out of heaven by
Jupiter (this fall of the Gyants perhaps an allusion to that of the Angells)
the chiefe called *Ophioneus*, which signifies Serpentine: having after made
use of that creature to poyson *Eve* with a false ambition.' Empson 175,
following Bentley, takes part of M.'s meaning to be that the serpent was
Eve's husband, and that she was *wide-Encroaching* (cp. *Eurynome* = wide-
ruling) in the sense that her children are all makind. But as Pearce cautions,
the tradition is presented by M. as a false slander of our parent. See ix 505–
10n above.   *purchase*] plunder, prey, spoil (*OED* II 8); but also 'annual
return or rent' (*OED* II 10) – alluding to the *annual* punishment of the devils
(ll. 575f).   *Dictaean*) The Cretan mountain where Jupiter spent his child-
hood was called Dicte, and Dictaeus was one of his surnames.
x *586–7*. Sin had already been present potentially (*in power*); but once com-
mitted (*once actual*) it was present in a fuller sense as a *body*–'the body of sin'
in St Paul's phrase. Cp. *Rom.* vi 6: 'Our old man is crucified with him, that
the body of sin might be destroyed, that henceforth we should not serve
sin.' *Actual* sin (the result of a free act of will) is to be distinguished from
original sin (the general state of sinfulness to which fallen man is subject).
See *De doctrina* i 11 (Columbia xv 199): 'The second thing in sin, after evil
concupiscence, is the crime itself, or the act of sinning, which is commonly
called Actual Sin.'
x *589–90*. Cp. *Rev.* vi 8: 'I looked, and behold a pale horse: and his name that
sat on him was Death, and Hell followed with him. And power was given
unto them over the fourth part of the earth; to kill with sword, and with
hunger, and with death, and with the beasts of the earth.' Death is *not
mounted yet* because the Last Things are not yet happening. The reason can-
not be (as Greenwood has it) because Death has not yet exercised his power,
since there were already perhaps dead animals at l. 217 above, and certainly
a dead plant at ix 893.

With travail difficult, not better far
Than still at hell's dark threshold to have sat watch,
595 Unnamed, undreaded, and thy self half starved?
  Whom thus the Sin-born monster answered soon.
To me, who with eternal famine pine,
Alike is hell, or Paradise, or heaven,
There best, where most with ravine I may meet;
600 Which here, though plenteous, all too little seems
To stuff this maw, this vast unhide-bound corpse.
  To whom the incestuous mother thus replied.
Thou therefore on these herbs, and fruits, and flowers
Feed first, on each beast next, and fish, and fowl,
605 No homely morsels, and whatever thing
The scythe of time mows down, devour unspared,
Till I in man residing through the race,
His thoughts, his looks, words, actions all infect,
And season him thy last and sweetest prey.
610 This said, they both betook them several ways,
Both to destroy, or unimmortal make
All kinds, and for destruction to mature
Sooner or later; which the almighty seeing,
From his transcendent seat the saints among,
615 To those bright orders uttered thus his voice.
  See with what heat these dogs of hell advance
To waste and havoc yonder world, which I
So fair and good created, and had still
Kept in that state, had not the folly of man

x 601. *unhide-bound*] (Only instance in *OED*): since Death is emaciated, he might be expected to be hidebound, like an emaciated horse; but on the contrary his skin is loose and capacious. See *OED* s.v. *Hidebound* I 1: 'Of cattle: Having the skin clinging closely to the back and ribs . . . as a result of bad feeding and consequent emaciation.'

x 602. *incestuous*] See ii 790ff.

x 606. Before the Fall, Raphael held out hope that 'tract of time' might improve man into spirit; but now time is a destroyer. On Time's scythe, and on the personification of Time generally, see Panofsky[2] 69–94.

x 611. *unimmortal*] First instance in *OED*. M. is probably coining negative forms, to emphasize the insubstantiality of Death. Cp. *unhide-bound* (l. 601), *unnamed, undreaded* (l. 595).

x 616. *dogs of hell*] Cp. the 'hell hounds' about Sin's middle at ii 653ff.

x 617. *havoc*] devastate, make havoc of. The order 'havoc!' was originally the signal for general pillage. Cp. *Julius Caesar* III i 270–3; 'And Caesar's spirit, ranging for revenge, / With Ate by his side come hot from hell, / Shall in these confines with a monarch's voice / Cry "Havoc!" and let slip the dogs of war'.

620 Let in these wasteful furies, who impute
     Folly to me, so doth the prince of hell
     And his adherents, that with so much ease
     I suffer them to enter and possess
     A place so heavenly, and conniving seem
625 To gratify my scornful enemies,
     That laugh, as if transported with some fit
     Of passion, I to them had quitted all,
     At random yielded up to their misrule;
     And know not that I called and drew them thither
630 My hell-hounds, to lick up the draff and filth
     Which man's polluting sin with taint hath shed
     On what was pure, till crammed and gorged, nigh
          burst
     With sucked and glutted offal, at one sling
     Of thy victorious arm, well-pleasing Son,
635 Both Sin, and Death, and yawning grave at last
     Through chaos hurled, obstruct the mouth of hell
     For ever, and seal up his ravenous jaws.
     Then heaven and earth renewed shall be made pure
     To sanctity that shall receive no stain:
640 Till then the curse pronounced on both precedes.
          He ended, and the heavenly audience loud

x *621*. God's providential use of evil is a frequent theme in *PL*: cp. i 162ff, 210ff; vii 613ff; xii 470ff; and see Lewis 66.

x *623. enter and possess*] Legal diction.

x *624. conniving*] taking no notice; pretending ignorance (*OED* 1).

x *627. quitted*] yielded, handed over (*OED* I 5 b).

x *630. draff*] refuse, dregs, lees. Often used figuratively, in such phrases as 'the draffs of filthy errors'.

x *633*. Cp. *1 Sam*. xxv 29: 'The souls of thine enemies, them shall he sling out, as out of the middle of a sling.'

x *635–6*. Cp. ii 734, 805ff, and see *Hos*. xiii 14 ('O death, I will be thy plagues; O grave, I will be thy destruction'), *1 Cor*. xv 54, and *Rev*. xx 14 ('death and hell were cast into the lake of fire. This is the second death').

x *638–9*. Alluding to the apocalyptic vision of *2 Pet*. iii 7–13: 'The heavens and the earth, which are now, by the same word are kept in store, reserved unto fire against the day of judgment. . . . We, according to his promise, look for new heavens and a new earth, wherein dwelleth righteousness.' *heaven and earth*] the universe. Burden 40 notes the positive activity in the darkest of God's speeches. Even the curse is imposed in order to cleanse the world.

x *640. curse*] Probably that of *Gen*. iii 17: 'Cursed is the ground for thy sake.'   *precedes*] not 'prevails' (as Bush) but 'goes before'.

Sung hallelujah, as the sound of seas,
Through multitude that sung: Just are thy ways,
Righteous are thy decrees on all thy works;
645 Who can extenuate thee? Next, to the Son,
Destined restorer of mankind, by whom
New heaven and earth shall to the ages rise,
Or down from heaven descend. Such was their song,
While the creator calling forth by name
650 His mighty angels gave them several charge,
As sorted best with present things. The sun

x *642*. Cp. v 872f, and see *Rev.* xix 6: 'I heard as it were the voice of a great multitude, and as the voice of many waters, and as the voice of mighty thunderings, saying, Alleluia: for the Lord God omnipotent reigneth.'

x *644*. Cp. *Rev.* xvi 7: 'True and righteous are thy judgments.' Note that M. reserves this explicit approval for perhaps the most appalling of all God's decrees.

x *645*. *extenuate*] disparage; diminish in honour (*OED* II 5).

x *647–8. the ages*] the millennium, the golden ages. Cp. xii 549, 'ages of endless date'.   *Or down*] see *Rev.* xxi 2: 'I John saw the holy city, new Jerusalem, coming down from God out of heaven.'

x *650*. Possibly the seven spirits of iii 648ff.

x *651*. Belief in nature's involvement in man's corruption was general in M.'s time; see ix 782–4n. The present passage may be regarded as a more detailed treatment of nature's 'signs of woe' at the Fall. On the microcosmic implication Svendsen writes: 'The first result was earth's wound; the next man's passion; then into the cosmos for the stupendous distortion (it was labor even for angels); and last back to earth and within Adam, now like Satan "inly racked". These tremendous arcs bind the universe and the poem together and contribute to the sense of visual image and cosmic rhythm.' More obviously, the repeated cutting has the effect of establishing the closest possible relation between macrocosm and microcosm.   *sorted*] associated; consorted (*OED* III 19).

x *651–706*. A passage of great importance for the understanding of the world picture of *PL*. It shows clearly that the cosmic system used throughout most of the poem is not–in spite of many scholarly statements to the contrary–the Ptolemaic system. Instead, it is a theoretical system, of ideal simplicity, in which the ecliptic and the equatorial circles coincide. On the earth of such a system, every point must be an equinoctial point, and there can be neither solstices nor seasons. Spring, in fact, is *perpetual*. The system we ourselves know, and try to describe in our Ptolemaic, Copernican, or other astronomies, is purely an accident of the Fall, and therefore obtains only in the part of the poem subsequent to the present passage. The originality and energy with which M. imagines a complete prelapsarian astronomy, and applies it throughout the larger part of *PL* with the most inventive consistency, are beyond praise. The physical implications of the initial assumption

Had first his precept so to move, so shine,
As might affect the earth with cold and heat
Scarce tolerable, and from the north to call
655   Decrepit winter, from the south to bring
Solstitial summer's heat. To the blank moon
Her office they prescribed, to the other five
Their planetary motions and aspects
In sextile, square, and trine, and opposite,
660   Of noxious efficacy, and when to join
In synod unbenign, and taught the fixed
Their influence malignant when to shower,
Which of them rising with the sun, or falling,
Should prove tempestuous: to the winds they set
665   Their corners, when with bluster to confound

about prelapsarian regularity are followed out even in quite minute details. The geographical location of Paradise, e.g., is conceived in terms of the 'special case' astronomy (see iv 209–16*n*). Other passages depending on the system include iii 555–61, iv 354f, 776–80, v 18–25 and x 328–9. Of particular importance are the many expressions of what I have called the equinoctial theme: balancings of night and day, light and darkness (see iv 997–1004*n*). This theme acquires a literal force and validity from the prelapsarian astronomical system. See Introduction, 'Milton's Universe'.

x *655.* The portrayal of Winter as an old man or woman was a commonplace of iconography; see, e.g., Ripa 475. It depended on the ancient correlation of ages of man with seasons of the year; on which see Klibansky 10 *et passim.*

x *656. blank*] white, pale.

x *675. other five*] i.e., planets; as at v 177.

x *658–61.* Astrological determinism has its beginning. For the terms used see Ptolemy, *Tetrabiblos* i 13: *sextile* is an aspect of 60°, *square* (or quartile) of 90°, *trine* of 120° and *opposite* (opposition) of 180°. Of these, trine and sextile are harmonious, quartile and opposition disharmonious. *Synod* (conjunction) is not formally recognized as an aspect by Ptolemy; hence its separate place here.   *aspects*] Stressed on the second syllable.

x *661–2.* Contrast the 'sweet influence' of the *fixed* stars when they were first created (vii 375). The present action is conceived as a detailed revision of the creation. Burden 184 observes that words such as *taught* constantly remind us that the changes in the macrocosm are neither random nor uncontrolled, but consequent on deliberate decrees of God.

x *663–4.* i.e., which cosmical risings and acronycal settings are signs of bad weather. Meteorological lore relating to the rising and setting of particular constellations was a considerable ingredient in such works as Aratus' *Phaenomena*, Ovid's *Fasti* and Manilius' *Astronomicon*.

x *665–6.* i.e., to *confound* the four elements; *thunder* implying Fire and *shore* Earth.

Sea, air, and shore, the thunder when to roll
With terror through the dark aerial hall.
Some say he bid his angels turn askance
The poles of earth twice ten degrees and more
670   From the sun's axle; they with labour pushed
Oblique the centric globe: some say the sun
Was bid turn reins from the equinoctial road
Like distant breadth to Taurus with the Seven
Atlantic Sisters, and the Spartan Twins
675   Up to the tropic Crab; thence down amain
By Leo and the Virgin and the Scales,
As deep as Capricorn, to bring in change
Of seasons to each clime; else had the spring
Perpetual smiled on earth with vernant flowers,
680   Equal in days and nights, except to those
Beyond the polar circles; to them day
Had unbenighted shone, while the low sun
To recompense his distance, in their sight
Had rounded still the horizon, and not known

x *668–80.* Starting from M.'s 'special case' cosmic system, the universe as
we now know it can be arrived at either by tilting the axis of earth about
23.5°, or else by altering the inclination of the sun's course by a correspon-
ding amount. (Not by 'shifting the centre of the sun's orbit' as Svendsen
71; only the *plane* of the orbit is moved, not its centre.) Naturally the first
alternative corresponds to the heliocentric theory and the second to the
geocentric; and M. avoids any decision between them.   *centric globe*]
earth.   *like distant breadth*] a similar number of degrees of declination.
The northern (summer) departure of the sun, which immediately followed
on the Fall, is traced out in detail: up to the tropic sign Cancer, when the
sun is 23.5° North, then back down again to the equator (*equinoctial road*),
reached when the sun enters Libra (*the Scales*). The winter departure is
indicated more summarily, by the mention of the southern tropic sign,
Capricorn. Aries is presumably omitted because the sun is already in that
sign (l. 329): the northern detour is *to* Taurus. M. could also have cited
Hyginus' description of Taurus (*Poet. astron.* iii 20): *Taurus ad ortum sig-
norum dimidia parte collocatus. . . . Genua eius a reliquo corpore dividit circulus
Aequinoctialis.*   *Seven / Atlantic Sisters*] the Pleiades, mythologically the
daughters of Atlas. Astronomically, they are situated in the constellation
Taurus. Their introduction in the present passage is to clinch an earlier
prolepsis; see vii 374–5*n* above.   *Spartan Twins*] the zodiacal sign Gemini;
mythologically Castor and Pollux, sons of King Tyndarus of Sparta.
amain] at full speed.
x *678–9. clime*] region. In the cosmography of M.'s day each hemisphere
was divided into seven horizontal strips called climes. For the perpetual
spring before the Fall, see iv 268*n.*

685   Or east or west, which had forbid the snow
       From cold Estotiland, and south as far
       Beneath Magellan. At that tasted fruit
       The sun, as from Thyestean banquet, turned
       His course intended; else how had the world
690   Inhabited, though sinless, more than now,
       Avoided pinching cold and scorching heat?
       These changes in the heavens, though slow, produced
       Like change on sea and land, sideral blast,
       Vapour, and mist, and exhalation hot,
695   Corrupt and pestilent: now from the north

x *686. Estotiland*] Modern N.E. Labrador. The name was sometimes used
vaguely.

x *687. Magellan*] In Heylyn's map of the Americas, modern Argentina is
called *Magellonica*, after the Portuguese explorer Magellan.

x *687-9.* Thyestes seduced Aerope, the wife of Atreus his brother. In
revenge, Atreus pretended to be reconciled and invited Thyestes to a
banquet, but served up to him the flesh of one of his children. The act was
thought so horrible that the sun was said to have changed course to avoid
observing it. See, e.g., Seneca, *Thyestes* 776ff. On the feast motif in *PL*, see
ix 9n above. Scan *Thyéstean*.

x *693. sideral*] coming from the stars (*OED* 2). Probably the *sideral blast is*
the malign blasting effect of the stars already referred to at l. 412.

x *694. exhalation hot*] Probably 'meteor'. Meteors were believed to be
ignited bodies of vapour.

x *695-706.* Repeating 'in miniature' the attack of Sin and Death upon the
abyss (MacCaffrey 90). Whiting 121f believes that the only wind-chart
giving all the winds mentioned by M. is in Jansson's *Novus atlas* (1647-62),
a splendid publication in eleven volumes, concerning which M. is known to
have made an enquiry. Here *Boreas* is the N.N.E. wind; *Caecias* E.N.E.;
Argestes N.W.; *Thrascias* N.N.W.; *Notus* S.; *Afer* (Africus) S.W.; *Eurus*
E.S.E.; *Zephir* (Zephirus) W.; *Sirocco* S.E.; *Libecchio* S.W.   *brazen
dungeon*] Alludes to the prison in which Aeolus keeps the winds enclosed, in
Virgil, *Aen.* i 50ff.   *flaw*] sudden squall of wind.   *Serraliona*] Modern
Sierra Leone.   *thwart*] Previously the winds have all been more or less N.
or S.; but now *lateral* (E.-W.) winds join the battle. Most of the names of the
winds are classical; but *Levant* is vernacular (in nautical jargon, a raw east wind
in the Mediterranean was a Levanter), *ponent* (setting, west) perhaps a Latini-
zing or Gallicizing coinage, and *Sirocco* and *Libecchio* Italian. The conflict of
all the winds was a reversion to chaos that had often been used as a symbol
of the chaotic state of human passion. Cp. Spenser, *F.Q.* IV ix 23, where the
conflict of four different erotic dispositions is compared to that of winds: 'As
when Dan Aeolus . . . / Sends forth the winds out of his hidden threasure, /
Upon the sea to wreake his fell intent; / They breaking forth with crude
unruliment, / From all foure parts of heaven doe rage full sore, / And tosse

Of Norumbega, and the Samoed shore
Bursting their brazen dungeon, armed with ice
And snow and hail and stormy gust and flaw,
Boreas, and Caecias and Argestes loud
700   And Thrascias rend the woods and seas upturn;
With adverse blast upturns them from the south
Notus and Afer black with thunderous clouds
From Serraliona; thwart of these as fierce
Forth rush the Levant and the ponent winds
705   Eurus and Zephir, with their lateral noise,
Sirocco, and Libecchio, thus began
Outrage from lifeless things; but Discord first
Daughter of Sin, among the irrational,
Death introduced through fierce antipathy:
710   Beast now with beast gan war, and fowl with fowl,
And fish with fish; to graze the herb all leaving,
Devoured each other; nor stood much in awe
Of man, but fled him, or with countenance grim
Glared on him passing: these were from without
715   The growing miseries, which Adam saw
Already in part, though hid in gloomiest shade,
To sorrow abandoned, but worse felt within,
And in a troubled sea of passion tossed,

the deepes, and teare the firmament, / And all the world confound with
wide uprore, / As if in stead thereof they Chaos would restore.' Cp. also ix
1122f above: 'high winds worse within / Began to rise, high passions.'

x 696. *Norumbega*] The name vaguely given to S.E. Canada and the N.E.
part of the U.S.A.; while *Samoedia*, which is mentioned in M.'s *Brief
History of Muscovia*, was a region corresponding to the extreme N.E. of
modern Siberia.

x 710–14. Contrast the unhurried play of the animals before the Fall, iv
340ff. For *herb* as the prelapsarian diet, see *Gen*. i 30: 'To every beast of
the earth, and to every fowl of the air, and to every thing that creepeth upon
the earth, wherein there is life, I have given every green herb for meat.'
but fled] Contrasting awe before the Fall with fear after it.

x 718. The correspondence between passion and macrocosmic disorder is
now introjected to become subjective metaphor. Cp. *Is*. lvii 20: 'The
wicked are like the troubled sea, when it cannot rest, whose waters cast up
mire and dirt.' The Sea of Troubles topic could be traced through St
Augustine's *Enarr. in Ps*. cvii (*Migne* xxxvii 1425f), Chaucer's *Man of Law's
Tale*, medieval and Renaissance Fortune iconography, *Hamlet* III i 59,
Quarles, *Emblemes* (Cambridge 1643) iii 11 (on *Ps*. lxix 15, 'Let not the water-
flood overflow me') and Vaughan's 'The Storm'. An erotic variant of the
topic, found e.g. in Petrarch, *Rime* clxxxix and Spenser, *F.Q*. III iv 8–10

       Thus to disburden sought with sad complaint.
720   O miserable of happy! Is this the end
       Of this new glorious world, and me so late
       The glory of that glory, who now become
       Accurst of blessed, hide me from the face
       Of God, whom to behold was then my highth
725   Of happiness: yet well, if here would end
       The misery, I deserved it, and would bear
       My own deservings; but this will not serve;
       All that I eat or drink, or shall beget,
       Is propagated curse. O voice once heard
730   Delightfully, *Increase and multiply*,
       Now death to hear! For what can I increase
       Or multiply, but curses on my head?
       Who of all ages to succeed, but feeling
       The evil on him brought by me, will curse
735   My head, Ill fare our ancestor impure,
       For this we may thank Adam; but his thanks
       Shall be the execration; so besides
       Mine own that bide upon me, all from me
       Shall with a fierce reflux on me redound,

('Huge sea of sorrow and tempestuous grief'), stems from Horace *Odes* I v.

x *720*. Broadbent 80 notices that 'the characters of *Paradise Lost* do not soliloquize until they have fallen; unfallen speech and gesture are directed always to another person, on the supreme model of light inter-reflected by Father and Son.' This the first of all complaints is made the subject of critical discriminations similar to those occasioned by the other genres worked into the poem (see ix 16*n*, 30–1*n*, etc.). Here, just causes of complaint are distinguished from unjust, Christian from unrepentant and unreasoning sorrow.

x *722*. Adam is probably meant here to have fallen into bad theology. He was not the glory of the world, but the 'glory of God' (*1 Cor*. xi 7).

x *728–9. propagated*] extended (*OED* 4); handed down from one generation to another (*OED* 1 d). Food prolongs life and thus extends the curse; while begetting children hands it on. Note also that eating and sex are jointly the concerns of the concupiscible faculty, which was often regarded as the especial field of operation of concupiscence or the 'body of sin' (*De doctrina* i 11, Columbia xv 193). Thus the eating and begetting itself might quite properly be called a *curse*.

x *730*. Cp. vii 530f, and see *Gen*. i 28.

x *736. For . . . Adam*] To Addison this seemed a colloquialism.

x *738–40. Mine own*] i.e., curses. On the repetition of *me* see l. 832*n*.   *redound*] Both in the physical sense 'flow back; overflow' (*OED* 4, 1 b) and the figurative 'recoil, come back' (of disgrace: *OED* 8).

740 On me as on their natural centre light
     Heavy, though in their place. O fleeting joys
     Of Paradise, dear bought with lasting woes!
     Did I request thee, Maker, from my clay
     To mould me man, did I solicit thee
745 From darkness to promote me, or here place
     In this delicious garden? As my will
     Concurred not to my being, it were but right
     And equal to reduce me to my dust,
     Desirous to resign, and render back
750 All I received, unable to perform
     Thy terms too hard, by which I was to hold
     The good I sought not. To the loss of that,
     Sufficient penalty, why hast thou added
     The sense of endless woes? Inexplicable
755 Thy justice seems; yet to say truth, too late,
     I thus contest; then should have been refused
     Those terms whatever, when they were proposed:
     Thou didst accept them; wilt thou enjoy the good,
     Then cavil the conditions? And though God
760 Made thee without thy leave, what if thy son
     Prove disobedient, and reproved, retort,

x 740–1. In the primary chain of discourse *light* means 'alight'; in the secondary, 'not heavy'. The curses might be expected to be light at their natural centre, since the force that returned them is there null. In view of the topicality of the science and the intricacy of the conceit we must suppose M. to have intended Adam's wit to seem positively Metaphysical.

x 743–4. The complaint condemned in *Is.* xlv 9: 'Woe unto him that striveth with his Maker! Let the potsherd strive with the potsherds of the earth. Shall the clay say to him that fashioneth it, What makest thou? or thy work, He hath no hands?'

x 748. *equal*] just.

x 754. *endless woes*] As Burden 186f remarks, it is unthinkable that such generalization of grief should have been approved by M., who always preferred to introduce rational discriminations. Adam, however, is not yet properly repentant.

x 758. *thou*] Adam takes first God's part, then his own, in an imaginary debate.

x 760–5. Cp. *Is.* xlv 10: 'Woe unto him that saith unto his father, What begettest thou? or to the woman, What hast thou brought forth?' Here, as at 743f, M. alludes to a Biblical curse, with an effect of dramatic irony. Even better than Adam, we can see how the curse of *Gen.* iii 14–19 will proliferate.   *election*] choice; but with the theological sense – predestination – as a strong overtone.

Wherefore didst thou beget me? I sought it not:
Wouldst thou admit for his contempt of thee
That proud excuse? Yet him not thy election,
765   But natural necessity begot.
God made thee of choice his own, and of his own
To serve him, thy reward was of his grace,
Thy punishment then justly is at his will.
Be it so, for I submit, his doom is fair,
770   That dust I am, and shall to dust return:
O welcome hour whenever! Why delays
His hand to execute what his decree
Fixed on this day? Why do I overlive,
Why am I mocked with death, and lengthened out
775   To deathless pain? How gladly would I meet
Mortality my sentence, and be earth
Insensible, how glad would lay me down
As in my mother's lap? There I should rest
And sleep secure; his dreadful voice no more
780   Would thunder in my ears, no fear of worse
To me and to my offspring would torment me

x 762. Following the punctuation of *Ed I*. *Ed II* has no point after *not*.

x 769. *doom*] judgment.

x 770. Alluding to the conclusion of God's curse on Adam at *Gen*. iii 19: 'Dust thou art, and unto dust shalt thou return.'

x 773. *this day*] Newton and Verity hold that this is a careless error, because the night of the day of the Fall was mentioned at l. 342; and the sun's subsequent rising at l. 329. But M. puts so much weight on the exact terms of the prohibition (both here and at ll. 49ff, 210f, and 1048ff) that we must count it extremely improbable that he should be vague about his chronology at precisely the stage most crucial from this point of view. Admittedly, the night following the Fall and Christ's judgment was mentioned at l. 342. But there is no reason why the present action should not be regarded as taking place on that same night, for l. 329 does not refer to a sunrise over Eden at all (see ll. 328–9n). Adam can speak of death delaying, since the day of the Fall *is* already over, reckoning in the Hebrew manner from sunset to sunset (see Introduction, 'Chronology'). But, lacking faith, he fears that God may be following some other system of reckoning whereby the day will not end until sunrise. Later, he overlooks a third system, whereby the 24-hour period starting with the noon of the Fall (ix 739) will not have run out until the 'hour precise' of the Expulsion, at xii 589. The completion of each period of reckoning of 'that day' brings with it a new peripeteia, and a fuller understanding of the depth of God's judgment. See ll. 49–53n, 854–9n, 923 and 1050n.

x 778. *mother's lap*] Cp. xi 536. Exclamation mark is probably intended after *lap*.

With cruel expectation. Yet one doubt
Pursues me still, lest all I cannot die,
Lest that pure breath of life, the spirit of man
785 Which God inspired, cannot together perish
With this corporeal clod; then in the grave,
Or in some other dismal place who knows
But I shall die a living death? O thought
Horrid, if true! Yet why? It was but breath
790 Of life that sinned; what dies but what had life
And sin? The body properly hath neither.
All of me then shall die: let this appease
The doubt, since human reach no farther knows.
For though the Lord of all be infinite,
795 Is his wrath also? Be it, man is not so,
But mortal doomed. How can he exercise
Wrath without end on man whom death must end?
Can he make deathless death? That were to make
Strange contradiction, which to God himself

x *783. all I*] all of me; cp. l. 792.

x *786–92.* Adam argues that since it was his spirit that sinned, and since death is the punishment for sin, it would be unjust for his body to die and not his spirit. See *De doctrina* i 13 (Columbia xv 227), where M. rejects 'the sophistical distinction, that although the whole man dies, it does not therefore follow that the whole of man should die'; also *ibid.* 219: 'What could be more absurd than that the mind, which is the part principally offending, should escape the threatened death; and that the body alone, to which immortality was equally allotted, before death came into the world by sin, should pay the penalty of sin by undergoing death, though not implicated in the transgression?' and *ibid.* 217–9: 'The death of the body is the loss or extinction of life. The common definition, which supposes it to consist in the separation of soul and body, is inadmissible. For what part of man is it that dies when this separation takes place? Is it the soul? This will not be admitted by the supporters of the above definition. Is it then the body? But how can that be said to die, which never had any life of itself? Therefore the separation of soul and body cannot be called the death of man.' M.'s belief in the joint extinction and joint resurrection of man's body and mind was not an eccentric heresy, but good Biblical theology; see the discussions in Kelley 13, G. Williamson, *SP* xxxii (1935) 553–79, corrected in N. H. Henry, *SP* xlviii (1951) 248. *living death*] *mors aeterna*, the fourth degree of death; on which see *De doctrina, ibid.* 251, also *De doctrina* i 33 *passim*. *yet why*] Why should this doubt (782) pursue me? *appease*] allay.

x *798–801.* Adam's theology is again at fault. While it is true that 'the power of God is not exerted in things which imply a contradiction' (*De doctrina* i 2, Columbia xiv 49), allowance should have been made for the possibility – which M. believed to be in fact the case – that man first dies, then is brought

800   Impossible is held, as argument
        Of weakness, not of power. Will he draw out,
        For anger's sake, finite to infinite
        In punished man, to satisfy his rigour
        Satisfied never; that were to extend
805   His sentence beyond dust and nature's law,
        By which all causes else according still
        To the reception of their matter act,
        Not to the extent of their own sphere. But say
        That death be not one stroke, as I supposed,
810   Bereaving sense, but endless misery
        From this day onward, which I feel begun
        Both in me, and without me, and so last
        To perpetuity; ay me, that fear
        Comes thundering back with dreadful revolution
815   On my defenceless head; both death and I
        Am found eternal, and incorporate both,

to life again at the day of judgment (e.g. *De doctrina* i 13, Columbia xv 249). *argument*] evidence, manifestation.

x *801*. In the early edns comma is wrongly inserted after *he*.

x *804–8*. As at ll. 798–801, Adam tries to comfort himself with an argument drawn from the Schools. Here the appeal is to an axiom, given in Stahlius' *Axiomata* (1651) xiv 4 in the form *Quod recipitur, per modum recipientis.* The axiom goes back through St. Thomas Aquinas (e.g. *Summa* I lxxxix 4) to Aristotle (*De anima* 424ᵃ); it was usually applied to the way in which things are received into the mind or the senses. Here Adam means that God would be going beyond a natural law about agents acting according to the capacities of their subjects, not their own.

x *810*. 'The second death, or the punishment of the damned, seems to consist partly . . . in eternal torment, which is called the punishment of sense' (*De doctrina* i 33, Columbia xvi 371).

x *813*. Cp. *Hamlet* III i 65–8: 'To sleep: perchance to dream: ay, there's the rub; / For in that sleep of death what dreams may come / . . . Must give us pause.'

x *816*. *Am*] Bentley objected to the use of a singular verb with a plural subject; but, as Darbishire² 305f points out, Adam is realizing that death has become one with himself. His own body and 'the body of this death' (*Rom.* vii 24) share a single identity and a single verb. M. had a precedent for the device in Spenser, *F.Q.* II xi 45f, where the antecedents of the pronouns are just uncertain enough to attract the attention momentarily. Arthur shares pronouns with Maleger, because Maleger is the body of sin in him.   *incorporate*] united in one body (*OED* I 1); also 'embodied, having a bodily form' (*OED* II 3); referring to the doctrine of the 'body of sin'; cp. l. 587, and see *n*.

Nor I on my part single, in me all
Posterity stands cursed: fair patrimony
That I must leave ye, sons; O were I able
820 To waste it all my self, and leave ye none!
So disinherited how would ye bless
Me now your curse! Ah, why should all mankind
For one man's fault thus guiltless be condemned,
If guiltless? But from me what can proceed,
825 But all corrupt, both mind and will depraved,
Not to do only, but to will the same
With me? How can they then acquitted stand
In sight of God? Him after all disputes
Forced I absolve: all my evasions vain,
830 And reasonings, though through mazes, lead me still
But to my own conviction: first and last
On me, me only, as the source and spring

x *817*. Not only are Death and I double, two in one, but so also am I, since I am both myself and my descendants. Cp. *2 Esdras* vii 48. *single*] 'one; solitary; unmarried; simple; free from duplicity'. In addition to the obvious resonances, there is a number symbolism: Adam reflects on his dyadic state (see vi 809–10n).

x *825*. Without holding the extreme Calvinist doctrine of Total Depravity, M. believed in a 'general depravity of the human mind', *communis . . . . mentis humanae pravitas* (*De doctrina* i 11, Columbia xv 194f).

x *826–7*. Cp. *Rom*. i 32: 'Who knowing the judgment of God, that they which commit such things are worthy of death, not only do the same, but have pleasure in them that do them.'

x *827*. *Ed I* omits *then*.

x *828–44*. Adam at last reaches full conviction of his sin; but being unable yet to pass to contrition, the next stage of repentance, he falls instead into despair. See *De doctrina* i 19 (Columbia xv 385): 'We may distinguish certain progressive steps in repentance; namely, conviction of sin, contrition, confession, departure from evil, conversion to good.' The present passage should be compared with Satan's similar fall into conscience-stricken despair, at iv 86–113; the progressive steps in repentance 'belong likewise in their respective degrees to the repentance of the unregenerate' (*De doctrina, ibid.*).

x *829*. It is didactically effective to have God's ways acknowledged to be just, by the man best placed of all to detect any injustice in the treatment accorded his species.

x *832*. Cp. Virgil, *Aen*. ix 427, where Nisus exposes himself to the Rutulians in an attempt to save Euryalus, acknowledging his own guilt with the cry *me, me, adsum, qui feci, in me convertite ferrum*; or 1 *Sam*. xxv 24, where Abigail to save Nabal cries 'Upon me, my lord, upon me let this iniquity be'. Broadbent 151f notes that Adam here repeats 'the central ploce on

Of all corruption, all the blame lights due;
So might the wrath. Fond wish! Couldst thou support
835   That burden heavier than the earth to bear
Than all the world much heavier, though divided
With that bad woman? Thus what thou desirest
And what thou fear'st, alike destroys all hope
Of refuge, and concludes thee miserable
840   Beyond all past example and future,
To Satan only like both crime and doom.
O conscience! into what abyss of fears
And horrors hast thou driven me; out of which
I find no way, from deep to deeper plunged!
845   Thus Adam to himself lamented loud
Through the still night, not now, as ere man fell,
Wholesome and cool, and mild, but with black air
Accompanied, with damps and dreadful gloom,
Which to his evil conscience represented
850   All things with double terror: on the ground
Outstretched he lay, on the cold ground, and oft
Cursed his creation, death as oft accused
Of tardy execution, since denounced
The day of his offence. Why comes not death,

"me"' in Christ's speech at iii 236 ('Behold me then, me for him, life for
life'): 'This is the spring of self-sacrifice which Adam and Eve draw on after
the Fall to recover sanity and love.' Cp. l. 738, and contrast the Satanic
travesty at ll. 494–8.

x *834*. i.e., would that the wrath, similarly, were confined to me.

x *835–6. world*] universe; not merely a repetition of *earth*.

x *840. future*] Stressed on the second syllable.

x *841*. Having heard God's distinction between Satan's sin and Adam's at
iii 129ff, we know this to be the false perspective of despair.

x *842*. But at iii 194–7 God said that he would place his 'umpire conscience'
within man 'as a guide', and that, if man listened, he would arrive safe in the
end. Conscience appears among the *dramatis personae* in M.'s drafts of a
tragedy on the Fall.

x *849–50*. 'Guiltiness'. . . is accompanied or followed by terrors of con-
science' (*De doctrina* i 12, Columbia xv 205).

x *853. denounced*] proclaimed as a warning, announced.

x *854–9*. Adam still thinks he can expect the terms of the prohibition to be
fulfilled literally, by his physical death. When this fails to occur, he begins
to discover the mysteriousness of divine justice. He is to learn that it is
tempered with mercy, but that its decrees are nevertheless eventually ac-
complished, though in an unexpected way. See l. 773n.   *acceptable*]
Stressed on the first syllable.

855   Said he, with one thrice acceptable stroke
To end me? Shall truth fail to keep her word,
Justice divine not hasten to be just?
But death comes not at call, justice divine
Mends not her slowest pace for prayers or cries.
860   O woods, O fountains, hillocks, dales and bowers,
With other echo late I taught your shades
To answer, and resound far other song.
Whom thus afflicted when sad Eve beheld,
Desolate where she sat, approaching nigh,
865   Soft words to his fierce passion she assayed:
But her with stern regard he thus repelled.
    Out of my sight, thou serpent, that name best
Befits thee with him leagued, thy self as false
And hateful; nothing wants, but that thy shape,
870   Like his, and colour serpentine may show
Thy inward fraud, to warn all creatures from thee
Henceforth; lest that too heavenly form, pretended
To hellish falsehood, snare them. But for thee
I had persisted happy, had not thy pride
875   And wandering vanity, when least was safe,
Rejected my forewarning, and disdained
Not to be trusted, longing to be seen
Though by the devil himself, him overweening
To over-reach, but with the serpent meeting
880   Fooled and beguiled, by him thou, I by thee,
To trust thee from my side, imagined wise,
Constant, mature, proof against all assaults,
And understood not all was but a show
Rather than solid virtue, all but a rib

x 860–1. The echo here is of the morning hymn of Adam and Eve; cp.
especially v 202–4.

x 867. Some commentators interpreted Eve's name etymologically in the
sense 'serpent'.

x 872. *pretended*] stretched in front as a covering (*OED* I 1).

x 873–4. Ed I has comma after *heart* and no comma after *dying*.

x 875–9 Adam takes a firm enough line now on Eve's wish to work sepa-
rately. With this harsh account of her motives, cp. ix 335–86 and *nn.*

x 884–8. *sinister*] left; corrupt, evil, base. Stressed on the second syllable.
For the true implication to be drawn from the side of Eve's origin, see
viii 465–6n. But here M. provides the recriminating Adam with fit ammu-
nition: mere stock antifeminist lore. Svendsen 184 illustrates the notion
that woman is formed from a bent rib, and therefore crooked, from such
misogynistic works as the *Malleus maleficarum* and Swetnam's *The Araign-
ment of Lewde, Idle, Froward, and Unconstant Women* (1615). Willet 38, citing

885 Crooked by nature, bent, as now appears,
     More to the part sinister from me drawn,
     Well if thrown out, as supernumerary
     To my just number found. O why did God,
     Creator wise, that peopled highest heaven
890 With spirits masculine, create at last
     This novelty on earth, this fair defect
     Of nature, and not fill the world at once
     With men as angels without feminine,
     Or find some other way to generate
895 Mankind? This mischief had not then befallen,
     And more that shall befall, innumerable
     Disturbances on earth through female snares,
     And strait conjunction with this sex: for either
     He never shall find out fit mate, but such
900 As some misfortune brings him, or mistake,
     Or whom he wishes most shall seldom gain
     Through her perverseness, but shall see her gained
     By a far worse, or if she love, withheld
     By parents, or his happiest choice too late
905 Shall meet, already linked and wedlock-bound
     To a fell adversary, his hate or shame:
     Which infinite calamity shall cause
     To human life, and household peace confound.
        He added not, and from her turned, but Eve

Mercerus and Calvin, argues that Eve must have been made from an extra
rib for Adam to have been perfectly created in the first instance. This rib
was 'supernumerarie ... above the usuall number or ribbes created of
purpose by the Lord, not as a superfluous or monstrous part, but as neces-
sarie for the creation of the woman, which God intended'. The supernumer-
ary syllable at the end of 887 may be intended mimetically; see Sprott 58f.
x 888–95. Another ancient piece of antifeminism; cp. Euripides, *Hippolytus*
616ff.   *defect / Of nature*] Aristotle had said in the *De generatione* (735^a25,
767^a35, 775^a15) that the female is a defective male. See Fletcher ii 177, and
Fr. W. T. Costello in *Ren N* viii (1955) 179–84, on a seventeenth-century
discussion of the point, in Keckermann's *Physica*. Keckermann discusses
whether the human female, being a defect of nature, is monstrous; but
decides not, on the grounds that women are common, monsters rare.
x 898–908. Those who attempt to find autobiographical allusions here ought
first to reckon with the exaggerated extremity of Adam's prognostications.
The almost comical multiplication of griefs accords with his present des-
pair, but hardly with M.'s own more rational view. Throughout the present
passage M. deliberately assigns to Adam culpable sentiments and erroneous
opinions.
x 899. *fit mate*] Contrast viii 450, and see *Gen.* ii 18.

910   Not so repulsed, with tears that ceased not flowing,
       And tresses all disordered, at his feet
       Fell humble, and embracing them, besought
       His peace, and thus proceeded in her plaint.
          Forsake me not thus, Adam, witness heaven
915   What love sincere, and reverence in my heart
       I bear thee, and unweeting have offended,
       Unhappily deceived; thy suppliant
       I beg, and clasp thy knees; bereave me not,
       Whereon I live, thy gentle looks, thy aid,
920   Thy counsel in this uttermost distress,
       My only strength and stay: forlorn of thee,
       Whither shall I betake me, where subsist?
       While yet we live, scarce one short hour perhaps,
       Between us two let there be peace, both joining,
925   As joined in injuries, one enmity
       Against a foe by doom express assigned us,
       That cruel serpent: on me exercise not
       Thy hatred for this misery befallen,
       On me already lost, me than thy self
930   More miserable; both have sinned, but thou
       Against God only, I against God and thee,
       And to the place of judgment will return,
       There with my cries importune heaven, that all
       The sentence from thy head removed may light
935   On me, sole cause to thee of all this woe,
       Me me only just object of his ire.
          She ended weeping, and her lowly plight,
       Immovable till peace obtained from fault
       Acknowledged and deplored, in Adam wrought
940   Commiseration; soon his heart relented

x *923*. See ll. 773*n*, 1050*n*.

x *926. doom*] The judgment of ll. 179–81. Appropriately it is Eve who re-
minds Adam of this, since the enmity was to be specifically between the
woman and the serpent. Cp. *Gen.* iii 15: 'I will put enmity between thee and
the woman.'

x *931*. Echoing iv 299, where the natures of man and woman are distin-
guished in similar terms: 'He for God only, she for God in him.' Cp. also
the Penitential Psalm, *Ps.* li 4: 'Against thee, thee only, have I sinned.'

x *936*. On an important resonance in the repeated *me*, see l. 832*n*.

x *937–40*. The difficulty in the syntax seems to arise from M.'s wish to
have *Immovable* qualify *plight* as well as *Adam*. In addition to the two chains
of discourse thus set up there is a third, in which *her lowly plight*=humbly
pledged herself. In that case it is Eve who cannot be moved from Adam's
feet, until he forgives her.

Towards her, his life so late and sole delight,
Now at his feet submissive in distress,
Creature so fair his reconcilement seeking,
His counsel whom she had displeased, his aid;
945 As one disarmed, his anger all he lost,
And thus with peaceful words upraised her soon.
   Unwary, and too desirous, as before,
So now of what thou know'st not, who desir'st
The punishment all on thy self; alas,
950 Bear thine own first, ill able to sustain
His full wrath whose thou feel'st as yet least part,
And my displeasure bear'st so ill. If prayers
Could alter high decrees, I to that place
Would speed before thee, and be louder heard,
955 That on my head all might be visited,
Thy frailty and infirmer sex forgiven,
To me committed and by me exposed.
But rise, let us no more contend, nor blame
Each other, blamed enough elsewhere, but strive
960 In offices of love, how we may lighten
Each other's burden in our share of woe;
Since this day's death denounced, if aught I see,
Will prove no sudden, but a slow-paced evil,
A long day's dying to augment our pain,
965 And to our seed (O hapless seed!) derived.
   To whom thus Eve, recovering heart, replied.
Adam, by sad experiment I know
How little weight my words with thee can find,
Found so erroneous, thence by just event
970 Found so unfortunate; nevertheless,

x *950–1.* Cp. ll. 834–7; Adam can grasp more clearly than Eve what the sentence of God may involve. Notice how he brings her back to rational discourse, to what she knows.

x *957.* Note the difference in Adam's attitude to the fault he denied at ix 1170ff. He may now be thought to exaggerate the degree of his own guilt.

x *959. elsewhere*] Either 'heaven' or the 'place of judgment' of l. 932 etc.

x *962–4.* Adam sees that the terms of the prohibition were not merely literal. Cp. ll. 854–9 and see *n*; also l. 773*n*.

x *965. derived*] imparted, passed on by descent, as in l. 77.

x *969. event*] consequence.

x *970. unfortunate*] Cp. l. 965, 'hapless seed'. Burden 181f comments on Adam's and Eve's concern for the ideology of the tragedy they see themselves as acting. Eve understands that the event is *just*, but wrongly imagines that the effect on posterity is a necessary or *certain woe* (l. 980). The necessitarian tragedy of pagan literature has become possible. Looked at from another

Restored by thee, vile as I am, to place
Of new acceptance, hopeful to regain
Thy love, the sole contentment of my heart
Living or dying, from thee I will not hide
975   What thoughts in my unquiet breast are risen,
Tending to some relief of our extremes,
Or end, though sharp and sad, yet tolerable,
As in our evils, and of easier choice.
If care of our descent perplex us most,
980   Which must be born to certain woe, devoured
By death at last, and miserable it is
To be to others cause of misery,
Our own begotten, and of our loins to bring
Into this cursed world a woeful race,
985   That after wretched life must be at last
Food for so foul a monster, in thy power
It lies, yet ere conception to prevent
The race unblest, to being yet unbegot.
Childless thou art, childless remain:
990   So death shall be deceived his glut, and with us two
Be forced to satisfy his ravenous maw.
But if thou judge it hard and difficult,
Conversing, looking, loving, to abstain
From love's due rights, nuptial embraces sweet,

point of view, the present phase is one in which God's justice is recognized, but not his mercy. Consequently the justice seems inflexible and rigid.

x *978. As in*] considering we are in. Possibly a Latinism; Richardson compares Cicero, *Epist. fam.* xii 2 (*nonnihil, ut in tantis malis, est profectum*) and iv 9.

x *979. descent*] descendants.   *perplex*] torment (a key word in *PL*: see ix 10–19*n*.)

x *982*. Some copies of *Ed I* have full stop after *misery*.

x *987. prevent*] cut off beforehand; preclude, render impossible (*OED* II 6, 8). At a time when the rate of puerperal and infant mortality was high and the expectation of life short, and when in consequence the begetting of as many children as possible was generally regarded as a sacred duty, Eve's sentiment would seem reprehensible, even shocking. M. uses violent strategies to bring home the seriousness of man's fallen state–and the cosmic role of hope.

x *989–90*. All previous editors have moved *So Death* back to the end of l. 989, in the interests of metrical regularity. But this may be philistinism. The line division as its stands in *Ed I*, *Ed II*, and three subsequent edns is perhaps intended to mime first the deficiency of childlessness (l. 989 defective), then the glut denied to Death (l. 990 hypermetrical).

995   And with desire to languish without hope,
        Before the present object languishing
        With like desire, which would be misery
        And torment less than none of what we dread,
        Then both our selves and seed at once to free
1000 From what we fear for both, let us make short,
        Let us seek death, or he not found, supply
        With our own hands his office on our selves;
        Why stand we longer shivering under fears,
        That show no end but death, and have the power,
1005 Of many ways to die the shortest choosing,
        Destruction with destruction to destroy.
            She ended here, or vehement despair
        Broke off the rest; so much of death her thoughts
        Had entertained, as dyed her cheeks with pale.
1010 But Adam with such counsel nothing swayed,
        To better hopes his more attentive mind
        Labouring had raised, and thus to Eve replied.
            Eve, thy contempt of life and pleasure seems
        To argue in thee something more sublime
1015 And excellent than what thy mind contemns;
        But self-destruction therefore sought, refutes
        That excellence thought in thee, and implies,
        Not thy contempt, but anguish and regret
        For loss of life and pleasure overloved.

x *995. without*] On the first-syllable accentuation, implying emphasis, see ii 892*n*. Cp. Dante, *Inf.* iv 42, 'without hope we live in desire'.

x *996. object*] Eve.

x *1007. vehement*] passionate; usually explained etymologically as *vehe-lacking + mens* mind. Cp. 'mindless' at ix 431, and see ix 358*n*.

x *1013–24.* In 'Milton and the Mortalist Heresy', *SP* xxxii (1935) 553–79, esp. 576f, G. Williamson relates these lines to a contemporary controversy about suicide; citing Charleton's defence of Epicurus on self-homicide and John Adams's *Essay concerning Self-Murther* (1700), where M. is said to have made 'the first man argue against self-murder from the Light of Nature'. The passage may also be taken more broadly, with Horrell 420f and perhaps also with Broadbent 98, as a discrimination between Stoic extremity (exemplified earlier by the devils of ii 562–9) and Christian patience. In his *Commonplace Book*, under the head 'Death self-inflicted', M. notes treatments of suicide in Dante (*Inf.* xiii) and in Sidney's *Arcadia* ('whether lawfull, disputed with exquisite reasoning': Yale i 371). M. himself regarded suicides as moved by a 'perverse hatred of self' (*De doctrina* ii 8, Columbia xvii 201), and thought they should be placed in the class denoted in *Ps.* lv 23: 'Bloody and deceitful men shall not live out half their days' (*ibid.* i 8, Columbia xv 93). Cp. also *SA* 505ff.

1020 Or if thou covet death, as utmost end
Of misery, so thinking to evade
The penalty pronounced, doubt not but God
Hath wiselier armed his vengeful ire than so
To be forestalled; much more I fear lest death
1025 So snatched will not exempt us from the pain
We are by doom to pay; rather such acts
Of contumacy will provoke the highest
To make death in us live: then let us seek
Some safer resolution, which methinks
1030 I have in view, calling to mind with heed
Part of our sentence, that thy seed shall bruise
The serpent's head; piteous amends, unless
Be meant, whom I conjecture, our grand foe
Satan, who in the serpent hath contrived
1035 Against us this deceit: to crush his head
Would be revenge indeed; which will be lost
By death brought on our selves, or childless days
Resolved, as thou proposest; so our foe
Shall scape his punishment ordained, and we
1040 Instead shall double ours upon our heads.
No more be mentioned then of violence
Against our selves, and wilful barrenness,
That cuts us off from hope, and savours only
Rancour and pride, impatience and despite,
1045 Reluctance against God and his just yoke
Laid on our necks. Remember with what mild
And gracious temper he both heard and judged
Without wrath or reviling; we expected
Immediate dissolution, which we thought
1050 Was meant by death that day, when lo, to thee

x *1024–8.* Adam delivers the fruits of the labouring of his 'more attentive mind' at ll. 786–816.   *doom*] judgment.   *make death in us live*] Cp. 'living death' l. 788 and see *n.*

x *1030–40.* The curse of ll. 164–81 is brought in here because (as Burden 178f remarks, citing Calvin, *Inst.* II xiii 2) it was pronounced in the first place in order to prevent Eve from giving way to despair. The dawning perception of man's (and implicitly Christ's) role is also a vital part of Adam's progression to true repentance and faith. Burden 31ff notes that Adam's rejection of suicide, and acceptance of the role predetermined by the curse, are experienced as free choices; whereas Satan's wilful serpent role is by x 510 involuntary.

x *1045. reluctance*] the act of struggling *against* something; resistance (OED 1).

x *1050.* Notice how Adam's understanding of the mysterious, figurative

Pains only in child-bearing were foretold,
And bringing forth, soon recompensed with joy,
Fruit of thy womb: on me the curse aslope
Glanced on the ground, with labour I must earn
1055 My bread; what harm? Idleness had been worse;
My labour will sustain me; and lest cold
Or heat should injure us, his timely care
Hath unbesought provided, and his hands
Clothed us unworthy, pitying while he judged;
1060 How much more, if we pray him, will his ear
Be open, and his heart to pity incline,
And teach us further by what means to shun
The inclement seasons, rain, ice, hail and snow,
Which now the sky with various face begins
1065 To show us in this mountain, while the winds
Blow moist and keen, shattering the graceful locks
Of these fair spreading trees; which bids us seek
Some better shroud, some better warmth to cherish
Our limbs benumbed, ere this diurnal star
1070 Leave cold the night, how we his gathered beams
Reflected, may with matter sere foment,

sense of Christ's sentence (ll.1031ff) is bound up with recognition of the figurative terms of the original prohibition (on which see viii 323–33*n*). He now grasps that the day of the Fall ended at sunset after all (see ll. 49–53*n*, 773*n*), and that it is now another day, Day 33. There is, however, a further surprise in store for him in this connection; see xii 588–9*n*.

x *1052–3. soon recompensed*] Alludes to *John* xvi 21: 'A woman when she is in travail hath sorrow, because her hour is come: but as soon as she is delivered of the child, she remembereth no more the anguish, for joy that a man is born into the world'–Christ's metaphor for the joy there will be at his victory.   *Fruit of thy womb*] A similar allusion to Christ, *via Luke* i 42.

x *1053–5.* Referring to Christ's words at ll. 201–5.

x *1060–81.* M. restores technology to its rightful context, by making it a matter of Christ's instruction, according to human needs. Adam's vision of a modest technological progress is sustained by the surrounding expressions of confidence in Christ's mercy: because God is merciful, life can continue and considerations of human convenience become appropriate. Nevertheless, as Broadbent 103 points out, it is only after the Fall that Adam has to think about applied science at all. See v 349*n*, 396*n*.

x *1060–1.* Biblical diction: cp. *Ps.* xxiv 4, cxix 36, 112; *1 Pet.* iii 12.

x *1066. shattering*] Cp. *Lycidas* 5.

x *1068. shroud*] shelter (*OED* sb[1]3); also 'loppings of a tree, branches cut off' (*OED* sb.[3]), continuing the thought of the preceding line more concretely.

x *1070–80.* M. blends hard primitivism and soft primitivism in his account of man's earliest state. The rationalistic explanation of the discovery of fire

Or by collision of two bodies grind
The air attrite to fire, as late the clouds
Justling or pushed with winds rude in their shock
1075   Tine the slant lightning, whose thwart flame driven
        down
Kindles the gummy bark of fir or pine,
And sends a comfortable heat from far,
Which might supply the sun: such fire to use,
And what may else be remedy or cure
1080   To evils which our own misdeeds have wrought,
He will instruct us praying, and of grace
Beseeching him, so as we need not fear
To pass commodiously this life, sustained

as a first step in civilization is characteristic of hard primitivism (see Panofsky[2] 41). But this whole logical development is made here to depend on a disturbance of the macrocosm caused by the Fall and the loss of the Golden Age, so that the world view is ultimately soft-primitivistic.

x *1070. how*] Follows *seek* (l. 1067).

x *1071. foment*] cherish; but alluding also to Lat. *fomes* (tinder). Adam's formidable intellect seems at first to be capable of envisaging quite a sophisticated method of making fire: focusing the sun's rays onto dry combustibles with a parabolic mirror. *Reflected*, however, could mean simply 'deflected' (*OED* I 1); in which case refraction through any transparent solid that will act as a lens need be all that is involved. (Cowley (81) could even imagine a 'Burning-Glass of Ice'.) Note the secondary sense in *Reflected*, appeased (*OED* I 2 b: see foll. *n*, and iv 30*n*).

x *1073. attrite*] Primarily 'ground down by friction' (*OED* 1); but the word had also a common technical theological sense which is highly appropriate in the present context: 'having an imperfect sorrow for sin, a bruising that does not amount to the utter crushing of contrition' (*OED* s.v. *Attrite* 2 and *Attrition* 4, citing Tucker: 'Three stages in the passage from vice to virtue: attrition, contrition, and repentance'). The diction of the present line shows the working of Adam's mind in the direction of true contrition, a stage that he has reached by ll. 1091 and 1103.

x *1074. Justling*] jostling. A spelling and perhaps a phonetic variant.

x *1075–8. Tine*] A variant form of *tind*: ignite.   *thwart*] transverse. Lightning is given as the origin of fire in Lucretius, v 1091–4.

x *1078–81. supply*] take the place of (*OED* 11).   *of*] for. Before the Fall man was 'guiltless of fire': see v 349*n*, 396*n*, ix 387–92*n*. M. has at several points found it hard to imagine prelapsarian mundane activities not dependent on technology; once he had even to invoke angels to get out of the difficulty. For he was committed to the view that arts as we know them exist to repair the damage caused by the Fall (a view that was commonplace in the Renaissance, though seldom more eloquently expressed than by Thomas Wilson in the Pref. to his *Arte of Rhetorique* (1560)).

By him with many comforts, till we end
1085   In dust, our final rest and native home.
What better can we do, than to the place
Repairing where he judged us, prostrate fall
Before him reverent, and there confess
Humbly our faults, and pardon beg, with tears
1090   Watering the ground, and with our sighs the air
Frequenting, sent from hearts contrite, in sign
Of sorrow unfeigned, and humiliation meek.
Undoubtedly he will relent and turn
From his displeasure; in whose look serene,
1095   When angry most he seemed and most severe,
What else but favour, grace, and mercy shone?
     So spake our father penitent, nor Eve
Felt less remorse: they forthwith to the place
Repairing where he judged them prostrate fell
1100   Before him reverent, and both confessed
Humbly their faults, and pardon begged, with tears
Watering the ground, and with their sighs the air
Frequenting, sent from hearts contrite, in sign
Of sorrow unfeigned, and humiliation meek.

THE END OF THE TENTH BOOK

---

x *1088–92.* Having passed on from conviction of sin Adam, now *contrite* (cp. 1103), is ready for confession, the third stage of repentance. See ll. 828–44n.   *Frequenting*] filling, crowding (*OED* 6; not a Latinism).

x *1090.* Cp. *Is.* xvi 9: 'I will water thee with my tears, O Heshbon'; and perhaps Virgil, *Aen.* xi 191, *spargitur et tellus lacrimis.*

x *1091.* Another allusion to the Penitential Psalm: 'The sacrifices of God are a broken spirit: a broken and a contrite heart, O God, thou wilt not despise' (*Ps.* li 17).

x *1096–7.* At last, explicit recognition of God's *mercy* is joined to recognition of his justice. God's mercy is the subject of the whole speech ll. 1046–96; but the word itself is held back until the last line. (See iii 134: 'mercy first and last shall brightest shine'.) In the next line, 1097, Adam is for the first time called *penitent.* No doubt M. wanted to draw attention to the sequence of phases: recognition of God's mercy leads to repentance, just as the latter leads to faith. See *De doctrina* i 19 (Columbia xv 387): 'Repentance, in re-generate man, is prior to faith.'. . . Therefore that sense of the divine mercy, which leads to repentance, ought not to be confounded with faith, as it is by the greater number of divines.'

x *1098–1104.* Repeating ll. 1086–92, modulated into narrative discourse (only the last two verses remain identical). The same device was used at iv 641–56.

Paradise Lost

BOOK XI

The Argument

The Son of God presents to his Father the prayers of our first parents now repenting, and intercedes for them: God accepts them, but declares that they must no longer abide in Paradise; sends Michael with a band of cherubim to dispossess them; but first to reveal to Adam future things: Michael's coming down. Adam shows to Eve certain ominous signs; he discerns Michael's approach, goes out to meet him: the angel denounces their departure. Eve's lamentation. Adam pleads, but submits: the angel leads him up to a high hill, sets before him in vision what shall happen till the flood.

> Thus they in lowliest plight repentant stood
> Praying, for from the mercy-seat above
> Prevenient grace descending had removed
> The stony from their hearts, and made new flesh
> 5 Regenerate grow instead, that sighs now breathed
> Unutterable, which the spirit of prayer
> Inspired, and winged for heaven with speedier flight

xi 1. *stood*] There is no literal contradiction of 'prostrate' at x 1099, since *stood* means 'remained' (*OED* I 15 d; cp. 'stand free', 'stand alone'). In a secondary chain of discourse, *in lowliest plight . . . stood* extends such idioms as 'stood in need' (*OED* s.v. *Stand* IV 46). The apparent contradiction is treated as a deliberate paradox by John E. Parish in *English Miscellany*, ed. M. Praz, xv (Rome 1964) 89–102. Adam and Eve are prostrate in sin, but raised by regeneration.

xi 2. *mercy-seat*] The solid gold covering laid on the Ark of the Covenant, God's resting-place. In *Exod*. xxv 18 it is described as having two cherubim of gold at its ends; and these were interpreted as a type of intercession in heaven. Cp. i 381–7 and see *n*.

xi 3. *Prevenient*] antecedent to human action (*OED* 2). Prevenient grace precedes the determination of the human will, which remains free, nevertheless, to accept or reject it. It is the condition and the initiation of all activity leading to justification. The doctrine was based on such texts as *Ps*. lix 10 (Vulg.: *Deus meus, misericordia eius praeveniet me*), *Rom*. viii 30 and *2 Tim*. i 9.

xi 4. Cp. *Ezek*. xi 19: 'And I will give them one heart, and I will put a new spirit within you; and I will take the stony heart out of their flesh, and will give them an heart of flesh.'

xi 5–7. Cp. *Rom*. viii 26: 'Likewise the Spirit also helpeth our infirmities: for we know not what we should pray for as we ought: but the Spirit itself maketh intercession for us with groanings which cannot be uttered.'

> Than loudest oratory: yet their port
> Not of mean suitors, nor important less
> 10 Seemed their petition, than when the ancient pair
> In fables old, less ancient yet than these,
> Deucalion and chaste Pyrrha to restore
> The race of mankind drowned, before the shrine
> Of Themis stood devout. To heaven their prayers
> 15 Flew up, nor missed the way, by envious winds
> Blown vagabond or frustrate: in they passed
> Dimensionless through heavenly doors; then clad
> With incense, where the golden altar fumed,

xi *8. port*] bearing.

xi *10–14.* Deucalion is a mythic analogue to Noah. Advised by his father Prometheus, he built a ship and escaped the universal flood. When the waters subsided, he and his wife Pyrrha consulted the oracle of Themis; and their prayers were effectual, for they were told how to repair the loss of mankind by throwing behind them stones, which became men and women. Bentley and Empson[2] 179f perversely take *less ancient* to imply that *Genesis* is an old fable too. But M. can hardly have meant that. What he says is that the pagan *ancient pair* is *less ancient* than the Biblical ancient pair. In narratives professing to describe the origin of the present human race, juniority brings discredit. The introduction of the Deucalion myth is particularly appropriate to the context of Adam's repentance, because it was allegorized as a symbol of conversion. See, e.g., the interpretation in George Sandys[2] 33: '*God is said in the Gospell* to be able of stones to raise up children unto Abraham: *the sence not unlike, though diviner; meaning the ingrafting of the Gentiles into his faith, hardned in sinne through ignorance and custome.* So the giving us hearts of flesh instead of those of stone, *is meant by our conversion*' (cp. esp. l. 4).

xi *14–16.* No doubt the 'violent cross wind' of iii 487, which 'blows . . . / Into the devious air', and from there into Limbo, those given to 'painful superstition and blind zeal' (iii 452).

xi *17–18. Dimensionless*] without physical extension (*OED* 1 a), because spiritual, not material. See *Ps.* cxli 2: 'Let my prayer be set forth before thee as incense; and the lifting up of my hands as the evening sacrifice'; also *Rev.* viii 3: 'And another angel came and stood at the altar, having a golden censer; and there was given unto him much incense, that he should offer it with the prayers of all saints upon the golden altar which was before the throne.' Dismissing M. M. Ross's complaint that the heaven of *PL* is too Catholic, Broadbent 157 points out that its equipment comes 'from the Jewish temple direct, not via a Roman cathedral'. Broadbent thinks that M. vacillates between an apocalyptic and an emblematic heaven. But if we grant M.'s initial premise about the corporeality of spirits, the appointments of his heaven will seem quite appropriate and consistent.

By their great intercessor, came in sight
20 Before the Father's throne: them the glad Son
Presenting, thus to intercede began.
    See Father, what first fruits on earth are sprung
From thy implanted grace in man, these sighs
And prayers, which in this golden censer, mixed
25 With incense, I thy priest before thee bring,
Fruits of more pleasing savour from thy seed
Sown with contrition in his heart, than those
Which his own hand manuring all the trees
Of Paradise could have produced, ere fallen
30 From innocence. Now therefore bend thine ear
To supplication, hear his sighs though mute;
Unskilful with what words to pray, let me
Interpret for him, me his advocate
And propitiation, all his works on me
35 Good or not good ingraft, my merit those
Shall perfect, and for these my death shall pay.
Accept me, and in me from these receive
The smell of peace toward mankind, let him live
Before thee reconciled, at least his days

xi *19. intercessor*] Christ; see *Heb.* ix 24; 'Christ is . . . entered . . . into heaven itself, now to appear in the presence of God for us.'
xi *24.* Cp. the 'golden vials full of odours, which are the prayers of saints' (*Rev.* v 8).
xi *26.* The 'sweet savour' of acceptable sacrifices or peace-offerings is a commonplace in the Bible (e.g. *Ezek.* xx 41). There is also a semantic resonance with *savoury* used of man's sacramental or forbidden fruit at v 84, 401, ix 741.
xi *26–30.* Varying the metaphor of the parable of the sower, in *Mark* iv 14–20, with the help of *Heb.* xiii 15: 'Let us offer the sacrifice of praise to God continually, that is, the fruit of our lips giving thanks to his name.' *manuring*] cultivating.
xi *31.* 'The Spirit itself maketh intercession for us with groanings which cannot be uttered' (*Rom.* viii 26).
xi *32–44.* The emphatic repetition of *me* (the rhetorical figure ploce) helps to connect the passage with Christ's similar offer of atonement at iii 236ff. See x 832*n*.
xi *32.* Some copies of *Ed I* omit comma.
xi *33.* Cp. *1 John* ii 1f: 'We have an advocate with the Father, Jesus Christ the righteous: And he is the propitiation for our sins.'
xi *35. engraft*] Keeps up the horticultural metaphor, and alludes to the Pauline allegory of regeneration and incorporation in Christ as a grafting, in *Rom.* xi 16ff.

40   Numbered, though sad, till death, his doom (which I
       To mitigate thus plead, not to reverse)
       To better life shall yield him, where with me
       All my redeemed may dwell in joy and bliss,
       Made one with me as I with thee am one.
45   To whom the Father, without cloud, serene.
       All thy request for man, accepted Son,
       Obtain, all thy request was my decree:
       But longer in that Paradise to dwell,
       The law I gave to nature him forbids:
50   Those pure immortal elements that know

xi *40–1. doom*] judgment. Cp. x 76, 'that I may mitigate their doom'.
From the divine stand-point, death is a mercy, not a punishment.   *num-*
bered] limited. But *at least his days numbered* is not entirely explicable as an
allusion to *Ps.* xc 12: 'teach us to number our days, that we may apply our
hearts unto wisdom.' The broad sense is Let man be reconciled with the
monad – made one with me (l. 44) – and belong with the numbered good,
instead of with the unnumbered evil (see vi 767*n*). In the Bible, 'numbered'
often means 'elect': see, e.g., *Exod.*, xxx 12, 'then shall they give every man
a ransom for his soul unto the Lord, when thou numberest them'. But one
suspects that M. here also hints at the number symbolism governing the
days of the poem's action.
xi *43–4*. Cp. *John* xvii 11, 21–3: 'Holy Father, keep through thine own name
those whom thou hast given me, that they may be one, as we are. . . . that
they also may be one in us.'
xi *45. without cloud*] without darkening of his countenance (*OED* s.v.
Cloud II 10; cp. iii 262 above); but alluding also to the clouds of mystery
from which God speaks to angels or to men (see *Num.* xi 25, *Mark* ix 7; and
cp. iii 378ff, vi 28). On the accentuation *wìthout*, implying emphasis, see ii
892*n*.
xi *49–57*. The Expulsion is not presented as a punishment, but as a further
physically inevitable consequence of the change in man's nature at the Fall.
Ironically, Adam earlier (x 805) appealed to 'nature's law' against what he
considered God's harshness; whereas now it turns out that God is merciful,
yet cannot change the harsh consequences of natural law.   *purge him off*]
Cp. ii 138–42, where Belial predicts that if the devils returned to heaven
'the ethereal mould / Incapable of stain would soon expel / Her mischief,
and purge off the baser fire'. Cp. *Lev.* xviii 25: 'The land is defiled: there-
fore I do visit the iniquity thereof upon it, and the land itself vomiteth out
her inhabitants.' On the 'purer air' of Paradise, see iv 153*n*. 'Of pure now
purer' there is countered by *of incorrupt / Corrupted* here.   *distempered*]
disturbed the proper proportion of humours or elements; disturbed the
condition of the air, weather, etc. Dissolution was thought to be held at bay
only by a proper tempering of conflicting qualities, so that decay and death
were physical consequences of sin.

No gross, no unharmonious mixture foul,
Eject him tainted now, and purge him off
As a distemper, gross to air as gross,
And mortal food, as may dispose him best
55 For dissolution wrought by sin, that first
Distempered all things, and of incorrupt
Corrupted. I at first with two fair gifts
Created him endowed, with happiness
And immortality: that fondly lost,
60 This other served but to eternize woe;
Till I provided death; so death becomes
His final remedy, and after life
Tried in sharp tribulation, and refined
By faith and faithful works, to second life,
65 Waked in the renovation of the just,
Resigns him up with heaven and earth renewed.
But let us call to synod all the blest
Through heaven's wide bounds; from them I will not
        hide
My judgments, how with mankind I proceed,
70 As how with peccant angels late they saw;
And in their state, though firm, stood more confirmed.
        He ended, and the Son gave signal high
To the bright minister that watched, he blew

xi 59. *fondly*] foolishly.

xi 64. *faithful works*] Cp. 'faith not void of works', xii 427. M. shared the
general Protestant belief in the doctrine of Justification by Faith. See *De
doctrina* i 22 (Columbia xvi 39): 'We are justified by faith without the works
of the law, but not without the works of faith.' In the long progression of
stages in regeneration, repentance has been achieved, and we are now enter-
ing the stage of faith. See x 828–44n, 1096–7n.

xi 65. Cp. 'the resurrection of the just', *Luke* xiv 14.

xi 66. 'Nevertheless we, according to his promise, look for new heavens
and a new earth, wherein dwelleth righteousness' (*2 Pet.* iii 13).

xi 67. *synod*] assembly. Cp. the synod of gods at vi 156, and the synod of
stars at x 661.

xi 73–6. Perhaps also the 'ethereal trumpet' that gave the signal for battle
at vi 60.   *Oreb*] Horeb; referring to the occasion when God descended
to the sound of a trumpet, to deliver the Ten Commandments on Mt Sinai
(*Exod.* xix 16; see vi 56–60n).   *general doom*] the Last Judgment; see *1
Thess.* iv 16: 'The Lord himself shall descend from heaven with a shout,
with the voice of the archangel, and with the trump of God: and the dead in
Christ shall rise first.' The concern with renovation in the passage immediate-
ly preceding accords with an allusion also to *1 Cor.* xv 52: 'The trumpet

His trumpet, heard in Oreb since perhaps
75   When God descended, and perhaps once more
To sound at general doom. The angelic blast
Filled all the regions: from their blissful bowers
Of amarantin shade, fountain or spring,
By the waters of life, where'er they sat
80   In fellowships of joy: the sons of light
Hasted, resorting to the summons high,
And took their seats; till from his throne supreme
The almighty thus pronounced his sovereign will.
    O sons, like one of us man is become
85   To know both good and evil, since his taste
Of that defended fruit; but let him boast
His knowledge of good lost, and evil got,
Happier, had it sufficed him to have known
Good by it self, and evil not at all.
90   He sorrows now, repents, and prays contrite,
My motions in him, longer than they move,

shall sound, and the dead shall be raised incorruptible, and we shall be changed.' Cp. *Nativity Ode* 157ff.

xi *77*. On the *regions* or layers of atmosphere distinguished in the meteorology of M.'s time, see i 515–16n, iii 562n.   *blissful bowers*] Empson 108 rightly compares the nuptial bower of Adam and Eve.

xi *78. amarantin*] On the unwithering amarant, symbol of immortality, see iii 353–7n.

xi *79. waters of life*] Cp. the 'fount of life' and 'river of bliss' at iii 357–9, and see *nn*.

xi *84–98*. Cp. *Gen*. iii 22f: 'And the Lord God said, Behold, the man is become as one of us, to know good and evil: and now, lest he put forth his hand, and take also of the tree of life, and eat, and live for ever: Therefore the Lord God sent him forth from the garden of Eden.' Empson 108 detects 'a mysterious tone of connivance'; but Burden's explanation (7f) is to be preferred: namely, that M. fears that the *Genesis* speech will sound like a confession of inadvertency, and so makes his God speak even more ironically. Cp. Willet (55), who believes 'with Mercerus and Calvin, that God speaketh ironically', or with Rupert of Deutz that Adam 'was so farre from being as God, but he was almost become as the divill'.

xi *86. defended*] forbidden (*OED* I 3 a).

xi *90. contrite*] Stressed on the second syllable. Sorrow for sin and contrition are separate stages of repentance; see x 828–44n, 1073n.

xi *91. motions*] inward promptings, stirrings of the soul, impulses. Used in a semi-technical way, in theological or homiletic contexts, of God's working in the soul (*OED* 9 b, citing Walton: 'God ... mark'd him with ... a blessing of obedience to the motions of his blessed Spirit').

His heart I know, how variable and vain
Self-left. Lest therefore his now bolder hand
Reach also of the tree of life, and eat,
95 And live for ever, dream at least to live
For ever, to remove him I decree,
And send him from the garden forth to till
The ground whence he was taken, fitter soil.
        Michael, this my behest have thou in charge,
100 Take to thee from among the cherubim
Thy choice of flaming warriors, lest the fiend
Or in behalf of man, or to invade
Vacant possession some new trouble raise:
Haste thee, and from the Paradise of God
105 Without remorse drive out the sinful pair,

xi 91–3. The syntax seems to be difficult because *I know* is held back, mimeti-cally, *longer* even than *His heart*. The sense is: 'I know his heart will outlast these impulses to good, and I know how variable and vain it will become if left to itself.'

xi 98. *fitter soil*] A curious expression, since it seems to imply the Scholastic distinction between the *donum supernaturale* of Adam's superadded 'original righteousness' and the *pura naturalia* or ordinary properties of human nature *per se* (see N. P. Williams, *The Ideas of the Fall and of Original Sin* (1927) 363). The ground from which Adam was taken (vii 535–8n above) is the dust of *pura naturalia*; from now on this is the nature he will have to work with.

xi 99. *Michael*] See vi 44n. 'It would not have been so proper for the *sociable spirit Raphael* to have executed this order: but as Michael was the principal Angel employ'd in driving the rebel Angels out of Heaven, so he was the most proper to expel our first parents too out of Paradise' (Newton). There is also the consideration that Michael is the apocalyptic angel; for the visions shown to Adam are essentially apocalyptic visions of history. Michael's name occurs in the *dramatis personae* of M.'s first draft of a tragedy on the Fall (see p. 419 above).

xi 102. *Or . . . or*] either . . . or.   *in behalf of man*] At first this seems surprising, and justly seized on by Empson([2] 165) as evidence of Satan's nobility in the eyes of God. But *in behalf of* quite usually meant 'with regard to; in respect of' in M.'s time (Adams 119). And in any case, the passage is ironic.

xi 102–3. *invade . . . possession*] encroach on my property while it has no possessor. In law, 'vacant effects' were 'such as are abandoned for want of an Heir, after the Death or Flight of their former Owner' (Bailey, 1730, *cit. OED* s.v. *Vacant* A 1 c). Continuing the ironic tone of the previous para-graph: see ll. 84–98n.

xi 105. *without remorse*] The angels feel pity readily, as v 566 and x 25 show. But Burden 36 points out that remorse would here be wrong, since it would imply injustice on the part of God.

From hallowed ground the unholy, and denounce
To them and to their progeny from thence
Perpetual banishment. Yet lest they faint
At the sad sentence rigorously urged
110 For I behold them softened and with tears
Bewailing their excess, all terror hide.
If patiently thy bidding they obey,
Dismiss them not disconsolate; reveal
To Adam what shall come in future days,
115 As I shall thee enlighten, intermix
My Covenant in the woman's seed renewed;
So send them forth, though sorrowing, yet in peace:
And on the east side of the garden place,
Where entrance up from Eden easiest climbs,
120 Cherubic watch, and of a sword the flame
Wide waving, all approach far off to fright,
And guard all passage to the tree of life:
Lest Paradise a receptacle prove
To spirits foul, and all my trees their prey,
125 With whose stolen fruit man once more to delude.
    He ceased; and the archangelic power prepared
For swift descent, with him the cohort bright
Of watchful cherubim; four faces each

xi *106. denounce*] proclaim, often with an implication of warning (*OED* 3).

xi *108. faint*] lose heart; become depressed (*OED* 1).

xi *111. excess*] transgression; outrage (*OED* 3, 4).

xi *115–16.* i.e., intermix the theme of the Covenant, the bond between the God of Israel and his people, whereby they paid sacrificial dues–later the spiritual bond, whereby righteousness, made perfect by the gift of grace, was the offering.

xi *118–22.* 'So he drove out the man; and he placed at the east of the garden of Eden Cherubims, and a flaming sword which turned every way, to keep the way of the tree of life' (*Gen.* iii 24); cp. xii 590ff. On cherubim as guards of Paradise, see iv 549–50*n*; on the *sword* see xii 643*n*.

xi *123. receptacle*] Stressed on the third syllable.

xi *128–9.* For the source of the four-faced cherubim in *Ezekiel*, see vi 749–59*n* above.   *double Janus*] *Ianus quadrifrons*, the four-headed variant of the ancient god Janus, who presided over gates. The comparison is particularly appropriate in view of the fact that man is going out into a world of change, seasonal and historical. For the four heads of Janus, like the four doors of his temple, were interpreted as meaning the four seasons of the year (Valeriano 384). See A. H. Gilbert in *PMLA* liv (1939) 1026–30, where St Augustine's connection of the four faces with the four quarters of the earth is cited.

Had, like a double Janus, all their shape
130 Spangled with eyes more numerous than those
Of Argus, and more wakeful than to drowse,
Charmed with Arcadian pipe, the pastoral reed
Of Hermes, or his opiate rod. Mean while
To resalute the world with sacred light
135 Leucothea waked, and with fresh dews embalmed
The earth, when Adam and first matron Eve
Had ended now their orisons, and found
Strength added from above, new hope to spring
Out of despair, joy, but with fear yet linked;
140 Which thus to Eve his welcome words renewed.
    Eve, easily may faith admit, that all
The good which we enjoy, from heaven descends;
But that from us aught should ascend to heaven
So prevalent as to concern the mind
145 Of God high-blest, or to incline his will,
Hard to belief may seem; yet this will prayer,
Or one short sigh of human breath, upborne
Even to the seat of God. For since I sought
By prayer the offended Deity to appease,
150 Kneeled and before him humbled all my heart,
Methought I saw him placable and mild,

xi *129–33.* Cp. *Ezek.* i 18, where the cherubim have rings 'full of eyes'.
Argus was set to guard Io, because he had a hundred eyes which watched by
turns; but Mercury lulled all the eyes to sleep with his reed pipe (Ovid, *Met.*
i 682–4) and finally with his *virga somnifera (ibid.* 671f, 716). Like Janus, Argus
was interpreted as a temporal or astronomical symbol; in the words of
Pontanus 'Argus is Heaven; aethereall fires his eyes, / That wake by turnes;
and Starres that set and rise' (Sandys[2] 37).
xi *134–5. Leucothea*] the Roman Mater Matuta, goddess of the dawn. She
is in place here because, as Ovid tells us, she 'keeps handmaidens afar from
the thresholds of her temple' (*Fasti* vi 479ff).   *embalmed*] Now with a
sinister overtone: the earth is decaying.
xi *137. Ed I* has comma after *found.*
xi *139.* Burden 199 remarks that M. balances cause for woe very carefully
against cause for joy. The idea of the 'fortunate Fall' does not cancel out
tragedy. Some copies of *Ed I* have comma after *linked.*
xi *141. faith*] The first mention, indicating a new phase in Adam's regener-
ation. For the previous phases, see x 828–44*n*, 1073*n*, 1096–7*n*; xi 3*n*, 91*n*.
xi *142.* Cp. *Jam.* i 17: 'Every good gift and every perfect gift is from above,
and cometh down from the Father of lights, with whom is no variableness,
neither shadow of turning.' *Ed I* has no point after *descends.*
xi *144. prevalent*] efficacious, influential, powerful (*OED* 1).
xi *148. seat*] The mercy-seat of l. 2 above.

Bending his ear; persuasion in me grew
That I was heard with favour; peace returned
Home to my breast, and to my memory
155 His promise, that thy seed shall bruise our foe;
Which then not minded in dismay, yet now
Assures me that the bitterness of death
Is past, and we shall live. Whence hail to thee,
Eve rightly called, Mother of all Mankind,
160 Mother of all things living, since by thee
Man is to live, and all things live for man.
      To whom thus Eve with sad demeanour meek.
Ill worthy I such title should belong
To me transgressor, who for thee ordained
165 A help, became thy snare; to me reproach
Rather belongs, distrust and all dispraise:
But infinite in pardon was my judge,
That I who first brought death on all, am graced
The source of life; next favourable thou,
170 Who highly thus to entitle me vouchsafest,
Far other name deserving. But the field
To labour calls us now with sweat imposed,
Though after sleepless night; for see the morn,
All unconcerned with our unrest, begins
175 Her rosy progress smiling; let us forth,
I never from thy side henceforth to stray,
Where'er our day's work lies, though now enjoined
Laborious, till day droop; while here we dwell,
What can be toilsome in these pleasant walks?

xi *154–8*. Referring to the curse on the serpent at x 175–81; the implication
of which—removal 'far off' of the 'instant stroke of death' (x 210f)–Adam
had been too dismayed to grasp, until the maturer reflections of x 962f and
1030–40. At first he expected to die, according to the literal terms of the
prohibition, on 'that day' when he transgressed. See viii 323–33*n*, x 773*n*.
Now, however, he errs on the other side; like Agag (who said 'surely the
bitterness of death is past' just before Samuel hewed him in pieces, *1 Sam.*
xv 32f) he has spoken too soon. The bitterness of the Expulsion and of the
historical consequences of the Fall lie ahead.
xi *158*. Adam addresses Eve with the 'holy salutation used / Long after to
blest Mary, second Eve' (v 386f), since it is as a type of Mary that Eve has the
promise applied to her.
xi *159*. 'And Adam called his wife's name Eve; because she was the mother of
all living' (*Gen.* iii 20).
xi *162. sad*] serious.
xi *165. help*] See x 899*n*.
xi *171–2*. Referring to the curse of Adam, x 205 and *Gen.* iii 19.

180   Here let us live, though in fallen state, content.
             So spake, so wished much-humbled Eve, but fate
         Subscribed not; nature first gave signs, impressed
         On bird, beast, air, air suddenly eclipsed
         After short blush of morn; nigh in her sight
185   The bird of Jove, stooped from his airy tower,
         Two birds of gayest plume before him drove:
         Down from a hill the beast that reigns in woods,
         First hunter then, pursued a gentle brace,
         Goodliest of all the forest, hart and hind;
190   Direct to the eastern gate was bent their flight.
         Adam observed, and with his eye the chase
         Pursuing, not unmoved to Eve thus spake.
             O Eve, some further change awaits us nigh,
         Which heaven by these mute signs in nature shows
195   Forerunners of his purpose, or to warn
         Us haply too secure of our discharge
         From penalty, because from death released
         Some days; how long, and what till then our life,
         Who knows, or more than this, that we are dust,
200   And thither must return and be no more.
         Why else this double object in our sight
         Of flight pursued in the air and o'er the ground
         One way the self-same hour? Why in the east
         Darkness ere day's mid-course, and morning light
205   More orient in yon western cloud that draws

xi *182–90. signs*] Not 'signs of the Fall; the blight now beginning to fall
on all nature' as Hughes (those signs were perceptible to Adam back at x
715), but specifically omens. In all three omens described, the sovereign of a
realm of creation displays his power in a changed and grimmer form. The
sun in eclipse darkens the air; the eagle (*bird of Jove*) stoops on two other birds;
and the lion pursues a hart and a hind (contrast the harmless lion of iv 343, but
cp. the earlier anticipation of fallen animality when Satan stalks his prey at
iv 402ff). The direction of the chase shows that the omens foreshadow the
Expulsion (cp. esp. xii 638f): the two beasts, like the two birds, correspond
to the human couple.
xi *185. stooped*] having swooped (a technical term in falconry); see viii 351*n*.
tower] lofty flight; soaring (but cp. *L'Allegro* 43). *Ed I* and *Ed II* have the form
'tour', common in the seventeenth century. A pun with tour = circuit
(*OED* 12) is possible.
xi *196. secure*] confident; over-confident.
xi *204.* Cp. *Is.* xvi 3: 'Execute judgment; make thy shadow as the night in
the midst of the noonday.'
xi *205. orient*] bright; but punning on the sense 'eastern', here paradoxical.
The light in the west is the glory of Michael's 'cohort bright' (l. 127),

O'er the blue firmament a radiant white,
And slow descends, with something heavenly fraught.
  He erred not, for by this the heavenly bands
Down from a sky of jasper lighted now
210 In Paradise, and on a hill made alt,
A glorious apparition, had not doubt
And carnal fear that day dimmed Adam's eye.
Not that more glorious, when the angels met
Jacob in Mahanaim, where he saw
215 The field pavilioned with his guardians bright;
Nor that which on the flaming mount appeared
In Dothan, covered with a camp of fire,
Against the Syrian king, who to surprise
One man, assassin-like had levied war,
220 War unproclaimed. The princely hierarch
In their bright stand, there left his powers to seize
Possession of the garden; he alone,
To find where Adam sheltered, took his way,
Not unperceived of Adam, who to Eve,
225 While the great visitant approached, thus spake.
  Eve, now expect great tidings, which perhaps
Of us will soon determine, or impose
New laws to be observed; for I descry
From yonder blazing cloud that veils the hill
230 One of the heavenly host, and by his gait
None of the meanest, some great potentate

already placed to drive Adam and Eve to the east gate. Note also that Michael was associated with the west wind (Valeriano 549).

xi *209. jasper*] See iii 363–4*n*, and *Rev.* iv 3, where God in judgment is 'to look upon like a jasper and a sardine stone'.   *lighted*] descended (*OED* v.¹ II 6), arrived (*OED* v.¹ II 10 b); but also 'shone' (*OED* v.² 1).

xi *210. alt*] a halt. A military term usually occurring only in the phrase 'to make alt'. (Alt = 'alto; high flight' was a different word.)

xi *212. carnal fear*] fleshly fear; the animal's terror of the spiritual.

xi *213–15.* See *Gen.* xxxii 1–2. On account of the meeting Jacob called the place *Mahanaim*, meaning 'Armies' or 'Camps' (cp. M.'s *pavilioned*).

xi *216–20.* See *2 Kings* vi 13–17.   *one man*] Elisha, whom the king of Syria besieged Dothan to catch. When Elisha's servant told him of this he was unconcerned; at his prayer God opened the servant's eyes 'and, behold, the mountain was full of horses and chariots of fire round about Elisha'.

xi *220. hierarch*] A title also of Raphael; cp. v 468.

xi *221. stand*] station, place of standing (*OED* II 11); but in view of the recent omen of the eagle (ll. 185f) the special application in falconry – 'an elevated resting place of a hawk' (*OED* II 14) – may have a grim relevance.

xi *227. determine*] make an end.

Or of the thrones above, such majesty
Invests him coming; yet not terrible,
That I should fear, nor sociably mild,
235 As Raphael, that I should much confide,
But solemn and sublime, whom not to offend,
With reverence I must meet, and thou retire.
He ended; and the archangel soon drew nigh,
Not in his shape celestial, but as man
240 Clad to meet man; over his lucid arms
A military vest of purple flowed
Livelier than Meliboean, or the grain
Of Sarra, worn by kings and heroes old
In time of truce; Iris had dipped the woof;
245 His starry helm unbuckled showed him prime
In manhood where youth ended; by his side
As in a glistering zodiac hung the sword,
Satan's dire dread, and in his hand the spear.
Adam bowed low, he kingly from his state

xi *232-3*. Cp. *Ps.* xciii 1: 'The Lord reigneth, he is clothed with majesty;
the Lord is clothed with strength, wherewith he hath girded himself: the
world also is stablished, that it cannot be moved.' The allusion suggests that
Michael's clothing, described at ll. 240-8, embodies aspects of deity.
xi *233*. The punctuation of *Ed I*; *Ed II* has question mark after *coming*.
xi *234*. Cp. v 221, where Raphael is called 'the sociable spirit'; and see l.
99*n* above.
xi *240-8*. Contrast the description of Raphael's wings at v 277-85, and see
n there. Raphael's wings were regal purple, gold and blue, but Michael's
vest is only purple. He comes without wings, because he is to talk about
terrestrial matters, about fallen mundane history, and because he is to
prepare Adam for a more lowly role. There is also the reason that spiritual
forms now frighten Adam (l. 212).   *Meliboean*] The vividness of purple
from Meliboea on the coast of Thessaly was anciently famous. A cloak of
purpura Meliboea is a prize of honour in Virgil, *Aen.* v 251.   *grain*] Cp.
v 285 and see *n*.   *Sarra*] Tyre, famous for its dye; see 2 *Chron.* ii 14.
Iris . . . woof] Cp. *Comus* 83, 'sky-robes spun out of Iris' woof'. *Iris*, because
the iris flower was the *lilium purpureum*; but also—as in *Nativity Ode* 143—
because the rainbow is a sign of God's Covenant or *truce* with his people.
See ll. 879ff.   *zodiac*] Michael's belt is compared with the belt of the
celestial sphere occupied by the zodiacal constellations. (Hughes's obscure
suggestion that *zodiac* meant 'belt' in Greek seems to be without founda-
tion). The zodiac is brought in because the belt, like the *helm*, is *starry*; but
also because the zodiac corresponds to the specifically post-lapsarian course
of the sun—Michael's mission relates to the new order of things. On the
sword, see vi 250-1*n*.
xi *249-51*. The abrupt beginning contrasts with the more leisurely meeting

250   Inclined not, but his coming thus declared.
       Adam, heaven's high behest no preface needs:
       Sufficient that thy prayers are heard, and Death,
       Then due by sentence when thou didst transgress,
       Defeated of his seizure many days
255   Given thee of grace, wherein thou mayst repent,
       And one bad act with many deeds well done
       Mayst cover: well may then thy Lord appeased
       Redeem thee quite from Death's rapacious claim;
       But longer in this Paradise to dwell
260   Permits not; to remove thee I am come,
       And send thee from the garden forth to till
       The ground whence thou wast taken, fitter soil.
       He added not, for Adam at the news
       Heart-strook with chilling gripe of sorrow stood,
265   That all his senses bound; Eve, who unseen
       Yet all had heard, with audible lament
       Discovered soon the place of her retire.
       O unexpected stroke, worse than of death!
       Must I thus leave thee Paradise? Thus leave
270   Thee native soil, these happy walks and shades,
       Fit haunt of gods? Where I had hope to spend,
       Quiet though sad, the respite of that day
       That must be mortal to us both. O flowers,
       That never will in other climate grow,
275   My early visitation, and my last
       At even, which I bred up with tender hand
       From the first opening bud, and gave ye names,

of Adam with Raphael, when it was Adam who spoke first. Cp. v 358–71
and see *n.*   *state*] dignity of demeanour (*OED* II 18).
xi *254. Defeated . . . seizure*] Either 'frustrated, cheated in his attempt to
seize' or (looking forward to *redeem* at 258) 'deprived, dispossessed of
what he had seized, his seizin' (*OED* s.v. *Defeat* 5 and 7a, b; *Seizure* 1 a and
2). The diction is legal. See viii 323–33*n*, x 773*n*.
xi *256–7.* Cp. *1 Pet.* iv 8.
xi *258. quite*] Either 'completely' or 'free, clear, rid of' (adj., since obsolete).
It is hard to say whether the adverb or the adjective forms the primary
chain of discourse.
xi *259–62.* In accordance with the solemnity of his commission, Michael
delivers the divine decree verbatim (see ll. 96–8). As Newton remarks, it is
on these words that the whole catastrophe of the poem depends.
xi *264. Heart-strook*] heart-stricken.   *gripe*] grip, spasm.
xi *267. retire*] withdrawal (*OED* 1).
xi *272. respite*] delay; extension (*OED* I 1).

Who now shall rear ye to the sun, or rank
Your tribes, and water from the ambrosial fount?
280   Thee lastly nuptial bower, by me adorned
With what to sight or smell was sweet; from thee
How shall I part, and whither wander down
Into a lower world, to this obscure
And wild, how shall we breathe in other air
285   Less pure, accustomed to immortal fruits?
Whom thus the angel interrupted mild.
Lament not Eve, but patiently resign
What justly thou hast lost; nor set thy heart,
Thus over-fond, on that which is not thine;
290   Thy going is not lonely, with thee goes
Thy husband, him to follow thou art bound;
Where he abides, think there thy native soil.
Adam by this from the cold sudden damp
Recovering, and his scattered spirits returned,
295   To Michael thus his humble words addressed.

xi *278-9.* On seventeenth-century interest in the naming and classification of species, see viii 343–56n.   *ambrosial fount*] More definite than iv 240, where we are told that the fountain of Paradise 'ran nectar'. In visual art, the fountain of Paradise was very often a Fountain of Life, shown as an architecturally elaborate well to connect it with the well of living water of *John* iv 10 (cp. l. 416 below). (See, e.g., Jan Gossart's *Adam and Eve* in the Queen's Collection; and the Bedford Book of Hours, B. M. Add. MS. 18850 fol. 14, where the fountain flows out as four distributaries.) On its significance see ix 71–5n above. Since the Expulsion must deprive Adam of natural access to immortality, the courses of the rivers are changed after the Fall; see iv 237–8n; ix 71–5n; xi 829–38n.
xi *283. to*] compared with.
xi *284-5. Less pure*] See ll. 49–57n above, on the need for 'gross [to be purged] to air as gross'. Bentley asked, more grossly still, what the fruits have to do with Eve's breathing; provoking a fine reply from Empson(2 162): 'In the tired repeated rhythm of the last two lines, she leaves floating, as things already far off, all that makes up for her the "atmosphere" of Paradise.' But M. may well have meant this nostalgic effect, moving as it is, to be yet another test of our discrimination. If it were true that Eve was *accustomed* exclusively to *immortal fruits*, she would not now be leaving Paradise (contrast i 2, 'mortal taste'). Michael's interruption, indeed, may be provoked by her insensitivity in venturing to mention fruit at this juncture.
xi *287. patiently*] See ll. 360–4n.
xi *289. over-fond*] Two words in *Ed I*.
xi *293-4. damp*] dazed or stupefied condition; depression of spirits (OED 4, 5). It was the scattering of Adam's animal *spirits*, the spirits controlling sensation (iv 805, v 484) that had 'his senses bound' at l. 265.

Celestial, whether among the thrones, or named
Of them the highest, for such of shape may seem
Prince above princes, gently hast thou told
Thy message, which might else in telling wound,
300   And in performing end us; what besides
Of sorrow and dejection and despair
Our frailty can sustain, thy tidings bring,
Departure from this happy place, our sweet
Recess, and only consolation left
305   Familiar to our eyes, all places else
Inhospitable appear and desolate,
Nor knowing us nor known: and if by prayer
Incessant I could hope to change the will
Of him who all things can, I would not cease
310   To weary him with my assiduous cries:
But prayer against his absolute decree
No more avails than breath against the wind,
Blown stifling back on him that breathes it forth:
Therefore to his great bidding I submit.
315   This most afflicts me, that departing hence,
As from his face I shall be hid, deprived
His blessed countenance; here I could frequent,
With worship, place by place where he vouchsafed
Presence divine, and to my sons relate;
320   On this mount he appeared; under this tree
Stood visible, among these pines his voice
I heard, here with him at this fountain talked:
So many grateful altars I would rear
Of grassy turf, and pile up every stone
325   Of lustre from the brook, in memory,

xi *296–8*. Only after the Fall does Adam bother about the social status of the different ranks of angels.

xi *307–10*. The first of Adam's many errors in his dialogue with Michael. We know from the parable of Luke xviii 5–7 that importunate prayers are in fact effective.   can] knows (*OED* I 1); the secondary sense 'is able' helps to make the irony clear.

xi *316*. Cp. Cain's response to his curse: 'Behold, thou hast driven me out this day from the face of the earth; and from thy face shall I be hid; and I shall be a fugitive and a vagabond in the earth' (*Gen.* iv 14).

xi *315–33*. Newton contrasts Adam's reasons for regret with Eve's. But this is unfair to Eve. Adam's speech is more considered, and in any case he has to make the necessary errors about local devotion, in order to provoke Michael's instruction of ll. 335ff.

xi *325–6*. The patriarchs were accustomed to raise altars wherever God appeared to them.

Or monument to ages, and thereon
Offer sweet smelling gums and fruits and flowers:
In yonder nether world where shall I seek
His bright appearances, or footstep trace?
330 For though I fled him angry, yet recalled
To life prolonged and promised race, I now
Gladly behold though but his utmost skirts
Of glory, and far off his steps adore.
　　　To whom thus Michael with regard benign.
335 Adam, thou know'st heaven his, and all the earth.
Not this rock only; his omnipresence fills
Land, sea, and air, and every kind that lives,
Fomented by his virtual power and warmed:
All the earth he gave thee to possess and rule,
340 No despicable gift; surmise not then
His presence to these narrow bounds confined
Of Paradise or Eden: this had been
Perhaps thy capital seat, from whence had spread
All generations, and had hither come
345 From all the ends of the earth, to celebrate
And reverence thee their great progenitor.
But this pre-eminence thou hast lost, brought down
To dwell on even ground now with thy sons:
Yet doubt not but in valley and in plain
350 God is as here, and will be found alike
Present, and of his presence many a sign

xi *327.* Burnt offerings would not be appropriate for Paradise. See x 1078–
81*n*; also *Gen.* iv 3, where Cain makes an offering of fruit.
xi *329.* Following *Ed I*: *Ed II* misplaces a hyphen: 'foot step-trace'.
xi *331. promised race*] the race whose destiny it is to bruise Satan; see x 175–92.
xi *332–3.* For the dazzling *skirts* of God cp. iii 380 and see iii 375–82*n*.
xi *335–54.* Michael corrects Adam's new-found fallacious enthusiasm for
local devotions, pious superstitions and tradition generally. In M.'s view
all such enthusiasm is definitely postlapsarian, and, it seems, to be closely
associated with depression of spirits. For the omnipresence of the God of
PL see vii 168f. Cp. *Jer.* xxiii 24, 'Do not I fill heaven and earth? saith the
Lord.'　　　*Not this rock only*] Alludes to Jesus' warning to the woman of
Samaria: 'The hour cometh, when ye shall neither in this mountain, nor
yet at Jerusalem, worship the Father' (John iv 21). But M.'s substitution of
rock for *mountain* (Vulg. *monte*, Gk. ὄρει) clearly strikes at the successors of
St Peter, the rock, for their excessive reliance on tradition and their belief
that God's presence is in some sense *confined* within the *narrow bounds* of the
institutional church.　　　*Fomented*] cherished, nurtured.　　　*virtual*] potent,
exerting influence. The omnipresence of God is the theme of *Ps.* cxxxix,
which tradition ascribed to Adam himself (see Charles ii 17).

Still following thee, still compassing thee round
With goodness and paternal love, his face
Express, and of his steps the track divine.
355 Which that thou mayst believe, and be confirmed
Ere thou from hence depart, know I am sent
To shew thee what shall come in future days
To thee and to thy offspring; good with bad
Expect to hear, supernal grace contending
360 With sinfulness of men; thereby to learn
True patience, and to temper joy with fear
And pious sorrow, equally inured
By moderation either state to bear,
Prosperous or adverse: so shalt thou lead
365 Safest thy life, and best prepared endure
Thy mortal passage when it comes. Ascend
This hill; let Eve (for I have drenched her eyes)
Here sleep below while thou to foresight wakest,

xi 355. The purpose of the vision is to *confirm* Adam's faith. In *De doctrina*
i 25 (Columbia xvi 67–9) M. traces the 'progressive steps' and the causes
leading to 'assurance of salvation, and the final perseverance of the saints':
'Both regeneration and increase are accompanied by confirmation, or
preservation in the faith, which is also the work of God.' Faith is the
theme of Bk xi, as repentance was the theme of Bk x. See x 828–44*n*, 1073*n*,
1096–7*n*.

xi 357. On the precedents for Adam's vision of the future, see l. 423*n*.

xi 360–4. *pious sorrow*] Burden (189) takes this to mean 'pity', and concludes
that the darker attitude to be learned is pity and terror: the correct response to
the series of tragedies Adam is shown.   *True patience*] By implication to be
distinguished from the false stubborn philosophical patience of ii 569 and
ix 920. Burden cites Calvin, *Inst.* III viii 8, where true Christian patience is
contrasted with the impracticable 'too exact and rigid patience' of the
Stoics and the puritans. Originally, however, *moderation* was itself a Stoic
and Aristotelian principle assimilated by Christianity. Hughes recalls that
Petrarch wrote a book *De remediis utriusque fortunae*.

xi 366. *mortal passage*] death. As Burden 189f remarks, the ascent of the
mount of contemplation and of truth is the legitimate ascent that contrasts
with the false easy ascent by flying (v 87).

xi 367. *drenched*] Probably 'administered medicine to' (*OED* 1); though
normally the word would refer to medicine drunk, as at ii 73–4. In view of
the other references earlier to Mercury's 'opiate rod' in connection with
Michael's cherubim (l. 133), it may be relevant that in Cabbalistic thought
Michael was sometimes identified with Mercury (Valeriano 549C; but see
vii 72*n* above.

xi 368–9. *foresight*] vision of the future. The resemblance with viii 40ff,
where Eve retired to leave Adam and Raphael alone, is superficial; in any case,

As once thou slept'st, while she to life was formed.
370   To whom thus Adam gratefully replied.
Ascend, I follow thee, safe guide, the path
Thou lead'st me, and to the hand of heaven submit,
However chastening, to the evil turn
My obvious breast, arming to overcome
375   By suffering, and earn rest from labour won,
If so I may attain. So both ascend
In the visions of God: it was a hill
Of Paradise the highest, from whose top
The hemisphere of earth in clearest ken
380   Stretched out to the amplest reach of prospect lay.
Not higher that hill nor wider looking round,
Whereon for different cause the tempter set
Our second Adam in the wilderness,
To show him all earth's kingdoms and their glory.
385   His eye might there command wherever stood
City of old or modern fame, the seat
Of mightiest empire, from the destined walls

Eve is here to have her own series of dreams (see xii 595). A deeper link, to which Michael himself draws attention, is with viii 452–78, where Adam slept yet remained conscious during the creation of Eve. This link is based on a typological correspondence. Earlier, Adam had a vision of the creation of the first Eve; now he is to have a vision of the 'race' leading up to the second Eve and the second creation. Burden 188 notes that the instruction of Adam makes him typical man, whereas before he was only archetypal. At the end of the poem he will go out into the world with the kind of historical knowledge ordinary fallen men have.

xi 372. *submit*] Broadbent (98) sees submission as a characteristic note of M.'s portrayal of Christian patience, distinguishing it from 'stoical apathy'. cp. xii 597.

xi 374. *obvious*] exposed, vulnerable (*OED* 2).

xi 375–6. Combining echoes of *Heb.* iv 11 and *Phil.* iii 11; with the implication that his aim is resurrection.

xi 377–84. MacCaffrey 61 includes this vista among the poem's series of synoptic godlike visions; noting that the episodes that follow are conceived as static tableaux. But see ll. 429–47n for a different opinion. M. here alludes to the ascent of Ezekiel: 'The hand of the Lord was upon me, and brought me thither. In the visions of God brought he me into the land of Israel, and set me upon a very high mountain, by which was as the frame of a city on the south' (*Ezek.* xl 1–2). Cp. *Matt.* iv 8, where the devil to tempt Christ 'taketh him up into an exceeding high mountain, and sheweth him all the kingdoms of the world, and the glory of them'; also *PR* iii 251ff.   *ken*] sight, view (*OED* 3).

xi 380. *Ed I* omits *the.*

> Of Cambalu, seat of Cathaian khan
> And Samarchand by Oxus, Temir's throne,
> *390*   To Paquin of Sinaean kings, and thence
> To Agra and Lahor of great mogul
> Down to the golden Chersonese, or where
> The Persian in Ecbatan sat, or since
> In Hispahan, or where the Russian czar

xi *387–8. Cambalu*] Stressed on the first syllable, Cambaluc, capital of Cathay. M. uses the popular form. Its walls are *destined* because they will exist, but do not yet.

xi *388–95*. The Asian kingdoms are arranged symmetrically according to an elaborately centralized Baroque pattern. *Chersonese*, the only place without a visible ruler, occupies nevertheless the central position of sovereignty. Next to it come the mogul's and the Persian's realms, each with a pair of capitals; then the Sinaean kings' and the czar's, each with a single capital. Finally, on each flank there is a pair of realms associated with the khans and the sultans respectively. Each of these except *Turchestan* has its capital. Thus: *Cambalu* and *Samarchand*; *Paquin*; *Agra* and *Lahor*; (CHERSONESE-OPHIR); *Ecbatan* and *Hispahan*; *Mosco*; *Bizance* and (*Turchestan*). Or: 1. Cathay and 2. Tartary; 3. China; 4. the mogul's empire; 5. (CHERSONESE-OPHIR); 6. Persia; 7. Russia; 8. Byzantium and 9. (Turkestan). The reason why the golden Chersonese should be assigned the place of sovereignty will only become evident when the pattern is repeated with the African realms that follow (see ll. 396–407*n*).

xi *389. Samarchand*] Samarkand, near the *Oxus* river, the capital of Timur, Marlowe's Tamburlaine.   *khan*] The title given to Chingiz Khan's successors, who during the Middle Ages ruled not only the Tartar and Mongol tribes but also Cathay. They were known in Europe as the great khans (chams) either of Cathay or (as in the case of Timur) of Tartary.

xi *390. Paquin*] Pekin, capital of China, which was regarded as a separate kingdom from Cathay (see x 289–93*n*).   *Sinaean*] Chinese.

xi *391*. Two areas of northern India.   *Agra*] A kingdom in the centre, whose capital, a city of the same name, is described by Heylyn as 'the Seat Royall, of late times, of the Great Moguls'.   *Lahor*] Lahore, in the Punjab, to the north-west.   *great mogul*] The designation, among Europeans, of the emperor of eastern India.

xi *392. golden Chersonese*, so called from its wealth, was in *India extra Gangem*, the extreme east part of the continent – what would now be called Malacca in the Malay Peninsula. Josephus identified it with the Ophir which supplied King Solomon with gold (*Antiq.* VIII vi 4); see ll. 396–407*n*, 400*n* below.

xi *393–4. Ecbatan*] Ecbatana, the ancient summer capital of the Persian kings; Ispahan became a capital city in the sixteenth century, when the Safavid dynasty moved their residence there from Kazvin.

395   In Mosco, or the sultan in Bizance,
       Turchestan-born; nor could his eye not ken
       The empire of negus to his utmost port
       Ercoco and the less maritime kings
       Mombaza, and Quiloa, and Melind,

xi 395–6. *Mosco*] Moscow.   *Bizance*] Byzantium, Constantinople, capital
of the Turkish sultan.   *Turchestan-born*] The sultans belonged to a tribe
that came originally from Turkestan, a region in central Asia between
Mongolia and the Caspian. Note that Turkestan, having no capital city
associated with it, falls into a somewhat separate category from the other
realms. See l. 405n below.

xi 396–407. *nor . . . ken*] Signalizes a transition to the African continent. Here
the kingdoms form a pattern which resembles that formed by the Asian
kingdoms in several respects (see ll. 388–95n). Again there are nine, and
again the last falls into a distinct category (here because it is European).
Thus: 1. Abyssinia; 2. Mombaza; 3. Quiloa; 4. Melind; 5. SOFALA-OPHIR;
6. Congo; 7. Angola; 8. Almanzor's Barbary; 9. (Rome). The central po-
sition is occupied by Sofala, which, like Chersonese in the earlier pattern,
is *thought Ophir*. It becomes clear that the idea underlying both patterns is the
attribution of secret sovereignty to Ophir. This is partly to be explained by
the connection between Ophir and King Solomon, the only Biblical ruler
named or implied anywhere in the passage. Solomon was the just divider,
so that he is associated here with the fifth position among the rulers, since the
fifth digit divides the others justly (Fowler 34, citing Iamblichus, etc.).
Moreover, the 'incorruptible' five, in its pentacle (pentagram) form, was
Solomon's mystic seal or knot. M.'s emphasis on the vacancy of the central
seat of sovereignty, however, suggests that his intention is also larger and
deeper. The pattern reflects both the absence of true sovereignty in the
natural world, and the unseen sovereignty of Christ. This symbolism
would be based on a verse in the Forty-fifth *Psalm*, which was interpreted
typologically as a prophecy of the majesty and grace of Christ's kingdom:
'upon thy right hand did stand the queen in gold of Ophir' (*Ps.* xlv 9);
cp. *Is.* xiii 12f: 'I will make a man more precious than fine gold; even a man
than the golden wedge of Ophir. Therefore I will shake the heavens, and the
earth shall remove out of her place, in the wrath of the Lord of hosts, and
in the day of his fierce anger.' Thus the centrality of Ophir here repeats the
structure of the poem as a whole (see Introduction, 'Numerology, p. 23
above). On the just centrality of Solomon's Temple *in meditullio mundi*,
see Giorgio 158ᵛ.

xi 397–8. The Abyssinian empire; *negus* was the hereditary title of the em-
perors. *Ercoco*, mod. Arkiko, is a port on the Red Sea. Scan *marìtime*. *Ed I*
spells 'Maritine', *Ed II* 'Maritim', both current forms until the eighteenth
century.

xi 399. *Mombaza*] Mombasa.   *Melind*] Malindi.   *Quiloa*] Kilwa.
The first two are on the coast of Kenya, the last, of Tanzania.

400   And Sofala thought Ophir, to the realm
      Of Congo, and Angola farthest south;
      Or thence from Niger flood to Atlas mount
      The kingdoms of Almansor, Fez and Sus,
      Morocco and Algiers, and Tremisen;
405   On Europe thence, and where Rome was to sway
      The world: in spirit perhaps he also saw
      Rich Mexico the seat of Motezume,

xi *400. Sofala*] (M. chooses to stress on the first syllable.) The name of a port in what is now Mozambique. From its wealth it was supposed (as Purchas and even the sceptical Heylyn inform us) to be the land of Ophir. The purity of the gold of Ophir was proverbial, and is given a typical moral application by Sir Thomas Browne in *Christian Morals* i 28: 'There is dross, alloy, and embasement in all human tempers; and he flieth without wings, who thinks to find ophir or pure metal in any.' Ophir gold is repeatedly mentioned in connection with the building of Solomon's Temple, so that it became endowed with the meaning 'wise sovereignty'. This symbolism was confirmed by *Gen.* ii 11 and x 29, where Ophir is connected through Havilah with Pison, the river of Paradise that according to Philo signifies Prudence (see Fowler[2] 290). Thus Adam's view is of the moral course of the river: a prospect of wise government and of the secret lordship of Christ through the ages (see ll. 396–407).

xi *402–4. Almanzor*] Mansur ('Victorious') was the surname of countless Mohammedan princes; but the one known to European writers as Almanzor was Ibn Abi'Amir Mahommed, the Caliph of Cordova (939–1002). The five territories named were all parts of Barbary.   *Sus*] Tunis.   *Tremisen*] Tlemcen, part of Algeria.

xi *405.* The numerological placement of Barbary and Rome in a position similar to that of Byzantium (New Rome) and Turkestan in the earlier array (see ll. 388–95*n*, 396–407*n*) probably implies an uncomplimentary analogy between Papal and Saracen empires. The point is made in a different way by the ambiguous *sway*. True sovereignty lies not in external secular power, but in the power of the invisible incorruptible 'true Church'.

xi *406. in spirit*] Even from this vantage-point Adam could not physically see the other hemisphere.

xi *407–11.* Montezuma's empire had been spoiled by Cortez and Atahuallpa's Peruvian empire, with its capital Cuzco, had been spoiled by Pizarro; but Manoa, the fabulous El Dorado (more gold of sovereignty), capital of Guiana, remained as yet unplundered by the Spanish. Three territories, because the monster *Geryon* that Hercules slew had three bodies and heads. Geryon was Dante's guardian of the fraudulent; but M. calls the Spanish his sons because Spenser had built up Geryon as a type of political tyranny in *F.Q.* V x 8ff: 'Geryon, / He that whylome in Spaine so sore was dred, / For his huge powre and great oppression.' Guiana would be of topical interest in 1667, when the British colony founded in 1663 between the

And Cusco in Peru, the richer seat
Of Atabalipa, and yet unspoiled
410   Guiana, whose great city Geryon's sons
Call El Dorado: but to nobler sights
Michael from Adam's eyes the film removed
Which that false fruit that promised clearer sight
Had bred; then purged with euphrasy and rue
415   The visual nerve, for he had much to see;
And from the well of life three drops instilled.
So deep the power of these ingredients pierced,
Even to the inmost seat of mental sight,
That Adam now enforced to close his eyes,
420   Sunk down and all his spirits became entranced:
But him the gentle angel by the hand
Soon raised, and his attention thus recalled.
    Adam, now ope thine eyes, and first behold

Copenam and Maroni rivers was ceded to the Netherlands by the Peace of Breda, in exchange for New York.   *Motezume*] A more correct form than the Spanish Montezuma.

xi *411–12*. So Homer's Pallas clears Diomedes' eyes (*Il.* v 127); Virgil's Venus, Aeneas' (*Aen.* ii 604); and Tasso's Michael, Goffredo's (*Gerus. Lib.* xviii 92f).

xi *413–15*. For Satan's promise to open Eve's eyes, see ix 706–9. The falsity of his comparison of the fruit to eye-quickening fennel at ix 581 is recalled by the need here for Michael to apply two herbs to *cure* its effects.   *euphrasy*] eyebright. Both euphrasy and *rue* are mentioned in Gerard's *Herball* as remedies for restoring or quickening the sight. But there were many such remedies, and M.'s selection of these particular ones is the result of a deliberate choice. The name 'euphrasy' is from Gk. εὐφρασία, 'cheerfulness', while the bitter 'rue' puns on rue = sorrow, pity, or repentance (a pun so common that no fewer than five instances are given in *OED* s.v. *Rue* sb.[2] I b). In other words the herbs are correlates of the 'joy' and 'pious sorrow' that Michael told Adam to temper, at ll. 361f. Note, however, that the tempering is connected with the operation of the *well of life*: true Christian patience depends on grace and repentance. See, however, a different interpretation in Svendsen 130f.

xi *416*. Cp. *Ps.* xxxvi 9: 'With thee is the fountain of life: in thy light shall we see light.'   *well of life*] See ll. 278–9n.   *three drops*] A masterfully assimilated structural signpost; see xii 5n.

xi *418*. Cp. M.'s appeal to his Muse to 'shine inward' and 'plant eyes' in his mind, at iii 51–5.

xi *421*. In *Dan.* x 8–14, one assisted by 'Michael, one of the chief princes' shows Daniel a 'great vision' of the future; positioning him first with 'an hand'.

xi *423*. Here the second of the poem's major episodes begins (the first being

The effects which thy original crime hath wrought
425   In some to spring from thee, who never touched
The excepted tree, nor with the snake conspired,
Nor sinned thy sin, yet from that sin derive
Corruption to bring forth more violent deeds.
His eyes he opened, and beheld a field,
430   Part arable and tilth, whereon were sheaves
New reaped, the other part sheep-walks and folds;
In the midst an altar as the landmark stood

Raphael's account of the war in heaven, in Bks v and vi; see v 563–4n).
Johnson commented: 'Both are closely connected with the great action;
one was necessary to Adam as a warning, the other as a consolation.' M.
deliberately challenges comparison with the closely comparable episode
in Virgil, *Aen.* vi 756ff, where Aeneas is shown a vision merely of Rome's
future. The kind of poetry to which the next part of *PL* belongs, namely
Biblical history or paraphrase, had often been attempted in English. Among
the most successful examples were Drayton's *Noahs Flood* and *Moses His
Birth and Miracles*; Sylvester's Du Bartas (from II i 4 onwards); Sandys's
Paraphrases; and Cowley's *Davideis*. By comparison with all of these except
the last, M.'s history is far more highly organized, both logically and theo-
logically.

ope thine eyes] Barbara K. Lewalski's 'Structure and the Symbolism of Vision
in Michael's Prophecy,' *PQ* xlii (1963) shows how M. uses improvement of
sight as a symbol of the different stages of faith (inner vision). Many of those
shown to Adam in his visions–Abel, Enoch, Noah, Abraham, Joseph,
Moses and David, for example–appear in the great roll-call of examples of
faith in *Heb.* xi.

xi *425.* Michael does not distinguish the sins of Adam and Eve; he addresses
an undifferentiated Adam-Eve, just as God refers to 'man' at iii 130 (Burden
77).

xi *427. sinned thy sin*] Biblical diction; cp. *Exod.* xxxii 30, *1 John* v 16. *Ed II*
omits the second *sin*; probably by an oversight, since the change makes the
line metrically defective.

xi *429–47.* The first of the six scenes shown to Adam is Cain's murder of
Abel (*Gen.* iv). On the general character of the visions, see ll. 377–84n.
It may be questioned, however, if MacCaffrey is right in likening them to
tableaux; they seem much more like brief tragedies, in which a single dra-
matic passage of intense movement is selected. As Burden 188 remarks,
Adam's role as observer exemplifies the role M.'s reader is expected to learn–
except that the reader will avoid, it is to be hoped, some of Adam's crasser
errors.

xi *432. an altar as the landmark*] Not merely because it is prominently visible,
but also because the landmark (boundary, mark, limit) was a symbol of the
Law and the Covenant (see ll. 115–16n). The spelling in the early edns,
'Ith' midst', probably gives a correct indication of the necessary elision.

Rustic, of grassy sward; thither anon
A sweaty reaper from his tillage brought
435   First fruits, the green ear, and the yellow sheaf,
Unculled, as came to hand; a shepherd next
More meek came with the firstlings of his flock
Choicest and best; then sacrificing, laid
The inwards and their fat, with incense strewed,
440   On the cleft wood, and all due rites performed.
His offering soon propitious fire from heaven
Consumed with nimble glance, and grateful steam;
The other's not, for his was not sincere;
Whereat he inly raged, and as they talked,
445   Smote him into the midriff with a stone
That beat out life; he fell, and deadly pale
Groaned out his soul with gushing blood effused.
Much at that sight was Adam in his heart
Dismayed, and thus in haste to the angel cried.
450   O teacher, some great mischief hath befallen
To that meek man, who well had sacrificed;
Is piety thus and pure devotion paid?
To whom Michael thus, he also moved, replied.
These two are brethren, Adam, and to come
455   Out of thy loins; the unjust the just hath slain,
For envy that his brother's offering found

xi 434. The omission of names is no doubt so that Adam will not know which of his sons is to turn out a murderer.   *sweaty*] in accordance with the curse of x 25.

xi 436. *unculled*] unselected; God's preference for Abel's 'choicest' sacrifice is not arbitrary.

xi 441. *fire from heaven*] An astonishingly common sign that a sacrifice was acceptable; see *Lev.* ix 24; *Judges* vi 21; *1 Kings* xviii 38; *1 Chron.* xxi 26; *2 Chron.* vii 1.   *nimble*] swift.   *glance*] oblique impact; flash.

xi 445. See Allen[2] 178, and cp. Cowley, *Davideis* i, note 16: 'Neither is it declared in what manner [Cain] slew his *Brother*: And therefore I had the Liberty to chuse that which I thought most probable; which is, that he knockt him on the head with some great stone, which was one of the first ordinary and most natural weapons of Anger. That this stone was big enough to be the *Monument* or *Tombstone* of *Abel*, is not so *Hyperbolical*, as what *Virgil* says in the same kind of *Turnus*, "*saxum circumspicit ingens, / Saxum antiquum ingens, campo qui forte jacebat / Limes agro positus.*"'

xi 450–2. Adam makes the wrong response to the first tragedy of death, distrusting God's justice (Burden 190).

xi 453. *he also moved*] The effect of tragedy is to move the spectator; see, e.g., Sidney, *An Apologie for Poetrie*, in G. Gregory Smith, *Elizabethan Critical Essays* (1904) i 177f.

From heaven acceptance; but the bloody fact
Will be avenged, and the other's faith approved
Lose no reward, though here thou see him die,
460   Rolling in dust and gore. To which our sire.
       Alas, both for the deed and for the cause!
But have I now seen death? Is this the way
I must return to native dust? O sight
Of terror, foul and ugly to behold,
465   Horrid to think, how horrible to feel!
       To whom thus Michael. Death thou hast seen
In his first shape on man; but many shapes
Of death, and many are the ways that lead
To his grim cave, all dismal; yet to sense
470   More terrible at the entrance than within.
Some, as thou saw'st, by violent stroke shall die,
By fire, flood, famine, by intemperance more
In meats and drinks which on earth shall bring
Diseases dire, of which a monstrous crew
475   Before thee shall appear; that thou mayst know

xi *457. fact*] crime (*OED* 1 c; the commonest meaning in the seventeenth century).

xi *458–9*. Throughout the visions, the theme of faith will be prominent; for their purpose is to confirm Adam. See l. 355*n*. With the thought here, cp. *Lycidas* 64–84.

xi *465*. As Burden 191 remarks, Adam is now feeling terror, part of the proper response to tragedy. See ll. 495–7*n*.

xi *466. Michael*] Here a trisyllable, in accordance with the slow gravity of the passage.

xi *469–70. his grim cave*] M.'s cave of death is like the underworld of the ancients. The classic description in Virgil, *Aen.* vi emphasized the access through a cavern (236ff) and the terrors *at the entrance* (*vestibulum ante ipsum primisque in faucibus Orci*, 273). Cp. also Sackville's Induction to *A Mirror for Magistrates* (1563).   *dismal*] dreadful.

xi *471–2*. The first vision showed the effect of the Fall on irascible passions, leading to death by 'violent deeds' (ll. 423, 428). The second is to show the effect on concupiscible appetites, leading to death by disease. At the entrance to Virgil's hell *pallentesque habitant Morbi . . . et malesuada Fames ac turpis Egestas, / terribiles visu formae* (vi 275ff). These are all on the opposite side of the threshold (*adverso in limine*) from War and Strife. (Spenser had made a similar psychological application of this dichotomy in *F.Q.* II vii 24ff.) All this does not, however, explain why the second vision should take the specific form of a catalogue of diseases. The reason seems to lie in a simple numerological decorum. For the second digit often symbolized the body; see Fowler 9, citing Valeriano 456: *Dualis numerus mystico significato corpoream indicat naturam.*

What misery the inabstinence of Eve
Shall bring on men. Immediately a place
Before his eyes appeared, sad, noisome, dark,
A lazar-house it seemed, wherein were laid
480 Numbers of all diseased, all maladies
Of ghastly spasm, or racking torture, qualms
Of heart-sick agony, all feverous kinds,
Convulsions, epilepsies, fierce catarrhs,
Intestine stone and ulcer, colic pangs,
485 Demoniac frenzy, moping melancholy
And moon-struck madness, pining atrophy,
Marasmus, and wide-wasting pestilence,
Dropsies, and asthmas, and joint-racking rheums.
Dire was the tossing, deep the groans, despair
490 Tended the sick busiest from couch to couch;
And over them triumphant death his dart
Shook, but delayed to strike, though oft invoked
With vows, as their chief good, and final hope.
Sight so deform what heart of rock could long
495 Dry-eyed behold? Adam could not, but wept,

xi 476. *inabstinence*] Perhaps a Miltonic coinage: *OED* gives no earlier
instance.
xi 477-90. In 'The Furies' (II i 3) Sylvester's Du Bartas describes several
regiments of personified diseases, but all under a military allegory.   *lazar-
house*] hospital; especially (but not necessarily) a leper-house.   *all feverous
kinds*] Careful diction, for the classification of fevers was a great question at
the time. See Svendsen 179 and cp. Sylvester's Du Bartas 265, where two
paragraphs are devoted to fever 'whose inconstant fury / Transforms her
ofter then Vertumnus can, / To *Tertian*, *Quartan*, and *Quotidian*, / And
Second too'.   *colic pangs*: paroxysmal griping belly pains.   *moon-
struck madness*] lunacy.   *pining*] causing to pine.   *Marasmus*] wasting
away of the body.
xi 485-7. Not in *Ed I*.
xi 491. For Death's dart see ii 672, 786.
xi 492. *oft invoked*] Cp. x 858 ('Death comes not at call'). Verity compares
Sophocles, *Phil.* 797f, Horace, *Odes* II xviii 38ff; but Pliny, *Nat. hist.* VII
I 167 is closer: *Tot morbi, tot metus, tot curae, totiens invocata morte ut nullum
frequentius sit votum.*
xi 493. *chief good*] An early use of the converted noun 'chief' in translating
summum bonum (Emma 43).
xi 494. For the stony heart of the unregenerate see l. 4.
xi 495-7. Echoing *Macbeth* V vii 42-7, where Macbeth, on hearing that
Macduff is not 'of woman born' exclaims: 'Accursed be that tongue that
tells me so, / For it hath cow'd my better part of man.' The echo is more than

Though not of woman born; compassion quelled
His best of man, and gave him up to tears
A space, till firmer thoughts restrained excess,
And scarce recovering words his plaint renewed.
500   O miserable mankind, to what fall
Degraded, to what wretched state reserved!
Better end here unborn. Why is life given
To be thus wrested from us? Rather why
Obtruded on us thus? Who if we knew
505 What we receive, would either not accept
Life offered, or soon beg to lay it down,
Glad to be so dismissed in peace. Can thus
The image of God in man created once
So goodly and erect, though faulty since,
510 To such unsightly sufferings be debased
Under inhuman pains? Why should not man,
Retaining still divine similitude
In part, from such deformities be free,
And for his maker's image sake exempt?
515   Their maker's image, answered Michael, then

a verbal reminiscence, for one of the chief themes of *Macbeth* is the drying-up of the 'milk of human kindness,' i.e., the hardening of the heart against *compassion*. Cp. also *Henry V* IV vi 31, 'all my mother came into my eyes'; and *Hamlet* IV vii 190, 'the woman will be out'. Compassion, or pity, is the second part of the response to tragedy. For the first part, terror, see l. 465.

xi *504–6*. See ll. 360–4n. Adam makes the wrong, Stoic response to tragedy. Cp. Seneca, *De consolat.* xxii 3: '*Non mehercules quisquam illam [vitam] accepisset, nisi daretur inscientibus.*' Also Drummond, *A Cypress Grove* (ed. Kastner ii 80): 'O! who if before hee had a beeing, hee could have knowledge of the manie-fold Miseries of it, would enter this woefull Hospitall of the World, and accept of life upon such hard conditiones?'

xi *509. erect*] See vii 505–11n.

xi *511–25*. Catholic theologians held that the *imago Dei* was obscured, but not lost, by the Fall; whereas the *similitudo Dei* was utterly destroyed, but restored by Baptism. (The *imago Dei* was often identified with man's intellectual nature.) Protestant theologians tended to emphasise the disfiguring of the *imago Dei* more strongly. M. himself held that 'some remnants of the divine image still exist in us' (*De doctrina* i 12, Columbia xv 209: a liberal version of the Protestant position). These he thought to be visible in the human understanding and free-will: he particularly instances the wisdom and holiness of many of the heathen. Here, *maker's image* (l. 515) seems to refer to the *similitudo Dei*, while *God's likeness* (which is also *their own*, l. 521) is the *imago Dei*. Contrast iv 291ff.

xi *515–19*. The account of the change in human nature at the Fall began at

Forsook them, when themselves they vilified
To serve ungoverned appetite, and took
His image whom they served, a brutish vice,
Inductive mainly to the sin of Eve.
520   Therefore so abject is their punishment,
Disfiguring not God's likeness, but their own,
Or if his likeness, by themselves defaced
While they pervert pure nature's healthful rules
To loathsome sickness, worthily, since they
525   God's image did not reverence in themselves.
          I yield it just, said Adam, and submit.
But is there yet no other way, besides
These painful passages, how we may come
To death, and mix with our connatural dust?
530   There is, said Michael, if thou well observe
The rule of not too much, by temperance taught
In what thou eat'st and drink'st, seeking from thence
Due nourishment, not gluttonous delight,
Till many years over thy head return:
535   So mayst thou live, till like ripe fruit thou drop
Into thy mother's lap, or be with ease
Gathered, not harshly plucked, for death mature:
This is old age; but then thou must outlive

ix 1013 (see *n*); the numerous diseases Adam has just seen are supposed the
proliferating consequences of that initial change.

xi *516. vilified*] reduced to a lower standing (*OED* 1).

xi *519. Inductive*] giving rise to (*OED* 2).

xi *526.* The need for submission and patience is a constant theme of the
present book; see above, Argument, 112 and 551.

xi *528. passages*] deaths (*OED* 2 b).

xi *531. rule . . . much*] Alludes to the ancient maxim μηδὲν ἄγαν, which is
said to have been written up in the temple at Delphi by Cleobulus. Plato
quotes it in *Protag.* 343B. M. writes often on the topic of moderation; see
Elegia VI 59f, *Il Penseroso* 46, *Comus* 762ff and *SA* 553ff.

xi *535–7.* The comparison goes back to Cicero, *De senectute* 19.   *mother's
lap*] Cp. Adam's use of the same phrase in a similar connection at x 778.

xi *538–46.* The description of old age is a highly traditional one; cp., e.g.,
Shakespeare's 'mere oblivion / Sans teeth, sans eyes, sans taste, sans every-
thing' (*As You Like It* II vii 165f); or Everyman's abandonment by Strength,
Beauty and Five-Wits. In the correlation of Ages of Man with humours,
melancholy was often assigned to the fourth period, old age; and the airy,
sanguine humour to the second, *youth*. See Klibansky 122, 149 and 293.
Sanguine was of course the preferred humour, supposed, usually, to have
prevailed before the Fall; whereas melancholy, the worst humour, was
regarded as especially characteristic of the corruption that followed (*ibid.*

Thy youth, thy strength, thy beauty, which will change
540 To withered weak and gray; thy senses then
Obtuse, all taste of pleasure must forego,
To what thou hast, and for the air of youth
Hopeful and cheerful, in thy blood will reign
A melancholy damp of cold and dry
545 To weigh thy spirits down, and last consume
The balm of life. To whom our ancestor.
    Henceforth I fly not death, nor would prolong
Life much, bent rather how I may be quit
Fairest and easiest of this cumbrous charge,
550 Which I must keep till my appointed day
Of rendering up, and patiently attend
My dissolution. Michael replied,
    Nor love thy life, nor hate; but what thou livest
Live well, how long or short permit to heaven:
555 And now prepare thee for another sight.
    He looked and saw a spacious plain, whereon

103, 105, 110f; see vi 331–4n above). According to one authority, melancholy was born out of the breath of the serpent (see Klibansky 79f). In this connection it is interesting that Satan entered the serpent as a 'midnight vapour' (ix 159); foreshadowing the *melancholy damp* that is to weigh Adam's spirits.   *damp*] depression of spirits (*OED* 5); but also, apparently, 'vapour' (in the physiological sense), an extension of the normal application of the word to external exhalations and vapours (*OED* 1, 2).

xi 551–2. *Ed I* has here only the one line, 'Of rendering up. Michael to him replied'. The insertion gives added emphasis to the thematic idea of patient resignation (see l. 526n).   *attend*] wait for. Cp. *Job* xiv 14: 'If a man die, shall he live again? all the days of my appointed time will I wait, till my change come.'

xi 553–4. Again a wrong response of Adam's – here his emotional embracing of death – is corrected by Michael; true patience is more detached (Burden 193). Cp. Martial, *Epig.* X xlvii 13, *summum nec metuas diem nec optes*; Horace, *Odes* I ix 9, *permitte divis cetera*; and Seneca, *Epist.* xxiv 29, lxv 18. The use of *permit* with an indirect object is not a departure from idiomatic English syntax (see *OED* s.v. *Permit* I 1).

xi 556–97. The third vision apparently shows mankind in a more fortunate condition. This is appropriate from the point of view of number symbolism, for three is fortunate. It is also a Marriage Number (being formed from the union of Odd and Even); hence much of the vision is taken up with nuptials.

xi 556–73. Cain's descendant Lamech had three sons: Jabal 'the father of such as dwell in tents, and of such as have cattle', Jubal 'the father of all such as handle the harp and organ', and Tubalcain 'an instructor of every artificer in brass and iron' (*Gen.* iv 19–22). Broadbent 105 notes that Tubalcain's smelting imitates that of the devils building Pandaemonium; and the same

Were tents of various hue; by some were herds
Of cattle grazing: others, whence the sound
Of instruments that made melodious chime
560 Was heard, of harp and organ; and who moved
Their stops and chords was seen: his volant touch
Instinct through all proportions low and high
Fled and pursued transverse the resonant fugue.
In other part stood one who at the forge
565 Labouring, two massy clods of iron and brass
Had melted (whether found where casual fire
Had wasted woods on mountain or in vale,
Down to the veins of earth, thence gliding hot
To some cave's mouth, or whether washed by stream
570 From underground) the liquid ore he drained
Into fit moulds prepared; from which he formed
First his own tools; then, what might else be wrought
Fusile or graven in metal. After these,
But on the hither side a different sort

point might be made in connection with Jubal and the organ (cp. i 708ff). The invention of the arts is given elaborate treatment in Sylvester's Du Bartas II i 4, 'The Handy-Crafts'; though from a point of view closer to Adam's than to Michael's–the characteristic tone is unreflecting exclamation: 'Happy device'! Cp. also Marvell's 'Musicks Empire', Sts 2f: '*Jubal* first made the wilder Notes agree; / And *Jubal* tuned Musicks *Jubilee*: / He call'd the *Ecchoes* from their sullen Cell, / And built the Organs City where they dwell. // Each sought a consort in that lovely place; / And Virgin Trebles wed the manly Base. / From whence the Progeny of numbers new / Into harmonious Colonies withdrew.'
xi *562–3*. Instinct] impelled, as at ii 937 (*OED* s.v. *Instinct* ppl. a; perhaps a Latinism).   proportions] The art of music was regarded as essentially based on numerical proportions. Perhaps M. alludes to the ancient accounts of the invention of music, which relate that Pythagoras discovered the proportions when he heard blacksmiths beating a hot iron (Macrobius, *In somn. Scip.* II i 9ff, ed. Stahl 186f, with refs).   fugue] Derived from Ital. *fuga*=flight. M. brings this out with *Fled*; no doubt to remind us that Jubal's race is the fugitive race of Cain; see ll. 608f.
xi *566–70*. casual] accidental, chance (*OED* 1). M. follows the account of the discovery of metals in Lucretius, *De rerum nat.* v 1241–68.
xi *573–80*. The descendants not of Cain but of Seth. According to Eutychius, they lived in the mountains *neighbouring* Paradise itself, and therefore on the *hither* side of the plain (whereas Cain dwelt 'on the east of Eden', *Gen.* iv 16). Josephus (*Antiq.* I ii 3) and others made them the inventors of physics and astronomy; hence their study is *God's works / Not hid*. Being children of light they presumably avoid meddling with God's secret hidden causes.
xi *573*. Fusile] able to be melted.

575 From the high neighbouring hills, which was their seat,
Down to the plain descended: by their guise
Just men they seemed, and all their study bent
To worship God aright, and know his works
Not hid, nor those things last which might preserve
580 Freedom and peace to men: they on the plain
Long had not walked, when from the tents behold
A bevy of fair women, richly gay
In gems and wanton dress; to the harp they sung
Soft amorous ditties, and in dance came on:
585 The men though grave, eyed them, and let their eyes
Rove without rein, till in the amorous net
Fast caught, they liked, and each his liking chose;
And now of love they treat till the evening star
Love's harbinger appeared; then all in heat
590 They light the nuptial torch, and bid invoke
Hymen, then first to marriage rites invoked;
With feast and music all the tents resound.
Such happy interview and fair event
Of love and youth not lost, songs, garlands, flowers,
595 And charming symphonies attached the heart
Of Adam, soon inclined to admit delight,
The bent of nature; which he thus expressed.
     True opener of mine eyes, prime angel blest,
Much better seems this vision, and more hope
600 Of peaceful days portends, than those two past;
Those were of hate and death, or pain much worse,
Here nature seems fulfilled in all her ends.
     To whom thus Michael. Judge not what is best
By pleasure, though to nature seeming meet,

xi *579. last*] lost *Ed I*, corrected in *Errata*.
xi *581-92.* Cp. *Gen.* vi 1f and see l. *622n.* M. treated the same subject again in a very similar fashion in *PR* 153ff.
xi *588-9. treat*] deal, discuss.   *evening star*] Venus, whose appearance was also the signal for the lighting of the 'bridal lamp' at viii 519f, at the nuptials of Adam and Eve. But the pagan god Hymen was not invoked by them.
xi *594. youth not lost*] Adam is particularly open to influence on this score, since Michael told him at ll. 538ff that he must lose his own youth.
xi *595. symphonies*] harmonies, concords; part-songs (*OED* 2, 4). Cp. the 'dulcet symphonies' that accompanied the building of Pandaemonium at i 712.
xi *599-602.* Burden 193f notes that Adam has again gone wrong by trusting his feelings. He fails to grasp the falsity of the god invoked, or to see that the marriages are based on *heat* (l. 589) and *delight* (l. 596), instead of on rational choice. As at viii 530 (after a scene not entirely dissimilar) he is 'transported'.

605 Created, as thou art, to nobler end
     Holy and pure, conformity divine.
     Those tents thou saw'st so pleasant, were the tents
     Of wickedness, wherein shall dwell his race
     Who slew his brother; studious they appear
610 Of arts that polish life, inventors rare,
     Unmindful of their maker, though his Spirit
     Taught them, but they his gifts acknowledged none.
     Yet they a beauteous offspring shall beget;
     For that fair female troop thou saw'st, that seemed
615 Of goddesses, so blithe, so smooth, so gay,
     Yet empty of all good wherein consists
     Woman's domestic honour and chief praise;
     Bred only and completed to the taste
     Of lustful appetance, to sing, to dance,
620 To dress, and troll the tongue, and roll the eye.
     To these that sober race of men, whose lives
     Religious titled them the sons of God,

xi 605–6. As the Catechism reminds us, the chief end of man is to know God and enjoy him. The joy of the third vision, however, is a delight at the fulfilment of merely natural ends – *Here Nature seems fulfilled*.

xi 607–8. 'I had rather be a doorkeeper in the house of my God, than to dwell in the tents of wickedness' (*Ps.* lxxxiv 10).

xi 611–12. The arts of the children of Cain provided an occasion for many commentators on *Genesis* to discuss the problems presented to the Christian theologian by the existence of secular culture. Calvin, e.g., applied his doctrine of General Grace to account for the inspiration of the heathen.

xi 618. *completed*] Perhaps 'accomplished; equipped'; but these senses seem to have been rare before *PL*. M. may intend an academic metaphor: 'graduated' (*OED* 13 b).

xi 619. *appetence*] desire.

xi 620. *troll*] wag.

xi 621–2. Referring to *Gen.* vi 1f: 'And it came to pass, when men began to multiply on the face of the earth, and daughters were born unto them, That the sons of God saw the daughters of men that they were fair; and they took them wives of all which they chose.' Some early commentators took these verses to mean that the fallen angels lay with the daughters of men (e.g. Philo, Clement of Alexandria and Tertullian), and M. himself allows us to dally with this surmise in an ambiguous passage at iii 461ff. But now, in the down-to-earth demythologizing Bk xi, it turns out that that was only another of the vanities and follies bound for Limbo. On the discarded theory, which certain later commentators treated as heretical, see D. C. Allen in *MLN* lxi (1946) 78. West 129f rightly rejects the idea that M. at any time seriously entertained the angel perversion theory; but he misses the joke of iii 461ff. See l. 642*n*.

Shall yield up all their virtue, all their fame
Ignobly, to the trains and to the smiles
625   Of these fair atheists, and now swim in joy,
(Erelong to swim at large) and laugh; for which
The world erelong a world of tears must weep.
      To whom thus Adam of short joy bereft.
O pity and shame, that they who to live well
630   Entered so fair, should turn aside to tread
Paths indirect, or in the mid way faint!
But still I see the tenor of man's woe
Holds on the same, from woman to begin.
      From man's effeminate slackness it begins,
635   Said the angel, who should better hold his place
By wisdom, and superior gifts received.
But now prepare thee for another scene.
      He looked and saw wide territory spread

xi *624. trains*] snares, enticements.

xi *625-7. swim in joy*] An idiomatic expression; cp. 'swim in mirth' at ix
1009 above. The word play in *swim* and in *The world . . . must weep* looks
forward to the Flood in the fifth vision, where it is repeated (l. 757).   Ere-
long] soon.

xi *631*. This line is numerologically in the *mid way* of the *Paths indirect* of the
first, destroyed world. For it is at the mid-point between the first line of the
first vision (l. 423) and the last line of the fifth (the Flood: l. 839).

xi *632-6*. Again Adam makes the wrong response, by putting the blame on
Eve. Burden 196 remarks how continuously the theme of the poem is applied
to marriage. It is true that M. gives a considerable place to marriage, both in
itself and as representative of the larger community. But here, as often
elsewhere, M. really intends a psychological statement about the relation
of intellect and emotions. The explanation of *woman* as meaning 'woe to
man' was proverbial, and is given by some of the commentators on *Gen.*
ii 23 or iii 20.

xi *638-711*. The tetrad commonly symbolized Friendship and Concord,
so that M.'s fourth vision shows the corresponding evil, Strife. Cp. Spen-
ser's treatment of Ate in his fourth book, and see Fowler 24-6 on the back-
ground of ancient number symbolism. M. repeats the point in miniature
by giving four separate vignettes within the vision: foraging (ll. 646-50);
tournament (ll. 651-5); siege (ll. 656-9); and council (ll. 660-71). The whole
vision bears a close relation to Homer's elaborate account of the shield of
Achilles (which had panoramic representations on it of conflict at a place of
assembly, a siege, an attack on shepherds and a battle; see *Il.* xviii 490-540),
as well as to Virgil's imitation in *Aen.* viii 626-728, a description of the shield
of Vulcan given to Aeneas by his mother, with its prophetic images of Rome's
future. Both ancient shields included representations of Discord or Strife
personified.

Before him, towns, and rural works between,
640   Cities of men with lofty gates and towers,
Concourse in arms, fierce faces threatening war,
Giants of mighty bone, and bold emprise;
Part wield their arms, part curb the foaming steed,
Single or in array of battle ranged
645   Both horse and foot, nor idly mustering stood;
One way a band select from forage drives
A herd of beeves, fair oxen and fair kine
From a fat meadow ground; or fleecy flock,
Ewes and their bleating lambs over the plain,
650   Their booty; scarce with life the shepherds fly,
But call in aid, which makes a bloody fray;
With cruel tournament the squadrons join;
Where cattle pastured late, now scattered lies
With carcasses and arms the ensanguined field
655   Deserted: others to a city strong

xi *641. concourse*] hostile encounter.

xi *642. Giants*] A shade more than a figure of speech, in view of the tradition that the offspring of the *sons of God* were Giants. See l. 622*n*.   *emprise*] chivalric enterprise, martial prowess.

xi *643–4.* Establishing an analogy with the warlike devils of ii 531f. As Broadbent 96 notes, M. has far more chivalry in hell and fallen earth than in heaven. He never loses an opportunity of chilling martial ardours.

xi *651. makes*] So *Ed II. Ed I* 'tacks' is almost certainly an error: tacks= 'attacks' (aphetic form) is syntactically difficult, while tacks='joins' would be unidiomatic with *fray*. On the other hand, if 'tacks' were idiomatic, as Adams 99 claims, the objection that it is too technical would carry little weight, in view of the high concentration of technical military terms in those parts of the poem that are concerned with the fallen world.

xi *654. ensanguined*] blood-stained (first instance in *OED*).

xi *655–71.* The just man is Enoch. From *Gen.* v 21–4, *Heb.* xi 5 and *Jude* 14 we learn that Enoch was 365 years of age (less than half the common patriarchal span) when he was translated by God. The details of Enoch's translation are not Scriptural, and it is possible that they may have been drawn from visual sources. The translation in a cloud agrees with the account of Enoch's vision translation in *Enoch* xiv 8f: 'Clouds invited me and a mist summoned me, and the course of the stars and the lightnings sped and hastened me, and the winds in the vision caused me to fly and lifted me upward, and bore me into heaven' (Charles ii 197). Unfortunately, however, these verses are not among the fragments of *The Book of Enoch* that could have been accessible to M. Nevertheless a good deal was known about *Enoch* in M.'s time, from quotations in patristic authors; indeed, the book was much discussed and quoted. This fact is of some importance as a key to the form of *PL* xi–xii. For the visions shown by Michael are from one

Lay siege, encamped; by battery, scale, and mine,
Assaulting; others from the wall defend
With dart and javelin, stones and sulphurous fire;
On each hand slaughter and gigantic deeds.
660   In other part the sceptred heralds call
To council in the city gates: anon
Gray-headed men and grave, with warriors mixed,
Assemble, and harangues are heard, but soon
In factious opposition, till at last
665   Of middle age one rising, eminent
In wise deport, spake much of right and wrong,
Of justice, of religion, truth, and peace,
And judgment from above: him old and young
Exploded and had seized with violent hands,
670   Had not a cloud descending snatched him thence
Unseen amid the throng: so violence
Proceeded, and oppression, and sword-law
Through all the plain, and refuge none was found.
Adam was all in tears, and to his guide
675   Lamenting turned full sad; O what are these,
Death's ministers, not men, who thus deal death
Inhumanly to men, and multiply
Ten thousand fold the sin of him who slew
His brother; for of whom such massacre
680   Make they but of their brethren, men of men?
But who was that just man, whom had not heaven
Rescued, had in his righteousness been lost?
    To whom thus Michael. These are the product
Of those ill mated marriages thou saw'st:

point of view a late contribution to the Enoch vision-literature tradition.
Enoch, too, was a prophet of the future, and his visions, like M.'s, foretold
the Deluge and God's judgments upon sin. M. would naturally have a
great interest in the *Book of Enoch* because it was very largely concerned
with the origin of evil. It also contained much useful angelic mythology.
See ll. 700–10*n.*   *exploded*] shouted down; drove away with hoots.

xi *656. scale*] ladder. Not a Latinism.

xi *661. city gates*] A common place for councils in Biblical times; see, e.g.,
Gen. xxxiv 20, *Zech.* viii 16.

xi *678.* Continuing the allusion to Enoch's visions. One of his prophecies
was that 'the Lord cometh with ten thousands of his saints, To execute
judgment upon all' (*Jude* 14f).

xi *683. Ed I* has semicolon after *Michael.*

xi *683–8.* For the Giant offspring of the sons of God and the daughters of
Cain, see ll. 621–2*n*, 642*n*. The subject is treated at length in *Enoch* vi–vii,
a passage that was paraphrased in many patristic authors.

685   Where good with bad were matched, who of themselves
       Abhor to join; and by imprudence mixed,
       Produce prodigious births of body or mind.
       Such were these giants, men of high renown;
       For in those days might only shall be admired,
690   And valour and heroic virtue called;
       To overcome in battle, and subdue
       Nations, and bring home spoils with infinite
       Manslaughter, shall be held the highest pitch
       Of human glory, and for glory done
695   Of triumph, to be styled great conquerors,
       Patrons of mankind, gods, and sons of gods,
       Destroyers rightlier called and plagues of men.
       Thus fame shall be achieved, renown on earth,
       And what most merits fame in silence hid.
700   But he the seventh from thee, whom thou beheld'st
       The only righteous in a world perverse,
       And therefore hated, therefore so beset
       With foes for daring single to be just,
       And utter odious truth, that God would come
705   To judge them with his saints: him the most high
       Rapt in a balmy cloud with winged steeds

xi *689–90*. A strong piece of evidence in support of Steadman's thesis that
M. systematically distinguishes two hierarchies of heroic virtues: the
Christian one based on goodness and the Satanic on might. See ii 5*n*, vi 41–
3*n*, 820–3*n*.

xi *692–3*. See ll. 643–4*n*.

xi *698*. Cp. *Gen.* vi 4: 'There were giants in the earth in those days; and
also after that, when the sons of God came in unto the daughters of men, and
they bare children to them, the same became mighty men which were of old,
men of renown.'

xi *700–10*. Enoch is called 'the seventh from Adam' in *Jude* 14. The cloud
with winged steeds is puzzling (see ll. 665–71*n*); though it may simply be
based on the description of Elijah's translation at *2 Kings* ii 11. (Enoch and
Elijah were often associated.)   *walk with God*) Cp. *Gen.* v 24.   *climes
of bliss*] Cp. the 'happy climes that lie / Where Day never shuts his eye',
of which the Attendant Spirit speaks in *Comus* 978f. Enoch's translation was
a controversial issue in M.'s time: commentators on Genesis discussed
whether Enoch escaped death, whether he was preserved in some terrene
paradise and whether he would come again to be slain by Antichrist. (The
various opinions are conveniently summarised in Willet 71f.) The trans-
lation was generally regarded as a type of Resurrection, or of the Ascension.
Thus the Geneva Bible gloss is that Enoch was taken 'to shew that there was
a better life prepared, and to be a testimonie of the immortalitie of soules and
bodies'.

Did, as thou saw'st, receive, to walk with God
High in salvation and the climes of bliss,
Exempt from death; to show thee what reward
710 Awaits the good, the rest what punishment;
Which now direct thine eyes and soon behold.
     He looked, and saw the face of things quite changed,
The brazen throat of war had ceased to roar,
All now was turned to jollity and game,
715 To luxury and riot, feast and dance,
Marrying or prostituting, as befell,
Rape or adultery, where passing fair
Allured them; thence from cups to civil broils.
At length a reverend sire among them came,

xi *708. High*] Cp. 665, 'rising'. Cope's thesis about a cycle of metaphoric rises and falls running through the poem is nowhere more evidently true. The just man Enoch is raised up on high, whereas the corrupt sons of God 'Down to the plain descended' (l. 576).

xi *710.* Punctuation as in *Ed I. Ed II* erroneously has question-mark after *punishment.*

xi *712–53.* Not only was five a Marriage Number (being the sum of two and three, the first female and the first male numbers in the Pythagorean system) but it was also the number of the senses and of sensuality. Consequently the fifth vision opens with the corruption of sexual manners. This point is reinforced by the series of five pairs of actions given in ll. 714–17. More important, however, is the symbolism whereby five stood for Justice (see Hopper 86, 115, 180; Fowler 34f). For it is in accordance with this symbolism that the Deluge now descends on human corruption.

xi *712. Ed I* semicolon after *changed* is preferable.

xi *714. luxury*] lust.

xi *717. passing fair*] Punning between 'surpassing, pre-eminent beauty' and 'woman passing by' (see *OED* s.v. *Passing* ppl. a. 3, 1; *Fair* sb.[2] 4, 2).

xi *719–53.* M.'s account of Noah and the Flood is faithful to *Gen.* vi 9– ix 17, with only a few divagations into the commentators; see Allen[2] 153f, where is is improbably suggested that the length and literal orthodoxy of M.'s account are due to the special doubts that had been cast on the historical truth of the Flood in his time. Noah's remonstrations with the rioters are mentioned in Josephus, *Antiq.* I iii 1. The loose sexual morals of antediluvian society are implied in *Luke* xvii 26f: 'As it was in the days of Noe, so shall it be also in the days of the Son of man. They did eat, they drank, they married wives, they were given in marriage, until the day that Noe entered into the ark, and the flood came.' They had occasionally provided a subject for visual representations, as in Hoet's engraving for the Cambridge Bible of 1660 (Fig. 15 in Allen[2]). The Flood itself, was, of course one of the great

720   And of their doings great dislike declared,
      And testified against their ways; he oft
      Frequented their assemblies, whereso met,
      Triumphs or festivals, and to them preached
      Conversion and repentance, as to souls
725   In prison under judgments imminent:
      But all in vain: which when he saw, he ceased
      Contending, and removed his tents far off;
      Then from the mountain hewing timber tall,
      Began to build a vessel of huge bulk,
730   Measured by cubit, length, and breadth, and highth,
      Smeared round with pitch, and in the side a door
      Contrived, and of provisions laid in large
      For man and beast: when lo a wonder strange!
      Of every beast, and bird, and insect small
735   Came sevens, and pairs, and entered in, as taught
      Their order: last the sire, and his three sons
      With their four wives; and God made fast the door.
      Meanwhile the south-wind rose, and with black wings

subjects of visual art; its prominence in that field, as in literature and theo-
logy, may be put down to the effectiveness with which it focused the apoca-
lyptic fears of the time. Its prominence in *PL* in particular, however, has this
additional reason, that it provides a complete analogue of the Fall: it too is
the loss of a world because of sin.

xi *721*. Cp. *Heb.* xi 7: 'By faith Noah, being warned of God of things not
seen as yet, moved with fear, prepared an ark to the saving of his house;
by the which he condemned the world.'

xi *723-5*. Cp. *1 Pet.* iii 18-21: Christ was 'put to death in the flesh, but
quickened by the Spirit: By which also he went and preached unto the
spirits in prison; Which sometime were disobedient, when once the long-
suffering of God waited in the days of Noah, while the ark was a preparing,
wherein few, that is, eight souls were saved by water. The like figure where-
unto even baptism doth also now save us . . . by the resurrection of Jesus
Christ.'

xi *730*. Cp. *Gen.* vi 15.

xi *734*. The inclusion of *insects* is not Biblical, and shows M. to be in agree-
ment with the more modern of the commentators on Genesis. In the most
elaborate of all treatments of the ark, Athanasius Kircher's *Arca Noe* (Am-
sterdam 1675), we still find the view that insects arise from putrefaction or
spontaneous generation; so that they could safely be excluded (Allen[2] 185,
153).

xi *738-53*. Based on Ovid's description of Deucalion's flood in *Met.* i 262-
347. The close relation between Deucalion and Noah was a commonplace of
Biblical Poetics. But it could be used either to prove or to disprove the truth
of pagan myth, either to prove or disprove the historicity of the Bible.

Wide hovering, all the clouds together drove
740 From under heaven; the hills to their supply
Vapour, and exhalation dusk and moist,
Sent up amain; and now the thickened sky
Like a dark ceiling stood; down rushed the rain
Impetuous, and continued till the earth
745 No more was seen; the floating vessel swum
Uplifted; and secure with beaked prow
Rode tilting o'er the waves, all dwellings else
Flood overwhelmed, and them with all their pomp
Deep under water rolled; sea covered sea,
750 Sea without shore; and in their palaces
Where luxury late reigned, sea monsters whelped
And stabled; of mankind, so numerous late,
All left, in one small bottom swum embarked.
How didst thou grieve then, Adam, to behold
755 The end of all thy offspring, end so sad,
Depopulation; thee another flood,
Of tears and sorrow a flood thee also drowned,
And sunk thee as thy sons; till gently reared
By the angel, on thy feet thou stood'st at last,

Allen[2] 176f discusses the modification that was currently taking place in the kind of truth attributed to the Flood narrative. The Ovidian passage has the south wind producing rain by its action on heavy clouds (implying a meteorological theory that, as Svendsen 97 shows, was still given credence in the seventeenth century); the image of the *sea without shore*; and a marvellous topsy-turvy panorama – very popular in M.'s time – of sea creatures taking the place of land creatures (*Met.* i 293–303). Sylvester's Du Bartas (I ii *ad fin.*; p. 57) develops the image at some length: 'The Sturgeon, coasting over Castles, muses / (Under the Sea) to see so many houses, / The *Indian* Manat and the Mullet float / O'r Mountain tops where yearst the bearded Goat / Did bound and brouz: the crooked Dolphin scuds / O'r th' highest branches of the hugest Woods,' etc. So does Drayton, but with more force: 'The Grampus, and the Whirlpoole, as they rove, / Lighting by chance upon a lofty Grove / Under this world of waters, are so much / Pleas'd with their wombes each tender branch to touch, / That they leave slyme upon the curled Sprayes, / On which the Birds sung their harmonious Layes' (*Noahs Floud* 729–34). Cp. also Cowley, *Davideis* i (ed. Waller 263).   supply] assistance (*OED* I 1).   *exhalation*] mist, vapour.   *stabled*] Punning between 'lived as in a stable' and 'stuck in the mud' (*OED* vb.[2] 2 b, vb.[3]). *bottom*] boat.

xi 750–2. As Broadbent 103 notices, this image brings to its logical conclusion a line of satire that began with the description of Pandaemonium's splendours.

xi 756–7. See ll. 625–7n.

760   Though comfortless, as when a father mourns
        His children, all in view destroyed at once;
        And scarce to the angel uttered'st thus thy plaint.
            O visions ill foreseen! Better had I
        Lived ignorant of future, so had borne
765   My part of evil only, each day's lot
        Enough to bear; those now, that were dispensed
        The burden of many ages, on me light
        At once, by my foreknowledge gaining birth
        Abortive, to torment me ere their being,
770   With thought that they must be. Let no man seek
        Henceforth to be foretold what shall befall
        Him or his children, evil he may be sure,
        Which neither his foreknowing can prevent,
        And he the future evil shall no less
775   In apprehension than in substance feel
        Grievous to bear: but that care now is past,
        Man is not whom to warn: those few escaped
        Famine and anguish will at last consume
        Wandering that watery desert: I had hope
780   When violence was ceased, and war on earth,
        All would have then gone well, peace would have
                crowned
        With length of happy days the race of man;
        But I was far deceived; for now I see
        Peace to corrupt no less than war to waste.
785   How comes it thus? Unfold, celestial guide,
        And whether here the race of man will end.
        To whom thus Michael. Those whom last thou saw'st
        In triumph and luxurious wealth, are they
        First seen in acts of prowess eminent
790   And great exploits, but of true virtue void;
        Who having spilt much blood, and done much waste
        Subduing nations, and achieved thereby
        Fame in the world, high titles, and rich prey,

xi 765–6. 'Take therefore no thought for the morrow: for the morrow shall
take thought for the things of itself. Sufficient unto the day is the evil there-
of' (*Matt.* vi 34).

xi 770–3. Adam now falls into the error of despair, brought on by a false
deterministic doctrine of Predestination.

xi 773–4. *neither . . . and*] Editors explain this as an imitation of the 'elegant'
Latin idiom *neque . . . et*. But is it likely that Adam would be elegant in his
despair? 'Neither . . . and' is good but ungrammatical English: see many
examples in *OED* s.v. *Neither* A 1 g.

xi 790. *true virtue*] See ll. 689–90n.

Shall change their course to pleasure, ease, and sloth,
795   Surfeit, and lust, till wantonness and pride
Raise out of friendship hostile deeds in peace.
The conquered also, and enslaved by war
Shall with their freedom lost all virtue lose
And fear of God, from whom their piety feigned
800   In sharp contest of battle found no aid
Against invaders; therefore cooled in zeal
Thenceforth shall practise how to live secure,
Worldly or dissolute, on what their lords
Shall leave them to enjoy; for the earth shall bear
805   More than enough, that temperance may be tried:
So all shall turn degenerate, all depraved,
Justice and temperance, truth and faith forgot;
One man except, the only son of light
In a dark age, against example good,
810   Against allurement, custom, and a world
Offended; fearless of reproach and scorn,
Or violence, he of their wicked ways
Shall them admonish, and before them set
The paths of righteousness, how much more safe,
815   And full of peace, denouncing wrath to come
On their impenitence; and shall return
Of them derided, but of God observed
The one just man alive; by his command
Shall build a wondrous ark, as thou beheld'st,
820   To save himself and household from amidst
A world devote to universal rack.
No sooner he with them of man and beast
Select for life shall in the ark be lodged,
And sheltered round, but all the cataracts

xi *797–806.* One of the few passages in the poem which editors are probably justified in regarding as direct topical allusion. See particularly Hughes, who thinks the passage can be read as 'an attack upon the time-servers in his own party . . . the record of disillusion from the mood in which he painted England in *Areopagitica*'. The lines about feigned zeal cooling in adversity, which sound particularly *ad hominem*, refer to a problem dealt with more fully in *SA.*   *contest*] Stressed on the second syllable.

xi *798. lose*] The *Ed I* and *Ed II* spelling 'loose' could indicate either 'lose' or 'loose' ('relax').

xi *815. denouncing*] proclaiming.

xi *821. devote*] doomed (*OED* s.v. Devoted 3).   *rack*] (Variant of 'wreck') destruction.

xi *824–7.* Cp. *Gen.* vii 11: 'The same day were all the fountains of the great deep broken up, and the windows of heaven were opened.'   *cataracts*]

825 Of heaven set open on the earth shall pour
    Rain day and night, all fountains of the deep
    Broke up, shall heave the ocean to usurp
    Beyond all bounds, till inundation rise
    Above the highest hills: then shall this mount
830 Of Paradise by might of waves be moved
    Out of his place, pushed by the horned flood,
    With all his verdure spoiled, and trees adrift
    Down the great river to the opening gulf,
    And there take root an island salt and bare,
835 The haunt of seals and orcs, and sea-mews' clang.
    To teach thee that God attributes to place
    No sanctity, if none be thither brought
    By men who there frequent, or therein dwell.
    And now what further shall ensue, behold.

where A.V. has 'windows' (marg. 'flood-gates'), Vulgate and Tremellius
have *cataractae*.
xi *829–38*. As Allen notes, the fate of Paradise was a topic much discussed
by the commentators. The Flood might naturally be expected to have
changed the landscape, and Pererius argued that Paradise must have been
destroyed altogether. Kircherus, on the other hand, held that it remained
exactly where it was: he ridicules the idea that it was carried off to the
Armenian mountains, or into the Antarctic, or to the Torrid Zone to be-
come the Isle of Zealand (see Allen² 153f, 191). The present passage helps
to explain the puzzling account of the entry of the Tigris into Paradise, at
ix 69ff ('There was a place, / Now not, though sin, not time, first wrought
the change'); though of course it would be simple-minded to conclude that
M.'s point was geological and not theological. The *great river*, then, is the
ordinary, mundane, present-day Tigris or Euphrates (cp. *Gen.* xv 18, 'the
great river, the river Euphrates'). After all the splendid exotic geographical
suggestions in such passages as iv 280ff, after all the esoteric theories about
the locations of the terrene Paradise, the matter is settled for us and we come
down to this: a bare island in the Persian Gulf. The lesson in the concluding
lines is a simple homiletic Protestant one, that the existence of Paradise is
inward and spiritual, and not to be superstitiously localized. MacCaffrey
88 rightly connects the *gulf* with the gulf of chaos, and finds analogues for the
uprooted mountain in those of hell (i 230ff, ii 539ff). The *horned flood* pro-
bably echoes a Virgilian description of the mighty Tiber, *corniger Hesperidum
fluvius regnator aquarum* (*Aen.* viii 77). But the phrase also occurs in Jonson,
as well as in Browne, *Britannia's pastorals* ii 5 (a copy of which is extant with
annotations thought by some to be M.'s holograph).   *orcs*] not merely
whales, but also leviathans, devouring monsters (*OED* 2, citing Sylvester's
Du Bartas: 'Insatiate Orque, that even at one repast / Almost all creatures
in the World would waste'). Cp. i 201ff above, where Satan is an orc.
sea-mew] gull.   *clang*] harsh scream; see vii 422–3n.

840   He looked, and saw the ark hull on the flood,
          Which now abated, for the clouds were fled,
          Driven by a keen north-wind, that blowing dry
          Wrinkled the face of deluge, as decayed;
          And the clear sun on his wide watery glass
845   Gazed hot, and of the fresh wave largely drew,
          As after thirst, which made their flowing shrink
          From standing lake to tripping ebb, that stole
          With soft foot towards the deep, who now had stopped
          His sluices, as the heaven his windows shut.
850   The ark no more now floats, but seems on ground
          Fast on the top of some high mountain fixed.
          And now the tops of hills as rocks appear;
          With clamour thence the rapid currents drive
          Towards the retreating sea their furious tide.

xi *840–69.* The appropriateness of the position of the sixth vision is obvious.
Six was the number of the days of Creation, so that it was generally a
creation symbol (see Bongo 264ff). This decorum is underlined by the
connection drawn with the first creation in ll. 852–4. Six was also the num-
ber of the ages of the world's duration; the sixth age being reckoned from
the coming of Christ to the Last Day. Consequently six symbolized the
salvation of man, of which the Covenant with Noah is the type (Bongo
280). See further in xii 1n below.

xi *840–3.* The diction may possibly reflect a recollection of phrases from
Sidney–'the carkas of the shippe . . . hulling there . . . bloud had (as it were)
filled the wrinckles of the seas visage'–in a chapter of the 1590 *Arcadia* (I i)
that sets out a myth of the Fall. See Tillyard in *TLS* (6 Mar. 1953) 153. Cp.
also Cowley's description of the Flood, in which 'The face of shipwrackt
Nature naked lay' (*Davideis* i, ed. Waller 263). More obviously, the wind is
the one that clears the clouds in *Gen.* viii 1, or in Ovid, *Met.* i 328 (where it is
specified to be the *north-wind*).   *hulling*] drifting.   *north-wind*] the
word was often hyphenated in the seventeenth century.

xi *844–6.* On the sun's drinking, see v 423–6n. Note the half-pun, whereby
face and *gazed* lead us to take *glass*=mirror, until *fresh . . . thirst* shows this
to be wrong. The shift in meaning is a profound one. As a self-reflecting
mirror (emblematic of vanity) the world is wrinkled and old, but as an
instrument of communion with God it becomes *fresh* again.

xi *849.* Cp. *Gen.* viii 2: 'The fountains also of the deep and the windows
of heaven were stopped, and the rain from heaven was restrained', and see
ll. 824–7n.

xi *851.* Deliberately avoiding the localization of *Gen.* viii 4, 'upon the
mountains of Ararat'.

xi *852–4.* Cp. the receding waters at the Creation, vii 285ff. The connec-
tion implies that 'one whole world' (l. 874) has been destroyed, and that
God is creating afresh a New Creation based on the Covenant.

855   Forthwith from out the ark a raven flies,
       And after him, the surer messenger,
       A dove sent forth once and again to spy
       Green tree or ground whereon his foot may light;
       The second time returning, in his bill
860   An olive leaf he brings, pacific sign:
       Anon dry ground appears, and from his ark
       The ancient sire descends with all his train;
       Then with uplifted hands, and eyes devout,
       Grateful to heaven, over his head beholds
865   A dewy cloud, and in the cloud a bow
       Conspicuous with three listed colours gay,
       Betokening peace from God, and Covenant new.
       Whereat the heart of Adam erst so sad
       Greatly rejoiced, and thus his joy broke forth.
870   O thou who future things canst represent
       As present, heavenly instructor, I revive
       At this last sight, assured that man shall live
       With all the creatures, and their seed preserve.
       Far less I now lament for one whole world
875   Of wicked sons destroyed, than I rejoice
       For one man found so perfect and so just,
       That God vouchsafes to raise another world
       From him, and all his anger to forget.
       But say, what mean those coloured streaks in heaven,
880   Distended as the brow of God appeased,
       Or serve they as a flowery verge to bind
       The fluid skirts of that same watery cloud,
       Lest it again dissolve and shower the earth?
         To whom the archangel, Dextrously thou aim'st;
885   So willingly doth God remit his ire,

xi *864.* On the pun in *Grateful* ('feeling gratitude' and 'pleasing') see Ricks 114.

xi *865–7.* See Svendsen 98.   *three . . . colours*] The primary colours red, yellow and blue.   *listed*] arranged in bands.   *Covenant*] See *Gen.* ix 13–15: 'I do set my bow in the cloud, and it shall be for a token of a covenant between me and the earth. . . . the waters shall no more become a flood to destroy all flesh.' For Michael's commission to 'intermix' God's Covenant in the visions, see ll. 115f above, with *n.*

xi *868. erst*] previously.

xi *870. who*] that *Ed I.*

xi *880. distended*] expanded (i.e., not contracted in anger).

xi *881.* In modern usage, *Or* might be preceded by a dash, to indicate that a sudden afterthought is being introduced.

Though late repenting him of man depraved,
Grieved at his heart, when looking down he saw
The whole earth filled with violence, and all flesh
Corrupting each their way; yet those removed,
890   Such grace shall one just man find in his sight,
That he relents, not to blot out mankind,
And makes a Covenant never to destroy
The earth again by flood, nor let the sea
Surpass his bounds, nor rain to drown the world
895   With man therein or beast; but when he brings
Over the earth a cloud, will therein set
His triple-coloured bow, whereon to look
And call to mind his Covenant: day and night,
Seed time and harvest, heat and hoary frost
900   Shall hold their course, till fire purge all things new,
Both heaven and earth, wherein the just shall dwell.

THE END OF THE ELEVENTH BOOK

---

xi *886–7.* Cp. *Gen.* vi 6, where God's reason for causing the Flood is that 'it repented [him] that he had made man on the earth, and it grieved him at his heart'.

xi *888–9.* Cp. *Gen.* vi 11: 'The earth also was corrupt before God, and the earth was filled with violence.'

xi *890.* 'But Noah found grace in the eyes of the Lord' (*Gen.* vi 8).

xi *892–901.* Cp. *Gen.* ix 14–16, viii 22. M. conspicuously omits the lifting of the curse on the ground (*Gen.* viii 21); probably not so much for the reason Burden gives–to avoid having God change his mind–as because the curse on the ground has in part been interpreted by M. as occasioning a macro-cosmic change to the mutable astronomical world of our own experience. See x 623–40, where we are told that mutability will continue until the last things: 'Till then the curse pronounced on both [heaven and earth] precedes.' That divine pronouncement was immediately followed by the movement of the sun, and by such other macrocosmic changes 'as sorted best with present things' (x 651).   *triple-coloured*] Cp. l. 866. Svendsen 98 mentions a belief that while the blue of the rainbow shows the Flood is past, the fiery colour shows what is yet to come. This idea stems ultimately from 2 *Pet.* iii 6f, which links the final conflagration with the Flood, in a criticism of those who take the continuance of the world too much for granted: 'The world that then was, being overflowed with water, perished: But the heavens and the earth, which are now, by the same word are kept in store, reserved unto fire against the day of judgment and perdition of ungodly men.' The verses that follow develop an apocalyptic vision of the Last Day when 'the elements shall melt with fervent heat', but when those within.

Paradise Lost

BOOK XII

The Argument

The angel Michael continues from the Flood to relate what shall succeed; then, in the mention of Abraham, comes by degrees to explain, who that seed of the woman shall be, which was promised Adam and Eve in the Fall;[1] his incarnation, death, resurrection, and ascension; the state of the Church till his second coming. Adam greatly satisfied and recomforted by these relations and promises descends the hill with Michael; wakens Eve, who all this while had slept, but with gentle dreams composed to quietness of mind and submission. Michael in either hand leads them out of Paradise, the fiery sword waving behind them, and the cherubim taking their stations to guard the place.

> As one who in his journey bates at noon,
> Though bent on speed, so here the archangel paused
> Betwixt the world destroyed and world restored,
> If Adam aught perhaps might interpose;

the Covenant may 'look for new heavens and a new earth, wherein dwelleth righteousness' (13f). The view that the present world will in a literal sense perish by fire was more general in M.'s time than in ours. He himself sets out what is known about the expected event from Scripture in *De doctrina* i 33 (Columbia xvi 369–71). Cp. viii 334–5*n*. It is fitting that an apocalypse should end the visions of the first 'world' (xii 6).

xii *Argument*[1]. *The angel Michael . . . in the Fall*] *Ed I* has 'thence from the Flood relates, and by degrees explains, who that seed of the woman shall be'.

xii *1–5*. Added when the tenth book of *Ed I* became the eleventh and twelfth of *Ed II*. Thus, *Ed II* xi 901 = *Ed I* x 896, and *Ed II* xii 6 = *Ed I* x 897. Note that *Ed I* does not even start a fresh paragraph to mark the pause in the archangel's journey. The paragraphs beginning at xii 1 and 6 are both new with *Ed II*.

xii *1. bates*] stops (*OED* v.[2] 1 b).   *noon*] the point of transition between one world and another, as the subsequent lines make clear. The transition is specifically like noon because noon is the 'sixth hour' of the Biblical day. A great deal of mystical speculation had been based on the tradition that the Fall, the Expulsion and the death of Christ all took place at the sixth hour. Bongo, who discusses the matter at some length (pp. 279–81) draws from these harmonies the conclusion that six is the number of salvation. See ll. 466–7*n*; also ix 739–40*n*. Note that the six visions which have just been shown to Adam correspond to the hours of Michael's journey in the exact metaphor of the present line. The visions cover the period of the Age of Adam (ll. 466–7*n*), so that the metaphorical noon here sees Adam's death, in

    5 Then with transition sweet new speech resumes.
          Thus thou hast seen one world begin and end;
       And man as from a second stock proceed.
       Much thou hast yet to see, but I perceive
       Thy mortal sight to fail; objects divine
   10 Must needs impair and weary human sense:
       Henceforth what is to come I will relate,
       Thou therefore give due audience, and attend.
       This second source of men, while yet but few;
       And while the dread of judgment past remains
   15 Fresh in their minds, fearing the Deity,
       With some regard to what is just and right
       Shall lead their lives, and multiply apace,
       Labouring the soil, and reaping plenteous crop,
       Corn wine and oil; and from the herd or flock,
   20 Oft sacrificing bullock, lamb, or kid,
       With large wine-offerings poured, and sacred feast,
       Shall spend their days in joy unblamed, and dwell
       Long time in peace by families and tribes
       Under paternal rule; till one shall rise

accordance with the terms of the prohibition; just as the real noon of l. 589 will see his expulsion from Paradise into the mortal world.

xii 5. Apparently M. felt it necessary to add an explicit commentary on the structure in *Ed II*. The *transition* is *sweet* in the sense that honey of doctrine can be extracted from it. It is a transition from the first to the second *world*, from the first to the *second stock* (l. 7) and from the first to the *second source* (l. 13). It corresponds to a movement from the first to the second of the 'three drops' instilled into Adam's eyes at xi 416, and it is marked formally by a change from vision to narration. See further in ll. 466–7n.

xii 7. *stock*] An ambiguity, referring not only to the literal replacement of one source of the human line of descent (Adam) by another (Noah), but also to the grafting of mankind onto the stem of Christ, according to the Pauline allegory of regeneration (*Rom*. xi). The covenant with Noah was a type of the New Covenant.

xii 13. Some copies *Ed I*, probably correctly, have comma after *few*.

xii 16–24. Since Richardson, editors have compared the Ovidian Age of Silver (*Met*. i 113ff); but the correspondence is not very close.

xii 18. *labouring*] tilling, cultivating (*OED* I 1).

xii 19. *Corn wine and oil*] Often associated in O.T. expositions of the law of tithes: see, e.g., *Deut*. xiv 23, *Neh*. x 39. But the phrase seems specifically to echo the Prayer Book version of *Ps*. iv 8 (7), as it was used in the Office of Compline: 'Thou hast put gladness in my heart: since the time that their corn and wine and oil increased.'

xii 24–63. Nimrod is not connected with the builders of the Tower in *Genesis*, which merely has 'Cush begat Nimrod: he began to be a mighty

25   Of proud ambitious heart, who not content
       With fair equality, fraternal state,
       Will arrogate dominion undeserved
       Over his brethren, and quite dispossess
       Concord and law of nature from the earth,
30   Hunting (and men not beasts shall be his game)
       With war and hostile snare such as refuse
       Subjection to his empire tyrannous:
       A mighty hunter thence he shall be styled
       Before the Lord, as in despite of heaven,
35   Or from heaven claiming second sovereignty;

one in the earth. He was a mighty hunter before the Lord: wherefore it is said, Even as Nimrod the mighty hunter before the Lord. And the beginning of his kingdom was Babel' (*Gen.* x 8–10). The connection is made, however, in Josephus, *Antiq.* I iv 2f, where we also learn the derivation of *Babel* (cp. l. 62), the composition of the Tower (ll. 41–3) and the fact that Nimrod 'changed the government into tyranny'. On this basis the commentators (especially St Jerome) developed Nimrod into an archetype of the tyrant, and made him replace the patriarchal *paternal rule* by *dominion* and *empire*. But M.'s presentation of Nimrod has also a republican tinge, for which we have been prepared by the preceding Senecan idyll of virtuous primitive governors (see Hughes in Yale iii 118f, citing Seneca, *Epist.* lxxxi). The appeal to Natural Law against the claim of the tyrannical ruler is republican (though by no means exclusively so), and so is the ideal of a *fraternal state*. Throughout the present passage there are resonances with *The Tenure of Kings and Magistrates*, some of which are noted below.

xii *29*. Cp. St Basil's definition of a tyrant, cited in *The Tenure*: 'A Tyrant whether by wrong or by right comming to the Crown, is he who regarding neither Law nor the common good, reigns onely for himself and his faction' (Yale iii 212). Cp. also *ibid.* 202, M.'s denial of the natural right of kings, and his insistence that their power is committed to them in trust by the people.

xii *30–3*. A metaphorical interpretation of Nimrod's hunting was frequent among the commentators. See, e.g., Willet 117, applying *Lam.* iv 18. Cp. *Eikonoklastes*: 'The Bishops could have told him, that *Nimrod*, the first that hunted after Faction is reputed, by ancient Tradition, the first that founded Monarchy; whence it appeares that to hunt after Faction is more properly the Kings Game' (Yale iii 466; similarly at 598). Cp. also Dryden, *The Hind and the Panther* i 282f.

xii *34–5*. The commentators found *Before the Lord* (*Gen.* x 9) a puzzling phrase. M. chooses to take it (with Vatablus and Mercerus) in a constitutional sense; cp. *The Tenure* (Yale iii 204): 'To say Kings are accountable to none but God, is the overturning of all Law.'

And from rebellion shall derive his name,
Though of rebellion others he accuse.
He with a crew, whom like ambition joins
With him or under him to tyrannize,
40   Marching from Eden towards the west, shall find
The plain, wherein a black bituminous gurge
Boils out from under ground, the mouth of hell;
Of brick, and of that stuff they cast to build
A city and tower, whose top may reach to heaven;
45   And get themselves a name, lest far dispersed
In foreign lands their memory be lost
Regardless whether good or evil fame.
But God who oft descends to visit men
Unseen, and through their habitations walks
50   To mark their doings, them beholding soon,
Comes down to see their city, ere the tower
Obstruct heaven towers, and in derision sets
Upon their tongues a various spirit to raze

xii 36. Starnes and Talbert (267) note that the explanation of *Nimrod* as
derived from Hebrew *mârad* and = Latin *rebellis* is given in Charles Estienne's
Dictionarium: perhaps the best prop to their shaky argument that M. drew
from there the material for the present passage.

xii 41-4. *The plain*] Shinar. For this and the direction of the journey cp.
Gen. xi 2, and see iii 466-8n above. The materials of the Tower – brick with
bitumen as mortar – are specified in *Gen*. xi 3; where A.V. translates the
Hebrew word rendered *bitumen* in Vulgate as 'slime' (a common syno-
nym at the time: see *OED* s.v. *Slime* 1 b). M.'s *hell* is not under the earth;
but bitumen has a symbolic connection with hell (see x 296-8 and *n*).
Bentley and Empson (²155) with an odd crassness insist on taking the loca-
tion literally.   *gurge*] whirlpool (first instance in *OED*; almost certainly a
Latinism: *gurges* = abyss, whirlpool).   *cast*] set themselves with resolu-
tion.

xii 45-6. 'And they said, Go to, let us build us a city and a tower, whose
top may reach unto heaven; and let us make us a name, lest we be scattered
abroad upon the face of the whole earth' (*Gen*. xi 4).

xii 52. *Obstruct heaven towers*] Ironic, surely; in spite of Empson² 155 to the
contrary.   *in derision*] Cp., e.g, *Ps*. ii 4: 'He that sitteth in the heavens
shall laugh: the Lord shall have them in derision.'

xii 53-8. In the seventeenth century it was generally believed that the separ-
ation of language into distinct individual languages had its beginning at the
confusion of tongues at Babel. At a time when synthetic universal languages
were much canvassed, the Babel story had a strong fascination. Sir Thomas
Urquhart, for example, presents his universal language as a return to a total
expression such as no language has been capable of since Babel; see his
Most exquisite Jewel and *Logopandecteision*. M. himself writes in his *Logic*

Quite out their native language, and instead
55 To sow a jangling noise of words unknown:
Forthwith a hideous gabble rises loud
Among the builders; each to other calls
Not understood, till hoarse, and all in rage,
As mocked they storm; great laughter was in heaven
60 And looking down, to see the hubbub strange
And hear the din; thus was the building left
Ridiculous, and the work Confusion named.
    Whereto thus Adam fatherly displeased.
    O execrable son so to aspire
65 Above his brethren, to himself assuming
Authority usurped, from God not given:
He gave us only over beast, fish, fowl
Dominion absolute; that right we hold
By his donation; but man over men
70 He made not lord; such title to himself
Reserving, human left from human free.
But this usurper his encroachment proud
Stays not on man; to God his tower intends
Siege and defiance: wretched man! What food
75 Will he convey up thither to sustain
Himself and his rash army, where thin air

(i 24, Columbia xi 220) that 'languages, both that first one which Adam spoke
in Eden, and those varied ones also possibly derived from the first, which the
builders of the tower of Babel suddenly received, are without doubt di-
vinely given'. See D. C. Allen in *PQ* xxviii (1949) 11.   *various*] causing
differences; unstable; going in different directions.   *jangling noise*]
Sylvester's phrase (Du Bartas 320).

xii 62. *Confusion named*] Cp. A.V. *Gen.* xi 9, 'Therefore is the name of it
called Babel'; marginal gloss 'that is, Confusion'. Josephus develops this
popular but false etymology in *Antiq.* I iv 3.

xii 66. Broadbent 112 compares Satan's establishment as king (e.g. ii 466f)
in spite of the republican sentiments he expresses at v 790ff.

xii 73-4. In *Antiq.* I iv 2 Josephus gives a relatively full account of Nimrod's
motives. He persuaded the people on the plain of Shinar not to ascribe their
happiness to God but to their own courage, because he wanted to turn them
from the fear of God and to 'avenge himself on God for destroying their
forefathers'.

xii 76-8. The upper air was not for mortals: see iii 562n. Throughout *PL*
the atmosphere is a symbol of degree–i.e., of both moral and natural
station. Cp., e.g., the 'purer air' of Paradise (iv 153) and the 'thinner air'
that fish are unable to breathe (viii 348). The importance of the idea to M.
may be gauged from its prominence in his Third Draft of a tragedy on the
Fall (see Introduction, 'Composition', p. 3 above).

Above the clouds will pine his entrails gross,
And famish him of breath, if not of bread?
    To whom thus Michael. Justly thou abhorr'st
80 That son, who on the quiet state of men
Such trouble brought, affecting to subdue
Rational liberty; yet know withal,
Since thy original lapse, true liberty
Is lost, which always with right reason dwells
85 Twinned, and from her hath no dividual being:
Reason in man obscured, or not obeyed,
Immediately inordinate desires
And upstart passions catch the government
From reason, and to servitude reduce
90 Man till then free. Therefore since he permits
Within himself unworthy powers to reign
Over free reason, God in judgment just
Subjects him from without to violent lords;
Who oft as undeservedly enthral
95 His outward freedom: tyranny must be,
Though to the tyrant thereby no excuse.
Yet sometimes nations will decline so low
From virtue, which is reason, that no wrong,

xii *80–101*. This whole passage may recall the style of the regicide tracts.
But it follows closely St Augustine's thought in *Civ. Dei* xix 15, where we
read that man was made lord 'only over the unreasonable, not over man,
but over beasts . . . justly was the burden of servitude laid upon the back of
transgression. And therefore in all the Scriptures we never read the word
servant, until such time as that just man Noah laid it as a curse upon his
offending son. So that it was guilt, and not nature that gave original unto
that name.' Hence the derivation of servitude, whose mother is sin, the
'first cause of man's subjection to man: which notwithstanding comes not to
pass but by the direction of the highest, in whom is no injustice' (*ibid.*,
alluding to *John* viii 34). For the connection between psychological and
political enslavement, cp. ix 1127–31 and see *n.*   *right reason*] conscience;
a great watch-word in seventeenth-century theological controversies (see
vi 41–3*n*). Cp. 'rectified' reason, *Articles of Peace* (Yale iii 330).   *Twinned*]
Implies not only a close relation but also a reflective relation in which free
will is a true image of reason. In Neoplatonic systems such as Pico's, the
mind (*intellectus*) was supposed to have such a reflective relationship with the
faculty of choice (*ratio*).   *dividual*] separate, distinct. The passage has an
obvious bearing on the separation of Adam and Eve immediately before the
Fall: without Adam's *reason*, Eve's *liberty* led only to *upstart passions*. Cp.
iii 108–10, ix 351f.
xii *95–6*. Cp. iv 393, where necessity is called 'the tyrant's plea'.

But justice, and some fatal curse annexed
100 Deprives them of their outward liberty,
Their inward lost: witness the irreverent son
Of him who built the ark, who for the shame
Done to his father, heard this heavy curse,
Servant of servants, on his vicious race.
105 Thus will this latter, as the former world,
Still tend from bad to worse, till God at last
Wearied with their iniquities, withdraw
His presence from among them, and avert
His holy eyes; resolving from thenceforth
110 To leave them to their own polluted ways;
And one peculiar nation to select
From all the rest, of whom to be invoked,
A nation from one faithful man to spring:
Him on this side Euphrates yet residing,
115 Bred up in idol-worship; O that men
(Canst thou believe?) should be so stupid grown,
While yet the patriarch lived, who scaped the flood,
As to forsake the living God, and fall
To worship their own work in wood and stone
120 For gods! Yet him God the most high vouchsafes

xii *101–14.* Because Ham the son of Noah looked on the nakedness of his drunken father, and told his brothers about it, his own son Canaan was cursed: 'Cursed be Canaan; a servant of servants shall he be unto his brethren' (*Gen.* ix 25).

xii *111–13.* Another new beginning from another faithful 'remnant'. In *De doctrina* M. distinguishes the 'general or national election' of Israel from the eternal predestination or election of an individual. (Hughes tells us that M. 'condemns the Calvinistic doctrine of individual election to personal salvation'. In fact what M. condemns is the doctrine of Reprobation, not of Election. There is nothing wrong with predestinating glory.) See especially *De doctrina* i 4, (Columbia xiv 96–100).   *peculiar*] special, particular; cp. *Deut.* xiv 2: 'For thou art an holy people unto the Lord thy God, and the Lord hath chosen thee to be a peculiar people unto himself, above all the nations that are upon the earth.'

xii *114–15.* On Abraham's origins, see *Joshua* xxiv 2: 'Thus saith the Lord God of Israel, Your fathers dwelt on the other side of the flood in old time, even Terah, the father of Abraham, and the father of Nachor: and they served other gods.'

xii *117. the patriarch*] Noah, who lived for 350 years after the Flood, according to *Gen.* ix 28.

xii *120. most high*] The name used in Melchizedek's blessing of Abraham, *Gen.* xiv 19.

> To call by vision from his father's house,
> His kindred and false gods, into a land
> Which he will show him, and from him will raise
> A mighty nation, and upon him shower

xii *121–34*. For the calling of Abraham and God's covenant with him, see *Gen.* xii and *Acts* vii. The departure from idolatry is stressed in *Judith* v 6–9.   *all nations*] Cp. *Gen.* xii 3: 'In thee shall all families of the earth be blessed.'   *firm believes*] Cp. Heb. xi 8, 'By faith Abraham, when he was called to go out into a place which he should after receive for an inheritance, obeyed; and he went out, not knowing whither he went.' The irony is strong in view of the imminence of Adam's expulsion: he will shortly be challenged by the need to have a similar faith.   *thou canst not*] the object is too divine for Adam in his present state; see l. 9. The *ford* is probably M.'s inference from the information given in *Gen.* xi 31: *Ur* was on one bank of the Euphrates and *Haran* (see iv 209–16*n*) on the other, to the N.W.   *servitude*] slaves and servants collectively (putting the abstract for the concrete). xii *135–51*. The account of the journey is based on *Gen.* xii 5f; of the promise, on *Josh.* xiii 5f.   *Hamath*] Marks the N. border, the 'great sea' the W. border, and the wilderness of Zin the S. border of the Promised Land in *Num.* xxxiv 3–8. *Josh.* xiii 5f itself mentions Mt *Hermon* and the district of *Hamath* as boundaries.   *as I point them*] In all his panoramic views, M. is most careful to establish a clear perspective: the places are not only visualized, but visualized from one particular standpoint.   *on the shore*] Mt *Carmel's* position, as certain as destiny, is something to swear an oath on in *Jer.* xlvi 18: 'As I live, saith the King, whose name is the Lord of hosts, Surely as Tabor is among the mountains, and as Carmel by the sea, so shall he come.' Thus the very landscape is prophetic of sure deliverance.   *double-founted*] The fallacious belief that the *Jordan* is formed by the confluence of two fountains Jor and Dan is still subscribed to in George Sandys's *Relation* (1615), which M. seems to have used (though the tradition went back to St. Jerome, as Hughes notes). The river is mentioned as the E. border of Canaan in *Num.* xxxiv 12. *Senir* seems to have been thought of by M. as a ridge running E. from Mt Hermon; the allusion is to *1 Chron.* v 23. Note that nine places are named in the Promised Land: the incorruptible number of heavenly things (see Fowler 270ff). Also, that among these nine Jordan has the eighth position – a position appropriate to its connection with baptism, since eight is the number of baptism and regeneration (*ibid.* 53; Bongo 330f). It may be for the purpose of drawing attention to this numerological arrangement that M. twice announces he is giving *names*, at ll. 140 and 142f (notice also, however, an echo of Virgil, *Aen.* vi 776). The central place of sovereignty is occupied by *Hermon*, because of its connection with King Solomon (see *Song of Sol.* iv 8, and cf. xi 396–407*n* above). See also St Augustine's mystical interpretation of the dew of Hermon (*Ps.* cxxxiii 3) as the grace of God: 'The light set on high is Christ, whence is the dew of Hermon.'

125 His benediction so, that in his seed
       All nations shall be blest; he straight obeys,
       Not knowing to what land, yet firm believes:
       I see him, but thou canst not, with what faith
       He leaves his gods, his friends, and native soil
130 Ur of Chaldaea, passing now the ford
       To Haran, after him a cumbrous train
       Of herds and flocks, and numerous servitude;
       Not wandering poor, but trusting all his wealth
       With God, who called him, in a land unknown.
135 Canaan he now attains, I see his tents
       Pitched about Sechem, and the neighbouring plain
       Of Moreh; there by promise he receives
       Gift to his progeny of all that land;
       From Hamath northward to the desert south
140 (Things by their names I call, though yet unnamed)
       From Hermon east to the great western sea,
       Mount Hermon, yonder sea, each place behold
       In prospect, as I point them; on the shore
       Mount Carmel; here the double-founted stream
145 Jordan, true limit eastward; but his sons
       Shall dwell to Senir, that long ridge of hills.
       This ponder, that all nations of the earth
       Shall in his seed be blessed; by that seed
       Is meant thy great deliverer, who shall bruise
150 The serpent's head; whereof to thee anon
       Plainlier shall be revealed. This patriarch blest,
       Whom faithful Abraham due time shall call,
       A son, and of his son a grandchild leaves,
       Like him in faith, in wisdom, and renown;
155 The grandchild with twelve sons increased, departs
       From Canaan, to a land hereafter called

xii *147–51*. The promise to Abraham (*Gen.* xii 1–3) renews the promise implicit in the curse on the serpent; see x 180ff.

xii *152*. *Abraham*] 'Father of a great multitude'; see *Gen.* xvii 5, with A.V. marg. gloss; and cp. *Gal.* iii 9: 'So then they which be of faith are blessed with faithful Abraham.'

xii *153*. The *son* is Isaac, the *grandchild* Jacob.

xii *155–63*. *Gen.* xlv and xlvi tell how Jacob went down to Egypt at the bidding of the *younger son* Joseph. The *seven mouths* of the Nile contrast with the nine places of the Promised Land (see ll. 135–51*n*), because seven is the number of mortality and mutability. The opposition between seven and nine was very common; and so was that between Egypt (symbolizing body, flesh, sin, this world) and the Promised Land (mind, spirit, regeneration, heaven). See Fowler, App. i *passim*.

Egypt, divided by the river Nile;
See where it flows, disgorging at seven mouths
Into the sea: to sojourn in that land
160   He comes invited by a younger son
In time of dearth, a son whose worthy deeds
Raise him to be the second in that realm
Of Pharao: there he dies, and leaves his race
Growing into a nation, and now grown
165   Suspected to a sequent king, who seeks
To stop their overgrowth, as inmate guests
Too numerous; whence of guests he makes them slaves
Inhospitably, and kills their infant males:
Till by two brethren (those two brethren call
170   Moses and Aaron) sent from God to claim
His people from enthralment, they return
With glory and spoil back to their promised land.
But first the lawless tyrant, who denies
To know their God, or message to regard,
175   Must be compelled by signs and judgments dire;
To blood unshed the rivers must be turned,
Frogs, lice and flies must all his palace fill
With loathed intrusion, and fill all the land;
His cattle must of rot and murrain die,
180   Botches and blains must all his flesh emboss,
And all his people; thunder mixed with hail,
Hail mixed with fire must rend the Egyptian sky
And wheel on the earth, devouring where it rolls;
What it devours not, herb, or fruit, or grain,
185   A darksome cloud of locusts swarming down
Must eat, and on the ground leave nothing green:
Darkness must overshadow all his bounds,
Palpable darkness, and blot out three days;

xii *164–8.* Following *Exod.* i.   *sequent king*] Named as Busiris at i 307,
in the comparison of the devils to the Pharaoh's 'Memphian chivalry'.
overgrowth] excessive growth (*OED* 1).
xii *172. spoil*] Jewels and clothes extorted as a 'loan' when the Egyptians
were anxious to see the Israelites leave as soon as possible (*Exod.* xii 36).
xii *173. denies*] refuses.
xii *173–90.* The brief account of the plagues is in general based on *Exod.*
vii–xii. The chariot image in l. 183, however, is M.'s own, and should be
referred to the central image of the poem, the chariot of cosmic justice (see
vi 749–59*n*, and cp. i 311). The locust plague has appeared earlier, in the
simile at i 338–43.
xii *188. palpable*] Cp. Vulgate *Exod.* x 21: *Sint tenebrae super terram Aegypti,
tam densae, ut palpari queant.*

        Last with one midnight stroke all the first-born
190   Of Egypt must lie dead. Thus with ten wounds
        The river-dragon tamed at length submits
        To let his sojourners depart, and oft
        Humbles his stubborn heart, but still as ice
        More hardened after thaw, till in his rage
195   Pursuing whom he late dismissed, the sea
        Swallows him with his host, but them lets pass
        As on dry land between two crystal walls,
        Awed by the rod of Moses so to stand
        Divided, till his rescued gain their shore:
200   Such wondrous power God to his saint will lend,
        Though present in his angel, who shall go
        Before them in a cloud, and pillar of fire,
        By day a cloud, by night a pillar of fire,
        To guide them in their journey, and remove
205   Behind them, while the obdurate king pursues:
        All night he will pursue, but his approach

xii *191. The*] This *Ed I*. Röstvig 187 remarks that the description of the
Pharaoh as 'the great dragon that lieth in the midst of his rivers' in *Ezek.*
xxix 3 is the foundation for his typological interpretation as Sin.

xii *192*. M. uses Pharaoh as the classic example of one whose heart was har-
dened, in *De doctrina* i 8 (Columbia xv 71), and compares his blindness to
that of King Charles, in *Eikonoklastes* (Yale iii 516).

xii *193–4*. Svendsen 99 notes that according to Swan's *Speculum mundi* snow
'melting on the high hilles, and after frozen againe, becommeth so hard, that
it is a stone, and is called Christall.'

xii *197*. Cp. the youthful *Psalm cxxxvi* 49f: 'The floods stood still like walls
of glass, / While the Hebrew bands did pass.' Both passages may have been
influenced by the phrase 'walls of crystal' in Sylvester's account of the
parting of the Red Sea (Du Bartas 454). But much more important is the
connection with the division of the waters at the Creation (vii 293 above:
'Part rise in crystal wall'). See *Exod.* xiv 16, 21f.

xii *199*. As the Nile 'divided' Egypt (l. 157), so Moses' rod *Divided* the
water. Division, when auspicious, was usually a symbol of justice and crea-
tive power; see Fowler 34, 206.

xii *200–5*. Cp. *Exod.* xiii 21f.   *present in his angel*] See *De doctrina* i 5
(Columbia xiv 287–9), where M. develops at length the point that God never
went himself with the Israelites, since that would have destroyed them;
but that he sent 'a representation of his name and glory in the person of
some angel'.   *saint*] Often applied, in the seventeenth century, to O.T.
personages.   *obdurate*] Stressed on the second syllable; there is elision or
synaloepha with *the*.

xii *206–14*. See *Exod.* xiv, and cp. i 306ff.   *defends*] wards off, averts

Darkness defends between till morning watch;
Then through the fiery pillar and the cloud
God looking forth will trouble all his host
210   And craze their chariot wheels: when by command
Moses once more his potent rod extends
Over the sea; the sea his rod obeys;
On their embattled ranks the waves return,
And overwhelm their war: the race elect
215   Safe towards Canaan from the shore advance
Through the wild desert, not the readiest way,
Lest entering on the Canaanite alarmed
War terrify them inexpert, and fear
Return them back to Egypt, choosing rather
220   Inglorious life with servitude; for life
To noble and ignoble is more sweet
Untrained in arms, where rashness leads not on.
This also shall they gain by their delay
In the wide wilderness, there they shall found
225   Their government, and their great senate choose
Through the twelve tribes, to rule by laws ordained:
God from the mount of Sinai, whose grey top
Shall tremble, he descending, will himself
In thunder lightning and loud trumpets' sound
230   Ordain them laws; part such as appertain
To civil justice, part religious rites

(*OED* I 1); hinders (*OED* I 2).   *war*] soldiers in fighting array (perhaps
poetic diction; first example in this sense in *OED*).

xii *216–19*. The explanation given in *Exod.* xiii 17f. The actual route took
a detour south to avoid the warlike Philistines. The Civil War is compared to
the wandering in the desert, in *Eikonoklastes* (Yale iii 580).

xii *224–6*. For the election of the Seventy Elders see *Num.* xi 16–25 and
Exod. xxiv.   *senate*] M.'s choice of the term probably implies that he saw
the Seventy as the beginning of the Sanhedrin, which he refers to as a senate
in *The Ready and Easy Way* (Columbia vi 128), and takes as a model for con-
temporary senates. The Jewish constitution was at the time fairly often
proposed as a pattern commonwealth; though such proposals by no means
met with general acceptance. Hobbes, e.g., 'expressly repudiated the view
of Moses as the institutor of a conciliar government' (Hughes, Yale iii 89*n*,
citing *Leviathan* iii 42).

xii *227–30*. Cp. *Exod.* xix 16–20.

xii *229*. In this case the modern spelling possibly obscures a piece of double
syntax. The early edns have 'trumpets' (without apostrophe), so that
sound may at first be felt as a verb.

Of sacrifice, informing them, by types
And shadows, of that destined seed to bruise
The serpent, by what means he shall achieve
235   Mankind's deliverance. But the voice of God
To mortal ear is dreadful; they beseech
That Moses might report to them his will,
And terror cease; he grants what they besought
Instructed that to God is no access
240   Without mediator, whose high office now
Moses in figure bears, to introduce
One greater, of whose day he shall foretell,
And all the prophets in their age the times
Of great Messiah shall sing. Thus laws and rites
245   Established, such delight hath God in men
Obedient to his will, that he vouchsafes
Among them to set up his tabernacle,

xii *232–4*. Cp. *Heb*. viii 5 : earthly priests 'serve unto the example and shadow of heavenly things, as Moses was admonished of God when he was about to make the tabernacle: for, See, saith he, that thou make all things according to the pattern showed to thee in the mount.'

xii *235–8*. See *Exod*. xx 19: frightened by the thunder and lightning and trumpeting, the Israelites said to Moses: 'Speak thou with us, and we will hear: but let not God speak with us, lest we die.'

xii *238*. *what they besought*] *Ed I* has 'them their desire' followed by comma.

xii *238–44*. 'For Moses truly said unto the fathers, A prophet shall the Lord your God raise up unto you of your brethren, like unto me; him shall ye hear in all things whatsoever he shall say unto you' (*Acts* iii 22, citing *Deut*. xviii 15–19. Moses was regarded as a *figure* of Christ in his capacity as mediator. Cp. *De doctrina* i 15 (Columbia xv 287): 'The name and office of mediator is in a certain sense ascribed to Moses, as a type of Christ.'   *laws and rites*] Described in typological terms in *Heb*. ix 19–23 (e.g. 'without shedding of blood is no remission').

xii *247–56*. The description of the Tabernacle in general follows *Exod*. xxv–xxvi; but mindful of his theme Michael adds from *Heb*. ix 4 the identification of the testimony as *The records of his Covenant*. The early edns indicate elision of the medial vowel of *Covenant*.   *cedar*] not in *Exod*.; the confusion between shittim-wood and cedar probably stems from A.V. *Is*. xli 19.   *mercy-seat*] see xi 2*n*.   *representing* / *The heavenly fires*] Josephus has several passages interpreting the details of the Tabernacle as cosmological symbols. See esp. *Antiq*. III vi 7, on the candlestick ('It terminated in seven heads, in one row, all standing parallel to one another; and these branches carried seven lamps, one by one, in imitation of the number of the planets'); *ibid*. III vii 7 ('By branching out the candlestick into seventy parts, he secretly intimated the *Decani*, or seventy divisions of the planets; and as to the seven lamps upon the candlesticks, they referred to the course

The holy one with mortal men to dwell:
By his prescript a sanctuary is framed
250   Of cedar, overlaid with gold, therein
An ark, and in the ark his testimony,
The records of his Covenant, over these
A mercy-seat of gold between the wings
Of two bright cherubim, before him burn
255   Seven lamps as in a zodiac representing
The heavenly fires; over the tent a cloud
Shall rest by day, a fiery gleam by night,
Save when they journey, and at length they come,
Conducted by his angel to the land
260   Promised to Abraham and his seed: the rest
Were long to tell, how many battles fought,
How many kings destroyed, and kingdoms won,
Or how the sun shall in mid heaven stand still
A day entire, and night's due course adjourn,
265   Man's voice commanding, sun in Gibeon stand,
And thou moon in the vale of Aialon,
Till Israel overcome; so call the third
From Abraham, son of Isaac, and from him
His whole descent, who thus shall Canaan win.
270   Here Adam interposed. O sent from heaven,
Enlightener of my darkness, gracious things
Thou hast revealed, those chiefly which concern
Just Abraham and his seed: now first I find

of the planets, of which that is the number'); and *De bellis* V v 5. These
passages would be precious to M., as providing a means of unifying the
astronomical and historical parts of his poem.

xii *256–8*. See *Exod.* xl 34–8.

xii *260*. For the promise to Abraham cp. ll. 137ff, and see *nn*.

xii *263–7*. See *Josh.* x 12f: 'Then spake Joshua to the Lord in the day when
the Lord delivered up the Amorites before the children of Israel, and he said
in the sight of Israel, Sun, stand thou still upon Gibeon; and thou, Moon,
in the valley of Ajalon. And the sun stood still, and the moon stayed, until
the people had avenged themselves upon their enemies. Is not this written in
the book of Jasher? So the sun stood still in the midst of heaven, and hasted
not to go down about a whole day.' The incident is often treated as an
example of the power of Faith; as in Spenser, *F.Q.* I x 20, where it is linked
(in the 1609 edn at least) with Moses' parting of the Red Sea – when Fidelia
wished, 'She would commaund the hastie Sunne to stay, / Or backward
turne his course from heauens hight; / Sometimes great hostes of men she
could dismay, / Dry-shod to passe, she parts the flouds in tway.' Note that
one of the themes projected in the *Trin. MS* is 'Joshua in Gibeon'.   *Israel*]
Jacob (see *Gen.* xxxii 28).

Mine eyes true opening, and my heart much eased,
275   Erewhile perplexed with thoughts what would become
Of me and all mankind; but now I see
His day, in whom all nations shall be blest,
Favour unmerited by me, who sought
Forbidden knowledge by forbidden means.
280   This yet I apprehend not, why to those
Among whom God will deign to dwell on earth
So many and so various laws are given;
So many laws argue so many sins
Among them; how can God with such reside?
285   To whom thus Michael. Doubt not but that sin
Will reign among them, as of thee begot;
And therefore was law given them to evince
Their natural pravity, by stirring up
Sin against law to fight; that when they see
290   Law can discover sin, but not remove,
Save by those shadowy expiations weak,
The blood of bulls and goats, they may conclude

xii *274. true opening*] Alludes to the serpent's false or ironic promise that the forbidden fruit will open man's eyes. Cp. xi 412ff.

xii *277.* The dramatic irony depends on familiarity with Christ's claim that 'before Abraham was I AM'. See *John* viii 56: 'Your father Abraham rejoiced to see my day: and he saw it, and was glad.' Adam means only that he can imagine the time of Abraham: he thinks the promise will be realised then. But he will learn that the blessing of ll. 147f contains another mystery still to be unfolded.

xii *285–306.* A statement of the relation of Law to Justification by Faith that covers central ground common to all Protestant theologians. This, together with the conciseness of the passage, puts the assigning of sources out of the question. The following texts, however, are somewhere in the background: *Rom.* iii 20, iv 22–5, v 1, 13, 17, 21, vii 7f, viii 15, x 5; *Heb.* vii 19, ix 13f, x 1–5; *Gal.* iii 4.

xii *287. evince*] Primarily 'make manifest' (*OED* 5), but secondarily 'overcome, subdue' (*OED* 1).

xii *288. pravity*] depravity.

xii *290.* Cp. *Rom.* iii 19f: The Law makes all guilty before God 'for by the law is the knowledge of sin'.

xii *291.* See ll. 238–44*n*. The Law being only a type, its sacrifices could not be efficacious like Christ's. See *Heb.* x 1: 'For the law having a shadow of good things to come, and not the very image of the things, can never with those sacrifices which they offered year by year continually make the comers thereunto perfect.'

Some blood more precious must be paid for man,
Just for unjust, that in such righteousness
295 To them by faith imputed, they may find
Justification towards God, and peace
Of conscience, which the law by ceremonies
Cannot appease, nor man the moral part
Perform, and not performing cannot live.
300 So law appears imperfect, and but given
With purpose to resign them in full time
Up to a better Covenant, disciplined
From shadowy types to truth, from flesh to spirit,
From imposition of strict laws, to free
305 Acceptance of large grace, from servile fear
To filial, works of law to works of faith.
And therefore shall not Moses, though of God
Highly beloved, being but the minister
Of law, his people into Canaan lead;
310 But Joshua whom the gentiles Jesus call,
His name and office bearing, who shall quell
The adversary serpent, and bring back
Through the world's wilderness long wandered man
Safe to eternal paradise of rest.
315 Meanwhile they in their earthly Canaan placed

xii *293*. Cp. *1 Pet.* i 18f: 'Ye know that ye were not redeemed with corrup-
tible things, as silver and gold, from your vain conversation received by
tradition from your fathers; But with the precious blood of Christ, as of
a lamb without blemish and without spot.'

xii *294*. Cp. *1 Pet.* iii 18.

xii *297-8*. Cp. *Gal.* ii 16.

xii *300-6*. The thought follows *Gal.* iii 22-6.   *but*] only.   *resign*]
consign; yield up with confidence (*OED* 2).

xii *307-11*. See *Deut.* xxxiv, *Josh.* i. In *De doctrina* i 26 (Columbia xvi 111)
we find what is almost a prose version of the present passage. The Law fails
to promise what faith in God through Christ has attained, eternal life:
'Thus the imperfection of the law was manifested in the person of Moses
himself; for Moses, who was a type of the law, could not bring the children
of Israel into the land of Canaan, that is, into eternal rest; but an entrance was
given to them under Joshua, or Jesus.'   *Jesus*] The Greek equivalent of
Joshua; appearing as such in *Acts* vii 45 etc. Starnes 261 compares the word-
ing of the entry on Joshua in Charles Estienne's *Dictionarium*: *Iosue, et Iesus,
idem est nomen . . . Iosue, Typum Iesu Christi non solum in gestis, verum etiam
in nomine genens, transiit Iordanem'.*

xii *313*. Clearly implying, like l. 190, a typological or mystical application
of the O.T.; see Röstvig 187.

Long time shall dwell and prosper, but when sins
National interrupt their public peace,
Provoking God to raise them enemies:
From whom as oft he saves them penitent
320   By judges first, then under kings; of whom
The second, both for piety renowned
And puissant deeds, a promise shall receive
Irrevocable, that his regal throne
For ever shall endure; the like shall sing
325   All prophecy, that of the royal stock
Of David (so I name this king) shall rise
A son, the woman's seed to thee foretold,
Foretold to Abraham, as in whom shall trust
All nations, and to kings foretold, of kings
330   The last, for of his reign shall be no end.
But first a long succession must ensue,
And his next son for wealth and wisdom famed,
The clouded ark of God till then in tents
Wandering, shall in a glorious temple enshrine.
335   Such follow him, as shall be registered
Part good, part bad, of bad the longer scroll,
Whose foul idolatries, and other faults
Heaped to the popular sum, will so incense
God, as to leave them, and expose their land,
340   Their city, his temple, and his holy ark
With all his sacred things, a scorn and prey
To that proud city, whose high walls thou saw'st
Left in confusion, Babylon thence called.

xii *316. but*] except.
xii *320*. Cp. *Judges* ii 16.
xii *321–4*. David received a promise from the prophet Nathan, that 'thine house and thy kingdom shall be established for ever before thee: thy throne shall be established for ever' (*2 Sam.* vii 16).
xii *324–30*. In many O.T. passages (such as *Is.* xi 10 and *Ps.* lxxxix 36), the royal line or the seed of David has a Messianic significance. *Luke* i 32 applies this to Jesus: 'He shall be great, and shall be called the Son of the Highest: and the Lord God shall give unto him the throne of his father David.' For the promise to Adam, see x 180ff; for the confirming of it to Abraham, xii 125f and 147ff.
xii *332–4*. i.e. Solomon, who built the Temple to give the ark its first fixed location (*1 Kings* v–viii; *2 Chron.* ii–v). The building of the Temple was the occasion of yet another divine Covenant (*1 Kings* ix 1–9): hence its relevance here.
xii *338. Heaped . . . sum*] added to the sum of the people's faults.
xii *339–43*. See *2 Chron.* xxxvi, *2 Kings* xvii 24ff.

> There in captivity he lets them dwell
> 345 The space of seventy years, then brings them back,
> Remembering mercy, and his Covenant sworn
> To David, stablished as the days of heaven.
> Returned from Babylon by leave of kings
> Their lords, whom God disposed, the house of God
> 350 They first re-edify, and for a while
> In mean estate live moderate, till grown
> In wealth and multitude, factious they grow;
> But first among the priests dissension springs,
> Men who attend the altar, and should most
> 355 Endeavour peace: their strife pollution brings
> Upon the Temple it self: at last they seize
> The sceptre, and regard not David's sons,
> Then lose it to a stranger, that the true
> Anointed king Messiah might be born
> 360 Barred of his right; yet at his birth a star

xii *344–7.* For the Babylonian captivity, see *Jer.* xxv 12 and xxxiii 20–6, where the return is related to the Covenant with David, and made as sure as the succession of day and night. Cp. the promise to David, *Ps.* lxxxix 29: 'His seed also will I make to endure for ever, and his throne as the days of heaven.' M.'s close juxtaposition of *seventy years* and *days of heaven* is possibly meant to recall Josephus' interpretation of the seventy parts of the candlestick of the Tabernacle as meaning 'the *Decani,* or seventy divisions of the planets' in the zodiac (see ll. 247–56n, and *Antiq.* III vii 7).

xii *348–50.* The rebuilding of Jerusalem is the subject of the Book of Ezra, and of *Neh.* i–vi; the Persian *kings* are Cyrus, Artaxerxes and Darius. *disposed*] put into a favourable mood (*OED* I 6).

xii *353–8.* 2 *Macc.* iv–vi relates the *strife* between the intriguing priests Jason (Joshua), Menelaus (Onias) and Simon, which led indirectly to Antiochus' sacking Jerusalem and polluting the Temple. Two years later Greek forms of worship were imposed and the Temple at Jerusalem was rededicated to Jupiter Olympius. M. would see these events as an exemplum of the Church's betrayal with an obvious bearing on the history of his own time.

xii *356. they*] Refers to the Asmonean family, who held the high priesthood 153–35 B.C. One of them seized *the sceptre* to become Aristobulus I, thus ending the Israelite theocracy (see Josephus, *Antiq.* XIII xi 1).

xii *357. David's sons*] The descendants of David whose genealogy is traced in *Matt.* i and *Luke* iii.

xii *358. a stranger*] Antipater the Idumean (father of Herod the Great), who was made Procurator of Judaea by Julius Caesar in 47 B.C. (Josephus, *Antiq.* XIV viii 5).

xii *360–9.* Combining details from *Matt.* ii and *Luke* ii.   *Barred*] Legal diction.   *solemn*] holy (*OED* 1); awe-inspiring (*OED* 7).   *thither*] To Bethlehem.   *squadroned*] Cp. *Nativity Ode* 21.   *power*] a deliberate

Unseen before in heaven proclaims him come,
And guides the eastern sages, who inquire
His place, to offer incense, myrrh, and gold;
His place of birth a solemn angel tells
365 To simple shepherds, keeping watch by night;
They gladly thither haste, and by a choir
Of squadroned angels hear his carol sung.
A virgin is his mother, but his sire
The power of the most high; he shall ascend
370 The throne hereditary, and bound his reign
With earth's wide bounds, his glory with the heavens.
He ceased, discerning Adam with such joy
Surcharged, as had like grief been dewed in tears,
Without the vent of words, which these he breathed.
375 O prophet of glad tidings, finisher
Of utmost hope! Now clear I understand
What oft my steadiest thoughts have searched in vain,
Why our great expectation should be called
The seed of woman: virgin Mother, hail,
380 High in the love of heaven, yet from my loins
Thou shalt proceed, and from thy womb the Son

formulation; cp. *De doctrina* i 14 (Columbia xv 281), where *Luke* i 35 ('The Holy Ghost shall come upon thee, and the power of the Highest shall overshadow thee') is taken to mean 'the power and spirit of the Father himself'.

xii *369–71*. The diction recalls Virgil's prophecy with respect to Augustus in *Aen.* i 287 (*imperium Oceano, famam qui terminet astris*), but the idea is probably of a terrestrial reign of Christ, prophesied in *Is.* ix 7, *Rev.* ii 25–7, etc. See particularly *Ps.* ii 8, where the kingdom stretches to 'the uttermost parts of the earth'; and *Dan.* vii 13–22, where its glory and dominion is everlasting. In *De doctrina* i 33 (Columbia xvi 359–63) M. writes at some length about this earthly kingdom of glory, which is to begin with Christ's second advent; he distinguishes it from the kingdom of grace, which began with the first advent. It is possible, however, that the present passage combines both kingdoms. See further in v 496–500*n*.

xii *373. Surcharged*] overwhelmed (*OED* 4).

xii *375–85*. As Burden 197f notes, Michael's first account of Christ is partly couched in epic terms, and Adam errs in his response by expecting an ordinary epic hero. To correct this response Michael will stress Christ's tragic role. *finisher*] 'one who reaches the end' (*OED* s.v. *Finish* v. 5); but there is also an irony, for Adam does not yet understand in what sense Christ is the 'finisher of our faith' (*Heb.* xii 2).

xii *379. seed of woman*] See x 179–81; still another facet of the promise becomes clear to Adam. *hail*] Cp. xi 158 and see *n*. Here ll. 379–82 is a catena of phrases from the angel's address to Mary at the Annunciation, *Luke* i 31–5.

Of God most high; so God with man unites.
Needs must the serpent now his capital bruise
Expect with mortal pain: say where and when
385 Their fight, what stroke shall bruise the victor's heel.
    To whom thus Michael. Dream not of their fight,
As of a duel, or the local wounds
Of head or heel: not therefore joins the Son
Manhood to Godhead, with more strength to foil
390 Thy enemy; nor so is overcome
Satan, whose fall from heaven, a deadlier bruise,
Disabled not to give thee thy death's wound:
Which he, who comes thy saviour, shall recure,
Not by destroying Satan, but his works
395 In thee and in thy seed: nor can this be,
But by fulfilling that which thou didst want,
Obedience to the law of God, imposed
On penalty of death, and suffering death,
The penalty to thy transgression due,
400 And due to theirs which out of thine will grow:
So only can high justice rest apaid.

xii *383. capital*] on the head (*OED* I 1); fatal (*OED* 2 d).
xii *386-7*. With the Fathers, and later with the medieval hymnists, the *duel*
was a favourite image for what led to Christ's victory on the cross. (The idea
has been studied by Bishop Aulén in *Den kristna försöningstanken*, of which
there is an abridged English version by A. G. Hebert, *Christus Victor* (1931).)
In M.'s view it is a misleading image, because insufficiently spiritual: there
can be no conflict so equal and uncertain as a duel, with a being so trans-
cendent as Christ (cp. *De doctrina* i 9, Columbia xv 104; also *PR* i 173ff).
xii *393. recure*] heal, cure.
xii *394-5*. Cp. *1 John* iii 8: 'For this purpose the Son of God was manifested,
that he might destroy the works of the devil.'
xii *395-465*. Cp. iii 208ff. A speech of some importance, since it sets out the
basis of the faith that Adam must have, before he can go out into the world
as a justified sinner. As an attempt to define the Faith and distil the definition
into a few lines, it must, perhaps inevitably, be considered a failure. There are
too many technical theological terms condensed into too little emotional
space. But if the passage is looked at in the context of the rest of Adam's
confirmation course, it will be seen to have the proper complementary,
even crowning, function. Its abstract and spiritual terms irrupt into the
Jewish history as if from another level of discourse. Notice, however, the
continuity of pace: Michael's narration has been steadily becoming more
summary.
xii *401. apaid*] satisfied.

The law of God exact he shall fulfil
Both by obedience and by love, though love
Alone fulfil the law; thy punishment
405   He shall endure by coming in the flesh
To a reproachful life and cursed death,
Proclaiming life to all who shall believe
In his redemption, and that his obedience
Imputed becomes theirs by faith, his merits
410   To save them, not their own, though legal works.
For this he shall live hated, be blasphemed,
Seized on by force, judged, and to death condemned
A shameful and accurst, nailed to the cross
By his own nation, slain for bringing life;
415   But to the cross he nails thy enemies,
The law that is against thee, and the sins
Of all mankind, with him there crucified,
Never to hurt them more who rightly trust
In this his satisfaction; so he dies,
420   But soon revives, Death over him no power
Shall long usurp; ere the third dawning light
Return, the stars of morn shall see him rise
Out of his grave, fresh as the dawning light,

xii *403–4.* 'Love worketh no ill to his neighbour: therefore love is the fulfilling of the law' (*Rom.* xiii 10).

xii *406. cursed death*] See *Gal.* iii 13, citing *Deut.* xxi 23.

xii *409–10.* In the Protestant doctrine of Justification by Faith Imputation had an important part to play. It was held that Christ's righteousness and obedience were *imputed* to the believer. Thus by a legal fiction the sinner's misdeeds were covered by the merits of Christ. See *De doctrina* i 22 (Columbia xvi 24ff).   *though legal*] though their works were in accordance with the law (there being no justification by works).

xii *412.* See iii 240*n*.

xii *416.* 'Blotting out the handwriting of ordinances that was against us, which was contrary to us, and took it out of the way, nailing it to his cross' (*Col.* ii 14).

xii *419. satisfaction*] Another theological term, meaning generally payment of a penalty due to God on account of man's sin. Here Christ's vicarious satisfaction is meant.

xii *422. stars of morn*] A complex phrase. Primarily, M. is using the morning star in a familiar way as an image of Christ's resurrection. (Based on the fact that the morning star is the same as the evening star that set to rise again, this symbolism goes back at least to Rabanus Maurus.) Secondarily, however, the stars may be angels; in which case *see* becomes literal and personal. Cp. v 708ff, where Satan has the face of the morning star. The opposition of true and false morning stars was also a patristic idea.

Thy ransom paid, which man from Death redeems,
425 His death for man, as many as offered life
Neglect not, and the benefit embrace
By faith not void of works: this Godlike act
Annuls thy doom, the death thou shouldst have died,
In sin for ever lost from life; this act
430 Shall bruise the head of Satan, crush his strength
Defeating Sin and Death, his two main arms,
And fix far deeper in his head their stings
Than temporal death shall bruise the victor's heel,
Or theirs whom he redeems, a death like sleep,
435 A gentle wafting to immortal life.
Nor after resurrection shall he stay
Longer on earth than certain times to appear
To his disciples, men who in his life
Still followed him; to them shall leave in charge
440 To teach all nations what of him they learned
And his salvation, them who shall believe
Baptising in the profluent stream, the sign
Of washing them from guilt of sin to life
Pure, and in mind prepared, if so befall,
445 For death, like that which the redeemer died.
All nations they shall teach; for from that day
Not only to the sons of Abraham's loins
Salvation shall be preached, but to the sons
Of Abraham's faith wherever through the world;
450 So in his seed all nations shall be blest.
Then to the heaven of heavens he shall ascend
With victory, triumphing through the air

xii 424. Thy] Implies that Adam is being addressed as representative of fallen
man.
xii 425–6. Hinting at the doctrine of Election. See iii 173–202 ('saved who
will').
xii 427. faith . . . works] See xi 64n.
xii 434. temporal death] The death of the body, which is described as a tem-
porary sleep in 1 Thess. iv 13–15.
xii 442. profluent] flowing in a full stream; often figuratively, 'abundant'.
M. thought baptism should be performed with running water; cp. De
doctrina i 28 (Columbia xvi 169): 'Baptism, wherein the bodies of believers
who engage themselves to pureness of life are immersed in running water [in
profluentem aquam], to signify their regeneration by the Holy Spirit, and their
union with Christ in his death, burial, and resurrection.'
xii 446–50. The promise to Abraham (ll. 25f and 147ff) is now given a more
precise spiritual interpretation, after Gal. iii 8 etc.
xii 452. triumphing] Stressed on the second syllable.

Over his foes and thine; there shall surprise
The serpent, prince of air, and drag in chains
455 Through all his realm, and there confounded leave;
Then enter into glory, and resume
His seat at God's right hand, exalted high
Above all names in heaven; and thence shall come,
When this world's dissolution shall be ripe,
460 With glory and power to judge both quick and dead,
To judge the unfaithful dead, but to reward
His faithful, and receive them into bliss,
Whether in heaven or earth, for then the earth
Shall all be paradise, far happier place
465 Than this of Eden, and far happier days.
    So spake the archangel Michael, then paused,
As at the world's great period; and our sire
Replete with joy and wonder thus replied.

xii 454. Cp. *Rev.* xx 1f.   *prince of air*] See *PR* i 39–41 and ii 117.

xii 458–65. Cp. the earlier account of the Second Coming, at iii 321ff. Empson (127) thinks that *Whether in heaven or earth* indicates that M. is doubtful about the idea of the Millennium. But the phrase hardly puts an alternative. It is rather equivalent to 'both in heaven and on earth'. There are, however, two chains of discourse. If a backward syntactic link is made, it is the comprehensiveness of the Last Judgment that is being expressed: angels as well as men are to be judged (iii 331–5), the living as well as the dead. But when we come to make the primary forward link, the point is that bliss will be general, so that the distinction between heaven and earth is insignificant. Some will be received here, others there.   *to judge both quick and dead*] Echoes the Apostle's Creed (or *Acts* x 42, *2 Tim.* iv 1 and *1 Pet.* iv 5).

xii 466–7. This is Michael's second pause: the first was at xii 2. The three divisions of Adam's instruction are meant to correspond to the 'three drops' of the well of life placed in his eyes (see xi 416, xii 5n). Here the pause is compared with the world's period, whereas at xii 1f the comparison was with noon, the sixth hour. The underlying connection between the two time indications is a number symbolism. See Cowley 184: 'The ordinary *Traditional opinion* is, that the world is to last six thousand years . . . and that the *seventh Thousand* is to be the *Rest* or *Sabbath* of *Thousands*.' Diurnal and millennial divisions correspond, because 'one day is with the Lord as a thousand years' (*2 Pet.* iii 8, where the context is a prophecy of the Last Judgment). The tradition of six periods of redemptive history went back to St Augustine, *Civ. Dei* xxii 30. There the ages run: (1) Adam to the Flood, (2) the Flood to Abraham, (3) Abraham to David, (4) David to the Captivity, (5) the Captivity to the Nativity of Christ, and (6) the present

O goodness infinite, goodness immense!
470   That all this good of evil shall produce,
       And evil turn to good; more wonderful
       Than that which by creation first brought forth
       Light out of darkness! Full of doubt I stand,

age, from the first to the second coming of Christ. M. adopts this scheme
almost exactly. Thus the structure of the episode may be expressed in the
form of a table:

Drop 1	Drop 2	Drop 3
xi 429–901	xii 1–467	xii 468–605
six-part vision	four narrations, divided by Adam's interposi-tions at xii 63, 270, 375, 469	narration
SIX DAYS OR AGES OF HISTORY		
Age of Adam	four ages, from the Flood to the coming of Christ	Age of Second Adam, ending with the Second coming

xii 469–78. In tracing the various aspects or 'causes' of the Fall, we have at
last come to the Final Cause or end of the Fall: namely a greater *glory* for
God and an opportunity for him to show his surpassing love through the
sacrifice of Christ (Howard 165). On God's power to turn evil to good, cf.
such passages as i 215ff, and see Lewis 66. The history of the idea of the For-
tunate Fall is traced by A. O. Lovejoy in 'Milton and the Paradox of the
Fortunate Fall', *ELH* iv (1937) 161–79. M.'s special contribution to the
idea is an infusion of hard realism. He never allows us to lose sight of the
plain misery brought by the Fall. We may rejoice in God's grace, not that
man gave him occasion to exercise it. From the classic statement in the
Hymn *O felix culpa* (Missal, *Exultet* for Holy Saturday), the idea of the
Fortunate Fall is often referred to as a paradox; but it is noticeable that M.
avoids paradox in its expression here. Contrast Salandra, *Adamo caduto*
ii 14, where the expression is extravagantly paradoxical. Addison was right,
however, to remark that at the end of the poem Adam is left triumphant in
the depth of misery, while Satan is miserable in the height of his triumph.
Some paradox is inherent in the story. Burden (37) notices the bearing of v
497–503, Raphael's prophecy of man's transmutation to spirit, on the present
passage. He draws the inference that fallen man is not better off than if he
had remained obedient; but perhaps the emphasis intended is rather that
God's will for man is to be fulfilled in spite of the Fall, though in a more

Whether I should repent me now of sin
475   By me done and occasioned, or rejoice
Much more, that much more good thereof shall spring,
To God more glory, more good will to men
From God, and over wrath grace shall abound.
But say, if our deliverer up to heaven
480   Must reascend, what will betide the few
His faithful, left among the unfaithful herd,
The enemies of truth; who then shall guide
His people, who defend? Will they not deal
Worse with his followers than with him they dealt?
485   Be sure they will, said the angel; but from heaven
He to his own a Comforter will send,
The promise of the Father, who shall dwell
His Spirit within them, and the law of faith
Working through love, upon their hearts shall write,
490   To guide them in all truth, and also arm
With spiritual armour, able to resist
Satan's assaults, and quench his fiery darts,
What man can do against them, not afraid,
Though to the death, against such cruelties
495   With inward consolations recompensed,
And oft supported so as shall amaze
Their proudest persecutors: for the Spirit
Poured first on his apostles, whom he sends

difficult and surprising way. The present passage ironically echoes i 162ff, where Satan announced his intention of opposing Providence's bringing forth of good out of evil. This is perhaps the most important of a long sequence of echoes between the first and second halves of the poem, discussed by J. R. Watson in *EC* xiv (1964) 148–55.

xii *478*. Cp. *Rom.* v 20 ('where sin abounded, grace did much more abound') and *2 Cor.* iv 15.

xii *486*. *Comforter*] The Holy Spirit. See *John* xiv 18 and xv 26: 'When the Comforter is come, whom I will send unto you from the Father, even the Spirit of truth, which proceedeth from the Father, he shall testify of me.' M. believed that the Holy Spirit was either God the Father himself, or his divine power; see *De doctrina* i 6.

xii *488–9*. Cp. *Rom.* iii 27 ('of works? Nay: but by the law of faith'); *Gal.* v 6 ('neither circumcision availeth any thing, nor uncircumcision; but faith which worketh by love'); and *Heb.* viii 10.

xii *491*. *spiritual armour*] Alluding to the allegory in *Eph.* vi 11–17. The most important part of the armour is Faith (vi 16): 'Above all, taking the shield of faith, wherewith ye shall be able to quench all the fiery darts of the wicked.'

xii *495*. Cp. *SA* 663–6: 'consolation from above: / Secret refreshings'.

xii *497–502*. Referring to events narrated, e.g., in *Acts* ii and x.

To evangelize the nations, then on all
500 Baptized, shall them with wondrous gifts endue
To speak all tongues, and do all miracles,
As did their Lord before them. Thus they win
Great numbers of each nation to receive
With joy the tidings brought from heaven: at length
505 Their ministry performed, and race well run,
Their doctrine and their story written left,
They die; but in their room, as they forewarn,
Wolves shall succeed for teachers, grievous wolves,
Who all the sacred mysteries of heaven
510 To their own vile advantages shall turn
Of lucre and ambition, and the truth
With superstitions and traditions taint,
Left only in those written records pure,
Though not but by the Spirit understood.

xii 505. The metaphor is Pauline: see *1 Cor.* ix 24, *2 Tim.* iv 7, *Heb.* xii 1.
xii 507–8. 'For I know this, that after my departing shall grievous wolves enter in among you, not sparing the flock' (*Acts* xx 29). Cp. the simile comparing Satan to a wolf in the fold, at iv 183–7 above; also *Lycidas* 113ff and *Cromwell* 14 ('hireling wolves whose gospel is their maw'). The whole passage that follows, down to l. 537, should be regarded, not as an attack on the Church of Rome or of England, but as a general condemnation of everything in the Church that is not built by Faith. See, however, Schultz 127, who argues that M.'s portrayal of Antichrist is specifically directed against Rome.
xii 511. See *1 Pet.* v 2: 'Feed the flock of God which is among you, taking the oversight thereof . . . not for filthy lucre, but of a ready mind.' M. wrote a tract on the subject, the *Considerations touching the likeliest means to remove hirelings out of the Christian Church* (Yale v).
xii 511–22. It was an important article of Protestant belief that in doctrinal matters the ultimate arbiter is individual conscience rather than mere authority. Those to the left of the Anglican position even held, with Henry Robinson, that 'there is no *medium* between an implicite faith, and that which a mans owne judgement and understanding leads him to' (*cit.* Yale ii 543*n*). (Implicit faith was unquestioning acceptance of the doctrines of the Church, on the authority of the higher clergy.) M. often expresses contempt for dependence on patristic and other authorities, the 'muddy pool of conformity and tradition' (*Areopagitica*, Yale *ibid.*) Cp. *De doctrina* i 30 (Columbia xvi 281): 'We are expressly forbidden to pay any regard to human traditions, whether written or unwritten' (citing *Deut.* iv 2 etc.). See also *1 Cor.* ii 14f: 'the natural man receiveth not the things of the Spirit of God: for they are foolishness unto him: neither can he know them, because they are spiritually discerned. But he that is spiritual judgeth all things.'

515 Then shall they seek to avail themselves of names,
 Places and titles, and with these to join
 Secular power, though feigning still to act
 By spiritual, to themselves appropriating
 The Spirit of God, promised alike and given
520 To all believers; and from that pretence,
 Spiritual laws by carnal power shall force
 On every conscience; laws which none shall find
 Left them enrolled, or what the Spirit within
 Shall on the heart engrave. What will they then
525 But force the spirit of grace it self, and bind
 His consort liberty; what, but unbuild
 His living temples, built by faith to stand,
 Their own faith not another's: for on earth
 Who against faith and conscience can be heard
530 Infallible? Yet many will presume:
 Whence heavy persecution shall arise
 On all who in the worship persevere
 Of spirit and truth; the rest, far greater part,
 Well deem in outward rites and specious forms
535 Religion satisfied; truth shall retire

xii 515-24. The corruption of the Church through its pursuit of *Secular power* is a subject M. had dealt with at large in *Of Reformation* (Yale i). In *De doctrina* i 30 (Columbia xvi 281) he condemns the enforcement of obedience to human opinions or authority (*sanctiones quascunque ... et dogmata*): no modern church or magistrate is entitled 'to impose on believers a creed nowhere found in Scripture, or which is merely inferred from thence by human reasons carrying with them no certain conviction.'   *laws which ... engrave*] laws neither written in Scripture nor in the individual conscience (*Jer.* xxxi 33). Cp. *Doctrine and Discipline*, Pref. (Yale ii 237), 'A Law not onely writt'n by *Moses*, but character'd in us by nature ... which Law is to force nothing against the faultles proprieties of nature.'
xii 526. Cp. *2 Cor.* iii 17: 'Now the Lord is that Spirit: and where the Spirit of the Lord is, there is liberty.'
xii 527. Cp. *1 Cor.* iii 17: 'The temple of God is holy, which temple ye are.'
xii 528-30. Not aimed exclusively at the Church of Rome. Infallibility was often held to reside in the edicts of the Oecumenical Councils and in articles of faith common to the whole Church. Yet, even though the doctrine of Papal Infallibility was not devised until 1870, there can be no doubt that Rome is M.'s *main* target here. In *A Treatise of Civil Power* he writes that the 'Pope assumes infallibility over conscience and scripture' (Columbia vi 8).
xii 532-3. Cp. *John* iv 23: 'True worshippers shall worship the Father in spirit and in truth.'
xii 534. *Well*] Will *Ed I.*

Bestuck with slanderous darts, and works of faith
Rarely be found: so shall the world go on,
To good malignant, to bad men benign,
Under her own weight groaning till the day
540   Appear of respiration to the just,
And vengeance to the wicked, at return
Of him so lately promised to thy aid
The woman's seed, obscurely then foretold,
Now amplier known thy saviour and thy Lord,
545   Last in the clouds from heaven to be revealed
In glory of the Father, to dissolve
Satan with his perverted world, then raise
From the conflagrant mass, purged and refined,
New heavens, new earth, ages of endless date
550   Founded in righteousness and peace and love
To bring forth fruits joy and eternal bliss.
   He ended; and thus Adam last replied.
How soon hath thy prediction, seer blest,
Measured this transient world, the race of time,
555   Till time stand fixed: beyond is all abyss,

xii *536. works of faith*] Cp. l. 427 and see *n.*

xii *537*. Some copies *Ed I* omit comma after *on.*

xii *539*. Cp. *Rom.* viii 22: 'For we know that the whole creation groaneth and travaileth in pain together until now.'

xii *539–51*. Note how *groaning* refers back to nature's groans at the Fall of Adam and Eve (ix 783, 1001), while *respiration* looks forward to a new breath, like that by which life was first inspired in man (vii 526, cf. i 7). The day of judgment is called *day . . . of respiration* because of *Acts* iii 19: 'Repent ye therefore, and be converted, that your sins may be blotted out, when the times of refreshing shall come from the presence of the Lord', where *refreshing* translates Gk. ἀνάψυξις (Vulg. *refrigerium*, but elsewhere sometimes transl. *respiratio*). M. may also, however, be thinking of A.V. *Esther* iv 14: 'Then shall there enlargement [marg. 'respiration'] and deliverance arise to the Jews from another place.'   *respiration*] opportunity for breathing again; rest (*OED* 3). The whole passage should be compared with ll. 446ff and with iii 321ff; all three are apocalyptic prophecies drawing on the same Biblical texts. The promise to Eve (x 179ff) is here given a final gloss, this time an eschatological one.

xii *546. dissolve*] annihilate, destroy (*OED* 6, 7).

xii *548. purged and refined*] Cp. xi 900f and see *n.*

xii *551*. Having begun with the immediate 'effects' of touching the forbidden tree (xi 424), Michael now ends with the final *fruits* Cp. i 1ff.

xii *555*. Cp. the vision of *Rev.* x 6, in which an angel swore 'that there should be time no longer'. Some copies *Ed I* have semicolon after *fixed.*

Eternity, whose end no eye can reach.
Greatly instructed I shall hence depart,
Greatly in peace of thought, and have my fill
Of knowledge, what this vessel can contain;
560 Beyond which was my folly to aspire.
Henceforth I learn, that to obey is best,
And love with fear the only God, to walk
As in his presence, ever to observe
His providence, and on him sole depend,
565 Merciful over all his works, with good
Still overcoming evil, and by small
Accomplishing great things, by things deemed weak
Subverting worldly strong, and worldly wise
By simply meek; that suffering for truth's sake
570 Is fortitude to highest victory,
And to the faithful death the gate of life;
Taught this by his example whom I now
Acknowledge my redeemer ever blest.
     To whom thus also the angel last replied:
575 This having learned, thou hast attained the sum
Of wisdom; hope no higher, though all the stars
Thou knew'st by name, and all the ethereal powers,
All secrets of the deep, all nature's works,
Or works of God in heaven, air, earth, or sea,
580 And all the riches of this world enjoyed'st,
And all the rule, one empire; only add

xii *559. vessel*] Not the Pauline metaphor for the body (as at *1 Thess.* iv 4);
implying rather the limitations of human nature as a created entity: cp.
Jer. xviii 4, xlviii 38, *Rev.* ii 27, etc. For the submission of the intellect, cp.
Adam's speech to Raphael, beginning viii 179ff.

xii *561–73.* Steadman 99f argues that Adam has learned the correct form of
the virtues of obedience and *fortitude* from the example of Messiah. Stripped
of virtue in the Fall (ix 1062f) he recovers it through regeneration.

xii *561. to obey is best*] Cp. *1 Sam.* xv 22, 'to obey is better than sacrifice'.

xii *565. Merciful*] Cp. *Ps.* cxlv 9, 'his tender mercies are over all his works.'

xii *566. overcoming evil*] Cp. *Rom.* xii 21, 'overcome evil with good'.

xii *567. things deemed weak*] Cp. *1 Cor.* i 27: 'God hath chosen the weak
things of the world to confound the things which are mighty'.

xii *576–81.* Cp. the exhortation of Raphael at viii 167–78.   *secrets of
the deep*] Recalls Uriel's speech about the impossibility of any created mind
comprehending the wisdom that hid the causes of God's works (iii 705ff).
Cp. also *Job* xxviii 28, 'the fear of the Lord, that is wisdom'.

xii *581–7.* Cp. *2 Pet.* i 5–7: 'Add to your faith virtue; and to virtue know-
ledge; And to knowledge temperance; and to temperance patience; and to
patience godliness; And to godliness brotherly kindness; And to brotherly
kindness charity.' M., however, subtracts godliness and brotherly love, and

> Deeds to thy knowledge answerable, add faith,
> Add virtue, patience, temperance, add love,
> By name to come called Charity, the soul
> 585 Of all the rest: then wilt thou not be loath
> To leave this Paradise, but shalt possess
> A paradise within thee, happier far.
> Let us descend now therefore from this top
> Of speculation; for the hour precise
> 590 Exacts our parting hence; and see the guards,
> By me encamped on yonder hill, expect

adds *deeds*; giving seven conditions of fruitfulness. These he arranges with some care; e.g. *virtue* is given fourth place, because the tetrad is a form of the *tetraktys*, which in Pythagorean symbolism is the fountain of virtue. Significantly, this puts virtue in the sovereign central place, so that we might say of Adam, as Cowley 195 of Brutus, 'Virtue was thy *Lifes Center*'–an emphasis which M. balances by asserting (after *1 Cor.* xiii) the primacy of *love* or *charity*. The seven qualities constitute a complete world or microcosm, which is seen as replacing the earthly Paradise (love as the animating soul of a world was a common idea in Platonic cosmogonies).

xii *587. paradise within*] contrast the 'hell within' of Satan, iv 20ff. G. C. Taylor, *PQ* xxviii (1949) 208, compares the title of Robert Croft's *A Paradice within us; or the Happie Mind* (1640), a book of consolation which gives pious and practical advice about how to attain an internal paradise of health and integration and spiritual comfort. Croft's exhortations are couched in terms not unlike Michael's: 'Let us possesse our minds with livelinesse, quicknesse, perspicacity, and gallantness of spirit, with moderation, Temperance, Humility, Meekenesse, Tranquility, Mildnesse, with Contentation, Fortitude, Cherefulnesse, with Humanity, Affability, Love, Kindnesse, and with all Joy and Happinesse. . . . So as to enjoy even a Paradice of delights and happinesse within us.'

xii *587.* Some copies *Ed I* omit comma after *thee.*

xii *588–9. top / Of speculation*] vantage-point (*OED* s.v. *Speculation* I 2 c); but also 'height of theological speculation'.   *hour precise*] The emphasis on the time (noon) is for two reasons. First, noon is the termination of the twenty-four-hour period beginning at the noon of the Fall (ix 739), so that the 'day' referred to in the Prohibition (viii 329–32) is in one sense only now accomplished. Hence, by a last bitter peripeteia, the terms of the Prohibition acquire yet another meaning: Adam and Eve die, in the sense of leaving Paradise for the mortal world, on 'that day' when they sinned. Secondly, noon was the sixth hour, the actual time of the Expulsion, according to Hugh of St-Victor; but also the hour of the Fall, as well as of the Crucifixion (see Bongo 280; also x 1050*n*, xii 1*n*). Thus the Expulsion becomes itself a Janus image, looking back to the Fall and forward to the Crucifixion and Redemption of man.

xii *591–3. expect / Their motion*] await deployment, transfer, marching

Their motion, at whose front a flaming sword,
In signal of remove, waves fiercely round;
We may no longer stay: go, waken Eve;
595 Her also I with gentle dreams have calmed
Portending good, and all her spirits composed
To meek submission: thou at season fit
Let her with thee partake what thou hast heard,
Chiefly what may concern her faith to know,
600 The great deliverance by her seed to come
(For by the woman's seed) on all mankind.
That ye may live, which will be many days,
Both in one faith unanimous though sad,
With cause for evils past, yet much more cheered
605 With meditation on the happy end.
      He ended, and they both descend the hill;
Descended, Adam to the bower where Eve
Lay sleeping ran before, but found her waked;

orders (military diction; see *OED* s.v. *Motion* 5).   *remove*] Sustains the
military diction: 'departure' (*OED* 5 b, citing Markham, 1622, 'he may then
cause the Drumme-major to beat a remove').   *flaming sword*] See l.
643*n*.

xii *594–605*. Michael's final summing-up emphasizes the two themes of the
visions: *submission* (or resignation) and *faith*. The two are balanced carefully
here in the single phrase *one faith unanimous though sad*: Adam is to look in
resignation at the Fall and its consequences, but in faith forward to Christ's
victory and the unification of God and man. Throughout the final books of
the poem, the opposition of the two themes has received a subtle and con-
stantly renewed expression at the formal level. For the terms of the Prohi-
bition and the terms of the promise to Eve have both received continual
reinterpretations and enlargements balanced one against the other. Thus
M. imitates the psychological process whereby Adam's understanding
of the curse and of the promise grows; yet at the same time imparts a nu-
minous sense of the mysteriousness of God's providence. Michael's last
speech gives each series of interpretations its final term, but with a difference.
The Expulsion is a matter of fact, the bruising of the serpent a matter of faith.
Hence M.'s balance of the two series is itself an expression of his faith in the
literal truth of the promise.

xii *601*. *(For by the woman's seed)*] for it will be by one born of a virgin
(l. 368). Some copies of *Ed I* have comma after *mankind*.

xii *602*. *many days*] Adam lived to be 930 years of age (*Gen.* v 5).

xii *603*. Some copies *Ed I* omit comma after *unanimous*.

xii *604*. *With cause for*] with good reason; in view of.

xii *607*. Some copies *Ed I* omit comma after *descended*.

xii *608*. Apparently in contradiction to the Argument, where 'Adam . . .
wakens Eve'.

And thus with words not sad she him received.
610   Whence thou return'st, and whither went'st, I know;
For God is also in sleep, and dreams advise,
Which he hath sent propitious, some great good
Presaging, since with sorrow and heart's distress
Wearied I fell asleep: but now lead on;
615 In me is no delay; with thee to go,
Is to stay here; without thee here to stay,
Is to go hence unwilling; thou to me
Art all things under heaven, all places thou,
Who for my wilful crime art banished hence.
620 This further consolation yet secure
I carry hence; though all by me is lost,
Such favour I unworthy am vouchsafed,
By me the promised seed shall all restore.
    So spake our mother Eve, and Adam heard
625 Well pleased, but answered not; for now too nigh
The archangel stood, and from the other hill
To their fixed station, all in bright array
The cherubim descended; on the ground
Gliding meteorous, as evening mist
630 Risen from a river o'er the marish glides,
And gathers ground fast at the labourer's heel
Homeward returning. High in front advanced,

xii *611.* Cp. *Num.* xii 6: 'If there be a prophet among you, I the Lord will make myself known unto him in a vision, and will speak unto him in a dream.' The authorities on the various types of dream were Artemidorus (*Oneirocritica*) and Macrobius (*In somn. Scip.* I iii 2–17). The prophetic vision (Lat. *visio*) was defined as a dream that 'actually comes true' (*ibid.* 9).

xii *615–23.* Cp. x 738–40 and see *n.* Eve has submissively assimilated Michael's exhortation at xi 292: 'where [Adam] abides, think there thy native soil'. There is also a resonance with Eve's song at iv 634–56 (every time of day is pleasing with, none without, Adam).

xii *626. archangel*] Two words in some copies *Ed I.*

xii *629–32. meteorous*] (=*meteoric*, from Gk μετέωρος): pertaining to the region of mid-air (*OED* 1 a). In the seventeenth century the term 'meteor' was applied to almost any atmospheric phenomenon, but especially to luminous bodies and exhalations such as fireballs, shooting stars, comets and the *ignis fatuus*.   *marish*] marsh. Richardson 533, with the approval of Ricks 109 returns to the derivative meaning of *meteorous* ('raised on high'), and contrasts the raised (and, one might add, luminous) mist of the good angels with the 'black mist low creeping' of Satan at ix 180. Clearly this is right, so far as it goes; but it is too simple. For, as Svendsen 107–12 points out in a fascinating if incompletely perspicuous discussion of the passage, Satan has also been compared to a delusively bright mist, at ix

The brandished sword of God before them blazed
Fierce as a comet; which with torrid heat,
535 And vapour as the Lybian air adust,
Began to parch that temperate clime; whereat
In either hand the hastening angel caught
Our lingering parents, and to the eastern gate
Led them direct, and down the cliff as fast
640 To the subjected plain; then disappeared.
They looking back, all the eastern side beheld
Of Paradise, so late their happy seat,
Waved over by that flaming brand, the gate

633-41. And the guardian cherubim almost seem like demons at l. 644 (see
n). As Svendsen 111 puts it: 'Adam's sin has made the Cherubim so, has
altered their relation to him.' Or, at least sin *may* make the cherubim seem
so, if they are not viewed with the eyes of faith. For Svendsen is wrong to
contrast the situation of the labourer with that of Adam and Eve. Fallen
man is indeed by God's curse a *labourer* (though the mention of *heel* balances
this curse as ever with the promise of *Gen.* iii 15). And the hour of the Ex-
pulsion is a time of transition from the immortal to the mortal world, just as
the labourer at *evening* passes from light to darkness. True, the mist is dread-
ful; but we know that 'to the faithful death [is] the gate of life' (l. 571):
Michael has shown Adam that, though he is exiled, he may eventually,
like the labourer, return home.
xii *633-6. adust*] scorched, burnt up; dried up with heat; parched. Swan and
Gadbury tell us that a comet in the shape of a sword signifies war and the
destruction of cities (Svendsen 92f). Again it requires faith to see a distinction
between this comparison with a comet and the comparison of Satan with a
comet at ii 706-11. The *Libyan air* simile alludes to a common gloss of the
'flaming sword' of *Gen.* iii 24, which explained it as the '*torrida zona*, the
parching countrie under the aequinoctiall' (Willet 54). This explanation
is not St Thomas Aquinas's (*pace* Hughes), but goes back to Tertullian; it
depended on a belief that the torrid zone was uninhabitable. On the equa-
torial location of the terrene Paradise, see iv 280-5*n* above. Cp. also the
separate account of the beginning of climatic extremes, at x 651ff.
xii *637-8*. The physical detail is transferred from Gen. xix 16, which de-
scribes the angels' conduct of Lot and his family from doomed Sodom.
There is a resonance also with l. 648.
xii *640*. 'We have descended with Adam and Eve to our own mundane
world' (MacCaffrey 59).   *subjected*] underlying, placed underneath
(*OED* s.v. *Subjected* 1); submissive, obedient (*OED* 2). On submission as a
theme of xii see ll. 594-605*n*.
xii *643*. Cp. *Gen.* iii 24, 'a flaming sword which turned every way'. M. here,
as at xi 120 ('of a sword the flame / Wide waving') follows the Chaldee
Paraphrast in understanding a literal sword 'which by the shaking seemeth
to glitter as the flame of fire' (Willet 57).

> With dreadful faces thronged and fiery arms:
> 645   Some natural tears they dropped, but wiped them
>   soon;
> The world was all before them, where to choose
> Their place of rest, and providence their guide:
> They hand in hand with wandering steps and slow,
> Through Eden took their solitary way.

THE END

---

xii *644*. W. B. Hunter in *MLR* xliv (1949) 89–91 cites John Petters, *Volatiles from the History of Adam and Eve* (1674): 'By this flaming sword etc. is meant an order of evil Angels, appointed also to guard the way to the tree of life'; and Svendsen (107) thinks that the *dreadful faces* make the cherubim 'strangely like Satan and his cohorts'. But it seems better to take 'dreadful' as a subjective description: guilt is a not uncommon cause of fear. Besides, even if the cherubim were objectively dreadful, that would not make them evil.

xii *645*. Burden 200 notes the careful balance of woe and joy.

xii *647*. Note that *providence* can be the object of *choose*: decisions of faith lie ahead.

xii *648*. The joining of hands is a hieroglyph of the pledging of faith. Svendsen 111f cites Camerarius, who 'in *The Living Librarie* collects numerous examples of such symbolism from Alexander of Alexandria, Numa Pompilius, and others to show the joining of hands as a consecration of faith.' She traces several earlier symbolic uses of hand imagery in *PL*, but perhaps the strongest echoes here are of iv 321 ('hand in hand they passed'), of the separation at ix 385f ('from her husband's hand her hand / Soft she withdrew') and of the corrupt sexuality in ix 1037 ('Her hand he seized'). There has been endless controversy about the propriety of the epithets; from which the main points to emerge are that *wandering* implies 'erring' and *slow* 'reluctant'. Thus the line could be said to counterbalance previous consolations and make terror the last passion left in the mind of the reader, were it not for the hope resting in the clasped hands. As often in *PL*, the positive aspect is the implicit one. The iconography of the Expulsion is discussed from a different point of view in M. Y. Hughes, 'Some Illustrators of Milton: the Expulsion from Paradise', in *JEGP* lx (1961). Some copies *Ed I* omit comma after *slow*.

xii *649*. Eden refers not to Paradise but to the country round it: see i 4 and iv 209–16*n*. Cp. *Ps.* cvii 4: 'They wandered in the wilderness in a solitary way; they found no city to dwell in.' But those who heard the echo of this psalm would also remember the continuation: 'Then they cried unto the Lord . . . And he led them forth by the right way, that they might go to a city of habitation.'

Bibliography of References Cited

Unless otherwise stated, the place of publication is London.

ADAMS, JAMES, ed. *The Republic of Plato.* 2 vols. Cambridge 1929.

ADAMS, ROBERT MARTIN. *Ikon: John Milton and the Modern Critics.* Ithaca, N.Y. 1955.

ALCIATI, ANDREA. *Emblemata.* Lyons 1600.

ALLEN, DON CAMERON. *The Harmonius Vision: Studies in Milton's Poetry.* Baltimore, Md. 1954.

ALLEN[2]. *The Legend of Noah: Renaissance Rationalism in Art, Science, and Letters.* Urbana, Ill. 1963.

ARTHOS, J. *On a Masque Presented at Ludlow Castle.* Ann Arbor, Mich. 1954.

AUERBACH, ERICH. *Mimesis: The Representation of Reality in Western Literature.* New York 1957.

BACON, FRANCIS. *The Philosophical Works,* ed. Ellis and Spedding, re-ed. John M. Robertson. 1905.

BANKS, T. H. 'The Meaning of "Gods" in *Paradise Lost*', *MLN* liv, 1939.

BARKER, ARTHUR E., ed. *Milton: Modern Essays in Criticism.* New York 1965.

BATESON, F. W. *English Poetry.* 1950.

BENTLEY, RICHARD. *Milton's Paradise Lost.* 1732.

BERNHEIMER, RICHARD. *Wild Men in the Middle Ages: A Study in Art, Sentiment and Demonology.* Cambridge, Mass. 1952.

BONGO, PIETRO. *Numerorum mysteria.* Bergamo 1591.

BRETT, R. L. *Reason and Imagination.* Oxford 1960.

BROADBENT, JOHN B. *Some Graver Subject: An Essay on 'Paradise Lost'.* 1960.

BROADBENT[2]. 'Milton's Hell', *ELH* xxi, 1954.

BROOKS, CLEANTH and HARDY, J. E. *Poems of Mr John Milton.* 1957.

BROWNE, WILLIAM. *Poems,* ed. G. Goodwin. 1894.

BURDEN, DENNIS. *The Logical Epic.* 1967.

BUSH, DOUGLAS. *Milton: Poetical Works.* 1966.

CARON, M. and HUTIN, S. *The Alchemists.* 1961.

CARTARI, VINCENZO. *Imagines deorum.* Lyons 1581.

CAXTON, WILLIAM. *Mirrour of the World,* ed. O. H. Prior. *EETS* 1913.

CHAMBERS, A. B. 'Chaos in *Paradise Lost*', *JHI* xxiv, 1963.

CHARLES, R. H. ed. *The Apocrypha and Pseudepigrapha of the Old Testament.* 2 vols. Oxford 1913.

CIRLOT, J. E. *A Dictionary of Symbols,* tr. Jack Sage. 1962.

CLARK, D. L. *John Milton at St Paul's School.* New York 1948.

COHN, NORMAN. *The Pursuit of the Millennium.* 1962.

COLUMBIA. *The Works of John Milton,* ed. F. A. Patterson *et al.* New York 1931–8.

CONDEE, R. W. 'The Formalized Openings of Milton's Epic Poems.' *JEGP* l, 1951.

CONTI, NATALE. *Mythologiae, sive explicationis fabularum, Libri decem.* Lyons 1653.

COPE, JACKSON I. *The Metaphoric Structure of 'Paradise Lost'.* Baltimore 1962.

CORCORAN, Sister M. I. *Milton's Paradise with Reference to the Hexaemeral Background.* Chicago, Ill. 1945.

CORMICAN, L. A. 'Milton's Religious Verse', in *From Donne to Marvell,* ed. Boris Ford. Pelican Guide to English Literature, vol. iii. 1956.

COWLEY, ABRAHAM. *Poems,* ed. A. R. Waller. Cambridge 1905.

CROMBIE, A. C. *Augustine to Galileo.* 2 vols. 1961.

CURRY. *Essays in Honour of Walter Clyde Curry,* ed. H. Craig. Nashville, Tenn. 1954.

CURTIUS, ERNST ROBERT. *European Literature and the Latin Middle Ages,* tr. Willard R. Trask. 1953.

DAICHES, DAVID. *Milton.* 1957.

DAICHES[2]. 'The Opening of *Paradise Lost*', in *The Living Milton,* ed. Frank Kermode. 1960.

DARBISHIRE, HELEN, ed. *The Early Lives of Milton.* 1932.

DARBISHIRE[2], ed. *The Poetical Works of John Milton.* 2 vols. Oxford 1952–5.

DARBISHIRE[3], ed. *The Manuscript of Milton's 'Paradise Lost' Book I.* Oxford 1931.

DAVIE, DONALD. *Articulate Energy: An Inquiry into the Syntax of English Poetry.* 1955.

DAVIE[2]. 'Syntax and Music in *Paradise Lost*', in *The Living Milton,* ed. Frank Kermode. 1960.

DIDRON, A. N. *Christian Iconography.* 2 vols. 1886.

DOBSON, ERIC. *English Pronunciation 1500–1700.* 2 vols. Oxford 1957.

DRAYTON, MICHAEL. *Works,* ed. J. William Hebel. Oxford 1961.

DREYER, J. L. E. *A History of Astronomy from Thales to Kepler.* 1953.

DRUMMOND, WILLIAM. *The Poems,* ed. W. C. Ward. 2 vols. n.d.

DU BARTAS. *Devine Weekes and Workes,* tr. Joshua Sylvester. 1613.

DU BARTAS[2]. *Devine Weekes and Workes,* tr. Joshua Sylvester. 1621.

DUNCAN, E. H. 'The Natural History of Metals and Minerals in the Universe of Milton's *Paradise Lost*', *Osiris* xi, 1954.

EISENSTEIN, S. *The Film Sense*, tr. and ed. J. Leyda. New York 1957.

EISLER, R. *The Royal Art of Astrology*. 1946.

ELLRODT, ROBERT. *Neoplatonism in the Poetry of Spenser*. Travaux d'Humanisme et Renaissance, xxxv. Geneva 1960.

EMMA, RONALD D. *Milton's Grammar*. The Hague 1964.

EMPSON, WILLIAM. *Milton's God*. 1961.

EMPSON². *Some Versions of Pastoral*. 1950.

EMPSON³. *The Structure of Complex Words*. 1952.

FICINO, MARSILIO. *Opera omnia*. Basel 1576.

FIXLER, M. *Milton and the Kingdoms of God*. 1964.

FLETCHER, HARRIS F. *The Intellectual Development of John Milton*. Vol. i: *The Institution to 1625: From the Beginnings Through Grammar School*. Vol. ii: *The Cambridge University Period 1625–32*. Urbana, Ill. 1956–61.

FLETCHER². *Milton's Rabbinical Readings*. Urbana, Ill. 1930.

FLETCHER³, ed. *Milton's Complete Poetical Works in Photographic Facsimile*. Urbana, Ill. 1943.

FOWLER, ALASTAIR D. S. *Spenser and the Numbers of Time*. 1964.

FOWLER². 'The River Guyon', *MLN* lxxv, 1960.

FOWLER³. 'The Image of Mortality: *The Faerie Queene*, II. i–ii', *HLQ* xxiv, 1961.

FREEMAN, ROSEMARY. *English Emblem Books*. 1948.

FRENCH, J. MILTON, ed. *The Life Records of John Milton*. New Brunswick, N.J. 1949–58.

FRYE, NORTHROP. 'The Typology of *Paradise Regained*', *MP* liii, 1956.

GILBERT, ALLAN H. *On the Composition of 'Paradise Lost': A Study of the Ordering and Insertion of Material*. Chapel Hill, N.C. 1947.

GIORGIO, FRANCESCO. *De harmonia mundi totius cantica tria*. Paris 1545.

GOULART, SIMON. *A learned summary upon the famous poeme of W. of Saluste* [i.e. Du Bartas], tr. T. L[odge]. 1621.

GRIERSON, H. J. C., ed. *The Poems of John Milton*. 1925.

HANFORD, JAMES HOLLY. 'That Shepherd, Who First Taught the Chosen Seed', *UTQ* viii, 1939.

HANFORD². *A Milton Handbook*. New York 1947.

HANFORD³. *John Milton, Englishman*. 1950.

HARDING, D. P. 'Milton and the Renaissance Ovid', *Illinois Studies in Language and Literature* xxx, 1946.

HENIGER, S. K. 'The Implications of Form for *The Shepheardes Calender*', *Studies in the Renaissance* ix, 1962.

HERRICK, ROBERT. *The Poetical Works of Robert Herrick*, ed. L. C. Martin. Oxford 1956.

HEYLYN, PETER. *Cosmographie In Four Bookes*. 1652.

HIEATT, A. KENT. *Short Time's Endless Monument: The Symbolism of the Numbers in Edmund Spenser's Epithalamion'*. New York 1960.

HOPPER, VINCENT F. *Medieval Number Symbolism*. New York 1938.

HORRELL, JOSEPH. 'Milton, Limbo, and Suicide', *RES* xviii, 1942.

HORWOOD, A. J., ed. *A Commonplace Book of John Milton*. Camden Society. 1876.

HOWARD, LEON. '"The Invention" of Milton's "Great Argument": A Study of the Logic of "God's Ways to Men"', *HLQ* ix, 1945.

HUGHES, MERRITT Y., ed. *John Milton: Complete Poems and Major Prose*. New York 1957.

HUIZINGA, J. *The Waning of the Middle Ages*. 1955.

HUNTLEY, FRANK L. 'Milton, Mendoza, and the Chinese Land-ship' *MLN* lxix, 1954.

HUNTLEY[2]. 'A Justification of Milton's "Paradise of Fools" (P.L. III 431–499)', *ELH* xxi, 1954.

JOHNSON, F. R. *Astronomical Thought in Renaissance England*. Baltimore, Md. 1937.

JONSON, BENJAMIN. *Works*, ed. C. H. Herford and P. and E. Simpson. Oxford 1925–50.

KELLEY, MAURICE. *This Great Argument: a Study of Milton's 'De Doctrina Christiana' as a Gloss upon 'Paradise Lost'*. Princeton, N.J. 1941.

KERMODE, FRANK. 'Adam Unparadised', in *The Living Milton*, ed. Frank Kermode. 1960.

KERMODE[2]. 'The Banquet of Sense', *Bulletin of the John Rylands Libr.* xliv, 1961.

KERMODE[3], ed. *The Living Milton*. 1960.

KERMODE[4]. 'Milton's Hero', *RES* iv, 1953.

KIRKCONNELL, WATSON. *The Celestial Cycle . . . with Translations of the Major Analogues*. Toronto 1952.

KLIBANSKY, RAYMOND, and others. *Saturn and Melancholy*. 1964.

LERNER, L. D. 'The Miltonic Simile', *EC* iv, 1954.

LEWALSKI, B. K. *Milton's Brief Epic*. Providence, R. I. 1966.

LEWIS, C. S. *A Preface to Paradise Lost*. 1942.

LEWIS[2]. *The Allegory of Love*. Oxford 1951.

LOVEJOY, ARTHUR O. *The Great Chain of Being: A Study of the History of an Idea*. New York 1960.

MACCAFFREY, ISABEL G. *'Paradise Lost' as 'Myth'*. Cambridge, Mass. 1959.

MCCOLLEY, GRANT. *'Paradise Lost': An Account of Its Growth and Major Origins*. Chicago 1940.

MÂLE, EMILE. *The Gothic Image: Religious Art in France of the Thirteenth Century*, tr. Dora Nussey. 1961.

MARLOWE, CHRISTOPHER. *Works*, ed. C. F. Tucker Brooke. Cambridge 1910.

MARTZ, L. *The Paradise Within*. New Haven, Conn. 1964.

MASSON, DAVID, ed. *The Poetical Works of John Milton*. 1890.

MASSON². *The Life of John Milton*. 1881.

MAXWELL, J. C. '"Gods" in *Paradise Lost*', *N & Q* cxciii, 1948.

MORE, HENRY, *Conjectura Cabbalistica. Or, a conjectural essay of Interpreting the minde of Moses, according to a Threefold cabbala.* 1653.

MORE². *The immortality of the soul*. 1659.

NELSON, L. *Baroque Lyric Poetry*. New Haven, Conn. 1961.

NICOLSON, MARJORIE H. 'Milton and the Conjectura Cabbalistica', *PQ* vi, 1927.

NICOLSON². 'A World in the Moon', *Smith College Studies in Modern Languages*, xvii, 1936.

NICOLSON³. *The Breaking of the Circle: Studies in the Effect of the 'New Science' Upon Seventeenth Century Poetry*. Evanston, Ill. 1950.

NICOLSON⁴. *Science and Imagination*. Ithaca, N.Y. 1956.

ORAS, ANTS. *Milton's Editors and Commentators from Patrick Hume to Henry John Todd 1695–1801: A Study in Critical Views and Methods*. Tartu 1930.

OVID. See under SANDYS².

PANOFSKY, ERWIN. *Meaning in the Visual Arts*. New York 1955.

PANOFSKY². *Studies in Iconology*. New York and Evanston, Ill. 1962.

PARKER, W. R. *Milton's Contemporary Reputation*. Columbus, Ohio 1940.

PARKER². *Milton's Debt to Greek Tragedy in 'Samson Agonistes'*. Baltimore, Md. 1937.

PEARCE, Z. *A Review of the Text of 'Paradise Lost'*. 1733.

PETER, JOHN. *A Critique of 'Paradise Lost'*. 1960.

PRICE, DEREK J., ed. *The Equatorie of the Planetis*. Cambridge 1955.

PRINCE, F. T. *The Italian Element in Milton's Verse*. Oxford 1954.

QVARNSTRÖM, G. *Poetry and Numbers: On the Structural Use of Symbolic Numbers. Scripta minora Regiae Societatis Humaniorum Litterarum Lundensis.* Lund 1966.

RAJAN, B. '*Paradise Lost' and the Seventeenth Century Reader*. 1962.

RAJAN², ed. *John Milton: 'Paradise Lost' Books I and II*. 1964.

RANDOLPH, THOMAS. *Works*, ed. W. C. Hazlitt. 1875.

READ. *Studies for William A. Read*, ed. N. M. Caffee and T. A. Kirby. Baton Rouge, La. 1940.

RÉAU, LOUIS. *Iconographie de l'art Chrétien*. 3 vols. Paris 1956.

RICCIOLI, GIOVANNI-BATTISTA, S. J. *Almagesti novi . . . tomus primus.* 2 parts. Bologna 1651.

RICHARDSON, JONATHAN, sen. and jun. *Explanatory Notes on 'Paradise Lost'.* 1734.

RICKS, CHRISTOPHER. *Milton's Grand Style.* Oxford 1963.

RIPA, CESARE. *Iconologia.* Rome 1603.

ROBIN, P. ANSELL. *Animal Lore in English Literature.* 1932.

ROBINS, HARRY F. *If This Be Heresy: A Study of Milton and Origen.* Illinois Studies in Lang. and Lit., No. li. Urbana, Ill. 1963.

ROBSON, W. W. 'The Better Fortitude', in *The Living Milton,* ed. Frank Kermode. 1960.

ROSEN, EDWARD, ed. *Three Copernican Treatises.* New York 1959.

RÖSTVIG, MAREN-SOFIE. *The Happy Man: Studies in the Metamorphoses of a Classical Ideal.* Vol. i: *1600–1700.* Oslo 1962.

RÖSTVIG[2]. *The Hidden Sense.* Oslo 1963.

SAMLA. *SAMLA Studies in English,* ed. J. Max Patrick. Gainesville, Fla. 1953.

SAMUEL, IRENE. *Plato and Milton.* Ithaca, N.Y. 1947.

SANDYS, GEORGE. *A relation of a journey.* 1615.

SANDYS[2]. *Ovid's Metamorphosis. Englished Mythologiz'd and Represented in Figures* by G[eorge] S[andys]. 1632.

SCHULTZ, HOWARD. *Milton and Forbidden Knowledge.* New York 1955.

SCOULAR, KITTY W. *Natural Magic: Studies in the Presentation of Nature in English Poetry from Spenser to Marvell.* Oxford 1965.

SELDEN, JOHN. *De Dis Syris.* 1617.

SIMS, JAMES H. *The Bible in Milton's Epics.* Gainesville, Fla. 1962.

SIMSON, OTTO VON. *The Gothic Cathedral: Origins of Gothic Architecture and the Medieval Concept of Order.* New York and Evanston, Ill. 1964.

SMITH, HALLETT. 'No Middle Flight', *HLQ* xv, 1951–2.

SPAETH, SIGMUND. *Milton's Knowledge of Music.* Ann Arbor, Mich. 1963.

SPROTT, S. ERNEST. *Milton's Art of Prosody.* Oxford 1953.

STARNES, DEWITT T. and TALBERT, ERNEST WILLIAM. *Classical Myth and Legend.* Chapel Hill, N.C. 1955.

STEADMAN, JOHN M. 'Heroic Virtue and the Divine Image in Paradise Lost', *JWI* xxii, 1959.

STEIN, ARNOLD. *Answerable Style: Essays on 'Paradise Lost'.* Minneapolis, Minn. 1953.

STEIN[2]. *Heroic Knowledge.* Minneapolis, Minn. 1957.

STEPHANUS, CAROLUS. *Dictionarium historicum, geographicum, poeticum.* Geneva 1621.

SVENDSEN, KESTER. *Milton and Science.* Cambridge, Mass. 1956.

SYLVESTER'S DU BARTAS. See DU BARTAS.

TAYLOR, GEORGE C. *Milton's Use of Du Bartas*. Cambridge, Mass. 1934.

TAYLOR². *A Tribute to George Coffin Taylor*, ed. A. Williams. Chapel Hill, N.C. 1952.

TERVARENT, GUY DE. *Attributs et symboles dans l'art profane 1450–1600* Travaux d'humanisme et renaissance, No. xxix. Geneva 1958.

TILLEY, M. P. *A Dictionary of Proverbs in England in the Sixteenth and Seventeenth Centuries*. Ann Arbor, Mich. 1950.

TILLYARD, E. M. W. *Milton*. 1930.

TILLYARD². *The Miltonic Setting, Past and Present*. Cambridge 1938.

TILLYARD³. *Studies in Milton*. 1951.

TODD, H. J., ed. *The Poetical Works of John Milton*. 1801.

TUVE, ROSEMOND. *A Reading of George Herbert*. 1952.

TUVE². *Images and Themes in Five Poems by Milton*. Oxford 1957.

VALERIANO, PIERIO. *Hieroglyphica, sive de sacris Aegyptiorum aliarumque gentium literis, Commentariorum Libri LVIII. ... Accesserunt loco auctarii, Hieroglyphicorum Collectanea, ex veteribus et recentioribus auctoribus descripta, et in sex libros digesta*. Frankfort 1613.

VERITY, A. W. ed. *Milton: 'Paradise Lost'*. Cambridge 1910.

WARTON, THOMAS, ed. *Poems upon Several Occasions ... by John Milton*. 1791.

WHALER, JAMES. 'Counterpoint and Symbol: An Inquiry into the Rhythm of Milton's Epic Style', *Anglistica* vi, 1956.

WHITE, T. H. *The Bestiary: A Book of Beasts*. New York 1960.

WHITING, GEORGE W. *Milton's Literary Milieu*. New York 1964.

WHITING². *Milton and this Pendant World*. Austin, Texas 1958.

WILLET, ANDREW. *Hexapla ... Sixfold Commentary upon Genesis*. 1608.

WILLIAMS, ARNOLD. *The Common Expositor: An Account of the Commentaries on Genesis 1527–1633*. Chapel Hill, N. C. 1948.

WILSON KNIGHT, G. *The Burning Oracle*. Oxford 1939.

WIND, EDGAR. *Pagan Mysteries in the Renaissance*. 1958.

WIND². *Bellini's Feast of the Gods*. Cambridge, Mass. 1948.

WITTKOWER, RUDOLF. *Architectural Principles in the Age of Humanism*. 1962.

WOODHOUSE, A. S. P. 'Theme and Pattern in *Paradise Regained*', *UTQ* xxv, 1956.

WRIGHT, B. A. '"Shade" for "Tree" in Milton's Poetry', *N & Q* cciii, 1958.

WRIGHT², ed. *Milton's Poems*. 1959.

YALE. *The Complete Prose Works of John Milton*, ed. Douglas Bush *et al.* New Haven, Conn. 1953–.